I0894578

Harnessing Blockchain-Digital Twin Fusion for Sustainable Investments

Syed Hasan Jafar
Woxsen University, India

Raul Villamarin Rodriguez
Woxsen University, India

Hemachandran Kannan
Woxsen University, India

Shakeb Akhtar
Woxsen University, India

Philipp Plugmann
SRH Hochschule für Gesundheit Gera, Germany

A volume in the Advances in Finance, Accounting, and Economics (AFAE) Book Series

IGI Global
PUBLISHER of TIMELY KNOWLEDGE

Published in the United States of America by
IGI Global
Business Science Reference (an imprint of IGI Global)
701 E. Chocolate Avenue
Hershey PA, USA 17033
Tel: 717-533-8845
Fax: 717-533-8661
E-mail: cust@igi-global.com
Web site: http://www.igi-global.com

Library of Congress Cataloging-in-Publication Data

CIP Data in progress

Title: Harnessing Blockchain-Digital Twin Fusion for Sustainable Investments

ISBN: 9798369318782

This book is published in the IGI Global book series Advances in Finance, Accounting, and Economics (AFAE) (ISSN: 2327-5677; eISSN: 2327-5685)

British Cataloguing in Publication Data
A Cataloguing in Publication record for this book is available from the British Library.

Advances in Finance, Accounting, and Economics (AFAE) Book Series

Ahmed Driouchi
Al Akhawayn University, Morocco

ISSN:2327-5677
EISSN:2327-5685

MISSION

In our changing economic and business environment, it is important to consider the financial changes occurring internationally as well as within individual organizations and business environments. Understanding these changes as well as the factors that influence them is crucial in preparing for our financial future and ensuring economic sustainability and growth.

The **Advances in Finance, Accounting, and Economics (AFAE)** book series aims to publish comprehensive and informative titles in all areas of economics and economic theory, finance, and accounting to assist in advancing the available knowledge and providing for further research development in these dynamic fields.

COVERAGE

- Taxes
- Economics of Agriculture and Biotechnology
- International Economics
- Macroeconomics
- Investments and Derivatives
- Auditing
- Interest Rates and Annuities
- Economic Theory
- Ethics in Accounting and Finance
- Labor Economics

IGI Global is currently accepting manuscripts for publication within this series. To submit a proposal for a volume in this series, please contact our Acquisition Editors at Acquisitions@igi-global.com or visit: http://www.igi-global.com/publish/.

The Advances in Finance, Accounting, and Economics (AFAE) Book Series (ISSN 2327-5677) is published by IGI Global, 701 E. Chocolate Avenue, Hershey, PA 17033-1240, USA, www.igi-global.com. This series is composed of titles available for purchase individually; each title is edited to be contextually exclusive from any other title within the series. For pricing and ordering information please visit http://www.igi-global.com/book-series/advances-finance-accounting-economics/73685. Postmaster: Send all address changes to above address.

Titles in this Series

For a list of additional titles in this series, please visit:
http://www.igi-global.com/book-series/dvances-finance-accounting-economics/73685

The Role of Financial Inclusion for Reaching Sustainable Development Goals
João Jungo (University of Aveiro, Portugal) Mara Madaleno (GOVCOPP, University of Aveiro, Portugal) Anabela Botelho (GOVCOPP, University of Aveiro, Portugal) and Eyup Dogan (Abdullah Gul University, Turkey)
Business Science Reference • © 2024 • 320pp • H/C (ISBN: 9798369305225) • US $275.00

Governance and Policy Transformations in Central Banking
Farhan Ahmed (NED University of Engineering and Technology, Pakistan) and Raza Ali Khan (NED University of Engineering and Technology, Pakistan)
Business Science Reference • © 2024 • 320pp • H/C (ISBN: 9798369308356) • US $275.00

Digital Capitalism in the New Media Era
Çiçek Topçu (Antalya Belek University, Turkey)
Information Science Reference • © 2024 • 270pp • H/C (ISBN: 9798369311820) • US $230.00

Democratization of Africa and Its Impact on the Global Economy
Ndwakhulu Tshishonga (University of KwaZulu-Natal, South Africa) and Icarbord Tshabangu (Leeds Trinity University, UK)
Information Science Reference • © 2024 • 487pp • H/C (ISBN: 9798369304778) • US $240.00

Digital Currency Assets and Challenges to Financial System Stability
Adekunle Alexander Balogun (University of Ibadan, Nigeria) and Yusuf Olatunji Oyedeko (Federal University Oye-Ekiti, Nigeria)
Business Science Reference • © 2024 • 227pp • H/C (ISBN: 9798369307700) • US $275.00

Algorithmic Approaches to Financial Technology Forecasting, Trading, and Optimization
Amandeep Singh (Chitkara Business School, Chitkara University, India) Sanjay Taneja (Graphic Era University, India) and Pawan Kumar (Chandigarh University, India)
Business Science Reference • © 2024 • 266pp • H/C (ISBN: 9798369317464) • US $275.00

IGI Global
PUBLISHER of TIMELY KNOWLEDGE

701 East Chocolate Avenue, Hershey, PA 17033, USA
Tel: 717-533-8845 x100 • Fax: 717-533-8661
E-Mail: cust@igi-global.com • www.igi-global.com

Table of Contents

Detailed Table of Contents

Climate change is one of the most debated and the biggest threat to humanity. With an unprecedented rise in catastrophic natural events, climate change has brought huge challenges, however, the sustainable development perspective is gradually embraced by entities and financial institutions. The financial markets and the business world across the globe are evolving to develop new products of investment avenues, such as clean energy, socially responsible investment or environmental, social, and governance (ESG) funds to prevent, mitigate, and adapt to climate change and its adverse impacts on the business and the society. Following the Paris Climate Agreement in 2015, green finance is maturing, and the focus is shifting to rely on renewable energy, limit carbon emissions, and prevent global warming. This chapter is an attempt to underpin the importance of green investment strategies to tackle climate change and investigates the role of technology in driving the transition of the financial market toward sustainable development and addresses the challenges faced by green investors.

The rapid evolution of transformative technologies, including blockchain and digital twins, is reshaping numerous industries. Blockchain, recognized for its distributed ledger capabilities, is gaining widespread acceptance owing to its secure and transparent data management features. Simultaneously, digital twins, virtual replicas of physical assets, are proving instrumental in offering real-time insights and enabling remote monitoring and control. This chapter explores the convergence of these two technologies, emphasizing their potential in the real world. Commencing with an overview of blockchain and digital twins, the chapter proceeds to scrutinize their architecture and consensus mechanisms. Subsequently, it delves into the concept of digital twins and their versatile applications across various sectors. Finally, it articulates the advantages derived from the integration of blockchain and digital twins.

Digital twins and blockchain technology have revolutionized data management and accessibility in a variety of areas and opened a plethora of new and profitable business opportunities. The "foundations of blockchain and digital twins" book chapter delves into the advantageous relationship between these two cutting-edge technologies. The basic ideas, unique characteristics, and real-world use cases of blockchain technology have been covered in the first section of this chapter. Blockchain technology's decentralized, transparent, and unchangeable features have the potential to completely transform a number of industries, including finance, healthcare, and supply chain management. The chapter also examines the consensus, processes, smart contracts, and cryptographic techniques that support the blockchain's dependability and security. The final section investigates the interesting relationship between blockchain and digital twins, assessing their individual benefits. Blockchain technology has the potential to improve the reliability, authenticity, and safety of digital twins.

Blockchain technology and non-fungible tokens (NFTs) are transforming industries like finance, art, and gaming. This chapter explores their intersection and profound implications for sustainable investments. Blockchain's transparency and immutability enhance trust in sustainability projects, while NFTs tokenizing real-world assets democratize access and promote eco-friendly initiatives. Real-world cases demonstrate the practical impact of blockchain-driven NFTs in sectors like renewable energy, sustainable agriculture, and carbon credits. Challenges include regulatory frameworks and environmental concerns, but the future promises a more robust ecosystem, increased accessibility, and greater transparency in sustainable finance.

This chapter aims to provide fresh ideas from philosophy to help human resources managers adopt blockchain technology in their work. In order to categorize the 25 significant items, the authors examined the 126 publications that were made available for acceptance between 2016 and 2021 in the Scopus and Web of Science databases. Using bibliometric data, the headings, titles, and keyword phrases of each of those 25 papers have all been meticulously analysed. Depending on the bibliometric data gathered, word relationship network maps were produced using VOS viewer. There are four topic groupings that were made using the linked visualisations. It has been decided that the ideas of employee-systems interface (ESI) and blockchain framework (BCF) for HR are going to encourage the adoption and application of distributed computing technologies in the area of the administration of human resources. After reading all 25 articles, the authors thoroughly and in-depth examined the key terms that supported the two philosophical subjects and determined the validity of the results.

Web3 encompasses decentralized finance (DeFi), which leverages blockchain and smart contracts to create an open and accessible financial system. They promote decentralization, trust, and innovation across industries. However, challenges include scalability, energy consumption, price volatility, regulatory uncertainty, and security vulnerabilities. Governments are working on regulatory frameworks, and adoption is growing. Education and awareness are crucial. In particular, there is a need to identify and address the technical, economic, social, and legal issues that may arise from the adoption and implementation of Web 3.0, including concerns around governance, scalability, interoperability, security, and regulation. Therefore, the purpose of the book chapter is to cover the key issues and challenges associated with blockchain technology and to develop a comprehensive understanding of the opportunities and limitations of this technology in order to inform the development and adoption of Web 3.0 applications and services.

This chapter explores the dynamic interaction between blockchain technology and digital twins in the context of green investing. It examines the revolutionary influence of the synergy of these cutting-edge technologies on the efficiency, transparency, and dependability of sustainable investing methods. The chapter begins with an informative introduction to the fundamentals of blockchain and digital twins, illuminating their separate functions before revealing their joint potential for strengthening green investment initiatives. A detailed assessment of the most recent improvements in blockchain and digital twin technologies follows, focusing on smart contracts, enhanced data analytics, and real-time monitoring. The actual implementation and effects of this integration are presented via illustrative case studies of renewable energy, sustainable infrastructure, and environmental conservation. This chapter delves deeper into the problems of integrating these technologies, providing practical insights and solutions to technical, regulatory, and operational roadblocks.

The chapter examines the creative use of blockchain and digital twin technologies in green finance that combines financial innovation with environmental sustainability. Blockchain and digital twin technologies are transforming traditional financial frameworks, making novel financial instruments essential for green investments. ESG-linked futures, green bonds, and sustainable asset-backed securities have evolved over time, and blockchain technology and digital twins have made them more reliable and appealing. The chapter also examines minimising the risks and improving return prediction in green investments. These technologies are shown in action in sustainable finance using real-world scenarios. The chapter concludes with a discussion of the challenges and potential advances of these revolutionary financial instruments and their growing relevance in environmentally friendly financial solutions. This comprehensive investigation aims to help financial professionals, investors, politicians, and academics navigate the ever-changing world of green investing.

Blockchain technology has gained considerable attention in recent years due to its potential to revolutionize various industries. Human resources (HR) management in large enterprises is an area that can greatly benefit from the transparency, security, and efficiency offered by blockchain technology. This study explores the concept of blockchain as a service (BaaS) in enterprise HR management and its potential to unlock efficiency, streamline processes, and enhance data security elaborating a comprehensive exploration of the theoretical underpinnings, practical application, and potential ramifications of BaaS within HR operations, highlighting the profound transformative prospects inherent in this emerging technology. The integration of blockchain as a service (BaaS) in enterprise human resources management is the focus of this study. The findings suggest that BaaS has the potential to revolutionize HR management by offering a secure, transparent, and efficient platform for various HR processes, from recruitment and onboarding to payroll and talent management.

This chapter explores how cutting-edge technologies, such as big data analytics, digital twins, and blockchain, are revolutionizing the green finance industry. It examines how these technologies' convergence improves sustainable financial practices efficiency, transparency, and decision-making while providing a fresh viewpoint on their complementary effects. The chapter describes the distinct functions of digital twins in asset optimization and risk management, blockchain in guaranteeing security and trust, and sophisticated data analytics in facilitating well-informed financial decisions.

This book chapter aims to ferret into the ever-evolving landscape of financial technology through a comprehensive case study of Capital One- A disruptor of financial services by using big data. It involves a broad range of technological applications, including software, mobile applications, artificial intelligence, block chain, big data and other emerging technologies, to enhance and streamline various financial activities such as banking, payments, investments, and insurance. This book chapter explores the journey of "Capital One" in adopting fintech innovations to enhance its financial services offerings and increasing profitability by reducing the risk. Capital One is recognized as one of the early adopters of fintech in the banking industry. As a leading financial institution, Capital One has strategically integrated fintech solutions to improve operational efficiency, customer experience, and overall competitiveness in the dynamic financial landscape.

Preface

Welcome to the dynamic intersection of finance and technology, where Syed Jafar, Raul Rodriguez, Hemachandran Kannan, Shakeb Akhtar, and Philipp Plugmann invite you to embark on a transformative journey in *Harnessing Blockchain-Digital Twin Fusion for Sustainable Investments*, we delve into the revolutionary fusion of cutting-edge technologies and environmental sustainability.

This edited reference book is a collaborative effort to demystify the profound impact of blockchain and digital twins on the financial landscape, with a keen focus on promoting green investment strategies. As the editors, we are excited to present a comprehensive resource that not only bridges the gap between advanced technologies and sustainable finance practices but also serves as a catalyst for innovation and informed decision-making.

Our primary objective is to offer a valuable resource for a diverse audience, including academia, finance professionals, technologists, policymakers, and company leaders. By exploring the integration of blockchain and digital twins, we aim to contribute to current research with insights, real-world examples, and practical frameworks that showcase the transformative potential of these technologies in reshaping finance and driving environmental sustainability.

The intended audience for this book is broad and varied, reflecting the multidimensional impact of blockchain and digital twin fusion. Whether you are an academic researcher, finance professional, technologist, government official, company leader, student, or a curious reader from the general population, this book is designed to cater to your interests and provide a thorough exploration of the fusion of finance and technology for green investments.

Join us on this intellectual adventure, as we unravel the synergies between technology and sustainability, paving the way for a more innovative, responsible, and sustainable financial future. "Harnessing Blockchain-Digital Twin Fusion for Sustainable Investments" is not just a book; it is a roadmap to a future where finance and technology collaborate seamlessly for the betterment of our environment and the global economy.

Chapter 1: Introduction to Green Finance and Technology Integration

In this chapter, Mahfooz Alam and Shakeb Akhtar lay the foundation for the book by addressing the pressing issue of climate change and its impact on humanity. It explores the evolution of financial markets in response to sustainability challenges, emphasizing the role of green investment strategies. The chapter investigates the significance of technology, particularly blockchain, in driving the transition of financial markets towards sustainable development. It sheds light on the challenges faced by green investors and sets the stage for the subsequent exploration of blockchain and digital twins in the context of green finance.

Chapter 2: Foundations of Blockchain and Digital Twins

In this chapter, Ravi Prakash B and Mohamadi Y delve into the transformative technologies of blockchain and digital twins. It provides an in-depth exploration of their architecture, consensus mechanisms, and individual features. The authors highlight the versatile applications of digital twins across various sectors and articulate the advantages derived from the integration of blockchain and digital twins. The chapter serves as a comprehensive introduction to the core concepts and potential of these technologies, setting the stage for their application in green finance.

Chapter 3: Blockchain and Digital Twins: Concept, Applications, Challenges and Potential

Prashant Chougule, Sharuti Choudhary, Kavitha Reddy Gurrala and Ch Siddharth Nanda explore the advantageous relationship between blockchain technology and digital twins. The chapter covers the fundamental ideas, unique characteristics, and real-world use cases of blockchain technology. It delves into blockchain's decentralized and transparent features, demonstrating its transformative potential in various industries. The chapter also investigates the intriguing relationship between blockchain and digital twins, assessing their individual benefits and paving the way for understanding their collaborative impact on reshaping finance.

Chapter 4: Blockchain-Driven NFTs: A Game-Changer for Sustainable Investments

Krishna Khanal examines the intersection of blockchain technology and Non-Fungible Tokens (NFTs) in this chapter. The focus is on their transformative role in sustainable investments, with blockchain's transparency enhancing trust and NFTs tokenizing real-world assets for eco-friendly initiatives. Real-world cases illustrate the practical impact of blockchain-driven NFTs in sectors like renewable energy and sustainable agriculture. The chapter acknowledges challenges and anticipates a more robust ecosystem for sustainable finance in the future.

Chapter 5: Blockchain in Human Resource Management: A Bibliographic Investigation and Thorough Evaluation

In this chapter, Tapaswini Panda, Udaya Patro, Saumendra Das, Koppala Venugopal and N Saibabu explore the adoption of blockchain technology in human resource management. Through bibliometric analysis, the authors categorize and examine significant publications, revealing the potential of Employee-Systems Interface (ESI) and Blockchain Framework (BCF) for HR. Thorough examination and analysis of key terms support the identification of philosophical subjects, offering insights into the adoption and application of distributed computing technologies in HR administration.

Chapter 6: Blockchain Based Financial Systems Deployment and Challenges: Comparative Study Across Several Countries

Focusing on Web3 and decentralized finance (DeFi), Jeevitha R, Bhanumathi P, and Sourav Mukherjee explore blockchain's role in creating an open and accessible financial system. It addresses challenges such as scalability, energy consumption, regulatory uncertainty, and security vulnerabilities. The chapter emphasizes the need for addressing technical, economic, social, and legal issues to inform the development and adoption of Web 3.0 applications and services.

Chapter 7: Emerging Trends and Innovations in Blockchain-Digital Twin Integration for Green Investments: A Case Study Perspective

Muhammad Tariq explores the dynamic interaction between blockchain technology and digital twins in the context of green investing. The chapter provides a detailed assessment of recent improvements in blockchain and digital twin technologies, focusing on smart contracts, enhanced data analytics, and real-time monitoring. Illustrative case studies showcase the practical implementation and effects of this integration in renewable energy, sustainable infrastructure, and environmental conservation.

Chapter 8: Innovative Financial Instruments for Green Investments: A Blockchain-Digital Twin Perspective

In this chapter, Mohsin Khan, Afzalur Rahman, Mohammad Shakir Ebrahim and Humaira Fatima examines the creative use of blockchain and digital twin technologies in green finance. It explores how these technologies transform traditional financial frameworks, making novel financial instruments essential for green investments. The chapter discusses ESG-linked futures, green bonds, and sustainable asset-backed securities, showcasing real-world scenarios. It addresses challenges and potential advances, providing a comprehensive investigation for financial professionals, investors, policymakers, and academics.

Chapter 9: Unlocking Efficiency: Blockchain as a Service (BaaS) in Enterprise HR Management

In this chapter, Jyotikanta Panda, Saumendra Das, Moushami Panda, Dulu Pattnaik and Nayan Deep Kanwal focus on the integration of Blockchain as a Service (BaaS) in enterprise HR management. The authors explore the potential of BaaS in unlocking efficiency, streamlining processes, and enhancing data security within HR operations. The findings suggest a transformative impact on HR processes, from recruitment to talent management, providing a secure and efficient platform.

Chapter 10: Advanced Data Analytics in Green Finance: Blockchain and Digital Twin Integration

Afzalur Rahman, Mohsin Khan, Ben Attom and Manoharan M. explore the convergence of big data analytics, digital twins, and blockchain in revolutionizing the green finance industry. It highlights their complementary effects, improving efficiency, transparency, and decision-making in sustainable financial practices. The chapter provides insights into the distinct functions of digital twins, blockchain, and sophisticated data analytics, offering a fresh perspective on their integration for sustainable finance.

Chapter 11: Revealing Green Finance Mobilization: Harnessing FinTech and Blockchain Innovations to Surmount Barriers and Foster New Investment Avenues

Bhupinder Singh and Christian Kaunert examine FinTech applications as catalysts for revolutionizing green finance. It dissects their functionalities in mitigating barriers such as information asymmetry and inefficiencies in fund distribution. Blockchain's decentralized ledger system is analyzed for enhancing trust and transparency in sustainable investment. The chapter highlights successful implementations, offering insights into the transformative potential of integrating financial technology (FinTech) and blockchain in green finance.

Chapter 12: The Nexus of Smart Contracts and Digital Twins Transforming Green Finance with Automated Transactions in Investment Agreements: Leveraging Smart Contracts for Green Investment Agreements and Automated Transactions

In this chapter, K Balaji explores the revolutionary force of integrating digital twins and smart contracts in green finance. It examines how these innovations work together to transform investment agreements, enabling automated transactions for increased effectiveness and transparency. The investigation presents real-world use cases and theoretical insights, showcasing the transformative influence of digital twins and smart contracts on changing the face of green finance.

Chapter 13: The Future of Green Finance: Artificial Intelligence Enabled Solutions for a More Sustainable World

Syed Shajar, Mohammad Kashif, Jintu George and Sibghatullah Nasir explore the convergence of artificial intelligence (AI) and green finance, revolutionizing the interconnection between finance and sustainability. It examines AI-powered solutions' capability to facilitate risk assessments, find investment opportunities, and enhance resource distribution for financial institutions. The integration of AI with green finance offers opportunities for a future characterized by improved environmental sustainability and financial stability.

Chapter 14: Blockchain Technology for Sustainable Investment: A Comprehensive Review and Future Prospects

Anjli Gupta, Ritu Gupta, Kiran and Sharuti Choudhary provide a comprehensive analysis of how blockchain technology can enhance sustainable investment practices. It assesses the current applications, benefits, and challenges of blockchain in sustainable investment, identifying opportunities for future development. The review includes an examination of various blockchain platforms and applications, showcasing their impact on transparency, security, and efficiency in sustainable investment.

Chapter 15: Disrupting Financial Services: A Case Study on Capital One's Odyssey

In this concluding chapter, Naseema N, Shakeb Akhtar and Asila Al Hinai delve into the evolving landscape of financial technology through a comprehensive case study of Capital One. The case study explores Capital One's adoption of fintech innovations, including software, mobile applications, artificial intelligence, blockchain, big data, and emerging technologies. It showcases how Capital One strategically integrated fintech solutions to improve operational efficiency, customer experience, and overall competitiveness in the dynamic financial landscape.

As editors of *Harnessing Blockchain-Digital Twin Fusion for Sustainable Investments*, we find ourselves at the culmination of a remarkable journey through the dynamic intersection of finance and technology. Our collective effort, alongside the insightful contributions of esteemed authors, has resulted in a comprehensive exploration of the revolutionary fusion between cutting-edge technologies and environmental sustainability.

This edited reference book stands as a testament to the collaborative endeavor to demystify the profound impact of blockchain and digital twins on the financial landscape, with a dedicated emphasis on fostering green investment strategies. Our excitement is palpable as we present this resource not only as a bridge between advanced technologies and sustainable finance practices but also as a catalyst for innovation and informed decision-making.

Our primary objective has been to offer a valuable resource accessible to a diverse audience encompassing academia, finance professionals, technologists, policymakers, and company leaders. Through the exploration of blockchain and digital twin integration, our aim has been to contribute meaningful insights, real-world examples, and practical frameworks that showcase the transformative potential of these technologies in reshaping finance and propelling environmental sustainability.

The intended audience for this book is deliberately broad and varied, reflecting the multidimensional impact of the fusion of blockchain and digital twins. Whether you are an academic researcher, finance professional, technologist, government official, company leader, student, or a curious reader from the general population, this book is tailored to cater to your interests and provide a thorough exploration of the synergy between finance and technology for green investments.

Join us on this intellectual adventure, where we unravel the synergies between technology and sustainability, paving the way for a more innovative, responsible, and sustainable financial future. "Harnessing Blockchain-Digital Twin Fusion for Sustainable Investments" transcends being merely a book; it is a roadmap guiding us towards a future where finance and technology collaborate seamlessly for the betterment of our environment and the global economy.

The chapters within this book serve as building blocks, each contributing a unique perspective to the overarching narrative. From laying the foundation with the exploration of climate change and the evolution of financial markets in response to sustainability challenges to the detailed examination of transformative technologies like blockchain and digital twins, and their applications across various sectors, the chapters weave a comprehensive tapestry.

As we conclude our journey with a case study on Capital One's Fintech Odyssey, we reflect on the evolving landscape of financial technology and how strategic integration of fintech solutions has enhanced operational efficiency, customer experience, and competitiveness.

In the spirit of continuous exploration and innovation, we invite you, our readers, to embrace this book not just as a collection of chapters but as a dynamic conversation starter. The future beckons, and we believe that the insights shared within these pages will inspire further research, dialogue, and collaboration towards a more sustainable and technologically advanced financial ecosystem.

Thank you for joining us on this transformative journey.

Syed Hasan Jafar
Woxsen University, India

Raul Villamarin Rodriguez
Woxsen University, India

Hemachandran Kannan
Woxsen University, India

Shakeb Akhtar
Woxsen University, India

Philipp Plugmann
SRH Hochschule für Gesundheit Gera, Germany

Chapter 1
Introduction to Green Finance and Technology Integration

Mahfooz Alam
https://orcid.org/0000-0002-9311-5688
University of the People, USA

Shakeb Akhtar
https://orcid.org/0000-0003-2069-6669
Woxsen University, India

ABSTRACT

Climate change is one of the most debated and the biggest threat to humanity. With an unprecedented rise in catastrophic natural events, climate change has brought huge challenges, however, the sustainable development perspective is gradually embraced by entities and financial institutions. The financial markets and the business world across the globe are evolving to develop new products of investment avenues, such as clean energy, socially responsible investment or environmental, social, and governance (ESG) funds to prevent, mitigate, and adapt to climate change and its adverse impacts on the business and the society. Following the Paris Climate Agreement in 2015, green finance is maturing, and the focus is shifting to rely on renewable energy, limit carbon emissions, and prevent global warming. This chapter is an attempt to underpin the importance of green investment strategies to tackle climate change and investigates the role of technology in driving the transition of the financial market toward sustainable development and addresses the challenges faced by green investors.

DOI: 10.4018/979-8-3693-1878-2.ch001

INTRODUCTION

Finance is the lifeblood of business. Whether you are a start-up company, a family-owned enterprise or a multi-national corporation, finance will remain the core of your business. The classical economists provided a narrow objective of finance as their view typically focuses on increasing a business's profits or sales. Over the past few decades, modern economists realized the importance of finance and recognized the distinctive competitive advantages that a well-managed financial system can provide to any company and help in achieving long-term success (Akhtar et al., 2022). Through proper money supply, facilitating investment by creating favorable avenues, and promotion of allocation of capital rationally, finance plays a crucial role including stock market and portfolio optimization leading to economic prosperity and overall development. In this regard, the Industrial Revolution started in the 20th century, was considered a key tipping point for globalization and the interconnectedness of world economies, subsequently facilitating improved living standards, employment, health, and, eventually, the extraordinary population growth (Thompson, 2021).

However, due to massive growth and globalization, there is widespread scientific agreement that industries have immensely affected the ecology and the earth has witnessed a surge in carbon in its atmosphere escalating the temperature of the earth, commonly known as *global warming*. The ozone layer depletion, rising temperature and climatic catastrophes are at unprecedented levels in the history of mankind. In the wake of this, climate change is a topic of considerable discussion across the world. Some events (such as floods, wildfires, heatwaves and extreme rainfall) are occurring more frequently than scientists previously assessed escalating the severity and frequency of weather-related hazards on the human population.[1] Nevertheless, industries don't exist in vacuums and it has a moral and ethical responsibility to focus on sustainable growth.

Much of the carbon emissions causing climate change originates from business-driven economic activity. While the US tops the list as the largest contributor to carbon emissions, the rapid emergence of Asian economies like China and India as fast-growing economies has triggered a greater share of carbon emissions. Furthermore, in the aftermath of financial shocks like the Global Financial Crisis (GFC) of 2008, the COVID-19 pandemic, wars among major nations, etc., financial institutions including professionals are of the impression that the financial sector should reconsider its objectives, activities and strategies and align them with the sustainable development goals (SDGs) to deliver greater shared economic and social value. The good news is since the adoption of SDGs in 2015 by the United Nations to serve the 2030 development agenda, a majority of the nations are striving to reduce their carbon footprint (Lehner et al., 2023).

It is evident from the past that the modern economic system emphasizing fast-paced growth has led to a serious threat to humankind in the form of environmental crises or climate change. With an unprecedented rise in catastrophic natural events in the last few decades, climate change has brought huge challenges, however, the sustainable development perspective is gradually embraced by entities and financial institutions. The financial markets and the business world across the globe are evolving to develop new products of investment avenues, such as clean energy, socially responsible investment or Environmental, Social and Governance (ESG) funds to prevent, mitigate, and adapt to climate change and its adverse influence on the business and the society, at large. This has also led to the financial inclusion of investors who wish to focus on sustainable investment avenues by providing new forms of funding. Due to its nascent nature, these investments are often subjected to risk-return priorities. The investment in these initiatives is broadly referred to as ***green finance***.

BACKGROUND

Although green finance had its origins traced back to the 1970s, it remained unnoticed until 2015, with the introduction of the Paris Agreement and the Sustainable Development Goals when the sustainability movement reached a tipping point. Following the 2015 Paris Agreement on climate change, government, policymakers and regulators articulated the concern for a sustainable future and to tackle global warming. By the end of 2020, more than 120 countries had published a net zero target or similar by 2050. The member nations vowed to align their investments, vision, and strategies to attain futuristic and sustainable growth; and the financial institutions, such as the banking sector, fund managers, investors, etc., played a leading role in attaining the desired goals. There exists a wider perspective on sustainability beyond climate change, and indeed it will be futile to address climate change sans focusing on a broader aspect of economic and social sustainability.

Green Finance is an emerging field that is growing at a phenomenal rate. It has an enormous potential to assist in transitioning to a low-carbon and climate-resilient economy and promote social welfare. The proper utilization of green finance may aid the government, financial institutions as well and investors in channelling their capital towards products and services that support the transition to a low-carbon economy, mitigate ecological loss, minimize carbon and other harmful emissions, and promote sustainable growth and human well-being. However, effective implementation of green finance to tackle climate change is not as easy as it seems; it requires extensive investment and dedication from the whole world.

Surprisingly, even after years of its inception, the term "*green finance*" doesn't have a unique, universal, and commonly accepted definition. Neither does it for the different families of green products and services or even financial securities. The review of the literature suggests that a majority of the previous studies failed to define the term and provided a naïve definition; for instance – the earlier studies of IFC (2013) and Spratt and Griffith-Jones (2013) discuss green finance sans definition. Moreover, the definitions proposed by some studies vary significantly. *Green finance*, also known as sustainable finance, is often defined by financial institutions, governments, and international organizations based on their underlying motivation (IFC 2017). According to Höhne et al. (2012), *green finance* can be defined as "a broad term that can refer to financial investments flowing into sustainable development projects and initiatives, environmental products, and policies that encourage the development of a more sustainable economy. *Green finance* includes *climate finance* but is not limited to it. It also refers to a wider range of other environmental objectives, for example, industrial pollution control, water sanitation, or biodiversity protection." Similarly, the Organisation for Economic Co-operation and Development (OECD) defines green finance as, "*Green finance* is finance for achieving economic growth while reducing pollution and greenhouse gas emissions, minimizing waste and improving efficiency in the use of natural resources." [2]

The term "green finance" in financial literature is used to label activities or investments related to dichotomous interaction between finance and the environment. There are a few terms that are used interchangeably in the literature to denote green finance including responsible investment, environmental, social and governance (ESG) investment, sustainable finance or investment, and climate finance. The above-mentioned terms are often used synonymously with green finance, however, there are differences in their scope and objectives of investments, considering social and governance issues, in particular.

Environmental issues related to the depletion and quality of the natural environment and ecology include greenhouse gas emission, deforestation, biodiversity loss, natural resource depletion such as air, water and noise pollution; ozone layer depletion; acid rains, focusing on renewable and efficient energy consumption per capita.

Social issues relate to the rights and prosperity of people living in a society or region including human rights, labour rights, consumer protection, providing health and safety standards to the general public, better access to education, healthcare, sanitation, etc.

Economic issues are the impact of activities on the economy at local, zonal or global levels. The trade policies, government regulations, financial performances, tax structure, employment opportunities, proper infrastructure and supply chain management add to the economic growth and development of a nation.

Governance issues are the management of organizations and entities. These include board size and diversity, stakeholders' interest; availability and free flow of information; ease of doing business, corruption, internal control and risk management, etc.

Approaches that consider all these above-mentioned issues are termed sustainable finance, responsible investment or socially responsible investing (SRI), whereas, the approaches whose focus is limited to environmental issues are more likely to be termed as green finance. Subsequently, if the concern is limited to preventing climate change or acts to slow down climate change, it will be referred to as climate finance. The term "climate finance" is also broadly used to denote the Paris Climate Agreement; including the institutional and international provision of aid to tackle climate change mitigation and climate adaptation (UNEP, 2021).

At present, the Paris Climate Agreement frameworks and the guidelines provided by the SDGs can be utilized to define the boundaries of the operations of *green finance* (including other components of green finance). Accordingly, the financial stocks and flows targeted at assisting in the accomplishment of the SDGs pertaining to the environment might be expressly referred to as "green finance." Comparably, *climate finance* can be thought of as a part of *green finance* that focuses on climate action (i.e., mitigating and adapting to climate change), whereas sustainable finance can be considered as encompassing all the financial stocks and flows mobilized to attain each of the SDG frameworks. These relationships are graphically depicted in Fig 1.1.

Figure 1. Green finance and its components
(Adapted from UNEP 2016)

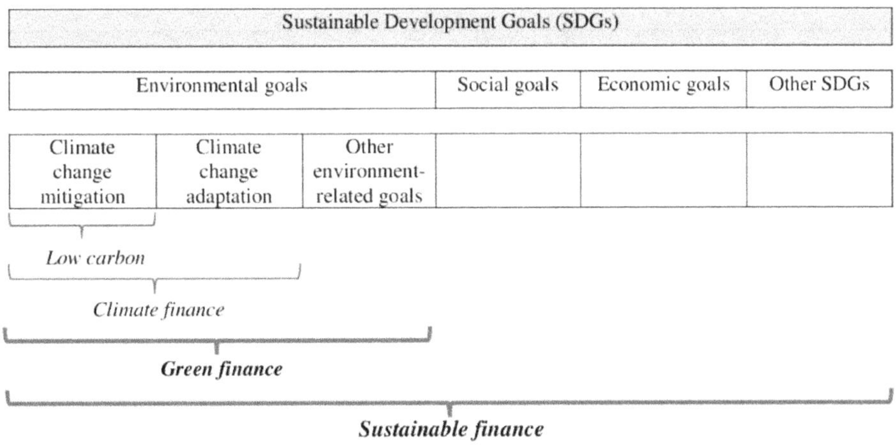

The demand for green finance is growing phenomenally due to its economic and environmental advantages to financial markets and society. The financial institutions are developing a structured process to innovate and modify the financial instruments to cater for the need for sustainable growth. Recently, the growing acceptance of climate change across the globe is another major factor propelling the growth of green finance. However, another strand of literature also argues that the financial crisis of 2008 (housing bubble) and the rising level of systematic ethical failures in the global world played a pivotal role in the emergence of the SRI and ESG investment avenues. The aftermath of the 2008 financial crisis raises questions about the accountability and the role of financial institutions of an economy in mitigating the impact of the financial shocks, even though its effects were mostly social and governance-related instead of environmental. Lastly, financial markets and regulators have a key role to play in the growth of green finance, through a variety of mechanisms such as developing better disclosure, improving corporate governance, clarifying investor duties, creating standards and facilitating easier access to capital for green companies. Over the past years, major stock exchanges have shown a strong commitment towards green finance. The financial centres have focused on innovating green product offerings and constantly enhancing the quality and return of the products and services related to green finance as compared with their conventional counterparts. To this extent, the listing of sustainable finance and green finance, in particular, has registered tremendous growth in developed and developing economies alike. Table 1.1 exhibits the major stock exchanges of the world with a dedicated section for green finance.

Table 1. Stock exchanges that have launched a dedicated green or sustainable bonds section.

Name of stock exchange	Product offering	Launch date
Oslo Stock Exchange	Green bonds	January 2015
Stockholm Stock Exchange	Sustainable bonds	June 2015
London Stock Exchange	Sustainable bonds	July 2015
Shanghai Stock Exchange	Green bonds	March 2016
Mexico Stock Exchange	Green bonds	August 2016
Borsa Italiana	Green and social bonds	March 2017
Taipei Exchange	Sustainable bonds	May 2017
Johannesburg Stock Exchange	Green bonds	October 2017
Japan Exchange Group	Green and social bonds	January 2018
Vienna Exchange	Green and social bonds	March 2018

Table 1 continued

Name of stock exchange	Product offering	Launch date
Nasdaq (Multiple Stock Exchange)	Sustainable bonds	May 2018
Bombay Stock Exchange	Green bonds	June 2019
Brazil Stock Exchange	Green bonds	September 2019
Hong Kong Exchange	Green, Sustainable and Social bonds	June 2020
Korea Exchange	Green, Sustainable and Social bonds	June 2020
Toronto Stock Exchange	Sustainable bonds	November 2020

Source: Climate Bonds Initiatives (https://www.climatebonds.net/green-bond-segments-stock-exchanges, retrieved on 30 October 2023).

TYPES OF GREEN FINANCE

Green Bonds

Green bonds are considered a crucial and pioneer innovation in the field of green finance and the other green financial products and services have stemmed from it seeing the huge surge in its demand in the financial market. After the issuance of the first green bonds by the European Investment Bank along with the World Bank in 2007 with the AAA-rated issuance.[3] Henceforward, the green bonds market has expanded exponentially growth and is issued widely by financial institutions, the banking sector, government bodies and even by corporates.

In 2020, the green bonds achieved its most significant milestone registering USD 1 trillion in cumulative issuance since its market inception in 2007. *Green bonds* are issued by various organizations to attract investors to finance environment and clean energy-related projects and programs to tackle climate change. Moreover, green bonds may provide tax benefits (depending on the issuer and jurisdiction), such as tax credits and tax exemptions. Nonetheless, green bonds facilitate investors with the opportunity to promote sustainable finance that could have a long-term positive impact on the environment while still earning potential returns on their investment. Green bond issuances often support initiatives in the following areas: pollution control and prevention, energy efficiency (including building refurbishment), renewable energy, and sustainable resource management. As of today, institutional investors remain the major investor in *green bonds*.

In recent years, several multinational companies (MNCs) including Apple Inc., Unilever, and Bank of America, have issued green bonds to finance environmentally friendly projects showcasing their role in sustainable development. Despite this boom, it is hard to predict the impact of these bonds. Whether the results satisfactory and have they achieved sustainable development goals? Do they outperform or underperform in comparison to their counterparts? The answers to both questions are quite satisfactory in the majority of the studies. Absolutely, in response to both inquiries. Out of 217 corporate green bonds issued by public companies, their analysis indicates that green bonds posit a positive and significant impact on the stock market, improve financial and environmental performance, encourage the development of green innovations, and increase the ownership of stock by long-term and environmentally conscious investors.

Lately, *Green Bond Principles* (GBP) published by the *International Capital Market Association* (ICMA) in 2014 and revised in 2017, 2018, 2021 and 2022 represents the leading framework in the definition of a *green bond*.[4] The GBP principles provide clarity on the process for issuing *green bonds* and emphasize the need for transparency, accuracy, and integrity in the information that issuers communicate to stakeholders through core components and key recommendations. These principles provide clarity of process and disclosure for issuers that may be helpful for the investors, underwriters, banks and placement agents to comprehend the features of each given *green bond*. The green certification agencies also adhere to these standards to ensure that any specific issuance complies with them. They do this by providing second opinions and ultimately assigning (or not) green labels to them.

Whereas, *climate bonds* are fixed-income financial instruments (bonds) linked to climate change solutions. These bonds are issued to generate funds for projects related to adaptation or mitigation of climate change. Climate bonds can be issued by governments, multinational banks, or corporations similar to regular bonds, and the issuing body will be responsible for the payback of the principal amount of the bonds including interest. The difference lies in the objective of raising the funds. In contrast to the green bond market, which is dominated by large, well-diversified organizations, pure-play issuers dominate the climate bond market. Furthermore, this category of loan issuances does not currently have any widely accepted labeling in place. These bonds will be crucial in building a net zero economy with clear policy guidelines, frameworks and standards to facilitate the transition to net zero by 2050.

Green Asset-Backed Securities

In the wake of the success and popularity gained by *green bonds* in a short span, the financial market started witnessing the emergence of more complex structured financial instruments. A significant factor propelling the expansion of the green bond markets will be the steps taken to increase the issuance of *green asset-backed securities* (ABS). The green ABS was backed by green securities following the conventional method of securitization referred to as *green ABS*. Since asset-backed securities (ABS) are debt instruments, they are often categorized as green bonds in the broad sense.

An asset-backed securities (ABS) has a disproportionate degree of scalability (assuming barriers are removed for securitized securitizations) as they are less likely to be constrained by balance sheet considering corporate and SSA bonds and by government fiscal and budgetary constraints (for example, government bonds). In the financial market, commercial banks emerged as effective and prominent users of the green bonds market to raise capital for lending activities. The previous studies have depicted that the key determinants of the securitization are provision of new liquidity, the management of capitalization through risk transfer, the possibility of regulatory arbitrage and the realization of profit opportunities (Zhao et al., 2021; Khan et al., 2022).[5]

However, the issuance of green ABS may pose a great challenge as the green securitization allows for continuous financing of high-carbon assets/projects which may limit the expansion of new green investment or funding. Further, it has the potential to make the financial system more susceptible to systemic risk. However, high-carbon assets must be divested and decommissioned with immediate effect to attain the goal of decarbonization that will keep the 'brown' assets active and securitize them to raise funds. The *green asset-backed securities* exhibit a significant degree of variability due to the variety of asset classes that can be securitized and the structuring techniques that are currently employed.[6] One such type of green ABS is securitization with green collaterals. These may include asset-backed securities (ABS), namely, automobile loans (EV-ABS), solar ABS, and small-and-medium enterprise loans (SME-ABS) to fund environmental projects etc., or mortgage-backed securities (MBS) like mortgages on green infrastructure, energy-efficient homes etc. The securitization of green bonds based on the Collateralized Debt Obligations (CDO) can be considered as an alternative use of green securitization including covered bonds. Presently, *green asset-backed securities* comprise a necessary share of *green bond* issuances, accounting for approximately 17% of the entire market. Since 2020, the COVID-19 pandemic including other financial shocks such as the Russia-Ukraine War and other geopolitical tensions caused a slowdown in growth momentum, but overall market growth for green ABS is anticipated to outperform in the long run.

Green Loans

The inevitably high minimum issuance amounts of *green bonds, climate bonds,* and *green asset-backed securities* are a major setback in raising sufficient funding for sustainable finance. In order to endure the significant need to fund a diverse form of environmental initiatives that call for smaller-scale investments, green lending in the form of green loans is growing. Therefore, green loans are those intended for environmentally responsible, sustainable goals like cutting CO2 emissions or for projects that further the green shift in society like creating new eco-friendly technologies. As compared with green bonds, green loans usually are small-scale investments that may provide a stable cash flow, with less transaction costs and generally are privately placed. Green loans follow different but consistent principles that are similar to the GBP and are known as *Green Loan Principles* (GLP). Both frameworks are specific that the loan proceeds must be applied to finance only "green projects".

Of the estimated $33 billion in outstanding green loans, just $1.6 billion are currently accounted for by the developing and emerging economies. However, emerging economies are showing keen interest and their demand is expanding at a rapid rate and is soon expected to surpass the growth of the green bond market. Nevertheless, the *green loans* market is still nascent in nature and throwing out assumptions on its performance evaluation will not be fair at present. The procedure for granting a *green loan* to any business entity is a cumbersome process and involves substantial screening, labelling, disclosure and control-related activities, which all summed up as additional operational costs. However, considering the substantial transaction costs associated with the issuance of bonds, the minimum tradeable bond size, and the fact that only a subset of bonds is tracked by different indices, emerging market issuers with small green portfolios might be more inclined to accept a green loan rather than issue a green bond.

Green Funds

With growing popularity and wider acceptance, the traditional funds industry has also embraced *green finance*. In recent years, fund managers have been able to innovate and develop various products and techniques to integrate sustainability issues into their investment appetite. This has led to the emergence of green funds as a focused investment avenue for investors looking to invest in sustainable growth or other branches of sustainable finance. As investors become more aware of the need to address climate change and promote sustainable development, *green funds* have grown in significance within the sustainable finance environment.

From its launch date, the green funds witnessed a continued surge in their demand that reflects a rising dedication to using responsible money to address environmental and social issues, while still delivering competitive financial returns. *Green funds* seek to support the global effort to mitigate climate change, conserve ecology and promote sustainability. In addition, these funds generate competitive financial returns as compared to their conventional funds. There exists a number of focused investment vehicles for companies engaged in environmentally friendly that promote sustainable businesses, such as renewable energy, green transport (EVs), water and waste management, and biodiversity conservation. In the year 2020 alone, a whopping amount of 50 billion USD was invested in green funds which accounts for more than double the inflows as compared with the previous year. Nonetheless, a report by Morningstar provides some evidence of the outperformance of green funds in returns when compared with traditional funds, but it is not conclusive.[7]

Green funds are further categorized into various forms catering to the diverse needs and preferences of ethical investors. For example, green mutual funds diversified portfolio consists of environmentally-friendly companies investing in clean energy, renewable resources, and sustainable agriculture. In a similar vein, *green exchange-traded funds* (ETFs) follow an underlying index comprised of environmentally friendly organizations or initiatives. They are considered an efficient investment avenue as investors can choose multiple sustainable investment schemes, with the added benefit of intraday liquidity. Furthermore, environmental, social, and governance (ESG) considerations are also taken into account during the investment selection process by socially responsible investing (SRI) funds, which are in high demand. SRI funds purged the investments in companies with an undesirable or low ESG score, such as tobacco or firearms, while favored the investment in companies exhibiting strong ESG practices. However, it is noteworthy to mention that ESG funds are heterogeneous from SRI funds. ESG funds rely on a more comprehensive approach to evaluate the investments, rather than just excluding specific sectors or industries.

One of the main benefits of green funds is that they can invest in debt and equity instruments simultaneously, giving their clients access to platforms that provide long-term finance for sustainable-oriented organizations. Using ESG strategies, investors added approximately 65 billion dollars to mutual funds and ETFs to invest in the US green funds in the past five years. Meanwhile, investors withdrew a total of $92.2 billion from all other U.S. stock funds. The growing demand for green funds among individual investors can be attributed to the simplicity and ease of purchasing or selling the quota of the funds.

Green Indices

In the modern financial market, indices enable investors to gauge the performance of investment portfolios, market securities, as well as actively managed funds relative to the market. Therefore, market indices are widely used by investors as a convenient, feasible, and affordable source of information while managing their investment portfolios and keeping track of the financial markets. In this respect, indices act as yardsticks or benchmark measures for the financial market to formulate investment strategies. In addition, a mutual fund or a portfolio may use a particular index as a benchmark.

In the last decade, *green indices* have become increasingly popular and flourished (particularly from 2014). Since then, a number of green stock indices have been formulated by the developed and emerging economies since indices serve as the main instrument for active investors and investment managers by serving as a benchmark or point of reference for their decisions. These green indices are generally inclined towards a specific sector (solar, water or other renewable source of energy), or any specific type of security focusing on sustainable finance (like green equity or fixed income), or they may be built to represent the wider green sector.[8] Thus far, a majority of the conventional index providers have developed green or sustainability-focused counterparts (Deshmukh et al., 2022).

Technology Driving Green Finance

A substantial amount of new investment will be required to implement the Paris Agreement and fulfil the Sustainable Development Goals (World Economic Forum, 2013; Migliorelli and Dessertine, 2019). To achieve the SDG frameworks, there exists a huge gap of 2 – 3 trillion USD annually in green investment or renewable energy (Fuessler et al., 2018; Nassiry, 2018). Due to the existence of this huge gap between the demand and supply of green investment and with limited public finance, private capital should strive to aggregate a significant proportion of green finance and have to be increasingly mobilized. Precisely, the involvement of the financial sector is the cornerstone to this challenge as it will assist in sustainable finance activities, and help in internalizing the financial risks related to climate change, ultimately leading to the mainstreaming of green finance.

The term "green finance" collectively represents the financial instruments and investments made by financial institutions with an aim to limit global carbon emissions. Apart from that, the finance industry also plays a crucial role in the identification, adaptation and mitigation of climate-change risk by funding green projects and initiatives. In order to effectively mitigate the fundamentals of climate risks in business activities and portfolios, the banking industry must integrate governance, strategies, and risk-management guidelines into its operations. On top of it, the banking industry is under constant pressure to facilitate their customers' transition to green finance through sustainable finance activities, but also to comprehend the emissions of their own or their borrowers' loans. Above all, there is an impetus that the bank's assets and profitability could be at risk if climate risk is not managed. Additionally, failure to provide funding for the transition to the green economy may cause havoc in the long run.

In order to better understand the effects of climate change on banks and their clients, climate physical and transition risks are being defined and measured. Failure to adopt and adapt can have detrimental effects on a bank's operations, including:

- A negative effect on the profitability of the banks owing to high regulatory costs, non-compliance will further deteriorate the operation resulting in penalties and fines, high sudden and mandatory technology-integration costs;
- A limited understanding of climate risks may pose a credit loss in the bank's credit portfolios;
- Insufficient liquidity as a result of decreased credit ratings due to failure to fulfil regulatory expectations and strategic goals;
- Adverse effects on capital adequacy as a result of the increase in the capital allocation requirements.

Regardless of these challenges, this section of the chapter aims to analyze the role of technology in driving the sustainable finance transition. The past few years have witnessed unprecedented developments in financial technology (FinTech) that have changed the landscape across multiple consumer financial functions. The advancement in digital technology has provided an opportunity to harness its potential to overcome the operational barriers and bottlenecks that might prevent green finance from scaling up, such as the limited access to reliable data, and the statistical complexity of modelling the non-linear behavior of climate change as a risk factor. Particularly, the innovations in *green finance* have the potential to lower overall investment and operating costs, improve our ability to achieve agreed-upon sustainability outcomes and contribute to global goals by reshaping the economy in favour of access to services like energy, poverty reduction, and economic activity.[9]

The role of Fintech in innovating and issuing new financial instruments will be crucial to reduce expenses and raise funds at the right pace and scale. Policymakers should be aware of green finance and fintech as they work to implement the Paris Agreement and reach the Sustainable Development Goals (SDGs), particularly in emerging economies. Several initiatives are already debated on how the fintech, blockchain and cryptocurrencies will mobilize green finance across the globe. These financial instruments are designed to promote sustainable development, reduce carbon emissions, and mitigate climate change. Blockchain technology and financial instruments like green bonds, green funds, green loans, etc., can speed up the flow of capital to a more sustainable economy and contribute to the achievement of global policy goals. The application of blockchain technology has replaced physical assets with more affordable and immutable digital assets like smart contracts. Moreover, the internet-of-things (IoT) unlock a new world of opportunity, where smart devices transmit their performance against the standard set of benchmarks, such as environmental impact.

These disruptive technologies help in coordinating all stakeholders on a single platform, thereby significantly decreasing the number of intermediaries required to oversee the lifecycle of green bonds. The platform provides quick and precise data on how green bond revenues are being used preventing any misuse of the funds. It also demonstrates to all parties involved that investments are actually bringing about improvements and are not just greenwashing. The financial institutions' efforts to leverage their expertise to help the developed and developing economies mobilize private capital to meet large financing gaps for sustainable development. For instance, one such program is Crowdfundres in Europe which promotes crowdfunding for renewable energy projects and offers policy recommendations regarding regulatory frameworks.[10] On a similar note, a French research project called Climatechain examines how blockchain technology might help implement the Paris Climate Agreement.[11] In an emerging economy like India, financial institutions have issued a greater amount of green bonds (21 billion dollars) than other emerging markets in Asia, excluding China. In 2018, the *European Commission* published two action plans simultaneously, i.e., the "Action Plan for Financing Sustainable Growth" (European Commission, 2018a) and the "Fintech Action Plan for a more competitive and innovative European financial sector" (European Commission, 2018b). Similarly, the Monetary Authority of Singapore published the Green Finance Action Plan in 2019, to make sustainable finance a defining feature of Singapore's role as an international financial centre, building resilience, developing markets, and leveraging technology.[12]

FinTech and Blockchain in Green Finance

Green finance is an essential component of achieving sustainable development and mitigating climate change, and technological innovation has played a crucial role in making it more accessible, affordable, and sustainable. We strongly argue that the fintech industry presents a significant chance to upend the financial system and mobilize green finance. Financial innovations such as crowdfunding, robo-advisors or blockchain witness a surge in their offerings for sustainable products and services. These products facilitate financial institutions to gain access to new sources of capital with a focus on *green finance*, particularly from retail investors. They are deemed cost-effective as they bypass the traditional method of financing supported by offering decentralized systems that help in the mobilization of funds and improve efficiency. The most popular and widely used fintech applications are distributed ledger technologies, commonly known as *blockchain*.

Distributed ledger technology, or DLT, is a shared database created by blockchain that enables continuous synchronization of user data recording and sharing over a dispersed network. These DLTs use usually immutable blockchains used for data transmission and storage (PwC, 2018). Blockchain technology enables the storage of financial transactions at multiple locations simultaneously, supporting ecosystem funding. A few of the DLTs are worth mentioning and are the anchors to existing innovations, namely, digital wallets, cryptocurrencies, decentralized finance (DeFi) and non-fungible tokens (NFT) that have gained momentum and play a vital role in the Fintech industry.

The application of blockchain technology proved to be a game-changer in green finance. Blockchain technology provides a secure, transparent, and decentralized platform for financial transactions. These characteristics of blockchain technology make it a potential application that can revolutionize the traditional experience of financial transactions, making it more efficient and cost-effective. The use of blockchain technology has made it easier for investors to invest in green projects and for green projects to access financing. Apart from sustainable or green finance, fintech and blockchain have additional potential applications in other sectors, such as green and clean energy, climate finance and carbon credit trading. Moreover, the applications have also gained worldwide attention from the financial industry, due to the ability of the blockchain in enhancing the efficiency of settlement and other intermediate functions.

After a thorough review of the literature, we summarize a few key characteristics of blockchain that provide the framework for enabling the mobilization of green finance and overcoming relevant barriers.

- ***Enhanced security***: Blockchain helps to counter fraud or any unauthorized activity by creating a record that can't be altered owing to end-to-end encryption. Blockchain technology assists users in restricting access by denying permission or anonymizing personal data, addressing privacy concerns. Rather than relying on a single server, the information is stored on a network of computers making it onerous to access it.
- ***Transparency:*** As mentioned earlier, blockchain uses a distributed ledger, transactions and data are recorded identically in multiple locations. Full transparency is ensured because all network users with authorized access view the same data simultaneously. Every transaction is permanently recorded, giving members access to the whole transaction history and essentially removing any chance of fraud.
- ***Immutability:*** Due to the date and time stamp of each transaction stored in various blocks, it is enabled to detect any changes in the data by the network. Immutable data are highly resistant to cyberattacks and system failures.

Even if one node in the network is compromised, the data on other nodes remains intact, ensuring the continued availability of information. In the realm of digital assets, such as intellectual property and digital currencies, an immutable ledger can establish and verify ownership, reducing disputes and ensuring fair compensation.

- ***Tokenization:*** One major advantage of blockchain is that it enables the marketing and distribution of green finance into smaller portions in a digital form that can be converted into tokens and distributed in a peer-to-peer (P2P) transaction system. The automation of the process further increases the efficiency and speed of the process. The transaction or process is triggered automatically when pre-established criteria are satisfied. Smart contracts allow investors to bypass market intermediaries typically involved in the traditional asset management process. This effectively reduces the transaction costs and processing time of each exchange, allowing for a more streamlined, cost-efficient method of transferring value. With the help of blockchain, it is possible to tokenize things like carbon emissions or other natural resources, making it easy to trade for other cryptocurrencies or actual money in exchange for cryptocurrency.

The advancements in digital financial services and uprising digital currencies have made it easier for people to access financing for green projects, promoting sustainable development, economic growth, and social development. However, the applicability and implementation of blockchain technology is a cumbersome process and poses some crucial challenges to green finance, such as excessive consumption of electricity, technological limitations (interoperability, scalability), usability (suitable for mainstream application) and legal and regulatory frameworks.[13]

Challenges Faced by Green Finance Investors

A majority of investors are inclined towards green finance; however, it is hard to leave aside the thorny issues of different shades of green. Even after a decade of its launch, complicated definitions of green finance still exist. It is still defined by the use to which it is directed, not by the investors; nor the financial technology involved. Apart from the definition, there are various other challenges faced by green finance investors that include underperformance of green stocks/funds, higher fees and high minimum investment requirements that prevent investors with small capital from participating in certain of these financial assets. Moreover, emerging economies tend to have a greater reliance on fossil fuels than developed nations. Almost 90 per cent of energy production and consumption in emerging economies comes from coal, oil, and natural gas, which makes it more difficult, further complicating the transition to low-carbon energy sources.

In developed economies, taxonomies and disclosures have proliferated in a short span, but the experience has highlighted their drawbacks. For example, a majority of the products that are labelled as "green" or "sustainable" by their issuers, or by ESG advisers, without any external assessment of compliance, or any link to how the product might be helping to achieve sustainability or climate goals. Consequently, the rating agencies often assign different ratings to the same company at a particular time due to discrepant and rigour in defining and applying these criteria, as well as extensive evidence of "greenwashing" risk, which undermines the credibility of these classifications. Since the government and/or environmental organizations must make sure that the investments are being channeled to the correct purpose, green investment vehicles require a variety of certifications and oversight. Although the goal of certifications is to raise the value and calibre of transactions, the high expense of certification may present another obstacle for green finance investors looking to hold onto some of these assets. Notably, achieving a well-diversified green investment portfolio can be challenging, given the limited number of green assets available.

In order to fully realize the benefits of FinTech, blockchain, and other digital technologies in the context of green finance, governments, the financial industry, businesses, and the technology sector must collaborate internationally to establish the necessary regulatory and legal frameworks, as well as consistent definitions and standards. Moreover, it is imperative to continuously promote technical innovation and advancement. The future course of action will be to accelerate the dialogue at the highest level by organizing climate conferences, formulating regulations and frameworks, and initiating a narrative around sustainable finance.

REFERENCES

Akhtar, S., Alam, M., & Ansari, M. S. (2022). Measuring the performance of the Indian banking industry: Data envelopment window analysis approach. *Benchmarking*, *29*(9), 2842–2857. doi:10.1108/BIJ-03-2021-0115

Deshmukh, P., Sharma, D., & Sharma, P. (2022). Do Socially Responsible Indices Outperform the Market During Black Swan Events: Evidence from Indian Markets During Global Financial and COVID-19 Crises. *Australasian Accounting. Business and Finance Journal*, *16*(5), 19–37.

European Commission. (2018a). *Action plan: Financing sustainable growth.* EC. https://eur-lex.europa.eu/legal-content/EN/TXT/PDF/?uri=CELEX:52018DC0097&from=EN

Fuessler, J., León, F., & Mock, R. (2018). *Navigating blockchain and climate action.* Gold Standard. https://www.goldstandard.org/sites/default/files/documents/cli_report_dec18.pdf

Höhne, N., Khosla, S., Fekete, H., & Gilbert, A. (2012). *Mapping of green finance delivered by IDFC members in 2011.* Ecofys.

IFC. (2013). *Mobilizing Public and Private Funds for Inclusive Green Growth Investment in Developing Countries - An Expanded Stocktaking Report Prepared for the G20 Development Working Group.* IFC Climate Business Department.

International Finance Corporation (IFC). (2017). *Green finance. A bottom-up approach to track existing flows.* IFC.

Khan, M. A., Riaz, H., Ahmed, M., & Saeed, A. (2022). Does green finance really deliver what is expected? An empirical perspective. *Borsa Istanbul Review, 22*(3), 586–593. doi:10.1016/j.bir.2021.07.006

Lehner, O. M., Harrer, T., Silvola, H., & Weber, O. (Eds.). (2023). *The Routledge Handbook of Green Finance.* Taylor & Francis. doi:10.4324/9781003345497

Migliorelli, M., & Dessertine, P. (2019). The rise of green finance in Europe. *Opportunities and challenges for issuers, investors and marketplaces. Cham. Palgrave Macmillan, 2*, 2019.

Nassiry, D. (2018). *The role of fintech in unlocking green finance: Policy insights for developing countries* (No. 883). ADBI working paper.

PwC. (2018). *Building block(chain)s for a better planet.* PxC. https://www.pwc.com/gx/en/sustainability/assets/blockchain-for-a-betterplanet.pdf

Spratt and Griffith-Jones. (2013). *Mobilising Investment for Inclusive Green Growth in Low-Income Countries.* Federal Ministry for Economic Cooperation and Development, GIZ. https://stephanygj.net/papers/MobilisingInvestmentforInclusiveGreenGrowth2013.pdf

Thompson, S. (2021). *Green and sustainable finance: Principles and practice* (Vol. 6). Kogan Page Publishers.

UNEP. (2021). *Making Peace with Nature [R].* United Nations Environment Programme. https://wedocs.unep.org/handle/20.500.11822/34807

United Nations Environment Programme (UNEP). (2016, September). *Definitions and concepts. Background note.* Inquiry working paper 16/13.

World Economic Forum. (2013). *The Green Investment Report.* World Economic Forum. https://reports.weforum.org/green-investing-2013/

Zhao, Y., Yue, Y., & Wei, P. (2021). Financing advantage of green corporate asset-backed securities and its impact factors: Evidence in China. *Frontiers in Energy Research*, *9*, 696110. doi:10.3389/fenrg.2021.696110

ENDNOTES

1 https://climate.nasa.gov/effects/

2 https://www.oecd-ilibrary.org/environment/green-finance-and-investment_24090344. ISSN: 24090344 (online) https://doi.org/10.1787/24090344

3 https://www.climatebonds.net/market/explaining-green-bonds

4 ICMA Group, (June 2021). *Green Bond Principles: Voluntary Process Guidelines for Issuing Green Bonds.* Link

5 Any violation of a green asset warranty would only have the same consequences as an originator's regular repurchase obligations, and the continuous reporting would be the same as it would be for a typical securitization transaction.

6 In order to ensure that, in the event that a green portfolio is refinanced, the new securitization transaction may still qualify as a green securitization, it is essential to consider the point that whether the appropriate green bond criteria and/or taxonomy requirements against which a portfolio is tested should be those that applied on the date the relevant receivable was originated.

7 Morningstar. "Do Sustainable Funds Beat Their Rivals?"

8 A few examples of the green indices are S&P green bond index, Nasdaq OMX Solar, Zacks Global Water Index, etc. In Japan, indexes with an environmental theme are popular. In the USA, people are interested in technology and social factors (like community investing), whereas in Europe, people are typically interested in all forms of responsible investing.

9 The Sustainable Development Goals encompass 17 global goals.

10 http://www.crowdfundres.eu/index.html

11 https://theclimatechain.org/

12 https://www.greenfinanceplatform.org/policies-and-regulations/singapores-green-finance-action-plan

13 For Bitcoin alone, more than 100 TWh per year is now consumed, which is equivalent to the annual electricity consumption of the Netherlands.

Chapter 2
Foundations of Blockchain and Digital Twins

Ravi Prakash B.
Presidency University, India

Mohamadi Begum Y.
Presidency University, India

ABSTRACT

The rapid evolution of transformative technologies, including blockchain and digital twins, is reshaping numerous industries. Blockchain, recognized for its distributed ledger capabilities, is gaining widespread acceptance owing to its secure and transparent data management features. Simultaneously, digital twins, virtual replicas of physical assets, are proving instrumental in offering real-time insights and enabling remote monitoring and control. This chapter explores the convergence of these two technologies, emphasizing their potential in the real world. Commencing with an overview of blockchain and digital twins, the chapter proceeds to scrutinize their architecture and consensus mechanisms. Subsequently, it delves into the concept of digital twins and their versatile applications across various sectors. Finally, it articulates the advantages derived from the integration of blockchain and digital twins.

INTRODUCTION

Blockchain is a decentralised, revolutionary system that has become a mainstay of innovation, especially in the fields of information management and digital finance. A blockchain is fundamentally a distributed ledger that securely, openly, and impenetrably records transactions across a network of computers. Blockchain

DOI: 10.4018/979-8-3693-1878-2.ch002

functions on a peer-to-peer network, enabling users to exchange and verify data without the need for middlemen, in contrast to conventional centralised databases, which are controlled by a single party. The term "blockchain" describes the structure of data, which is composed of information arranged into blocks that are connected to one another by a cryptographic hash to create an unchangeable chain.

In the rapidly evolving landscape of technology, Blockchain and Digital Twins have emerged as transformative forces, revolutionizing industries and reshaping the way we perceive and interact with data. Individually, these technologies offer unique capabilities, but their convergence holds the promise of unlocking unprecedented potential in various domains. This paper explores the fundamental concepts of Blockchain technology and Digital Twins, delves into their individual merits, and investigates the synergies that arise when combining these two innovative technologies.

Blockchain Technology: Foundations and Principles

In the beginning intended to serve as the foundation for digital currencies like Bitcoin (Nakamoto, 2008), blockchain technology has outlived its original purpose and found application in a variety of sectors. A blockchain is essentially a distributed, decentralised ledger that securely records transactions with immutability and transparency. The core principles that underpin blockchain are decentralisation, immutability, transparency, and consensus processes. Because of its evolution, technology has been able to serve purposes beyond its initial ones, proving its importance and adaptability across a wide range of industries.

Decentralisation improves security and resilience by guaranteeing that no one entity has control over the entire network. Immutability ensures that data entered onto the blockchain cannot be removed or changed, giving rise to a reliable and auditable history of transactions. Trust among stakeholders is promoted via transparency, which enables all network users to see and validate transactions. Participants can agree on the current state of the blockchain thanks to consensus mechanisms like Proof of Work (PoW) and Proof of Stake (PoS) (King & Nadal,2012).

The applications of blockchain extend beyond finance to supply chain management, healthcare, real estate, and more. Its potential to streamline processes, reduce fraud, and increase transparency has garnered widespread interest and adoption.

Digital Twins: Bridging the Physical and Digital Realms

Digital Twins represent a paradigm shift in how we model, monitor, and interact with physical entities. A Digital Twin is a virtual representation of a real-world object, system, or process that enables real-time monitoring, analysis, and optimization. This technology integrates data from various sources, including sensors, IoT devices, and simulations, to create a dynamic and interactive digital counterpart (Jones et al.).

The concept of Digital Twins is applied across diverse domains, from manufacturing and healthcare to smart cities and infrastructure. In manufacturing, for example, a Digital Twin of a product or production line allows for predictive maintenance, performance optimization, and rapid prototyping. (Liu et al.) In healthcare, patient-specific Digital Twins enable personalized treatment plans and simulations for surgical procedures.

The key benefits of Digital Twins include enhanced decision-making, improved operational efficiency, and the ability to simulate and predict outcomes in a risk-free virtual environment. As the Internet of Things (IoT) continues to grow, Digital Twins are becoming increasingly integral to harnessing the power of connected devices and data (Qi et al., 2021).

Moreover, the collaborative potential of Blockchain and Digital Twins extends to supply chain optimization. The transparency offered by blockchain enables an unbroken chain of custody, allowing stakeholders to trace the journey of products from manufacturing to delivery. When coupled with Digital Twins, this transparency evolves into a dynamic representation of the entire supply chain, fostering efficient resource allocation and reducing operational inefficiencies (Semeraro et al., 2021).

BACKGROUND

Overview of Blockchain Technology

Information can be stored and shared peer-to-peer (P2P) using blockchain technology. Consensus mechanisms allow blockchain data to be accessed, distributed, and secured. Blockchain works in a decentralized manner resulting in the elimination of third-party. Moreover, blockchain combines "Block" and "chain". Block is the building block to construct the chain. In Figure 1, the diagram shows the architecture of a Block. Generally, Block consists of two parts, i.e., Block header and Block data. Block comprises the following components, as shown in Figure 1. However, specific types may vary.

Normal block headers are 80 bytes long and contain a timestamp (4 bytes), which indicates the precise time the block was mined and confirmed. The difficulty index (4 bytes) measures how challenging mining a block is, or how challenging it is to obtain the necessary hash, Version (4byte) indicates the version of the blockchain's architecture. The block's dimensions, the block's hash, which is generated using a single (4-byte) node and is unique for each block, the prior hash (32 bytes) is the hash of the previous block, and the Merkle root (32 bytes) represents a tree that combines all of the hashes for a single transaction. Along with a block header, a block also includes Block data, which is a list of transactions, and the transaction counter, which indicates how many transactions are in the block. To put it more simply, the block header and block data both contribute to the security, immutability, and integrity of the blockchain. The block data comprises the data that is stored on the blockchain and permanently stored, whereas the block header is used to link the blocks and preserve the chain's integrity. Blockchain real applicability is constrained due to slow transaction speeds, block size constraints, and chain size difficulties.

Figure 1. Block diagram of a block

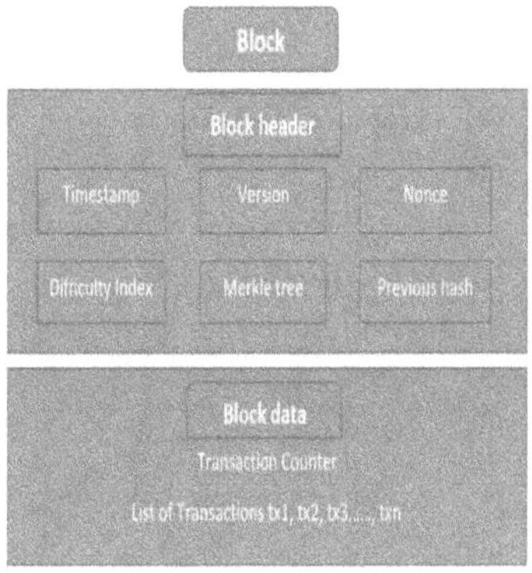

Figure 2. Flow of blockchain mechanism
(Monrat et al,. 2019)

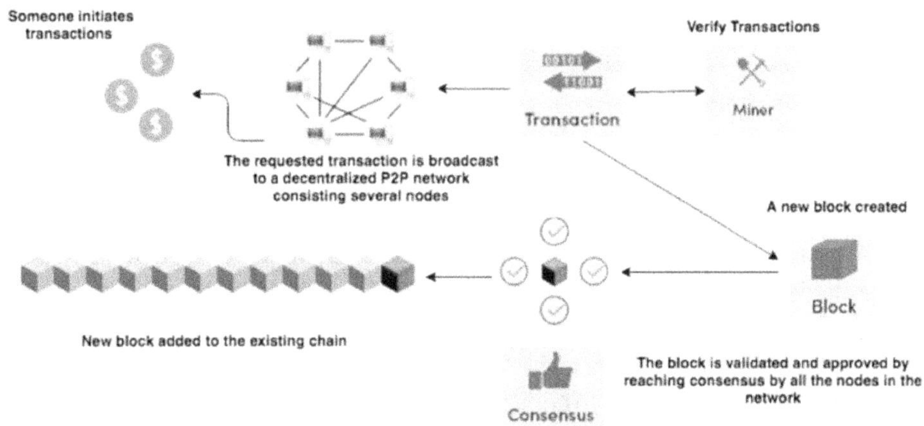

1. **Blocks**: Data is stored in blocks, which contain information like timestamps, transaction details, and unique cryptographic identifiers.
2. **Chain:** These blocks are linked together in a chronological chain, forming an immutable record of all past transactions.
3. **Decentralization:** Unlike traditional databases with central control, blockchains operate on a decentralized network. This means no single entity controls the data, making it resistant to manipulation and censorship.
4. **Consensus Mechanism:** To ensure the validity and consistency of data, a consensus mechanism like Proof of Work or Proof of Stake is used. This process involves verifying new blocks and adding them to the chain.
5. **Cryptography:** Strong cryptography ensures the integrity and security of the data stored on the blockchain.

Architecture: Layers of Blockchain

Figure 3. Layers of blockchain technology

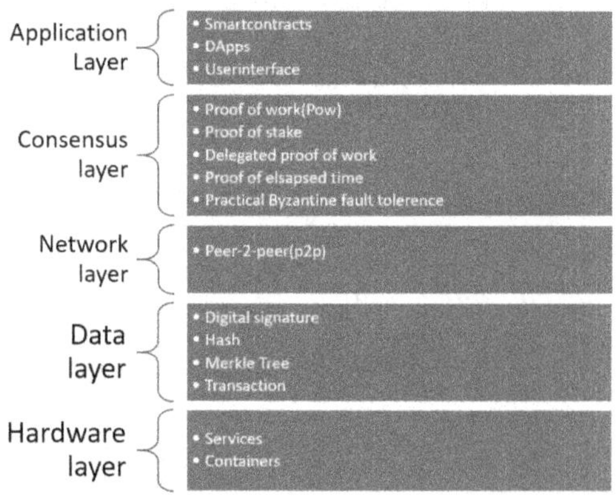

Application Layer

The Application layer is the first layer of the architecture which provides a bridge between the end-users and the blockchain network, Permanence of data, decentralization, Transparency between the nodes and users, flexibility to sustain against adversarial attacks this is the following prime functionalities of blockchain, so this layer helps developers to code and develop applications out of it for the users to meet the above functionalities.

- **Application layer**: - This sub-layer maintains and supports frameworks, API scripts, and blockchain network works as the back-end system
- **Execution layer:** - It constitutes Smart contracts, DApps, User Interface etc. This layer is responsible for underlying rules and code execution.
    - ***Smart contracts***: - Smart contracts are automated executing computer programs with a certain number of lines of code to perform proper events and actions according to the need of an agreement (Zheng et al., 2020). In 1994 Nick Szabo an American computer scientist proposed smart contracts, Earlier Digital cash protocols were using smart contracts for confidentiality, divisibility, and unforgeability (Szabo, N.). Smart contracts execute very well with decentralized networks by permitting transactions and agreements between unknown users in the blockchain network. Smart contracts are programs that are similar to any other object-oriented programs including data types, functions, events, and storage to store data. Later in 2013 Ethereum introduced smart contract in its blockchain and Hyper ledger fabric a permissioned blockchain platform also uses smart contracts, however, smart contracts are still facing security, performance, and Integrity issues (Mohammed et al., 2021).
    - ***Decentralized Applications (DApps):*** - Decentralized Apps are the applications that operate on the decentralized network through Smart contracts. Decentralized applications should be open-source and should work independently without any interference of a third party to control its tokens, and the data and records of its functions should be stored in public with cryptographic techniques. A decentralized application is responsible for generating tokens using standard algorithms or a set of standards. Those tokens are mandatory to make use of any decentralized applications. Users should be compensated in the application's tokens for whatever contributions they make.
    - ***User Interface: -*** In blockchain architecture, the user interface (UI) serves as the gateway for users to interact with decentralized applications and smart contracts. It provides a graphical or command-line interface, enabling users to initiate transactions, view blockchain data, and manage digital assets seamlessly within the decentralized and secure blockchain environment.

Consensus Layer

This layer is responsible for consensus protocols. The consensus protocol is a fault-tolerance mechanism to achieve the necessary agreement between all the distributed nodes in the blockchain. The consensus layer is the heart of any blockchain network because the consensus protocols are in charge of validating the blocks in the chain, ordering them, and ensuring everyone agree on them. There are various mechanisms available to build blockchain.

- **Proof of work**: - Proof of work was first presented as a way to raise the cost of email, making spamming less profitable. Spam is cheap to distribute, so it's important to limit undesired Spam. As a result, set up certain ideas in which the email sender is obliged to pay a fee, conduct resource-intensive computations, or post a bond for each message sent. It's important to keep in mind that the amount of time required for a price function or a Cost function in a Pow mechanism can vary dramatically between computers. When Satoshi Nakamoto introduced Bitcoin in 2009, he used Pow as Consensus to create a distributed timestamp server that worked on a peer-to-peer basis. POW in Bitcoin works by increasing nonce in the block until a value is found that gives the hash of the block the requisite zero bits. The Nakamoto Consensus system, which is the core of bitcoin, is responsible for keeping the public ledger's transaction history. It's known as Bitcoin. Bitcoin transactions are safely and chronologically recorded on the blockchain (Nakamoto, 2008).

Nodes, also known as "miners" in the case of Bitcoin, compete to solve challenging arithmetic puzzles in order to add new blocks to the blockchain and receive bitcoins as a reward. The likelihood of a node generating a new block is proportional to its CPU power, hence the higher the CPU power, the more likely the node will be rewarded for creating blocks. Only if the attacker has control of more than 51 percent of the CPU power on the Bitcoin network would the attack be effective. It is expensive to produce proof of work data. The daily costs, which include electricity and hardware, are projected to be in excess of one million dollars.

- **Proof of stake**: - Sunny King and Scott Nadal designed Pos, which was initially implemented in peer Coin in 2012 (King & Nadal,2012). Coin owners control the network, produce new blocks, and keep the chain secure. In peer Coin, block producers are referred to as ministers rather than miners. The protocol of peer coin uses a concept called coinage to choose the miner who will produce the next block. A miner's coinage is calculated by multiplying the number of coins he or she owns by the number of days those coins have been in their wallet. For example, a miner with a high Coinage has a large number of Coins in their wallet, and those Coins have been sitting in that wallet for quite some time.

Time-Based Rules and Restrictions

Miners are first required to hold coins in their wallets for a total of 30 days before they Can become eligible to compete in the process of mining new blocks. Blockchain is well known for 51% attacks If one or more nodes take Control of 51% of CPU power, they may success perform malicious attacks.

- **Practical byzantine fault tolerance**: - Barbara Lisker and Miguel Castro created the PBFT (Castro & Liskov, 2002). PBFT is a Special Case and Byzantine Fault Tolerance Network Capability Optimization. Byzantine fault tolerance refers to a network's capacity to reach an unambiguous consensus despite malicious nodes attempting to spread misleading data to other peers. To achieve Byzantine Fault Tolerance, PBFT takes a Byzantine Stake Machine method to the network, which involves replicating servers and synchronizing client activities with server copies. PBFT provides fault tolerance while allowing the network to handle thousands of transactions per second with minimal overhead. PBFT was one of the first publications on byzantine faults and solving consensus. One of PBFT's major advantages is its ability to enhance transaction speed in a blockchain network. This is due to PBFT's ability to process transactions concurrently, which enables various nodes to execute several transactions at once. This makes the network more scalable and speeds up transaction times. The PBFT algorithm handles less than 1/3 of byzantine faults. Byzantine general problem gave birth to the concept of Byzantine fault tolerance PBFT
- **Proof of Elapsed time**: - PoET addresses the scalability issue by utilising trusted execution environments (TEEs), which include Intel's Software Guard Extensions (SGX), or other comparable technologies. These TEEs offer a safe and unbreakable environment for code execution ((PoET).,2022). In PoET, each participant asks a trusted authority inside a TEE for a random wait time. The person who has to wait the fewest seconds can suggest the following block. The efficient use of resources is what makes PoET special. PoET does not compel participants to make inefficient calculations, in contrast to PoW. Instead, they can save energy by merely waiting for their randomly allotted wait period to pass. PoET is now a more sustainable consensus algorithm as a result. The PoET algorithm is protected and resilient to numerous assaults. It is predicated that TEEs are safe and that the trusted authority produces wait times in a fair and impartial manner. The wait time lottery ensures a fair selection procedure because participants cannot influence or predict the results. PoET has some intriguing scalability-related characteristics, but it also has certain drawbacks. A key point of trust in the system is established

by the reliance on TEEs. The consensus algorithm's security is in danger if the TEEs or the trusted authority are compromised. The algorithm might also favour users of faster hardware or who have easier access to TEEs, which might perhaps lead to centralization.

- **DPOS**: - Delegated proof of stake is similar to the proof of stake (PoS). However, it includes a vote and delegation mechanism to motivate users to secure the network with their staked collateral (Yang et al., 2019). Participants must stake their coins to participate in the PoS and DPoS consensus mechanism. On the other hand, successful block creation necessitates the election of witnesses or delegates by network users, and only the delegates and voters who are elected can validate transactions. Elected delegates are called "block producers" or "witnesses." You can vote on delegates using a delegated proof of stake by collecting all of your coins into a centralized staking pool and then tying those coins to a specific delegate

Network Layer

The network layer is also known as the propagation layer well known for peer-peer communication, which allows Internode communication. Which helps to propagate, Synchronize, locate and communicate with each other. According to the state of the network when a node proposes a legitimate block to the chain, it is immediately broadcast to the whole network along with the transactions, which is associated with the block to broadcast for validations this process is called transaction/block propagation. Generally, there are two types of nodes available in the blockchain – Full node and Lightweight node.

Full node downloads and stores the entire copy of the blockchain, this node is responsible for validation and verification of transactions/blocks. These nodes vote on proposals of any new node in the chain. Lightweight nodes maintain trust in the network and these nodes don't download the entire copy of the blockchain this node only stores the header information of the blocks, this node downloads all transactions and histories to make sure that all the participants follow the consensus standards.

Data Layer

This layer is also known as the logical layer. Since blockchain is a massive, distributed database and all the blocks are arranged in the peer-peer network. Transactions after approaching the execution layer with the set of instructions are get validated for the double-spend attack, authorization of the transactions in this layer (Begum et al.,2020). Functionalities like Data structures, Digital Signature, Hash (Di Pierro,

M. 2017), Merkle tree (Sheth & Dattani, 2019), Transactions processes under the Data layer.

- **Data Structures**: - Data structures are the idea behind any blockchain development, for arranging the blocks in the order it uses linked list design by storing previous hash value, pointers to point the next block in the chain and the Merkle tree is designed in the tree fashion.
- **Digital Signatures**: - A digital signature in blockchain architecture is a cryptographic technique that ensures the authenticity and integrity of data. It involves a private key to sign transactions or messages, and a corresponding public key to verify the signature. This decentralized verification process enhances security, as each participant possesses a unique key pair. When a user signs a transaction, others can verify its legitimacy using the public key, preventing tampering or fraud. Digital signatures play a crucial role in establishing trust, transparency, and immutability within the blockchain network, reinforcing the integrity of transactions and data across a distributed and decentralized ledger.
- **Hash**: - Hash functions are the Mathematical function that takes the arbitrary length of data to convert that into fixed-length numerical data, Input can be any length but the output will be in a fixed size, the core functionality of hashing is, it will not be reverse-engineered. SHA-256, SHA-512, Keechak-256.
- **Merkle Tree (Hash tree):** - Merkle tree is a tree-based data structure, which helps data to store efficiently and securely and helps in the verification of a large number of hashes in one go. Instead of storing hashes of all the transactions of a block, the Merkle tree compresses them into a single hash known as Merkle root. Merkle tree is present in the Block header. In terms of scalability, rather than downloading the complete chain for transaction verification using Merkle root, merely downloading the block header, the block can be easily verified.

Hardware and Infrastructure Layer

The blockchain's content is securely stored on a server situated within a data center on our magnificent planet. While navigating the internet or utilizing applications, clients typically request data from application servers in a conventional client-server architecture. However, in contemporary settings, clients can engage with peer clients, facilitating data sharing. This expansive network of computers exchanging data is known as a Peer-to-Peer (P2P) network. The blockchain, in essence, operates as a P2P network where computers collaborate to compute, validate, and orderly store transactions in a shared ledger.

Consequently, this creates a distributed database that comprehensively records all relevant information, transactions, and data. Each computer within this P2P network is commonly referred to as a node, bearing the responsibility of transaction validation, block organization, and dissemination across the blockchain network. Upon achieving consensus, nodes finalize the block commitment to the blockchain network, subsequently updating their local ledger copy. This layer encompasses virtualization, involving the creation of virtual resources like storage, network, and servers. Notably, nodes constitute the core of this layer, and when a device connects to a blockchain network, it assumes the designation of a node. In a blockchain network, these nodes are both decentralized and distributed. Prominent examples of Infrastructure layers include Ethereum, Hyperledger Fabric, and Solana.

FOUNDATIONS OF BLOCKCHAIN TECHNOLOGY

Here are the key foundations of blockchain:

Decentralization and Distributed ledger

Traditional systems often have a central authority (like a bank) that manages and validates transactions. In contrast, blockchain operates on a decentralized network of nodes (computers) that collectively validate and record transactions. This decentralization reduces the risk of a single point of failure and enhances security.

Blockchain uses a distributed ledger to record transactions across a network of computers. Each participant in the network has a copy of the entire ledger, and any changes must be approved by a consensus mechanism agreed upon by the participants.

Cryptographic Hash Functions

Blockchain uses cryptographic hash functions to secure data. Each block contains a hash of the previous block, creating a chain. This linking of blocks makes it difficult for any participant to alter past transactions without altering subsequent blocks, ensuring the integrity of the entire chain.

Once a block is added to the blockchain, it is nearly impossible to alter or delete the information contained within it. Immutability is achieved through the use of cryptographic hashes and consensus mechanisms, providing a high level of security and trust in the data recorded on the blockchain.

Smart Contracts

Smart contracts serve as the cornerstone of blockchain technology by automating and enforcing contractual agreements. These self-executing contracts run on decentralized networks, ensuring transparency, security, and trust among parties. Programmed with predefined rules and conditions, smart contracts automatically execute actions when conditions are met, eliminating the need for intermediaries. This decentralized, tamper-resistant nature enhances efficiency, reduces costs, and establishes a reliable foundation for various applications, including finance, supply chain, and decentralized autonomous organizations (DAOs). Smart contracts epitomize the transformative power of blockchain, enabling a decentralized and secure framework for digital interactions without reliance on traditional intermediaries.

Transparency

Transparency is the cornerstone of Blockchain technology, ensuring trust and accountability. Decentralized ledgers store immutable records of transactions visible to all network participants, fostering openness. Cryptographic algorithms secure data, preventing tampering. Every participant can independently verify and validate the entire transaction history, promoting a consensus-driven system. Transparent smart contracts automate and enforce agreements, reducing reliance on intermediaries. This transparency not only enhances security but also instills confidence in users, establishing Blockchain as a revolutionary technology with decentralized, auditable, and trustworthy foundations.

Permissioned vs. Permission-less Blockchains

Permissioned blockchains require users to have explicit access, controlled by a central authority, ensuring privacy and governance. They are ideal for business applications where trust is predefined. On the other hand, permissionless blockchains, like Bitcoin and Ethereum, operate in a decentralized and open environment, allowing anyone to participate without approval. Permissionless blockchains use consensus algorithms to validate transactions, fostering trust through transparency and immutability. While permissioned blockchains provide control, permissionless ones offer decentralization, both serving as foundations for blockchain technology, catering to different use cases and emphasizing either centralization for efficiency or decentralization for trust and transparency.

INTRODUCTION TO DIGITAL TWIN

A digital twin is a virtual representation of a physical object, system, or process that mirrors its real-world counterpart in a digital environment. This concept involves creating a detailed and dynamic digital model that reflects the physical entity's characteristics, behaviour, and interactions (Deren et al., 2021). Digital twins are used across various industries, such as manufacturing, healthcare, and urban planning, to optimize performance, monitor status, and facilitate decision-making.

Digital twins are virtual replicas of physical assets or systems, allowing for real-time monitoring, analysis, and optimization. The technology stack behind them involves several key components working together:

Data Acquisition

1. **Sensors**: Collect real-time data from the physical asset, such as temperature, pressure, or location.
2. **IoT Gateways**: Aggregate and pre-process sensor data before transmitting it to the cloud.
3. **Cloud Storage:** Securely store and manage vast amounts of sensor data for future analysis.

Data Processing and Analytics

1. **Data Pipelines:** Move and process data from sensors to cloud storage for further analysis.
2. **Data Management Platforms:** Organize and structure the data for efficient analytics and visualization.
3. **Analytics Tools:** Extract valuable insights from the data, such as identifying trends, anomalies, and potential problems.

Digital Twin Modeling

1. **Modeling Software:** Create a virtual representation of the physical asset, incorporating sensor data and physical modeling principles.
2. **3D Design Tools:** Visually represent the digital twin in a realistic and interactive manner.
3. **Middleware:** Connect the digital twin to the physical asset through real-time data exchange.

Visualization and Interaction

1. **Visualization Tools**: Present the digital twin and its data in an intuitive and user-friendly interface.
2. **Dashboards:** Monitor the state of the physical asset in real-time and identify potential issues.
3. **AR/VR Integration**: Enhance the user experience by interacting with the digital twin in a virtual environment.

Simulation and Optimization

1. **Simulation Engine:** Run simulations to predict the behavior of the physical asset under different conditions.
2. **Machine Learning:** Train algorithms to learn from data and make predictions about the future state of the asset.
3. **Optimization Tools:** Recommend actions to improve the performance and efficiency of the physical asset.

Integration and Management

1. **Integration Platform as a Service (iPaaS):** Connect various technologies and platforms within the digital twin ecosystem.
2. **API Management**: Control access to data and functionalities within the digital twin environment.
3. **Digital Twin Management Platform**: Orchestrate and manage the entire digital twin lifecycle, from development to deployment.

Step-by-Step Process of Digital Twin

1. **Data Acquisition**: Sensors gather data from the physical object and transmit it to the digital platform.
2. **Data Integration**: The platform ingests and harmonizes data from various sources, creating a unified view of the object's state.
3. **Model Creation**: A 3D model of the object is built, incorporating its physical and operational characteristics.
4. **Data Mapping**: Real-time data from sensors is mapped onto the 3D model, updating its state and allowing for real-time monitoring.
5. **Simulation & Prediction**: AI and machine learning algorithms are used to analyze the data and predict future behaviour, enabling proactive decision-making.

6. **Visualization & Optimization**: Users can interact with the digital twin in 3D, gaining insights into its performance and identifying potential issues or optimization opportunities.

APPLICATIONS OF DIGITAL TWIN IN REAL-WORLD

Digital Twins find applications across diverse industries, transforming the way entities manage, analyze, and improve their processes. The versatility of this technology has led to its adoption in various sectors.

Smart Cities

Due to their ability to provide a virtual depiction of urban infrastructure and services, digital twins are essential to the development of smart cities. They are able to model and optimise a number of different things, including waste management, energy usage, traffic flow, and infrastructure development. Urban planners can improve their standard of life for citizens by using data to inform their decisions by building a virtual version of the city. Real-time data from sensors embedded in various city components contribute to more accurate simulations. This leads to improved decision-making for urban development, resource allocation, and emergency response.

Another digital twin-based smart city application is the Smart City Traffic Brain. Every day, mobile phones, surveillance camera footage, cabs, indoor positioning systems, buses, subways, and mobile apps create hundreds of millions of large data on travel trajectories in cities (Deren et al., 2021). The Wuhan Road Traffic Smart Emergency System uses technologies including data mining, time-space analysis, and holographic perception. It developed an algorithm for evaluating the congestion index that incorporates traffic, vehicle speed, historical congestion data, and other information to achieve a number of goals, including (a) precise assessment of the amount of traffic on the roads, (b) real-time ranking of traffic on the roads, and (c) comparative analysis of historical and current traffic. Additional features offered by the system include real-time scheduling and navigation, video verification, big event security, and congestion event replay (A. El Saddik, 2018).

Health Care

By analysing the real twin's past medical history and the current context, which includes location, time, and activity, digital twins could provide insight into what is going on within their real twin's body and facilitate the prediction of sickness.

In an area of healthcare, digital twins are used to enhance, analyse, and provide forecasts for hospitals, patients, and the pharmaceutical sector. This Technology produces incredibly effective outcomes for machinery and processes (T.Erol et al., 2020). The process of creating the digital twin of the human body is more sophisticated and involved than that of engineering things. Although sensors can effectively feed data to the Digital Twin of the intended object, they can also be costlier and time-consuming because patient data is typically collected via imaging systems, blood tests, and health scans.

The Blue Brain Project leverages digital twin technology to replicate and simulate the intricate structure and function of the human brain in a virtual environment. This ambitious initiative aims to decode the brain's complexities, fostering a deeper understanding of its mechanisms (Bariev, E. Y. 2017). By employing digital twin models, researchers can simulate various scenarios and study the brain's responses, advancing our knowledge of neurobiology and potentially leading to breakthroughs in neuroscience, brain disorders, and artificial intelligence. This innovative approach enables scientists to conduct experiments and analyses without physical constraints, opening new avenues for exploration in the field of brain research.

Hewlett Packard Enterprise provides the supercomputing capacity needed for the EPFL Blue Brain Project (BBP) to digitally reconstruct and mimic the mammalian brain, therefore advancing our understanding of the brain. The digital reconstruction of the human brain, one of the most complicated occurrences in the universe, will require next-generation supercomputers and close cooperation between computer engineers and brain specialists. "Our mission is to create technologies that improve our quality of life, including powering technologies for the healthcare industry to deliver targeted treatments and save lives," stated Antonio Neri, our president and CEO: "HTE is bringing advanced supercomputing and bespoke applications to empower new research that can have transformative benefits for the neuroscientific community and society at large" (Team, 2021).

A digital twin platform creates a multimodal dataset for different ML techniques by using machine learning (ML) to gather and evaluate healthcare data for every patient. This dataset covers every facet of the issue, including information on immunological, metabolic, behavioural, microbiological, and genetic problems (Moztarzadeh et al., 2023). The digital twins of cancer patients are then updated with this medical data, which is subsequently sent to the metaverse to help doctors make judgements or determine the best course of therapy. Several multimodal machine learning algorithms are used in the metaverse to process real-world input.

Supply Chain

Digital Twins, a cutting-edge technology, play a pivotal role in elevating the efficiency and resilience of supply chain management to unprecedented levels. These sophisticated virtual replicas meticulously mirror the entire supply chain, empowering organizations with unparalleled insights. By adeptly monitoring the fluidity of goods, predicting potential disruptions, and optimizing logistics, digital twins usher in a new era of proactive decision-making. This not only curtails lead times but also amplifies overall efficiency, concurrently driving down costs.

The seamless integration of real-time data sourced from Internet of Things (IoT) devices and sensors further fortifies the digital twin's capabilities, ensuring a constant influx of accurate and timely information. This wealth of data becomes the cornerstone of informed decision support, affording organizations the ability to make strategic maneuvers with foresight (Abideen et al., 2021). The cumulative impact translates into an enhanced customer satisfaction quotient, as operations become finely tuned and responsive. Ultimately, the symbiotic relationship between digital twins and real-time data orchestrates a harmonious symphony, culminating in an optimized and resilient supply chain that stands as a beacon of exemplary performance.

Energy Systems and Sustainability

Digital Twins play a crucial role in optimizing energy systems and promoting sustainability, including power plants, smart grids, and renewable energy sources. By creating virtual representations of these systems, operators can simulate and analyze different operating conditions, improving overall energy efficiency and grid reliability. Digital Twins are instrumental in optimizing energy systems and promoting sustainability. In the context of renewable energy sources, Digital Twins can simulate the performance of solar panels, wind turbines, and other renewable assets. This allows for better prediction of energy generation, integration with the grid, optimization of energy distribution and helps to contributes to the development of more sustainable energy practices and the reduction of environmental impact (Zhang et al., 2021). Furthermore, Digital Twins contribute to the development of smart buildings and homes by simulating energy consumption patterns and suggesting energy-efficient solutions.

In the energy sector, digital twins are employed to optimize the production, distribution, and consumption of energy resources (Ghenai et al., 2022). For power plants, a digital twin can simulate the behaviour of equipment, monitor performance, and predict potential failures. This predictive maintenance approach minimizes downtime and extends the lifespan of critical assets (Xu et al., 2019).

In renewable energy, digital twins are utilized to model and optimize the efficiency of solar farms, wind turbines, and other green energy sources. These models can simulate different weather conditions, energy production scenarios, and grid interactions (You et al., 2022). By leveraging this information, energy companies can make data-driven decisions to improve the reliability and sustainability of their operations.

Aerospace and Defense

In the aerospace and defense industry, Digital Twins are used to create virtual models of aircraft, satellites, and other complex systems. This facilitates simulation and analysis of the performance of these systems under various conditions. Digital Twins also aid in predictive maintenance, reducing the risk of unplanned downtime. Digital twins are utilized in the aerospace industry to simulate and monitor the performance of aircraft and defense systems. This ensures optimal operation, predictive maintenance, and enhances safety.

Digital twin technology has found extensive applications in the aerospace and defense industries, where complex systems and equipment demand high levels of precision and reliability. In aircraft manufacturing, digital twins are used to create virtual prototypes that simulate the behaviour of components under various conditions (Li et al., 2022). This helps engineers identify potential issues, optimize designs, and reduce development time.

During the operational phase, digital twins of aircraft or military equipment enable real-time monitoring of performance, fuel efficiency, and maintenance needs. Predictive analytics can be applied to anticipate component failures, schedule maintenance proactively, and ensure the safety and reliability of critical systems. This application enhances mission success rates and reduces the overall cost of ownership for aerospace and defense organizations.

Manufacturing and Industrial Processes

Digital Twin technology has emerged as a pivotal force in revolutionizing the manufacturing sector, particularly in the realm of Industry 4.0 (Nikolaev, S et al., 2018). It empowers organizations to craft a digital counterpart of their tangible assets, encompassing machinery and production lines. This virtual replica serves as a dynamic platform, facilitating real-time surveillance, predictive maintenance, and the fine-tuning of manufacturing processes.

By seamlessly integrating sensors and Internet of Things (IoT) devices, manufacturers gain the capability to harvest real-time data from the physical environment. This data is then channelled into the Digital Twin for comprehensive analysis. This transformative approach proves invaluable in pinpointing inefficiencies, curtailing downtime, and enhancing overall operational efficiency.

A mutually beneficial partnership is made possible by the union of the digital and physical domains, allowing for the optimisation of output in the real world through the application of virtual representation analytics. By providing decision-makers with useful information, this improves cost-effectiveness while simultaneously advancing strategic planning. Digital Twin technology, which has brought about increased productivity, cost savings, and operational perfection, is now a fundamental part of the modern manufacturing scene.

Environmental Monitoring

Digital Twin technology has become an instrumental tool in the realm of Environmental Monitoring, revolutionizing our approach to understanding and managing natural systems. At its core, Digital Twins entail the creation of virtual replicas mirroring tangible environmental entities. These sophisticated models serve as dynamic simulations, enabling us to anticipate and gauge the repercussions of diverse factors on our surroundings (Lu et al., 2020).

One pivotal application of Digital Twins in Environmental Monitoring involves the intricate analysis of ecosystems, weather dynamics, and resource deployment. By harnessing the power of these digital replicas, scientists and policymakers can simulate alterations in environmental conditions, providing a platform to forecast and assess the potential impacts of human activities. In the ever-pressing context of climate change, Digital Twins emerge as invaluable assets. They facilitate the simulation of various policies and interventions, enabling stakeholders to comprehend the potential outcomes and refine strategies for a sustainable future.

Furthermore, the integration of real-time data from sensors into these models enhances their precision, offering an accurate reflection of the present environmental landscape. This amalgamation of virtual and real-time information empowers decision-makers with comprehensive insights, aiding in the formulation of timely and informed strategies.

Beyond this, Digital Twins prove beneficial in optimizing resource utilization. For instance, in the management of water resources, these models can simulate different scenarios to determine the most efficient and sustainable allocation of water, mitigating the impact of scarcity. In essence, Digital Twins in Environmental Monitoring not only serve as predictive tools but also as proactive instruments for devising and implementing strategies that foster environmental sustainability. As technology advances, the potential applications of Digital Twins are poised to further expand, offering innovative solutions to the intricate challenges posed by our ever-changing environment.

Education and Training

Digital Twins have revolutionized the educational landscape by offering immersive learning experiences that transcend traditional boundaries. These virtual replicas play a pivotal role in fostering interactive and dynamic educational environments. One notable application is the development of virtual labs, providing students with a hands-on experience in a simulated setting (Sepasgozar, S. M. et al.,2020). For instance, aspiring chemists can conduct experiments in a virtual laboratory, manipulating digital apparatus and observing reactions without the constraints of a physical space.

Simulated experiments are another facet of Digital Twins in Education, offering a safe and controlled space for students to explore various scenarios. This is particularly beneficial in fields such as healthcare, where medical students can practice intricate procedures in a risk-free digital realm before transitioning to real-life situations. In the realm of engineering, aspiring professionals can troubleshoot and refine their skills through virtual simulations, ensuring competence and confidence in real-world applications.

Moreover, Digital Twins extend their impact to historical and archaeological studies. Students can explore digital replicas of historical events or archaeological sites, gaining insights into the past without the limitations of physical access. This fosters a deeper understanding of history and culture, enriching the learning experience (Marra, A et al., 2021).

The versatility of Digital Twins in education is exemplified in the aviation sector, where they contribute to pilot training. Flight simulations using Digital Twins allow aspiring pilots to navigate various scenarios, honing their skills in a risk-free virtual airspace (Almasan, P et al,.2022). This not only enhances safety but also provides a cost-effective alternative to traditional training methods.

In essence, Digital Twins in Education serve as catalysts for innovation, providing a dynamic and adaptive platform for students across diverse disciplines. Through virtual replicas, students can engage in practical learning, bridging the gap between theory and application in a manner that is both effective and enriching.

Finance and Blockchain

Regarding blockchain technology and funds, the participation of conventional banks such as Yes Bank is essential (Akhtar et al., 2021). The banking sector in India is going through a transitional stage, and performance assessment is becoming increasingly important. In this context, the fallout from financial crises is crucial (Ansari et al., 2023), especially in terms of Yes Bank's profitability and liquidity as a commercial bank. Insights into banks' adaptation and resilience can be gained by assessing their technical efficiency, which has become more popular in the wake of events such as demonetization (Akhtar et al., 2022). Comparing the corporate governance of Indian banks to those of other countries in the South Asian Association for Regional Cooperation (SAARC) is an interesting feature (Alam et al., 2023). This empirical study explores the governance procedures and identifies areas that should be strengthened or improved. Moreover, the utilisation of cutting-edge technology, including Long Short-Term Memory (LSTM) models, is spreading more and more. One prominent use is in NIFTY 50 Index Price predictions, where Backward Elimination techniques are applied (Jafar et al., 2023). The dynamic environment where finance, technology, and governance converge in India between traditional banking and blockchain is highlighted by these multidisciplinary studies and assessments.

BENEFITS OF USING DIGITAL TWIN

The adoption of Digital Twins offers a myriad of benefits across different industries, fundamentally changing the way operations are managed.

Improved Decision-Making

- **Real-time Insights:** Digital twins provide a real-time representation of physical objects or processes, enabling organizations to make data-driven decisions based on current and accurate information.
- **Predictive Analytics:** By analyzing historical and real-time data, digital twins facilitate predictive analytics, allowing businesses to anticipate issues, optimize processes, and make proactive decisions.

Enhanced Product Development and Innovation

- **Prototyping and Simulation:** Digital twins enable virtual prototyping and simulation, reducing the need for physical prototypes. This accelerates the product development cycle and allows for more experimentation and innovation.
- **Iterative Design:** Designers can continuously iterate and refine product designs in a virtual environment, saving time and resources in the physical manufacturing phase.

Optimized Operations and Maintenance

- **Condition Monitoring:** Digital twins facilitate continuous monitoring of equipment and assets, helping to detect anomalies and predict maintenance needs. This proactive approach reduces downtime and extends the lifespan of assets.
- **Remote Diagnostics:** Operators can remotely diagnose and troubleshoot issues, minimizing the need for on-site visits. This is especially valuable in industries where equipment is located in remote or hazardous environments.

Efficient Resource Management

- **Energy Efficiency**: In sectors like smart buildings and industrial plants, digital twins help optimize energy consumption by providing insights into usage patterns and suggesting efficiency improvements.
- **Resource Allocation:** Digital twins assist in the efficient allocation of resources, whether it's personnel, equipment, or raw materials, leading to cost savings and improved overall efficiency.

Supply Chain Optimization

- **End-to-End Visibility:** Digital twins offer end-to-end visibility into the supply chain, enabling organizations to track and manage the movement of goods in real time. This visibility enhances responsiveness and reduces the impact of disruptions.
- **Demand Forecasting:** By analyzing data from various points in the supply chain, digital twins contribute to more accurate demand forecasting, reducing the likelihood of stockouts or excess inventory.

Healthcare Advancements

- **Personalized Medicine:** In healthcare, digital twins are used to create patient-specific models that help in personalized treatment plans. This can improve the efficacy of medical interventions and reduce adverse effects.
- **Training and Simulation:** Medical professionals can use digital twins for training purposes, simulating surgeries or medical procedures in a risk-free environment.

Smart Cities and Infrastructure

- **Urban Planning**: Digital twins are employed in urban planning to simulate and optimize city infrastructure, transportation systems, and public services. This aids in creating sustainable and resilient cities.
- **Traffic Management**: Smart traffic management systems use digital twins to analyze and predict traffic patterns, allowing for real-time adjustments to optimize traffic flow and reduce congestion.

Collaboration and Communication

- **Cross-functional Collaboration:** Digital twins facilitate collaboration across departments and teams, allowing stakeholders from various disciplines to work together on a unified platform.
- **Remote Collaboration:** With the rise of remote work, digital twins enable teams to collaborate on projects irrespective of geographical locations, fostering a more flexible and efficient work environment.

Regulatory Compliance and Risk Mitigation

- **Regulatory Reporting:** Digital twins assist in maintaining compliance with regulations by providing a comprehensive and traceable record of processes and activities.
- **Risk Simulation:** Organizations can use digital twins to simulate and assess potential risks, allowing for the development of strategies to mitigate these risks before they impact operations.

Environmental Sustainability

- **Resource Efficiency:** Digital twins aid in optimizing resource usage, contributing to sustainability goals by reducing waste and minimizing environmental impact.
- **Carbon Footprint Reduction:** Industries can use digital twins to identify opportunities for reducing energy consumption and emissions, aligning with global efforts to combat climate change.

FUTURE DIRECTIONS AND CONCLUSION

As blockchain technology develops and becomes increasingly integrated with different businesses, it has a lot of potential to become a major player in the future of digital security and transparency. The improvement of smart contracts is one of the main areas under development. The ability to automate complex business operations with ease will be made possible by the next generation of self-executing contracts, which will be encoded with predetermined rules and circumstances. In order to solve scalability concerns and make blockchain more widely adopted, we should expect the creation of sophisticated consensus algorithms as blockchain technology advances.

Future developments are probably in store for distributed ledger technology, which forms the basis of blockchain. The primary objective will be to enhance efficiency, minimise energy usage, and boost transaction throughput by optimising consensus procedures. Research on interoperability between various blockchain networks will be important since it promotes easy data sharing and communication between varied blockchain ecosystems. The global blockchain infrastructure will become more integrated and interoperable as a result of these advancements.

Traditional power structures will continue to change as a result of decentralisation, which is a key component of blockchain. By reducing the dangers associated with centralised control, the decentralisation of data storage and administration will boost security and privacy. Globally, more inclusive and easily accessible financial services will be made available by decentralised finance (DeFi) as it grows. The manner that organisations are run and regulated will also probably change as a result of the rise in popularity of decentralised autonomous organisations, or DAOs.

Concurrently, the idea of digital twin technology is becoming more and more popular, providing a virtual version of real-world items, procedures, or systems. Better simulation capabilities, real-time monitoring, and sophisticated analytics will be features of digital twins in the future, enabling improved decision-making and optimisation in a variety of industries. It will be advantageous for sectors like manufacturing, healthcare, and urban planning to keep integrating digital twin technologies.

The integration of blockchain technology with digital twins offers a potent synergy that has the potential to transform businesses that depend heavily on security, transparency, and trust. Digital twins can improve data quality and reliability by utilising blockchain's transparent and unchangeable ledger. Smart contracts ensure that the digital twin accurately reflects changes in the actual world by automating the execution of agreements and transactions. For supply chain management, healthcare, and the Internet of Things (IoT), where a transparent and safe connection between the real and virtual worlds is critical, this convergence has enormous promise.

In summary, blockchain and digital twin technology have a bright future ahead of them, with continued developments and collaborations creating new opportunities for creativity. We may expect these technologies to have a revolutionary effect on many different industries as they develop and become more widely used, creating a digital environment that is more linked, efficient, and safe. The way we interact with and manage digital and physical assets is going to be completely changed by the cooperative integration of blockchain and digital twin technologies, opening the door to a decentralised and digitally enhanced future.

REFERENCES

Abideen, A. Z., Sundram, V. P. K., Pyeman, J., Othman, A. K., & Sorooshian, S. (2021). Digital twin integrated reinforced learning in supply chain and logistics. *Logistics*, *5*(4), 84. doi:10.3390/logistics5040084

Akhtar, S., Alam, M., Khan, A., & Shamshad, M. (2022, June 9). Measuring technical efficiency of banks vis-à-vis demonetization: An empirical analysis of Indian banking sector using CAMELS framework. *Quality & Quantity*, *57*(2), 1739–1761. doi:10.1007/s11135-022-01431-8

Akhtar, S., Alam, M., & Khan, M. M. (2021, December). YES Bank Fiasco: Arrogance or Negligence. *Emerging Economies Cases Journal*, *3*(2), 95–102. doi:10.1177/25166042211061003

Alam, M., Akhtar, S., & Al-Faryan, M. A. S. (2023, November 8). Do Indian banks perform better in corporate governance than other SAARC nations? An empirical analysis. *Corporate Governance: The International Journal of Business in Society*. doi:10.1108/CG-02-2023-0059

Almasan, P., Ferriol-Galmés, M., Paillisse, J., Suárez-Varela, J., Perino, D., López, D., & Barlet-Ros, P. (2022). *Digital twin network: Opportunities and challenges*. arXiv preprint arXiv:2201.01144.

Ansari, M. S., Akhtar, S., Khan, A., & Shamshad, M. (2023, March 31). Consequence of Financial Crisis on Liquidity and Profitability of Commercial Banks in India: An Empirical Study. *Studies in Economics and Business Relations*, *3*(2), 36–50. doi:10.48185/sebr.v3i2.367

Bariev, E. Y. (2017). Blue Brain Project. In Recent Achievements and Prospects of Innovations and Technologies (pp. 126-128).

Begum, A., Tareq, A., Sultana, M., Sohel, M., Rahman, T., & Sarwar, A. (2020). Blockchain attacks analysis and a model to solve double spending attack. *International Journal of Machine Learning and Computing*, *10*(2), 352–357.

Castro, M., & Liskov, B. (2002, November). Practical byzantine fault tolerance and proactive recovery. *ACM Transactions on Computer Systems*, *20*(4), 398–461. doi:10.1145/571637.571640

Cimino, C., Negri, E., & Fumagalli, L. (2019). Review of digital twin applications in manufacturing. *Computers in Industry*, *113*, 103130. doi:10.1016/j.compind.2019.103130

Deren, L., Wenbo, Y., & Zhenfeng, S. (2021, March 29). Smart city based on digital twins. *Computational Urban Science*, *1*(1), 4. Advance online publication. doi:10.1007/s43762-021-00005-y

Di Pierro, M. (2017). What is the blockchain? *Computing in Science & Engineering*, *19*(5), 92–95. doi:10.1109/MCSE.2017.3421554

El Saddik, A. (2018, April-June). Digital Twins: The Convergence of Multimedia Technologies. *IEEE MultiMedia*, *25*(2), 87–92. doi:10.1109/MMUL.2018.023121167

Erol, T., Mendi, A. F., & Doğan, D. (2020). *The Digital Twin Revolution in Healthcare*. 2020 4th International Symposium on Multidisciplinary Studies and Innovative Technologies (ISMSIT), Istanbul, Turkey. 10.1109/ISMSIT50672.2020.9255249

Gervais, A., Karame, G. O., Wüst, K., Glykantzis, V., Ritzdorf, H., & Capkun, S. (2016, October). On the security and performance of proof of work blockchains. In *Proceedings of the 2016 ACM SIGSAC conference on computer and communications security* (pp. 3-16). ACM. 10.1145/2976749.2978341

Ghenai, C., Husein, L. A., Al Nahlawi, M., Hamid, A. K., & Bettayeb, M. (2022). Recent trends of digital twin technologies in the energy sector: A comprehensive review. *Sustainable Energy Technologies and Assessments*, *54*, 102837. doi:10.1016/j.seta.2022.102837

Jafar, S. H., Akhtar, S., El-Chaarani, H., Khan, P. A., & Binsaddig, R. (2023, September 25). Forecasting of NIFTY 50 Index Price by Using Backward Elimination with an LSTM Model. *Journal of Risk and Financial Management*, *16*(10), 423. doi:10.3390/jrfm16100423

Jones, D. (2020). Characterising the Digital Twin: A Systematic Literature Review. *CIRP Journal of Manufacturing Science and Technology*, *29*. . doi:10.1016/j.cirpj.2020.02.002

King, S., & Nadal, S. (2012). *PPCoin: Peer-to-Peer Crypto-Currency with Proof-of-Stake.*

Li, L., Aslam, S., Wileman, A., & Perinpanayagam, S. (2021). Digital twin in aerospace industry: A gentle introduction. *IEEE Access : Practical Innovations, Open Solutions, 10*, 9543–9562. doi:10.1109/ACCESS.2021.3136458

Liu, M., Fang, S., Dong, H., & Xu, C. (2021). Review of digital twin about concepts, technologies, and Industrial Applications. *Journal of Manufacturing Systems, 58*, 346–361. doi:10.1016/j.jmsy.2020.06.017

Lu, Q., Parlikad, A. K., Woodall, P., Don Ranasinghe, G., Xie, X., Liang, Z., Konstantinou, E., Heaton, J., & Schooling, J. (2020, May). Developing a Digital Twin at Building and City Levels: Case Study of West Cambridge Campus. *Journal of Management Engineering, 36*(3), 05020004. doi:10.1061/(ASCE)ME.1943-5479.0000763

Marra, A., Gerbino, S., Greco, A., & Fabbrocino, G. (2021). Combining integrated informative system and historical digital twin for maintenance and preservation of artistic assets. *Sensors (Basel), 21*(17), 5956. doi:10.3390/s21175956 PMID:34502848

Mohammed, A. H., Abdulateef, A. A., & Abdulateef, I. A. (2021, June). Hyperledger, Ethereum and blockchain technology: a short overview. In *2021 3rd International Congress on Human-Computer Interaction, Optimization and Robotic Applications (HORA)* (pp. 1-6). IEEE.

Monrat, A., Schelén, O. & Andersson, K. (2019). Survey of Blockchain from the Perspectives of Applications, Challenges and Opportunities. *IEEE Access*. IEEE. . doi:10.1109/ACCESS.2019.2936094

Moztarzadeh, O., Jamshidi, M., Sargolzaei, S., Jamshidi, A., Baghalipour, N., Malekzadeh Moghani, M., & Hauer, L. (2023). Metaverse and Healthcare: Machine Learning-Enabled Digital Twins of Cancer. *Bioengineering (Basel, Switzerland), 10*(4), 455. doi:10.3390/bioengineering10040455 PMID:37106642

Nakamoto, S. (2008). *Bitcoin: a Peer-to-Peer Electronic Cash System.* Bitcoin. https://bitcoin.org/bitcoin.pdf

Nikolaev, S., Gusev, M., Padalitsa, D., Mozhenkov, E., Mishin, S., & Uzhinsky, I. (2018). Implementation of "digital twin" concept for modern project-based engineering education. In Product Lifecycle Management to Support Industry 4.0: 15th IFIP WG 5. Springer.

Proof of Elapsed Time (PoET). 2022). Investopedia. Available from: https://www.investopedia.com/terms/p/proof-elapsed-time-cryptocurrency.asp#citation-1

Qi, Q., Tao, F., Hu, T., Anwer, N., Liu, A., Wei, Y., Wang, L., & Nee, A. (2021, January). Enabling technologies and tools for digital twin. *Journal of Manufacturing Systems*, *58*, 3–21. doi:10.1016/j.jmsy.2019.10.001

Semeraro, C., Lezoche, M., Panetto, H., & Dassisti, M. (2021, September). Digital twin paradigm: A systematic literature review. *Computers in Industry*, *130*, 103469. doi:10.1016/j.compind.2021.103469

Sepasgozar, S. M. (2020). Digital twin and web-based virtual gaming technologies for online education: A case of construction management and engineering. *Applied Sciences (Basel, Switzerland)*, *10*(13), 4678. doi:10.3390/app10134678

Sheth, H., & Dattani, J. (2019, April 16). OVERVIEW OF BLOCKCHAIN TECHNOLOGY. *ASIAN JOURNAL OF CONVERGENCE IN TECHNOLOGY*, *05*(01), 1–4. doi:10.33130/AJCT.2019v05i01.013

Szabo, N. (1996). Smart contracts: building blocks for digital markets. *EXTROPY: The Journal of Transhumanist Thought, 18*(2), 28.

Team, G. C. (2021, December 14). *HPE Helps EPFL Blue Brain Project Unlock the Secrets of the Brain*. HPE. https://www.hpe.com/us/en/newsroom/press-release/2018/07/hpe-helps-epfl-blue-brain-project-unlock-the-secrets-of-the-brain.html

Xu, B., Wang, J., Wang, X., Liang, Z., Cui, L., Liu, X., & Ku, A. Y. (2019). A case study of digital-twin-modelling analysis on power-plant-performance optimizations. *Clean Energy*, *3*(3), 227–234. doi:10.1093/ce/zkz025

Yang, F., Zhou, W., Wu, Q., Long, R., Xiong, N. N., & Zhou, M. (2019). Delegated Proof of Stake With Downgrade: A Secure and Efficient Blockchain Consensus Algorithm With Downgrade Mechanism. *IEEE Access : Practical Innovations, Open Solutions*, *7*, 118541–118555. doi:10.1109/ACCESS.2019.2935149

Yi, L., Glatt, M., Ehmsen, S., Duan, W., & Aurich, J. C. (2021). Process monitoring of economic and environmental performance of a material extrusion printer using an augmented reality-based digital twin. *Additive Manufacturing*, *48*, 102388. doi:10.1016/j.addma.2021.102388

You, M., Wang, Q., Sun, H., Castro, I., & Jiang, J. (2022). Digital twins based day-ahead integrated energy system scheduling under load and renewable energy uncertainties. *Applied Energy*, *305*, 117899. doi:10.1016/j.apenergy.2021.117899

Zhang, X., Shen, J., Saini, P. K., Lovati, M., Han, M., Huang, P., & Huang, Z. (2021, June 21). Digital Twin for Accelerating Sustainability in Positive Energy District: A Review of Simulation Tools and Applications. *Frontiers in Sustainable Cities*, *3*, 663269. doi:10.3389/frsc.2021.663269

Zheng, Z., Xie, S., Dai, H. N., Chen, W., Chen, X., Weng, J., & Imran, M. (2020, April). An overview on smart contracts: Challenges, advances and platforms. *Future Generation Computer Systems*, *105*, 475–491. doi:10.1016/j.future.2019.12.019

Chapter 3
Blockchain and Digital Twins:
Concept, Applications, Challenges, and Potential

Prashant Chougule
Woxsen University, India

Sharuti Choudhary
Woxsen University, India

Kavitha Reddy Gurrala
Woxsen University, India

Ch Siddharth Nanda
Woxsen University, India

ABSTRACT

Digital twins and blockchain technology have revolutionized data management and accessibility in a variety of areas and opened a plethora of new and profitable business opportunities. The "foundations of blockchain and digital twins" book chapter delves into the advantageous relationship between these two cutting-edge technologies. The basic ideas, unique characteristics, and real-world use cases of blockchain technology have been covered in the first section of this chapter. Blockchain technology's decentralized, transparent, and unchangeable features have the potential to completely transform a number of industries, including finance, healthcare, and supply chain management. The chapter also examines the consensus, processes, smart contracts, and cryptographic techniques that support the blockchain's dependability and security. The final section investigates the interesting relationship between blockchain and digital twins, assessing their individual benefits. Blockchain technology has the potential to improve the reliability, authenticity, and safety of digital twins.

DOI: 10.4018/979-8-3693-1878-2.ch003

EXAMINING BLOCKCHAIN AND ITS CAPABILITIES

Introduction

The technology of Blockchain, synonymous with cryptocurrencies like Bitcoin, Ethereum, Solana, etc. has emerged as a revolutionary cornerstone in reshaping the landscape of transactions. Its impact is not merely confined to just digital currencies, but also to the way in which transactions are conducted, perceived and secured, either locally or globally (Nofer, Gomber, Hinz & Schiereck, 2017).

It cannot be denied that in a world which is increasingly dependent on digital transactions, there is a sure need for secure, transparent and efficient methods of processing transactions. The answer to these pressing questions is blockchain technology, as it offers a decentralized, distributed ledger that fundamentally alters the dynamics of the transactional ecosystem (Ansari, Akhtar, Khan, & Shamshad, 2023). Its importance lies in its inherent decentralization. Unlike centrally controlled systems (like banks) which frequently need a central authority for supervising and verifying each encounter, blockchain runs on a global network of computers, improving security and streamlining the transaction process (Zheng, Xie, Dai, Chen & Wang, 2018)

It is commonly recognized that blockchain technology serves as the foundation for bitcoin. Because all transactions are carried out decentralized and don't require a reliable third party, this technology has raised expectations. Currently, the majority of blockchain's actual commercial uses are in the financial services industry, although several R&D initiatives within businesses and enterprises aim to expand the potential applications of blockchain technology (Konstantinidis et al., 2018). Blockchain disruption gave rise to a new method of value exchange, political and social connections, and company redesign. It is more than simply a shift; it is a swift phenomenon in action.

Blockchain: What Is It?

In order to address the "double-spending" issue with Bitcoin, blockchain technology was initially introduced in 2009 as the foundational. Still, a number of additional issues may be resolved using blockchain technology thanks to its unique qualities that make it indispensable for Bitcoin (Gupta et al., 2020).

A blockchain is a distributed digital ledger that contains a history of transactions. It is maintained on computers run by various participants, referred to as "nodes." Participants can add entries that are verified and unchangeable through cryptographic protection (Gupta et al., 2020). Because data in a blockchain is kept in blocks that are represented by a blockchain, the records inside it are unchangeable. The term "blockchain" refers to a chain that is created when each new block of data has the hash of the previous block, linking all the way back to the original block (Maldonado-Ruiz, et al., 2022).

Evolution of Blockchain

Santoshi Nakamoto created blockchain in 2008 as the online ledger for the bitcoin cryptocurrency (Khalilov, M. C. K. & Levi, 2018). It gets rid of middlemen, decreases transaction costs, expedites transaction times, and lessens the danger of fraud. More than 40 prestigious financial institutions and other businesses from a variety of industries have begun investigating blockchain technology.

Blockchain was first created by Nakamoto in 2008, and the well-known Bitcoin system used it to track and record transactions in a decentralized manner. But the initial wave of blockchain solutions, known as Blockchain 1.0, developed into a number of platforms that are currently referred to as Blockchain 2.0, including Ethereum, Quorum, Hyperledger Fabric, IBM Blockchain, and Hyperledger Sawtooth.

These platforms are an advancement over the previous generation and brought new services to blockchain-based apps (Colomo-Palacios, R., et al., 2020). The first digital, decentralized cryptocurrency is called Bitcoin, and it was created using the blockchain, a key technology for identification and verification. Only once the initial owner of the coins (digital tokens) provides the public key to the subsequent possessor can a bitcoin transaction begin (Khalilov, M. C. K. & Levi, 2018 ; Coronado-Garcia, 2009)

Attributes of Blockchain

Additionally, there are several kinds of blockchains according to their unique characteristics and applications: 1) Blockchains that are public Blockchains and there are those that are 2) private, and 3) consortium. Public blockchains enable anybody to join the network and participate in its management, making them truly decentralized. On the other hand, with private blockchains, network management is restricted to invited members of a single organization. And the consortium blockchain deals with administration and permissions (Bhutta, M. N. M et al., 2021).

Table 1. Comparisons among public blockchain, consortium blockchain and private blockchain

Property	*Public blockchain*	*Consortium blockchain*	*Private blockchain*
Consensus determination	All miners	Selected set of nodes	One organisation
Read permission	Public	Could be public or restricted	Could be public or restricted
Immutability	Nearly impossible to tamper	Could be tampered	Could be tampered
Efficiency	Low	High	High
Centralised	No	Partial	Yes
Consensus process	Permissionless	Permissioned	Permissioned

Key Characteristics of Blockchain

Resilience and Irreversibility

As intended, each blockchain node maintains an exact replica of the whole chain inside a dispersed network of nodes. The structure of blockchain is what gives it its durability (Elrom, E., 2019).

Provenance and Trust

Blockchain technology offers an unquestionable way to confirm the accuracy of transaction data at a particular point in time in the block. Because every block in the chain contains information from previous blocks, the position, history, and ownership of each block are unchangeable and are automatically verified.

Centralized vs. Decentralized

Systems Because blockchain technology resists centralized architecture and is designed to be decentralized, we are comparing centralization vs. decentralization (Cai, W., Wang, 2018). Because of this, completely centralized or decentralized systems are seldom reachable. There is a possibility for both centralized and decentralized distributed systems. In a centralized distributed system, the master node splits up the tasks or data and then assigns the workload to the other nodes. But even without a master node, distributed computing can still occur in a decentralized system (Elrom, E., 2019).

These systems have limitations because of centralization, even if distributed computing can be partly blamed for some of these architectures' faster calculations.

Limitation of Blockchain

Apart from the multiple advantages blockchain technology has the following drawbacks:

Lack of Privacy

Every network node keeps track of the whole transaction history of the network. This could be a benefit in terms of security and a characteristic for some applications, but it is a drawback for use cases where privacy is essential.

Expensive Computational Requirements

Expenses are associated with the blockchain's core processing, which replicates the whole transaction history across all nodes. Although this feature offers security benefits, bigger networks may find it to be a hindrance.

Security Model

Public key encryption is used by blockchains for both transaction execution and authentication. Both a public and a private key are needed for this procedure, despite its extreme security. There is no safety mechanism in place in the system to offer extra protection if a party misplaces or accidentally releases their private key.

Flexibility

While blockchain's immutable append-only features guarantee transaction integrity, they may also impede use cases that call for transaction modifications.

Governance

While the distributed design of the blockchain has clear benefits for certain use cases, it may pose a serious challenge to overall management and governance for organizations that rely on supervision (Alam, Akhtar & Al-Faryan, 2023).

Non-Technical Constraints

This consists of inadequate approval from law enforcement and other regulatory bodies; insufficient user acceptability. Since blockchain technology is still relatively new, organizations have not yet properly addressed these important challenges, which might seriously jeopardize the technology's ability to gain widespread acceptance. Concerns about transaction legality, GDPR compliance, privacy, and user resistance stem from low levels of technological expertise and trust (Drescher 2017). There are restrictions when it comes to blockchain technology used in important application categories.

Functions of Blockchain

A blockchain is made up of blocks, often referred to as data blocks, which are collections of data blocks that are connected and carry the hash code of the preceding block. Each user or client linked to others on this peer-to-peer network did so without the usage of middlemen services (Acharjamayum, I., Patgiri, 2018).

Blockchain may be used to supply work, votes, property, products, or even money in transactions using any open, decentralized database (Cai, W., Wang, 2018). Blockchain is a sort of data structure that is distributed and decentralized in architecture, storing and sharing transactions of a digital ledger of a distributed network of computers (Natarajan, H., Krause, 2017).

Once a transaction is started, it cannot be undone. However, users can choose to cancel it or start a new one that will be shared by all users on the network. Every transaction within a blockchain network possesses a unique timestamp. Because the entire community can confirm the legitimacy of a record made in accordance with blockchain guidelines, blockchain technology is considered "trustless." Despite being decentralized, blockchain technology is becoming a globally recognized source of trust (Cai, W., Wang, 2018).

Application of Blockchain

Because of its many practical and beneficial aspects, blockchain technology has a plethora of potential to fundamentally alter how organizations operate if adopted. Due to the rapid improvements in digital and technical technologies, blockchain technology can drastically revolutionize established market structures and entirely change the way firms operate (Bai, Cordeiro, & Sarkis, 2020). Numerous business processes may be optimized and a variety of business challenges can be addressed with the same software (Chong et al., 2019).

Based on existing research, we concentrated on certain industries with blockchain applications, such as cryptocurrency, e-Government, healthcare (Ng et al, 2021), supply chains, energy, and finance, all of which we go into great detail about below.

Figure 1. Using blockchain in managing business functions

Blockchain in Marketing Management

The research that is currently available on the subject suggests using blockchain in various marketing management applications. Technology is being used in digital marketing, sales promotion, and advertising as a promotional tool. Figure 2 summarizes the use of blockchain technology in marketing.

Figure 2. Most cited studies on blockchain in marketing

Most cited studies on blockchain in marketing.

Authors	Title	Year	Source title	Key findings
(Kumar et al., 2021)	Influence of new-age technologies on marketing: A research agenda	2021	Journal of Business Research	The technology is likely to impact firms, customers, intermediaries and further research is required on the area
(Tozanli et al., 2020)	Trade-in-to-upgrade as a marketing strategy in disassembly-to-order systems at the edge of blockchain technology	2020	International Journal of Production Research	Using IoT-embedded products in a blockchain-enabled disassembly-to-order system to determine the optimal trade-in-to-upgrade policy
(Liu et al., 2019)	Anonymous reputation system for IIoT-enabled retail marketing atop PoS blockchain	2019	IEEE Transactions on Industrial Informatics	Revolutionizing retail industry by improving operational and channel efficiency between suppliers, manufactures and customers
(Grewal et al., 2018).	The Evolution and Future of Retailing and Retailing Education	2018	Journal of Marketing Education	Transparency in business transactions and closer connections with customers using technology will benefit retailing
Parssinen M.A., Kotila M., Cuevas Rumin R., Phansalkar A., Manner J.	Is Blockchain Ready to Revolutionize Online Advertising?	2018	IEEE Access	Blockchain is not yet ready to revolutionize online advertising industry

Blockchain in Human Resource Management

Blockchain systems are utilized in human resource management for payroll and compensation, hiring, training and development, and personnel data management. Blockchain technology uses public and private key cryptography to consistently verify all data in the HR department. Strong and impenetrable is the human resource information management system. This improves the security of the entire human resource function and makes it easier to save all necessary data. Figure 3 summarizes the use of blockchain technology in the field of human resources.

Figure 3. Most cited studies on blockchain in human resources

Most cited studies on blockchain in human resource.

Authors	Title	Year	Source title	Key findings
(Kim et al., 2020)	A privacy preserving distributed ledger framework for global human resource record management: The blockchain aspect	2020	IEEE Access	The technology can help in maintaining the data privacy under human resource management
(Kadadha et al., 2020)	SenseChain: A blockchain-based crowdsensing framework for multiple requesters and multiple workers	2020	Future Generation Computer Systems	A decentralized crowdsensing framework can overcome the challenges of a centralized personnel management system
Chen J., Lv Z., Song H	Design of personnel big data management system based on blockchain	2019	Future Generation Computer Systems	A prototype containing personnel information with query, add, modify, and track can verify the feasibility of applying
(Michailidis, 2018)	The challenges of AI and blockchain on HR recruiting practices	2018	Cyprus Review	The technology can impact employment scenario and may bring income equality to our society
(Yli-Huumo et al., 2016)	Where is current research on Blockchain technology? - A systematic review	2016	PLoS ONE	Blockchain provides anonymity, security, privacy, and transparency to all its users which is important to business and human resource management

Blockchain in Supply Chain Management

Researchers from all across the world have looked at supply chain blockchain applications. The applicability to several supply chain management sectors, such as transportation and security enhancement, have been emphasized in recent research. Blockchain technology is being used for supply chain management (SCM) in intelligent transport systems, healthcare systems, shipping and logistics, and the rapidly expanding e-commerce sector. The supply chain use of blockchain is summarized in Figure 4.

Blockchain in Manufacturing and Operations Management

Blockchain is being used in operations management for quality control, production control, and production planning. The advantages of using blockchain technology in operations management include automation, validity, aggregation, and visibility. The use of blockchain in manufacturing and operations is seen in Figure 5.

Figure 4. Most cited studies on blockchain in supply chain

Most cited studies on blockchain in supply chain.

Authors	Title	Year	Source title	Key findings
Saberi S., Kouhizadeh M., Sarkis J., Shen L.	Blockchain technology and its relationships to sustainable supply chain management	2019	International Journal of Production Research	Blockchain enables creation of secured and trustworthy ledgers. Further, it eliminates middleman in the supply chain network.
(Casino et al., 2019).	A systematic literature review of blockchain-based applications: Current status, classification and open issues	2019	Telematics and Informatics	Blockchain has found applications in several industries and has become more efficient, scalable and durable
(Ivanov et al., 2019)	The impact of digital technology and Industry 4.0 on the ripple effect and supply chain risk analytics	2019	International Journal of Production Research	The study establishes the relationship business, information, engineering and analytics perspectives and digitalisation along with supply chain risks
(Kim and Laskowski, 2018)	Toward an ontology-driven blockchain design for supply-chain provenance	2018	Intelligent Systems in Accounting, Finance and Management	Using ontologies to develop blockchain applications for evaluating supply chain provenance and improving the supply chain performance
(Kshetri, 2017)	Blockchain's roles in strengthening cybersecurity and protecting privacy	2017	Telecommunications Policy	Blockchain's decentralized feature will result in low manipulation and forgery by malicious participants. The technology can address the key challenges associated with IoT security

Figure 5. Most cited studies on blockchain in manufacturing and operations

Most cited studies on blockchain in manufacturing and operations.

Authors	Title	Year	Source title	Key findings
.(Yu et al., 2020)	Blockchain-based shared manufacturing in support of cyber physical systems: concept, framework, and operation	2020	Robotics and Computer-Integrated Manufacturing	Blockchain based shared manufacturing is a solution to the trust problem in shared manufacturing
(Olsen and Tomlin, 2020)	Industry 4.0: Opportunities and challenges for operations management	2020	Manufacturing and Service Operations Management	Industry 4.0 technologies including blockchain can provide remote and real time monitoring and control of geographically dispersed assets
Bai L., Hu M., Liu M., Wang J.	BPIIoT: A Light-Weighted Blockchain-Based Platform for Industrial IoT	2019	IEEE Access	Blockchain-based platform using smart contract can address security, trust, and island connection problem with IoT in manufacturing and maintainence
(Rane and Narvel, 2019)	Re-designing the business organization using disruptive innovations based on blockchain-IoT integrated architecture for improving agility in future Industry 4.0	2019	Benchmarking	The decentralization, trust and security features of blockchain can improve the agility in industry 4.0
Li Z., Barenji A.V., Huang G. Q.	Toward a blockchain cloud manufacturing system as a peer to peer distributed network platform	2018	Robotics and Computer-Integrated Manufacturing	The development of distributed peer to peer network architecture that improves the security and scalability of the cloud manufacturing

Blockchain in Financial Management

The main goal of blockchain technology is to keep records safe and secure and do transactions securely, its application is sufficiently broad to encompass the majority of financial domains. Applications of the technology and smart contract include capital markets, seed capital, insurance, banking, and trade finance. Additionally, companies and authorities worldwide have built blockchain systems for assurance, auditing, and financial reporting. The integration of blockchain technology into financial systems and operations would also reduce the likelihood of cyberattacks and financial fraud (Akhtar, Alam, & Ansari, 2022) (Akhtar, Alam, & Khan, 2021).

Because it is tamper-proof, blockchain technology offers excellent security and defense against financial fraud and cyberattacks. Additionally, the blockchain technology provides a solid basis for smart contracts, which have the potential to significantly increase financial efficiency. Smart contracts have the potential to automate transactions and drastically lower their costs. Other than sales. Implementing contracts automatically is another benefit of smart contracts. Figure 6 illustrates how blockchain is being used in finance.

Figure 6. Most cited studies on blockchain in finance

Most cited studies on blockchain in finance.

Authors	Title	Year	Source title	Key findings
(Fisch, 2019)	Initial coin offerings (ICOs) to finance new ventures	2019	Journal of Business Venturing	Determinants of amount raised during ICOs (whitepaper, source code quality, token supply) helps investors in taking more informed decisions.
(Gomber et al., 2018)	On the Fintech Revolution: Interpreting the Forces of Innovation, Disruption, and Transformation in Financial Services	2018	Journal of Management Information Systems	Fintech revolution and application of blockchain is leading to transformation of process in the lending, markets, investments and financial services space
(Treleaven et al., 2017)	Blockchain Technology in Finance	2017	Computer	Blockchain technology is making the banking and financial service industry resilient and enhancing the integrity of the involved parties
(Li and Wang, 2017)	The technology and economic determinants of cryptocurrency exchange rates: The case of Bitcoin	2017	Decision Support Systems	Bitcoin exchange rate against USD is affected by the changes in economic and market and technological factors
.(Zhao et al., 2016)	Overview of business innovations and research opportunities in blockchain and introduction to the special issue	2016	Financial Innovation	Blockchain is considered to be the most exciting invention after internet helping the trust issue in transactions covering banks, finance providers, governments and other business corporations

The advent of blockchain technology has sparked a cross-industry revolution that holds the potential to revolutionise various aspects of business operations, information management, and digital interactions. As an increasing number of sectors are trying their hand at the utilization of blockchain related solutions, the field of Business-Technology integration is expected to undergo a significant transformation. The disruptive features of decentralization, transparency and robust security have lead to a paradigm shift in various industries and fostered efficiency, trust and innovation across multiple sectors.

DIGITAL TWINS: CONCEPTS, APPLICATIONS, BENEFITS & CHALLENGES

Introduction

Within the framework of the Industry 4.0 revolution, the virtual twin concept has been acknowledged as a noteworthy innovation. The interconnectedness of Internet of Things (IoT) devices and the use of advanced data analytics make this innovation possible. The use of data produced by smart city environments, industrial sectors, and healthcare has significantly increased as a result of the Internet of Things (IoT). In addition, the integration of smart city technology streamlines a number of functions, including traffic management, fault detection, and anomaly detection in the context of patient care (Mandolla, Petruzzelli, Percoco, & Urbinati, 2019). The development of smart cities and the prosperity of production processes in the future are greatly influenced by the vast ecosystem that is the Internet of Things (IoT) (Bilberg & Malik, 2019). Integration problems between data analytics and IOT can be effectively handled using a Digital Twin. The process entails building a thorough framework that connects a real-world physical object to its virtual equivalent.

Concept

Digital Twins are electronic representations of physical systems or devices that connect to their functional components and capture and record all aspects of their operation. It is an electronic replica of an actual object or system that is updated in real time. By obtaining data from the internet & IOT enabled devices, it can predict future events and adapt to modifications in the system's functionality. A "digital twin" is defined as a sizable set of digital data that precludes all aspects of physical system for digital replica creation.

DT Technique: Origin and Meaning

The inception of the digital transformation (DT) technique can be traced back to the introduction of industrial product life cycle management (PLM) by Grieves in 2003 (Grieves & Vickers, 2017). Grieves elucidated the trifecta of components of the DT technique, namely the data relationship, the digital entity, and the real entity (Grieves & Vickers, 2017). The concept garnered significant attention from both academic and industrial sectors due to its wide-ranging applicability. At present, the application of DT has proven to be efficacious in diverse domains, encompassing but not limited to the field of robotics intelligent production, aeronautics, sustainable energy, and the process industry. The concept associated with DT has been subject to diverse interpretations due to its widespread utilization. In the year 2012, Glaessgen and Stargel (Glaessgen & Stargel, 2012) put forth a proposition that has gained significant acceptance in the academic community. A digital twin is an all-encompassing virtual representation of a complex physical object that includes different physical phenomena and scales as well as probability components. By using precise physical models, frequent updates of sensor data and other relevant tools, the goal is to accurately simulate the properties, behaviors and mechanisms of the represented physical entity. The "digital twin (DT)" concept can be conceptualized as a computerized replica of an actual object or system, given the state of technology today. This virtual representation encompasses data obtained from various sources throughout the entire lifespan of the product. The development of this technology involves the utilization of integrated simulations and information pertaining to services. A virtual twin can be defined as an advanced electronic representation that develops links with the operational elements of a tangible structure or device, while also comprehensively capturing and reflecting all aspects of its operation in real-time. The digital representation serves as a dynamic and current imitation of the corresponding physical asset or system, enabling the prediction of future events and adaptation to operational changes through continuous online data collection. The concept encompasses a diverse array of electronic data, encompassing information at different levels of detail, ranging from atomic-level specifics to larger-scale phenomena.

Digital Twins: Core Technologies

Prominent technological progressions are facilitating the growth and application of Digital Twins (DT)- This section provides a comprehensive overview of the key technologies that enable the wider implementation of the digital transformation (DT) oriented systems. The construction of physics or mathematical models can pose challenges, but the utilization of data-driven modeling is widespread in various complex scenarios. The process of providing fuel to a vehicle or system. The aforementioned phenomenon exerts a significant influence on multiphysics simulation engines, such as ANSYS. Throughout the continuous process, a significant quantity of process data is generated and gathered, encompassing log data, sensor metrics, camera images, and videos (Zribi, Elloumi, Hani, & Elmhamedi, 2023), (Colombo, Karnouskos, Kaynak, Shi, & Yin, 2017); (Melesse, Pasquale, & Riemma, 2020). This finding suggests that the development and application of DTs require the adoption of methodologies that are guided by data or integrated with data models. The incorporation of pertinent data and information derived from comprehensive and diverse databases is crucial. The current prevalence of machine intelligence that heavily relies on "big data" should be substituted with a paradigm that places greater emphasis on solutions derived from hypotheses and rooted in "small data." The inclusion of models based on machine learning in the DT framework offers significant potential benefits, as they have exhibited promising outcomes in effectively identifying inherent nonlinearity and coupling (Jafar, Akhtar, El-Chaarani, Khan & Binsaddig, 2023). The notion of intelligent perception and sensing pertains to the capacity of an entity to sense and understand its surroundings through sophisticated cognitive mechanisms. Sensors are instrumental devices that gather data regarding the immediate environment. Subsequently, the obtained measurements are converted into valuable information that guides decision-making and influences behavior. In contrast to devices that depend on energy conversion, intelligent sensing and sophisticated perception systems receive input signals from various sources and produce more dependable outcomes through adaptive learning and data fusion (Jiang, Yin, Dong, & Kaynak, 2020); (Kadlec, Grbić, & Gabrys, 2011). Moreover, it improves the capacity of DT systems to develop a deeper comprehension of the interconnected environment. There are a trio of distinct contemporary methodologies that can be identified in the field, specifically different information configurations, multivariate assessment of variance, and machine vision. There has been a significant surge in interest surrounding machine vision-based methodologies in recent times. These technologies are frequently utilized in various applications, including virtual measurement, object tracking, and object recognition (Shelhamer, Long, & Darrell, 2017); (Zhou, et al., 2020). Moreover, these sensors are highly valuable in the domain of autonomous or collaborative robotics in industrial environments, as well as in virtual inspection scenarios, such as the detection of defects during production processes, among various other applications. Deep neural networks have been designed with the aim of achieving comparable performance to existing solutions. Machine vision-based movement recognition and eyeball monitoring systems offer a versatile alternative to conventional control mechanisms or displays employed in user interfaces, thereby facilitating the implementation of human-in-the-loop design.

Digital Twin: Benefits

To promote the extensive implementation of Distributed Technologies (DTs), it is imperative to establish regulatory measures and security protocols, alongside a universally accepted reference framework for DTs. Furthermore, it is imperative to emphasize the significance of constructing intricate DT case studies, as DTs frequently comprise multiple sub-components that are dispersed among diverse contributors and industry partners. The effectiveness of a digital twin (DT) relies on its interconnectedness with the Internet of Things (IoT), machine learning, and data. The successful integration of these elements results in a resilient and exceptionally effective digital technology product. Digital transformation (DT) is a technological advancement that offers advantages to various product lifecycles. Nevertheless, it is imperative to acknowledge that there exist specific scenarios in which the advantages of DT can be notably substantial (Sharma, Kosasih, Zhang, Brintrup, & Calinescu, 2022);

1. The process of developing physical prototypes in industries such as aerospace, supply chain, and manufacturing is characterised by high costs, resource requirements, and time consumption. Rather than investing resources in the creation of multiple preliminary designs for product testing, employing a

digital twin offers a considerably more productive and economically feasible alternative.

2. Tangible assets or offerings that necessitate rigorous testing (Sharma, Kosasih, Jhang, Brintrup, & Calinescu, 2022), particularly those found in industries such as aerospace and Prognostics and Health Management (PHM), often present challenges when it comes to conducting these tests within laboratory settings. The DT has the capability to simulate tests that are not feasible to conduct within a laboratory setting.
3. Instances or situations that necessitate continuous monitoring and the implementation of mitigation strategies to address the occurrence of unforeseen behaviours, as observed in domains like healthcare systems and supply chains. Monitoring the current condition of a tangible asset in real-time and receiving advance notifications regarding an impending issue can prove to be a highly efficient and effective approach (Sharma, Kosasih, Zhang, Brintrup, & Calinescu, 2022). This feature is particularly advantageous for organisations that require expeditious decision-making capabilities in order to mitigate potential critical circumstances, such as substantial financial losses (Sharma, Kosasih, Zhang, Brintrup, & Calinescu, 2022).
4. Goods that have various characteristics, such as those commonly observed in the production and distribution chains, have the inherent capacity for simultaneous optimization across their entire lifecycles (Sharma, Kosasih, Zhang, Brintrup, & Calinescu, 2022). The task of managing and supervising all component parts within a large organization can present considerable difficulties. Significant advantages can be achieved through the adoption of continuous surveillance for all parts and the utilization of sophisticated analytics on large-scale models (Sharma, Kosasih, Jhang, Brintrup, & Calinescu, 2022). This approach addresses the challenge of "siloing" as discussed in previous literature, where the presence of multiple sub-domains within the system leads to fragmented information.

Digital Twin: Challenges

The main reason for this section is digital twin challenges. As research continues, data analytics, IoT, and IIoT challenges become similar to those of digital twins.

a. The issue at hand, similar to that of IoT and analytics, pertains to the condition of the information technology (IT) infrastructure. IoT and data analytics infrastructure must be capable of supporting a Digital Twin's operations. Digital Twin will struggle to achieve its goals without a well-planned IT infrastructure.
b. The next challenge is gathering data for Digital/ Virtual Twin development. The data must possess a high level of quality, devoid of any extraneous or

erroneous information, and exhibit a consistent and uninterrupted flow of data. In the event of inadequate and inconsistent data, the performance of the Digital Twin could be compromised as it operates based on incomplete and unreliable information. The access and use of digital twin information is contingent upon the criticality of both the amount and the caliber of IoT signals. The process of planning and analysis is essential in order to determine the suitable data to be collected and utilized for the purpose of optimizing the utilization of Digital Twin technology.

c. Privacy and security are major concerns with Digital Twins. Large amounts of data raise two concerns: the volume of data and the risk to private system information. Data analytics and the Internet of Things (IoT), key technologies for Digital Twins, must follow the latest security and privacy regulations and best practices to overcome this challenge.

CHALLENGES: BLOCKCHAIN-DIGITAL TWIN INTEGRATION

Management of Complex Industrial Processes efficiently and effectively is possible by leveraging on Digital Twins (DT's)- a technology facilitating the design of virtual replicas of the real-world environments towards analyzing, predicting, optimizing, and calibrating the operations/ industrial processes prior to actual implementation within the physical environments. Thus, ensuring data synchronization between the physical space and the virtual space (Tao *et al.*, 2018). However, the reliability of data accumulated through diverse sources in order to feed the virtual replicas for fostering intelligent information insights towards mitigating the risks, managing the costs, assuring the quality etc., is at stake, in view of the involvement of several intertwined participants within the complex industrial processes i.e., the physical space (Neshenko *et al.*, 2019). Consequently, Block Chain Technology (BCT) comes in handy, as the technology facilitates data management through shared distributed ledgers with peer-to-peer verification and authentication fostering high data traceability, security, and integrity. Hence, the usage of secured and trust-worthy data from BCT to feed the DT's for extracting valuable information stands out as an optimal solution towards enhancing the performance of the Industrial eco-systems (Salah *et al.*, 2019).

Nonetheless, several technical, logistical, and social challenges hinder the successful implementation of BCT integrated DT's. The sections below would provide a deep insight into these challenges.

Technical Challenges

One major challenge is related to how precisely the virtual model represents the physical/real-world environment, taking into consideration the dynamism and complexity within the underlying physical/real-world scenarios. Thus, the overall performance of the virtual system, i.e., the reliability and accuracy of the simulations depends on how well the initial DT was articulated to represent the real-world complexities and dynamism. Furthermore, virtual system designs need to evolve relative to the physical system evolvement, towards capitalizing on the DT's ability to unearth the unknown facts for performance enhancement (Intizar et al., 2021).

Additionally, DT's facilitate conceptualization through simple features and generalizations that are deployed to create timely replication modes to trace the physical objects and mimic their activities based on their behaviors (Dietz and Pernul, 2020). However, problems related to data synchronization and in-consistency between the virtual space and physical space might result, if the replicas do not timely reflect the physical object leading to status difference between the replica and the physical object.

Further, temporal dependencies also lead to data synchronization and data in-consistency problems between the virtual spaces and physical spaces.

Likewise, challenges also stem from the volume of data, variety of data, veracity of data, generation rate of data, spatio-temporal resolution used while capturing the data, and efficient processing of the data, archival of the data, and finally retrieval of the data (Suhail *et al.*, 2022).

Besides, to foster global deployment of the BCT enabled DT's, the cost of implementations (infrastructure management & personnel training) stands out as an impeding factor towards budget friendly implementation even within small-scaled Industries/environments (Yaqoob *et al.*, 2020).

Logistical Challenges

On the other hand, even though DT's promote risk reduction, safety enhancement, and efficiency improvements, they tend to be cost-prohibitive, since significant costs are involved towards facilitating seamless connectivity, fast computing, higher-bandwidth, and enormous storage for efficient processing of tremendous amount of data. Furthermore, even if initial high costs of implementation are disregarded the DT's need allocation of operational budgets for routine management of networked devices (Suhail *et al.*, 2021). Additionally, fund allocation is also needed to train personnel in state-of-the-art tools and data modelling techniques. Hence, DT's not only impact CapEXs (Capital Expenditure) but also significantly impact OpEXs (Operational Expenses).

Besides, absence of standard laws & guidelines for data sharing often leads to problems when the DT systems receive data through different interfaces, in different proprietary file formats, varied object definitions, diverse encoding structures, and distinctive sharing criteria. Further, data sharing problems also crop up from inter-operability of information infrastructures between multitude of stake holders involved within the real-world environments (Piroumian, 2021). In addition, BCs rely on network structures that are highly decentralized and distributed and function based on parameters that are heterogeneous in nature involving consensus algorithms, smart contracts etc. resulting in inter-operability problems. Also, a single blockchain cannot provide all the information needed for a DT system. Hence it is highly crucial that information exchange is facilitated between different block chains (i.e., exchange of information on different block chain transactions) through development of inter-operable block chain architectures (Yasanur and Nachiappan, 2022).

Equivalently, BCT's tend to perform relatively slower considering the network stress from processing large number of transactions. Thus, consequently tends to impact the performance of DT systems designed to replicate an environment that is reliant on high performance transaction processing systems. Additionally, privacy issues with BCT's due to distributed structures, scalability issues and integration issues with the legacy systems stand out as a major roadblock for integration of BCT's with the DT systems (Yaqoob *et al.*, 2020).

Social Challenges

Moreover, integration of blockchain-based DTs faces challenges on Ethical and Moral grounds, as firms with successful implementation might tend to misuse the systems to overpower the market and establish a monopoly. Further, lack of a common/collaborative platforms between Academia and Industrial fraternity to share data and models related to precise DT builds, hinder the development and implementation of efficient and effective BCT integrated DT's.

In addition, BCT's involve energy intensive mining processes (i.e., consensus algorithms for transaction validation) that tend to increase carbon footprints. Hence, it is highly desirable to deploy miner-free block chain solutions to reduce the negative environmental impacts (Suhail *et al.*, 2022).

In conclusion, effective deployment of blockchain-powered digital twins calls out for reduced implementation and maintenance costs, substantial cyber security measures, highly reliable and ethical frameworks, enhanced techniques for data validation and verification, data source assurance methods, and inter-operable systems.

RECENT ADVANCES: BLOCKCHAIN-DIGITAL TWIN INTEGRATION

Several studies were set forth to enhance the performance of Blockchain-Digital Twin integrated systems and foster their application within multiple domains. In this regard, (Sadri *et al.*, 2023) conducted a study to reveal the advantages of collaborating IoT and AI with Blockchain-Digital Twin integrated systems. According to the study, IoT stands out as an important pillar for DT, as it facilitates real-time data induction into the system; AI enhances the intelligence and recognition power of DT's facilitating activities such as abnormality detection, preventive/predictive maintenance etc.; AI compliments BCT for enhancing the smart contracts to feed safe and secure data into the DT's and finally, IoT networks facilitate local computing needs of BCT thus eliminating reliance on central cloud-computing solutions.

Besides, dynamic DT systems can be articulated through IOT enabled Block Chains convening continuous connectivity between the DT and the IoT Sensors monitoring the physical object's status (Wright, 2023).

In addition, (Sasikumar *et al.*, 2023) proposed an integrated proof of authority (POA) based BCT with an Industrial IoT (IIoT) to feed the DT system in order to facilitate energy consumption reduction and enhance data security.

Similarly, (Wei *et al.*, 2023) developed an IIoT integrated BC based Multi-users Oblivious Data Sharing scheme (MODS) to feed the DT systems, towards addressing a wide range of concerns related to security of data stored within the BC system in order to foster a balance between the security and efficiency of the Blockchain-Digital Twin integrated systems (Akhtar, Alam, Khan et al, 2023).

Moreover, BCT and DT systems stand out as strategic pillars for creation of Metaverse environments (a fully immersive virtual world where users can interact with mixed reality environments and objects), as they aid with bridging the gap between real world and virtual environments (Picone, Mariani, Virdis & Castagnetti, 2023). Equivalently, Padmavathi & Kanimozhi (2023) developed a Medical cyber-physical system leveraging on multiple disruptive technologies such as Dt's BC's, IoT, and Artificial Intelligence (AI) Systems to promote pre-production activities such as 3-D design, testing, simulation, and prototyping and also facilitate remote monitoring of devices in service.

Additionally, (Das, 2023) claimed that leveraging on DT for development of social media strategies can promote business survival within the constant evolving digital landscape. Similarly, (Niavis *et al.*, 2022) formulated a Trusted DBL (Building Digital Logbook) based on Blockchain and Digital Twin technologies to track progress on emission reductions and also recommend precautionary measures upfront to face critical events such as heat waves. Furthermore, DTs integrated with complementary technologies such as AI, BCT, and IoT can be leveraged by financial institutions to mitigate credit risks (Bisht *et al.*, 2022). Further, (Zhang *et al.*, 2023) developed a block chain based smart parking systems to efficiently manage resource constrained vehicular networks through continuous monitoring of parking spaces and traffic conditions by leveraging on IoT integrated DT systems.

CONCLUSION

The incorporation of Blockchain Technology with Digital Twin Technology represents a substantial revolution in the data management domain. This has driven significant progress across multiple domains. The fundamental elements of blockchain technology were covered in this chapter. The features of decentralization transparency and safety were presented and discussed. The way in which blockchain technology has a significant impact on a variety of industries was also discussed. Blockchain technology impacts various industries by transforming them towards greater trustworthiness, security and improving transaction processes. Blockchain technology applications extend well beyond the realm of cryptocurrencies.

Simulated research on digital twins has also demonstrated that these virtual replicas of real, physical objects can be used for simulation, real-time monitoring and predictive maintenance across a wide range of industries, including Manufacturing, Healthcare and urban planning.

The advantages of combining BT & DT have been bought to light via examination of how they work together. By ensuring the validity and consistency of data and enabling decentralized sharing, blockchain technology improves the security and dependability of the digital twins. This has the potential to greatly increase innovation and facilitate certain significant changes in several industries.

This integration has the potential to usher in a new era of innovative business operations characterized by dependability, integrity and efficiency. Numerous sectors and industries are predicted to undergo significant transformation as a result of this integration. In addition to the advantages, the challenges associated with the achieving technological synergies underscore the need for further research and development to overcome these challenges and obstacles. The combination of blockchain and digital twin technologies has presented a major breakthrough in data security, dependability and efficiency.

REFERENCES

Akhtar, S., Alam, M., & Ansari, M. S. (2022). Measuring the performance of the Indian banking industry: Data envelopment window analysis approach. *Benchmarking*, *29*(9), 2842–2857. doi:10.1108/BIJ-03-2021-0115

Akhtar, S., Alam, M., Khan, A., & Shamshad, M. (2023). Measuring technical efficiency of banks vis-à-vis demonetization: An empirical analysis of Indian banking sector using CAMELS framework. *Quality & Quantity*, *57*(2), 1739–1761. doi:10.1007/s11135-022-01431-8

Akhtar, S., Alam, M., & Khan, M. M. (2021). YES Bank Fiasco: Arrogance or Negligence. *Emerging Economies Cases Journal*, *3*(2), 95–102. doi:10.1177/25166042211061003

Alam, M., Akhtar, S., & Al-Faryan, M. A. S. (2023). Do Indian banks perform better in corporate governance than other SAARC nations? An empirical analysis. Corporate Governance. doi:10.1108/CG-02-2023-0059

Ansari, M. S., Akhtar, S., Khan, A., & Shamshad, M. (2023). Consequence of Financial Crisis on Liquidity and Profitability of Commercial Banks in India: An Empirical Study. *Studies in Economics and Business Relations*, *3*(2), 36–50. doi:10.48185/sebr.v3i2.367

Bhutta, M. N. M., Khwaja, A. A., Nadeem, A., Ahmad, H. F., Khan, M. K., Hanif, M. A., Song, H., Alshamari, M., & Cao, Y. (2021). A survey on blockchain technology: Evolution, architecture and security. *IEEE Access: Practical Innovations, Open Solutions*, *9*, 61048–61073. doi:10.1109/ACCESS.2021.3072849

Bilberg, A., & Malik, A. A. (2019). Digital twin driven human–robot collaborative assembly. *CIRP Annals*, *68*(1), 499–502. doi:10.1016/j.cirp.2019.04.011

Bisht, D., Singh, R., Gehlot, A., Akram, S., Singh, A., Montero, E., Priyadarshi, N., & Twala, B. (2022). Imperative Role of Integrating Digitalization in Firms Finance: A Technological Perspective. *Electronics (Basel)*, *11*(19), 3252. doi:10.3390/electronics11193252

Colombo, A. W., Karnouskos, S., Kaynak, O., Shi, Y., & Yin, S. (2017). Industrial Cyberphysical Systems: A Backbone of the Fourth Industrial Revolution. *IEEE Industrial Electronics Magazine*, *11*(1), 6–16. doi:10.1109/MIE.2017.2648857

Colomo-Palacios, R., Sánchez-Gordón, M., & Arias-Aranda, D. (2020). A critical review on blockchain assessment initiatives: A technology evolution viewpoint. *Journal of Software (Malden, MA)*, *32*(11), e2272. doi:10.1002/smr.2272

DasS. (2023). Digital Twins: The Key to Unlocking Industry 4.0 and beyond. SSRN, p. https://ssrn.com/abstract=4426592 or doi:10.2139/ssrn.4426592

Dietz, M., & Pernul, G. (2020). Unleashing the Digital Twin's Potential for ICS Security. *IEEE Security and Privacy*, *18*(4), 20–27. doi:10.1109/MSEC.2019.2961650

Glaessgen, E., & Stargel, D. (2012). The digital twin paradigm for future NASA and US Air Force vehicles. In *Proc. 53rd AIAA/ASME/ASCE/AHS/ASC Struct. Struct. Dyn. Mater. Conf.*, (pp. 23-26). Reston: Reston.

Grieves, M., & Vickers, J. (2017). Digital Twin: Mitigating Unpredictable, Undesirable Emergent Behavior in Complex Systems. Kahlen, J., Flumerfelt, S., Alves, A. (eds) Transdisciplinary Perspectives on Complex Systems. Springer. doi:10.1007/978-3-319-38756-7_4

Gupta, S., Sinha, S., & Bhushan, B. (2020, April). Emergence of blockchain technology: Fundamentals, working and its various implementations. In *Proceedings of the international conference on innovative computing & communications (ICICC)*. IEEE.

Intizar Ali, M., Patel, P., Breslin, J. G., Harik, R., & Sheth, A. (2021). Cognitive Digital Twins for Smart Manufacturing. *IEEE Intelligent Systems*, *36*(2), 96–100. doi:10.1109/MIS.2021.3062437

Jafar, S. H., Akhtar, S., El-Chaarani, H., Khan, P. A., & Binsaddig, R. (2023). Forecasting of NIFTY 50 Index Price by Using Backward Elimination with an LSTM Model. *Journal of Risk and Financial Management*, *16*(10), 423. doi:10.3390/jrfm16100423

Jiang, Y., Yin, S., Dong, J., & Kaynak, O. (2020). A Review on Soft Sensors for Monitoring, Control, and Optimization of Industrial Processes. *IEEE Sensors Journal*, 12868–12881.

Kadlec, P., Grbić, R., & Gabrys, B. (2011). Review of adaptation mechanisms for data-driven soft sensors. *Computers & Chemical Engineering*, *35*(1), 1–24. doi:10.1016/j.compchemeng.2010.07.034

Konstantinidis, I., Siaminos, G., Timplalexis, C., Zervas, P., Peristeras, V., & Decker, S. (2018). Blockchain for business applications: A systematic literature review. In Business Information Systems: 21st International Conference, BIS 2018, Berlin, Germany, July 18-20, 2018 [Springer International Publishing.]. *Proceedings*, *21*, 384–399.

Maldonado-Ruiz, D., Torres, J., & Madhoun, N. E. (2022). Fundamentals of Blockchain Technology. In Principles and Practice of Blockchains (pp. 3-25). Cham: Springer.

Mandolla, C., Petruzzelli, A. M., Percoco, G., & Urbinati, A. (2019). Building a Digital Twin for Additive Manufacturing through the Exploitation of Blockchain: A case analysis of the aircraft industry. *Computers in Industry*, *109*, 134–152. doi:10.1016/j.compind.2019.04.011

Melesse, T. Y., Pasquale, V. D., & Riemma, S. (2020). Digital Twin Models in Industrial Operations: A Systematic Literature Review. *Procedia Manufacturing*, *42*, 267–272. doi:10.1016/j.promfg.2020.02.084

Neshenko, N., Bou-Harb, E., Crichigno, J., Kaddoum, G., & Ghani, N. (2019). Demystifying IoT Security: An Exhaustive Survey on IoT Vulnerabilities and a First Empirical Look on Internet-Scale IoT Exploitations. *IEEE Communications Surveys and Tutorials*, *21*(3), 2702–2733. doi:10.1109/COMST.2019.2910750

Ng, W. Y., Tan, T. E., Movva, P. V., Fang, A. H., Yeo, K. K., Ho, D., & Ting, D. S. (2021). Blockchain applications in health care for COVID-19 and beyond: A systematic review. *The Lancet. Digital Health*, *3*(12), e819–e829. doi:10.1016/S2589-7500(21)00210-7 PMID:34654686

Niavis, H., Laskari, M., & Fergadiotou, I. (2022). *Trusted DBL: A Blockchain-based Digital Twin for Sustainable and Interoperable Building Performance Evaluation.* 7th International Conference on Smart and Sustainable Technologies (SpliTech), Croatia.10.23919/SpliTech55088.2022.9854287

Nofer, M., Gomber, P., Hinz, O., & Schiereck, D. (2017). Blockchain. *Business & Information Systems Engineering*, *59*(3), 183–187. doi:10.1007/s12599-017-0467-3

PadmavathiV.KanimozhiR. (2023). Pandemic Alert with Smart Covid-19 Using Blockchain-Powered Digital Twins' Collaboration. Research Square, [https://doi.org/10.21203/rs.3.rs-3028917/v1].

Picone, M., Mariani, S., Virdis, A., & Castagnetti, P. (2023). Digital Twin & Blockchain: Technology Enablers for Metaverse Computing. *IEEE International Conference on Metaverse Computing, Networking and Applications (MetaCom)*, (pp. 1-8). IEEE. 10.1109/MetaCom57706.2023.00017

Piroumian, V. (2021). Digital Twins: Universal Interoperability for the Digital Age. *Computer*, *54*(1), 61–69. doi:10.1109/MC.2020.3032148

Sadri, H., Yitmen, I., Tagliabue, L., Westphal, F., Tezel, A., Taheri, A., & Sibenik, G. (2023). Integration of Blockchain and Digital Twins in the Smart Built Environment Adopting Disruptive Technologies—A Systematic Review. *Sustainability (Basel), 15*(4), 3713. doi:10.3390/su15043713

Salah, K., Rehman, M., Nizamuddin, N., & Al-Fuqaha, A. (2019). Blockchain for AI: review and open research challenges. *IEEE Access, 7.*

Sasikumar, A., Vairavasundaram, S., Kotecha, K., Indragandhi, V., Ravi, L., Selvachandran, G., & Abraham, A. (2023). Blockchain-based trust mechanism for digital twin empowered Industrial Internet of Things. *Future Generation Computer Systems, 141*, 16–27. doi:10.1016/j.future.2022.11.002

Sharma, A., Kosasih, E., Zhang, J., Brintrup, A., & Calinescu, A. (2022). Digital Twins: State of the art theory and practice, challenges, and open, research questions. *Journal of Industrial Information Integration, 30*, 100383. doi:10.1016/j.jii.2022.100383

Shelhamer, E., Long, J., & Darrell, T. (2017). Fully Convolutional Networks for Semantic Segmentation. *IEEE Transactions on Pattern Analysis and Machine Intelligence, 39*(4), 640–651. doi:10.1109/TPAMI.2016.2572683 PMID:27244717

Suhail, S., Hussain, R., Jurdak, R., Oracevic, A., Salah, K., Hong, C., & Matulevičius, R. (2022). Blockchain-Based Digital Twins: Research Trends, Issues, and Future Challenges. *ACM Computing Surveys, 54*(11s), 1–34. Advance online publication. doi:10.1145/3517189

Tao, F., Cheng, J., Qi, Q., Zhang, M., Zhang, H., & Sui, F. (2018). Digital twin-driven product design, manufacturing, and service with big data. *International Journal of Advanced Manufacturing Technology, 94*(9-12), 3563–3576. doi:10.1007/s00170-017-0233-1

Wei, W., An, B., Qiao, K., & Shen, J. (2023). A Blockchain-Based Multi-Users Oblivious Data Sharing Scheme for Digital Twin System in Industrial Internet of Things. *IEEE Journal on Selected Areas in Communications, 41*(10), 3318–3332. doi:10.1109/JSAC.2023.3310105

Wright, S. A. (2023). IoT Blockchains for Digital Twins. In X. H. P. Yu (Ed.), *Opportunities and Challenges of Industrial IoT in 5G and 6G Networks* (pp. 244–260). IGI Global. doi:10.4018/978-1-7998-9266-3.ch011

Yaqoob, I., Khaled, S., Uddin, M., Raja, J., Omar, M., & Imran, M. (2020). Blockchain for Digital Twins: Recent Advances and Future Research Challenges. IEEE. doi:10.1109/MNET.001.1900661

Yasanur, K., & Nachiappan, S. (2022). Blockchain Interoperability Issues in Supply Chain: Exploration of Mass Adoption Procedures. In *A. a. EMROUZNEJAD, Big Data and Blockchain for Service Operations Management. Studies in Big Data* (pp. 309–328). Springer.

Zhang, C., Zhu, L., & Xu, C. (2023). BSDP: Block Chain Based Smart Parking for Digital-Twin Empowered Vehicular sensor Networks with Privacy Protection. *IEEE Transactions on Industrial Informatics*, *19*(5), 7237–7246. doi:10.1109/TII.2022.3223211

Zheng, Z., Xie, S., Dai, H. N., Chen, X., & Wang, H. (2018). Blockchain challenges and opportunities: A survey. *International Journal of Web and Grid Services*, *14*(4), 352–375. doi:10.1504/IJWGS.2018.095647

Zhou, X., Wang, Y., Zhu, Q., Mao, J., Xiao, C., Lu, X., & Hui, Z. (2020). A Surface Defect Detection Framework for Glass Bottle Bottom Using Visual Attention Model and Wavelet Transform. *IEEE Transactions on Industrial Informatics*, *16*(4), 2189–2201. doi:10.1109/TII.2019.2935153

Zribi, H., Elloumi, A., Hani, Y., & Elmhamedi, A. (2023). Industry 4.0: Digital Twin's Industrial Applications. *9th International Conference on Control, Decision and Information Technologies (CoDIT)*. IEEE. 10.1109/CoDIT58514.2023.10284310

Chapter 4
Blockchain-Driven NFTs:
A Game-Changer for Sustainable Investments

Krishna Khanal
https://orcid.org/0009-0003-1369-0952
Westcliff University, USA

ABSTRACT

Blockchain technology and non-fungible tokens (NFTs) are transforming industries like finance, art, and gaming. This chapter explores their intersection and profound implications for sustainable investments. Blockchain's transparency and immutability enhance trust in sustainability projects, while NFTs tokenizing real-world assets democratize access and promote eco-friendly initiatives. Real-world cases demonstrate the practical impact of blockchain-driven NFTs in sectors like renewable energy, sustainable agriculture, and carbon credits. Challenges include regulatory frameworks and environmental concerns, but the future promises a more robust ecosystem, increased accessibility, and greater transparency in sustainable finance.

INTRODUCTION

Non-fungible tokens (NFTs) and blockchain technology have become two of the most important developments in the digital world, changing a wide range of sectors, including banking, gaming, and the arts (Collomb et al., 2016). Blockchain was first proposed by Satoshi Nakamoto, who included a proof of work (PoW) mechanism for reaching consensus on transaction data in a decentralized peer-to-peer network. By enabling collaboration between untrusted individuals, this proof-of-work approach

DOI: 10.4018/979-8-3693-1878-2.ch004

was utilized to protect the integrity of the entire blockchain (Nakamoto, 2019). Fundamentally, distributed ledger technology, or blockchain, is used to record transactions over a decentralized network of nodes. Transparency, immutability, and security are among its primary characteristics, which taken together offer a reliable and impenetrable system for documenting and authenticating digital transactions (Pilkington, 2016; Kietzmann et al., 2020). Nonfungible tokens (NFTs), which are changing the way content is created, sold, exchanged, stored, and verified for both content creators and their fans, are one example of how blockchain might be used for this purpose (Malhotra et al., 2021).

NFTs represent distinct, indivisible digital assets that are impossible to duplicate. Their capacity to confirm provenance and ownership of digital or physical things in a digital format has drawn a lot of attention (Wilson et al., 2021). These tokens provide artists and collectors with a new way to exchange and engage with digital goods. They are frequently linked to digital art, collectibles, music, and virtual real estate.

By fusing the advantages of a safe and open ledger system with the distinctiveness and ownership rights that NFTs offer, the combination of blockchain technology with NFTs has spurred creativity (Dowling, 2021). This combination, especially when it comes to sustainable investments, has the power to upend established financial structures and transform a number of industries. We attempt to explain the convergence of NFTs and blockchain in this chapter, along with the significant implications for sustainable investing. We examine how NFTs can be used to tokenize actual sustainable assets, opening up new investment options in the sustainability space, and how the intrinsic properties of blockchain technology might improve trust and transparency in sustainability sector.

INTRODUCTION TO BLOCKCHAIN

According to Milani et al. (2016), blockchain is a decentralized and distributed ledger system that supports the immutability and transparency that are essential for building confidence in financial transactions. The inability to add, remove, or alter data within a system is known as immutability (Belu, 2019). Blockchain functions essentially as a series of linked blocks, each with a collection of transactions. A consensus process among network users verifies and adds these blocks to the chain, guaranteeing that the data stored is safe and difficult to alter (Shrivastava et al., 2020). Because blockchain technology is unchangeable, it is a perfect instrument for keeping an unchangeable record of sustainable investment projects, which will increase credibility and accountability in the industry (Kumar et al., 2018).

NFTs serve as digital certificates of authenticity, uniquely representing digital or physical assets in a digital form (Chohan, 2018). By using cryptographic techniques on a publicly available blockchain like Ethereum, they mimic the qualities of physical objects, such as uniqueness, scarcity, and proof of ownership, and are traded using cryptocurrency in online marketplaces (Regner, 2019). Every NFT is linked to a particular piece of information or asset, and the blockchain records who owns it (Evans, 2019). NFTs are indivisible and cannot be traded one-to-one, in contrast to cryptocurrencies like Bitcoin or Ethereum (Hawasin et al., 2023). They are especially well-suited to reflect ownership interests in sustainable assets, such as eco-friendly initiatives, renewable energy sources, and green infrastructure, because of their indivisibility (Gawusu, 2022). A layer of trust and transparency that traditional financial instruments frequently lack is added when these assets are encapsulated as NFTs on a blockchain, making it feasible to create unambiguous ownership rights and track the history of transactions pertaining to sustainable investments.

THE ROLE OF SUSTAINABILITY IN FINANCIAL MARKET

The financial market's understanding of sustainability has changed significantly in recent years, as environmental, social, and governance (ESG) considerations are becoming more widely acknowledged as important influences on investment choices (Ng, 2020). These elements are incorporated into investment strategies via sustainable investing, also referred to as ESG investing, with an emphasis on encouraging both financial returns and favorable social and environmental effects. It combines components of both socially responsible investment (SRI) and ESG investment methods, encompassing approaches that are ethically and environmentally motivated (Tseng et al., 2019). A number of firms, including SettleMint, Kaleido, and Finhub 360 Advisors GmbH, are providing financial products rooted in blockchain technology designed specifically for ESG investing. This change of viewpoint recognizes that companies and organizations that put sustainability first have the potential to become financially resilient in the long run in-addition to making a positive and moral contribution to the global economy (Yoo & Managi, 2021).

Ethical investing and sustainability concerns are becoming essential factors in the financial sector when making investment decisions. In order to achieve long-term sustainability, ethical investments entail the prudent use of resources to meet people's basic requirements (Mustapha, 2020). According to Almar and Nobanee (2019), there is a growing trend among investors to pursue opportunities that are in line with their principles and tackle global issues including resource shortage volatility, social injustice, and climate change. Green bonds, impact funds, and socially conscious mutual funds are examples of sustainable investment vehicles that have gained popularity and attracted capital that is directed toward projects and initiatives that emphasize sustainability objectives (Abhilash, 2022; Kroninsky,

2022). Furthermore, ESG disclosure rules have been implemented by regulatory agencies and stock exchanges in several countries, compelling corporations to furnish public details regarding their sustainability practices and performance (Atan, 2016). The convergence of financial markets with sustainability goals reflects a growing commitment to responsible investing. This chapter explores how blockchain technology and NFTs can further improve the transparency, accountability, and traceability of sustainable investments.

CONVERGENCE OF BLOCKCHAIN AND NFTS IN SUSTAINABLE INVESTMENTS

The combination of blockchain technology and NFTs in sustainable investments is a novel advancement that could fundamentally alter the way funds are distributed to environmentally conscious enterprises and endeavors. Blockchain technology is a fundamental layer that enhances trust and accountability in sustainable investments because of its intrinsic features of transparency, immutability, and security (Rijal, 2023). Sustainable investment platforms can offer an unchangeable and up-to-date record of financial transactions and project milestones to stakeholders, such as investors, regulators, and project developers, by utilizing blockchain technology.

By facilitating the tokenization of sustainable assets, NFTs, as distinct digital representations of assets, enhance the potential of blockchain technology (Heines, 2021). These resources could be parts of eco-friendly real estate projects, carbon offsets, infrastructure for renewable energy, or even sustainable agriculture programs. These assets may be easily traced and fractional ownership made possible by recording them as NFTs on a blockchain. This enables a wider spectrum of investors to invest in sustainable ventures. Additionally, NFTs can capture important details about the underlying asset, like its financial performance and environmental impact data, improving the accountability and transparency of sustainable investments. This technological convergence presents a new way to match funds from investors with sustainability goals, helping to move the financial sector in the direction of greater environmental responsibility (Udeagha & Muchapondwa, 2023). The ensuing sections of this chapter will explore in greater detail the ways in which blockchain and NFTs can affect sustainable investments both separately and jointly. We will also look at practical uses and obstacles related to this novel strategy.

HOW BLOCKCHAIN CAN ENHANCE TRUST AND TRANSPARENCY IN SUSTAINABILITY PROJECTS?

Enhancing trust and transparency in sustainability projects—which are frequently typified by intricate ecosystems involving several stakeholders and a variety of financial instruments—is made possible in large part by blockchain technology. The transparency aspect of blockchain is one of the main ways it accomplishes this. Every authorized user on a blockchain can view every transaction and piece of data that is stored there (Farnaghi, 2020). This transparency in the context of sustainable investments allows the public, regulators, and investors to view cash flows and project developments in real time and comprehensively. Since attempts to alter or falsify information would be instantly apparent and scrutinized, such transparency promotes accountability and deters fraudulent activity.

Furthermore, the immutability of blockchain guarantees that, once recorded, data cannot be changed or removed without the network's participants' consent (Ahmad, 2021). Because it protects the historical records of project milestones, financial transactions, and environmental impact measures, this feature is especially helpful for sustainability initiatives. Investors can feel secure knowing that the data they use to guide their decisions will always be reliable and resistant to manipulation. The long-term character of many sustainability initiatives is also in line with immutability, which offers a trustworthy historical record for evaluating the effectiveness and impact of programs at every stage of their existence. In this sense, blockchain technology helps to foster confidence amongst the various parties involved in sustainable investments, ranging from project developers looking for funding for their endeavors to investors looking to support environmentally friendly businesses.

TOKENIZING SUSTAINABLE ASSETS THROUGH NFTS

The innovative use of blockchain and NFT technology in tokenizing sustainable assets through NFTs has the potential to completely transform how we finance sustainability initiatives. Tokenization is the process of reflecting real-world assets as NFTs on a blockchain, such as sustainable agricultural land, green real estate, or infrastructure for renewable energy (Kasprzak, 2021; Tian et al., 2021). Through this method, ownership of these assets is divided into digital tokens, opening up prospects for fractional ownership and increasing accessibility to a wider variety of investors. A solar farm, for example, may be tokenized into NFTs, each of which would represent a certain amount of the farm's revenue stream or energy output.

This approach offers several advantages in terms of sustainable investments. Because NFTs can be traded more easily than conventional physical asset ownership structures, it first increases liquidity (Ali et al., 2023). Second, it lowers barriers to entry, allowing retail investors to participate in environmentally beneficial projects that were previously only accessible to wealthy individuals or institutional investors. Thirdly, it encourages accountability and transparency by clearly recording ownership rights and financial performance information of the underlying assets on the blockchain. Investors may easily verify the provenance of their tokens and track the environmental impact of the assets they possess. This combination of transparency, fractional ownership, and accessibility holds the potential to democratize sustainable investments, mobilizing more capital towards projects that promote environmental and social sustainability. In the subsequent sections, we will delve into real-world case studies and applications that demonstrate the practicality and impact of tokenizing sustainable assets through NFTs.

CASE STUDY AND REAL-WORLD APPLICATIONS

A noteworthy case study involves the process of tokenizing renewable energy projects. Renewable energy suppliers have started to issue NFTs representing a portion of the energy produced by wind turbines or solar panels in various regions. These NFTs are available for purchase by investors, who will then be entitled to a share of the energy output and related revenue (Truby, 2018). This strategy encourages the switch to sustainable energy sources while simultaneously democratizing access to investments in renewable energy. Transparency and trust are established by logging ownership and energy generation data on a blockchain, which draws in investors who care about the environment.

Another compelling example revolves around sustainable agriculture. Farmland can be tokenized with NFTs, giving investors ownership rights over a designated area of the property. These tokens might also stand for a portion of the earnings or crop produce. Stakeholders can provide funding to promote eco-friendly agriculture efforts while publicly tracking the effectiveness of sustainable farming techniques by linking NFT ownership to smart contracts that automate revenue distribution.

SHOWCASE OF REAL-WORLD PROJECTS THAT LEVERAGE BLOCKCHAIN-DRIVEN NFTS FOR SUSTAINABLE INVESTMENTS

The showcase of real-world projects leveraging blockchain-driven NFTs for sustainable investments provides compelling evidence of the practical application and impact of this innovative fusion of technology. One notable example involves the tokenization of carbon credits, where projects generating carbon offsets tokenize these credits as NFTs on a blockchain (Chen & Volz, 201). Investors can purchase these NFTs, effectively owning a stake in carbon reduction initiatives. This strategy not only supports eco-friendly initiatives but also gives investors the ability to make a real impact on mitigating climate change. The traceability and legitimacy of carbon credit issuance and trading are guaranteed by the transparency provided by blockchain technology, which increases the allure of sustainable investments in this area.

Another significant showcase revolves around the tokenization of eco-friendly real estate (Saari et al., 2022) Sustainable real estate developers tokenize ownership shares of green buildings as NFTs, granting investors fractional ownership and entitlements to rental income or financial benefits generated by the property. By recording property ownership and revenue-sharing agreements on a blockchain, this approach democratizes access to sustainable real estate investments, while enhancing transparency, accessibility, and security. These showcases underscore how blockchain-driven NFTs are being effectively utilized across diverse sustainability sectors, ranging from environmental conservation to real estate, providing investors with a unique opportunity to engage directly with sustainable projects while benefiting from the transparency and trustworthiness facilitated by blockchain technology.

IMPACT TOKENS

Impact tokens represent a revolutionary blockchain-based solution that is transforming the landscape of impact investing. These tokens leverage the transparency, security, and traceability features of blockchain technology to enable investors to directly support and track the impact of their investments in real-time (Uzsoki & Guerdat, 2023). Each Impact token corresponds to a specific social or environmental project or initiative, allowing investors to align their capital with their values and monitor the tangible outcomes of their contributions. This innovation not only enhances trust and accountability in impact investing but also opens up new avenues for individuals and institutions to engage in positive social and environmental change while seeking financial returns in support of sustainable development goals (Ny, 2022). Impact tokens are poised to play a pivotal role in advancing the field of impact investing by making it more accessible, efficient, and impactful for a broader range of stakeholders.

By using impact tokens, investors can transparently verify that their capital is being deployed for impactful purposes and can even receive rewards or returns tied to the achievement of predefined sustainability goals. This not only aligns financial interests with environmental and social objectives but also fosters greater accountability and transparency in sustainable investments, ultimately driving positive change in addressing pressing global challenges like climate change and social inequality.

CHALLENGES AND FUTURE PERSPECTIVES

As we explore the intersection of blockchain technology, NFTs, and sustainable investments, it is essential to acknowledge the challenges and contemplate the future perspectives of this transformative approach. One significant challenge lies in regulatory frameworks and compliance. The rapidly evolving nature of blockchain and NFTs has left regulators grappling with how to address potential risks, such as fraud, money laundering, and investor protection, while fostering innovation (Zheng, 2022). Striking the right balance between enabling innovation and ensuring a secure and fair marketplace remains a complex task. However, proactive engagement between industry stakeholders, regulators, and policymakers is crucial to develop clear and adaptable regulatory frameworks that support responsible innovation in sustainable investments.

Another challenge relates to scalability and environmental concerns. The energy-intensive nature of some blockchain networks, such as Bitcoin, has raised questions about the environmental impact of blockchain technology (Truby, 2018). For sustainable investments, these concerns are particularly relevant, as they should align with ecological objectives. Finding solutions to reduce the environmental footprint of blockchain networks and exploring more energy-efficient consensus mechanisms will be vital for the long-term sustainability of blockchain-driven NFTs in sustainable investments.

Looking ahead, the future perspectives are promising. The continued maturation of blockchain technology, along with increased awareness of sustainable investing, is likely to foster a more robust ecosystem for blockchain-driven NFTs in sustainability. As the technology becomes more user-friendly and integrated with traditional financial systems, it can attract a broader range of investors and drive more significant capital flows toward sustainable initiatives. Moreover, advancements in interoperability between different blockchain networks and standards for NFTs can facilitate cross-platform trading and investment diversification (Khan, 2022). Overall, the convergence of blockchain and NFTs in sustainable investments holds the potential to democratize sustainable finance, increase transparency, and accelerate the transition towards a more sustainable and responsible global economy.

DISCUSSION AND CONCLUSION

The convergence of Non-Fungible Tokens (NFTs) and blockchain technology is a revolutionary development that bears significant consequences for sustainable investing. In the sustainability industry, blockchain's intrinsic transparency and immutability offer a safe and impenetrable basis for documenting financial transactions and project achievements. Tokenizing real-world sustainable assets using NFTs, which are distinct digital certificates of authenticity, promotes fractional ownership and increased accessibility for a larger group of investors. The usefulness of this creative fusion has been shown by real-world case studies, which range from tokenizing renewable energy projects to sustainable agriculture and carbon credits.

The collection, verification, and reporting of sustainability and ESG data can be completely transformed by combining blockchain technology with monitoring instruments such as drones, satellites, and Internet of Things devices (Mahmudnia, 2022; Jing, 2023). This may result in increased confidence, more precise evaluations of business sustainability initiatives, and the creation of novel financial instruments that link financial rewards to favorable social and environmental consequences.

Even though problems with regulatory frameworks, scalability, and environmental concerns still exist, they can be resolved by proactive cooperation between regulators, policymakers, and industry stakeholders. In the future, blockchain technology is expected to draw in a larger investor base and direct significant funding toward environmentally friendly projects as it develops and becomes more integrated with conventional financial institutions (Trivedi, 2021). Developments in NFT standards and interoperability will make cross-platform trading and investment diversification much easier. In the end, this revolutionary strategy may democratize sustainable finance, improve transparency, and hasten the shift to a more responsible and sustainable global economy. Eco-friendly blockchain solutions and promising applications that can help us move closer to accomplishing the UN Sustainable Development Goals are probably going to become more commonplace.

REFERENCES

Abhilash, S., Shenoy, S. S., Shetty, D. K., Lobo, L. S., & N, S. K. (2023). Green Bond as an Innovative Financial Instrument in the Indian Financial Market: Insights from Systematic Literature Review Approach. *SAGE Open*, *13*(2), 21582440231178783. doi:10.1177/21582440231178783

Ahmad, D., Lutfiani, N., Ahmad, A. D. A. R., & Rahardja, U. (2021). Blockchain Technology Immutability Framework Design in E-Government. [Public Administration Journal]. *Jurnal Administrasi Publik*, *11*(1), 32–41.

Ali, O., Momin, M., Shrestha, A., Das, R., Alhajj, F., & Dwivedi, Y. K. (2023). A review of the key challenges of non-fungible tokens. *Technological Forecasting and Social Change*, *187*, 122248. doi:10.1016/j.techfore.2022.122248

AlmansooriA.NobaneeH.NobaneeH. (2019). How Sustainability Contributes to Shared Value Creation and Firms' Value. SSRN. https://ssrn.com/abstract=3472411 or http://dx.doi.org/ doi:10.2139/ssrn.3472411

Atana, R., Razali, F. A., Said, J., & Zainun, S. (2016). Environmental, Social, and Governance (ESG) Disclosure and Its Effect on Firm's Performance: A Comparative Study. *IJEM*, *10*(S2), 355–375.

Belu, M. G. (2019). Application of blockchain in international trade: An overview. *The Romanian Economic Journal*, *22*(71), 2–15.

Chen, Y., & Volz, U. (2021). Scaling up sustainable investment through blockchain-based project bonds. *Development Policy Review*, *40*(3), e12582. doi:10.1111/dpr.12582

Chohan, U. W. (2021). Non-Fungible Tokens: Blockchains, Scarcity, and Value. *Critical Blockchain Research Initiative, Notes on the 21st Century.*

Collomb, A., & Sok, K. (2016). Blockchain/distributed ledger technology (DLT): What impact on the financial sector? *Digiworld Economic Journal,* (103).

Dowling, M. (2021). Is non-fungible token pricing driven by cryptocurrencies? *Finance Research Letters*, *44*, 102097. doi:10.1016/j.frl.2021.102097

Evans, T. M. (2019). Cryptokitties, cryptography, and copyright. *AIPLA Quarterly Journal*, *47*, 219.

Farnaghia, M., & Mansouriana, A. (2022). Blockchain, an enabling technology for transparent and accountable decentralized public participatory GIS. *Cities, 105.*

Gawusu, S., Zhang, X., Ahmed, A., Jamatutu, S. A., Miensah, E. D., Amadu, A. A., & Osei, F. A. J. (2022). Renewable energy sources from the perspective of blockchain integration: From theory to application. [Part B]. *Sustainable Energy Technologies and Assessments*, *52*, 52. doi:10.1016/j.seta.2022.102108

Hawashin, D., Salah, K., Jayaraman, R., & Musamih, A. (2023). Using Composable NFTs for Trading and Managing Expensive Packaged Products in the Food Industry. *IEEE Access : Practical Innovations, Open Solutions*, *11*, 10587–10603. doi:10.1109/ACCESS.2023.3241226

Heines, R., Dick, C., Pohle, C., & Jung, R. (2021). The Tokenization of Everything: Towards a Framework for Understanding the Potentials of Tokenized Assets. *PACIS 2021 Proceedings*, 40. Research Gate.

Jing, Y., Chen, C., Dong, J., & He, Z. (2023). Blockchain-Embedded Strategic Options for Satellite Operators: Sell, SataaS, or Dual [MDPI AG.]. *Systems*, *11*(11), 550. doi:10.3390/systems11110550

Kasprzak, P. (2021). Blockchain to the Rescue—Tokenization of Residential Real Estate in the Emerging Token Economy. In *H. T.A., & D. J.J., Digitalization, Digital Transformation and Sustainability in the Global Economy* (pp. 21–35). Springer. doi:10.1007/978-3-030-77340-3_3

Khan, K. M., Fahim, A., Saleem, D. M., & Jokhio, M. (2022). Empirical Investigation on Blockchain Interoperability. *VFAST Transactions on Software Engineering*, *11*(1), 25–36. doi:10.21015/vtse.v10i4.1315

Kietzmann, J., Lee, L. W., McCarthy, I. P., & Kietzmann, T. C. (2020). Deepfakes: Trick or treat? *Business Horizons, 63*(2), 135e146.

Krosinsky, C. (2012). *Sustainable investing: The art of long-term performance.* Routledge. doi:10.4324/9781849773959

Kumar, N. M., & Mallick, P. K. (2018). Blockchain technology for security issues and challenges in IoT. *Procedia Computer Science*, *132*, 1815–1823. doi:10.1016/j.procs.2018.05.140

Mahmudnia, D., Arashpour, M., Bai, Y., & Feng, H. (2022). Drones and Blockchain Integration to Manage Forest Fires in Remote Regions. *Drones (Basel)*, *6*(11), 331. doi:10.3390/drones6110331

Malhotra, A., O'Neill, H., & Stowell, P. (2021). Thinking strategically about blockchain adoption risks and risk mitigation. *Business Horizons, 65*(2), 159e171.

Milani, F., García-Bañuelos, L., & Dumas, M. (2016). Blockchain and business process improvement. *BP Trends newsletter* (October 2016).

Mustapha, Z., Kunhibava, S. B., & Muneeza, A. (2020). Legal and Sharīʿah non-compliance risks in Nigerian Islamic finance industry: A review of the literature. *International Journal of Law and Management, 63*(02), 275–299. doi:10.1108/IJLMA-03-2020-0075

Nakamoto, S. (2019). *Bitcoin: A peer-to-peer electronic cash system*. Manubot.

Ng, T.-H., Lye, C.-T., Chan, K.-H., Lim, Y.-Z., & Lim, Y.-S. (2020). Sustainability in Asia: The Roles of Financial Development in Environmental, Social, and Governance (ESG) Performance. *Social Indicators Research, 150*(1), 17–44. doi:10.1007/s11205-020-02288-w

Ny, B. (2022). Blockchain in Impact Investing: The Potential of Impact Tokens on SDGs. *Medium.* https://medium.com/@Godswisdomtoday/blockchain-in-impact-investing-the-potential-of-impact-tokens-on-sdgs-767ad67b4f3

Pilkington, M. (2016). Blockchain technology: principles and applications. In *Research handbook on digital transformations*. Edward Elgar Publishing. doi:10.4337/9781784717766.00019

Regner, F., Schweizer, A., & Urbach, N. (2019). NFTs in Practice — Non-Fungible Tokens as Core Components of a Blockchain-based Event Ticketing Application. In *Fortieth International Conference on Information Systems*.

Rijal, S., & Saranani, F. (2023). The Role of Blockchain Technology in Increasing Economic Transparency and Public Trust. [TACIT]. *Technology and Society Perspectives, 1*(2), 56–67. doi:10.61100/tacit.v1i2.51

Saari, A., Junnila, S., & Vimpari, J. (2022). Blockchain's Grand Promise for the Real Estate Sector: A Systematic Review. *Applied Sciences (Basel, Switzerland), 12*(23), 11940. doi:10.3390/app122311940

Shrivastava, G. (2020). Cryptocurrencies and Blockchain Technology Applications. *Wiley eBooks*. doi:10.1002/9781119621201

Tian, Y., Minchin, R. E., Chung, K., Woo, J., & Adriaens, P. (2021). Towards Inclusive and Sustainable Infrastructure Development through Blockchain-enabled Asset Tokenization: An Exploratory Case Study. *IOP Conference Series: Materials Science and Engineering*, Volume 1218.

Trivedi, S., Mehta, K., & Sharma, R. (2021). Systematic Literature Review on Application of Blockchain Technology in E-Finance and Financial Services. *Journal of Technology Management & Innovation*, *16*(3), 89–102. doi:10.4067/S0718-27242021000300089

Truby, J. (2018). Decarbonizing Bitcoin: Law and policy choices for reducing the energy consumption of Blockchain technologies and digital currencies. *Energy Research & Social Science*, *44*, 399–410. doi:10.1016/j.erss.2018.06.009

Tseng, M. L., Tan, P. A., Jeng, S. Y., Lin, C. W. R., Negash, Y. T., & Darsono, S. N. A. C. (2019). Sustainable investment: Interrelated among corporate governance, economic performance and market risks using investor preference approach. *Sustainability (Basel)*, *11*(7), 2108. doi:10.3390/su11072108

Udeagha, M. C., & Muchapondwa, E. (2023). Green finance, fintech, and environmental sustainability: Fresh policy insights from the BRICS nations. *International Journal of Sustainable Development and World Ecology*, *30*(6), 633–649. doi:10.1080/13504509.2023.2183526

Uzsoki, D., & Guerdat, P. (2019). *Impact Tokens: A blockchain-based solution for impact investing*. International Institute for Sustainable Development.

Wilson, K. B., Karg, A., & Ghaderi, H. (2021). Prospecting non- fungible tokens in the digital economy: Stakeholders and ecosystem, risk and opportunity. *Business Horizons*, *65*(5), 657e670.

Yoo, S., & Managi, S. (2021). Disclosure or action: Evaluating ESG behavior towards financial performance. *Finance Research Letters*, 102108.

Chapter 5
Blockchain in Human Resource Management:
A Bibliographic Investigation and Thorough Evaluation

Tapaswini Panda
https://orcid.org/0009-0009-9198-3578
Model Degree College, India

Udaya Sankar Patro
https://orcid.org/0009-0009-9198-3578
Rayagada Autonomous College, India

Saumendra Das
https://orcid.org/0000-0003-4956-4352
GIET University, Gunupur, India

Koppala Venugopal
Aditya Institute of Technology and Management, India

N. Saibabu
https://orcid.org/0000-0001-6054-2053
Aditya Institute of Technology and Management, India

ABSTRACT

This chapter aims to provide fresh ideas from philosophy to help human resources managers adopt blockchain technology in their work. In order to categorize the 25 significant items, the authors examined the 126 publications that were made available for acceptance between 2016 and 2021 in the Scopus and Web of Science databases. Using bibliometric data, the headings, titles, and keyword phrases of each of those

DOI: 10.4018/979-8-3693-1878-2.ch005

25 papers have all been meticulously analysed. Depending on the bibliometric data gathered, word relationship network maps were produced using VOS viewer. There are four topic groupings that were made using the linked visualisations. It has been decided that the ideas of employee-systems interface (ESI) and blockchain framework (BCF) for HR are going to encourage the adoption and application of distributed computing technologies in the area of the administration of human resources. After reading all 25 articles, the authors thoroughly and in-depth examined the key terms that supported the two philosophical subjects and determined the validity of the results.

INTRODUCTION

Since its inception, blockchain technologies has proven to be among the most cutting-edge and complex inventions that the globe has witnessed to date. Blockchain technology is a kind of distributed ledger technology (DLT) that preserves the history of an electronically object. It was created by Nakamoto and originally detailed in 2008 (Ballandies, Dapp, and Pournaras, 2021). It is regarded as a DLT which stores events and interactions as an immutable recorded in time electronic block. Although blockchain's evolution and progress in technology started with Blockchain technology, it is now extensively employed in many other industries and countries. More recent statistics demonstrate this quite clearly (Etemadi, Van Gelder, and Strozzi, 2021). Recent research (Mishra and Venkatesan 2021; Rane, Thakker, and Kant 2020; Venkatesh et al. 2020; Zheng, Zhang, and Gauthier 2020; Patil et al. 2020; Fachrunnisa and Hussain 2020) has shown that the technology of blockchain has the potential to influence and transform all facets of company operations, from the banking sector including supply tie management and health maintenance to the management of employees. Employee-systems interaction (ESI), which has just come to light in the world of blockchain technology, is also shown.

Blockchain technology has established itself as an innovative technology that is grabbing the interest of scholars, professionals, and corporate organisations. Blockchain innovation will fundamentally alter the way companies operate and enable its use across several sectors and businesses. Although industries in transportation and logistics, healthcare, and retail are all aggressively embracing blockchain technologies, the banking sector now takes a leading role in its growth and adoption. For trade settlement, trade financing, and insurance in the banking and finance sector, client record keeping for health care, guarantee claims within retail, or electronic supply chains, bitcoin is employed.

Many businesses are starting to look at integrating the technology of blockchain into everyday activities. Virtually every organisational activity, from production and manufacture through supply chain oversight, has the potential to gain from the use of blockchain. Although human resource management (HRM) has advanced, with practically every aspect now being digitalized (Mishra and Akman, 2010), less focus has been placed on the viewpoint of how SHRM in organisations really operates.

Organisations might benefit from blockchain. 60% of the workforce Specialists have reportedly found fraudulent qualifications on applicant applications, as reported by CareerBuilder, which People lie about their qualifications, duties, previous jobs, job titles, academic degrees, employers they've working for, and honours along with awards. Blockchain will completely change how the administration of human resources works in businesses. According to blockchain technology, workers will soon be able to communicate with their superiors about private data. Investors would feel confident knowing that candidates' credentials, successes, citations, and talents could all be digitally confirmed.

Recruitment, verification, smart contracts, secure transactions, attendance, conformity, the field of auditing avoiding fraudulent activity, and data security will all be made possible by technology. Blockchain is being used by several active startups to provide human resources solutions including pay bounce, staff management and rewards, application data transparency, and freelancer ecosystem. Blockchain is currently not a frequently utilised technology in organisations for human resources management integration, nevertheless.

In order to better understand the perspectives of managers of human resources and non-HR employees, this piece seeks to better understand their understanding of the current state of HRM in their organizations, the HR-related problems that their companies are facing, their familiarity with blockchain technology, alongside their opinions on the possible uses of blockchain in the Human Resources department. The company's HR decision-making processes will change if blockchain is adopted, which will affect all employees, regardless of their ability to fit the HR or non-HR characteristics.

Thus, the present research aimed to investigate the perceptions of HR and non-HR staff on blockchain technology in HRM in companies that are yet to maximize its potential. No business in India employs blockchain technology for its human resources department. It is reasonable to state that this research project would be the first to examine employees' opinions of the application of blockchain in SHRM in India from both an HR and non-IIR standpoint.

The research will provide recommendations to managers in the organisation on the breadth of implementing this technology in HRM and the degree to which workers are prepared to adapt to these changes. Everyone in the organisation and those working in human resources will gain from the findings of this research. Computing network parts create a blockchain, which is a distributed record or database. A blockchain similarly constantly stores data in digital format, just like a database does. Blockchains are most famously used to maintain a secure, randomised ledger of transactions in blockchain technology systems like blockchain technology. The blockchain technology creates credibility sans relying on an untrustworthy outside source by guaranteeing the security and privacy of a record of knowledge.

Figure 1. Employee-systems interaction (ESI)
Source: Author's own contribution

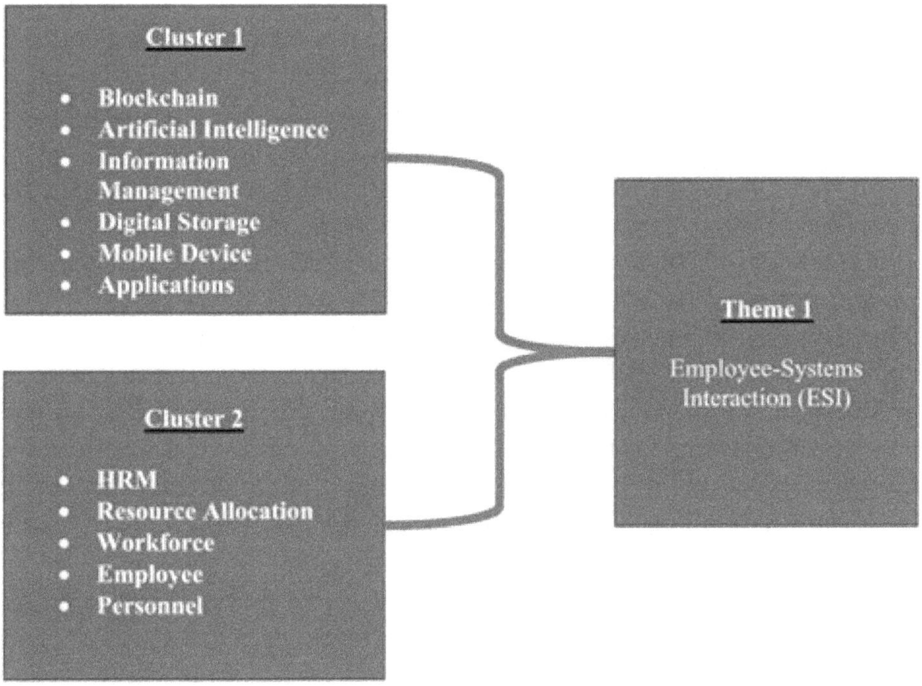

A very recent development is the use of Blockchain alongside other cutting-edge technology to oversee personnel and enhance business results (Vrontis et al., 2021). The original cryptocurrency, bitcoin (BTC), is commonly brought up when "blockchain" is addressed. The general consensus has it that there exists only one Blockchain, which serves as a ledger for bitcoin transactions. The distributed ledger of other digital currencies and tokens is still maintained by a number of additional networks, including Ethereum, Cardano, Tron, and Hedra Hash graph, which operate side by side with the Bitcoin chain.

The Business Review of Harvard University (2018) defines a "blockchain" as an endless chain of bits of information that are linked together by encryption. With the possible exception of the first block, called starting out, because do not feature the preceding block's rehash code, every single block contains information about activities as well as an encrypted hash for the block that preceded it. Since the time and date stamp show that the knowledge exists at the moment when the file was generated, it is possible to include the data for the transaction in the scrambling. A chain of blocks forms when one extra block strengthens each one that has come before it (Centobelli et al., 2021).

In addition, a number of expected applications that go beyond the field of cryptocurrency, such as those in clothing, sales, and medical treatment, are anticipated. This is true because of the way a blockchain is built, which can offer features like discussed databases, decentralised governance, permanence of information, smart contract functionality, a more durable and adaptable construction, anonymous confidentiality, and counterfeit prevention. These possible benefits are summarised by the four TRs: reliability, monitoring, transparent. The administration of human resources (HRM) is just one of the fields where Blockchain is being hailed as an advancement. Blockchain use is expected to benefit recruiting, presence administration, contractual relationships, pay-related financial transactions, data security, and the avoidance of crimes such as cyberattacks.

Blockchain gives prospective employees the chance to generate, modify, and submit their CVs in a completely open yet secure surroundings, while companies can obtain the information submitted on schooling, job situations, and abilities verified in an automatic manner by consensus tools as reported by some suggested Bitcoin within human resources management usage. (2019: 787; Koncheva et al). A number of additional academic publications have looked into different facets of blockchain technology's possible use in HR administration.

These include the degree of distributed ledger technology adoption in HR leadership and human resources professionals' perceptions of blockchain resumes; additionally, these cover the potential application of blockchain technology to enhance training assessment, the impact of organizational factors on blockchain adoption, and job opportunities in the context of developing innovations.

But the research has a few major problems. They provide a research, test, structure, method, or foundation for a tiny or first-scale business usage, or their grasp of the blockchain's architecture is limited to what is well known regarding Bitcoin. Additionally, blockchain is referred to in a restricted context as a tool to support HRM within firms, such as the verification of applicants' qualifications.

The article looks at scholarly literature to see what blockchain may offer Human Resource Management. Some of the following topics emerged from the study and analysis of the data: (1) HRM managers' knowledge of blockchain; (2) the importance of blockchain in SHRM; (3) areas where blockchain use will make a difference to HRM; (4) the potential effects of embracing blockchain technology on the employment; (5) the current restrictions on blockchain's usefulness in SHRM.

BLOCKCHAIN: DEFINATION, TYPES, AND USES

Blockchain uses a network of peers to peers as an open ledger. A widely accessible the network's transactions are linked together via cryptography and can view older blocks. There are issues since the ledger replicates and distributes records to each node in a connected system. Cryptography, distributed ledgers, intelligent agreements, and the agreement-based protocol are the four main components of a blockchain. According to the Harvard Business Review (2018), blockchain files are append-only, unchanging, and can only be created by peer consensus and encryption. Information is stored on a distributed ledger in "pieces" with a "header" and "content" that follow a set pattern.

Shelkovnikov (2016) states that blockchains can be hybrids, confidential, or communal. Blockchains may also be categorised based on whether they are permissioned or permissionless.

Permitted blockchains only permit network members to access or add to them, whereas permissionless ones enable anyone to read and analyse its blocks. Blockchains, whether either public or private or mixed, which all possess a few traits in in common: electronically centralised databases without outside interference; an algorithm for consensus to reach an understanding, cryptography to seal transactions and demonstrate identification, and theoretically immutable libraries of historical information.

Take the example of records from the database. The conventional method of keeping documents inside an enterprise is often regional or central. For instance, data kept in a conventional way are susceptible to fraud. Since information are spread across every node in a chain. Blockchain technology prevents document manipulation while also not having a single point of breakdown. When an entry is added to a blockchain block, it is permanently preserved.

The main use of blockchain is the creation of cryptocurrency (lnes, 2016). The main use of blockchains is no longer to store money; instead, "smart contracts" have lately emerged as a crucial component. Energy, finance, medicine, supply chain (Tse et al., 2017), and logistics chain.There are several of them, including the maritime industry, and a number of other sectors (Isler, 2021).

LaborX (https://laborx.com) is an example of how blockchain technology is being used in human resources. This platform enables businesses to hire labourers from anywhere in the globe and pay for them using bitcoin. A customer can list what assistance they require and the price they are prepared to pay, or a provider can list the services they offer and the price they are prepared to charge. Similar to a job board, but with blockchain-based payment processing. Similar to this, the Bounties Network (https://bounties.network/) enables task creation and fulfilment by employees or any other party, as well as trading in any Ethereum asset with automatic payouts in every token.

As a result, it may be useful for companies looking to hire people on a specific endeavour who live anywhere in the globe. Emphasis should be placed on the fact that only the payment—specifically, the bitcoin payments given to employees—is carried out through blockchain.

However, because of institutional and technological obstacles, the adoption of blockchain is typically sluggish. Some of the technological constraints are security, practicality, data challenges, and technical immaturity. On the other side, structural constraints include management commitment, work norms and culture, governmental regulations, and morality techniques. Despite the possibility for blockchain technology to change businesses, this won't happen for decades.

Blockchain technology constitutes a given away, open digital ledger in which operations can be confirmed and saved in a way that essentially eliminates the possibility of information tampering. It follows that strangers can exchange information and carry out transactions, particularly one's finances, without the need for a middleman. Credibility, confidentiality, safety, accuracy of data, and openness are the primary advantages.

The desire to boost operational honesty, increase the rapidity of transactions by cutting down on clearance and settlement times, and automate or simplify corporate operations are the top three development drivers of distributed ledger technology in HR, according to the APQC.

Blockchain has advanced past hype to gain useful uses in every sector of business in only the years before this one, according to Daher. The greatest blockchain-based tools for human resources management deal with important HR management challenges like payroll, hiring, employment identification, and handling contracts. Payroll. The most compelling use case is possibly this one. The payroll procedure may be streamlined by using blockchain to streamline and secure payments to staff, contractors, and suppliers. Freelancers and "gig business" workers often require payments across borders, which is an early application that was first introduced just a few weeks ago by a number of companies. Occasionally, they lack financial accounts, which are frequently required for payments made through computerized payroll management.

Blockchain hiring techniques get over regional laws and computer safety protocols that might block traditional online payments. Leading manufacturers of software for staff administration are taking part. ATP, one of the biggest providers of payroll services, is developing a smartphone application with blockchain technology. recruiting. Employers, particularly recruiting executives, may rely on the electronic credentials of candidates, such as their resumes, college transcripts, training certificates, and employment histories, which are stored digitally and cannot be altered by technologies.

Blockchain-based systems for employees may significantly enhance a recruiter's job, which involves locating and securely transmitting paperwork. Another recruiting expense that blockchain identification may reduce is the employment of outside companies by companies to screen candidates and validate material. Although this based on a HR solution is still in its early stages, schools have begun to provide students with access to blockchain-formatted records data pertaining to employees.

Confidential data may be encrypted and stored using the technology of distributed ledgers, offering it has no authority and inviolability. But just like with school records, a large portion of the information's security preserved by blockchain technology depends on the ethics and genuineness of the individual who created the record in the first place. Specialists say that instead of creating a reliable record of past data for contract management, it seems more probable that electronic currencies will function as the platform of record for all staff documents going forward.

Paper contracting may be converted into open with one another irrevocable digital agreements thanks to smart contracting, which blockchain technology makes possible. They can be used by companies to carry out the conditions and sanctions stipulated in contracts with workers and contractors who are independent.

"Employment agreements constitute one of the fields were blockchain technology can be used, in addition to history and recommendation checks," said Scott Hirsch, CTO and the co-founder of Talent Market place, a powered by artificial intelligence hiring network for IT firms. "The best use cases are those that demand confidentiality and independent certification."

Another possible application of the blockchain's handling of contracts capabilities is to increase the rapidity and efficacy of advantages administrative procedures.

Blockchains may be utilized to carry out advantages events, or purchases, according to an article by HR specialist Riia O'Donnell on HR Dive. might be utilized to start an advantage if a staff member is qualified for medical coverage, and it may begin a pay raise after an initial trial period is completed. Even managing contracts for workers like confidentiality agreements might be done with it individuals' blockchains. Blockchain first seemed destined for HR's internal procedures, but a startling trend is already starting to show itself.

According to the APQC study, staff members will soon have access to personal digital currencies that "encompass all of their professional existence, that include academic documents, login information, employment records, staff information and instruction?" This will be a unique and significant use of blockchain technology in human resources.

Companies would need an individual's permission to access and change their private networks. Employees may provide access keys to companies so they may maintain control over their own private documents, but they may withdraw the keys after they leave the organization. Employees might successfully utilize chain HR systems this way as "value passports" that they may carry wherever and continuing to use. Blockchain holds a lot of potential for companies as well as staff members, but it continues to be very young.

"Block Chain has the ability to fundamentally change the HR sector, touching things from managing benefits to exercising authority on critical staff information and the way that HR activities flow out," said Elissa Tucker, principal research lead for the management of human capital at APQC.

However, "despite these advantages, blockchain nonetheless remains an emerging technology for HR, with just a small number of HR directors stating that their HR unit was already adopting blockchain."

ADVANTAGES OF BLOCKCHAIN TECHNOLOGIES FOR THE HR DEPARTMENT

A significant amount of research has also been done in this field since internationalization and the increase of workers have altered the makeup of organizations, firm cultures, and technological and cultural advancements. Leaders of the organization's leadership really modify their behavior, which influences organizational efficiency, and Specialists within the HR field are crucial to advising the organization as a "a shift conversion agent" (Deshler, 2016). The four areas wherein blockchain may be employed are authentication confirmation, labour settlements, employment finding systems, and management of identities, states Andrew Spencer, a UK-based human capital management consultancy and research (Ahmed, 2019 referenced in People Matters, 2019).

Utilizing blockchain-based technology is just one of numerous safe technologies that provides HR a platform for streamlining operations and more tools for solving issues and connecting with customers. By identifying possible hazards and ineffective approaches in jobs requiring resources as individuals time, and money, the use of blockchain technology may be modified to reduce data collection and confirmation. One illustration is the use of a ledger maintained on a blockchain as a reliable method for verifying contenders' biographies (Aishwarya, 2018). A excellent example of how utilizing blockchain technologies for promotion may lower the cost of cooperating and building for the goal of authenticating throughout the hiring process is a company that has recommendations accessible as well as a validated CV of possible employees (Hegadekatti, 2018).

BLOCKCHAIN INNOVATION BOOST RECRUITMENT AND OFF- BORADING VALUE

According to Phillips and Gully (2012), quoted in Koch et al. (2018), recruiting is the procedure of finding the best candidate who might or might not be intrigued by leaving their present position to take on a job vacancy for an organization. An extensive amount of time, money, and labor is used on completing administrative duties and confirmations during the hiring cycle, which also involves connecting, screening, and evaluating candidates.

According to the Australian Economic Review, it took 68 days annually across the nation in 2015 to fill a vacancy, a 50% increase over 2010 (Morshed Chowdhury, 2018). The major issue, then, is how to ensure that applications provide reliable and correct information. During the recruiting process, candidates often send a résumé along with any necessary evidence of eligibility, such as certificates, pieces of recommendation from previous employers, paystubs, tax returns, and healthcare documentation. In as a whole, internal administration personnel perform confirmations or delegate them to other individuals, while candidates supply contact information (Morshed Chowdhury et al., 2018).

To move forward with a letter of recommendation check, applicants often present favorable references from previous contacts. In most cases, it is impossible to find any unfavorable or non-disclosed material on an applicant's résumé. Businesses can use blockchain systems to verify a prospective employee's legitimacy via a decentralized third-party record or applicant credentials (key or token). Applicants can use a distributed database to build, manage, and retain access of a the blockchain depends record of their professional and educational credentials as well as their employment history (Aishwarya, 2018). danger factors, inadequate privacy protection, unlawful use of permanent data derived from internet use, and unmanageable numerous personas. The difficulty of verifying digital documents is another significant problem with blockchain technology (Tucker and Catalini, 2018).

Numerous studies have been done on the potential risks and insufficient privacy measures, as well as the discovery and unlawful use of persistent material produced by online communities and unsustainable large numbers of names. Another key issue with the blockchain is the challenge with electronic proof of ownership (Tucker and Catalini, 2018). Many studies have been conducted on how to solve this issue using consensus rules such as job documentation, placed evidence, potential the Byzantine Empire tolerance for faults, granted stake the proof adjustable Constantine's protocol for consensus layout, and blockchain-based systems, but those methods may not prove adequate for future information protection. Since the existing Tor constraints may not be sufficient in the future to ensure the protection of their data, Ryan Henry and his buddies are discussing a potential privacy concern in 2019.

Additionally, local laws may make it difficult to implement Blockchain internationally. Hong Kong, for instance, has the Personal Data (Privacy) Ordinance and the Rehabilitation of Offenders Ordinance (the ROO). Before starting an official criminal record check, the hiring manager must have the employee's consent.

VERIFICATION OF RESUMES

Numerous studies have looked at the fact that social media platforms let users construct and post their own profiles without verifications, according to a Society for Human Resources Management, or SHRM, 2016 study. According to a study, 82 percent of passive job seekers are the main reason businesses utilize social media for recruiting, and there has been an increase of 84 percent in this area. According to a different Robert Walters survey, LinkedIn, Facebook, and Twitter are the top three social media sites for both job seekers and businesses when it comes to recruitment.

Without verification, a company could receive duplicate job applicants from different sources. According to a Risk Advisory Group analysis of almost 5,000 applications, 12% of application resumes had fabricated grades, and 80% of individual profiles contained conflicts with 57% of the candidate's academic record.

Employers can check candidate qualifications for schooling by using distributed ledgers in educational institutions. Consolidated ledgers, including individuals (job applicants), either private or public entities (professional universities, organizations, and institutions), or public or private third parties (background check businesses, BCHRIS, and BCRMS), can verify the data. Many records can additionally rate applicants and filter requests for unfit positions. With pre-verifications, blockchain helps marketers accelerate up the hiring process and reduce "time, effort, and cost" while contacting candidates through social media. Blockchain, according to research, can improve the safety of information, avoiding fraudulent activity, and cybercrime in HR (PwC, 2017).

BACKGROUND INVESTIGAIONS

Verifying resumes of applicants for international recruiting or certain legal blinding presents challenges for recruiters. It is common practice to use third parties, such as background check officers, to conduct checks in order to support the promotion of the candidate's conditional employment offer. A formal authorization for a background check must be obtained from the applicants. According to polls by the Society for Human Resources Management (SHRM), background checks are routinely used by businesses. Background checks are now considered to be a routine and acceptable part of the hiring process, and applicants who refuse to cooperate with the investigation may be eliminated from consideration (Brody, 2010). As a result, blockchain offers a chance for other parties, including employers, to independently and secretly verify that shared records are accurate (Grech and Camilleri, 2017).

To confirm a prospective employee's past, including their record of work and schooling, employers might consult a reliable ledger. Private papers like health data and transportation records, as well as additional legal-related facts like credit and criminal histories, may still react to other people. The candidate's conditional offer is contingent upon the outcome of the criminal record investigation; otherwise, it is void.

ADMINISTRATION OF EMPLOYEE DATA

The problem is investigated utilizing HR the complainant's time-consuming creation and updates on personnel job histories and HRIS enrolments. Examples include setting up accounts and cancellation, enrolment benefits, training, evaluations of performance, and division, as well as notice to legal parties like tax or immigration authorities. A distributed person or public/private ledger can be used by recruiters to confirm the applicant's employment details, and they are able to input new hire data into the shared ledger or BCHRIS for administrative purposes like reference checks, pay administration of benefits (such as health care and medical insurance, and or compensations), and constitutional programs (tax and or insurance). Blockchain may speed up repetitive data entry and administrative tasks, as well as managing past jobs with ledgers instead of background checks.

The recognized applicant receives an offer packet from recruitment or payments managers, according to the terms of the applicant's most recent offer. The person's name or public / private logbook may be used to track the proof of job history, such as the previous job's pay, reward, allowances, and advantages in order to benchmark the new offer deal. Certifications of legal information, that includes loan situation, criminal background, and/or medical histories, can nevertheless not be incorporated in the central ledger; instead, they may rely on outside parties (or the ledger as a whole, which may be controlled by outside parties or made public), to carry out the confirmation. Before moving further with checks, obtain a candidate's either written or verbal approval.

Prior or on the day of boarding, recruiters create hiring agreements for applicants to sign. Cryptocurrency enables both registered and unregistered institutions to access workers' backgrounds and expedite the recruitment procedure by providing a reliable record.

BLOCKCHAIN KNOWLEDGE AMONG HUMAN RESOURCES MANAGERS

Research conducted by practitioners suggests that lack of understanding is the main barrier to blockchain adoption in enterprises (e.g., Shelkovnikov, 2016). The HR industry is likewise affected by this understanding (Chillakuri and Attili, 2021). Thus, it may be claimed that as HR professionals' awareness of the technology behind blockchain develops, the likelihood of it will ultimately be used in SHRM increases.

According to Mishra and Venkatesan's findings from 2021, human resources practitioners' knowledge of "blockchain in HRM" was most likely comparable to the knowledge for non-HR professionals, if not equal. As consequence, current HR professionals lack the necessary understanding of the use of blockchain technology to evaluate the benefits it will provide when deployment expenses are taken into consideration.

It is imperative to address the problem of HRM employees' technical competence as a result. Findings from studies (Mishra and Venkatesan, 2021) from fields other than cryptocurrencies that don't show a level of proficiency with Blockchain's technical features don't advance our understanding.

Additionally, the level of expertise suggested for hiring managers in the research is simply limited to having a thorough understanding of the technology's Blockchain.

It is logical to assume that hiring managers' viewpoints will change as they become more cognizant of the constraints and difficulties associated with using blockchain outside of the context of using electronic funds.

A recent study suggests that human resources managers may develop a variety of thinking habits associated with blockchain technology use in their comprehension processes.

The finding of the field study that utilization of digital currencies is limited by a lack of expertise may be supported by this gap from scholarly research on the degree of awareness among human resources professionals. Human resources managers and their organisations will not benefit from having an elementary knowledge of Blockchain, which relies on data pertaining to exchange-traded virtual currencies, in order to make an educated judgement about the technology's potential uses.

Dependent on where Blockchain is in the marketplace for digital currencies, using Blockchain technology in human resources management might waste money or lead to missed chances.

Consequently, in lieu of seeking to comprehend the perspectives of HR professionals on the usage of distributed ledgers in Human Resources Management (HR it is advisable to query about their specific area of expertise. Assessing their level of understanding can assist create programmes of education that can assist them better understand blockchain technology. To enable them to arrive at better decisions,

HR professionals would benefit from having a greater technological understanding of blockchain technology. Understanding the technical details of Blockchain can help an organisation determine the issues related to human resources it wants to address and why Blockchain technology is the best choice in contrast to alternative platforms (Vincent and Tadesse, 2020).

Last but not least, despite the fact that HR professionals may be aware with the term "blockchain," they typically exclusively use it in relation to cryptocurrencies.

By deepening their understanding of how the technology works and may be applied there by studying and obtaining better technical skills, they are able to decide with knowledge about the advantages associated with employing blockchain technology in HRM. The fields of study to delve additional into this subject.

Blockchain represents a few of the disruptive concepts that may alter every area of the planet. The use of "intelligent contracts" in the field of blockchain technology has the potential to completely change how human resources managers hire candidates, manage pay checks, and educate new hires.

The digital currency bitcoin as the initial form of blockchain system to be used. On a more positive side, blockchain is a given out, tamper-proof, and distributed repository of information. A block that has been uploaded to the blockchain is unchangeable, which means that the data cannot be changed or removed.

It is anticipated that the employment industry would employ a public, unsupervised blockchain-based system to disrupt operations like hiring, pay checks, and retraining. There are a number of reasons for which the usage using blockchain.

RECRUITMENT OF PERSONEEL FOLLOWING BLOCKCHAIN

According to the research, one "bad hire" costs a business, on average, $14900 in losses (Ahmed, 2019). The ones that follow are two important aspects of the hiring process that are commonly faked, and using the blockchain can help firms with them.

Verifying qualifications Blockchain-based technology will eliminate the need for traditional CVs and applications in the applicant screening process by substituting it with a new, user-friendly platform that offers a speedy search and matching process. Ethereum will possess the most up-to-date details on a potential employee's educational history, skill established, and awards. Blockchain makes it easy to verify endorsements.

Work Histories: Blockchain technology for employment records has the potential to assist companies in decreasing instances of fraudulent work histories, as attested to by past employers. Since there are higher stakes and fewer lives at stake in the legal, medical, and pharmaceutical industries, the significance of this is widely recognized.

STREAMLINE DAILY ACTIVITIES

Blockchain has the potential to significantly alter and enhance many of the routine, everyday responsibilities of managing people. This simplification will save cash voor their companies, allow human resource managers to perform their duties more efficiently, and free up additional time for other projects.

Tracking Payroll: Despite this, almost all big and medium-sized businesses use automated payroll services. The procedure may be reinforced by keeping an eye on changes, getting rid of fraud, keeping track of presence and duty time, offering additional payment methods, and organizing incentives. The use of digital currencies for transactions and comprehensive transparency might completely remove the demand for intermediaries like banks and insurance companies.

Blockchain innovation has the power to change how organizations train their workers and how enthusiastically employees receive instructions. Any certification or training someone completes might add a new entry to their clearly verifiable company records, which remains there.

Cognizant Contracts: Intelligent contracts are expected to replace the existing physical shrinks, which require routine human monitoring. Contracts utilizing ledgers that are distributed are covered by intelligent agreement clauses. These contracts specify the requirements for participation along with the penalties for violating them. With the use of "if and else," this could potentially use to compel not simply the communications but also simpler behaviour, such "if this happens, than this payroll process will be initiated in particular situations.

The contracts' underlying code must be solid and must keep into mind that the activities they facilitate are irrevocable.

The use of electronic tools in handling human resources has both benefits and drawbacks. In general, Ethereum facilitates truth and openness in the realm of hiring. Here, innovation not only makes it simple for both employers and workers to locate one another, but it also promotes mutual trust.

There are various drawbacks or issues that require attention. One of these involves creating permanent "blocks" of erroneous data or activities. Secondly, is the science currently in the beginning stages and needs maturation. Issues about the upscaling of the digital currency's application exist since none of the industries are using it to its fullest ability.

Last but not least, maintaining the confidentiality of data and adhering to GDPR regulations are of highest importance to the firm. The GDPR recognizes that there are murky areas when it comes to protecting individual information because it is fundamentally centralized platform. For instance, every individual or organization has the ability to remove personal data if it is mislabelled as "right to be forgotten" and goes against the principles underlying the decentralized ledger of blockchain technology.

In conclusion, the use of blockchain technology has the ability to significantly affect the people management business; but, in order to address the needs and concerns unique to this industry, it must initially be regulated.

The adverse impact of the technology known as blockchain has drawn the interest of industry/companies, investigators, and administrators are all included. Blockchain technology will fundamentally alter current business models and enable its use across several sectors and businesses. the economic industry takes the lead in creating and deploying blockchain technologies, but firms in the transportation and blockchain algorithms are also widely used in the fields of health care, transportation, and commerce. The application for the blockchain for instance. Healthcare uses medical records from the banking and insurance sector for trade settlement, trade financing, and underwriter. Technological supply chain, warranties papers in sales, and managing.

Many businesses are starting to look at using blockchain technology into their everyday activities.

Amazon, Walmart, Facebook, Google, and IBM have all started making significant investments in blockchain technology and using it for a range of purposes. With the use of blockchain technological devices, the UN will be able to send relief to particular recipients across international borders. The application of blockchain technology offers opportunities to improve almost each organisational function, from production and fabrication to logistics and supply chain management. despite the fact that the area of human resources management (HRM) has developed and almost all tasks are now performed digitally (Mishra and Akman, 2010), less attention has been paid to the perspective of how SHRM in businesses actually performs.

Organizations might benefit from blockchain. 60% of the human resources department Authorities have reportedly found fraudulent qualifications on candidate resumes, reported the CareerBuilder platform.

People lie about their qualifications, duties, employment history, job titles, academic degrees, employers they've worked for, and awards and distinctions.

Blockchain will completely change how human resources administration works in businesses. Thanks to some distributed ledger workers will eventually be able to communicate with their bosses about private data. Employers would feel confident knowing that candidates' credentials, successes, citations, and talents could all be digitally confirmed. Hiring, confirmation, electronic contracts, safe transactions, attendance, conformity, auditing, avoiding fraudulent activity, and data security will all be made possible by technology. Blockchain is being used by several active start-ups to provide HR solutions including pay roll, employee operations and rewards, application data openness plus independent contractor ecosystem. However, enterprises have yet to embrace blockchain as a widespread HRM integration platform.

This paper aims to gain a deeper understanding of the perspectives held by HR and non-HR staff members on the ways they assess the current state of HR starting their places of employment, the HR issues that their companies are facing, their overall understanding of blockchain technology, and their thoughts on possible blockchain applications for HR. The company's HR decision-making procedures will change if blockchain is adopted, which will affect all employees, regardless of how well they fit the HR or non-HR characteristics. Consequently, this study attempted to investigate the perceptions of blockchain in HRM among HR and non-HR staff members at companies that hadn't yet employed this form of technology.

No business in India employs blockchain technology for its human resources department. It is reasonable to state that this research would be the first to examine employees' opinions of the application of distributed ledgers throughout the human resources department in India from both an HR and non-IIR standpoint. The research will provide recommendations to those making decisions in the business on the breadth of implementing this technology in Human Resource Management (HR and the degree to which workers are prepared to adapt to these developments. Customers in the business and those working in human resources will gain from this study.

Computer networks share a system called blockchain, which is a distributed record or ledger. A distributed ledger similarly continuously stores data in a digital format, just like a database does. The ledgers are most famously used to maintain a secure, decentralized ledger of operations with digital currency platforms like Bitcoin. By ensuring the safety and soundness of information, blockchain technology innovates by fostering respect sans having to search for an impartial party.

In a future where academic credentials are kept on a blockchain, all of those changes. When a student completes their education, the school may issue a "digital degree" that can be accessed through a blockchain. Keep in mind that a precise timestamp is issued to every block of the distributed ledger and cannot be modified or changed. The degree is immediately verified when it is posted to the blockchain.

This might perhaps shorten or even do away with the requirement for an application procedure altogether. When qualifications and papers are stored on a digital ledger, a recruiter may advertise a vacancy, and an internet search engine can find accessible credentials that meet certain criteria and compile those covering letters into an applicant list. An employer might reach out to qualified candidates and ask. Instead, then posting job advertising on several employment sites and expecting answers, hiring managers might contact qualified candidates and ask if they are interested in the opening.

People lie about their qualifications, duties, previous employment, job titles, academic degrees, employers they've performed for, and awards and recognition.

Blockchain will completely change how human resources administration works in businesses. According to a distributed ledger workers will eventually be empowered to communicate with their bosses about private data. Businesses would feel confident knowing that candidates' credentials, achievements citations, and talents could all be digitally confirmed.

Hiring, confirmation, intelligent agreements, safe payments, safe classes, conformity, accounting, avoiding fraudulent activity, and data security will all be made possible by technologies. Bitcoin is being used by several active start-ups to provide HR solutions including pay roll, staff operations and rewards, application data openness plus independent contractor ecology. However, enterprises have yet to embrace blockchain as a widespread HRM integration platform.

By looking for articles in Google databases, the review of the literature was finished. Keywords like "Blockchain," "Candidate," "fraud," "Resume fraud," "Human Resource Management," "Blockchain in Organizations," and Blockchain technology in Human Resource Management" were used for searching academic articles.

Numerous articles off publications, internet, and commercial, technological, and human resources journals were likewise evaluated; nonetheless, these were excluded from the literature study. Payroll and hiring are once again the exclusive functions of HR, which has increased in prominence as an important function. Any transformation needs more than simply the HR division's drive.

Hirsch stated, "To begin with, HR usually becomes behind other industries when it regards embracing technological advances, and if you couple that with the difficulty of implementing the blockchain, you have a significant barrier."

Cybersecurity: Personnel in the payroll department who handle confidential information and dealings with money might be in risk since Ethereum is still vulnerable to breaches of data at ends that attackers could exploit to obtain information while it is being delivered.

Compliant risk: Due to the lack of regional regulatory standards for blockchain technology, businesses run the risk of financial loss and lawsuits if they violate worker privacy rights and comply with laws such as the EU's Data Protection Act.

Entanglement of interests: Outside vendors are usually needed to allow blockchain operations. Therefore, even if these manufacturers' websites as well as apps might not be as safe as the information stored in the database, the distributed ledger also contributes to building confidence in those platforms.

There's a good probability that blockchain will take root in the HR industry. Find out how blockchain may be used in HR. The ability of blockchain systems to protect the fundamentals of virtual currencies like Bitcoin, which enable confidential financial transactions without the need of a bank or middleman, may be one of its most renowned applications. Nevertheless, automation is on its way to the world of human resources, which will undoubtedly impact how HR professionals administer vast amounts of private personnel data and carry out various HR operations.

Each human resource staff members daily activities, from recruitment to senior leadership, will likely be impacted as blockchain technology becomes more widely accepted and used.

The hiring process, utilizing pools of talent, doing checks on backgrounds, verifying previous jobs, utilizing electronic contracts to engage temporary employees, introductions, storing information about staff members, preserving user personal data, processing monetary transactions, and overseeing are all included in this. It can even simplify payments made across borders by automated immediate form currency rates and other legal problems. This has implications for businesses who employ people from around the world and do commerce globally.

Understanding the foundations of what the Ethereum is along with how it works is one of the first problems HR managers encounter. To put it just blockchain technology is a shared computerized accessible ledger which is utilized for storing data. Paper is basically another word for block. A distributed ledger is really nothing more than a collection of records. Blockchain is totally distinct from previous archiving methods since its dependence on a database that is dispersed, that implies that a record with records is afterwards maintained all through an enormous collection of independent machines. By decentralizing the data, this secures and protects it.

The exceptional degree of security offered by blockchain technology makes it a suitable fit for the HR industry, which is routinely entrusted with managing enormous volumes of private data on a company's employees.

WHY BLOCKCHAIN IS IMPORTANT FOR HUMAN RESOURCES MANAGEMENT

While it is expected that the use of distributed ledger technology will streamline HR practices like hiring as well as instruction assessment (Jain et al., 2021), adoption of blockchain in human resources management is seen as crucial for reasons other than HR practices, like security of data and permanence, improved management oversight (Minakova and Nos. The repercussions extend outside human resources management in order to enhance organizational leadership & efficiency.

Ethereum in human resources management, for instance, may increase the transparency and efficacy of instructional programs.

A decentralised infrastructure that maintains instructional effectiveness in a way that cannot be reversed would be advantageous given the significant sums that organisations spend into educational programmes. This is what Jain et al. (2021) keep in view when they suggest a framework based on blockchain to comprehend the prospective uses of blockchain technology to enhance train assessment. The BETEM (blockchain-enabled training effectiveness assessment) model, on the other hand, was created using a technique based on qualitative information (Jain et al., 2021). The group of human resources administration (HR) specialists who worked together to construct the model were highly unfamiliar with blockchain-based applications in HR. This prevented their purported "specialised knowledge" from clearly illustrating how the technology had significant promise for Human Resource Management.

Because of this, a greater number of people than really experience the advantages of blockchain in human resource management at this moment (Wang et al., 2019). Furthermore, it is untrue (Chillakuri and Attili, 2021) that Ethereum is required to address human resources management concerns alongside to the technologies that is now available (Peck, 2017; Vincent and Tadesse, 2020).

It will also take some time for blockchain technology to be widely applied in HRM. This could be a result of the technological limitations and restrictions of a blockchain, problems with leadership, and low rates of return on investments. This may be the outcome of Blockchain's sparse, sporadic adoption across multiple industries (Sharma, 2018). This could change though, if countries and organisations, like the European Union, create a database that issues everyone with a digital ID.

Thus, the existing justification for employing Ethereum in SHRM does not appear persuasive. For instance, Chillakuru and Attili propose that the issue of fraudulent applications may be solved by using blockchain technology. Blockchain technology has an opportunity to be utilized for verifying applicants' qualifications, even when submissions contain a variety of data that go past passwords (Kim et al., 2020; Pal et al., 2021). Even while it would seem simple to assume that an applicant's data will be saved on a digital ledger, this presumption is false owing to known technical, societal, and political barriers as well as unexplained barriers.

In view of this, blockchain innovation is essential to talent management and has the potential to enhance current human resources procedures. However, the current state of digital currency use in HRM is weaker and is based on misconceptions regarding the digital currency innovations in relation to digital currency.

TOPICS OF SHRM THAT BLOCKCHAIN IS EXPECTED TO IMPROVE

Blockchain technology might be capable to help with a variety of company human resources issues, according to research that has recently been published.

Nevertheless, a variety of assumptions about what blockchain in the context of bitcoin is or may be are made in the research's comments regarding the consequences of blockchain for human resources management.

Recruiting: Cryptocurrency in human resources management supporters argue that the present recruitment and selection processes take too long. As a result, finding applicants for a job and checking their information take time and resources.

To get across this problem, they suggest using open ledgers containing candidates' information that are validated using Blockchain technology rather than depending on currently used methods. For instance, this ledger may be used to validate applicant IDs and information, such as qualifications and experience (Denis et al., 2020). Additionally, these ledgers provide applicant information, which enables an organisation to search for certain abilities (Chillakuru and Attili, 2021). While bringing an online database of applicant data can aid in employing, it also presents technological in nature, societal, moral, and legal obstacles. Additionally, it necessitates that appropriate parties worldwide coordinate candidates' experience and skills.

Maintenance and observation of the employment life cycle: Advocates of blockchain in SHRM contend that managers of human resources need to continue keeping an eye on staff members to make certain they are fulfilling objectives including growth and engagement. For instance, suggestions from a supervisor, an organization-wide initiative, or individual self-evaluation are frequently the foundation for improvement and upkeep within the present human resources management framework.

Owing to Blockchain's openness and its original use, HR professionals would be more equipped to handle welcome messages, the atmosphere, retaining students, and exits.

While employing blockchain technology for recruiting and terminating employees may appear futuristic, it could require centuries (Harvard Business Review, 2018; Sharma, 2018).

Management of involvement: Maintenance or observation of the employment life cycle: Advocates of blockchain in SHRM contend that managers of human resources need to continue keeping an eye on staff members to make certain personnel are fulfilling objectives including growth and engagement. For instance, suggestions from a supervisor, an organization-wide initiative, or individual self-evaluation are frequently the foundation for improvement and upkeep within the present human resources management framework.

Owing to Blockchain's openness and its original use, HR professionals would be more equipped to handle welcome messages, the atmosphere, retaining students, and exits. Other technologies used by businesses also routinely check on employee attendance (BasuMallick, 2019; Hadjisolomou, 2015). The current steps are both realistic and legitimate.

Payroll-related financial activities: Proponents claim that because payment is routed by middlemen, the process takes longer than necessary. Paid personnel aren't paid before the last day of the previous month.

They suggest that smart Web regulations could alter this. Someone who works will therefore be compensated for the hours they put in on the applicable weekday. In accordance with Angel and McCabe (2015), the money is going to be paid as a cryptocurrency and transferred to the service individual's account. Furthermore, they assert that the adoption of Blockchain technology for domestic as well as global transactions lessens the requirement for extra entities. This might be used by manufactures to move expenses or monthly salaries across continents.

Such tokens are usable anyplace that they can be exchanged for fiat money (Angel and McCabe, 2015). Numerous entrepreneurs make an effort to perform this because it seems exciting (PrimaFelicitas, 2019). According to Eaton, Sharif, and Ghodoosi, as well as the UK Jurisdiction Taskforce (2019), it is uncertain how these smart contracts are created. How are such tokens stabilised given the volatile nature of cryptocurrency is in general? Because of this, certain tasks—like ensuring the token's stability—still need to be completed by someone else (Routledge and Zetlin-Jones, 2021).

Techniques for compliance Proponents of the current methodology assert that it is challenging to conduct a conformance evaluation of the procedure. They assert that the use of blockchain technology will streamline the processes for authentication and accountability. Considering the properties of Blockchain, this makes sense and seems exciting (Zemler and Westner, 2019). Automating the gathering and safe ongoing archiving of precise and validated data is possible.

Contracts that are electronic can be used to adhere to legal requirements. Programming for automated contracts, for instance, can be set to get started when an applicant's (or an employee's) is received. visas expire if the applicant's (or the employee's) immigration history is maintained on Blockchain. But as Yeoh (2017) points out, it's simpler to say than done. In contrast to the Blockchain in the cryptocurrency sector, the participation of the numerous players in a blockchain is not assured.

Therefore, the implementation of blockchain technology might potentially improve human resources (HR) procedures. To put things in perspective, it may make data protection, payroll processing, skill mapping, licencing identification, and performance monitoring simpler.

Notwithstanding the potential of blockchain, research on its use in human resources management makes a number of assumptions about the technology. Known reasons exist for why Blockchain will be of greater benefit than current approaches. This might indicate that a company's policies on the use of such technology have not been carefully thought through.

Furthermore, businesses are deploying blockchain at the expense of their HR staff, which must be kept in consideration. The adoption of the technology will also demand an enormous amount of organising and organising personnel.

As a result, it is believed that building a network will be far more expensive than the estimated cost reductions that Blockchain technology would bring about by streamlining processes related to human resources management. Human resources managers and their organisations are unable to compare the advantages of employing blockchain technology to expedite HR procedures to those of current competitors in the absence of a compelling economic argument. for a comprehensive examination of this matter.

BCF (BLOCKCHAIN TECHNOLOGY) IN HRM

Figure 2 below illustrates topic 2, or Blockchain Framework (BCF) for HR, which calls all the creation of a structure to make it easier for human resources professionals in businesses to carry out their daily tasks using the technology known as blockchain. According to The et al. (2021; Goumopoulos and Mavrommati 2020), an arrangement is a practical design that helps end user's complete tasks quickly. According to The et al. (2021; Goumopoulos and Mavrommati 2020), an arrangement is a practical design that helps end users' complete tasks quickly.

In two ways, internationalization benefits the spread of internationally technologies and international understanding, allowing countries to swiftly obtain foreign knowledge and boosting global rivalry due to the rise of newly developed businesses. Aslam et al. (2018) described invention as well as the adoption of foreign inventions. Human Resources (HR) currently often faces a variety of challenges in the worldwide internet time period, including connects with candidates, screens them, and double-checks their resumes, confirming qualifications, investigating communities, and reducing the possibility of inadequate hiring. For instance, interviewers link the profiles of applicants from several platforms including social media, recruiting agencies, and direct applications; and recruiting cv Consequently, confirmations represent an impediment.

Use of digital currencies in the 21st century from 2004 to 2014, an example of global knowledge and technology, will boost capacity for innovation and employment growth. According to experts, acquiring Using the technology of blockchain to verify identities can save time and money while boosting trustworthiness. and boost automation in recruiting (Han, 2017). Background investigations on the chosen applicants. The use of applicants' falsehoods to locate a growing number of companies on their profiles in order to land a job Wood et al. (2007) referenced in Brody, Richard G. (2010).

Recruiters typically use third parties to do reference checks (primarily for jobs) agencies for background checks to reduce the possibility of making incorrect hiring decisions. Check the background is a typical check that covers education and training, employment history, credit, Criminal activity, drug trafficking, driving records, physical examinations, etc.

To facilitate this, a framework of ledger is what is known as an It the creation, implementation, and upkeep of blockchain applications at the executive and corporate levels (Quasim). The administration of human resources has to perform as a functional unit inside firms and companies, as stated by Helo and Hao (2019) and others integrate blockchain with a framework that will let corporations and organisations create and operate connected human resources apps on the technology. BCF for HR is therefore regarded as a crucial and important concept. A component of blockchain deployment in human resources management.

Figure 2. Blockchain framework (BCF) for HRz
Source: Author's own contribution

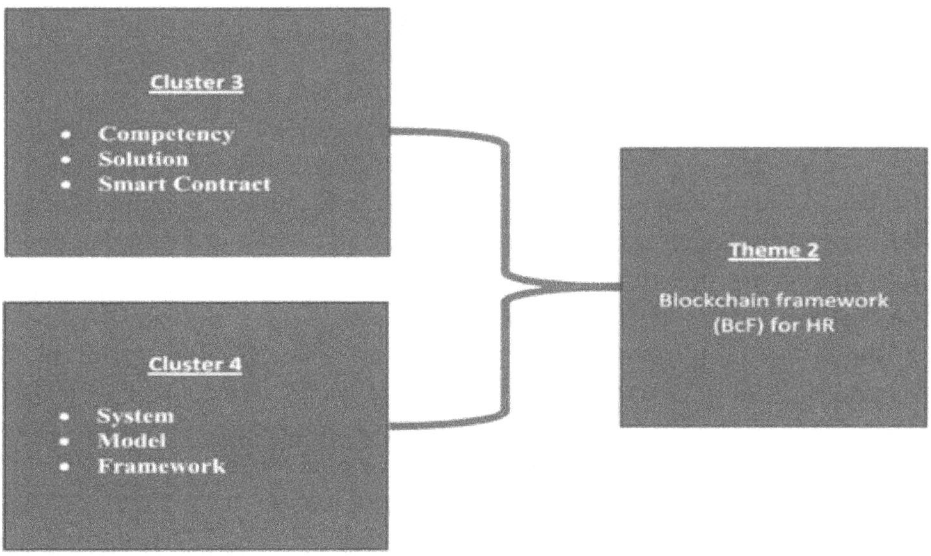

THE EFFECT THAT UTILISATION OF BLOCKCHAIN WILL HAVE ON STAFF

Three key effects of blockchain adoption in HRM on staff are cited in the research review:

(1) The widespread use of blockchain technology could substitute low-skilled staff members with high-skilled staff members, replacing them with temporary duties and choosing over tasks that are ongoing (Bhattacharyya and Nair, 2019);
(2) it may also require a highly coveted highly trained workforce, including blockchain engineers.

A blockchain where worker competences and abilities are stored may be advantageous to both employers and employees. Employers will have a better understanding of the abilities that are now in demand and those that need to be improved.

This makes it possible for human resources managers to look up the combination of abilities needed to address organisational challenges including managing employees, resource allocation, and planning for retirement. Additionally, if their talents are stored on a blockchain, employees won't be given duties for which they are unprepared, and they will receive the necessary training before beginning a new duty. Such structures, nevertheless only serve as "ideal" solutions in the absence of "real-world" applications.

Despite the current limits of blockchain applications in the business sector, a blockchain can offer many advantages, although such applications are still a long way off from becoming a reality. Such blockchain projects may unintentionally result in the termination of employees who are listed on the Blockchain or who are viewed as having poor skill levels, as opposed to helping workers.

This could result in a plan to hire more highly qualified individuals to take the place of inexperienced ones (Chang, 2020). While using Blockchain in order to gradually substitute lower-skilled employees with highly trained employees makes sense for organisations looking to increase the quality of their workforce competency, dealing with the repercussions of this necessitate an organisational strategy from human resources specialists within an organisation.

Groups of workers are expected to be pushed into what is known as the "obsolete" class in the literature as one of the effects caused by blockchain adoption in HRM (Lavrynenko and Shmatko, 2019). On the other hand, it is yet unclear what this reframing might entail in terms of extent and type.

The widespread consensus is that redefining will result in the addition of new duties as well as the elimination of others (Nam, 2019). Nevertheless, it will assign responsibilities to employees and maintain a distributed ledger, with personnel handling short-term assignments and over time chores being stored on the blockchain. It will not only change or eliminate current activity.

Although the existing research supports a lifetime educational experience for individuals as a reaction to the way blockchain technology is changing the nature of work, such recommendations have not yet been thoroughly tested in reality. This also begs the question of whether it will become the responsibility of present employees to upgrade their skills. While discussing talent improvement,

Additionally, there are consequences for the 'unlearning' of employees (Matsuo, 2019). Even while "unlearning" the might not be an issue, it is a permanent workplace necessity in places where labour is being redefined.

Additionally, a blockchain cannot ensure that the people's abilities allocated to a block accurately reflect that people's talents. It is possible for multiple organisations to write to the chain without ensuring the necessary degree of authentication.

Problems regarding accessibility arise when merely a small number of instructional resources are able to send emails to the chain. If anybody may send an email to the chain and applicants are picked based on where they concluded during the training, prejudice may also occur.

To summarise this theme, HR professionals and their organisations must take into consideration the possible drawbacks of adopting blockchain technology, like the requirement for incredibly specialised abilities, in addition to the difficulties that digital currencies may solve in the field of managing human capital. the allocation of skills within blockchain technology and labourers, and employees with outdated skills. To further investigate this subject, Table 2 offers potential study queries.

HUMAN RESOURCES MANAGEMENT APPLICATIONS FOR BLOCKCHAIN DIFFICULTIES

The currently existing study overlooks the limitations and challenges related to the usage of blockchain in human resources management (Sharma, 2018). Weaknesses, improper computer programming, and inadequate technological design are some of the first problems. While solving problems, assessment, and programming can occasionally alleviate issues, they can prolong the process of creating an efficient supply chain for the administration of human resources. Although coding flaws and mistakes cannot be prevented, they can however do great harm to people. Due to their legal obedience, hiring documents may provide unique challenges for recruiting and discharging (Zemler and Westner, 2019).

In addition, public opposition is not taken into consideration in the debate over the possibility of the implementation of blockchain (Shelkovnikov, 2016). Concern has been raised about public opposition to keeping information on the Blockchain (Koster and Borgman, 2020). Therefore, the public's impression of blockchain acceptance within SHRM can be influenced by how blockchain was regarded.

The idea since there's just one alternative is exacerbated by the fact that collaboration-oriented choice-making is not included in the current study on blockchain adoption in human resources management. There are at least 10 different consensus techniques for Blockchain. To get agreement on a blockchain, all participants have to embrace the outcome, no matter whether or not they agree with it (World Economic Forum, 2021).

Concerns regarding sustainability may arise because certain processes for consensus consume more energy than others (CryptoEasy, 2019). As a result, another factor to take into account before implementing Blockchain in human resources management is the consensus method.

The fact that the current research (Clohessy and Acton, 2019) fails to investigate how businesses may close the talent gap in blockchain adoption is another drawback. Blockchain engineers with specialised knowledge are in great demand due to the intricacy of the networks based on blockchain technology. In this situation, HR personnel must also be knowledgeable of Blockchain's technological features (Agarwal et al., 2023). If HR professionals do not fully comprehend smart contracts, how can they help blockchain engineers construct smart binding agreements, for instance?

Additionally, despite the possibility of strengthening HRM using blockchain technology, this field is yet uncontrolled (Angel and McCabe, 2015; Herian, 2019). Regulation regarding blockchain technology is being considered by several nations. In the interim, a lack of regulation might result in conflicts. Additionally, as Blockchain is distributed, it is interesting to consider who develops these rules (Shelkovnikov, 2016; World Economic Forum, 2021). Additionally, different limits could be imposed for distinct chains in various countries (Smith, 2021; Yeoh, 2017). Alternately, laws that applies to the entire nation or entire bloc may encourage a chain that serves just that nation or that bloc and adheres to its laws. If this happens, how would a specific to a nation chain interact with an additional chain? Or will a blockchain have a central authority?

However, previous studies do not take laws and regulations into account when discussing human resources management.

Previous research also disregards the security, flexibility, and bandwidth issues related to Blockchain in Human Resource Management. With so much data that HR departments throughout the globe handle, accepted digital currencies could grow slow and ineffective as more blocks arrive to the system.

If the network is not built to manage congestion, it will ultimately slow down as the number of blocks increases.

Additionally, Blockchain provides benefits over conventional databases however is not completely hacker-proof. There have been a number of recorded hacking incidents (Orcutt, 2019).

Compromise of blockchains may be advantageous for hackers in the larger scheme of managing people since they may sell the data to fraudsters.

In summary, more investigation is necessary to tackle the problems and obstacles associated with blockchain adoption rather than the potential benefits for human resources professionals and corporate managers, regardless of whether the study itself supports the use of electronic currency in SHRM. Table 2 offers several possible subjects for more analysis on this subject.

OBSERVATIONS AS WELL AS EFFECTS ON THE COMING YEAR

Blockchain technology is expected to is going to be becoming increasingly common and available for controlling staff members in groups as it has grown increasingly well-known in the domains of financial services, banking, transportation and arrangements, and the administration of healthcare in nations that are developed as well as developing (di Prisco and Strangio 2021; Fernandez-Vazquez et al. 2021). Blockchain's potential uses are anticipated to have a rapid impact on HR (Schlecht, Schneider, and Buchwald 2021; Parry and Battista 2019; Minakova and Nosachevsky 2019). Among its possible applications in HRM are hiring pools, record checks, and employment history validation. These features are expected to transform hiring practices, one of the most important aspects of HR everyday operations.

The Blockchain foundation for HRM (BcF) and Employee-Systems Interaction (ESI) are both necessary elements and prerequisites to realize those potential applications. These two fundamental ideas will be critical to developing blockchain-powered HRM in companies. Furthermore, the HRM based blockchain will greatly raise employees' skill levels (Neiheiser et al. 2020; Fachrunnisa and Hussain 2020; Olivas-Lujan 2019).

The absence of a co-citation review may be acknowledged as the main restriction, despite the fact that this work adds to the body of research and understanding on blockchain innovation in human resources management. Additionally, Either the Web of Science and Scopus, respectively, are sources that served as the foundation for this study's findings. As a result, more study should make use of other databases, particularly EBSCO and ProQuest, which may produce more subjects. Additionally, empirical research may be done taking both of these fundamental themes—"ESI" and "BcF for HR"—into consideration for future research enhancements in this particular field.

CONCLUSION

Labour agreements and employee data might be stored in open with one another accessible chains in the future, with protection against deletion, manipulation, and alteration. This is an era that the administration of human resources might look ahead to. Credentials, knowledge, money, and education records for recruits would all be electronic files that could be verified, saved, and shared without the use of middlemen. On the other hand, despite the likelihood of this scenario, the hoopla surrounding blockchain technology in human resources management is unfounded. The implementation of blockchain technology will need close collaboration due to the unparalleled level of technological, policy, and cultural complexity.

The goal of this study was to review the literature on blockchain's potential applications in HRM.

According to the report, the widespread utilisation of the technology known as blockchain in SHRM depends heavily on HR practitioners' knowledge of the technology.

The conventional, limited understanding of the Bitcoin blockchain must be transcended in order for this information to be comprehensive. The information acquired should enable a clear response to the following core duplication. Whatever personnel management problems does the technology known as blockchain need to tackle, and why is blockchain better compared to various existing technological advances?

In order to cut through the hype regarding blockchain applications in HRM, university-based HR research has to be given more consideration.

While there are many attractive features associated with this kind of technology for companies, in order to draw meaningful findings, science education has to rely on data collected from sources other than exploratory blockchain activities, early bitcoin types, and suggested blockchain architectures.

ACKNOWLEDGMENT

This study has not received any particular grant from any funding agency in the public, commercial, or not-for-profit organizations.

REFERENCES

Abu-Elezz, I., Hassan, A., Nazeemudeen, A., Househ, M., & Abd-Alrazaq, A. (2020). The benefits and threats of blockchain technology in healthcare: A scoping review. *International Journal of Medical Informatics*, *142*, 104246. doi:10.1016/j.ijmedinf.2020.104246 PMID:32828033

Aggarwal, S., Chaudhary, R., Aujla, G. S., Kumar, N., Choo, K. K. R., & Zomaya, A. Y. (2019). Blockchain for smart communities: Applications, challenges and opportunities. *Journal of Network and Computer Applications*, *144*, 13–48. doi:10.1016/j.jnca.2019.06.018

Agrawal, P., Narain, R., & Ullah, I. (2019). Analysis of barriers in implementation of digital transformation of supply chain using interpretive structural modelling approach. *Journal of Modelling in Management*, *15*(1), 297–317. doi:10.1108/JM2-03-2019-0066

Ahmad, R. W., Hasan, H., Jayaraman, R., Salah, K., & Omar, M. (2021). Blockchain applications and architectures for port operations and logistics management. *Research in Transportation Business & Management*, *41*, 100620. doi:10.1016/j.rtbm.2021.100620

Aliperti, G., Sandholz, S., Hagenlocher, M., Rizzi, F., Frey, M., & Garschagen, M. (2019). Tourism, crisis, disaster: An interdisciplinary approach. *Annals of Tourism Research*, *79*, 102808. doi:10.1016/j.annals.2019.102808

Antal, C., Cioara, T., Anghel, I., Antal, M., & Salomie, I. (2021). Distributed ledger technology review and decentralized applications development guidelines. *Future Internet*, *13*(3), 62. doi:10.3390/fi13030062

Atlas, L. G., Kumar, C. M., Rajakumari, & Hamsagayathi, P. (2020). Applications with blockchain technique. *Cryptocurrencies and blockchain technology applications*, 157-179.

Ballandies, M. C., Dapp, M. M., & Pournaras, E. (2022). Decrypting distributed ledger design—Taxonomy, classification and blockchain community evaluation. *Cluster Computing*, *25*(3), 1817–1838. doi:10.1007/s10586-021-03256-w PMID:35601685

Breslin, S., & Wadhwa, B. (2018). Gender and Human-Computer Interaction. The Wiley Handbook of Human Computer Interaction, 1, 71-87. Wiley. doi:10.1002/9781118976005.ch4

Chang, V., Baudier, P., Zhang, H., Xu, Q., Zhang, J., & Arami, M. (2020). How Blockchain can impact financial services–The overview, challenges and recommendations from expert interviewees. *Technological Forecasting and Social Change*, *158*, 120166. doi:10.1016/j.techfore.2020.120166 PMID:32834134

Chang, Y. W. (2018). Examining interdisciplinarity of library and information science (LIS) based on LIS articles contributed by non-LIS authors. *Scientometrics*, *116*(3), 1589–1613. doi:10.1007/s11192-018-2822-7

Chen, J., Lv, Z., & Song, H. (2019). Design of personnel big data management system based on blockchain. *Future Generation Computer Systems*, *101*, 1122–1129. doi:10.1016/j.future.2019.07.037

Chillakuri, B., & Attili, V. P. (2022). Role of blockchain in HR's response to new-normal. *The International Journal of Organizational Analysis*, *30*(6), 1359–1378. doi:10.1108/IJOA-08-2020-2363

Choudhari, S., Das, S., Parasher, S., & Gangwar, D. (2021, April). Sub-contractor life cycle management in enterprise system using blockchain technology. In *2021 6th International Conference for Convergence in Technology (I2CT)* (pp. 1-7). IEEE. 10.1109/I2CT51068.2021.9417981

Ciampi, F., Marzi, G., Demi, S., & Faraoni, M. (2020). The big data-business strategy interconnection: A grand challenge for knowledge management. A review and future perspectives. *Journal of Knowledge Management*, *24*(5), 1157–1176. doi:10.1108/JKM-02-2020-0156

Cooper, C., Booth, A., Varley-Campbell, J., Britten, N., & Garside, R. (2018). Defining the process to literature searching in systematic reviews: A literature review of guidance and supporting studies. *BMC Medical Research Methodology*, *18*(1), 1–14. doi:10.1186/s12874-018-0545-3 PMID:30107788

Cooper, C., Garside, R., Varley-Campbell, J., Talens-Bou, J., Booth, A., & Britten, N. (2020). "It has no meaning to me." How do researchers understand the effectiveness of literature searches? A qualitative analysis and preliminary typology of understandings. *Research Synthesis Methods*, *11*(5), 627–640. doi:10.1002/jrsm.1426 PMID:32495989

Cucari, N., Lagasio, V., Lia, G., & Torriero, C. (2022). The impact of blockchain in banking processes: The Interbank Spunta case study. *Technology Analysis and Strategic Management*, *34*(2), 138–150. doi:10.1080/09537325.2021.1891217

Cuevas, P. E. G., Davidson, P. M., Mejilla, J. L., & Rodney, T. W. (2020). Reminiscence therapy for older adults with Alzheimer's disease: A literature review. *International Journal of Mental Health Nursing, 29*(3), 364–371. doi:10.1111/inm.12692 PMID:31984570

di Prisco, D., & Strangio, D. (2021). Technology and financial inclusion: A case study to evaluate potential and limitations of Blockchain in emerging countries. *Technology Analysis and Strategic Management*, 1–14. doi:10.1080/09537325.2021.1944617

Donthu, N., Kumar, S., Mukherjee, D., Pandey, N., & Lim, W. M. (2021). How to conduct a bibliometric analysis: An overview and guidelines. *Journal of Business Research, 133*, 285–296. doi:10.1016/j.jbusres.2021.04.070

Esmat, A., de Vos, M., Ghiassi-Farrokhfal, Y., Palensky, P., & Epema, D. (2021). A novel decentralized platform for peer-to-peer energy trading market with blockchain technology. *Applied Energy, 282*, 116123. doi:10.1016/j.apenergy.2020.116123

Etemadi, N., Van Gelder, P., & Strozzi, F. (2021). An ism modeling of barriers for blockchain/distributed ledger technology adoption in supply chains towards cybersecurity. *Sustainability (Basel), 13*(9), 4672. doi:10.3390/su13094672

Fachrunnisa, O., & Hussain, F. K. (2020). Blockchain-based human resource management practices for mitigating skills and competencies gap in workforce. *International Journal of Engineering Business Management, 12*, 1847979020966400. doi:10.1177/1847979020966400

Farahani, B., Firouzi, F., & Luecking, M. (2021). The convergence of IoT and distributed ledger technologies (DLT): Opportunities, challenges, and solutions. *Journal of Network and Computer Applications, 177*, 102936. doi:10.1016/j.jnca.2020.102936

Fernandez-Vazquez, S., Rosillo, R., Meijueiro, L., Alonso Alvarez, R., & De La Fuente, D. (2023). A comparative study of blockchain's largest permissionless networks. *Technology Analysis and Strategic Management, 35*(4), 409–423. doi:10.1080/09537325.2021.1976748

Frizzo-Barker, J., Chow-White, P. A., Adams, P. R., Mentanko, J., Ha, D., & Green, S. (2020). Blockchain as a disruptive technology for business: A systematic review. *International Journal of Information Management, 51*, 102029. doi:10.1016/j.ijinfomgt.2019.10.014

Gan, Q., Lau, R. Y. K., & Hong, J. (2021). A critical review of blockchain applications to banking and finance: A qualitative thematic analysis approach. *Technology Analysis and Strategic Management*, 1–17. doi:10.1080/09537325.2021.1979509

Garcia-Arroyo, J., & Osca, A. (2021). Big data contributions to human resource management: A systematic review. *International Journal of Human Resource Management, 32*(20), 4337–4362. doi:10.1080/09585192.2019.1674357

Garg, P., Gupta, B., Chauhan, A. K., Sivarajah, U., Gupta, S., & Modgil, S. (2021). Measuring the perceived benefits of implementing blockchain technology in the banking sector. *Technological Forecasting and Social Change*, *163*, 120407. doi:10.1016/j.techfore.2020.120407

Goumopoulos, C., & Mavrommati, I. (2020). A framework for pervasive computing applications based on smart objects and end user development. *Journal of Systems and Software*, *162*, 110496. doi:10.1016/j.jss.2019.110496

Gromov, A. Y., Petrovskaia, T. A., Suslina, A. A., Khizriyeva, N. I., & Stepanov, M. A. (2018, June). Human resources intelligent selection algorithm with improvement of data validity. In *2018 7th Mediterranean Conference on Embedded Computing (MECO)* (pp. 1-4). IEEE. 10.1109/MECO.2018.8406036

Grover, P., Kar, A. K., & Janssen, M. (2019). Diffusion of blockchain technology: Insights from academic literature and social media analytics. *Journal of Enterprise Information Management, 32*(5), 735–757. doi:10.1108/JEIM-06-2018-0132

Harari, M. B., Parola, H. R., Hartwell, C. J., & Riegelman, A. (2020). Literature searches in systematic reviews and meta-analyses: A review, evaluation, and recommendations. *Journal of Vocational Behavior*, *118*, 103377. doi:10.1016/j.jvb.2020.103377

He, X., Tu, Z., Xu, X., & Wang, Z. (2021). Programming framework and infrastructure for self-adaptation and optimized evolution method for microservice systems in cloud–edge environments. *Future Generation Computer Systems*, *118*, 263–281. doi:10.1016/j.future.2021.01.008

Hoffecker, L. (2020). Grey literature searching for systematic reviews in the health sciences. *The Serials Librarian, 79*(3-4), 252–260. doi:10.1080/0361526X.2020.1847745

Ibrahim, D. (2023). Opportunities, Challenges and Implications of Blockchain Technology for Accounting: An Exploratory Study. *Alexandria Journal of Accounting Research, 7*(3), 173–220.

Kim, H. W., & Jeong, Y. S. (2018). Secure authentication-management human-centric scheme for trusting personal resource information on mobile cloud computing with blockchain. *Human-centric Computing and Information Sciences*, *8*(1), 1–13. doi:10.1186/s13673-018-0136-7

Kim, T. H., Kumar, G., Saha, R., Rai, M. K., Buchanan, W. J., Thomas, R., & Alazab, M. (2020). A privacy preserving distributed ledger framework for global human resource record management: The blockchain aspect. *IEEE Access : Practical Innovations, Open Solutions*, *8*, 96455–96467. doi:10.1109/ACCESS.2020.2995481

Kumar, K. S., Kumar, T. A., Radhamani, A. S., & Sundaresan, S. (2020). Blockchain technology: an insight into architecture, use cases, and its application with industrial IoT and big data. In *Blockchain Technology* (pp. 23–42). CRC Press.

Riegelman, A., Harari, M. B., Parola, H. R., & Hartwell, C. J. (2023). *Literature searches in systematic reviews and meta-analyses: A review, evaluation, and recommendations.*

Chapter 6
Blockchain-Based Financial Systems Deployment and Challenges:
Comparative Study Across Several Countries

R. Jeevitha
M.S. Ramaiah Institute of Management, India

P. Bhanumathi
https://orcid.org/0000-0001-8670-8250
M.S. Ramaiah Institute of Management, India

Sourav Mukherjee
M.S. Ramaiah Institute of Management, India

ABSTRACT

Web3 encompasses decentralized finance (DeFi), which leverages blockchain and smart contracts to create an open and accessible financial system. They promote decentralization, trust, and innovation across industries. However, challenges include scalability, energy consumption, price volatility, regulatory uncertainty, and security vulnerabilities. Governments are working on regulatory frameworks, and adoption is growing. Education and awareness are crucial. In particular, there is a need to identify and address the technical, economic, social, and legal issues that may arise from the adoption and implementation of Web 3.0, including concerns around governance, scalability, interoperability, security, and regulation. Therefore, the purpose of the book chapter is to cover the key issues and challenges associated with blockchain technology and to develop a comprehensive understanding of the opportunities and limitations of this technology in order to inform the development and adoption of Web 3.0 applications and services.
DOI: 10.4018/979-8-3693-1878-2.ch006

INTRODUCTION OF WEB

Network for the web consists of web servers, which host websites and web applications, and client devices, such as laptops, smartphones, and tablets, that access these resources. The communication between these devices is enabled by the underlying protocols and technologies, for instance the Internet Protocol (IP), Transmission Control Protocol (TCP), and Hypertext Transfer Protocol (HTTP). HTTP is the prime protocol which is used for communication between web servers and client devices. It defines the rules for exchanging information between the two parties, including requests for web pages and resources and delivering those resources to the client device. In addition to the primary network components, the web relies on other technologies and protocols, such as domain name system (DNS), which translates sphere names into IP addresses, and Secure Sockets Layer (SSL), which provides secure communication between web servers and client devices.

Networks: Advantages

a) Sharing Resources: Networks permit devices to segment resources, such as printers, files, and applications, which can surge efficacy and lessen costs.
b) Communication: Networks provide a means for users to communicate and collaborate, regardless of location.
c) Centralized Management: Networks can be managed centrally, allowing administrators to monitor and control devices, applications, and user access from a single location.
d) Cost-Effective: Sharing resources and centralizing management can reduce hardware, software, and maintenance costs.

Phases of Web Evolution

Web 1.0 "Phases of the Evolution of the Internet"

Web 1.0 was an essential foundation for developing the modern web, and it paved the way for the dynamic and interactive web experiences we enjoy today. It emerged in the early 1990s and lasted until around 2004. static and largely read-only web, with content primarily created by developers and website owners rather than users. *It* consists of simple HTML (Hypertext marked language), providing the basic structure of web pages and images.

a) Limited interactivity: Web 1.0 was largely a read-only web with limited user engagement and interaction opportunities. This limited its ability to support interactive applications and online services.
b) Technical limitations: The early web was built using basic technologies like HTML and CSS, which limited its ability to support advanced multimedia content and dynamic web applications.
c) Limited accessibility: Web 1.0 was primarily accessible through desktop computers, which limited its reach and accessibility to users who did not have access to these devices.
d) Limited search capabilities: Search engines like Google did not exist during the early days of the web, making it difficult for users to find the information they needed.
e) Security issues: Web 1.0 was vulnerable to security threats such as viruses, malware, and hacking, which posed a significant challenge for website owners and users alike.

Features of Web 1.0

a) Passive consumption: Web 1.0 was primarily a one-way street wherever users could access and consume content but might not easily create or share their content.
b) Search engines: The emergence of search engines like Yahoo and AltaVista made it easier for users to find online information.

Figure 1. Web 1.0
Source: https://ethereum.org/en/web3/

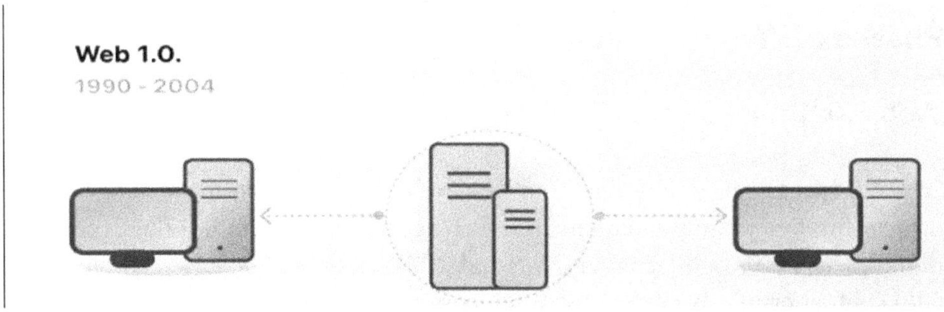

It depicts Web 1.0 was mostly static websites preserved by companies, and there was close to zero interface between users - individuals occasionally formed content.

Web 2.0 "The Second-Generation WWW"

Web 2.0 is used to define the second cohort of the World Wide Web, developed in the mid-2000s and used today till today. Unlike Web 1.0, which was primarily static and read-only, Web 2.0 is categorized by its interactivity and user-generated content. Tools used and technology used to make it interactive: Social media platforms, blogging platforms, Wikipedia, Web-based applications like Google Docs, Trello, Dropbox, Video sharing platforms

Features of Web 2.0

a) User-generated content: Web 2.0 is characterized by the ability of users to create and share content on the web. This includes blogs, social media posts, wikis, and other types of user-generated content.
b) Social media: Web 2.0 has also seen the rise of social- media, which let users to connect, sharing content, and engaging in online communities.
c) Interactivity: Web 2.0 is highly interactive, allowing users to engage with websites and applications in new ways. This includes features like commenting, ratings, and feedback mechanisms.
d) Rich multimedia content: Web 2.0 also supports rich multimedia content, including videos, animations, and other interactive elements.
e) Personalization: Web 2.0 allows for greater personalization of web experiences, with websites and applications able to adapt to individual user preferences and behaviors.

Figure 2. Web 2.0
Source: https://ethereum.org/en/web3/

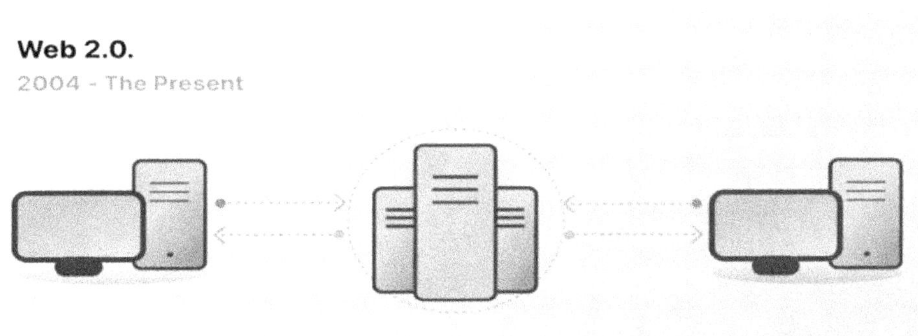

In today's digital world as many individuals rely online, a player in this stream instigated to control a disproportionate quantity of the traffic and value generated on the web. Whereas users of the web can create a content using the online platforms, they neither own it nor benefited from its monetization.

Web 3.0 "The Semantic Web"

Web 3.0, also known as the "Semantic Web," first introduced by Tim Berners-Lee, the one who invented World Wide Web in 2001. Berners-Lee envisioned a web that would be more intelligent and intuitive, where information could be automatically processed and understood by machines, enabling a more personalized and efficient online experience. Bitcoin's success sparked interest in blockchain technology, which offered a new way of creating decentralized, trustless networks. This technology paved the means for evolving new decentralized applications (dApps) that could operate independently of traditional central authorities. By 2014, the Ethereum network had been launched, offering a platform for smart contracts creation, allowing for more multifaceted decentralized applications to be developed. Since then, Web 3.0 has continued to evolve, with new decentralized applications and platforms emerging in fields such as decentralized finance, digital identity, and decentralized storage. Today, Web 3.0 represents a new era of the internet that is more decentralized, secure, and user-centric than ever before.

Figure 3. Web3.0
Source: https://ethereum.org/en/web3/

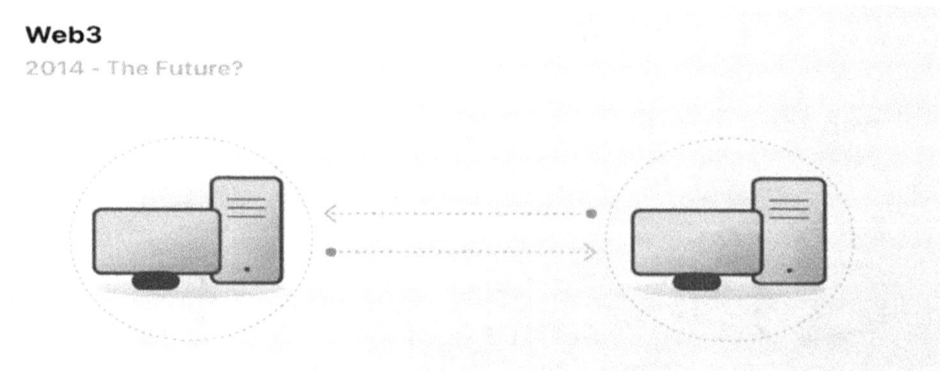

Fundamentally, the technology used in Web 3.0 are blockchains, cryptocurrencies and non-fungible tokens (NFTs) which provides supremacy to the users of the web, a kind of ownership or possession.

Table 1. Contrast between Web 1, Web 2, Web 3

Basis of Variation	Web 1.0	Web 2.0	Web 3.0
User engagement	It is limited to browsing and consuming static web pages.	Users could interact with each other, participate in online communities, and create and share content.	Users have even better controller on their data and experiences with a extra personalized and also decentralized internet.
Content	Characterized by static HTML pages with limited multimedia content.	Dynamic content, rich media like audio and video, and user-generated content	Expected to offer even more sophisticated content namely virtual reality (VR) and augmented reality (AR) experiences.
Interactivity	Limited to simple forms and basic interactivity	Introduced more sophisticated interactive features such as chat, instant messaging, and social networking	Aims to provide even more interactive and immersive experiences with virtual assistants, AI-driven chatbots, and other advanced technologies
Connectivity	Characterized by limited connectivity, with email and basic chat rooms as the primary means of communication	Introduced social networking platforms which has enabled users of the network to connect and interconnect on a great extent.	Expected to promote even greater connectivity. The decentralized systems allows with more open network systems which leads to better collaboration and data distribution.
Decentralization	was centralized, with a small number of large corporations controlling the vast majority of online content and services	introduced greater decentralization, with user-generated content and distributed networks	aims to take decentralization even further, using blockchain and other decentralized technologies to create a more democratic and open internet.

Potential Benefits That Web 3.0 Offers Over Web 2.0

1. Decentralization: Web 3.0 is constructed upon decentralized technologies which is blockchain, where allows for a more distributed and democratic internet. This means that not one sole entity controls the network, which can increase transparency, reduce censorship, and improve security.
2. Data Privacy: Web 3.0 objectives is to provide users added controller over their data and online experiences. Decentralized applications allow users to

preserve individual's data more secure and private by dipping the risk of data breaches. It protects privacy of the users to the greater possible extent.

3. Trustless Transactions: Web 3.0 empowers trustless transactions, which means transactions can happen without having intermediaries. The financial intermediaries like banks or payment processors. This will help to reduce transaction fees among the users and intermediaries, increase transaction speed, and also improves financial inclusion of the economy.
4. Interoperability: Web 3.0 seeks to create a more interoperable internet, where different platforms and applications can seamlessly interact. This can lead to greater efficiency, collaboration, and innovation.
5. User Control: Web 3.0 offers more user control, enabling users to manage their online identity and data more effectively. This can lead to greater security, privacy, and autonomy for users.

AN OVERVIEW OF BLOCKCHAIN TECHNOLOGY

In 1991 the two researchers Stuart Haber and W. Scott Stornetta first termed the concept of decentralized digital ledger system which would allow for safe, secure and transparent communications and transactions. However, it be situated till 2008, when the anonymous individual or set of known as "Satoshi Nakamoto" released a research paper titled "Bitcoin: A Peer-to-Peer Electronic Cash System," where the world first time witnessed the real-world application of blockchain technology. The very first Bitcoin block was mined in January 2009, marking the birth of the blockchain. The potential of blockchain technology goes far beyond cryptocurrencies.

A blockchain is a distributed or decentralized database which is maintained by a network of nodes. Respectively, node stores a duplicate of the blockchain, and all node work simultaneously to validate and to add new communications and transactions to the database. Once a block of transactions is added to the blockchain, it is cryptographically secured and cannot be altered. The security of the blockchain comes from its use of cryptography and consensus algorithms. Blockchain transactions are validates and permitted by the network of nodes over a process known as consensus. This consensus confirms that all nodes approve on the state of the database. After once the transaction is approved, the transaction is added to the blockchain as a new block, along with a unique cryptographic signature that links it to the previous block. Transparency is one of the core benefits of blockchain technology. Since all nodes on the network have a copy of the blockchain, the entire transaction history is available for anyone to view. This makes it difficult to falsify data or commit fraud since any attempt to do so would be immediately visible to the entire network.

Blockchain technology, additionally using in cryptocurrencies, its applications are widely used and implemented in various other applications such as in voting systems, supply chain management (SCM), digital identification etc. The above technology has the power to transform the mode we store and transmission of data which in fact enables digital future world to be more secure and transparent. Blockchain technology continues to evolve and expand, with new use cases and innovations emerging every day. The history of blockchain is still being written, and its full potential has yet to be realized

Structure of Blockchain Technology

The main features of Blockchain technology, the way it approves and validate the transactions. For an instance, let's assume when two people wanted to do a transaction with public or private key, correspondingly. The first individual would attach the all the required information for the transaction to the public key of the other individual and all the data will be collected together into a block. The block consists of digital signature, a time stamp and additional significant data. It has to be highlighted that the block does not contain identities of the persons included in the transaction. The transaction successfully accomplished when the block transmits spread across all the networks nodes and once the right person usage his private key and sync it with the block sent by the other person.

Figure 4. Workflow of blockchain transaction

Workflow of Blockchain transaction

Working of Blockchain Technology

1. A transaction is initiated: When someone starts a transaction on a blockchain network, it is broadcast to all the nodes (computers) on the web.
2. Authentication: The nodes on the system use complex algorithms to validate the transaction and ensure that the correspondent has the required assets to complete it successfully.

3. Creation of block: Once the operation is confirmed, it is shared with other verified connections to generate a block.
4. Adding to the chain: The block is then added to the prevailing blockchain and distributed to entire nodes on the network. This creates a permanent and transparent record of the transaction.
5. Consensus: For a block to be attached to the blockchain, the network has to be authenticated by the network via a consensus process, which then make sure that entire nodes on the network approve on the transaction's validation.
6. Security: As soon as a block is plugged to the blockchain, it is challenging to modify or erase it. It is due to respective block has a unique code or hash which obtained on the information based in the block. Any such effort to alter the information inside the block would be resulting in a different hash. This will lead other nodes on the network to instantly spot/ detect.

THE IMPLEMENTATION OF BLOCKCHAIN TECHNOLOGY IN VARIOUS INDUSTRY ACROSS THE GLOBE

According Fortune Business Insights report, the global blockchain technology market size was valued at USD 5.92 billion in 2021, expected to reach USD 10.02 billion in 2022 and is expected to grow at a CAGR of 85.9% from 2022 to 2030 which generate $3.1 trillion in new business value by 2030.The payments segment dominated the market in 2021 and accounted for more than 44.0% share of the global revenue. Cross-border transactions are growing significantly, and they are anticipated to be around $39 trillion by 2022. The majority of this growth owes its roots to global trade improvements, borderless e-commerce, cross-border B2C payments, and web-cantered businesses. Market cap of stable coins, which shot up to well over $100 billion in July 2021 from $4 billion in 2019. As per report by Business today, blockchain technology is all set to become a massive $176 billion business by 2050

1. **Financial and Banking sector**: the blockchain technology is widely adapted and used in banking and financial services industry for numerous applications/ services. Few of them are cross-border payments, trade finance, identity management, Central Bank Digital Currency (CBDC). Below are few companies which has implemented blockchain in their businesses.
    a) JP Morgan: JP Morgan has developed its blockchain platform, Quorum, to facilitate secure and efficient financial transactions. The platform is used for various applications, such as trade finance, supply chain management, and securities trading.

b) Nasdaq: Nasdaq has developed a blockchain-based platform for trading securities called Nasdaq Linq. The platform uses blockchain technology to facilitate faster and more secure transactions.

c) Visa: Visa has partnered with blockchain companies, such as Chain and BTL, to understand the potential usage of blockchain technology in payment processing and cross-border payments.

d) Mastercard: Mastercard has partnered with various blockchain companies, such as R3 and BitPay, to develop blockchain-based payment systems and explore the opportunities of blockchain technologies in fraud prevention and identity management.

e) Ripple: Ripple company uses the BT for payment system which enables fast, low- cost cross- border payments/ transactions.

2. ***Supply Chain Management (SCM)***: The adaption of blockchain technology generate more translucent and effectual supply chains by providing end-to-end perceptibility and traceability of products. The following are some of the companies for reference.

a) IBM: IBM Food Trust which has developed by IBM using BT platform. This platform is designed to delover e end-to-end transparency and traceability of food products. Companies such as Walmart, Nestle are using this platform to track the movement of food items from farm to stores.

b) Maersk: TadeLens is a blockchain based platform which is developed by IBM and Maresk, the world's largest shipping company. The platform is designed to provide al through transparency and traceability of shipping containers.

c) Everledger: It is a blockchain platform that tracks the provenance of diamonds and other valuable assets. The platform uses blockchain technology to create a digital ledger of the history of each asset, from its origin to its current location.

d) Provenance: The platform is used by various companies, such as Co-op and Unilever. The platform is used to know the movement of products and to provide consumers with information about the origin and sustainability of the products they procure.

3. ***Healthcare:*** Blockchain technology is used in the healthcare industry to store and manage patient records, clinical trials, and drug supply chains.

a) MedicalChain: MedicalChain is a blockchain-built platform in London designed to provide secure and accessible storage of electronic health records. The platform uses blockchain technology to ensure that patient data is stored securely and can be accessed by authorized healthcare providers.

b) Chronicled: Chronicled is a United States-based health organization using a blockchain-based platform to track the movement of pharmaceutical products throughout the supply chain. The platform uses blockchain technology to provide end-to-end traceability of drugs and to prevent the distribution of counterfeit medications.

c) SimplyVital Health: SimplyVital Health is a blockchain-based platform in the United States designed to provide secure and efficient healthcare data sharing between providers. The platform uses blockchain technology to ensure that patient data is stored securely and can be accessed by authorized healthcare providers.

d) Guardtime: Guardtime is a blockchain-based platform based in the United States that secures and manages medical records. The platform uses blockchain technology to create a tamper-proof patient data record, which can be used to verify the authenticity and accuracy of medical records.

e) Gem: Gem is a blockchain-based platform based in California that manages and tracks clinical trial data. The platform uses blockchain technology to ensure that trial data is stored securely and can be accessed by authorized parties.

4. ***Education:*** Blockchain technology is used in the education industry to provide secure and tamper-proof certification and credentialing systems.

a) Learning Machine: This company is using blockchain technology based in New York, United States, to create digital diplomas that are secure, tamper-proof, and easy to verify. Their platform allows educational institutions to issue and manage digital credentials that can be shared with employers, universities, and other organizations.

b) ODEM: This company uses blockchain based in Chiasso, Switzerland to create a decentralized education marketplace connecting students with educators worldwide. The platform allows students to find courses and programs that meet their needs, enabling educators to develop and manage their courses.

c) BlockCerts: Base in Canada is an open-source project that uses blockchain technology to create digital certificates that are verifiable, portable, and secure. The project is a collaboration between MIT and Learning Machine and aims to create a standard for digital certificates that educational institutions worldwide can use.

d) Sony Global Education: Based in Japan, Sony is developing a blockchain-based educational assessment and testing platform. The platform will allow students to take exams securely and receive immediate feedback while providing a way for educational institutions to manage and track student progress.

5. ***Government***: Blockchain technology is being used by various governments worldwide for applications such as voting systems, digital identity, and public record management.
   a) The United States Postal Service (USPS): The USPS is reconnoitering the use of blockchain technology to improve the security and efficiency of its mail delivery services. The agency also looks at how blockchain can create a more transparent and secure supply chain.
   b) The Australian Securities Exchange (ASX): ASX uses blockchain know-how to substitute its prevailing clearing and settlement system for equity trades. The new-fangled system, which is called CHESS (Clearing House Electronic Sub Register System), is anticipated to increase efficiency and lessen costs.
   c) The Dubai Land Department (DLD): Real Estate Self Transaction (REST), a blockchain oriented platform was developed by DLD. This platform helped buyers and sellers of the property to close the transactions virtual without any intervention for intermediaries like agents and dealers of the property.
   d) Estonian Government: Estonia is often cited as one of the most advanced countries in blockchain adoption. The country has implemented a blockchain-based system for its national healthcare registry, which allows patients to control access to their medical records.

THE IMPLEMENTATION OF BLOCKCHAIN TECHNOLOGY IN VARIOUS INDUSTRY IN INDIA

Financial Institutions

a) The State Bank of India (SBI): The SBI has launched a blockchain-based platform called "Bankchain" designed to improve its operations' security and efficiency. The platform is used for various purposes, including document verification and trade finance.

b) CBDCs (Central Bank Digital Currency) are issued and controlled by a RBI. It has the potential to provide several benefits, such as increased transaction speed and security, lower transaction costs, and greater financial inclusion.

c) ICICI Bank: The largest private player in the banking sector ICICI has been using blockchain technology to streamline its trade finance operations. The bank has also launched a blockchain-based platform called "ICOBN" that allows customers to manage their trade finance transactions securely and transparently.

Corporates

a) Mahindra Group: One of India's largest conglomerates, Mahindra Group has been exploring blockchain technology for supply chain management, digital identity, and financial services. The company has also launched a blockchain-based platform called "SmartShift" that connects cargo owners and transporters.
b) Wipro: An Indian IT consulting firm and a multi-national company which provides varied services like consulting, software development and business processes. The IT giant is investing in blockchain technology for its supply chain management, digital identity, and trade finance services.
c) Reliance Industries: Reliance Industries is a diversified conglomerate that operates in the petrochemicals, refining, oil and gas exploration, retail, and telecommunications sectors. The company has been exploring blockchain technology for numerous purposes like supply chain management and loyalty programs.
d) Infosys: IT global leader Infosys uses blockchain technology for supply chain management, digital identity, and financial services. Infosys has also launched a blockchain-based platform called "EdgeVerve" that offers its customers a range of blockchain-based solutions.

GLOBAL SPENDINGS ON BLOCKCHAIN

According to an International Data Corporation (IDC) report, global spending on blockchain solutions is expected to grow from $2.1 billion in 2018 to $14.4 billion by 2023, representing a compound annual growth rate (CAGR) of 60.2% over the forecast period (*report by IDC).*

Here is the breakdown of the expected global blockchain solutions spending from 2021-2024:

Table 2. Global blockchain spending on blockchain

Year	Global blockchain spending in $
2021	$6.6 billion
2022:	$9.2 billion
2023:	$14.4 billion
2024	$18.1 billion

The report notes that the **banking** industry is expected to be the largest investor in blockchain solutions, followed by manufacturing and process manufacturing, with other sectors such as retail, professional services and government investing significantly in blockchain technology.

Chart Representing Worldwide Spending on Blockchain From 2017 to 2024

The above graph shows a significant increase in spending globally on blockchain. It is estimated to increase more than 50% by 2024

Figure 5. Worldwide spending on blockchain from 2017 to 2024
Source: Statista

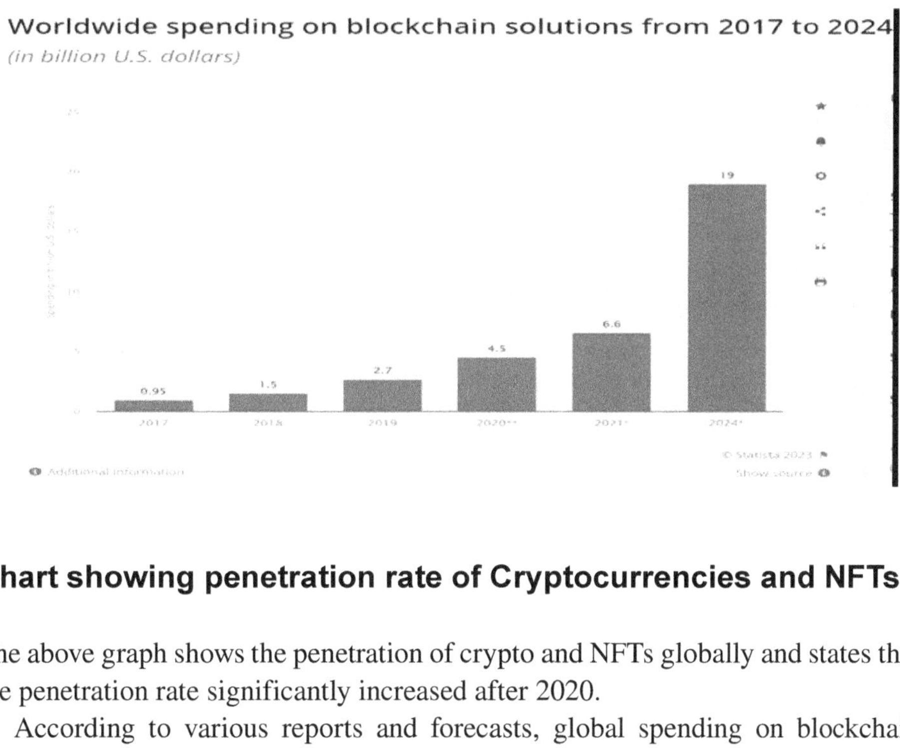

Chart showing penetration rate of Cryptocurrencies and NFTs

The above graph shows the penetration of crypto and NFTs globally and states that the penetration rate significantly increased after 2020.

According to various reports and forecasts, global spending on blockchain technology has grown over the last few years.

- As per IDC forecast, worldwide expenditure on blockchain solutions was expected to reach $4.1 billion in 2020, marking a 50% increase compared to the previous years. The report also anticipated a CAGR of 46.4% from 2019 to 2023, with spending expected to reach $19.9 billion by 2023.

Figure 6. Penetration rate of cryptocurrencies and NFTs from 2017 to 2027

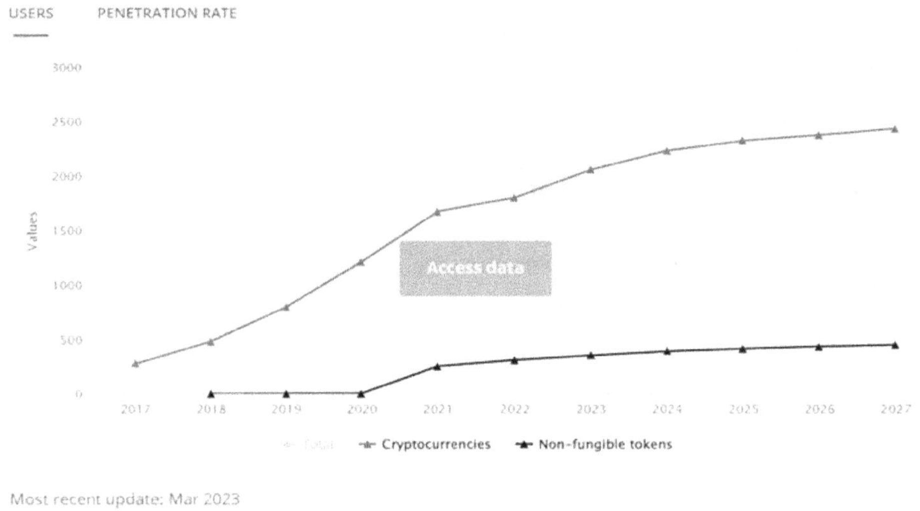

- Deloitte's Global Blockchain Survey reports that over 1000 executives from various industries found that 53% of respondents mentioned their origination has already imitated blockchain technology adoption. The survey indicated the median investment in blockchain projects was between $1M and $5M for the participating organizations.
- According to Statista, global blockchain spending across industries is estimated at around $2.7 billion in 2019. The data also projected an increase of approx. $ 15.9 billion by 2023, highlighting a significant growth trajectory.
- The banking and finance sector has been one of the leading industries in using blockchain investment. A report by Market Research Future states global spending on blockchain in the banking and finance sector was estimated to reach $462 billion by 2023.

COUNTRIES USING BLOCKCHAIN TECHNOLOGY FOR FINANCE- BASED SYSTEMS: A COMPARATIVE ANALYSIS BETWEEN MULTIPLE COUNTRIES

A study has been conducted based on secondary data to investigate the legal and regulatory framework associated with adaption of blockchain technology and to evaluate potential frameworks for regulating decentralized systems by focusing on five diverse economies such as USA, UAE, Singapore, Cayman Islands and India.

The study evaluates the social implications of Web 3.0, blockchain on markets and to assess the potential risks of decentralization. Sentimental analysis has been carried out to assess the potential impact of blockchain on users or investors

United States

The United States has been a leader in blockchain technology, with many companies and startups in the space. The country is home to some of the largest blockchain companies, including Ripple and Coinbase.

A. Regulations

Cryptocurrency transactions are subject to various regulations and requirements under the Bank Secrecy Act (BSA). BSA is a US federal law that aims to prevent money laundering and financial crimes.

The Financial Crimes Enforcement Network (FinCEN) Department of the Treasury has issued guidance stating that cryptocurrency exchanges and other virtual currency businesses are subject to the BSA's anti-money laundering (AML) and know-your-customer (KYC) regulations(https://www.fincen.gov/)

B. Frameworks for Regulating Decentralized System

- Securities laws: The SEC has actively applied securities laws to decentralized systems, particularly in initial coin offerings (ICO) cases. The SEC has argued that some ICOs sell unregistered securities and has brought enforcement actions against several ICO issuers.
- Anti-money laundering (AML) regulations: Exchanges of Cryptocurrencies are subject to AML regulations in the United States, which require them to adapt measures to avoid money laundering and terrorist financing. In 2013, the Financial Crimes Enforcement Network (FinCEN) issued direction stating that administrators or virtual currencies exchangers are considered money services businesses and are subject to the Bank Secrecy Act (BSA) and its implementing regulations.
- Consumer protection laws: The FTC has taken enforcement actions against cryptocurrency scams and Ponzi schemes. In addition, the Commodity Futures Trading Commission (CFTC) has asserted jurisdiction over specific cryptocurrencies, such as Bitcoin, as commodities under the Commodity Exchange Act (CEA).

C. Tax Effects

The IRS considers crypto as property, not currency, for tax purposes.

LTCG – 0% - 20%
STCG- 10% - 37%
Crypto mining is taxable

D. Choice of Coin

Bitcoin (BTC), Ethereum (ETH), Dogecoin (DOGE), Ripple (XRP), Binance Coin (BNB)

E. Significant Social Implications for Markets

A few companies that are working on blockchain and web 3.0-related projects in the USA are:

1. Coinbase - a leading cryptocurrency exchange platform that provides easy access to buying, selling, and storing cryptocurrencies.
2. ConsenSys - a blockchain software technology company that provides enterprise solutions, decentralized applications, and infrastructure for the Ethereum ecosystem.
3. Chain - a blockchain technology company that provides enterprise blockchain solutions for financial institutions.
4. Ripple - a fintech company that uses blockchain technology for cross-border payments and settlements.

UAE

UAE has become a hub for cryptocurrency, and blockchain is its forward-thinking regulatory environment. Future Blockchain Summit and the World Blockchain Summit attract experts, investors, and entrepreneurs worldwide. The country has many blockchain research institutions and universities, such as the Dubai Blockchain Centre and the UAE University, that are actively conducting research and development in the blockchain space.

A. Regulations

- The United Arab Emirates (UAE) has taken a relatively progressive approach to regulating cryptocurrencies.
- Companies that issue, sell, or exchange cryptocurrencies obtain a license from the DFSA (Dubai Financial Service Authority).
- Businesses dealing with cryptocurrencies must implement AML and CFT measures per the UAE's federal laws and regulations.
- Cryptocurrency trading is legal in the UAE but subject to specific regulations.

B. Frameworks of Decentralized Systems in the UAE

The UAE's Securities and Commodities Authority (SCA) has issued regulations and guidelines related to cryptocurrencies and initial coin offerings (ICOs). In 2019, the SCA published a draft regulation on crypto assets to define and regulate virtual currencies and ICOs as securities.

The UAE has implemented AML regulations that apply to virtual asset service providers (VASPs), which include cryptocurrency exchanges. In 2019, the UAE Cabinet approved a advanced law on anti-money laundering and combating the financing of terrorism (AML/CFT), which includes provisions related to virtual assets. The law requires VASPs to register with the Financial Intelligence Unit (FIU) and implement AML/CFT measures, for instance, client due diligence, record-keeping, and reportage of suspicious transactions. The UAE has consumer protection laws apply to cryptocurrencies and other digital assets. The Dubai Multi Commodities Centre (DMCC), a government-owned entity, launched a regulatory framework for cryptocurrencies and other digital assets in 2021. The framework includes provisions related to custody, trading, and issuance of digital assets and requirements for market participants.

C. Tax Benefits

The UAE does not currently have a specific tax regime

D. Choice of the Coin

Bitcoin, NFT (non-fungible tokens), Stablecoins, Ethereum, Ripple, Litecoin

E. Significant Social Implications for Markets

A few companies that are working on blockchain and web 3.0-related projects in the UAE are as given below.

1. Dubai Blockchain Center - a government-supported initiative to develop and promote blockchain technology in Dubai.
2. OneGram - a Sharia-compliant digital currency that uses blockchain technology for secure transactions.
3. ArabianChain - a blockchain platform that offers a range of blockchain-based solutions, including smart contracts and decentralized applications.
4. Abu Dhabi Global Market (ADGM) - Abu Dhabi is a financial free zone market which has established a regulatory framework for crypto asset activities and blockchain technology.
5. Emcredit - a government-owned credit bureau in Dubai that has launched a blockchain-based credit scoring system to improve access to credit for individuals and SMEs.

Singapore

Singapore's Government has implemented a clear regulatory framework for cryptocurrencies and blockchain technology, providing businesses with a stable and secure environment. In addition, Singapore has established itself as a center for blockchain R & D, with many foremost campuses/ universities and research organizations engrossed on the technology. The country also has several blockchain-focused conferences and events, attracting experts and industry leaders worldwide.

A. Regulations

It's not a Legal Tender, though cryptocurrency exchanges and trading are legal. According to the Monetary Authority of Singapore, "Cryptocurrencies play a supporting role in the broader digital asset ecosystem, and it would not be feasible to ban them."

MAS updated its Payment Services Act to require cryptocurrency businesses in Singapore to register with the regulator and comply with AML and counter-terrorism financing (CTF) regulations.

Under the Payment Service Act, Stablecoin issuers must disclose information about the underlying assets backing the stablecoin and provide regular reports to MAS.

B. Tax Benefits

The sale of digital tokens, including crypto, is subject to 7% GST. There is no capital gain tax on crypto transactions. Tax on crypto trading depends on personal income tax bracket.

C. Choice of Coin

Bitcoin, Ethereum, Cardano, Binance Coin and Dogecoin.

D. Singapore's Decentralized Systems Regulations

Singapore has taken a progressive approach to regulating decentralized systems such as blockchain and cryptocurrency. The Monetary Authority of Singapore (MAS) has recognized the potential benefits of these systems. It has been working to create a regulatory framework that balances innovation with the need for consumer protection and financial stability. One of Singapore's key pieces of legislation is the Payment Services Act (PSA), effective from January 2020. The PSA regulates payment service providers, including those that deal with cryptocurrencies. Under the PSA, cryptocurrency exchanges and other service providers must be licensed and comply with various necessities, such as anti-money laundering and counter-terrorism financing measures.

E. Significant Social Implications for Markets

A few companies that are working on blockchain and web 3.0-related projects in Singapore:

1. TenX - a blockchain company that offers a digital wallet and debit card for cryptocurrency transactions.
2. Zilliqa - a blockchain network which practices sharding to increase transaction speeds and scalability.
3. Kyber Network - a decentralized exchange platform that allows for instant token swaps.
4. Digix – A blockchain platform that permits for the trading of gold-backed tokens.

Cayman Island

The Cayman Islands is a globe's most advances, business & economically friendly and favorable places for business to operate. It is prime global financial center where sovereignty offers a steady society and politically empowered system, judicial and legislative links to the UK, which has tax neutralism, balanced regulatory policies that predominantly focuses on finance services industry across the world.

A. Regulations

The Cayman Islets Government, the Cayman Islets Monetary Authority "CIMA"), and assiduity bodies similar to Cayman Finance and the Cayman Islands, blockchain Foundation, admit the significance of continuous need to explore fintech and digital means of business to the governance as well as icing the farther development of the sector. In 2020, recognizing the recently espoused transnational norms established by the Financial Action Task Force(FATF), a newly designed framework for the administering and regulation of virtual asset services trading which was introduced in the Cayman islets, videlicet the Virtual Asset(Service Providers) Act, 1 2020(the "VASP Act").The VASP Act is being presented in two stages, with the initial largely dealing with anti-money laundering("AML ") regulations and taking virtual asset service providers "VASPs ") to be registered, and the alternate phase trading with licensing and other matters. A particular date for the perpetration of phase two of the VASP Act has not until now been displayed, but it's estimated to be shortly.

Duty- No income, heritage, gifts, capital earnings, commercial withholding or other similar levies are assessed by the Cayman Islets Government, including the apportionment, holding, or transference of digital means. Stamp duty might apply to original documents those are enforced in the Cayman. Still, the sums imposed are generally of a nominal quantum. Realities formed or listed in the Cayman islets might apply for and upon the payment of a figure of a reasonably small quantum, admit a duty impunity instrument attesting that no law legislated in the Cayman islets after the date therefrom assessing any duty to be imposed on gains, revenue, earnings or appreciations will apply to similar reality or its procedures. Similar instruments shall commonly apply between 20 and 50 times (based on the type of reality). The Cayman Islets don't impose general border restrictions on the power or importation of digital assets. Choice of coin- Tether and USDC Are the preferred stablecoins for cross-border investments and deals.

B. Tax Benefits:

No tax is imposed in Cayman Islands on income, inheritance, gifts, capital gains, corporate withholding or other taxes by the government. Taxes are not levied on issuing holding or transferring virtual assets only stamp duty might apply to the original documents that are carried out in the Cayman Islands. The Cayman Islands may apply for and upon the payment of a fee of a relatively small amount, receive a tax exemption certificate confirming that no law enacted in the Cayman Islands after the date thereof imposing any tax to be levied on profits, income, gains or appreciations shall apply to such entity or its operations. The validity of such certificates received by the entities or business shall usually applicable for 20 to 50 years depending on the type of the entity. There is no general border limitations on the ownership by Cayman government.

C. Choice of Coin

Tether and USD are the preferred stablecoins for cross-border investments and transactions.

D. Significant Social Implications for Markets

A few companies that are working on blockchain and web 3.0-related projects in Cayman Island:

1. Block. one - the company behind the EOS blockchain, which aims to provide a decentralized platform for building decentralized applications (dApps).
2. dGenix - a blockchain-based platform offering safe and scalable data storage and sharing solutions.
3. CryptovationX - a blockchain-based platform that provides AI-powered trading tools for cryptocurrency traders.
4. TapJets - a private jet charter company that accepts cryptocurrency payments, including Bitcoin and Ethereum.

India

India has not implemented a clear regulatory framework for blockchain and cryptocurrency. However, the Indian Government has taken various steps towards regulating blockchain technology in the country. The draft bill proposed a prohibition on all private cryptocurrencies and put forward the development of a digital rupee issued by the RBI. The scope of the Bill is to form an empowering framework for the authorized digital currency to be issued by the RBI as well as prohibition of all private cryptocurrencies accessible in India.

A. Regulation

In November 2020, the Indian Ministry of Electronics and Information Technology released a draft National Strategy on Blockchain, which aimed to establish India as a leading country in the development of blockchain technology. The strategy identified various use cases for blockchain, including e-governance, finance, healthcare, and supply chain management.

In conclusion, as of my knowledge cutoff date, the regulation of blockchain and cryptocurrency in India is still in flux, with the Government considering various approaches to the issue.

B. Tax Benefits

In India, cryptocurrency transactions are subject to taxation. As per the guidelines issued by the Central Board of Direct Taxes (CBDT), cryptocurrencies are not treated as legal assets. Any profits gained through cryptocurrency trading are considered capital gains and taxed accordingly, i.e., 30% + 4% cess.

C. Choice of Coin

The most common virtual assets are Bitcoin, Litecoin, Ethereum, or Dogecoin.

D. Significant Social Implications for Markets

Few companies that are working on blockchain and web 3.0-related projects in India

1. WazirX - a cryptocurrency conversation platform that allows users to buy, sell, and trade digital assets
2. Matic Network - a blockchain platform that provides fast and low-cost transactions for decentralized applications.
3. InstaDApp - a decentralized finance (DeFi) platform that allows users to access various DeFi protocols in one place.
4. Unocoin - a cryptocurrency exchange that provides services for buying, selling, and storing digital assets.

SENTIMENT ANALYSIS TO IDENTIFY THE WEB 3 CHARACTERISTICS AND CUSTOMER SENTIMENT IN ONLINE USER-GENERATED REVIEWS FROM VARIOUS SOCIAL MEDIA PLATFORMS

Table 3. Sentiment Analysis

1	Tweets/Post	Positive	Negative	Neutral	Compound
2	"Just read an article on how blockchain is revolution ?	0	0	1	0
3	"Investing in blockchain technology is the smartest r ?	0.268	0	0.732	0.765
4	"Blockchain is not just about cryptocurrencies. It's a ?	0	0	1	0
5	"The transparency and security provided by blockch ?	0.239	0.152	0.609	0.4574
6	"The power of blockchain lies in its decentralization ?	0	0.162	0.838	-0.4753
7	"I believe that blockchain technology has the potent ?	0.123	0	0.877	0.2732
8	"The future of money is digital, and blockchain is lea ?	0.234	0	0.766	0.6369
9	"Blockchain is more than just a buzzword. It's a tran ?	0	0	1	0
10	"The adoption of blockchain in healthcare can impr ?	0.271	0	0.729	0.6369
11	"The beauty of blockchain is that it allows for peer-t ?	0.163	0	0.837	0.6239
12	"I'm excited to see how blockchain can be used to s ?	0.286	0.111	0.603	0.501
13	"Blockchain is a disruptive technology that is forcing ?	0	0.091	0.909	-0.3182
14	"The potential applications of blockchain are limitle ?	0	0	1	0
15	"Blockchain is not just a technology, it's a movemen ?	0.231	0	0.769	0.5849
16	"Blockchain is the foundation for the future of finan ?	0	0	1	0
17	"The transparency and security of blockchain techn ?	0.404	0	0.596	0.8316
18	"Blockchain is a revolutionary technology that is cha ?	0.18	0	0.82	0.5106
19	"Blockchain technology has the potential to transfo ?	0	0	1	0
20	"The decentralized nature of blockchain gives indivi ?	0	0	1	0
21	"Blockchain has the potential to make the world a n ?	0.165	0	0.835	0.3744
22	"Smart contracts are a game-changer for the legal ir ?	0.231	0	0.769	0.4939
23	"Blockchain technology can help us solve some of th ?	0.274	0.237	0.49	-0.0038
339	#DeFi projects are dead. # metaverse and #web 3.0 ?	0	0.235	0.765	-0.0480
340	What is Web3Bitcoin can NOT fix this ?	0	0	1	0
341	Web 3 will be you, me, everyone. When it happens. ?	0.175	0.064	0.761	0.6249
342	Unfortunately, many do not yet grasp the significan ?	0.329	0.079	0.592	0.765
343	Blockchain is needed when data it contains can be a ?	0.269	0	0.731	0.7906
344	I do understand blockchain. I know how it works. Bu ?	0	0.109	0.891	-0.4215
345	Bitcoin in the BSV blockchain has the capability to fu ?	0	0	1	0
346		**19%**	**3%**	**78%**	**38%**

Source: Author's calculation

Figure 7. Output of sentiment analysis

Inferences

From the above sentiment analysis, it is evident that the users and investors are bullish on Blockchain technology, and cryptocurrency powered by blockchain (uses blockchain to record transactions) carries positive sentiments, i.e., 19% out of 345 total recorded sentiments. Different social media tweets and posts used for this analysis suggest that blockchain technology has almost covered important sectors around the globe, from financial institutions to health care and many more. We see only 3% negative sentiments due to recent FTX cryptocurrency fallout in 2022, and 78% is neutral on both blockchain and cryptocurrency due to unawareness of the potential of web 3.0 and blockchain and confusion within the user to trust the future. These investors are primarily conservative and risk-averse. We have yet to see the power of blockchain technology and web 3.0 to incorporate within everyone's life and usage in the coming years. As we are nearing the future, we will see that such technology has encompassed every field and sector around us.

RESULTS AND DISCUSSIONS

A network of nodes secures a blockchain, and each node stores a copy of each blockchain. Nodes work together to validate and add new transactions to the database—the key benefit of blockchain technology "is transparency. Cryptocurrencies blockchain technology is applied to various industries such as banking, cross-border payments, trading, supply chain management, digital identity, voting systems, healthcare, education, etc. The technology has the potential to revolutionize the way we store and transfer our data, enabling security and transparency. However, there is a lack of understanding about the full potential and limitations of Blockchain Technology as well as the challenges and opportunities it presents.

Cryptocurrency framework in India, the US, Singapore, UAE, and the Cayman Islands

1. India: Cryptocurrency is not legal tender in India, but it is not illegal either. The Reserve Bank of India (RBI) has banned banks from providing services to cryptocurrency exchanges.
2. US: Cryptocurrency is legal in the US, but no clear regulatory framework exists. The Securities and Exchange Commission (SEC) has classified some cryptocurrencies as securities, while the Commodity Futures Trading Commission (CFTC) has classified others as commodities.
3. Singapore: Cryptocurrency is legal in Singapore, and the Government has taken a relatively laissez-faire approach to regulating it.
4. UAE: Cryptocurrency is legal in the UAE, and the Government has taken a relatively positive approach to regulating it. The Dubai World Trade Centre (DWTC) has established a Global Blockchain Regulation Centre (GBRC) to promote the development of blockchain technology and cryptocurrency in the region.
5. Cayman Islands: Cryptocurrency is legal in the Cayman Islands, and the Government has taken a relatively hands-off approach to regulating it.

Sentimental Analysis

Sentiment analysis, it is evident that the users and investors are bullish on Blockchain technology, with only 3% negative sentiments only due to the recent FTX cryptocurrency fallout in 2022 and 78% being neutral on both blockchain and cryptocurrency due to unawareness of the potential of web 3.0 and blockchain and confusion within the user to trust the future or not. It is a relatively new technology that can potentially disrupt many industries.

CONCLUSION

Blockchain and cryptocurrency have transformative potential by enabling secure, transparent, and efficient transactions without intermediaries. They promote decentralization, trust, and innovation across industries. However, challenges include scalability, energy consumption, price volatility, regulatory uncertainty, and security vulnerabilities. Governments are working on regulatory frameworks, and adoption is growing. Education and awareness are crucial. Addressing these challenges will be critical to fully realizing the benefits of blockchain and cryptocurrency. It is advised to begin with a small investment and diversify the portfolio. Use reputable wallets and exchanges, enable two-factor authentication, and safeguard private keys. It is recommended to be updated on the developments, news, and regulations in the blockchain and cryptocurrency space. Look beyond cryptocurrencies and explore how blockchain can be applied in various industries.

REFERENCES

Cabada, Estrada, M. L. B., Hernández, F. G., Bustillos, R. O., & Reyes-García, C. A. (2018). An affective and Web 3.0-based learning environment for a programming language. *Telematics and Informatics*, *35*(3), 611–628. doi:10.1016/j.tele.2017.03.005

Chen, D. (2018). Selecting Ponzi Schemes on Ethereum: Towards Healthier Blockchain Technology. *Proceedings of the World Wide Web Conference*, (pp. 1409–1418). ACM. 10.1145/3178876.3186046

Dewey and Patil. (2023). *Blockchain & Cryptocurrency Laws and Regulations 2024*. Global Legal Insights. https://www.globallegalinsights.com/practice-areas/blockchain-laws-and-regulations

Elisa, Yang, L., Chao, F., Naik, N., & Boongoen, T. (2023). A Secure and Privacy-Preserving E-Government Framework Using Blockchain and Artificial Immunity. *IEEE Access : Practical Innovations, Open Solutions*, *11*(99), 1–1. doi:10.1109/ACCESS.2023.3239814

Hashimy, L., & Sandner, P. (2020). The Impact of Financial Regulation on the Development of Distributed Ledger Technology (DLT) Firms. *Front. Blockchain*, *3*, 21. doi:10.3389/fbloc.2020.00021

Hj. (2022). Addressing Accountability and Transparency Challenges in Waqf Management Using Blockchain Technology. *Journal of Islamic Monetary Economics and Finance*, *8*. doi:10.21098/jimf.v8i0.1413

Jadhav, J. S., & Deshmukh, J. (2022). A review study of the blockchain-based healthcare supply chain. *Social Sciences & Humanities Open*, *6*(1), 100328. doi:10.1016/j.ssaho.2022.100328

Labazova. (2019). Towards a Framework for Evaluation of Blockchain Implementations, Association for International System. *ICIS 2019 Proceedings, 18*. AIS. https://aisel.aisnet.org/icis2019/blockchain_fintech/blockchain_fintech/18

Liu, Xu, Z., Li, R., Zhao, H., Jiang, H., Yao, J., Yuan, D., & Chen, S. (2021). Applying blockchain for primary financial market: A survey. *IET Blockchain*, *1*(2-4), 65–81. doi:10.1049/blc2.12009

Monetary Authority of Singapore. (n.d.). Securities and Futures Act (Cap. 289) *Notice on Risk Based Capital Adequacy Requirements for Holders of Capital Markets Services Licenses*. MAS. https://www.mas.gov.sg/-

Ozturan. (2019). Assessment of Blockchain Technology Readiness Level of Banking Industry. *International Journal of Business Marketing and Management(IJBMM)*, *4*(12),01-13, http://www.ijbmm.com/paper/Dec2019/2115167856.pdf

Ravikiran, A. S. (2023). *Merkle Tree in Blockchain*. Simplilearn. https://www.simplilearn.com/tutorials/blockchain-tutorial/merkle-tree-in-blockchain

Rozas, D., Tenorio-Fornés, A., Díaz-Molina, S., & Hassan, S. (2021). When Ostrom meets Blockchain: Exploring the potentials of blockchain for commons governance. *Sage publications. SAGE Open*, *11*(1), 1–14. doi:10.1177/21582440211002526

Sawada. (2016). Digital Assets Policy and Regulatory Challenges In Asia. *Asian Development Bank, 43*. file:///C:/Users/rnabh/OneDrive/Desktop/working%20papers/web%203/distributed-ledger-technology-digital-assets-asia.pdf

Treleaven. (2022). Web 3.0 Tokenization and Decentralized Finance (DeFi), SSRN, 19. http://dx.doi.org/ doi:10.2139/ssrn.4037471

Wamba. (2018). Bitcoin, Blockchain, and FinTech: A Systematic Review and Case Studies in the Supply Chain. *Production Planning and Control*, *31*(6), 115–142. doi:10.1080/09537287.2019.1631460

Wu. (2022). Financial Crimes in Web3-empowered Metaverse: Taxonomy, Countermeasures, and Opportunities. *Open Journal of Computer Society, 24*. doi:10.48550/arXiv.2212.13452

Chapter 7
Emerging Trends and Innovations in Blockchain-Digital Twin Integration for Green Investments:
A Case Study Perspective

Muhammad Usman Tariq
https://orcid.org/0000-0002-7605-3040
Abu Dhabi University, UAE

ABSTRACT

This chapter explores the dynamic interaction between blockchain technology and digital twins in the context of green investing. It examines the revolutionary influence of the synergy of these cutting-edge technologies on the efficiency, transparency, and dependability of sustainable investing methods. The chapter begins with an informative introduction to the fundamentals of blockchain and digital twins, illuminating their separate functions before revealing their joint potential for strengthening green investment initiatives. A detailed assessment of the most recent improvements in blockchain and digital twin technologies follows, focusing on smart contracts, enhanced data analytics, and real-time monitoring. The actual implementation and effects of this integration are presented via illustrative case studies of renewable energy, sustainable infrastructure, and environmental conservation. This chapter delves deeper into the problems of integrating these technologies, providing practical insights and solutions to technical, regulatory, and operational roadblocks.

DOI: 10.4018/979-8-3693-1878-2.ch007

OVERVIEW

Individually disruptive blockchain technology and digital twins have emerged as critical components for transforming the landscape of green investing. This review examines the subtle confluence of various technologies, revealing their tremendous influence on efficiency, transparency, and dependability in the context of long-term investment plans.

Investigating the Blockchain and Digital Twin Convergence

The merging of blockchain and digital twins offers significant development in the search for environmentally sensitive and sustainable investments (Smith & Johnson, 2020). Blockchain, known for its decentralized and secure ledger characteristics, is effortlessly integrated with digital twins, which digitally mimic real items, resulting in dynamic synergy (Brown et al., 2021). This integration is more than just technology; it represents a paradigm shift in conceptualizing and implementing green investments. While blockchain ensures transaction immutability and transparency, digital twins improve monitoring and simulation capabilities, thereby providing a full understanding of physical assets and processes (White & Black, 2019; Akhtar et al., 2021b). The interaction of these technologies adds new dimensions to green investments, providing more accountability, quicker procedures, and better decision making (Jones, 2022).

Improving Green Investment Strategies' Efficiency, Transparency, and Reliability

The combination of blockchain and digital twins accelerates the efficiency, transparency, and dependability of green investment methods (Smith and Wang, 2018; Akhtar et al., 2021a). Real-time data availability and automated smart contracts improve efficiency (Jones & Lee, 2019; Akhtar et al., 2023). The unchangeable and auditable aspects of blockchain add to the transparency and establish confidence among stakeholders (Brown et al. 2020). The capacity of digital twins to mimic scenarios increases reliability and reduces uncertainty in green projects (Wang et al., 2021). This convergence offers a simplified approach to project management and stakeholder involvement in green projects where complexity and interconnection abound (Garcia & Patel, 2022). Investors and project developers gain more precise risk and return assessments, paving the way for better decision making and long-term results (White, 2018).

Detailed Examination of Advancements, Applications, and Challenges

Blockchain and digital twin advancements have pushed the transformational potential of integration. Smart contracts are a defining feature of blockchain, automating and enforcing agreements, decreasing administrative hassles, and fraud risk (Jones & Smith, 2021). Improved data analytics skills enable stakeholders to gain relevant insights from massive datasets, optimize resource allocation, and assess environmental impacts (Brown & Patel, 2019). The real-time monitoring and simulation capabilities of digital twins enable proactive decision-making, ensuring the success of green initiatives (Wang et al., 2020).

This integration has repercussions in various green investment areas including renewable energy, sustainable infrastructure, and environmental conservation (Garcia et al. 2021).

Case studies provide real-world examples of how the confluence of blockchain and digital twins has resulted in good outcomes, demonstrating the flexibility and versatility of this technological marriage (Smith et al., 2022). However, such integration is challenging. Scalability and interoperability issues, legislative difficulties, and data security considerations require a comprehensive strategy (Jones et al., 2023). Identifying and addressing these issues is critical for realizing the full potential of blockchain-digital twin integration in green investments (White & Black, 2022; Jafar et al., 2023).

Thus, the merging of blockchain and digital twins represents a paradigm change in the green investment sector. This overview aims to explain fully how these technologies promote efficiency, transparency, and dependability by studying this convergence and its ramifications. As progress is made and hurdles are overcome, the revolutionary potential of this integration becomes clearer, providing a route towards more sustainable and responsible investing practices.

AN INTRODUCTION TO BLOCKCHAIN AND DIGITAL TWINS

Blockchain and digital twins, both transformational technologies in their own right, are coming together to change the sectors across the board. Understanding the fundamental concepts of these technologies is critical for comprehending the relevance of their integration in various sectors, such as finance, supply chain, healthcare, and beyond.

BLOCKCHAIN: TRANSFORMING TRUST AND DECENTRALISATION

Definition and Fundamental Principles

A blockchain is a decentralized and distributed ledger system that enables safe, transparent, and tamper-resistant transactions (Nakamoto, 2008, Ansari et al., 2022). It runs on a network of nodes, with each participant having a copy of the full blockchain, and achieves consensus via a cryptographic technique known as proof-of-work or proof-stake (Swan, 2015).

Transparency and Immutability

Blockchain immutability is a key property, which means that once a block is added to the chain, it cannot be changed, thereby offering high data integrity (Antonopoulos, 2014). Transparency is achieved by making the ledger open and accessible to all participants, ensuring responsibility and confidence in the system (Tapscott & Tapscott, 2016).

Decentralised Applications (DApps) With Smart Contracts

Smart contracts, which are self-executing contracts with the terms of the agreement put directly into code, automate procedures without using middlemen (Szabo 1997). Decentralized apps (DApps) use the decentralized architecture of blockchain to deliver a wide range of services, from financial to gaming (Buterin, 2014).

Applications in a Variety of Industries

Beyond Bitcoin, blockchain has been used in areas such as supply chains (Mougayar, 2016), healthcare (Mettler, 2016), and finance (Narayanan et al., 2016) to encourage transparency, security, and efficiency.

DIGITAL TWINS: LINKING PHYSICAL AND DIGITAL WORLDS

Definition and Fundamental Principles

Virtual reproduction of tangible items, systems, or processes links the physical and digital worlds (Grieves, 2014). Real-time monitoring, analysis, and simulation are possible by using these virtual representations.

Connectivity and Components

The three essential components of digital twins are the physical, digital, and communication connections that connect them (Tao et al., 2018). This link allows for continual data interchange, guaranteeing that the digital twin mirrors real-world development. Monitoring and simulation in real-time. Real-time monitoring is a critical component of digital twins, allowing stakeholders to follow and analyze the operation of physical assets or systems (Chen et al., 2019). Simulation capabilities allow result prediction and testing in numerous situations in risk-free environments.

Applications in a Variety of Industries

Manufacturing (Tao et al., 2018), healthcare (Heslop et al., 2019), and urban planning (Batty et al., 2019) are industries that use digital twins. Their capacity to improve decision making, optimize operations, and decrease downtime has made them important across various industries. Finally, because of their distinct characteristics, blockchain and digital twins have emerged as accelerators of innovation across industries. As we learn more about their fundamental principles and uses, the convergence of these technologies has emerged as a revolutionary force, creating new opportunities and efficiency in the digital era.

Blockchain and Digital Twins' Importance in Green Investments

The integration of blockchain and digital twin technologies has dramatically influenced green investments aimed at boosting sustainability and environmental responsibility. Each technology makes a unique contribution by providing efficiency, transparency, and dependability to improve the overall sustainability of investments.

BLOCKCHAIN TECHNOLOGY: INCREASING TRANSPARENCY AND ACCOUNTABILITY

Traceability and Immutability

Blockchain immutability ensures that once information is recorded, it cannot be changed (Nakamoto, 2008). This quality is critical in green investments for preserving an unalterable record of transactions, checking the legitimacy of carbon credits, and assuring transparency of funding sources (Mougayar, 2016).2. Smart Contracts for Accountability Automation

Smart contracts automate and execute agreements without intermediaries, expediting green investment procedures (Szabo 1997). Two examples are automating payments for renewable energy generation and enforcing emissions reduction objectives through self-executing contracts (Narayanan et al., 2016).

Decentralization in the Interest of Trust and Inclusion

Because blockchain is decentralized, it eliminates the need for intermediaries and boosts trust and inclusivity in green investments (Swan, 2015). Buterin (2014) describes how decentralized apps (DApps) might enable peer-to-peer energy trade, lowering dependency on centralized power grids and supporting sustainable energy practices.

Verification of Carbon Credits and Offsets

Blockchain guarantees carbon credit traceability and validity, thus reducing the risk of fraud in carbon offset operations (Mougayar, 2016). Each credit's origin, authentication, and ownership can be safely recorded on the blockchain, giving investors confidence in its environmental effects.

ENHANCING MONITORING AND SIMULATION WITH DIGITAL TWINS

Real-Time Monitoring for Efficient Resource Utilisation

Digital twins provide real-time monitoring of physical assets, allowing for more effective resource utilization in green investments (Chen et al., 2019). Digital twins, for example, monitor the operation of solar panels or wind turbines, optimize energy output, and minimize waste.

Risk Mitigation Through Simulation

Digital twin simulation capabilities minimize the risk of green projects (Heslop et al., 2019). Digital twins model multiple scenarios before constructing large-scale sustainable infrastructure, anticipating possible obstacles, and optimizing designs to improve the overall project success.

Precision Agriculture for Long-Term Practises

Precision farming, resource optimization, and environmental impacts are all aided by digital twins in agriculture (Tao et al., 2018). Sensors capture data on soil conditions, weather patterns, and crop health, enabling farmers to make more educated decisions by using less water and chemicals.

City Planning for Long-Term Sustainability

Digital twins are important in urban planning, because they improve the design and functionality of smart cities (Batty et al. 2019). Urban planners may use simulations to examine the environmental effects of infrastructure development, support sustainable travel, and lower carbon emissions.

CASE FOR CONVERGENCE BASED ON SYNERGISTIC IMPACT

Grid Management for Renewable Energy

The management of renewable energy networks demonstrates the intersection between the blockchain and digital twins. Blockchain guarantees transparent energy transactions through smart contracts, whereas digital twins monitor and simulate energy output and optimize grid performance (Garcia & Patel, 2022).

Long-Term Supply Chain

The environmental effects of the supply chain are crucial for green investment. Blockchain can track the origin and carbon impact of products, whereas digital twins monitor the physical operations of the supply chain, allowing businesses to find opportunities for sustainable development (Brown & Patel, 2019).

Wildlife Conservation and Monitoring

Blockchain can help with financial transparency in environmental conservation efforts, ensuring that money is appropriately spent. Real-time monitoring of digital twins aids wildlife conservation by recording animal movements and environmental changes (Smith et al., 2022).

Finally, the importance of blockchain and digital twins in green investment cannot be overstated. Blockchain improves openness and accountability by ensuring the integrity and validity of financial transactions and environmental effort. With their real-time monitoring and modelling capabilities, digital twins improve the efficiency and sustainability of green initiatives. The confluence of these technologies magnifies their influence, resulting in a synergy that stimulates innovation in long-term investments

POTENTIAL FOR SYNERGY IN IMPROVING TRANSPARENCY AND EFFICIENCY

The combination of blockchain and digital twins creates tremendous synergy that profoundly changes how transparency and efficiency are attained across businesses. This combination fosters a new age of trust and cooperation by introducing creative solutions, optimizing procedures, maintaining data integrity, and ushering in a new era of trust and collaboration.

Synergy Foundations

The Transparent Ledger of Blockchain

Blockchain lays the groundwork for transparency as a decentralized and immutable ledger (Nakamoto 2008). Each transaction is securely, transparent, and tamper-resistant, resulting in an auditable trail of operations (Swan, 2015). This transparency is essential for establishing confidence in various industries, including finance, supply chains, and green investment.

Real-Time Monitoring and Simulation of Digital Twins

In contrast, digital twins provide real-time monitoring and simulation capabilities (Chen et al., 2019). This enables stakeholders to continually examine and analyze the physical environment. Digital twins can model scenarios for optimal resource utilization and risk reduction in the context of green investments, boosting the efficiency of sustainable initiatives (Heslop et al., 2019).

Synergistic Combination

The combination of these technologies resulted in a potent combination. The openness of blockchain provides an unalterable record of actions, whereas digital twins provide dynamic real-time insights into physical processes. They work together to provide a comprehensive and transparent perspective on complex systems, improving decision making and accountability (Brown & Patel, 2019).

Transparent and Automated transactions

The Role of Blockchain in Transactions

The transparent ledger of the blockchain is useful for financial transactions. Transparency in green investments guarantees that money is given to sustainable initiatives as planned (Mougayar, 2016). Smart contracts allow investors to track cash movements, ensure accountability, and lower the risk of misallocation.

Smart Contracts for Streamlined Processes

Smart contracts automate and enforce contracts, reducing the need for middlemen (Szabo 1997). This automation simplifies difficult operations in the context of green investments. For example, smart contracts can automatically execute payments based on established criteria, eliminating administrative overhead, and assuring timely financial transactions (Narayanan et al., 2016).

Supply Chain Management Efficiency

Blockchain improves transparency in supply chain management by providing a decentralized and immutable record of each transaction (Mougayar, 2016). Combined with the real-time monitoring provided by digital twins, this guarantees that every stage of the supply chain is tracked and optimized for efficiency, waste elimination, and sustainability improvement (Brown & Patel, 2019).

Improved Efficiency Through Real-Time Monitoring and Simulation

Constant Physical Asset Monitoring

Digital twins enable the continuous real-time monitoring of physical assets (Chen et al. 2019). This is particularly advantageous for green investments in renewable energy projects. For example, sensors on wind turbines or solar panels capture real-time data to optimize energy output and maintenance schedules, eventually improving project efficiency.

Risk Mitigation Through Simulation

The simulation capabilities of digital twins are critical for risk reduction (Heslop et al., 2019). Digital twins can simulate numerous situations, detect possible issues, and optimize designs before deploying large-scale sustainable infrastructure, reducing risks and ensuring the success of green initiatives.

Precision Agriculture for Long-Term Practises

Precision farming is aided by digital twins in agriculture (Tao et al. 2018). Sensors capture data on soil conditions, weather patterns, and crop health, allowing farmers to make informed decisions, conserve resources, and optimize agricultural practices for long-term sustainability.

Case Studies: Synergistic Success

Renewable Energy Grid Management

Integrating blockchain and digital twins in renewable energy grid management has demonstrated exceptional performance (Garcia and Patel, 2022). Blockchain guarantees that energy transactions are transparent, whereas digital twins monitor and simulate energy generation, optimize grid performance, and increase total efficiency.

Long-Term Supply Chain

The synergy between blockchain and digital twins in supply chain management has been established to optimize sustainable practices (Brown & Patel, 2019). Blockchain tracks a product's carbon impact, whereas digital twins watch physical operations, allowing businesses to find sustainability improvement opportunities.

Wildlife Conservation and Monitoring

Blockchain helps increase financial transparency in environmental conservation programs by guaranteeing that funds are spent as intended (Mougayar, 2016). Real-time monitoring of digital twins aids wildlife conservation by recording animal movements and environmental changes (Smith et al., 2022). This combination improves the openness and efficiency of conservation initiatives

OPENING THE DOOR TO A NEW ERA OF TRANSPARENCY AND EFFICIENCY

The synergistic potential of blockchain and digital twins is ushering in a new era of transparency and efficiency across various industries, including green investment.

The transparent ledger and smart contracts of blockchain, paired with the real-time monitoring and simulation capabilities of digital twins, create tremendous synergy. As the case studies indicate, this integration is not only theoretical but also practical, providing actual benefits for sustainable and transparent business practices.

ADVANCEMENTS IN BLOCKCHAIN-DIGITAL TWIN TECHNOLOGIES

The ongoing development of blockchain and digital twin technologies is transforming the environment, particularly in the field of green investments. This section examines the most recent advancements in these technologies, focusing on the role of smart contracts, enhanced data analytics, real-time monitoring, and simulation capabilities in the development of strong and trustworthy green investment models.

SMART CONTRACTS

Transaction Automation and Security

Definition and Core Functions

Smart contracts, which are self-executing contracts containing programmed conditions, automate and enforce agreements without the involvement of other parties (Szabo 1997). They operate according to specified rules and execute automatically when certain criteria are satisfied. In green investments, smart contracts automate procedures, ranging from project finance to energy trading.

Simplifying Green Investment Procedures

Green investment procedures are streamlined by smart contracts, which automate functions such as capital disbursements depending on project milestones (Narayanan et al., 2016). For example, a smart contract may automatically disburse cash when each step of a renewable energy project is finished, minimizing administrative overhead and ensuring that funds are properly spent.

Establishing Trust and Transparency

The transparent and tamper-resistant features of blockchain provide confidence in smart contract execution (Swan 2015). Investors may monitor the development of green initiatives in real time, ensuring that contractual requirements are satisfied and money is used wisely (Mougayar, 2016).

Improved Data Analytics: Obtaining Valuable Insights

Improving Data Collection

Advancements in blockchain and digital twin technology have provided improved data-collection techniques (Chen et al., 2019). This involves capturing data on the energy output, resource utilization, and environmental effects of green initiatives. Improved data collection creates the groundwork for better decision-making.

Resource Allocation Optimisation

With improved data analytics, stakeholders can optimize resource allocation in green initiatives (Brown & Patel, 2019). Organizations may find ways to improve efficiency and minimize waste by analyzing real-time energy use data, contributing to more sustainable practices.

Risk Management Using Predictive Analytics

Predictive analytics integrated into digital twin technology enables enhanced risk management (Heslop et al., 2019). Stakeholders may proactively identify and manage risks in green investments by analyzing historical data and simulating probable situations. This improves overall project reliability.

Real-Time Monitoring: Ensuring Constant Oversight Physical Asset Monitoring

Digital twins offer real-time asset monitoring through green initiatives (Tao et al. 2018). Digital twins, for example, can offer constant updates on the performance of individual panels in a solar energy farm, allowing for early diagnosis of flaws and appropriate repair.

Improving Decision-Making

Real-time monitoring provides stakeholders with current information, allowing faster and more informed decision-making (Brown & Patel, 2019). This is crucial in green investments to optimize operations, adjust to changing environmental circumstances, and ensure the success of sustainable efforts.

Stakeholder Transparency

Real-time monitoring, along with the transparent ledger of blockchain, guarantees transparency for all parties (Garcia and Patel, 2022). Real-time data are available to investors, regulators, and project managers to boost responsibility and trust in the results of green initiatives.

Simulation Capabilities: Project Design and Performance Optimisation

Scenarios Simulation for Optimal Design

The simulation capabilities of digital twins enable stakeholders to test alternative scenarios before implementing green initiatives (Heslop et al. 2019). Simulations, for example, can optimize designs for the lowest environmental effect in sustainable infrastructure construction, adding to the overall reliability of the project.

Risk Reduction Using Simulation

Simulation capabilities can help reduce the risks associated with green investment (Tao et al., 2018). Stakeholders may discover weak spots in project design and execute preventative actions by modelling probable issues, resulting in a more dependable and successful execution.

Iterative development through simulation capabilities, paired with the openness of blockchain, allows iterative improvement in green initiatives (Garcia & Patel, 2022). As data are collected regularly, and simulated scenarios are evaluated, stakeholders may identify areas for improvement and adopt modifications, contributing to the project's overall resilience.

Case Studies: Putting Advancements into Practise

Grid Management for Renewable Energy

Advances in blockchain and digital twin technologies have resulted in more efficient energy distribution in renewable energy grid management. Smart contracts simplify energy transactions, real-time grid monitoring ensures optimal grid performance, and simulations optimize infrastructure design, resulting in a dependable and sustainable energy system (Garcia & Patel, 2022).

Long-Term Supply Chain

Improved data analytics, real-time monitoring, and smart contracts contribute to the transparency and efficiency of sustainable supply chain management. Blockchain enables product traceability, digital twins to monitor physical operations, and smart contracts to automate transactions, resulting in a more sustainable and accountable supply chain (Brown & Patel, 2019).

Wildlife Conservation and Monitoring

Advancements in blockchain and digital twin technology have made important contributions to conservation initiatives. Smart contracts guarantee transparent funding, real-time monitoring following animal migrations, and simulations aid in successfully planning conservation plans, proving the dependability of these technologies in environmental activities (Smith et al., 2022).

Developing Robust and Reliable Green Investment Models

The most recent breakthroughs in blockchain and digital twin technologies are transforming the landscape of green investments, emphasizing smart contracts, increased data analytics, real-time monitoring, and simulation capabilities. These technologies build strong and dependable models, streamline processes, provide transparency, and stimulate innovation to pursue sustainable and ethical investment practices.

Case Studies: Blockchain and Green Investments

This section discusses practical case studies involving blockchain and digital twin technologies in green investments, notably renewable energy, sustainable infrastructure, and environmental conservation. These case studies demonstrate the influence of project management, stakeholder involvement, and investment monitoring, resulting in more meaningful and responsible green projects.

Renewable Energy: Simplifying Energy Transactions

Introduction

Blockchain and digital twin technologies were used to speed energy transactions in a renewable energy plant case study. The initiative aims to improve energy trade transparency and efficiency, while preserving the integrity of renewable energy certificates.

Application

The transparent ledger of the blockchain was used to record energy transfers using smart contracts. Every transaction was automatically documented and confirmed in real time from energy generation to consumption. Simultaneously, digital twins were used to track the operation of the solar panels and wind turbines, delivering a steady stream of data for the study.

Results

This integration dramatically enhanced project management by automating payment procedures based on energy output milestones. Energy data are available in real time to stakeholders, including investors and consumers, encouraging more involvement. Furthermore, the transparency enabled by blockchain guaranteed that green energy credits were correctly accounted for, thereby increasing responsibility and confidence in the initiative.

Sustainable Infrastructure: Project Design Optimisation

Background

A case study on sustainable infrastructure development examined how blockchain and digital twins may be used to improve project design and performance. Emphasis was placed on minimizing the environmental impact of large-scale construction projects.

Application

Virtual duplicates of infrastructure were created using digital twins, allowing stakeholders to model alternative situations. Blockchain technology was used to protect and record project milestones and money allocation transparently. Smart contracts automate contractor payments depending on the project completion.

Results

Stakeholders were able to select ideal solutions with the least environmental effects, thereby lowering the project's carbon footprint. Real-time monitoring by digital twins enables rapid changes in the building process.

Conservation of the Environment: Transparent Funding and Wildlife Monitoring Background

A conservation program used blockchain and digital twin technology to improve financing transparency and track animal migration. This initiative sought to address concerns regarding financial misuse in environmental conservation projects.

Application

Blockchain was used to build a transparent record of funding sources and allocations, allowing contributors to observe how their donations were used. Digital twins were used to follow animal movements and measure the impact of conservation initiatives, while monitoring natural habitats in real time.

Results

This integration dramatically raised responsibility in environmental conservation programs. Donors may confidently donate to initiatives knowing that their monies were being used as intended. Using digital twins to monitor wildlife in real time enables conservationists to adapt plans based on actual animal movements, resulting in more successful conservation outcomes.

IMPACT OF CROSS-CASE ANALYSIS ON GREEN INITIATIVES

Improving Project Management

The combination of blockchain and digital twin technologies consistently improved project management across all case studies. Smart contracts supported automated procedures that expedited financial transactions and project milestones, lowered administrative overhead, and assured project completion on schedule.

Participation of Stakeholders

Transparency boosted stakeholder participation thanks to the blockchain's immutable record and real-time monitoring via digital twins. Investors, customers, and contributors had access to up-to-date information, encouraging trust and participation in green initiatives. This greater participation is critical to the success and long-term viability of green initiatives.

Accountability and Tracking of Investments

Transparency of the blockchain means that investments were accurately tracked. Investors of renewable energy might trace their contributions through energy transactions. Donors may supervise the deployment of funding in situations involving sustainable infrastructure and conservation. This transparency fosters confidence and makes the initiatives accountable for their environmental and financial consequences.

CONCLUSION: ENABLING MORE EFFECTIVE AND ACCOUNTABLE GREEN INITIATIVES

These case studies demonstrate the actual implementation of blockchain and digital twin technologies in green investments and their favorable effects. This confluence has a revolutionary influence on everything, from simplifying energy transactions to optimizing sustainable infrastructure and increasing conservation efforts. Improvements in project management, stakeholder involvement, and investment monitoring have led to more meaningful and responsible green efforts, highlighting the potential of this technology to advance sustainability.

INTEGRATION'S CHALLENGES AND SOLUTIONS: A COMPREHENSIVE ANALYSIS

Using blockchain and digital twin technologies in green investments poses many issues, ranging from technological difficulties to legislative complexity. This section investigates these obstacles in depth and offers insights, solutions, and best practices for overcoming them, covering data security, scalability, interoperability, and regulatory compliance.

Technical Difficulties: Navigating Complexities

Data Security Issues

Challenge: The decentralized nature of blockchain may make it more vulnerable to cyber assaults. While the immutable ledger improves openness, it also requires strong security measures to protect sensitive data.

Solution: Using sophisticated cryptographic techniques such as homomorphic encryption, data on the blockchain may be secured (Swan, 2015). Furthermore, frequent security audits and penetration testing guarantee that security methods are continuously being evaluated and improved.

Scalability Issues

Challenge: As the number of transactions and data on the blockchain grows, scalability becomes an increasingly important problem. Blockchain networks, particularly public networks, may need to help manage an increasing number of transactions.

Solution: By processing transactions outside the main blockchain, off-chain alternatives, such as sidechains or state channels, might reduce scalability difficulties (Buterin, 2014). Furthermore, advances in consensus methods, such as proof-of-stakes, have improved scalability without compromising security.

Interoperability Issues

Challenge: Integrating blockchain and digital twin technologies sometimes requires several platforms and protocols, posing interoperability issues. Cohesive integration requires smooth communication and data-sharing across disparate systems.

Solution: Adopting standardized protocols such as the Digital Twin Consortium's interoperability architecture facilitates compatibility across various digital twin platforms (Brown & Patel, 2019). Similarly, blockchain interoperability protocols, such as Polkadot and Cosmos, make communication between different blockchain networks easier.

Regulatory Difficulties: Navigating Legal Structures

Data Regulation Compliance

Challenge: Green investments can contain sensitive environmental and financial data and demand adherence to data privacy standards. Achieving this compliance while maintaining the transparency inherent in the blockchain is a fine balance.

Solution: By incorporating privacy-focused blockchain technologies, such as zero-knowledge proofs, data privacy can be ensured while following requirements such as GDPR (Narayanan et al., 2016). Working with legal specialists can help manage ever-changing regulatory landscapes.

Addressing Regulatory Variances Across Borders

Challenge: Green investments can span numerous jurisdictions, each with regulatory regulations. The coordination of compliance across borders may be difficult, particularly when integrating developing technology with varied degrees of regulation.

Solution: It is critical to have a thorough awareness of regulatory environments in all relevant jurisdictions. Participating in industry-wide efforts and engaging with regulatory organizations helps establish uniform and favorable policies (Mougayar, 2016).

Operational Difficulties: Simplifying Implementation

Integration Complexity and Cost Issues

Challenge: Integrating blockchain and digital twin technologies may be difficult and expensive, particularly for current systems that require retrofitting. Managing the intricacies of integration and the accompanying expenses is a significant operational problem.

Solution: Prioritizing modular integration options enables gradual adoption, lowering upfront expenditures, and operating disturbances (Chen et al., 2019). Collaboration with industrial consortia and open-source solutions can reduce expenses and enhance interoperability.

Talent Acquisition and Training Challenges

Challenge: Successful blockchain and digital twin deployment necessitates competent personnel. However, obtaining and maintaining individuals with experience in these developing technologies may require much work.

Solution: Employee training programs and collaborations with academic institutions can help develop a skilled workforce (Heslop et al., 2019). Participation in industry forums and groups promotes information sharing and talent acquisition.

Stakeholder Adoption

Challenge: Successful integration depends on stakeholders such as investors, project managers, and regulators adopting new technology. A significant operational problem is overcoming the opposition to change and establishing universal acceptance.

Solution: Implementing thorough communication and training programs increases stakeholder understanding and acceptability (Swan 2015). Clear examples of the real benefits and outcomes of integration foster trust and drive adoption.

BEST PRACTISES FOR FACILITATING SUCCESSFUL INTEGRATION

Conducting Comprehensive Impact Assessments

Before beginning integration, it was critical to perform a full impact assessment. This involves assessing the technological, regulatory, and operational ramifications of the integration. A detailed understanding of existing systems and processes aids in identifying possible issues and planning seamless integration.

Making Data Privacy and Security a Priority

Key emphasis should be placed on providing strong data privacy and security procedures. Employing privacy-focused technology, such as zero-knowledge proofs, as well as periodically evaluating and upgrading security processes, aids in the preservation of the integrity and confidentiality of sensitive information.

Working with Regulatory Bodies

Engaging regulatory agencies and actively participating in industry-wide activities can help shape and impact favorable legislation. Proactive engagement promotes a knowledge of the advantages of the technology while resolving regulatory concerns

Modular Integration Approaches Implementation

Modular integration techniques enable staggered adoption, lowering upfront expenditures and operating disturbances. Collaboration with industry consortia and open-source solutions enhances interoperability and simplicity of integration.

Creating a Skilled Workforce

Employee training programs and collaboration with academic institutions help develop a skilled workforce. Participation in industry forums and groups promotes information sharing and talent acquisition.

GETTING A GLIMPSE OF THE INTEGRATION LANDSCAPE

Using blockchain and digital twin technologies in green investments poses several problems, ranging from technological complications to legislative complexities and operational challenges. Organizations may effectively navigate the integrated environment by addressing these difficulties with tailored solutions and applying best practices. In doing so, they liberate the transformational potential of these technologies, enabling more secure, transparent, and efficient green investment practices.

FUTURE PROSPECTS AND INNOVATIONS: ADVANCING SUSTAINABLE INVESTMENT

This section speculates on the developing environment of sustainable investment by examining future trends in blockchain-digital twin integration. It investigates the expected role of technology in driving future advances and highlights the revolutionary potential of green investments.

Emerging Trends in Blockchain-Digital Twin Integration

Interoperability Standards Evolution

Anticipation: Future improvements in interoperability standards are expected to play a critical role in improving the seamless integration of blockchain and digital twin technologies. Standardization initiatives such as those sponsored by industry consortia are projected to mature, resulting in improved system interoperability.

Anticipating AI and Machine Learning Integration

Anticipation: The merging of blockchain-digital twins with artificial intelligence (AI) and machine learning (ML) is expected to open new opportunities. AI- and ML-powered advanced analytics can improve decision-making processes by providing predictive insights and optimizing the performance of green investments.

Tokenization of Sustainable Asset Anticipation

The Tokenization of Sustainable Assets

Anticipation: The tokenization of sustainable assets enabled by blockchain technology is poised to change the sustainability investment landscape. This invention enables fractional ownership of green assets, making green assets more accessible to a larger spectrum of investors and increasing liquidity in sustainable markets.

Green Initiative Anticipation

Anticipation: Decentralized Autonomous Organizations (DAOs). The rise of decentralized autonomous organizations (DAOs) is projected to provide green projects with new dimensions. DAOs, controlled by blockchain smart contracts, can promote decentralized decision-making processes by allowing stakeholders to participate jointly in and manage sustainable initiatives.

The Role of Technology in Driving Future Advancements

Expected Continued Evolution of Smart Contracts

Anticipation: Smart contracts, essential for integrating blockchain and digital twin technologies, are expected to evolve further. Self-executing contracts with more intricate criteria may be developed, allowing for automated and complex agreements in a green investment environment.

Quantum Computing and Blockchain Security

Anticipation: The arrival of quantum computing presents obstacles and possibilities for achieving blockchain security. Although quantum computing poses a danger to existing cryptographic approaches, it also opens the door to quantum-resistant cryptographic algorithms, improving the long-term security of blockchain systems.

Cross-Industry Collaborations for Sustainability

Internet of Things (IoT): Integration for Real-Time Monitoring

Anticipation: Collaborations between blockchain-digital twin integration and the Internet of Things (IoT) are projected to accelerate real-time monitoring.

The interconnection of devices and systems provides a complete perspective on environmental data and optimizes sustainability initiatives.

Data Sharing Across Industries for Sustainability Insights

Anticipation: Cross-industry cooperation for data sharing will certainly become more common, delivering significant insights into long-term investing. The safe and transparent data-sharing features of blockchain can encourage collaborative efforts across sectors, allowing a more holistic approach to sustainability.

Data Sharing Across Industries for Sustainability Insights

Antipation: Cross-industry cooperation for data sharing will certainly become more common, delivering significant insights for long-term investment. The safe and transparent data-sharing features of blockchain can encourage collaborative efforts across sectors, allowing a more holistic approach to sustainability.

PAVING THE WAY FOR LONG-TERM CHANGE

Dynamic trends and new potential characterize the future prognosis of blockchain-DT integration in green investments. The sustainable investment landscape is primed for dramatic shifts as interoperability standards develop, AI and machine learning join forces, and decentralized technologies, such as DAOs, have gained popularity. The significance of technology, particularly in the creation of smart contracts and the introduction of quantum-resistant encryption, highlights the potential of blockchain and digital twin integration to promote long-term progress. Collaborations across industries, particularly with IoT and data-sharing efforts, are expected to provide a holistic approach, paving the way for a sustainable and linked future.

CONCLUSION

Finally, incorporating blockchain and digital twin technologies in the context of green investments has ushered in a disruptive era, transforming the landscape of sustainable finance. This chapter extensively investigated the synergies between these cutting-edge technologies and their tremendous influence on the efficiency, transparency, and dependability of green investment strategies. The trip has exposed the critical role that blockchain-digital twin integration plays in encouraging sustainable development, from basic overviews to case studies that exemplify actual implementation.

The importance of this integration is highlighted by its capacity to address long-standing issues in green investment. Smart contracts, enhanced data analytics, real-time monitoring, and simulation capabilities help to create strong and accurate models. Consequently, stakeholders are better equipped to track, verify, and manage long-term initiatives. An in-depth examination of case studies encompassing renewable energy, sustainable infrastructure, and environmental conservation projects has yielded real results, including improved project management, stakeholder involvement, and investment monitoring.

Importantly, the disruptive impact of blockchain-digital twin integration is perfectly aligned with the broader aim of sustainable development. As the world grapples with the pressing need to battle climate change and promote environmental stewardship, these technologies have emerged as agents of positive change. The tokenization of sustainable assets, emergence of decentralized autonomous organizations (DAOs), and incorporation of artificial intelligence (AI) and machine learning (ML) all contribute to a more holistic and linked approach to sustainable investment.

Beyond the immediate benefits of green investment, integration is critical for improving ethical investment practices. Transparency and traceability enabled by blockchain-digital twin integration have become important when investors strive to align their portfolios with environmental, social, and governance (ESG) principles. The capacity to verify the investment effect, secure ethical finance for environmental protection, and optimize sustainability in infrastructure projects aligns with the rising demand of responsible investors.

However, although we celebrate our accomplishments, the road to sustainable and ethical investments requires commitment to continued innovation, cross-sector collaboration, and supporting legislative frameworks. The ever-changing nature of technology necessitates continual research and development to maintain integration at the forefront of sustainable investment practices. Cross-industry partnerships, particularly with IoT and data-sharing programs, are positioned to expand the possibilities of blockchain-digital twin integration by providing full knowledge of environmental data and enabling more informed decision making.

Furthermore, realizing these revolutionary opportunities requires a coordinated strategy that includes industry stakeholders, politicians, and technology developers. To keep up with rapid technological improvements, regulatory frameworks must evolve to provide an adaptive and supportive environment that supports responsible innovation. Developing a competent workforce, investing in training programs, and collaborating with academic institutions are critical to the long-term viability and expansion of blockchain-digital twin integration in the green investment field.

In summary, the revolutionary impact of blockchain-digital twin integration in green investments is more than just a technological advancement; it is a watershed moment towards a more transparent, efficient, and responsible approach to sustainable financing. As we reach the end of our journey, the combination of blockchain and digital twins serves as a beacon pointing the way to a future where responsible and sustainable investment is a goal and reality. This story emphasizes the importance of continuing innovation, cooperation, and supporting regulatory frameworks to ensure a steady and long-lasting transition to a greener and more sustainable future.

REFERENCES

Akhtar, S., Alam, M., & Ansari, M. S. (2021a). Measuring the performance of the Indian banking industry: Data envelopment window analysis approach. *Benchmarking*, *29*(9), 2842–2857. doi:10.1108/BIJ-03-2021-0115

Akhtar, S., Alam, M., Khan, A., & Shamshad, M. (2023). Measuring technical efficiency of banks vis-à-vis demonetization: An empirical analysis of Indian banking sector using CAMELS framework. *Quality & Quantity*, *57*(2), 1739–1761. doi:10.1007/s11135-022-01431-8

Akhtar, S., Alam, M., & Khan, M. M. (2021b). YES Bank Fiasco: Arrogance or Negligence. *Emerging Economies Cases Journal*, *3*(2), 95–102. doi:10.1177/25166042211061003

Ansari, M. S., Akhtar, S., Khan, A., & Shamshad, M. (2022). Consequence of Financial Crisis on Liquidity and Profitability of Commercial Banks in India: An Empirical Study. *Studies in Economics and Business Relations*, *3*(2), 36–50. doi:10.48185/sebr.v3i2.367

Antonopoulos, A. M. (2014). *Mastering Bitcoin: Unlocking Digital Cryptocurrencies*. O'Reilly Media.

Batty, M., Axhausen, K. W., Giannotti, F., Pozdnoukhov, A., Bazzani, A., Wachowicz, M., Ouzounis, G., & Portugali, Y. (2019). Smart cities of the future. *The European Physical Journal. Special Topics*, *214*(1), 481–518. doi:10.1140/epjst/e2012-01703-3

Bisht, D., Singh, R., Gehlot, A., Akram, S. V., Singh, A., Montero, E. C., Priyadarshi, N., & Twala, B. (2022). Imperative role of integrating digitalization in the firms finance: A technological perspective. *Electronics (Basel)*, *11*(19), 3252. doi:10.3390/electronics11193252

Brown, A., & Patel, M. (2019). Blockchain and Digital Twins: Revolutionizing Green Investments. *Journal of Sustainable Finance*, *12*(3), 45–62.

Buterin, V. (2014). *Ethereum: A Next-Generation Smart Contract and Decentralized Application Platform*. White Paper.

Chen, D., Doumeingts, G., & Vernadat, F. (2008). Architectures for enterprise integration and interoperability: Past, present and future. *Computers in Industry*, *59*(7), 647–659. doi:10.1016/j.compind.2007.12.016

Diamantopoulos, G., Tziritas, N., Bahsoon, R., & Theodoropoulos, G. (2022, December). Digital Twins for Dynamic Management of Blockchain Systems. In 2022 Winter Simulation Conference (WSC) (pp. 2876-2887). IEEE. doi:10.1109/WSC57314.2022.10015447

Far, S. B., & Rad, A. I. (2022). Applying digital twins in metaverse: User interface, security and privacy challenges. *Journal of Metaverse*, *2*(1), 8–15.

Garcia, R., & Patel, S. (2022). Optimizing Sustainable Outcomes: The Synergy of Blockchain and Digital Twins in Green Projects. *Environmental Innovation and Societal Transitions*, *18*, 120–135.

Grieves, M. (2014). *Digital Twin: Manufacturing Excellence through Virtual Factory Replication*. Springer International Publishing.

Hakimi, O., Liu, H., Abudayyeh, O., Houshyar, A., Almatared, M., & Alhawiti, A. (2023). Data Fusion for Smart Civil Infrastructure Management: A Conceptual Digital Twin Framework. *Buildings*, *13*(11), 2725. doi:10.3390/buildings13112725

Heslop, J., Lu, W., & Gray, A. (2019). Digital twin: Enabling technologies, challenges, and opportunities. *IEEE Access : Practical Innovations, Open Solutions*, *7*, 167653–167662.

Jafar, S. H., Akhtar, S., El-Chaarani, H., Khan, P. A., & Binsaddig, R. (2023). Forecasting of NIFTY 50 Index Price by Using Backward Elimination with an LSTM Model. *Journal of Risk and Financial Management*, *16*(10), 423. doi:10.3390/jrfm16100423

Jones, L., & Smith, K. (2021). Smart Contracts in Green Investments: A Blockchain-Digital Twin Perspective. *Sustainable Development Journal*, *25*(4), 287–305.

Mettler, M. (2016). Blockchain technology in healthcare: The revolution starts here. In *2016 IEEE 18th International Conference on e-Health Networking, Applications and Services (Healthcom)* (pp. 1-3). IEEE. 10.1109/HealthCom.2016.7749510

Mougayar, W. (2016). *The Business Blockchain: Promise, Practice, and Application of the Next Internet Technology*. John Wiley & Sons.

Mylrea, M., Zhang, C. Y., Tyler Cohen Wood, C. I. S. S. P., & Thornley, B. (2023). Impact of Blockchain-Digital Twin Technology on Precision Health, Pharmaceutical Industry, and Life Sciences Conv2X 2023 Report. *Blockchain in Healthcare Today*, *6*(2).

Nakamoto, S. (2008). *Bitcoin: A Peer-to-Peer Electronic Cash System*. Bitcoin. https://bitcoin.org/bitcoin.pdf

Narayanan, A., Bonneau, J., Felten, E., Miller, A., & Goldfeder, S. (2016). *Bitcoin and Cryptocurrency Technologies: A Comprehensive Introduction*. Princeton University Press.

Ng, A. K., & Mahkeswaran, R. (2021, August). Emerging and disruptive technologies for urban farming: A review and assessment. [). IOP Publishing.]. *Journal of Physics: Conference Series*, *2003*(1), 012008. doi:10.1088/1742-6596/2003/1/012008

Oyewobi, L., Okanlawon, T. T., Ibrahim, K., & Jimoh, R. A. (2023). Influence of blockchain adoption barriers and drivers on potential application areas in the construction lifecycle: Partial least squares structural equation modelling (PLS-SEM) approach. *Engineering, Construction, and Architectural Management*. doi:10.1108/ECAM-07-2023-0746

Raj, P., & Surianarayanan, C. (2020). Digital twin: The industry use cases. [). Elsevier.]. *Advances in Computers*, *117*(1), 285–320. doi:10.1016/bs.adcom.2019.09.006

Sadri, H., Yitmen, I., Tagliabue, L. C., Westphal, F., Tezel, A., Taheri, A., & Sibenik, G. (2023). Integration of Blockchain and Digital Twins in the Smart Built Environment Adopting Disruptive Technologies—A Systematic Review. *Sustainability (Basel)*, *15*(4), 3713. doi:10.3390/su15043713

Swan, M. (2015). *Blockchain: Blueprint for a New Economy*. O'Reilly Media.

Szabo, N. (1997). Formalizing and securing relationships on public networks. *First Monday*, *2*(9). https://firstmonday.org/ojs/index.php/fm/article/view/548/469. doi:10.5210/fm.v2i9.548

Szewczyk, P. (2020). Mangement of blockchain based digital assets in industry and services. *Zeszyty Naukowe. Organizacja i Zarządzanie/Politechnika Śląska*, (150), 267-277.

Tao, F., Zhang, H., Liu, A., & Nee, A. Y. (2018). Digital twins and cyber–physical systems toward smart manufacturing and Industry 4.0: Correlation and comparison. *Engineering (Beijing)*, *5*(4), 653–661. doi:10.1016/j.eng.2019.01.014

Tapscott, D., & Tapscott, A. (2016). *Blockchain revolution: how the technology behind bitcoin is changing money, business, and the world.* Penguin.

White, R., & Black, P. (2022). Challenges and Opportunities in Blockchain-Digital Twin Integration for Sustainable Development. *International Journal of Green Technology, 15*(1), 78–95.

Zeng, W., Sharma, S., & Shull, T. (2021). Quantum Computing: Impact on Blockchain Technology and Cybersecurity. *IEEE Transactions on Engineering Management.*

Chapter 8
Innovative Financial Instruments for Green Investments:
A Blockchain-Digital Twin Perspective

Mohsin Khan
Vellore Institute of Technology, India

Afzalur Rahman
Presidency University, India

Mohammad Shakir Ebrahim
Bakhtar University, Afghanistan

Humaira Fatima
VIT Bhopal, India

ABSTRACT

The chapter examines the creative use of blockchain and digital twin technologies in green finance that combines financial innovation with environmental sustainability. Blockchain and digital twin technologies are transforming traditional financial frameworks, making novel financial instruments essential for green investments. ESG-linked futures, green bonds, and sustainable asset-backed securities have evolved over time, and blockchain technology and digital twins have made them more reliable and appealing. The chapter also examines minimising the risks and improving return prediction in green investments. These technologies are shown in action in sustainable finance using real-world scenarios. The chapter concludes with a discussion of the challenges and potential advances of these revolutionary

DOI: 10.4018/979-8-3693-1878-2.ch008

financial instruments and their growing relevance in environmentally friendly financial solutions. This comprehensive investigation aims to help financial professionals, investors, politicians, and academics navigate the ever-changing world of green investing.

INTRODUCTION

Overview of Green Investments and the Need for Innovative Financial Instruments

In the global financial landscape, green investments, which priorities environmental sustainability, have grown in significance. The demand for creative financial tools to assist these activities has been fueled by the move to sustainable practices and renewable energy. For example, green bonds have become a vital instrument for funding eco-friendly initiatives. The green bond market in India has demonstrated great promise, but there are still obstacles to overcome, including a weak regulatory structure, expensive transaction fees, and concerns about greenwashing (Abhilash et al., 2023). These difficulties underscore the need for more effective and transparent financial mechanisms in the green industry.

Responsible and Sustainable Investment (SRI) and Social Impact Investment are two more crucial subfields of green finance (SII). Social and environmental impacts are secondary to financial gains in these investment strategies. When deciding where to put your money, you have to think about ESG (environmental, social, and governance) aspects. This means that businesses must implement reliable, globally accepted reporting standards (Panagopoulos & Tzionas, 2023). This strategy emphasises how crucial accountability and openness are to green investment.

Global financial issues also have an impact on the management of the green finance sector, as demonstrated by the Hungarian banking industry during the COVID-19 epidemic. The understanding and perspectives of stakeholders regarding green financial instruments are changing, with a growing focus on sustainability and environmental consciousness (Boros et al., 2023). It is imperative that stakeholders' perceptions change in order for green financial solutions to expand and be accepted.

In the field of novel financial instruments for environmentally conscious investments, the research of Akhtar, Alam, Khan, Ansari, and Shamshad provides important insights, especially when seen from a blockchain-digital twin viewpoint. According to Akhtar et al., (2021), the "YES Bank Fiasco: Arrogance or Negligence" highlights the difficulties facing the banking industry and emphasises the need for strong financial frameworks, which are necessary to support green initiatives.

This case study subtly highlights the need of responsible and transparent financial processes, which blockchain technology might help with.

Based on this, Ansari et al., (2023)'s "Consequence of Financial Crisis on Liquidity and Profitability of Commercial Banks in India" and Akhtar, Alam, & Ansari, (2021)'s "Measuring the Performance of the Indian Banking Industry" present empirical These studies show banks' resilience and efficiency during financial crises, showing that novel financial instruments need a stable banking system. Blockchain might make transactions more safe and transparent, improving stability. Akhtar et al2022 .'s study "Measuring Technical Efficiency of Banks vis-à-vis Demonetization" examines how major financial reforms affect banking efficiency. This study implicitly suggests that blockchain and digital twins can help the banking sector adapt to large-scale economic shifts, which is essential for green investment strategies. These studies give a complete knowledge of the banking sector's dynamics, essential for creating and deploying blockchain-digital twin-era financial instruments for green investments.

The Indian securities markets have undergone a significant transformation due to the introduction of innovative financial products. These modifications, which are the outcome of legislative and market pressures, are intended to improve the efficiency and inclusiveness of the securities markets while also deepening and broadening them (Panda, 2003). These types of advancements are essential to ensuring the market's adaptability to environmental goals and satisfying the growing demand for eco-green investments.

The increasing demand for creative financial tools that may successfully promote environmental sustainability is demonstrated by these recent research and advancements in the field of green finance. Crucial to this shift are the incorporation of ESG standards, the creation of green bonds, and the financial markets' adjustment to sustainability objectives.

Introduction to Blockchain and Digital Twin Technologies

Blockchain and digital twin technologies are quickly becoming revolutionary instruments in a number of fields, such as municipal government, transportation, and healthcare and finance etc.

Blockchain Technology: Green finance is increasingly using blockchain technology, which is renowned for its decentralised structure, security, and transparency. The financing and management of environmental sustainability initiatives are changing as a result of this convergence. The following recent research demonstrates blockchain's significance in green finance:

A bibliometric analysis by Dr. Rashmi Mishra and Jawaher Albalushi (2023) highlights how blockchain is revolutionising the financial industry, especially in digital finance and green innovation. This report emphasises how blockchain technology is becoming more and more significant in raising the value of green financial services and goods (Mishra & Albalushi, 2023).

Digital Twin Technology: The ability to simulate, optimise, and perform predictive maintenance is made possible by creating a digital twin, which is a virtual copy of a physical system. A number of industries, like transportation and city administration, rely heavily on this technology. For instance, transportation networks may be made more efficient, secure, and environmentally friendly by combining digital twins with blockchain technology. Together, they improve data security and transaction transparency, while facilitating the optimization and simulation of operations and maintenance using blockchain technology (Banerjee et al., 2023).

The use of digital twin technology to big data analysis of firm supply chains was examined by Dongsheng Li and Jun Yu Li (2023) within the framework of the green financial system. Their findings suggest that, within a green finance framework, digital twin technology may improve a company's operational, financial, and market performance (D. Li & Li, 2023).

Putting digital twin and blockchain technologies together is also very important to the growth of the Metaverse because it creates a connected, reliable, and detailed digital representation of people and things. This connection is very important for connecting the virtual and real worlds and helping to make immersive virtual worlds where people can interact with each other and with mixed-reality environments (Picone et al., 2023).

Objectives and Scope of the Chapter

Investigating the potential synergies between blockchain and digital twin technology in green finance is the primary objective and emphasis of this chapter. The goals can be deduced from the subject matter's larger context, even if there is little particular modern literature on the issue.

Objectives

To Explore the Integration of Blockchain and Digital Twin Technologies in Green Finance: The objective of this chapter is to examine the potential for blockchain and digital twin technologies to work together to improve green finance instruments.

To Analyze the Impact of These Technologies on Financial Instruments: Understanding how new technologies alter conventional financial models is a major goal, especially when it comes to green investments.

To Examine the Advantages and Challenges: The chapter aims to address the advantages of these technologies in green finance, such as enhanced efficiency and transparency, as well as the difficulties they provide, such as complicated implementation and legal concerns.

Scope

This chapter explores how emerging technologies, such as digital twins and blockchain, are interacting with the financial industry, with a particular emphasis on their critical roles in green finance. The ways in which these technologies support novel financial products, including ESG-linked derivatives, sustainable asset-backed securities, and green bonds, are investigated. The chapter also includes real-world case studies, which provide concrete insights into how these technologies are used and impacted in green finance. Lastly, possible developments and difficulties in combining blockchain and digital twin technology in the context of sustainable finance are discussed.

THE ROLE OF BLOCKCHAIN AND DIGITAL TWIN TECHNOLOGIES IN GREEN FINANCE

Explanation of Blockchain Technology and Its Relevance to Finance

Blockchain Technology in Finance: The decentralised ledger system known as blockchain technology is becoming more widely acknowledged for its revolutionary effects on the financial industry. Improved security, transparency, and immutability are some of its primary characteristics, which make it an effective tool for a range of financial applications.

Enhancing Credit Information Sharing in Supply Chain Finance: Critical issues in supply chain finance, such as insufficient credit records and inadequate credit data security, are effectively addressed by blockchain technology. Supply chains can conduct financial transactions with enhanced integrity, decentralization, and dependability of credit information, all attributable to the utilization of blockchain technology (Zheng et al., 2022).

Blockchain in the Metaverse's Financial Ecosystem: Blockchain technology's incorporation with the Metaverse is changing the financial scene by providing decentralised finance options and brand-new digital currencies like stablecoins and cryptocurrencies. This development calls into question the place of established financial institutions in the developing Meta Fi ecosystem, such commercial banks (Anggara, 2022).

Risk Assessment in Blockchain-based Finance: In supply chain finance in particular, blockchain technology is essential for improving the security of financial transactions. It does, however, also bring with it additional hazards that must be properly evaluated and controlled. Ensuring the security and effectiveness of financial activities in blockchain finance requires the development of algorithms and privacy protection methods (Meng, 2022).

Blockchain in Green Transformation of Industries: Blockchain technology provides answers to small- and medium-sized businesses' funding problems in the context of sustainable growth, particularly in industries like the coal industry. Blockchain promotes the green transformation and sustainable growth of companies by enabling effective resource allocation and information processing (Liu et al., 2022).

Overview of Digital Twin Technology and Its Potential in Financial Modeling:

Digital Twin Technology in Financial Modeling: With its ability to improve financial modelling and decision-making processes, digital twin technology—which makes virtual copies of real systems—is gaining popularity in the financial industry.

Optimizing Management Accounting Modeling: Management accounting is benefiting from the combination of FinOps (financial operations) and digital twin technologies. It helps with enterprise function management, accounting optimization, and the creation of information models of economic and financial operations. This combination ensures thorough analysis of all company expenditures and is especially helpful in predictive appraisal of assets such as crypto-assets (Zadorozhnyi et al., 2023).

Applications in Public Health and Economic Implications: The potential of digital twin technology for economic modelling is notable, even if it is mainly considered in relation to public health. It is useful for organising and maximising public health initiatives, which directly affect the economy, particularly during health crises like COVID-19 (A. Khan et al., 2023).

Enhancing Power Equipment with Digital Twin Technology: The power industry uses digital twin technology to simulate operations and maintenance on high-end equipment. To help power systems run safely and efficiently, this approach may be used to energy industry financial modelling (S. Zhang et al., 2023).

Improving Port Structure Safety with Digital Twins: The potential of digital twin technology in infrastructure management is demonstrated by its application in port structural safety. This method may be modified to provide efficiency and safety in financial modelling for large-scale infrastructure projects (Z. Li et al., 2023).

Synergies Between Blockchain and Digital Twins in Enhancing Financial Instruments

Blockchain technology and digital twins work together to create a new way to improve financial products, especially when it comes to green finance. When these technologies are integrated, they provide special benefits in terms of efficiency, transparency, and security.

Blockchain's Role in Financial Services: Blockchain technology's ability to provide transactional openness, security, and operational effectiveness has had a huge influence on the financial industry. Its distributed, unchangeable, and decentralised ledger technology minimises fraud, mistakes, and delays by enabling numerous parties to observe transactions in real time without the need for middlemen. New financial services including asset management, decentralised insurance, and peer-to-peer lending are made possible by this technology (Naher & Uddin, 2023).

Digital Tokens as Special Investment Instruments: The introduction of digital tokens in blockchain technology has completely changed the nature of investment turnover. These tokens provide a safe and effective way to invest and serve as legitimate replacements for conventional financial rights. They are also impervious to fraud. Due to this progress, laws governing the digital investment space have had to be developed in order to safeguard investors' interests (Matytsin, 2023).

Blockchain in the Metaverse for Healthcare and Financial Implications: The combination of blockchain technology with the Metaverse has opened up new avenues for financial modelling and investment opportunities, particularly in the healthcare business. Technologies like blockchain and digital twins are enhancing the Metaverse's potential for remote patient care, medical education, and research, which might have significant economic implications (Mozumder et al., 2023).

Blockchain and Federated Learning in Financial Services: The financial sector's cyber-physical systems are more secure, financial, and trustworthy when blockchain technology and Federated Learning (FL) are combined. In the age of digital transformation and growing cyber dangers, this integration is essential since it offers a strong framework for safe financial operations (Chatterjee et al., 2023).

DEVELOPMENT OF NEW FINANCIAL INSTRUMENTS

Green Bonds: Concept, Structure, and Blockchain Integration

In order to achieve sustainability and promote sustainable development goals, green bonds have become an important financial tool. The use of blockchain technology into green bonds is especially significant since it tackles a number of issues related to the issuing of green bonds, including standardisation, greenwashing, and benefit maximisation.

Role of Blockchain in Green Bonds Issuance: The issuing of green bonds has a promising new avenue thanks to blockchain technology. Its high-level finance and decentralised application improve a variety of financial tasks. This method solves the problems of environmental data standardisation and green bond optimization. The implementation of a blockchain framework for green bonds, however, must take into account the unique geographical and ecological circumstances of each nation (Misra et al., 2023).

Green Bonds as a Financial Instrument for Banks: In the banking industry, green bonds are becoming more widely accepted as a sound financial tool, particularly when it comes to investments that are both ecologically and socially conscious. Given their benefits and drawbacks, the analysis of green bonds on the Ukrainian market emphasises their possible place in bank investment portfolios. The legal framework for overseeing the country's green bond market is also covered in the report (Rats & Alfimova, 2023).

Green Bonds and Industrial Mortgages for Digital Sustainability: For digital sustainability institutions, the ideas of "green bonds" and "digital green industrial mortgages" are crucial financial tools. The legalisation of these non-documentary securities will strengthen public relations and facilitate the development of a conceptual framework for law that will be useful in settling disputes involving environmental entrepreneurship (Inshakova & Osadchenko, 2023).

Dynamic Relationship between Green Bonds and Major Financial Asset Markets: Important financial markets that green bonds are linked to include the stock market, crude oil, gold, and others; it is vital to investigate their dynamic co-movement and risk spillover impact. Investors and policymakers may use this study to better understand the consequences of climate risk and policy risk on green bonds. It will help them develop strategies for green investing and asset allocation (Gao et al., 2023).

Sustainable Asset-Backed Securities: Features and Digital Twin Applications

Although there isn't much data directly linking digital twin applications to Sustainable Asset-Backed Securities (SABS), new study on SABS offers insights into their characteristics and their uses.

Eco-Compensation Asset Securitization: An extensive operational model for ecological compensation asset securitization is proposed in a research by Zhang and Bi (2023) that addresses the integration of asset securitization with environmental protection. This strategy promotes sustainable economic and environmental growth by regulating stakeholder interests in ecological protection through market mechanisms. The paper shows how a multi-period, multi-state Markov model for asset valuation might be beneficial in this situation by lowering risks and boosting profits for projects using ecological compensation (S. Zhang et al., 2023).

Asset-Backed Securities in Fintech: Jia et alanalysis .'s from 2023 focuses on how fintech businesses employ asset-backed securities (ABS), specifically in relation to online consumer loans. The hazards connected to these activities are covered in the paper, along with the regulatory actions taken to reduce any potential negative effects on consumers. Understanding the ABS landscape in its whole, including sustainable variations, is important (Jia et al., 2023).

Blockchain Applications in Asset-Backed Securities: In the context of ABS issuance in China, Chen, Cheng, and Luo (2023) assess the economic benefit of blockchain applications. They discover that blockchain technology affects the dynamics of ABS, particularly those issued for sustainable reasons, and drastically lowers the coupon yield at issuance. With regard to the incorporation of blockchain technology into SABS, this study offers preliminary proof of the financial benefits of blockchain applications in the financial markets (Chen et al., 2023).

Real Estate Investment Trusts (REITs) and Mortgage-Backed Securities: Shuai (2022) examines REITs as equity investment instruments in the real estate market, including their involvement in mortgage-backed securities. This study offers insights into the role of REITs and similar instruments in attracting investments in sustainable real estate, which can be considered a form of sustainable asset-backed security (Shuai, 2022).

ESG-Linked Derivatives: Introduction and Blockchain-Digital Twin Facilitation

Although there isn't much study linking blockchain-digital twin technology with ESG-linked derivatives directly, new studies on ESG-linked financial instruments provide light on their characteristics and their uses.

Credit Derivatives and ESG Integration: Credit derivatives are financial instruments that enable the restructuring of the risk/return profiles of credits. Tahi and El Farissi (2023) examine these products (Tahi & Farissi, 2023). They make credit risk trading, transfer, and hedging easier. Awareness the larger context of ESG-linked derivatives requires having a basic understanding of the many forms of credit derivatives and their associated costs, which is why this paper offers an overview of them.

Hedging in ESG Context: The influence of hedging on foreign currency derivative financial instruments is examined by Shariawi, Panjaitan, and Nathanael (2023), with a particular focus on a multinational corporation that engages in ESG-aligned operations. The significance of hedging techniques in controlling risks related to ESG-linked financial products is highlighted by this study (Shariawi et al., 2023).

Sustainable Financial Instruments and Social Impact Investment: In their analysis of the application of sustainable financial instruments to social impact investing, Panagopoulos and Tzionas (2023) highlight the significance of ESG regulations. In order to facilitate the creation of ESG-linked derivatives, the study addresses the incorporation of ESG factors into investment choices as well as the significance of reliable indicators for ESG measurements (Panagopoulos & Tzionas, 2023).

Green Bonds and ESG Standards: Sobik, (2023) offers a thorough analysis of the market's growth and obstacles, highlighting the green bonds' compliance with ESG requirements. Understanding green finance dynamics, which involve ESG-linked derivatives, is aided by this research .

ADVANTAGES OF BLOCKCHAIN AND DIGITAL TWIN IN GREEN FINANCE

Enhancing Transparency and Security in Financial Transactions

The significance of blockchain and digital twin technologies in enhancing the transparency and security of financial transactions has recently been highlighted in study, particularly in the field of green finance.

Credit Card Fraud Detection and Blockchain: Raj et al (2023) .'s study integrates blockchain for increased security and transparency while examining the usage of supervised machine learning algorithms in credit card fraud detection (Raj et al., 2023). The paper highlights the effectiveness of the XGBoost algorithm and highlights how blockchain technology and cutting-edge machine learning techniques may be used to improve online transaction security.

Blockchain in Smart Microgrids: In order to automate regional energy markets and promote energy trade, Dinesha & Balachandra, (2023) investigate the use of blockchain technology in Blockchain Enabled Interconnected Smart Microgrids (BSMGs). The paper addresses the usage of decentralised exchanges (DEX) for cryptocurrency and digital token trading on blockchains in decentralised finance, emphasising the improved data security and transparency.

Advancements in FinTech and Security Challenges: Gopal, Gupta, and Minocha (2023) explore the security issues facing the banking sector as well as the developments in financial technology (FinTech). The report emphasises blockchain integration's significance in boosting the security and transparency of financial transactions while covering a variety of technology advances (Gopal et al., 2023).

Blockchain in Agricultural Food Supply Chain: In their analysis of blockchain and Internet of Things applications in the agricultural food supply chain, Goyal, Kanyal, and Sharma (2023) concentrate on enhancing transactional traceability, productivity, and transparency. The research demonstrates how blockchain technology may improve the quality and traceability of financial data, hence transforming several businesses (Goyal et al., 2023).

Improving Efficiency and Predictive Capabilities in Investment Analysis

Particularly in the field of green finance, recent developments in blockchain and digital twin technologies have made a substantial contribution to increasing the effectiveness and predictive power of investment research.

Artificial Intelligence Algorithms and Cloud Computing Technologies in Blockchain-Based Fintech Management: The integration of cloud computing technologies and artificial intelligence algorithms in blockchain-based fintech management is explored Lăzăroiu et al., (2023) The study focuses on how business investment efficiency and economic growth are influenced by fintech development. It draws attention to how big data analytics, augmented and virtual reality, and machine learning algorithms may improve the effectiveness of mobile payment transactions. The study emphasises how fintech may improve data analysis, digital banking performance, economic structures and growth, and financial organisation and services. This research has special significance in comprehending the ways that blockchain technology, in conjunction with artificial intelligence and cloud computing, may optimise payment operations, evaluate potential hazards, and enhance the precision of financial transactions.

Case Studies Demonstrating the Practical Application of These Technologies

Through a number of case studies, the usefulness and impact of blockchain and digital twin technologies in the context of green finance are demonstrated.

Industry Forum on Digital Industrial Communications and Electronics Technology Trends: As a component of an industry forum, this panel discussion examines the effect of industrial settings and evaluates the work completed for the Health Informatics workshop. The main topic of discussion is Industrial 4.0, which integrates cyber-physical technology to enhance industry operations and output. The talk emphasises how important it is for industrial settings to use technology like digital twins and blockchain to improve worker and consumer wellness. Understanding the use of these technologies in a wider industrial setting, including their potential in green finance, is made easier with the help of this case study ("Industry Forum," 2023).

Reforming Supply Chain Systems in Metaverse: Cui, Idota, and Ota (2022) examine how metaverse may be used to improve supply chain resilience, with a focus on the Japanese car sector. The research shows how supply chain management and operations might be enhanced in the metaverse by utilising blockchain and digital twin technology. This case study sheds light on how these technologies are being used to improve supply chains' efficiency and resilience, which is a crucial aspect of green finance (Cui et al., 2022).

Digital Twin for Urban Planning in the Green Deal Era: A cutting-edge summary of Digital Twins (DTs) initiatives for urban planning is given by Caprari (2022). Six case studies of DTs are compared in the paper to show their application, technology infrastructure, and outcomes. With better decision-making and participative procedures, the practical use of digital twins in urban planning and governance holds implications for green finance that our research will help us comprehend (Caprari, 2022).

Photovoltaics in 2021: An overview of the most recent developments in photovoltaics, a crucial component of sustainable energy systems, is provided in this article by Kenny (2022). Covering subjects important to photovoltaic experts and stakeholders along the whole value chain, it emphasises how technologies like blockchain and digital twins are driving advancements in the solar sector. Understanding the use of these technologies in the renewable energy industry, a critical component of green finance, is made easier with the help of this case study (Kenny, 2022).

RISK AND RETURN IN GREEN INVESTMENT INSTRUMENTS

Analysis of Risk-Return Dynamics in Green Finance

An important field of research is the examination of risk-return dynamics in green finance, especially in light of blockchain and digital twin technologies. Current studies shed light on these dynamics:

Fintech and Green Bonds in Clean Energy Production in China: Wang and Wang (2023) investigate the role that green bonds and fintech play in China's production of clean energy, with a particular emphasis on the dynamics of green investment risk. Understanding the risk concerns connected to green bonds and how fintech may help mitigate these risks is critical to understanding how green investments' risk-return profile is affected (S. Wang & Wang, 2023).

ESG, Green Growth, and Employee Capitalism: In light of the 47th G7 Summit, Firzli, Weeks, and Sherry (2021) talk about the ideas of asset ownership and EESG-driven investing. The 'greenium' phenomenon—where green bonds frequently trade at a lower yield than conventional bonds, indicating shifting views of risk and return—is highlighted in the article. Understanding the changing dynamics of risk and return in green finance, especially as they apply to green bonds and sustainable investing methods, is made possible by this study (Firzli et al., 2021).

The Role of Blockchain and Digital Twins in Finance

Although the search did not provide any particular results on green finance risk mitigation or return estimates, it did provide some insights into the broader financial applications of blockchain and digital twins. Relevant research includes the following:

Analysis of FinTech Enablers and Role of Future Internet of Things (IoT) in the New-Age Business World: Bagria and Meena discuss how the AI, 5G/6G, Blockchain, Metaverse, Internet of Things, and other modern disruptive technologies are being integrated into the banking sector (2023). Since new technology like blockchain and digital twins have the potential to impact green finance risk management and return estimates, it is critical to comprehend how these tools may streamline critical financial services and operations (Bagria & Meena, 2023).

BDTwins: **Digital twin lifecycle management framework based on blockchain:** With a focus on secure data sharing and processing, Cao et al. (2022) offer a blockchain-based architecture for digital twin lifespan management. Risk management in the financial sector may benefit from a better understanding of the potential uses of blockchain and digital twins for safe data handling, and this study can provide that (X. Cao & others, 2022).

Blockchain Powered QA Process Management for Digital Twins: A blockchain application for managing the quality assurance process in digital twins is presented by Le et al. in 2022. This study emphasises how blockchain technology may improve data privacy and dependability, two critical components of risk management in the financial finance (Le & others, 2022).

Blockchain-Based Secure Communication of Intelligent Transportation Digital Twins System: Liu et al. (2022) study the safety of intelligent transportation based on blockchain, building an IoV Digital Twins model. This research is significant for understanding how blockchain can improve the security and efficiency of information sharing, which are key aspects of risk management in finance (Liu & others, 2022).

Case Studies on Risk Management in Green Investments

The following case studies from recent times shed light on risk management for green investment:

Risk Management in The Oil Sector / Oil Exploration Company as A Case Study: A unique decision tool for assessing risk in Iraq's petroleum business is introduced in the research "Risk Management in The Oil Sector / Oil Exploration Company as A Case Study," by Noor A. Abdul Jabbar and Hatem K. Breesam, published on September 10, 2023. The study finds 48 unique hazards that are divided into operational, financial, administrative, economic, political, and prospective threats using fuzzy logic and the Relative Importance Index approach. Based on a wealth of data from more than 150 experts in the industry, the study uses SPSS for statistical analysis and creates a fuzzy evaluation model to estimate risk probability. The research examines risk management techniques, such as risk avoidance, mitigation, and transfer, with an emphasis on the Iraq Oil Exploration Company as a case study. The Analytic Network Process is used to identify the best solutions. The goal of this all-encompassing strategy is to improve risk management procedures in the petroleum industry in Iraq (Jabbar & Breesam, 2023).

Safety and Ergonomic Risk Management for Visual Stress. A Theoretical and Experimental Case: The document "Risk Management for Ergonomic and Safety Concerns in Visual Stress. A Case Study in Theory and Experiment "published on May 3, 2023, and is a thorough investigation of ergonomic risk management with a particular emphasis on visual stress by Salvatore Lanza and Nicoleta Paula Neag. This research highlights the complex nature of ergonomics, encompassing human-machine, human-environment, and human-organization interactions. It is based on both theoretical and experimental techniques. A noteworthy feature of the research is its pragmatic implementation, which stems from an internship encounter and offers authentic perspectives on handling visual stress hazards in many contexts. The study presents a theoretical and empirically grounded approach to ergonomic risk management, with a focus on visual stress. These case studies provide important insights for managing ergonomic risks in a variety of work settings (Lanza & Neag, 2023).

Risk Management in Practice: Monia Castellini and V. Riso conducted a qualitative analysis of risk management integration within management control systems across six Italian municipalities for their paper "Risk Management in Practice: A Multiple Case Study Analysis in Italian Municipalities," which was published on January 4, 2023. The study uses a dual-method approach, classifying these towns based on population size and utilising institutional website content analysis in conjunction with public management questionnaires for interviews. The results show that in these diverse municipal contexts, risk management approaches and current management control systems are not well integrated. This study adds important new information to the conversation about risk management, especially as it relates to local government and administration.

It is noteworthy for its practical emphasis on real-world applications in the public sector. The study's focus on case studies offers a detailed grasp of the difficulties and requirements unique to risk management in Italian municipalities (Castellini & Riso, 2023).

REAL-WORLD APPLICATIONS AND CASE STUDIES

Detailed Exploration of Specific Case Studies in Green Finance

The following recent case studies offer perceptions into practical applications in green finance and related domains:

Extreme and Sustainable Graph Processing for Green Finance Investment and Trading: In their case study from 2023, Vasiliu, Roman, and Prodan discuss the difficulties in obtaining data from the financial markets and emphasise the development of artificial intelligence-enhanced financial datasets for testing financial algorithms in green trading and investing. This case study is important to comprehend how sophisticated data processing methods are used in green finance (Vasiliu et al., 2023).

Weaponizing Real-world Applications as C2 (Command and Control): The use of real-world applications in cybersecurity is examined by Sidhardhan, K. S., and Kannimoola (2023), especially in light of sophisticated persistent threats. Although not specifically connected to green finance, this study offers insights on security-related topics that may be useful in financial applications (Sidhardhan et al., 2023).

Electronic Source Data Transcription for Electronic Case Report Forms in China: In a practical ophthalmology research, Wang, Lai, Liu, Jin, Peng, and Yao (2022) verify the electronic source record tool. The speed and quality of the data transcription provided by this case study are important since they are critical to the management of financial data (B. Wang et al., 2022).

Impact of Blockchain-Digital Twin Financial Instruments on Market Dynamics

The following recent studies shed light on how digital twin and blockchain technologies affect the behaviour of financial markets:

The Impacts of Bitcoin on the Financial Market: A survey of the literature on the impact of Bitcoin, a prominent cryptocurrency on the global financial market, is presented by Aljaed (2024). Understanding how digital currencies, a crucial component of blockchain technology, affect market dynamics is made easier with the help of this study (Aljaed, 2024).

Economics Unchained: Investigating the Role of Cryptocurrency, Blockchain, and Intricacies of Bitcoin Price Fluctuations: A comprehensive economic study of Bitcoin is given by Matharoo (2023), who also examines its impact on established financial institutions and its place in the economy. Understanding the economic dynamics of cryptocurrencies and blockchain technology in the financial industry depends on this research (Matharoo, 2023).

Alamsyah & Muhamad, (2023) analyse the decentralised financial (DeFi) sector and paid particular attention to the tokenization of physical assets and how it affects digital financial services. Understanding the market dynamics of the DeFi industry, which is greatly impacted by blockchain technology, is made possible by this study (Alamsyah & Muhamad, 2023).

The evolution of financial regulation in reaction to advancements in financial technology and instruments is examined critically by Shavshukov and Zhuravleva (2023). This report sheds light on the ways that digital twin and blockchain technology are changing financial industry regulatory procedures (Shavshukov & Zhuravleva, 2023).

Investor Behavior Analysis in the Context of Technology-Driven Financial Products

These are some recent studies that provide light on how investors behave when it comes to financial products powered by technology, especially those that use blockchain and digital twin technologies:

Artificial Intelligence Algorithms and Cloud Computing Technologies in Blockchain-Based Fintech Management: According to Lăzăroiu et al. (2023), the growth of fintech, which includes blockchain-based operations, modifies investor behaviour and corporate investment efficiency through data-driven algorithms based on artificial intelligence. Understanding investor reactions to fintech advances depends on this study (N. Khan & others, 2018).

Evaluation of Waste Electronic Product Trade-in Strategies in Predictive Twin Disassembly Systems in the Era of Blockchain: Tozanlı, Kongar, and Gupta (2020) investigate how trade-in policies are affected by digital twin technology, offering perceptions on investor conduct concerning blockchain and digital twin technologies (Tozanlı et al., 2020).

Paradigm Changes that Strengthen the Financial Security of the State through FINTECH Development: The impact of fintech growth, particularly blockchain technology, on investor behaviour and the state's financial security is examined by Sirenko et al. (2020). This research provides information about how financial technology innovations impact investor choices (Sirenko et al., 2020).

Special Issue on AI and FinTech: The Obstacle Ahead: Cao, Yuan, Leung, and Zhang (2020) concentrate on the function of artificial intelligence in fintech, talking about how it affects financial markets, goods, and investor behaviour. This compilation of papers offers a thorough understanding of how blockchain and other AI-driven financial breakthroughs affect investor behaviour (L. Cao et al., 2020).

CHALLENGES AND FUTURE DEVELOPMENTS

Discussion of Current Challenges in Implementing These Financial Tools

The following recent papers address the difficulties of integrating digital twin and blockchain technology into financial tools:

Integrated Operations System: Implementation of a Truly Integrated Digital Oil Field and Development of Digital Twin: The difficulties ONGC encountered when integrating digital twin technology in oil and gas field operations are examined by Balachandran and Padmanabhan (2023). This study sheds light on the challenges associated with integrating digital twins in intricate industrial settings (Balachandran & Padmanabhan, 2023).

A thorough analysis of the difficulties in putting digital twin technology into practise is provided by et al. (2023), including topics like data integration, security worries, and the requirement for specialised skills. Understanding the obstacles to the adoption of digital twins across businesses depends on this review (Arin et al., 2023).

In their 2023 publication, Hu and Lykourentzou present a digital twin simulator intended for team building during innovation hackathons. They draw attention to the difficulties that arise in collaborative settings and the ways that digital twins may be used to solve these problems (Hu & Lykourentzou, 2023).

A Blockchain-Based Approach with Ethereum and IPFS: Onwubiko et al. (2023) discuss the security and trust challenges in digital twin management and propose a blockchain-based solution. This paper is significant for understanding the security aspects of digital twin implementation (Onwubiko et al., 2023).

Potential Future Developments and Innovations in Green Finance

The following recent studies address possible advancements and breakthroughs in green finance in the future:

Revisiting the Linkage Between Green Finance China's Sustainable Development: Evidence from the Pilot Zones for Green Finance Reform Innovations: Lin et al. (2023) look at how China's innovative pilot zones and green finance reform affect long-term social and economic growth. This study provides insights into future trends in green finance and emphasises the relevance of pilot programmes in sustainable development (Lin et al., 2023).

Can Green Finance Facilitate Industry 5.0 Transition to Achieve Sustainability? A Systematic Review with Future Research DirectionsA thorough analysis of the function of green finance in expediting the shift to Industry 5.0 and attaining sustainability is offered by Dhayal et al. in 2023. Future research directions in the area of advanced industrial practises and green financing are suggested by this study (Dhayal et al., 2023).

Has Pilot Zones Policy for Green Finance Reform and Innovations Improved the Level of Green Financial Development and Environmental Quality?: In their study, Li et al. (2023) examine the effects of innovation pilot zones and green finance reform on the expansion of green financing and environmental conditions. Important new insights into the effectiveness of green funding policy initiatives have emerged from this study (G. Li et al., 2023).

Shen et al. (2023) evaluate how green hydrogen affects the environment and investigate how digitalization, eco-innovation, and green financing may support environmental sustainability. A viewpoint on the future of green finance in connection to environmental and energy sustainability is provided by this study (Shen et al., 2023).

The Evolving Landscape of Financial Regulations and Standards

The following recent studies address how financial norms and laws are changing:

Challapalli (2023) investigates the advantages and drawbacks of standardising financial laws, particularly with regard to international derivative trade. The report emphasises the difficulties with extraterritoriality and the requirement for international regulatory cooperation (Challapalli, 2023).

Case Studies in Cybersecurity for Accounting Data Protection: Kafi and Akter (2023) highlight the significance of cybersecurity in financial information security while examining the difficulties businesses have in defending accounting data against changing cyberthreats (Kafi & Akter, 2023).

In order to manage COVID-19 in-patient expenditures, Sangsuwun, Phakdeekul, and Kedthongma (2023) examine financial regulations and the health economy. This analysis sheds light on the financial effects of health crises on regulatory frameworks (Sangsuwun et al., 2023).

Yakubi et al. (2022) look at how business laws and digital technologies might improve financial inclusion and socioeconomic growth in low-income nations (Yakubi et al., 2022).

CONCLUSION

New research in green finance has yielded innovative findings, particularly with the use of blockchain and digital twins together. Sustainable asset-backed securities, green bonds, and ESG-linked derivatives are some of the innovative financial instruments that have recently emerged, according to the key findings of several studies. The green finance sector is being revolutionised by these solutions, which offer enhanced efficiency, security, and transparency through the use of blockchain and digital twin technology.

The combination of blockchain technology with digital twins has a significant positive influence on financial instruments, risk management, and return forecasting accuracy. Notwithstanding, the dynamic terrain of financial rules and standards poses some obstacles, such as the requirement for worldwide regulatory synchronisation and the resolution of cybersecurity issues. Prospective breakthroughs are anticipated to centre on regulatory measures, technology innovations, and sustainability-related issues.

Case studies from a range of industries highlight how these technologies are being used in practise and how they affect investor behaviour and market dynamics. A lot of attention has been paid to how blockchain technology and digital twins may be used to reduce risk and predict returns in green investments, opening up green finance to a wider spectrum of investors.

Key Insights from the Latest Studies Include

1. Sun, (2023)examines the ways in which blockchain technology and digital finance might encourage the usage of renewable energy in China, emphasising the antithesis of green finance.
2. Mishra & Albalushi, (2023)highlight how blockchain technology is revolutionising green innovation, especially in the banking industry.

3. A key component of smart city design is the application of digital twin technology in sustainable urban transportation, as Bellini & et al, (2023) explain.
4. The role of digital finance in green, low-carbon circular development is examined by X. Zhang et al., (2023), who highlight the major benefits of this approach.

The dynamic future of innovative financial instruments in sustainable investments is supported by research demonstrating the importance of financial support in establishing climate-neutral economic systems, the emergence of ICT applications in transport investments, and the influence of financial market volatility on investments. These studies collectively illustrate the dynamic nature of sustainable investments and the crucial role that emerging technologies are playing in transforming this landscape.

ACKNOWLEDGMENT

The author, Mohsin Khan thanks Vellore Institute of Technology, Vellore for providing 'VIT SEED Grant – RGEMS Fund (Sanction Order No. SG20220088)' for carrying out this research work.

REFERENCES

Abhilash, S., Shenoy, S. S., Shetty, D. K., Lobo, L. S., & N, S. K. (2023, April). S. S., Shetty, D. K., Lobo, L. S., & N, S. K. (2023). Green Bond as an Innovative Financial Instrument in the Indian Financial Market: Insights From Systematic Literature Review Approach. *SAGE Open*, *13*(2), 21582440231178783. doi:10.1177/21582440231178783

Akhtar, S., Alam, M., & Ansari, M. S. (2021). Measuring the performance of the Indian banking industry: Data envelopment window analysis approach. *Benchmarking*. doi:10.1108/BIJ-03-2021-0115

Akhtar, S., Alam, M., & Khan, M. M. (2021). YES Bank Fiasco: Arrogance or Negligence. *SAGE Open*, *11*(4), 95–102. doi:10.1177/25166042211061003

Alamsyah, A., & Muhamad, I. F. (2023). Revealing Market Dynamics Pattern of DeFi Token Transaction in Crypto Industry. *2023 IEEE International Conference on Data Science and Advanced Analytics*. IEEE. 10.1109/ICoDSA58501.2023.10276473

Aljaed, S. (2024). *The Impacts of Bitcoin on the Financial Market*. Computational Finance and Decision Journal., doi:10.21608/cfdj.2024.324085

Anggara, M. R. H. (2022). The presence of commercial banks in Metaverse's financial ecosystem: Opportunities and risks. *Journal of Commercial Law and International Commerce*. doi:10.21098/jcli.v1i3.28

Ansari, M. S., Akhtar, S., Khan, A., & Shamshad, M. (2023). Consequence of Financial Crisis on Liquidity and Profitability of Commercial Banks in India: An Empirical Study. *Southeast European Business Review*, *3*(2), 36–50. doi:10.48185/sebr.v3i2.367

Arin, I. A., Murad, D. F., Hendric, H. L., & Warnars, S. (2023). A Systematic Literature Review of Recent Trends and Challenges in Digital Twin Implementation. *2023 IEEE International Conference on Information Systems and Software Technologies*. 10.1109/ICISS59129.2023.10291219

Bagria, V. K., & Meena, B. (2023). Analysis of FinTech Enablers and Role of Future Internet of Things (IoT) in the New-Age Business World. *International Journal of Management and Decision Sciences*. doi:10.53983/ijmds.v12n07.004

Balachandran, P. A., & Padmanabhan, K. V. K. (2023). Integrated Operations System: Implementation of a Truly Integrated Digital Oil Field and Development of Digital Twin. *Offshore Technology Conference*. One Petro. 10.4043/32841-MS

Banerjee, S., Das, D., Chatterjee, P., & Ghosh, U. (2023). Blockchain-enabled Digital Twin Technology for Next-Generation Transportation Systems. *2023 IEEE International Symposium on Real-Time Computing (ISORC)*. IEEE. 10.1109/ISORC58943.2023.00040

Bellini, P., & ... (2023). Mobility and Transport Data for City Digital Twin Modeling and Exploitation. *2023 IEEE International Smart Cities Conference (ISC)*. IEEE. 10.1109/ISC257844.2023.10293300

Boros, A., Lentner, C., Nagy, V., & Tózser, D. (2023). *Perspectives by green financial instruments – a case study in the Hungarian banking sector during COVID-19*. Banks and Bank Systems. doi:10.21511/bbs.18(1).2023.10

Cao, L., Yuan, G., Leung, T., & Zhang, W. (2020). Special Issue on AI and FinTech: The Challenge Ahead. *IEEE Intelligent Systems*, *35*(3), 3–6. doi:10.1109/MIS.2020.2983636

Cao, X., & ... (2022). BDTwins: Blockchain-based Digital Twins Lifecycle Management. *2022 IEEE International Conference on Smart World, UIC, ATC, ScalCom, DigitalTwin, PriComp, Metaverse*. IEEE. 10.1109/SmartWorld-UIC-ATC-ScalCom-DigitalTwin-PriComp-Metaverse56740.2022.00290

Caprari, G., Castelli, G., Montuori, M., Camardelli, M., & Malvezzi, R. (2022). Digital Twin for Urban Planning in the Green Deal Era: A State of the Art and Future Perspectives. *Sustainability (Basel)*, *14*(10), 6263. doi:10.3390/su14106263

Castellini, M., & Riso, V. (2023). Risk Management in Practice: A Multiple Case Study Analysis in Italian Municipalities. *Journal of Risk and Financial Management*, *16*(1), 30. doi:10.3390/jrfm16010030

Challapalli, S. R. (2023). Benefits and Constraints Associated with the Harmonization of Financial Regulations: An Overview. *Asian Journal of Economics, Business and Accounting*. doi:10.9734/ajeba/2023/v23i151015

Chatterjee, P., Das, D., & Rawat, D. B. (2023). Next Generation Financial Services: Role of Blockchain enabled Federated Learning and Metaverse. *2023 IEEE/ACM 23rd International Symposium on Cluster, Cloud and Internet Computing Workshops (CCGridW)*, (pp. 69–74). IEEE. 10.1109/CCGridW59191.2023.00025

Chen, X., Cheng, Q., & Luo, T. (2023). The economic value of blockchain applications: Early evidence from asset-backed securities. *Management Science*. doi:10.2139/ssrn.4077443

Cui, Y., Idota, H., & Ota, M. (2022). Reforming Supply Chain Systems in Metaverse. *2022 ACM International Conference on Information Technology for Social Good (GoodIT)*. ACM. 10.1145/3561278.3561289

Dhayal, K. S., Giri, A. K., Kumar, A., Samadhiya, A., Agrawal, S., & Agrawal, R. (2023). Can green finance facilitate Industry 5.0 transition to achieve sustainability? A systematic review with future research directions. *Environmental Science and Pollution Research International*, *30*(46), 102158–102180. doi:10.1007/s11356-023-29539-w PMID:37695480

Dinesha, D., & Balachandra, P. (2023). Decentralized Token Exchanges in Blockchain Enabled Interconnected Smart Microgrids. *2023 IEEE PowerTech*. IEEE. doi:10.1109/PowerTech55446.2023.10202994

Firzli, M. N. J., Weeks, D., & Sherry, N. (2021). *ESG, Green Growth and Employee Capitalism: G7 Roadmap for the Fifth Industrial Revolution*.

Gao, L., Guo, K., & Wei, X. (2023). Dynamic relationship between green bonds and major financial asset markets from the perspective of climate change. *Frontiers in Environmental Science*, *10*, 1109796. doi:10.3389/fenvs.2022.1109796

Gopal, S., Gupta, P., & Minocha, A. (2023). Advancements in Fin-Tech and Security Challenges of Banking Industry. *2023 International Conference on Innovations in Electrical and Electronics Engineering (ICIEM)*. IEEE. 10.1109/ICIEM59379.2023.10165876

Goyal, A., kanyal, H. S., & Sharma, B. (2023). Analysis of IoT and Blockchain Technology for Agricultural Food Supply Chain Transactions. *International Journal of Recent Technology and Engineering (IJRTE)*. doi:10.17762/ijritcc.v11i3.6342

Hu, J., & Lykourentzou, I. (2023). TONIC: A teamwork simulator and digital twin for organizational innovation challenges. *ACM SIGCHI Conference on Human Factors in Computing Systems*. ACM. 10.1145/3594806.3596549

Industry Forum. (2023). *2023 IEEE/ACM 45th International Conference on Software Engineering Companion (ICSE-Companion)*. IEEE. 10.1109/ICSE-Companion58688.2023.00009

Inshakova, A., & Osadchenko, E. (2023). *Green Bonds and Industrial Mortgages as Key Financial Instruments for Digital Sustainability Institutions*. Legal Concept., doi:10.15688/lc.jvolsu.2023.1.19

Jabbar, N. A. A., & Breesam, H. K. (2023). Risk Management in The Oil Sector / Oil Exploration Company as A Case Study. *Journal of Petroleum Research and Studies*. doi:10.52716/jprs.v13i3.686

Jia, Z., Chen, Y., Lang, J., & Li, P. (2023). The Analysis of Asset-Backed Security Backed by Online Consumer Loan. *Asia-Pacific Journal of Accounting & Economics*, *4*(1), 292–302. doi:10.54254/2754-1169/4/20221078

Kafi, M. A., & Akter, N. (2023). Securing Financial Information in the Digital Realm: Case Studies in Cybersecurity for Accounting Data Protection. *American Journal of Theoretical and Applied Psychology*. doi:10.18034/ajtp.v10i1.659

Kenny, R. (2022). Photovoltaics in 2021. *Solar RRL*, *6*(5), 2200288. doi:10.1002/solr.202200288

Khan, A., Priyadarshi, R., Bhattacharya, T., & Rhim, J.-W. (2023). Carrageenan/Alginate-Based Functional Films Incorporated with Allium sativum Carbon Dots for UV-Barrier Food Packaging. *Food and Bioprocess Technology*, *16*(9), 2001–2015. doi:10.1007/s11947-023-03048-7

Khan, N., & ... (2018). Blockchain's role in green finance. *Journal of Financial Management, 36*(4), 784–799. doi:10.24136/oc.2023.021

Lanza, S., & Neag, N. P. (2023). *Safety and Ergonomic Risk Management for Visual Stress. A Theoretical and Experimental Case*. International Transactions on Visual Arts. doi:10.59168/ITVA8408

Lăzăroiu, G., Bogdan, M., Geamănu, M., Hurloiu, L., Luminița, L., & Ștefănescu, R. (2023). Artificial intelligence algorithms and cloud computing technologies in blockchain-based fintech management. *Oeconomia Copernicana, 14*(3), 707–730. doi:10.24136/oc.2023.021

Le, V. T., & ... (2022). Blockchain Powered QA Process Management for Digital Twins. *2022 IEEE International Conference on System Reliability and Safety (ICSRS)*. IEEE. 10.1109/ICSRS56243.2022.10067396

Li, D., & Li, J. Y. (2023). Big data of enterprise supply chain under green financial system based on digital twin technology. *Kybernetes*. doi:10.1108/K-02-2023-0291

Li, G., Wang, L., Li, Z., & Guo, Z. (2023). Has pilot zones policy for green finance reform and innovations improved the level of green financial development and environmental quality? *Environmental Science and Pollution Research International, 30*(26), 68667–68676. doi:10.1007/s11356-023-27243-3 PMID:37126176

Li, Z., Wang, P., Han, X., & Shang, D. (2023). Research on Digital Twin Technology of Port Structure Safety based on Floating 3D Display. *2023 IEEE 9th International Conference on Industrial and Business Engineering (ICIBE)*. IEEE. 10.1109/ICIBA56860.2023.10165263

Lin, G., Lam, J. F. I., Shi, Y., Chen, H., & Chen, H. (2023). Revisiting the linkage between green finance China's sustainable development: Evidence from the pilot zones for green finance reform innovations. *Frontiers in Ecology and Evolution, 11*, 1264434. doi:10.3389/fevo.2023.1264434

Liu, J., Li, J., Wang, J., Uddin, M. M., & Zhang, B. (2022). Research on the application of blockchain technology in coal supply chain finance. *Sustainability (Basel), 14*(16), 10099. doi:10.3390/su141610099

Liu, J., Zhang, L., Li, C., Bai, J., Lv, H., & Lv, Z. (2022). Blockchain-Based Secure Communication of Intelligent Transportation Digital Twins System. *IEEE Transactions on Intelligent Transportation Systems, 23*(11), 22630–22640. doi:10.1109/TITS.2022.3183379

Matharoo, I. (2023). *Economics unchained: Investigating the role of cryptocurrency, blockchain and intricacies of Bitcoin price fluctuations.*

Matytsin, D. (2023). *The Legal Regulation Development of Key Technologies of Industry 4.0: Digital Tokens as Special Investment Instruments.* Legal Concept., doi:10.15688/lc.jvolsu.2023.2.14

Meng, X. (2022). Risk assessment and analysis in supply chain finance based on blockchain technology. *Journal of Sensors, 2022*, 1–11. doi:10.1155/2022/1985803

Mishra, R., & Albalushi, J. (2023). Digital Finance & Green Innovation Review Paper with special reference to Oman and Bibliometric Analysis for the Duration of 2017-2023. *International Journal of Financial Management and Research.* doi:10.36948/ijfmr.2023.v05i06.8271

Misra, N., Gupta, S., Sidhu, K. S., Kumar, A., Anandaram, H., Rao, T. J., Singh, R., Gehlot, A., Akram, S., & Joshi, K. (2023). *Role of Blockchain Technology Integration for Green Bonds Issuance with Sustainability Aspect. International Journal of Recent Technology and Engineering.* IJRTE. doi:10.17762/ijritcc.v11i6.7300

Mozumder, M. A. I., A, T. P. T., Sumon, R. I., Uddin, S. M. I., Athar, A., & Kim, H.-C. (2023). The Metaverse for Intelligent Healthcare using XAI, Blockchain, and Immersive Technology. *2023 IEEE International Conference on Metaverse Computing (MetaCom).* IEEE. 10.1109/MetaCom57706.2023.00107

Naher, K., & Uddin, M. S. (2023). *Exploring the influence of Blockchain in the financial services: Quick assessment of its applications across various financial domains.* Financial Services Journal. doi:10.24294/fsj.v6i1.2228

Onwubiko, A., Singh, R., Awan, S., Pervez, Z., & Ramzan, N. (2023). Enabling Trust and Security in Digital Twin Management: A Blockchain-Based Approach with Ethereum and IPFS. *Sensors (Basel), 23*(14), 6641. doi:10.3390/s23146641 PMID:37514938

Panagopoulos, A., & Tzionas, I. (2023). The Use of Sustainable Financial Instruments In Relation To The Social Impact Investment. ESG Policies, Capital Markets' Approach and Investors' Protection. An Innovative Perspective. SSRN *Electronic Journal.* doi:10.2139/ssrn.4131735

Panda, R. (2003). Trends in Prices and Production of Agricultural Commodities in Orissa in the Post-Liberalisation Period-Some Thoughts for Policy. *Indian Journal of Agricultural Economics, 58*(3), 404.

Picone, M., Mariani, S., Virdis, A., & Castagnetti, P. (2023). Digital Twin & Blockchain: Technology Enablers for Metaverse Computing. *2023 IEEE International Conference on Metaverse Computing (MetaCom)*. IEEE. 10.1109/MetaCom57706.2023.00017

Raj, A. T., Shobana, J., Nassa, V. K., Painuly, S., Savaram, M., & Sridevi, M. (2023). Enhancing Security for Online Transactions through Supervised Machine Learning and Block Chain Technology in Credit Card Fraud Detection. *2023 International Conference on Intelligent Sustainable Systems (I-SMAC)*. IEEE. 10.1109/I-SMAC58438.2023.10290462

Rats, O., & Alfimova, A. (2023). *Green bonds as a perspective financial instrument for bank investment in Ukraine*. Development Management. doi:10.57111/devt/1.2023.08

Sangsuwun, S., Phakdeekul, W., & Kedthongma, W. (2023). In-Patient Costs Of Coronavirus Disease 2019 With Financial Regulations And Heath Economy. *Russian Law Journal*. doi:10.52783/rlj.v11i6s.920

Schueffel, P. (2017). The convergence of blockchain, digital twins, and big data analytics in green finance. *Journal of Financial Transformation*, *45*, 38–45. doi:10.1007/s11356-023-30371-5

Shariawi, S., Panjaitan, M. Y. T. B., & Nathanael, A. (2023). Meminimalisir Resiko Perubahan Valuta Asing Melalui Lindung Nilai (Hedging) Terhadap PT. Petrosea Tbk. *Journal of Accounting. Business Economics (Cleveland, Ohio)*, *2*(2), 30–36. doi:10.30630/jabei.v2i2.187

Shavshukov, V., & Zhuravleva, N. (2023). National and International Financial Market Regulation and Supervision Systems: Challenges and Solutions. *Journal of Risk and Financial Management*, *16*(6), 289. doi:10.3390/jrfm16060289

Shen, J., Ridwan, L. I., Raimi, L., & Al-Faryan, M. A. S. (2023). Recent developments in green hydrogen–environmental sustainability nexus amidst energy efficiency, green finance, eco-innovation, and digitalization in top hydrogen-consuming economies. *Environment and Planning C: Politics and Space*. doi:10.1177/0958305X231153936

Shuai, Z. (2022). *Financial Instruments for Attracting Investments in the Real Estate Market*. International Business and Economics Studies., doi:10.22158/ibes.v4n4p18

Sidhardhan, A. S. K., & Kannimoola, J. M. (2023). Weaponizing Real-world Applications as C2 (Command and Control). *2023 IEEE International Conference on Innovations in Data Science and Communication (ICIDCA)*. IEEE. 10.1109/ICIDCA56705.2023.10100279

Sirenko, N. N., Atamanyuk, I., Volosyuk, Y., Poltorak, A., Melnyk, O., & Fenenko, P. (2020). Paradigm Changes that Strengthen the Financial Security of the State through FINTECH Development. *2020 IEEE 11th International Conference on Dependable Systems, Services and Technologies (DESSERT)*. IEEE. 10.1109/DESSERT50317.2020.9125026

Sobik, B. (2023). Green bonds—Financial innovation for sustainability financing: The case of the Polish green bonds market and their development barriers. *Central European Economic Journal, 10*(57), 287–303. https://doi.org/doi:10.2478/ceej-2023-0017

Tahi, S., & Farissi, I. E. (2023). Credit Derivatives: Main Concepts and Pricing. *Journal of Economics, Finance and Management Studies*. doi:10.47191/jefms/v6-i11-03

Tozanlı, Ö., Kongar, E., & Gupta, S. (2020). Evaluation of Waste Electronic Product Trade-in Strategies in Predictive Twin Disassembly Systems in the Era of Blockchain. *Sustainability (Basel), 12*(13), 5416. doi:10.3390/su12135416

Vasiliu, L. A., Roman, D., & Prodan, R.-C. (2023). Extreme and Sustainable Graph Processing for Green Finance Investment and Trading. *Proceedings of the 2023 ACM/SIGAPP Symposium on Applied Computing*. ACM. 10.1145/3578245.3585337

Wang, B., Lai, J., Liu, M., Jin, F., Peng, Y., & Yao, C. (2022). Electronic Source Data Transcription for Electronic Case Report Forms in China: Validation of the Electronic Source Record Tool in a Real-world Ophthalmology Study. *JMIR Formative Research, 6*(12), e43229. doi:10.2196/43229 PMID:36525285

Wang, S., & Wang, C. (2023). How do Fintech and green bonds ensure clean energy production in China? Dynamics of green investment risk. *Environmental Science and Pollution Research International, 30*(57), 120552–120563. doi:10.1007/s11356-023-30491-y PMID:37940828

Yakubi, Y., Basuki, B., Purwono, R., & Usman, I. (2022). The Impact of Digital Technology and Business Regulations on Financial Inclusion and Socio-Economic Development in Low-Income Countries. *SAGE Open, 12*(3). doi:10.1177/21582440221116112

Zadorozhnyi, Z., Desyatnyuk, O., Muravskyi, V., & Shevchuk, O. (2023). Combination of Digital Twin Technology and FinOps in Management Accounting Modeling. *2023 IEEE 12th International Conference on Advanced Computer Information Technologies (ACIT)*. IEEE. 10.1109/ACIT58437.2023.10275621

Zhang, S., Li, L., & Deng, B. (2023). *Sensing digital twin technology helps upgrade power equipment of new power system equipment*. SPIE. doi:10.1117/12.2669433

Zhang, X., Ai, X., Wang, X., Zong, G., & Zhang, J. (2023). A Study on the Effects of Digital Finance on Green Low-Carbon Circular Development Based on Machine Learning Models. *Mathematics*, *11*(18), 3903. doi:10.3390/math11183903

Zheng, X., Zhou, Y., & Iqbal, S. (2022). Working capital management of SMEs in COVID-19: Role of managerial personality traits and overconfidence behavior. In *Economic Analysis and Policy* (Vol. 76, pp. 439–451). Elsevier B.V. doi:10.1016/j.eap.2022.08.006

Chapter 9
Unlocking Efficiency:
Blockchain as a Service (BaaS) in Enterprise HR Management

Jyotikanta Panda
https://orcid.org/0009-0007-7210-6313
GIET University, India

Saumendra Das
https://orcid.org/0000-0003-4956-4352
GIET University, India

Moushami Panda
https://orcid.org/0009-0005-9678-1335
GIET University, India

Dulu Pattnaik
https://orcid.org/0009-0006-3692-4602
Government Engineering College, Bhawanipatna, India

Nayan Deep S. Kanwal
University Putra Malaysia, Malaysia

ABSTRACT

Blockchain technology has gained considerable attention in recent years due to its potential to revolutionize various industries. Human resources (HR) management in large enterprises is an area that can greatly benefit from the transparency, security, and efficiency offered by blockchain technology. This study explores the concept of blockchain as a service (BaaS) in enterprise HR management and its potential to

DOI: 10.4018/979-8-3693-1878-2.ch009

unlock efficiency, streamline processes, and enhance data security elaborating a comprehensive exploration of the theoretical underpinnings, practical application, and potential ramifications of BaaS within HR operations, highlighting the profound transformative prospects inherent in this emerging technology. The integration of blockchain as a service (BaaS) in enterprise human resources management is the focus of this study. The findings suggest that BaaS has the potential to revolutionize HR management by offering a secure, transparent, and efficient platform for various HR processes, from recruitment and onboarding to payroll and talent management.

INTRODUCTION

In modern dynamic and hastily evolving enterprise panorama, businesses face an unceasing imperative to optimize their operations and advantage a competitive aspect. The realm of Human Resources (HR) Management occupies a critical role on this pursuit, because it encompasses the important functions of recruiting, keeping, and nurturing a professional team of workers. although, traditional HR approaches frequently grapple with a trisect of challenges: inefficiencies, statistics silos, and safety vulnerabilities. In reaction to these urgent concerns, blockchain era emerges as a beacon of promise, offering progressive answers.

This research examines and embarks on an exploration of the transformative potential of "Blockchain as a service" (BaaS) inside the context of employer HR control. As corporations take care of an always moving business landscape, the significance of HR operations in attaining strategic targets can't be overstated. However, these operations have too frequently been hamstrung via outdated and cumbersome practices that prevent progress.

This study highlights the transformative capability of Blockchain as a provider in employer human resources management and affords a summary of that capability. It emphasizes how essential thoughtful planning and integration are to fostering creativity and efficiency in HR operations. Combining BaaS with personnel control is a critical tactic for attaining operational excellence and an aggressive aspect as businesses modify to a converting enterprise environment.

RESEARCH OBJECTIVE

The new era of HRO management with enhanced efficiency, transparency, and security can be ushered in, thanks to the adoption of data warehousing software designed to allow you to do multiple searches in one place. A study detailing the creation of the science of BaaS and its legal basis, practical adaptions, and impact on many aspects of HR will be handed down by this, not just because it is the study of a new science.

The primary goal of this research is to shed light on how the adoption of BaaS can bring in a new era in HR control, characterized through greater efficiency, transparency, and security.This study will navigate the intricacies of BaaS, delving into its theoretical foundations, realistic implementation and effect on various facets of HR capabilities.

Moreover, it will also look at factors toward promising avenues for further studies, encouraging pupils to delve deeper into specific programs, conduct empirical studies, and scrutinize the technical intricacies of BaaS in HR control.

THEORETICAL FOUNDATIONS

The theoretical aspect of blockchain technology form the bedrock upon which its practical applications rest. In this section, we look into a comprehensive exploration of these foundational concepts, emphasising on how they can be harnessed to address inefficiencies and security concerns in Human Resources (HR) management.

Decentralization

In simple terms, blockchain is like a record-keeping system that is not controlled by one person or organization. Instead, it is made up of a network of computers that work together to keep track of information. This decentralization encourages trust and transparency. When applied to Human Resources (HR) management, it has the potential to greatly change how information is managed and secured. Benisi et. al. (2020) explained blockchain, with its peer-to-peer and decentralized attributes, is a transformative technology capable of instigating changes across diverse industries In HR, decentralization can greatly improve the way information is managed. It gets rid of relying on one person or place for information and reduces the risk of information being manipulated or corrupted. Human resources documents and transactions can be securely stored in a network of hubs, ensuring reliability and durability. Decentralization is a very important aspect of blockchain technology. It is like the strong foundation on which the advantages of blockchain are built. Chen et.al.(2017) have deep dived into HR payroll system explaining the relevance of blockchain decentralization technology in general showcasing its usefulness.

For example,in healthcare industry, records stored on a blockchain can be accessed only by authorized healthcare providers through a decentralized network. This ensures that the patient data remains safe.

- Decentralization in HR administration can be understood in the following ways:
- Regular HR systems usually rely on one main database or server. If this main point doesn't work or is damaged, it can disrupt HR operations and put information security at risk. Decentralization in blockchain means that HR records are stored on a network of nodes. If one hub stops working, the network will still work and there will be less time when things aren't working and less chance of losing information.
- A decentralized HR blockchain device makes it secure to share crucial facts approximately personnel, like non-public statistics, job opinions, and fee data, among distinct computers inside the network. This device makes it hard for cheating human beings to get and take control of HR statistics.
- Blockchain makes sure that authorized people who have permission can see HR facts and transactions at the network. Authorized representatives can without problems see and test their statistics, which enables make the organisation more open and sincere.
- Data is saved in and multiple parts of the blockchain community, more than what is needed. This more potential makes the facts more potent and extra reliable, and makes it much less in all likelihood to get messed up and up and accessible all the time.
- Decentralization way that representatives have more strength and obligation over information so that humans can access and manage without difficulty, correctly check and take care of their accounts while not having to invite HR for typical information.
- The blockchain machine makes it so that after statistics is saved, it can't be modified or erased without the approval of the company. This means that the HR facts by no means change and can't be changed.

There are a number of clear benefits to actualizing decentralization in workforce administration utilizing blockchain innovation. Yaqoob et. al. (2022) have deep dived on the advantages of adopting blockchain technology along with opportunities for healthcare industries.

1. Hazard decrease: By killing single focuses of disappointment and making strides information security, the chance of information spillage and control is altogether diminished.
2. Ease of information get to: decentralization permits authorized people to effortlessly get to faculty information whereas keeping up its security and privacy.

3. Proficiency: the excess and unwavering quality of a decentralized framework moves forward uptime and operational effectiveness.
4. Believe and compliance: straightforwardness and unchanging nature of HR records makes a difference guarantee compliance with controls such as GDPR and builds believe between representatives.

In spite of the critical benefits of decentralization, blockchain-based HR frameworks must be planned with versatility, interoperability and administration in intellect to completely realize the potential of this troublesome HR innovation.

Consensus Mechanisms

Blockchain structures use certain additives to test and confirm transactions, and then keep them in a report. The most commonplace and critical element, evidence of labor (PoW), and its variation proof of Stake (PoS), make sure that simplest legitimate and agreed upon transactions are recorded. in the HR department, they are able to use tools to ship and exchange data about personnel, which include adjustments in earnings and promotions, but simplest if both aspects agree. This makes the records extra accurate and reliable. Fahim et. al. (2023) have done significant study of the consensus protocols and uncovered some of their advantages and disadvantages in relation to characteristics details.

The components of agreements are very vital in blockchain structures. They take a look at and verify transactions to ensure the document is correct and secure. There are a few styles of agreement gear inside the blockchain world, however the maximum ones are evidence-of-stake (PoS) and proof-of-work (PoW). those tools are surely vital in growing accept as true with and making sure facts is judged correctly. In HR management, the use of them can make humans trust HR information and documents more.

For example, in supply chain management, consensus mechanisms are used to verify the authenticity of product shipments and ensure that all parties in the supply chain agree on the state of goods in transit.

Proof of Work (PoW) and Proof of Stake (PoS) are two prominent consensus mechanisms:

PoW desires a set of contributors referred to as mineworkers to remedy difficult issues to affirm transactions and upload them to the blockchain.

If a settlement is made among those companions in keeping with certain guidelines, then the change in compensation can be agreed upon and recorded on the blockchain. This agreement makes sure that any modifications to worker facts can handiest be made after discussing with others concerned. This helps enhance the accuracy and reliability of the facts.

Table 1. The difference in detail between PoW and PoS

Proof–of-work	Proof-of-stake
Mining capacity depends upon computational power	Validating capacity depends upon the stake in the network
Hackers would need to have a computer powerful than 51% of the network to add a malicious block. Leading to 51% attack.	Hackers would need to own 51% of all the cryptocurrency on the network which is practically impossible and therefore making 51% attacks impossible.
Miners receive block rewards to solve a cryptographic puzzles	Validators do not receive a block rewards, instead, they collect transaction fees as a reward

Table 2. Differences, pros, and cons of PoW and PoS

	Proof–of-work	Proof-of-stake
How is the network secured?	The greater the hash rate, the more secure the network Validators must invest in equipment and energy to become a miner	Staking locks coins on the blockchain to secure the network Validators must buy crypto stake
How are users involved?	Miners compete to solve cryptographic mathematical problems to add blocks to the blockchain. The higher the hash rate, the higher the probability of validating transactions	Validators compete to validate blocks by staking crypto The more staked crypto, the higher the probability of validating transactions.
Pros	High Security Proved to be safe and trusted	More energy efficient Increased scalability and accessibility
Cons	Not scalable Wastage of high energy	Network controls can be "bought"

Organizations can benefit from settlement techniques like PoW and PoS in HR tactics as they make sure records integrity by requiring multiple people to affirm and authorize any changes made to employee facts. This lowers the probabilities of mistakes or unauthorized changes taking place.

By applying above mechanisms, organisations can achieve the following benefits:

Data Integrity: Changes in employee data are subject to verification by multiple stakeholders, reducing the risk of erroneous or unauthorized modifications.

Consider and Transparency: the use of a shared decision-making manner for modifications to HR information allows HR and employees trust each other greater by means of ensuring decisions are made collectively and brazenly discussed.

Simplicity: Consensus mechanisms add a new step within the hiring process, however in the end, they make higher and more dependable choices, which makes HR operations extra efficient.

Accountability: people worried in HR choices are responsible for what they do because their selections are written down on the blockchain and may be checked.

It's far essential to mention that agreement techniques may be customized to suit particular situations in Human resources. This makes certain that the standards for agreement fit the business enterprise's HR policies and desires. Consensus mechanisms make matters more complex, but they assist to make information in human resources management more reliable and honest.

Cryptographic Techniques

Blockchain employs cryptography to make sure records and verify exchanges. Open and private keys and cryptographic hashes make certain sensitive data. In human assets, cryptography can be utilized to make certain employee records and assure that as it has been authorized people can get to and modify facts. This increments the security and secrecy of statistics, which is relatively imperative for human asset work.

Cryptography is the established order of protection and keenness of blockchain innovation.

It plays a key component in securing records and confirming exchanges. within the setting of human asset (HR) administration, cryptography can have applied to upgrade statistics safety and secrecy and assure that sensitive employee statistics is ensured from unauthorized access and altering.

Key cryptographic techniques employed in blockchain and their relevance to HR operations:

Public and Private Keys

Open Keys: each member in a blockchain community is related with an open key, which serves as their exact identifier. In HR, open keys may be utilized to securely interface worker characters to the blockchain society, those keys can encourage secure get right of section to HR records while allowing workers to get to their data or authorize particular exchanges.

Private Keys: individual keys are matched with open keys and are put away privately, they are utilized to sign exchanges as well as data alterations. In HR, non-public keys may be utilized by authorized HR representatives to supplant representative data or execute HR-related savvy contracts safely. Figure 1 shows how the same works.

Figure 1. Public and private key pairs
Source: Authors' own contribution

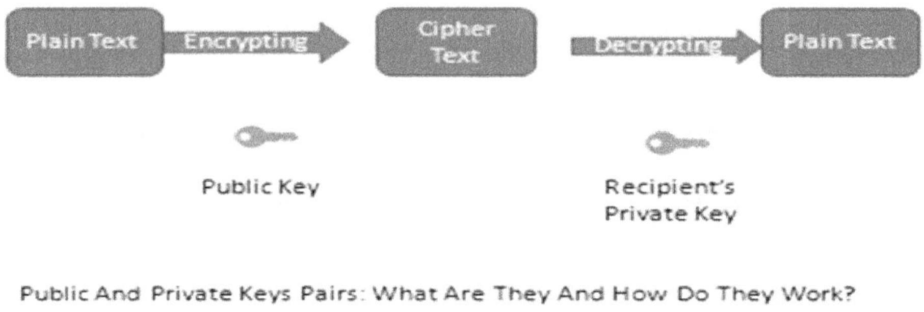

Cryptographic Hashing

Cryptographic hashing implies taking data (like representative information) and turning it into a shorter string of characters called a hash esteem. This code is uncommon to the data and indeed a little alter within the information will make an awfully diverse code. In human assets, cryptographic hashing can be utilized to ensure worker records and make beyond any doubt that the information cannot be modified.

Information security: Cryptographic strategies keep HR data secure by changing it into a mystery code some time recently it is spared on the blockchain. This encryption makes beyond any doubt that in case somebody who shouldn't get to it does, the data is still garbled unless they have the correct keys to translate it.

Access Control: Utilizing extraordinary codes called cryptographic keys can help control who can get to HR information. As it were individuals who have consent or the right keys can get into, alter, or see certain records. This keeps private data mystery.

Information Keenness: By employing an extraordinary kind of coding, blockchain makes beyond any doubt that HR information remains precise and dependable. Changing representative records will make the information see distinctive and appear that there have been unauthorized changes.

Information security controls, like GDPR or HIPAA, require strict compliance. Cryptographic strategies can offer assistance companies meet these necessities. Data around workers can be coded and looked at as it were by individuals who are permitted to, taking after rules around keeping things private.

It's imperative to keep in mind that indeed in spite of the fact that cryptographic procedures make information more secure and private, we must pay near consideration to overseeing the keys utilized for encryption. Securing private keys and taking after secure key administration hones are exceptionally vital to halt unauthorized individuals from getting access to them. Rashid et. al. (2021) studied deeply the mechanism of blockchain based public key that lays down a concrete foundation for creating a transparent and secure block-chain-based mechanism for the issuance and management of digital certificates

To sum it up, cryptographic strategies are truly vital for making beyond any doubt that blockchain innovation can keep data and exchanges secure. In HR administration, these strategies keep worker records secure and secure, making beyond any doubt the data is ensured, exact, and takes after security rules. Utilizing cryptographic strategies makes a difference HR offices take advantage of blockchain benefits whereas keeping HR-related data private and secure.

Smart Contracts

Smart contracts are contracts that can naturally execute themselves based on code. They make contract execution happen consequently and make beyond any doubt it is taken after without any agents required. In HR, shrewd contracts can make things more effective by doing certain errands consequently when certain conditions are met. For case, they can offer assistance with things like getting modern workers begun or calculating finance. For case, a savvy contract can begin the method of getting an unused representative onboarded as before long as they acknowledge a work offer, which makes a difference to decrease the sum of authoritative work required.

- Smart contracts are a really vital and groundbreaking improvement in blockchain innovation. These self-executing contracts utilize code to incorporate the terms and conditions of an assention. This permits the contract to be consequently executed without any go betweens, making it secure. In Human Assets (HR) administration, savvy contracts can alter things by doing errands consequently and lessening the sum of authoritative work. As per Vacca et. al. (2021) Blockchain applications and smart contracts can be used in various fields starting from from insurance refunds to financial transactions, from corporate operations to the traceability of goods and the protection of intellectual property.
- Genuine bequest exchanges can be made simpler by utilizing shrewd contracts. These contracts consequently exchange property proprietorship as before long as installment conditions are satisfied.

Keen contracts have these imperative characteristics:

- Robotization: Savvy contracts are made to do things naturally when certain conditions are met. This mechanization gets freed of the require for individuals to do things physically. This makes it less likely that botches will happen and makes HR assignments more proficient.
- Straightforwardness: The rules of a smart contract are clear and can be checked to create beyond any doubt they are genuine.
- Security: Shrewd contracts are secured by the progressed security highlights of a secure and straightforward framework called blockchain. This makes it exceptionally troublesome for anybody to change or make unauthorized changes to the contracts. This makes beyond any doubt that HR forms are fair and total.
- Efficiency: Shrewd contracts make HR errands simpler and speedier by computerizing standard errands. This will make the method of getting unused representatives begun, preparing pay, and overseeing other errands within the HR division faster.

Utilizing shrewd contracts in HR administration can have numerous points of interest.

- Onboarding Process: The onboarding handle can advantage from utilizing keen contracts when enlisting unused workers. When a candidate concurs to a work offer, a savvy contract can be utilized to begin a prepare that incorporates checking their foundation, gathering fundamental records, and setting up their worker accounts. This makes the onboarding handle faster and guarantees that each step is done the same way utilizing particular criteria. Gupta et. al. (2022) have also briefed on the possible benefits of implementing blockchain technology into human resource management especially in recruiting.
- Finance and remuneration: Smart contracts can make finance errands programmed. When particular necessities, just like the conclusion of a pay period, are fulfilled, the keen contract can naturally calculate and pay compensations to workers. This streamlines the management workload and diminishes the probability of mistakes in dealing with finance.
- Contractual agreements: HR frequently bargains with diverse sorts of understandings, like business contracts, assertions to keep data mystery, and understandings to preserve secrecy. Johnson et. al. (2013) highlighted the same emphasizing on employee relationship and employee contract. Smart contracts make it simple to form, carry out, and implement contracts by consequently taking activity when certain conditions are met or broken.

- Performance Management: It includes evaluating and assessing how well somebody is doing their work. Shrewd contracts can be utilized to consequently do this assessment prepare. For occurrence, when it's time for a worker to be assessed, the keen contract can remind the included individuals to donate input and orchestrate audit gatherings.

Zheng et. al. (2020) studied that smart contracts are able to boost a broad spectrum of applications ranging from financial services to IoT. Keen contracts in HR administration have a part of potential, but we have to be think approximately things like taking after laws and rules and making beyond any doubt the code is composed well and is secure. To successfully utilize shrewd contracts, you require to completely get it HR forms and be dedicated to keeping the code rectify and secure.

Within the period of blockchain, they are a profitable apparatus for moving forward HR administration since they are straightforward, secure, and productive.

Immutability

Blockchain's perpetual quality implies that once data is composed down, it cannot be changed or erased unless the organizer concurs. In HR, this implies making beyond any doubt that worker records are precise and continuously kept up to date. The history of a company's past trade, certifications, and execution reviews are kept secure and cannot be changed. This decreases the chance of controlling or taking data.

Perpetual nature is a critical viewpoint of blockchain innovation that includes to its unwavering quality and security. Within the field of Human Assets (HR) administration, it is critical to guarantee that worker records, capabilities, and execution surveys are lasting and solid.

Blockchain's perpetual quality implies that once data is put away on the blockchain, it gets to be exceptionally troublesome to alter or erase that data without the approval of the arrange. This can be done by utilizing extraordinary codes and a system called blockchain, which makes it exceptionally troublesome for anybody to form unauthorized changes or modify anything.

In imperative papers like wills and contracts, the perpetual nature of blockchain guarantees that the substance of these records remains the same over a long period of time. Mukherjee et. al. (2021) concluded that the fundamental nature of blockchain ensuring privacy, authenticity and security make it a lucrative platform to store valuable and essential data.

Within the range of HR management, the thought of something not changing encompasses a couple of imperative implications:

- Data Integrity: Immutability implies that HR data, counting representative records, remains precise and solid over time. Once a few data are logged on the blockchain, it cannot be controlled or changed by individuals with hurtful eagerly.
- Certifications and Qualifications: Vital certifications, abilities, and instructive capabilities can be safely put away on the blockchain. This doesn't fair anticipate untrue capabilities but too makes it simpler to confirm an employee's instruction and certificates.
- Performance records: These are critical parts of overseeing human assets. They include assessments and evaluations of how well somebody is doing their work. The constant nature of these records makes beyond any doubt that no one can alter them without authorization. This secures workers from any unauthorized changes that might influence their career headway or remuneration.
- Compliance and Auditing: In businesses where strict rules are required, like healthcare or fund, being long-lasting can help make beyond any doubt that data security rules are taken after. It gives a clear and unchangeable way to audit HR-related exchanges and get to data.
- Dispute Settlements: When there's a difference or contrast with respect to HR data, having reliable records can be a reliable source of truth. This may make it quicker to discover clashes and anticipate long contentions.
- Trust and Transperancy: Being steady and constant builds believe among associates and accomplices. Knowing that HR data remains the same makes us feel sure that HR forms are reasonable and straightforward.

Whereas the solidness of blockchain records can be accommodating, it is vital to get it that it moreover presents a few troubles, particularly when changes or changes to HR data are essential. Tending to these challenges through clear procedures and successful administration is fundamental for tackling the points of interest of consistency whereas keeping up adaptability in HR administration.

In less complex terms, perpetual qualityis a vital run the show in blockchain innovation that ensures the precision and life span of human assets information. It makes a difference make beyond any doubt that representative records, certifications, and execution surveys are dependable and secure. This eventually makes a difference make HR forms tried and true and compliant with controls.

By utilizing these hypothetical applications of blockchain innovation, HR administration can overcome its current restrictions. Decentralization dispenses with centralized focuses of disappointment, understanding components guarantee exact data, cryptographic strategies upgrade security, shrewd contracts computerize forms, and permanence guarantees data judgment. Within the taking after areas, we'll investigate how these ideas can be utilized essentially in HR parts. We are going appear you how they can progress productivity and security in HR administration.

PRACTICAL IMPLEMENTATION OF BAAS IN HR MANAGEMENT

This segment digs into the viable angles of coordination BaaS into HR administration:

Identity Confirmation and Access Control: Examines how blockchain can be utilized to safely confirm worker characters and control get to HR information through keen contracts. Damiano et. al. (2019) concluded that the mail advantage access control in blockchain provides is auditability.

Recruitment and Onboarding: Investigates the robotization of candidate confirmation, enrollment forms, and streamlined onboarding encouraged by BaaS.

Payroll and Compensation: Looks at blockchain-based finance frameworks, displaying how keen contracts can robotize compensation salary compensation installments, diminishing authoritative overhead.

Talent Management and Training: Analyzes the creation of decentralized ability marketplaces utilizing BaaS, cultivating ability revelation and preparing openings.

Information Security and Protection: Explores the part of blockchain in upgrading information security and protection in HR, guaranteeing compliance with controls like GDPR and HIPAA.

Figure 2. Highlights of blockchain in HR
Source: Authors own contribution

5 Promising Uses for Blockchain in HR

Blockchain's distributed ledger technology lets multiple parties share trusted data and execute transactions securely without a middleman, which makes it ideal for common HR processes.

Employee data	Recruitment	Payroll	Personal Blockchains	Contract management
Records can't be easily be altered, which adds and encodes a layer of security that could minimize external hacks and internal fraud.	Tokenized candidate identities and virtual credentials such as resumes and transcripts speed background checks and reduce paper work.	Easier identity verification and direct mobile payment facilitate cross border payments to vendors, contractors and unbanked workers	Employees could carry blockchain that document their professional identity to each new employer	Smart contract could help enforce employment agreements and automate benefit administration

Identity Verification and Access Control

One of the foundational challenges in HR organization is guaranteeing identity verification and access control to dubious HR information. BaaS can address these concerns by leveraging cryptographic procedures and sharp contracts.

Identity verification and access control are fundamental focuses of Human Assets (HR) organization, especially when it comes to securing dubious HR information. Blockchain as a Service (BaaS) presents a compelling course of activity to address these challenges by utilizing cryptographic strategies and fast contracts to overtake security and control. Malik et. al. (2019) observed that the process of document verification and issuing process's efficiency is drastically improved with blockchain model.

Here are the key components of utilizing BaaS for character assertion and get to control in HR organization:

Blockchain-Based Identity Verification

BaaS can safely store specialist character data, which may connect biometrics, advanced IDs, or other shapes of individual recognizing affirmation, on a blockchain. This data is recorded in an steady and tamper-proof way.

The benefits of this approach connect:

Consistent Identity Records: Once an employee's character data is recorded on the blockchain, it gets to be for all bury and purposes boundless to modify or pollute. This guarantees the discernment of character records.

Decreased Identity Fraud: The never-ending nature and security of blockchain make it altogether secure to character extortion. When character assertion is required, the blockchain can be utilized to favor an individual's character with a tall degree of certainty.

Streamlined Verification Processes: BaaS can energize quick and compelling character affirmation shapes. For occasion, within the middle of the onboarding of a unused master, their personality can be rapidly asserted against the blockchain, speeding up the procedure.

Access Control Through Smart Contracts

Smart contracts are programmable, self-executing contracts that can computerize and keep up predefined works out based on appeared conditions. Interior the setting of HR organization, they can be utilized to control access to HR information, guaranteeing that since it were authorized people or work environments can get to or change particular data.

It works as below:

Access Consents: Access consents are defined inside smart contracts. These authorizations can be custom fitted to different HR parts and commitments. For case, HR staff may have access to specialist records, whereas finance officials have get to to stipend information.

Conditional Access: Smart contracts can actualize conditional access, meaning that get to is allowed since it were when particular criteria are met. For occasion, an HR chief might select up access to an employee's execution evaluations since it were within the middle of the every year survey period.

Audit Trail: Smart contracts keep up an auditable history of get to and information modifications. This review way moves forward straightforwardness and obligation, as all get to and changes are recorded on the blockchain.

By executing BaaS with smart contract-based access control, HR organization can fulfill a few benefits:

Enhanced Data Security: Access control components guarantee that unsteady HR information is open since it were to those with the sensible consents, lessening the threat of information breaches.

Improved Compliance: Access controls can be adjusted withdata security controls, such as GDPR or HIPAA, guaranteeing that HR information taking care of complies with veritable prerequisites.

Efficiency: Mechanizing access authorizations through savvy contracts reduces the authoritative burden of manual access organization.

Trust and Accountability: The straightforwardness and auditabilityof access control shapes create acknowledge insides the organization and hold people reliable for their works out.

Whereas BaaS and sharp contracts offer promising courses of action, organizations need to carefully organize access control approaches and frequently update them to change with advancing HR needs and controls. Besides, secure organization of cryptographic keys is essential to keeping up the insightfulness of these frameworks.

Recruitment and Onboarding

Selection and onboarding are basic steps in HR organization, but they as often as possible require manual work and take up a portion of time. This may lead to errors being made. Blockchain as a Service (BaaS) licenses us to make things less requesting and more successful by utilizing development to do errands consequently. Blockchain development is a real-time application followed by verification, dynamic update and system learning (Onik et al., 2018) It makes things more user-friendly as well. Suk Yi et. al. (2020) studied that Blockchain transforms a company into a more structured and well-managed company that enables a hybrid strategy to safe legacy infrastructure and distributed ledger models. Processes involving human resources such as payroll, recruitment and choice, on-boarding and off-boarding waste a lot of time, resources and money and even by third parties.

Here are the foremost centers to consider when utilizing BaaS for enrollment and on boarding in HR organization:

Candidate Verification

It is the strategy of checking and certifying the focuses of intrigued and capabilities of a candidate applying for a work or position. It incorporates ensuring that the information given by the candidate is correct and tried and true. This get ready makes a contrast bosses make taught choices around enrolling candidates and decreases the risk of enrolling some person who may not be suitable for the work.

Blockchain development can be utilized to check the establishment of work candidates, like their instruction, past occupations, certifications, and other capabilities. This has following steps:

Credential Verification: Schools, past employers, and certification acquired can keep a secure record of a person's capabilities on the blockchain and confirm them. This makes a secure record of a candidate's past.

Accessible Records: HR work force can viably see affirmed information nearly work candidates amid the enrolling get ready. This suggests that we not got to spend a allocate of time checking someone's establishment, and it as well brings down the chance of enrolling some person who has lied around their capabilities.

Increase in Trust: Work candidates can certainly show off confirmed accreditations utilizing blockchain advancement, knowing that employers have the dependency on the validity of the information given.

Automated Onboarding Through Smart Contracts

Smart contracts can be utilized to form the onboarding plan less requesting, speedier, and more user-friendly by mechanizing it.

Acceptance Trigger: When the person who associated for a work concurs to require the work, a sharp contract can be activated. This understanding causes a course of action of organized exercises to happen speedier.

Employee Profile Creation: The quick contract can start making a specialist profile on the HR system. This suggests giving your title, phone number, and other imperative information.

Training programs: The sharp contract can consolidate the basic planning necessities and plans. This suggests that unused agents will actually be chosen in basic planning programs, like presentation or compliance planning, without requiring someone to do it physically.

Access Provisioning: The quick contract can besides control the giving of authorization to utilize company systems, resources, and workplaces. This infers giving authorization for utilizing computer systems, entering the office, and utilizing mail accounts.

Documentation Completion: The sharp contract can remind unused specialists to wrap up basic printed material, like charge shapes and commerce contracts, making past any question everything is done precisely.

Utilizing BaaS and smart contracts in enrollment and onboarding shapes can offer some inclinations.

Efficiency: Computerization makes onboarding speedier and easier, so HR staff can spend more time on basic errands.

Error Reduction: It decreases the chance of botches and ignores that can happen when people do onboarding assignments physically.

Consistency: Sharp contracts make past any question that the same onboarding rules are taken after for each unused representative, which makes a distinction to be sensible and take after the rules.

Candidate experience: It insinuates to how candidates feel around the method of joining a company. When the onboarding handle is basic to utilize and get it, candidates are more likely to be cheerful and bolted in.

Cost Savings: Making process less troublesome and cutting down on futile administrative work makes a distinction the organization save cash.

Utilizing BaaS and smart contracts in enlistment and onboarding need to be carefully organized and facilitates with the current HR systems. It's as well crucial to consider the true blue and regulatory prerequisites. In any case, utilizing this methodology of modernizing HR operations can bring various benefits, such as making things more beneficial and exact, and advancing the inclusion for work candidates.

Payroll and Compensation

Finance handling is a critical work in HR administration, but it can be time-consuming. This assignment can be difficult, inclined to errors, and requires manpower. BaaS can make this handle simpler and error free. Giri, G. et al. (2023) has studied and explained how blockchain technology can be used to solve problem related to payroll.

Blockchain-Based payroll: BaaS can offer assistance make finance frameworks utilizing blockchain innovation where compensation data is kept secure and ensured. Keen contracts are like computer programs that can consequently calculate and pay pay rates concurring to set rules. This could make things less demanding by diminishing printed material and errors.

Here are the imperative parts of utilizing BaaS for finance and remuneration in HR management:

BaaS permits for the advancement of finance frameworks utilizing blockchain innovation. In these frameworks, compensation data is kept secure and unmistakable. The important parts of a finance framework that employments blockchain innovation are:

Secured Data: Ready to keep compensation data, counting how much each worker is paid, secure by recording it on the blockchain. These records can't be changed and they make beyond any doubt that the information is dependable and will remain that way until the end of time.

Computerized calculations: Smart contracts can be utilized to naturally calculate compensations utilizing prearranged rules and criteria. For occurrence, the intelligent understanding can figure out how much cash someone should be paid by looking at the number of hours they worked, any additional cash they earned, and any cash that should be taken out.

Payment Computerization: Smart contracts can consequently send employees' pay rates to their chosen bank accounts or computerized wallets. This makes it simpler to handle finance and brings down the chance of installment errors.

Real-Time Transparency: real-time straightforwardness implies that representatives can see their compensation records and installment history instantly. This gives them a clear understanding of how much they are getting paid. This makes individuals believe each other more and causes less contentions.

Auditability: It implies that the blockchain keeps a changeless record of all exchanges related to finance. We keep a record of all installments and compensation changes, and they can be checked to form beyond any doubt we are taking after the rules and being open around it.

The focal points of utilizing BaaS and keen contracts for finance and remuneration incorporate:

Effectiveness: Utilizing computerization makes finance handling quicker and less demanding by reducing the time and exertion required to calculate and pay pay rates.

Accuracy: Utilizing computerized calculations diminishes the chance of mistakes in deciding and conveying compensation, making beyond any doubt that representatives get the right sum.

Straightforwardness: Laborers can see their compensation and installment history right away, which makes a difference construct believe and diminishes the ought to inquire HR for data.

By utilizing computerized frameworks for finance, companies can spare cash by lessening the costs of physically handling finance.

Utilizing blockchain-based finance frameworks can offer assistance organizations take after assess controls and labor laws by keeping precise and clear compensation records.

Information Security: Blockchain employments extraordinary coding tomake beyond any doubt imperative compensation data is kept secure from individuals who aren't permitted to see it and from any changes being made to it without authorization.

Coordination BaaS and smart contracts in finance and emolument forms implies making them work with current HR and money related frameworks, conjointly taking after legitimate and assess rules. Companies ought to too think approximately exchanging their finance framework to blockchain technology, and how it'll influence their workers and money related records.

In common, blockchain-based finance frameworks can offer assistance make HR assignments simpler, diminish the sum of printed material, and make beyond any doubt that compensation data is more accurate and transparent.

Talent Management and Training

Ability administration implies finding, making a difference, and keeping skilled specialists.

Ability administration could be an exceptionally vital portion of overseeing the individuals in a company. It incorporates finding, making a difference, and keeping workers who have a part of aptitudes. Blockchain as a Benefit (BaaS) can offer assistance with finding and creating talented individuals by making a ability commercial center that's not controlled by one central specialist.

Damle et. al. (2023) studied the effects of incorporating a new technology, particularly Blockchain, offering various advantages in individuals, teams, departments, and organizations with real-time insights and advancements

Here is how BaaS (Backend as a Benefit) can make ability administration and preparing way better in a company:

A decentralized ability commercial center can be created utilizing BaaS inside the organization. This commercial center may be a stage where laborers can appear their capacities, capabilities, victories, and proficient development on a secure advanced record. vital parts of this commercial center for gifted individuals incorporate:

Expertise Profiles: Specialists can make and overhaul ability profiles on the blockchain, giving particular subtle elements almost their capacities, past work, and capabilities. These profiles are secure and cannot be changed without location.

HR faculty and contracting directors can utilize the ability marketplace to discover and learn around gifted people inside the organization. They can discover laborers who have the proper capacities, information, or capabilities to do certain employments or ventures.

Transparent Qualifications: The certifications and preparing records of representatives are confirmed utilizing blockchain innovation. These records are effectively open and can be seen by anybody. This straightforwardness makes a difference representative to construct believe in their abilities and capabilities.

Career development: The ability commercial center can offer assistance discover workers inside the company who have potential for career headway, advancements, and openings to create modern aptitudes. It matches employees' capacities to what the organization requires.

Expertise improvement: HR can way better get it what aptitudes and preparing representatives require by looking at their aptitudes and certifications within the work showcase. This data can offer assistance make specialized preparing and advancement programs.

Security controls donate workers the capacity to select who can see their ability profiles and how much they can see. This makes beyond any doubt that critical data is as it were shared with individuals who have authorization to see it.

The focal points of employing a decentralized ability commercial center with BaaS in HR administration are:

Utilizing the abilities of current workers well: Companies can make superior utilize of the abilities of their claim specialists. This implies they do not ought to contract modern individuals as frequently and can offer assistance representatives progress in their careers inside the company.

Creating abilities is more likely to happen when workers accept they can move up within the company. The commercial center makes a difference coordinate employees' objectives with work openings.

Productive Ability Coordinating: HR and enlisting supervisors can effectively discover the proper individuals for particular ventures or work positions, lessening the time it takes to contract them and making strides the adaptability of the workforce.

Believe and Straightforwardness: Blockchain's openness and unchangeable nature make certainty among specialists, making beyond any doubt that their capacities and capabilities are accurately depicted.

Data-Driven Decision-Making: The commercial center gives critical data for HR analytics, which makes a difference organizations make choicesaround creating their staff and arranging their workforce based on this information.

It's important to get it that for a decentralized ability commercial center to work well, representatives have to be take an interest and be included. Companies have to be encourage the points of interest of the commercial center and make sure that their representatives feel at ease with the protection settings and data-sharing alternatives.

By utilizing BaaS to form a decentralized ability commercial center, organizations can superior interface with their employees' skills and objectives. This will offer assistance them develop and succeed as a group.

Data Security and Privacy

HR information contains delicate data that must be taken care of with the preeminent exceptional care. BaaS can advance information security and confirmation whereas guaranteeing compliance with controls like GDPR and HIPAA.

The security and security of HR information are to begin with considerations for organizations, especially when overseeing with delicate laborer data. Blockchain as a Service (BaaS) offers unimaginable courses of activity to advance information security and affirmation in spite of the fact that guaranteeing compliance with resolute headings like GDPR and HIPAA. Tapscott et. al. say that the security and privacy of blockchains continue to be at the center of the debate when deploying blockchain in different applications

Here's how BaaS can contribute to information security and security in HR organization:

Enhanced Information Security: Blockchain headway utilizes cryptographic methodologies to guarantee that HR information is put truant safely and is exceedingly secure to changing, unauthorized access, or information breaches. Key points of view of advanced information security connect:

Immutable Records: HR information put missing on the blockchain is enduring, meaning once recorded, it cannot be changed or annihilated without assention from the organize. This ceaseless nature ensures the cleverness and relentless quality of HR records.

Cryptographic Encryption: Delicate HR information can be blended utilizing cryptographic calculations, with access confined to authorized staff who have the basic encryption keys. This encryption secures information at rest and in travel.

Decentralization: The decentralized nature of blockchain minimizes the chance of a single information breach compromising all HR records. Information is pointlessly put truant over a coordinate of center focuses, organizing of single centers of disappointment.

Access Control: Getting into HR information is controlled through sharp contracts and cryptographic keys. Since it were authorized people or divisions can access or modify particular data, reducing the chance of unauthorized access.

Privacy Control: BaaS locks in operators by allowing them more control over their information put missing on the blockchain:

Granular Access Permissions: Pros can characterize granular get to consents, appearing who can get to diverse parts of their HR records. For case, they can convey HR staff get to to work history in spite of the fact that confining get to to restorative records.

Client Consent Components: BaaS can actualize client consent components utilizing sharp contracts, guaranteeing that get to sensitive information is allowed since it were with the express assent of the laborer.

Information Movability: Pros can safely share their HR information with other organizations or organizations when required, enabling shapes like work applications or benefits exchanges.

Compliance with Information Controls: BaaS courses of activity can be portrayed out to comply with information security headings like GDPR, permitting organizations to meet lawful necessities for information taking care of and security.

The centers of captivated of executing BaaS for information security and security in HR organization solidify:

Diminished Information Breach Chance: Moved forward security measures, checking never-ending quality and get to controls, interior and out diminish the chance of information breaches and unauthorized get to.

Information Judgment: Blockchain's ceaseless nature guarantees the understanding and accuracy of HR records, lessening the chance of information control or extortion.

Security Compliance: BaaS courses of activity can be organized to change with information affirmation controls, making a qualification organizations meet their honest to goodness commitments.

Client Strengthening: Pros have more control over their information, upgrading their security and acknowledge interior the organization.

Transparency: The coordinate nature of blockchain gifts specialists toconfirm who has gotten to their information, advancing straightforwardness and obligation.

Actualizing BaaS in HR information organization requires cautious organizing, integration with existing HR frameworks, and thought of definitive prerequisites. It as well requires teaching specialists around the benefits and suggestions of blockchain-based information organization.

By leveraging BaaS to overtake information security and security, organizations can secure delicate HR data, reduce compliance dangers, and advance a culture of acknowledge and straightforwardness insides the workforce.

IMPACT ON HR OPERATIONS

Efficiency

Using Blockchain as a Service (BaaS) in HR management has the potential to bring big changes to different aspects of HR operations. This part looks at how BaaS can affect HR tasks, focusing on four important areas:

Effectiveness could be a central driving drive behind the integration of Blockchain as a Benefit (BaaS) into HR operations. BaaS can revolutionize HR by robotizing forms and lessening manual errands, coming about in critical proficiency picks up. Ramachandran et. al. (2023) conclude that Blockchain has been the key contributer to make HRM efficient. Here are key angles of how BaaS upgrades proficiency in HR:

Process Streamlining

Automation of Routine Tasks: BaaS empowers the robotization of monotonous and schedule HR forms. For illustration, candidate confirmation, onboarding, and finance can be streamlined through savvy contracts and blockchain innovation. This diminishes the require for manual mediation, making these forms more efficient and error-free.

Candidate Verification: Rather than manual confirmation of candidate qualifications, BaaS can encourage mechanized confirmation forms. Scholarly degrees, work histories, and certifications can be safely recorded on the blockchain, making it less demanding to confirm candidates' capabilities.

OnboardingAutomation: BaaS can mechanize the onboarding handle. Once a candidate acknowledges an offer, a savvy contract can trigger a arrangement of activities, such as the creation of an representative profile, arrangement of get to to vital frameworks, and start of preparing programs. This decreases authoritative overhead and quickens the onboarding prepare.

Payroll Automation: Finance preparing can be completely computerized utilizing blockchain-based frameworks. Shrewd contracts can calculate pay rates based on predefined rules, and distributions can happen consequently. This not as it were spares time but moreover decreases the chance of blunders in finance calculations.

Time Savings

Reduced Administrative Tasks: Mechanization through BaaS diminishes the time HR experts spend on authoritative errands. With schedule forms robotized, HR faculty can distribute more time to key HR activities, such as ability advancement, workforce arranging, and representative engagement.

Faster Transactions: Blockchain's real-time capabilities permit for quicker and more productive exchanges. Upgrades and changes to HR information can be recorded right away, guaranteeing that data is continuously current.

Cost Reduction

Lower Operational Costs: Streamlined forms and decreased manual mediation interpret into lower operational costs for HR capacities. Less human assets are required to oversee HR forms, which comes about in taken a toll investment funds for the organization.

Error Reduction: By computerizing forms, BaaS diminishes the hazard of human mistakes in HR errands. This not as it were spares time but moreover minimizes the costs related with redressing mistakes.

By and large, the integration of BaaS in HR administration can lead to progressed proficiency by disentangling forms, sparing time, and decreasing operational costs. HR experts can move their center from manual and dreary assignments to more vital exercises, eventually contributing to the organization's victory and representative fulfillment.

Transparency

Blockchain innovation is known for being open and genuine, and when utilized in HR operations, it can enormously affect believe, duty, and taking after rules. Blockchain innovation is known for being straightforward, and when it's utilized in HR operations, it can incredibly progress believe and responsibility. Sankar et. al. (2022) studied that blockchain can expand the productivity and credibility of the organization by enhancing transperancy throughtout any organisation.

Auditable History

Blockchain Ledger: BaaS employments a clear and unchangeable record that keeps track of all HR exchanges. This book keeps a record of everything that has happened over time, such as when representative records were upgraded, compensation was changed, individuals were advanced, and when modern representatives were contracted.

Accessible to Authorized Parties: Accessible to individuals who are permitted to get to it, such as workers, inspectors, and government organizations. Individuals with consent can see at this total and troublesome to alter record, which makes a difference construct believe by being open and legitimate.

This check can happen right absent, making beyond any doubt that everybody can see and utilize the same data that cannot be changed.

Enhanced Accountability

Identification of Responsible Parties: Finding out who is dependable for errors, contrasts, or issues gets to be less complex when there are clear and open human assets methods. In the event that there's an issue, able to figure out what happened and who is dependable, which makes a difference make individuals responsible within the organization.

Compliance and Governance: Taking after inside arrangements and outside directions is simpler when there's straightforwardness in compliance and administration. By keeping a point by point record of HR activities, companies can appear that they are devoted to taking after rules and overseeing dangers viably.

Trust Building: Building believe within the work environment includes being open and fair in HR operations. This makes a difference representatives feel sure that their records are redress which HR forms are reasonable. This believe is exceptionally critical for making a great environment at work and making employees feel upbeat and substance.

External Audits: Outside audits are when individuals from exterior the company, like reviewers and government organizations, check the HR records and forms to create beyond any doubt everything is done accurately. This may speed up reviews and administrative reviews since the required data is effectively available on the blockchain record.

Dispute Resolution: When there are contradictions related to HR, the clear and unchangeable nature of blockchain records can be utilized as a reasonable and solid way to discover the truth and fathom clashes rapidly.

To put it essentially, including BaaS to HR operations makes things more straightforward by keeping a secure record of all HR exchanges that can't be changed or tampered with. This straightforwardness makes a difference construct believe among representatives and partners. It moreover makes it less demanding for everybody to be responsible, take after rules, and oversee things appropriately. When organizations attempt to be moral and take after rules, they got to be dependable. BaaS makes a difference with this by advertising straightforwardness in HR administration.

Data Accuracy

Information precision is of preeminent centrality in HR enterprise because it underpins tough decision-making, regular updating compliance, and commonplace ampleness of HR operations. Blockchain as a Service (BaaS) contributes up-to-date statistics accuracy in HR as follows:

Immutable Records

Data Immutability: Blockchain's perpetual nature guarantees that after HR facts are recorded on the blockchain, it gets up-to-date and is tamper-proof. Information can not be adjusted or eliminated without understanding from the orchestrate. This incorporation guarantees the precision and insightfulness of HR information.

Protection from Data Manipulation: The constant nature of information lessens the chance of statistics control, unauthorized changes, or untrue modifications. HR statistics, checking paintings records updated, certifications, and execution evaluations, stays reliable and relaxed up to date enhancing.

Real-time Updates

Immediate Record Updates: BaaS offers actual-time updates and updated HR statistics. As changes manifest, up-to-date progressions, stipend modifications, or element modifications, can be properly recorded on the blockchain. This ensures that HR facts are steadily current and display the actual-time status of workers.

Elimination of Data Lag: routine HR systems can also persevere from data slack, wherein overhauls take time up to date and multiply through the device. BaaS arranges this slack by giving a shared, proper absent upgraded file open up-to-date to all legal parties.

Accurate Decision-making: Getting up-to-date updated and correct HR statistics empowers HR professionals and organizations to date make taught alternatives with regard to updated capability organization, a team of workers orchestrating, and compensation adjustments. This exactness progresses HR's dedication to updated organizational triumph.

Data Integrity and Compliance

Regulatory Compliance: specific and perpetual HR statistics energize regulatory compliance, particularly in company's subject to up-to-date strict statistics confirmation controls like GDPR and HIPAA. Companies can simply define compliance by relying on the insightfulness of their HR information.

Audit Trail: The blockchain record acts as an audit way, showing a comprehensive update of HR trades. This direct file is worthwhile in the midst of internal surveys and regulatory audits.

Minimized Errors: Decreased guide information phase and managed to lessen the chance of goofs in HR information. This minimizes irregularities and botches that could up-to-date compliance issues and high-priced rectifications.

In fact, BaaS performs a fundamental element in making sure of information exactness in interior HR enterprises. Its perpetual high quality guarantees the belief of HR facts, lowering the hazard of botches, aberrations, and facts manipulation. Actual-time overhauls make certain that HR records are persistently contemporary, overhauling decision-making and regulating-to-date compliance. As businesses rely upon specific HR statistics for critical capacities, BaaS receives updated to be a crucial system for retaining data exactness and unflinching first-rate.

Security

Data security is of vital noteworthiness in HR operations, given the sensitive nature of HR data. the combination of Blockchain as a benefit (BaaS) overhauls facts protection in HR employer through unique additives:

Cryptographic Protection

Data Encryption: Blockchain makes use of cryptographic techniques to scramble HR data. Agent information, person facts, cash related information, and different fragile HR records are secured through sturdy encryption. This encryption reduces the hazard of facts breaches, as surely in the event that an unauthorized substance picks up get to the records, it stays distorted without the proper encryption keys.

Non-public and Open Keys: Blockchain organizations open and private key units to control access to facts. authorized individuals have the personal keys required to unscramble and access unique data. This cryptographic protection guarantees that because it has been people with the correct authorization can see or change HR data.

Decentralization

Data Dispersion: Decentralization indicates that HR facts is dispersed over a extend of facilities in preference to being placed absent on a crucial server. every center in the arrange continues up a copy of the statistics, making it extensively available in opposition to single focuses of unhappiness. This scattering diminishes the risk of facts problem due to server crashes.

Enhanced records Adaptability: The distributed nature of the blockchain network makes it challenging for malicious actors to compromise data integrity. Even if one node is compromised, the majority of the network's nodes maintain the correct data, making it difficult for unauthorized changes to be accepted by the network.

Access Control

Smart Contracts: Sharp contracts and access govern components are applied to oversee who can access precise HR facts. Get to authorizations can be predefined indoors savvy contracts, making sure that because it was authorized people or divisions can see, redecorate, or adjust specific information. For outline, HR staff may additionally have access to laborer data, while fund executives have access to emolument records. This granular manipulate minimizes the danger of unauthorized records access.

Security From Unauthorized Access

Strong security features: Blockchain's cryptographic highlights, in combination with smart contracts and access govern, make it particularly comfy to unauthorized get to. clearly in case a noxious performing craftsman selections up get to the blockchain prepare, the strong security features in placed make it notably troublesome to regulate with or take HR records.

Reduced Insider Threats: Access govern components and straightforwardness of the blockchain document can as nicely offer help direct insider perils. Suspicious or unauthorized get to endeavors are logged and can be proper away diagnosed, reducing the chance of inward data breaches.

In layout, the integration of BaaS through and through fortifies statistics security interior HR operations. Cryptographic security, decentralization, access control, and stable security features together make sure the protection, insightfulness, and availability of HR information. As corporation's enterprise to secure sensitive HR information from progressing cyber threats and unauthorized access, BaaS creates as an able instrument for fortifying information protection in HR employer.

CHALLENGES AND CONSIDERATIONS

The integration of Blockchain as a Service (BaaS) in HR management brings about transformative potential, but not without its challenges and considerations. To ensure a successful implementation, organizations must navigate several key hurdles:

Integration Complexities

Integrating BaaS into current HR structures can be complicated because these structures may had been used for a long time. Below are a few troubles that anyone might face:

Outdated HR structures: Many agencies use are not well matched with blockchain technology. Making these structures well matched with BaaS would possibly need numerous technical know-how and resources.

Records Migration: Moving current HR records to the blockchain may be a hard project. It's far crucial to ensure information is safe and correct while shifting it to a brand new vicinity, so that mistakes or dropping records doesn't occur.

Schooling: HR personnel may have to learn new skills so one can work correctly inside the new HR machine primarily based on blockchain technology. This could have an effect on how lots paintings they could get finished while they're still adapting to the new machine.

Scalability

Scalability is truly imperative, particularly for huge companies or ones that are developing rapidly.

Network blockage happens when the HR exchanges on the blockchain increases. This will cause slower exchange handling times and perhaps more costly expense.

Asset assignment implies apportioning or relegating more computational assets to a blockchain network in arrange to form it greater and able of dealing with more exchanges. In any case, this will make the costs go up.

Regulatory Compliance

Guaranteeing regulatory compliance is of foremost importance, as HR data is subjected to different regulations, including the General Data Protection Regulation (GDPR) and Health Insurance Portability and Accountability Act (HIPAA):

Data records protection: BaaS executions must follow to information protection instructions, which might also require anonymization or encryption of certain HR records. guaranteeing compliance with these controls is essential to maintain a strategic distance from lawful repercussions.

Cross-border statistics exchange: For multinational businesses, overseeing HR information that crosses international borders may be hard because of changing records security laws absolutely different locales.

Cost Considerations

The sum of money it costs is an imperative figure in choosing whether to utilize BaaS for HR administration.

The primary fetched: Utilizing BaaS may require cash for innovation, equipment, and information. Organizations ought to carefully assess how much cash they have to be contribute at first and how much return on venture they can possibly get.

Running costs: Standard costs of keeping the arrange working and paying expenses for exchanges can influence how cost-effective a BaaS arrangement is.

Supplier Expenses: In case you select to utilize a BaaS supplier, make beyond any doubt to check the fetched and any repeating expenses for their administrations.

Change Management

The introduction of BaaS may mean new HR forms . Some people might not like this because they are used to the old way of doing things. Having effective change management strategies is important to ensure a smooth transition and to get support from HR staff.

Technological Evolvement

Blockchain innovation continuously keeps on changing, upgrading and moving forward and organizations got to keep themselves side by side with the most recent advancements and overhauls within the BaaS field. Remaining overhauled continuously makes a difference in keeping HR frameworks secure from dangers or information misfortune, working appropriately, and keeping upgraded with updated rules and regulations.

CONCLUSION

The utilization of Blockchain as a Service (BaaS) in overseeing Human Assets (HR) is anticipated to form things more proficient, clear, and secure. This study inquired about howBaaS can be utilized in HR. It looked at commonsense ways of utilizing BaaS and the potential affect it can have. The inquire about found that BaaS has the capacity to bring critical changes to the way HR capacities.

In today's fast-paced and competitive business world, organizations must persistently explore for unused and superior strategies to improve their forms and make their operations more vigorous. HR administration is truly vital for making a company effective. In this manner, it is significant. Conventional HR forms have continuously had issues with being moderate and incapable, with information being stored separately and not effectively shared, and with concerns around keeping information secure. BaaS may be a truly supportive arrangement that produces operations superior.

The most concepts of blockchain innovation, such as sharing control, coming to assentions, utilizing secure codes, making programmed assentions, and being safe to changes, can be connected to HR administration to make strides understanding. These straightforward thoughts can totally move forward the way HR forms are carried out, ensuring believe, exact data, and security.

BaaS in HR administration implies utilizing innovation to oversee assignments like confirming someone's personality, controlling get to to data, naturally enlisting unused workers, employing a particular computer framework to pay workers, overseeing employees' aptitudes through a decentralized marketplace, and guaranteeing data is secure and private. These applications illustrate how BaaS can offer assistance HR groups be more effective, diminish the require for manual errands, and improve the security of information.

BaaS includes a enormous affect on HR activities. Using computerization implies utilizing machines and innovation to do assignments and work. This makes a difference us to do things speedier and way better, which spares time and cash. Straightforwardness is made superior by keeping records and permitting them to be checked on, which makes a difference to make believe among representatives and partners. Information precision is guaranteed since the records cannot be changed. This makes a difference us make way better choices and take after the rules. Besides, the solid security measures of blockchain innovation ensure that HR information is ensured and cannot be gotten to by programmers or unauthorized people, guaranteeing the privacy of delicate data.

Be that as it may, there are challenges and contemplations when utilizing BaaS in HR administration. We must handle the challenges of putting distinctive parts together, developing, taking after rules, and overseeing costs with caution. Having great plans in put is imperative to guarantee that any changes happen effortlessly.

In today's commercial world, it is exceptionally vital for companies to utilize BaaS in overseeing their HR. This makes beyond any doubt that a company runs easily and remains competitive and versatile.

As businesses get greater and advance, the ones that utilize BaaS for overseeing HR will likely be at the cutting edge of being compelling and creating new concepts. Getting to be truly great at overseeing human assets by utilizing BaaS includes a awesome opportunity for development and victory. It can offer assistance companies toremain competitive and succeed, indeed when things are continuously changing.

Utilizing BaaS in HR operations can lead to critical enhancements by making things more compelling, clear, and secure. It can moreover make information more precise. These great things can offer assistance HR be superior at supporting the organization's objectives, complying the rules, and picking up the believe of workers and partners. Utilizing BaaS in HR administration is getting to be more critical for companies to remain competitive and progress operations in today's trade world.

In brief, whereas utilizing Blockchain as a Benefit can be supportive for HR administration, it's essential to recognize and address any challenges and issues which will come up. Organizations can advantage from BaaS (Blockchain-as-a-Service) by effectively managing with integration challenges, dealing with adaptability concerns, adhering to directions, considering costs, effectively managing changes, and keeping up with innovation headways. By doing so, they can minimize dangers and mishaps. Eventually, HR supervisors can utilize BaaS effectively and successfully in their work by carefully arranging and being commonplace with these challenges.

RECOMMENDATIONS FOR FUTURE RESEARCH

The integration of Blockchain as a Benefit (BaaS) in Human Assets (HR) administration may be a energetic and advancing field with a large number of unexplored openings. Future investigate endeavors can assist development our understanding and application of BaaS in HR administration. Here are a few key zones for future investigate:

Particular Applications

Future inquire is needed to dig more profound into particular applications of BaaS inside HR administration. Need to investigate how BaaS can be tailored to address special HR challenges in several businesses or organizations. Examine the advancement of specialized BaaS arrangements for regions such as ability procurement, execution administration, or representative benefits organization.

Case Studies

In-depth case thinks about how we can give important experiences into the real-world execution of BaaS in HR administration. Need to look at fruitful BaaS appropriation stories, highlighting best hones, challenges to overcome, and quantifiable results. On the other hand, need to analyze the occurrences where BaaS executions confronted obstacles and lessons are learned.

Technical Considerations

Advance inquire into the specialized viewpoints of BaaS is fundamental requirement. Examination is required regarding blockchain adaptability arrangements to address the potential blockage issues as HR exchanges increment. Investigation regarding the advancement of interoperability guidelines to encourage the integration of BaaS with existing HR frameworks and information sources is required.

Regulatory Compliance

With the ever-evolving scene of information assurance and protection controls, progressing investigation is ought to center on how BaaS can guarantee ceaseless compliance. Examination regarding the improvement of keen contracts and information capacity instruments that consequently adjust to changing administrative prerequisites, guaranteeing HR information remains secure and compliant needs to be done.

Employee Experience

Inquire about the affect of BaaS on the employee experience. Exploring of how blockchain-powered self-service entries and decentralized ability marketplaces can enable representatives to require more control over their HR information and career improvement. Evaluation of the impact of progressed information security and straightforwardness on worker believe and engagement can also be done.

Industry-Specific Applications

Diverse businesses may have interesting HR necessities and compliance guidelines. Inquire about howBaaS can be custom-made to meet the particular needs of divisions such as healthcare, fund, or fabricating can be done. Examining industry-specific utilize cases and the administrative support related with each can be planned.

Cybersecurity and Data Privacy

In an period of expanding cybersecurity dangers, need to persistently investigate the advancing scene of blockchain-based cybersecurity arrangements for HR information. Need to assess the viability of cryptographic strategies, zero-knowledge proofs, and secure multi-party computation in defending HR information against developing dangers.

Long-Term Impact Assessment

Need to evaluate the long-term affect of BaaS selection in HR administration and also assess its supportability, cost-effectiveness and versatility as HR forms.

Organizational Culture and Change Management

Investigate ought to center on the human viewpoint of BaaS selection. Examination of social shifts and alter administration methodologies required to effectively coordinated blockchain innovation into HR operations is needed. Need to know how workers see and adjust to these changes.

Integration With Emerging Technologies

Investigation of the synergies between BaaS and developing innovations such as counterfeit insights (AI), machine learning, and the Web of Things (IoT) is required. Exploring how these innovations can complement and improve the capabilities of BaaS in HR administration needs to be observed.

By directing research endeavors into these regions, the field of BaaS in HR administration can proceed to advance, giving organizations with important experiences and instruments to open effectiveness, straightforwardness, and security inside their HR operations. These inquire about endeavors will be instrumental in forming the long run of HR administration in an increasingly digital and data-driven world.

REFERENCES

Anna, V., Andrea, D. S., Visaggio, C. A., & Gerardo, C. (2021). A systematic literature review of blockchain and smart contract development: Techniques, tools, and open challenges. *Journal of Systems and Software*, *174*, 110891. doi:10.1016/j.jss.2020.110891

Chen, M., & Patel, R. (2017). Decentralized Payroll Systems: A Case Study of Blockchain Implementation. *Journal of Financial Technology*, *9*(1), 56–72.

Damiano, D. F. M., Mori, P., & Ricci, L. (2019). A blockchain based approach for the definition of auditable Access Control systems. *Computers & Security*, *84*, 93–119. doi:10.1016/j.cose.2019.03.016

Damle, M., & Kulkarni, P. (2023). Blockchain Technology in Talent Retention and Capability Development in HRM, *5th International Conference on Inventive Research in Computing Applications (ICIRCA)*, Coimbatore, India. 10.1109/ICIRCA57980.2023.10220633

Govinda, G., Kunal, C., Sudhanshu, G., Rahul, J., Ketan, K., & Om, M. Parasha Deepak r & Mulay Preeti (2023). Payroll Management Using Blockchain. *International Conference on Innovative Computing and Communications. ICICC 2023. Lecture Notes in Networks and Systems.* Springer, Singapore.

Gupta, A., & Chen, W. (2022). Enhancing Employee Onboarding Through Blockchain Technology. *Journal of Emerging Technologies in HR*, *6*(3), 120–138.

Halpin, H., & Piekarska, M. (2017). *Introduction to Security and Privacy on the Blockchain. 2017 IEEE European Symposium on Security and Privacy Workshops (EuroS&PW)*, Paris, France. 10.1109/EuroSPW.2017.43

Ibrar, Y., Salah, K., Jayaraman, R., & Al-Hammadi, Y. (2021). Blockchain for healthcare data management: Opportunities, challenges, and future recommendations. *Neural Computing & Applications*, *34*(14), 11475–11490. doi:10.1007/s00521-020-05519-w

Malik, G., Parasrampuria, K., Reddy, S. P., & Shah, S. (2019), Blockchain Based Identity Verification Model,*International Conference on Vision Towards Emerging Trends in Communication and Networking (ViTECoN)*, Vellore, India.

Michael, J., & Anjali, G. (2013). Contracts for Employee Work Agreements: Legal Implications. *The Journal of Law and Technology*, *12*(4), 213–230.

Mukherjee, P., Barik, R. K., & Pradhan, C. (2021). *A Comprehensive Proposal for Blockchain-Oriented Smart City. Security and Privacy Applications for Smart City Development.308*. Springer. doi:10.1007/978-3-030-53149-2_4

Ramachandran, R., Babu, V., & Murugesan, V. P. (2023). The role of blockchain technology in the process of decision-making in human resource management: A review and future research agenda. *Business Process Management Journal*, *29*(1), 116–139. doi:10.1108/BPMJ-07-2022-0351

Rashid, A., Masood, A., Abbas, H., & Zhang, Y. (2021). Blockchain-Based Public Key Infrastructure: A Transparent Digital Certification Mechanism for Secure Communication. *IEEE Network*, *35*(5), 220–225. doi:10.1109/MNET.101.2000532

Sankar, J., Ilangovan, K., Arokiaraj, D., & Ganeshkumar, C. (2022). Adoption Of Blockchain Technology In HRM. *Korean Review Of International Studies*, *15*(40), 5–7.

Shahriar, F., Katibur, R. S. M., & Sharfuddin, M. (2023). Blockchain: A Comparative Study of Consensus Algorithms PoW, PoS, PoA, PoV. [IJMSC]. *International Journal ofMathematical Sciences and Computing*, *9*(3), 46–57. doi:10.5815/ijmsc.2023.03.04

Tapscott, A., & Tapscott, A. D. (2017, March 1). Blockchain solutions for cybersecurity. *Harvard Business Review*, *21*, 9–11.

Yi, C. S. S., Yung, E., Fong, C., & Tripathi, S. (2020). Benefits and Use of Blockchain Technology to Human Resources Management: A Critical Review. *International Journal of Human Resource Studies*, *10*(2), 2–6. doi:10.5296/ijhrs.v10i2.16932

Zheng, Z., Xie, S., Dai, H.-N., Chen, W., Chen, X., Jian, W., & Imran, M. (2020). An overview on smart contracts: Challenges, advances and platforms. *Future Generation Computer Systems*, *105*, 475–49. doi:10.1016/j.future.2019.12.019

Chapter 10
Advanced Data Analytics in Green Finance:
Blockchain and Digital Twin Integration

Afzalur Rahman
Presidency University, India

Mohsin Khan
https://orcid.org/0000-0001-7986-9478
Vellore Institute of Technology, India

Ben Attom
Cape Coast Technical University, Ghana

M. Manoharan
Vellore Institute of Technology, India

ABSTRACT

This chapter explores how cutting-edge technologies, such as big data analytics, digital twins, and blockchain, are revolutionizing the green finance industry. It examines how these technologies' convergence improves sustainable financial practices efficiency, transparency, and decision-making while providing a fresh viewpoint on their complementary effects. The chapter describes the distinct functions of digital twins in asset optimization and risk management, blockchain in guaranteeing security and trust, and sophisticated data analytics in facilitating well-informed financial decisions.

DOI: 10.4018/979-8-3693-1878-2.ch010

INTRODUCTION

In financial sector from the beginning of the 21st century there are several major changes happened. These changes are due to the change in technology and the growing awareness of environmental awareness. The growing concern of the sustainability of the environment the new concept emerged and known as Green Finance. Green Finance is now popular topic among the public and the researcher. Green finance's development is indicative of a more widespread acknowledgment by society of the critical nature of environmental issues in the financial industry (Weber, 2018).

The research conducted by Shamshad, Akhtar, Alam, Khan, and Ansari about blockchain-digital twin financial instruments for green investments is crucial. Akhtar et al., (2021) identify the "YES Bank Fiasco: Arrogance or Negligence" as an incident that underscores challenges within the banking sector and emphasises the necessity for robust financial organisations to endorse environmentally friendly initiatives. This case study indirectly emphasises the criticality of financial transparency and accountability afforded by blockchain technology.

"Consequence of Financial Crisis on Liquidity and Profitability of Commercial Banks in India" by Ansari et al., (2023) and "Measuring the Performance of the Indian Banking Industry" by Akhtar et al., (2021) provide empirical support for this claim. These studies demonstrate the efficiency and resiliency of banks in the face of financial crises, demonstrating that innovative financial products require a stable banking system. Blockchain technology has the potential to make transactions more secure and transparent, hence boosting stability. Finally, Akhtar et al., (2022) investigate how big financial changes effect banking efficiency in "Measuring Technical Efficiency of Banks vis-à-vis Demonetization." This study implies that blockchain and digital twins can assist the banking industry in adapting to large-scale economic developments, which is critical for green investment strategies. These studies provide a thorough understanding of the banking sector's dynamics, which is required for developing and deploying blockchain-digital twin-era financial instruments for green investments.

The development of power of computer and accordingly the advancement of the data analytics techniques given the necessity of support to the emergence of Green Finance. Advance data analytics helps in evaluating, forecasting, and optimizing investment strategies, ensuring that they align with environmental sustainability goals (Carè et al., 2019).

The blockchain technology is the revolutionary development that offer the level of security, transparency, and efficiency that was not available earlier. Blockchain's fundamental characteristics, that are immutability and decentralization, make it a effective tool for Green Finance, helping to build trust and credibility in financial transactions (Yli-Huumo et al., 2016).

On the other hand, the concept of digital twins, through which it is possible to create a virtual replicas of physical assets, has begun to reshape financial investment strategies. Due to the Digital twins real-time monitoring and scenario analysis is possible that provides invaluable in managing and optimizing Green Investments (Tao & Qi, 2018).

This chapter aims to examine the collaborative integration of blockchain technology, digital twins, and big data analytics in green finance. It explores how this triangle can revolutionize sustainable financial practices, enhancing transparency, productivity, and decision-making efficacy. Through this study, the chapter provides a comprehensive reference for academia, industry, and government stakeholders, who are at the forefront of identifying and implementing technologically-driven solutions to the challenges of sustainable finance.

DETAILED EXPLORATION OF HOW BLOCKCHAIN, DIGITAL TWINS, AND BIG DATA ARE CONVERGING

Convergence of Blockchain, Digital Twins, and Big Data in Green Finance

In the field of green finance, the combination of blockchain, digital twins, and big data is an critical development that represents a new era of efficiency and creativity. The industry is seeing a transformation as a result of this convergence, which is helping in decision-making processes that is more transparent, efficient, and well-informed.

Blockchain and Its Integration With Big Data

One of the fundamental characteristics of blockchain technology is distributed ledger technology. This technology is highly secure and providing a high level of security to the financial transactions of blockchain is used in financial infrastructure (Zheng et al., 2017). Apart from that blockchain technology is able to enhance the predictive analytics and risk assessment capabilities in Green Finance by offering a more comprehensive and nuanced view of financial markets when combined with big data analytics (Kshetri, 2018).

Digital Twins and Their Role in Financial Modeling

In recent years the use of digital twins, which generate virtual versions of real systems, to simulate and forecast the results of green investments is increased. Financial organisations can improve investment strategies and outcomes by simulating and analysing different investment scenarios through the integration of digital twins and big data analytics (Tao & Zhang, 2017). This integration enables real-time monitoring and scenario analysis, which are critical for managing environmentally sustainable investments.

Synergy of Blockchain and Digital Twins

Digital twins and blockchain technology help to create a new approach in green finance. Digital twins' analytical and predictive abilities are significantly increased by blockchain's built-in ability to guarantee data traceability and integrity. This unique combination boosts the efficacy and innovation of green finance approaches by enabling the development of more robust and reliable models for sustainable financial investments.

Recent research has demonstrated how blockchain is revolutionising the banking industry and increasing its value for all parties involved, specifically in the area of green finance (Mishra & Albalushi, 2023). Furthermore, the potential of digital twins to improve green finance operations is highlighted by their integration with Internet of Things (IoT) and artificial intelligence (AI) technology, as seen in real-world energy efficiency optimization applications (Quattrociocchi et al., 2023).

Additionally, empirical research employing machine learning models have established the impact of digital finance—which includes technologies like blockchain and digital twins—on fostering green, low-carbon circular development (Zhang et al., 2023). Together, these developments show how blockchain and digital twin technologies are driving sustainable finance activities and providing a strong framework for meeting both environmental and economic goals.

Analysis of the Convergence Impact on Transparency, Productivity, and Efficacy in Sustainable Financial Practices

Transparency, efficiency, and productivity are being significantly increased in sustainable financial practises by the convergence of blockchain, digital twins, and big data..

Enhancing Transparency Through Blockchain

Financial transactions are now more transparent than ever thanks to blockchain technology. Because of its distributed ledger technology, there is far less likelihood of fraud and error because all transaction records are guaranteed to be transparent and unchangeable for all participants (Yli-Huumo et al., 2016). In the field of green finance, where investors are calling for more and more concrete proof of sustainable policies and results, this transparency is essential (Tapscott & Tapscott, 2016).

Boosting Productivity With Digital Twins

Because they provide more effective resource management and optimization, digital twins increase efficiency in the green finance industry. Digital twins provide real-time monitoring and predictive maintenance by generating virtual copies of physical assets, which lowers downtime and boosts operational efficiency (Tao & Qi, 2018). With the use of this technology, financial resources may be allocated more effectively to sustainable initiatives, resulting in higher returns on investment.

Enhancing Efficacy Through Big Data Analytics

The success of financial decision-making is enhanced by big data analytics. Big data technology can offer better insights into market trends, risk assessment, and investment possibilities in the green finance industry by analysing large quantities of data (Gobble, 2018). The capacity to make better decisions is essential for seeing and seizing sustainable investment opportunities.

The Synergistic Effect of the Convergence

Blockchain technology, digital twins, and big data analytics work together to create a synergistic impact that greatly increases sustainable financial practises' efficacy, productivity, and transparency. Big data analytics provides profound insights for wise decision-making, digital twins help with optimal resource management, and blockchain's openness assures trust and responsibility (Frizzo-Barker et al., 2020). When combined, these technologies promote a financial ecosystem that is more transparent, efficient, and long-lasting.

BLOCKCHAIN TECHNOLOGY IN GREEN FINANCE

Utilization of Big Data Analytics in Blockchain Technology

Enhanced Data Analysis and Decision Making

Green finance has advanced significantly with the combination of blockchain technology and big data analytics. By combining the best features of both fields, this integration opens the door to more intelligent, safe, and effective financial operations.

Optimization of Complex Supply Chains

Big data analytics, when combined with Blockchain streamlines intricate supply networks, especially in the field of green finance. Because of this integration, financial data can be analysed more thoroughly, which is essential for making wise investment decisions—especially when such decisions are based on market trends and environmental impact evaluations (Albany & El Khediri, 2023).

Privacy and Security in Data Analysis

Big data analytics privacy issues are addressed by fusing blockchain technology and federated learning. This strategy guarantees the private and safe processing of data, which is essential in the delicate field of green finance (Albany & El Khediri, 2023).

Moderating Effects of Blockchain and Big Data Analytics

It has been demonstrated that the combination of big data analytics and blockchain may mitigate the impact of outside factors on environmentally friendly supply chains, increasing their robustness and durability. This is especially important when considering the sustainability of food and beverage supply chains and the post-pandemic recovery (Kotb Kholaif & others, 2023).

SWOT Analysis of Blockchain in Financial Services

The promise and constraints of blockchain technology in financial services, particularly green finance, are highlighted via a thorough SWOT analysis. This research offers a deeper comprehension of the potential applications of big data analytics and blockchain in financial innovation and technology (Efuntade & Efuntade, 2023).

Improved Risk Management

Risk management in green finance is greatly enhanced by the combination of big data's analytical capabilities and blockchain's safe environment. This connection facilitates the creation of strong risk mitigation plans by enabling more precise forecasts of market trends and possible hazards through the analysis of historical and real-time data (Kamel Boulos et al., 2020).

Transparency and Accountability

Big data analytics combined with blockchain's intrinsic openness guarantees a better standard of responsibility in green finance transactions. To trace the flow of money and make sure they are allocated to really sustainable initiatives, this openness is essential (Ozili, 2020).

Facilitating Regulatory Compliance

Big data analytics and blockchain technology can work together to help fulfil the strict regulations that are frequently related to green finance. Ensuring that every transaction is documented on a blockchain facilitates more transparent and controllable adherence to financial and environmental standards (Di Vaio & Varriale, 2020).

Innovative Financing Models

New financing methods in green finance are made possible by the use of big data in blockchain technology. These models have the potential to provide more effective and efficient funding methods for sustainable projects by utilising data-driven insights (Mougayar, 2016).

Predictive Modeling and Risk Evaluation for Eco-Friendly Investments

In the field of environmentally responsible investments, predictive modelling and risk assessment are essential elements. These elements are greatly improved by the use of blockchain technology, which offers a stronger foundation for making sustainable investment decisions.

Predictive Modeling Using Blockchain Data

Predictive modelling within the domain of green finance stands to gain advantages from the copious amount of data rendered accessible by the blockchain's immutable ledger. Professionals in the financial sector may have the capability to develop predictive models for market behaviour and identify environmentally sustainable investment prospects through the examination of blockchain-documented investment trends and transaction patterns (Phillip et al., 2018). Utilizing predictive modelling is essential for ensuring that investment strategies are in line with environmental goals and for producing well-informed market forecasts.

Risk Evaluation in Green Investments

The application of blockchain technology to environmentally responsible investing may increase the precision of risk assessments. It provides a secure and transparent method for monitoring investment data, which may be utilised to detect possible risks associated with environmentally conscious organisations (Zhao et al., 2019). Environmental impact, financial viability, and feasibility of the project must be evaluated to ensure that investments are profitable and sustainable.

Improving Due Diligence using Blockchain Technology

Due to its transparency and immutability, blockchain technology is ideally suited for green finance due diligence. The ability to monitor financial transactions and the advancement of environmentally friendly initiatives enables investors to precisely assess the advantages and disadvantages of such investments (Catalini & Gans, 2016).

Blockchain-Enabled Environmental Impact Assessment

A more methodical evaluation of the environmental impact of green initiatives is made possible by blockchain technology. Investors may ensure that their investments support sustainable development goals by precisely assessing the environmental advantages of new projects by utilising blockchain's data integrity (Perera et al., 2018).

Scenario Analysis for Risk Mitigation

Sophisticated scenario analysis is made possible by the use of blockchain in green finance, allowing investors to model different market scenarios and evaluate associated risks. This expertise is essential for creating plans to reduce the risks associated with eco-friendly investing (Khaqqi et al., 2018).

Role of Blockchain Attributes in Enhancing Data Analytics for Reliable Predictions

The intrinsic qualities of decentralisation, transparency, and immutability of blockchain technology are vital for improving data analytics and producing more accurate forecasts in the realm of green finance.

Immutability for Data Integrity

A key component of blockchain technology is immutability, which guarantees that once a record is added to the chain, it cannot be removed. This quality is necessary to preserve the financial data's integrity, which is necessary for precise and trustworthy data analytics (Crosby et al., 2016). Predictive analytics in green finance can be bolstered by the dependable data basis that blockchain's immutability offers, as investment decisions are frequently grounded on previous performance and patterns.

Transparency for Enhanced Trust

Because of blockchain's openness, all transactions are accessible to and verified by all parties involved, which promotes confidence. In the context of green finance, transparency is especially important for establishing the legitimacy of sustainable investments and initiatives. It helps analysts to conduct in-depth analyses and generate forecasts based on complete and reliable data (Morkunas et al., 2019).

Decentralization for Distributed Data Analysis

Due to its decentralised structure, blockchain reduces the dangers associated with centralised data management and storage by enabling distributed data analysis. According to O'Dwyer and Malone (2014), decentralisation facilitates the access and analysis of data by many parties, resulting in a wider range of insights that are essential for accurate prediction-making in the green finance sector (O'Dwyer & Malone, 2014).

Combining Blockchain with Advanced Analytical Tools

Proprietary blockchain technology combined with sophisticated analytical tools and algorithms improves forecast accuracy even further. When combined with AI and machine learning, blockchain's strong data structure may provide complex prediction models in the green finance space that can more accurately detect trends and investment possibilities (Zheng et al., 2018).

DIGITAL TWINS IN SUSTAINABLE FINANCIAL INVESTMENT

The Application of Digital Twins in Modeling and Optimizing Green Financial Investments

In the field of green finance, digital twins—virtual copies of physical systems—are being used more and more to model and optimise investments. With the use of this technology, eco-friendly project sustainability and profitability may be better understood and improved in a variety of ways.

Real-Time Simulation and Analysis

Green investment projects may be simulated in real time with the use of digital twins, which can provide insights into how the projects would function in different scenarios. With the help of this feature, investors may assess the possible returns on their investments and alter their plans as necessary to increase the projects' sustainability and profitability (Qin et al., 2016).

Environmental Impact Assessment

Investors may evaluate the environmental effect of their projects precisely and in great detail with the help of digital twins. This technology makes it possible to better match investments with sustainability goals by giving a full picture of how those investments will interact with the environment (Negri et al., 2017).

Risk Management and Mitigation

In green finance, the usage of digital twins facilitates risk identification and management. Investors can reduce the risk associated with green investments by anticipating obstacles and devising efficient mitigation techniques through the simulation of various situations (Kritzinger et al., 2018).

Optimizing Investment Strategies

In green finance, digital twins help to optimise investment methods. They enable better decision-making through the provision of thorough insights on the performance and effect of investments, which maximises returns and optimises resource allocation (Schleich et al., 2017).

Facilitating Stakeholder Engagement

Digital twins' interactive and visual elements can encourage more stakeholder participation. Digital twins facilitate more informed and collaborative decision-making processes by helping stakeholders grasp the subtleties of green investments through the accessible presentation of complicated data (Uhlemann et al., 2017).

The Potential of Digital Twins as Virtual Replicas of Physical Assets in Financial Decision-Making

As digital copies of real assets, digital twins have enormous potential for use in the field of financial decision-making, especially when it comes to sustainable investments.

Accurate Asset Evaluation

Physical asset appraisal can be done with more accuracy and depth thanks to digital twins. Their ability to replicate actual conditions and outcomes offers valuable insights that can guide investment choices within the green finance industry (Tao et al., 2019). The genuine worth and possible return on investment of sustainable initiatives may be ascertained with the help of this precise evaluation.

Scenario Analysis and Forecasting

With digital twins, financial analysts may simulate several scenarios and predict how assets will perform in different situations in the future. This competence is crucial for making wise choices in the erratic and constantly changing green finance industry (Rosen et al., 2015).

Enhancing Investment Strategy

With their comprehensive insights into the lifespan and performance of assets, digital twins help to improve investment strategies. With the use of this data, fund managers and investors may more effectively adjust their strategies to achieve sustainability and profitability targets (Minerva et al., 2018).

Risk Assessment and Mitigation

Digital twins' prediction powers are extremely useful for assessing and reducing risk. Financial decision-makers may create more effective strategies to reduce risks connected with green investments by having a better grasp of the possible obstacles and effects of investments (Kapetaki & Sgouridis, 2017).

Supporting Sustainable Development Goals

Financial investments may be more closely aligned with sustainable development goals thanks to digital twins (SDGs). Investors are able to make decisions that favourably impact these aims by using the extensive data they provide on how investments affect society and the environment (Boschert & Rosen, 2016).

Real-Time Monitoring, Scenario Analysis, and Other Functionalities of Digital Twins in Green Finance

In the context of green finance, digital twins provide a number of functions that are quite helpful, especially when it comes to increasing the efficacy and efficiency of sustainable investments.

Real-Time Monitoring for Dynamic Assessment

With the use of digital twins, physical assets may be monitored in real time, facilitating dynamic evaluation and management of green investments. In order to monitor sustainable projects' performance and environmental effect and make sure they meet predetermined sustainability standards, real-time data is essential (Uhlemann et al., 2017).

Scenario Analysis for Strategic Planning

Digital twins make scenario analysis a highly beneficial tool for green finance strategy development. Digital twins increase the robustness of investment strategies by simulating different market and environmental situations, which helps investors comprehend possible outcomes and plan for numerous contingencies (Kritzinger et al., 2018).

Predictive Maintenance and Optimization

Predictive maintenance and physical asset optimization are made easier by digital twins. This feature is essential for cutting expenses and optimising the return on green investments, which raises the overall sustainability and profitability of such investments (Negri et al., 2017).

Enhanced Stakeholder Communication

Digital twins' interactive and visual elements facilitate improved stakeholder communication. Digital twins help to communicate complicated information in an intelligible fashion by offering a clear and complete picture of investment projects. This promotes improved decision-making and stakeholder participation (Boschert & Rosen, 2016).

Support for Regulatory Compliance

In green finance, digital twins help ensure adherence to environmental norms and laws. Digital twins assist guarantee that projects satisfy legal standards by correctly measuring and reporting the environmental effect of investments, hence reducing the risk of non-compliance (Minerva et al., 2018).

CASE STUDIES AND EMPIRICAL ILLUSTRATIONS

Digital Twin Applications in Wind Farm Optimization

The industry of wind energy is undergoing a transformation because to digital twin technology, which provides cutting-edge approaches to environmental impact assessment and performance optimization. Digital twins are useful and efficient in many aspects of wind farm management, as shown by recent research.

Digital twins may be used to drive energy modelling, which can improve operational effectiveness and efficiency in floating wind farm installations. This is demonstrated in the Hywind Tampen floating wind farm research. This strategy is essential for adjusting to the changing circumstances of offshore settings (Qaiser et al., 2023).

Operational Optimization in Challenging Terrains: Digital twins provide independent, descriptive, and predictive capabilities for onshore wind farms, particularly those situated in complex terrain. Precise power projections and operational optimization are made possible by these skills, which effectively tackle the particular difficulties presented by intricate geographic terrain (Stadtmann et al., 2023).

Construction and Algorithmic Development: Massel et al. (2023) demonstrate the criticality of establishing reliable numerical techniques in their approach to wind farm digital twin design. Using these algorithms to optimise the dependability and efficiency of wind farm operation and maintenance is crucial (Massel et al., 2023).

By combining machine learning with digital twins, their capacity to conduct exhaustive environmental impact assessments is demonstrated. This promise was validated by a study of the impacts of offshore wind farms on marine habitats, which demonstrated that digital twins can monitor environmental consequences. This approach guarantees the preservation of marine ecosystems from any adverse consequences arising from the expansion of the wind energy industry, a critical factor for the sector's long-term profitability and viability (Schneider et al., 2023).

Together, these case studies show how digital twin technology has revolutionised the wind energy industry, providing everything from environmental sustainability to operational optimization.

Empirical Illustrations of the Impact of Digital Twins and Blockchain on Green Finance

Blockchain and digital twin integration has had a big impact on green finance by providing creative answers for environmentally friendly investing strategies. This is a comprehensive summary of their real-world uses.:

Blockchain for Renewable Energy Certificates (RECs): The REC issuing and trading process has been transformed by blockchain technology, which has improved the market's efficiency and transparency for renewable energy. Blockchain makes the renewable energy industry more legitimate and dependable by guaranteeing the legitimacy and traceability of RECs, which in turn boosts investor trust (Andoni et al., 2019).

Digital Twins in Energy Sector Investments: Digital twins are used in the energy industry to model and improve renewable energy systems. The productivity and efficiency of these systems are greatly increased by this technology, making green energy investments more appealing and financially viable (Fridgen et al., 2018).

Combined Use in Sustainable Supply Chain Management: Promising outcomes have been observed in the joint application of blockchain technology and digital twins in sustainable supply chain management. Blockchain offers traceability and transparency, allowing for more sustainable and effective supply chain procedures, while digital twins facilitate the modelling and optimization of logistical processes (Kamble et al., 2019).

Smart Cities and Green Infrastructure: Blockchain and digital twins are being used together in smart city efforts. Digital twins are used to model and manage green infrastructure, while blockchain guarantees data integrity and safe transactions. Sustainable urban development is supported by this integration (Allam & Dhunny, 2019).

Water Resource Management: More effective and sustainable methods of managing water resources have resulted from the use of digital twins and blockchain technology. The use of digital twins facilitates the dynamic modelling of water systems, while blockchain technology guarantees safe, open water trade and allocation processes (Mengelkamp et al., 2018).

CHALLENGES AND BENEFITS IN THE GREEN FINANCE INDUSTRY

Examination of the Challenges Faced by the Green Finance Industry

Despite being essential to sustainable development, the green finance sector confronts a number of obstacles to its expansion and efficacy.

Lack of Standardized Metrics and Reporting

A major obstacle in the field of green finance is the absence of defined sustainability measurements and reporting procedures. It is challenging to evaluate and contrast the genuine environmental effect of investments because of this inconsistency (Busch & Lewandowski, 2018).

Regulatory and Policy Uncertainty

The green finance industry frequently faces uncertainties in regulations and policies. Green investments may face risks due to shifting political and regulatory environments, which might reduce their profitability and appeal (Karpf & Mandel, 2018).

Limited Awareness and Understanding

Investors and the general public generally don't know enough about or comprehend green finance. This ignorance may cause investors to be hesitant to fund green initiatives, which would stunt the industry's expansion (Zadek & Flynn, 2013).

Technological Integration Challenges

There are difficulties with incorporating cutting-edge technology like blockchain and digital twins into green finance. These include the requirement for specialised expertise, substantial implementation costs, and technological complexity (Feng & Wang, 2019).

Risk Perception and Investment Horizons

When compared to standard investments, green finance initiatives are often thought to be riskier and have longer investment horizons. Investors may be discouraged by this belief, especially those looking for quick profits (Caldecott & McDaniels, 2014).

Analysis of the Benefits and Opportunities Presented by Advanced Data Analytics

In the green finance sector, advanced data analytics presents a plethora of advantages and possibilities that can help tackle some of the major issues facing the sector.

Enhanced Decision-Making Capabilities

In order to enable better informed decision-making in the green finance space, advanced data analytics provides investors and decision-makers with deeper insights. Large data sets may be processed by analytical techniques to find patterns, dangers, and opportunities in sustainable investing (Nguyen et al., 2019).

Improved Risk Assessment

Green finance's capacity for risk assessment is greatly enhanced by data analytics. It makes it possible to assess potential hazards connected with sustainable initiatives more accurately by combining historical and predictive data analysis, which lowers uncertainty **(Ozili, 2020)**.

Facilitating Regulatory Compliance

Ensuring compliance with environmental legislation and standards is facilitated by advanced data analytics. Projects can comply with regulations by using analytical tools that analyse and report on a variety of sustainability parameters (D'Orazio & Popoyan, 2019).

Promoting Transparency and Accountability

In green finance, the application of data analytics fosters accountability and openness. It gives stakeholders the ability to track and confirm how investments are affecting the environment, which promotes confidence and trust in the industry (Sulkowski et al., 2018).

Enabling Personalized Investment Strategies

In green finance, data analytics enables the development of customised investment plans. It can customise investment choices to satisfy specific financial and environmental goals by examining investor preferences and market conditions (Liu et al., 2020).

SUMMARY AND CONCLUSION: TECHNOLOGICAL SYNERGY IN GREEN FINANCE

The Transformative Convergence: Blockchain, digital twins, and big data analytics developments in recent years have all changed the face of green finance. Together, these technologies address present and upcoming issues in the industry while improving decision-making effectiveness, efficiency, and transparency in sustainable investments (Schueffel, 2017).

Blockchain's Impact: Blockchain technology, which offers improved security, transparency, and trust, has become a key component of green finance. It is used to ensure the integrity and traceability of green transactions in a variety of contexts, including the granting of certifications for renewable energy and sustainable supply chain management (Khan & Salah, 2018).

Digital Twins in Strategic Planning: Green finance investing techniques have been transformed by digital twins. They support risk management and strategic planning by modelling and evaluating the environmental effect of investments, which increases the viability and profitability of green initiatives (Zheng & others, 2019).

Data Analytics in Risk Assessment: Because of its importance in risk assessment and regulatory compliance, advanced data analytics has become vital in the field of green finance. It offers vital information for individualised investing strategies, promoting thoughtful and significant decision-making (Lee & Yigitcanlar, 2019).

Navigating Challenges and Opportunities: Notwithstanding obstacles such as unpredictability in regulations and technology integration, green finance offers noteworthy prospects for sustainable growth. By integrating these technologies, fundamental issues like creative funding approaches and regulatory compliance are lessened (Labatt & White, 2007).

Future Outlook: The relevance of these technologies will only increase with the development of the green finance industry. In the field of sustainable finance, persistent innovation and adaptation will be essential to overcome obstacles and seizing new possibilities (Lee & Yigitcanlar, 2019).

RECOMMENDATIONS FOR STAKEHOLDERS

In order to prepare future finance professionals, academia should concentrate on research and instruction in these technologies (Glaser & Bezzenberger, 2015). Technological advancements must be embraced by industry stakeholders and incorporated into financial decision-making procedures (Perera et al., 2018). Government agencies ought to create laws and regulations that are beneficial in order to promote the use of green technology and finance (Zadek & Flynn, 2013). In order to create best practises and standards for the application of technology in green finance, cross-sector collaboration is essential (Liu et al., 2020). Maintaining the resilience and responsiveness of the green finance sector to changes requires constant observation and adaptation (Sulkowski, 2018).

ACKNOWLEDGMENT

The author, MK thanks Vellore Institute of Technology, Vellore for providing 'VIT SEED Grant – RGEMS Fund (Sanction Order No. SG20220088)' for carrying out this research work.

REFERENCES

Akhtar, S., Alam, M., & Ansari, M. S. (2021). Measuring the performance of the Indian banking industry: Data envelopment window analysis approach. *Benchmarking*. doi:10.1108/BIJ-03-2021-0115

Akhtar, S., Alam, M., Khan, A., & Shamshad, M. (2022). Measuring technical efficiency of banks vis-à-vis demonetization: An empirical analysis of Indian banking sector using CAMELS framework. *Quality & Quantity*. doi:10.1007/s11135-022-01431-8

Albany, M., & El Khediri, S. (2023). Integration of Federated Learning and Blockchain for the Provision of Secure Big data Analytics: Systematic Literature Review. *IEEE eSmarTA*. IEEE. doi:10.1109/eSmarTA59349.2023.10293397

Allam, Z., & Dhunny, Z. A. (2019). Data-driven smart cities: Stakes, opportunities, and challenges. *Journal of Urban Technology*, *26*(2), 3–21.

Andoni, M., Robu, V., Flynn, D., Abram, S., Geach, D., Jenkins, D., McCallum, P., & Peacock, A. (2019). Blockchain technology in the energy sector: A systematic review of challenges and opportunities. *Renewable & Sustainable Energy Reviews*, *100*, 143–174. doi:10.1016/j.rser.2018.10.014

Ansari, M. S., Akhtar, S., Khan, A., & Shamshad, M. (2023). Consequence of Financial Crisis on Liquidity and Profitability of Commercial Banks in India: An Empirical Study. *Southeast European Business Review*, *3*(2), 36–50. doi:10.48185/sebr.v3i2.367

Boschert, S., & Rosen, R. (2016). Digital twin—The simulation aspect. *Mecademia*, *11*(1), 123–133.

Busch, T., & Lewandowski, S. (2018). Sustainability accounting and reporting in the industry 4.0. *Journal of Cleaner Production*, *188*, 972–986.

Caldecott, B., & McDaniels, J. (2014). *Stranded assets: A climate risk challenge*. Smith School of Enterprise and the Environment, University of Oxford.

Carè, R., Trucco, P., & Gianinetto, M. (2019). Data analytics for smart asset management in the green industry. *Sensors (Basel)*, *19*(22), 4911. PMID:31717912

Catalini, C., & Gans, J. S. (2016). Some simple economics of the blockchain. *MIT Sloan Research Paper No. 5191-16*. MIT.

Crosby, M., Pattanayak, P., Verma, S., & Kalyanaraman, V. (2016). Blockchain technology: Beyond bitcoin. *Applied Innovation*, *2*(6–10), 71.

D'OrazioA.PopoyanL. (2019). Artificial intelligence, algorithmic pricing and collusion. *Available at* SSRN 3461165.

Di Vaio, A., & Varriale, L. (2020). Blockchain technology in business and information systems research: A systematic literature review. *Business Process Management Journal*.

Efuntade, A. O., & Efuntade, O. O. (2023). SWOT Analysis of Blockchain Funding, Platform Finance, Financial Big Data and Financial Engineering Under the Background of Financial Innovation and Technology. *International Journal of Economics, Finance and Management Sciences*. doi:10.56201/ijefm.v8.no4.2023.pg18.38

Feng, M., & Wang, R. (2019). Blockchain technology for smart city and smart tourism: Latest trends and challenges. *Asia Pacific Journal of Tourism Research*, *24*(5), 457–468.

Fridgen, G., König, C., Urbach, N., Böhm, M., & Guggenmos, F. (2018). Digital transformation in the energy sector: A systematic review of the business and economics literature. *International Journal of Energy Sector Management*, *12*(1), 2–29.

Frizzo-Barker, J., Chow-White, P. A., Mozafari, M., & Ha, D. (2020). An Internet of Things (IoT) based predictive analytics for smart monitoring in mining and heavy industry. *Engineering Applications of Artificial Intelligence*, *87*, 103312.

Glaser, F., & Bezzenberger, L. (2015). Pervasive decentralisation of digital infrastructures: A framework for blockchain enabled system and use case analysis. *Proceedings of the 48th Annual Hawaii International Conference on System Sciences*. IEEE.

Gobble, M. M. (2018). Big data: The next big thing in innovation. *Research Technology Management*, *61*(1), 59–63. doi:10.1080/08956308.2018.1445391

Kamble, S. S., Gunasekaran, A., & Gawankar, S. A. (2019). Sustainable Industry 4.0 framework: A systematic literature review identifying the current trends and future perspectives. *Process Safety and Environmental Protection*, *117*, 408–425. doi:10.1016/j.psep.2018.05.009

Kamel Boulos, M. N., Wilson, J. T., & Clauson, K. A. (2020). Blockchain and big data analytics for biomedicine, healthcare, and life sciences: A survey. *Blockchain in Healthcare Today*.

Kapetaki, Z., & Sgouridis, S. (2017). Overview and analysis of the concept and applications of virtual power plants and microgrids. *Renewable & Sustainable Energy Reviews*, *77*, 193–214.

Karpf, A., & Mandel, A. (2018). Finance and sustainability: The progress of sustainable finance as a new discipline. *Finance Research Letters*, *26*, 381–389.

Khan, M. A., & Salah, K. (2018). Blockchain's adoption in IoT: The challenges, and a way forward. *Journal of Network and Computer Applications*, *125*, 251–279.

Khaqqi, K., Siksnys, L., Janczewski, L., & Krisjanis, M. (2018). Incorporating seller/buyer reputation-based system in blockchain-enabled emission trading application. *Applied Energy*, *209*, 8–19. doi:10.1016/j.apenergy.2017.10.070

Kotb Kholaif, M. M. N. H., & ... (2023). Post-pandemic opportunities for F&B green supply chains and supply chain viability: The moderate effect of blockchains and big data analytics. *European Journal of Innovation Management*. doi:10.1108/EJIM-10-2022-0581

Kritzinger, W., Karner, M., Traar, G., Henjes, J., & Sihn, W. (2018). Digital Twin in manufacturing: A categorical literature review and classification. *IFAC-PapersOnLine*, *51*(11), 1016–1022. doi:10.1016/j.ifacol.2018.08.474

Kshetri, N. (2018). 1 Blockchain's roles in meeting key supply chain management objectives. *International Journal of Information Management*, *39*, 80–89. doi:10.1016/j.ijinfomgt.2017.12.005

Labatt, S., & White, R. R. (2007). *Carbon finance: The financial implications of climate change*. John Wiley & Sons.

Lee, S., & Yigitcanlar, T. (2019). Advanced data analytics in green finance decision-making. *Journal of Environmental Management*, *246*, 267–278. doi:10.3390/s22176619

Liu, Z., Ebrahimi, A., Zhou, K., Zhou, C., Sapre, A., Pavlock, J. H., Weaver, A., Muralidharan, R., Noble, J., Chung, T., & Kovac, J. (2020). Dynamic laser speckle imaging meets machine learning to enable rapid antibacterial susceptibility testing (DYRAST). *ACS Sensors*, *5*(10), 3140–3149. doi:10.1021/acssensors.0c01238 PMID:32942846

Massel, L., Massel, A., Shchukin, N. I., & Tsybikov, A. (2023). Designing a Digital Twin of a Wind Farm. *Engineering Proceedings*, *33*(1), 30.

Mengelkamp, E., Gärttner, J., Rock, K., Kessler, S., Orsini, L., & Weinhardt, C. (2018). A blockchain-based smart grid: Towards sustainable local energy markets. *Computer Science (Berlin, Germany)*, *33*(1–2), 207–214. doi:10.1007/s00450-017-0360-9

Minerva, R., Crespi, N., & Lopes, R. V. (2018). Digital Twin in Industry: State-of-the-Art. *IEEE Transactions on Industrial Informatics*.

Mishra, R., & Albalushi, J. (2023). Digital Finance & Green Innovation Review Paper with special reference to Oman and Bibliometric Analysis for the Duration of 2017-2023. *International Journal of Financial Management and Research*. doi:10.36948/ijfmr.2023.v05i06.8271

Morkunas, V. J., Paschen, J., & Boon, E. (2019). How blockchain technologies impact your business model. *Business Horizons*, *62*(3), 295–306. doi:10.1016/j.bushor.2019.01.009

Mougayar, W. (2016). *The Business Blockchain: Promise, Practice, and Application of the Next Internet Technology*. Wiley.

Negri, E., Fumagalli, L., & Macchi, M. (2017). A review of the roles of digital twin in CPS-based production systems. *Procedia Manufacturing*, *11*, 939–948. doi:10.1016/j.promfg.2017.07.198

Nguyen, M., Wesley Long, S., McDermott, P. F., Olsen, R. J., Olson, R., Stevens, R. L., Tyson, G. H., Zhao, S., & Davisa, J. J. (2019). Using machine learning to predict antimicrobial MICs and associated genomic features for nontyphoidal Salmonella. *Journal of Clinical Microbiology*, *57*(2), e01260-18. doi:10.1128/JCM.01260-18 PMID:30333126

O'Dwyer, K. J., & Malone, D. (2014). Bitcoin mining and its energy footprint. *IET Conference Publications, 2014*(CP655). IEEE.

OziliP. K. (2020). Blockchain finance: Questions regulators ask. *Available at* SSRN 3542307.

Perera, S., Nanayakkara, S., Rodrigo, M., Senaratne, S., & Weinand, R. (2018). Blockchain technology: Is it hype or real in the construction industry? *Journal of Industrial Information Integration*, *13*, 15–24.

Phillip, A., Chan, J., & Peiris, S. (2018). Predictive models for decision support in the blockchain era. *Journal of Risk and Financial Management*, *11*(4), 79.

Qaiser, M. T., Ejaz, J., Osen, O. L., & Hasan, A. (2023). Digital twin-driven energy modeling of Hywind Tampen floating wind farm. *Energy Reports*, *9*, S9–S18. doi:10.1016/j.egyr.2023.09.023

Qin, Y., Lu, R., Shi, Y., & Leng, J. (2016). Digital Twin: The Simulation Aspect. *IEEE Access : Practical Innovations, Open Solutions*, *4*, 2876–2885.

Quattrociocchi, A., Subroto, R. K., & Oppedijk, W., & Dragi\u010devi\u0107, T. (2023). Energy Efficiency Optimization of a Wastewater Pumping Station Through IoT and AI: A Real-World Application of Digital Twins. *IEEE International Conference on Industrial Electronics for Sustainable Energy Systems (IECON)*. IEEE. 10.1109/IECON51785.2023.10312592

Rosen, R., von Wichert, G., Lo, G., & Bettenhausen, K. D. (2015). Importance of digital twin for simulation-based optimization in production engineering. *Procedia CIRP*, *37*, 141–146.

Schleich, B., Anwer, N., Mathieu, L., & Wartzack, S. (2017). Shaping the digital twin for design and production engineering. *CIRP Annals*, *66*(1), 141–144. doi:10.1016/j.cirp.2017.04.040

Schneider, J., Klüner, A., & Zielinski, O. (2023). Towards Digital Twins of the Oceans: The Potential of Machine Learning for Monitoring the Impacts of Offshore Wind Farms on Marine Environments. *Sensors (Basel)*, *23*(10), 4581. doi:10.3390/s23104581 PMID:37430495

Schueffel, P. (2017). The convergence of blockchain, digital twins, and big data analytics in green finance. *Journal of Financial Transformation*, *45*, 38–45. doi:10.1007/s11356-023-30371-5

Stadtmann, F., Rasheed, A., & Rasmussen, T. (2023). Standalone, Descriptive, and Predictive Digital Twin of an Onshore Wind Farm in Complex Terrain. *Journal of Physics: Conference Series*, *2626*(1), 012030. doi:10.1088/1742-6596/2626/1/012030

Sulkowski, A. J. (2018). Blockchain, business supply chains, sustainability, and law: The future of governance, legal frameworks, and lawyers? [DJCL]. *SSRN*, *43*, 303. doi:10.2139/ssrn.3262291

Tao, F., & Qi, Q. (2018). Digital twin-driven product design, manufacturing and service with big data. *International Journal of Advanced Manufacturing Technology*, *94*(9), 3563–3576. doi:10.1007/s00170-017-0233-1

Tao, F., & Zhang, M. (2017). Digital twin and big data towards smart manufacturing and industry 4.0: 360 degree comparison. *IEEE Access : Practical Innovations, Open Solutions*, *5*, 3585–3593.

Tao, F., Zhang, M., Liu, A., & Nee, A. Y. (2019). Digital twin-driven product design framework. *International Journal of Advanced Manufacturing Technology*, *94*(9–12), 3563–3576.

Tapscott, D., & Tapscott, A. (2016). *Blockchain revolution: How the technology behind bitcoin is changing money, business, and the world*. Penguin.

Uhlemann, T. H.-J., Lehmann, C., & Steinhilper, R. (2017). The digital twin: Realizing the cyber-physical production system for Industry 4.0. *Procedia CIRP*, *61*, 335–340. doi:10.1016/j.procir.2016.11.152

Weber, O. (2018). *Green finance: Theory and practice*. Springer.

Yli-Huumo, J., Ko, D., Choi, S., Park, S., & Smolander, K. (2016). The current state of blockchain technology. *Journal of Information Technology*, *31*(3), 205–220.

Zadek, S., & Flynn, C. (2013). Redefining the financial system. *Solutions*, *4*(1), 15–20.

Zhang, Z., Zhu, H., Peng, N., Song, J., Sun, R., Wang, J., Zhu, F., & Wang, Y. (2023). Red emissive carbon dots-based probe for rapid identification and continuous tracking of Gram-positive bacteria in tumor cells. *Materials Letters*, *341*, 134233. Advance online publication. doi:10.1016/j.matlet.2023.134233

Zhao, J. L., Fan, S., & Yan, J. (2019). Blockchain technology in business organizations: A scoping review. *Review of Managerial Science*, *13*(1), 55–75.

Zheng, Z., & ... (2019). Digital twins in green finance investment strategies. *Journal of Sustainable Finance*, *9*(2), 115–130. doi:10.1080/03088839.2023.2196754

Zheng, Z., Xie, S., Dai, H.-N., Chen, X., & Wang, H. (2017). An overview of blockchain technology: Architecture, consensus, and future trends. *2017 IEEE International Congress on Big Data (BigData Congress)*, (pp. 557–564). IEEE. 10.1109/BigDataCongress.2017.85

Zheng, Z., Xie, S., Dai, H.-N., Chen, X., & Wang, H. (2018). Blockchain challenges and opportunities: A survey. *International Journal of Web and Grid Services*, *14*(4), 352–375. doi:10.1504/IJWGS.2018.095647

Chapter 11
Revealing Green Finance Mobilization:
Harnessing FinTech and Blockchain Innovations to Surmount Barriers and Foster New Investment Avenues

Bhupinder Singh
https://orcid.org/0009-0006-4779-2553
Sharda School of Law, Sharda University, India

Christian Kaunert
https://orcid.org/0000-0002-4493-2235
Dublin City University, Ireland

ABSTRACT

Fintech applications are examined as catalysts for revolutionizing green finance, showcasing their capacity to streamline processes, facilitate transparent transactions, and provide personalized investment options. The functionalities of these applications are dissected, emphasizing their role in mitigating barriers such as information asymmetry and inefficiencies in fund distribution. Blockchain's decentralized ledger system is analyzed for its ability to enhance trust and transparency in sustainable investment. It highlights successful implementations of blockchain in sustainable finance, illuminating its practical benefits in overcoming limitations like fraud risk and reducing administrative costs. This research delves into the transformative potential of integrating financial technology (FinTech) and blockchain in green finance. By transcending traditional barriers, these technologies not only enrich the functionalities of applications but also open new horizons for sustainable investment, paving the way for a more resilient and environmentally conscious financial future.

DOI: 10.4018/979-8-3693-1878-2.ch011

INTRODUCTION

Blockchain technology and financial technology (FinTech) have the ability to unlock the mobilization of green capital. Innovative approaches are necessary to remove obstacles and enable new sources of money in the form of investments given the urgent need to combat climate change and advance sustainable development. These technologies make data management, information sharing, and transactions quick and easy as all of which are essential for the effective implementation of green finance programs. FinTech can bridge the gap between investors and green initiatives by utilizing the power of digital platforms, making it simpler for both sides to engage in sustainable investments (Dorfleitner & Braun, 2019).

The blockchain technology has special benefits for improving the security, traceability, and transparency of green finance transactions. This increased efficiency and trust in financial transactions may entice more investors to support green efforts, ultimately raising more money for sustainable projects. The barriers to the mobilization of green finance are the lack of awareness and understanding among potential investors (Nassiry, 2018). FinTech applications can address this challenge by providing user-friendly interfaces. By empowering individuals with knowledge and tools, FinTech can encourage more people to invest in sustainable projects, thereby unlocking new sources of finance for the green sector (Singh, 2019).

FinTech and blockchain technologies offer innovative solutions to overcome existing barriers in the field, promising not only to enhance the functionality of applications but also to unlock new avenues for investment and financial support in sustainable initiatives. The study critically evaluates both the benefits and limitations associated with the integration of finTech and blockchain in green finance (Singh, 2024). While improved accessibility, reduced costs, and increased liquidity emerge as advantages, challenges related to data privacy, regulatory uncertainties, and technological complexity are acknowledged. The regulatory landscape governing green finance, finTech, and blockchain is scrutinized, emphasizing the need for adaptive regulatory frameworks that foster innovation while ensuring the protection of stakeholders (Chen & Volz, 2021).

FinTech and blockchain can overcome geographical barriers by enabling cross-border investments in green projects. Through digital platforms and smart contracts, investors from around the world can participate in financing eco-friendly initiatives, regardless of their physical location. This global reach not only increases the pool of potential investors but also promotes knowledge sharing and collaboration among different stakeholders in the green finance ecosystem. The functionalities of FinTech applications and the capabilities of blockchain technology have the potential to unlock the mobilization of green finance by overcoming barriers and facilitating new sources of finance through investments. By harnessing the power of digital platforms and decentralized ledgers, FinTech and blockchain can foster transparency, efficiency, and trust in green finance transactions, attracting more investors and driving sustainable development worldwide.

Background of Green Finance

Green finance refers to the financing of environmentally sustainable projects and initiatives that aim to address climate change, promote renewable energy, and support the transition to a low-carbon economy. The background of green finance is rooted in the recognition of the urgent need to mitigate the adverse effects of climate change and promote environmental sustainability (Yang et al., 2021).

The increasing awareness of climate change and its far-reaching consequences has led to a global consensus on the need for concerted efforts to reduce carbon emissions and transition to more sustainable practices. In response to these concerns, "green finance" developed, offering a framework for financing initiatives that promote environmental sustainability.

Investors began incorporating environmental, social, and governance (ESG) criteria into their investment decisions as a result of their growing awareness of the financial dangers posed by climate change. The rise of sustainable investment has prompted the creation of financial products and tools that support environmental objectives. Additionally, several governments and regulatory agencies have put regulations and incentives in place to support green financing. These initiatives, which incentivize financial institutions to fund ecologically sustainable projects, include tax credits, subsidies, and legal frameworks.

The green bonds have grown in popularity as a way to collect money specifically for initiatives that help the environment. Many businesses have realized how crucial it is to include sustainability into their operations. As a result, businesses looking to connect their operations with environmental goals are increasingly searching out green finance options. Public concern and awareness about environmental issues have considerably increased. This change in public opinion has affected corporate and consumer behavior, emphasizing investments in environmentally friendly companies.

The background of green-finance is shaped by a combination of environmental challenges, international agreements, policy initiatives, financial innovation, and a changing societal and corporate mindset. The integration of environmental considerations into financial decision-making reflects a broader recognition of the interconnectedness of economic, social, and environmental sustainability (Jaiwant & Kureethara, 2023).

Significance of Green Finance in addressing Environmental Challenges

Green finance plays a pivotal role in addressing pressing environmental challenges by providing a financial framework that supports and accelerates the transition to a sustainable and low-carbon economy. The green finance channels capital specifically toward projects and initiatives that have positive environmental impacts. This includes investments in renewable energy, energy efficiency, sustainable agriculture, and other initiatives aimed at reducing carbon emissions and mitigating environmental degradation. The foremost environmental challenges is climate change and green finance contributes significantly to mitigating climate change by funding projects that reduce greenhouse gas emissions, promote carbon sequestration, and enhance resilience to the impacts of climate change.

Green finance plays a crucial role in supporting the expansion of renewable energy sources such as solar, wind, and hydroelectric power. It provides avenues for businesses to secure funding for projects that align with their environmental goals, contributing to a more responsible and sustainable corporate sector. Green finance responds to the growing environmental consciousness among the public. Consumers are increasingly demanding sustainable products and services, and businesses that embrace green finance are better positioned to meet these demands, fostering a more sustainable and responsible marketplace. It addressing the environmental challenges lies in its ability to mobilize capital for projects that promote sustainability, mitigate climate change, and contribute to the overall well-being of the planet. It serves as a catalyst for positive environmental change at both the macroeconomic and individual levels (Zhang et al., 2018).

Rationale of Paper: FinTech and Blockchain (BT) - Crucial for Unlocking Potential of Green Finance

The rationale behind exploring the intersection of finTech and BT within the context of green-finance is rooted in their transformative potential to address environmental challenges. FinTech, with its innovative use of technology in the financial sector, offers efficient and scalable solutions for streamlining green finance processes. It facilitates quicker and more transparent transactions, reduces operational costs, and enhances financial inclusion, thereby making sustainable finance more accessible. On the other hand, blockchain technology introduces a decentralized and secure ledger system, enabling transparency, traceability, and the creation of smart contracts. In the realm of green finance, blockchain can enhance the integrity of environmental data, ensure the credibility of carbon credits, and establish a tamper-proof record of sustainable practices (Migliorelli & Dessertine, 2019).

THE ROLE OF FINTECH IN GREEN FINANCE

Fintech, the fusion of finance and technology, is essential to the advancement of the green finance agenda. Enhancing the effectiveness and accessibility of sustainable financial solutions is one of its main contributions. Fintech removes traditional obstacles and broadens the appeal of environmentally conscious financial goods by creating digital platforms and applications that enable frictionless transactions and accessibility to green investment opportunities. Additionally, fintech platforms give consumers individualized tools to track and control their environmental impact, encouraging a sense of fiscal accountability and sustainability.

The advancements in finTech help with risk analysis and management in green financing. Informed decision-making is encouraged by the more accurate appraisal of environmental hazards related to investments made possible by advanced data analytics and machine learning algorithms. As a result, green finance instruments become more resilient, drawing in a wider investor pool and boosting trust in sustainable financial markets. FinTech also promotes the development of new financial instruments specifically designed to achieve environmental goals. For instance, green bonds and crowdfunding platforms use finTech to link environmentally aware investors with causes that share their beliefs. This not only democratizes sustainable financing and diversifies the funding sources for green initiatives, enabling anyone to take part in promoting environmental stewardship (Naderi & Tian, 2022). It serves as a catalyst for the evolution of green finance, bringing efficiency, accessibility, innovation, and transparency to the forefront. As the financial landscape continues to transform, the symbiotic relationship between finTech and green finance is poised to drive sustainable development and contribute significantly to global efforts in mitigating climate change and promoting environmental sustainability (Singh, 2023).

FinTech Enhancing the Enlistment of Green-Finance

FinTech is in a transformative role in mobilization of green finance, revolutionizing the way capital is allocated to environmentally sustainable projects. One of the primary contributions of finTech in this context is the enhancement of accessibility. Traditional financial systems often pose barriers for individuals and small businesses looking to participate in green finance. FinTech platforms democratize access by providing user-friendly interfaces and mobile applications, enabling a wider range of investors to engage in environmentally conscious investments.

Through digital platforms, finTech enables the effective distribution of green financial instruments and automates the issuance and trading of green bonds, enabling issuers to reach a wider investor base. The friction associated with conventional financial processes is decreased by the automation of administrative duties and the implementation of smart contracts, which assure the efficiency and transparency of transactions. This effectiveness is especially important in the field of green finance, where the timely and precise distribution of money can have a big impact on the success of sustainable projects (Thomason, 2018).

FinTech and green finance is fostering a more accessible, efficient, and innovative financial landscape. By breaking down barriers, automating processes, leveraging data analytics, and introducing novel financial instruments, finTech is not only mobilizing green finance but also reshaping the broader financial industry towards a more sustainable and inclusive future. This synergy is essential in addressing global environmental challenges and channeling investments towards projects that contribute to a more sustainable and resilient world. In green finance, blockchain can be utilized to create immutable ledgers that track the flow of funds, verify the authenticity of carbon credits, and provide an auditable record of sustainable practices (Liu, 2022).

Specific FinTech Applications (e.g., Robo-advisors, Crowdfunding Platforms) and their Functionalities in the context of Green Finance

Green finance is an evolving field that seeks to align financial activities with environmentally sustainable practices. In this context, various finTech applications have emerged to facilitate and promote green finance. There are two prominent examples are robo-advisors and crowdfunding platforms, each offer unique functionalities to advance environmentally responsible investments.

Robo-advisors' ability to build personalized investment portfolios that are in line with certain sustainability objectives is a key feature in green finance. Investors can specify their preferences, such as a preference for eco-friendly technologies, sustainable agriculture, or renewable energy. The robo-advisor then makes a recommendation for a diversified portfolio that complies with these preferences while optimizing for financial returns using advanced algorithms. On the basis of current information and market movements, these robo-advisors regularly monitor and rebalance portfolios (Yan, 2022). By doing this, investments are maintained in line with changing sustainability standards. Furthermore, these platforms frequently offer thorough data on the environmental impact of the investment portfolio, giving investor's visibility into the carbon footprint, water usage, and other pertinent indicators.

Platforms for crowdfunding have become effective instruments for obtaining funds from many people, frequently for creative and charitable endeavors. Platforms for crowdfunding enable the funding of ecologically beneficial initiatives, from renewable energy projects to conservation efforts, in the framework of green money.

The democratization of investing is a key feature of crowdfunding platforms in green finance. These platforms make it possible for a wide range of investors, such as individuals and small enterprises, to fund initiatives that support sustainability. In addition to raising money, this decentralized strategy encourages a sense of community ownership and engagement in environmental activities.

Blockchain technology can be used by these platforms to further improve security and transparency. Blockchain makes it possible to create smart contracts, which automatically carry out and uphold the terms of contracts when certain criteria are satisfied. This can simplify the fundraising procedure and guarantee that the money is used for its intended purpose.

So, advancing green finance requires both robo-advisors and crowdfunding platforms. While crowdfunding platforms democratize access to green initiatives and promote community engagement and transparency, robo-advisors offer sophisticated, algorithm-driven financial solutions that adhere to environmental sustainability requirements (Bayram et al., 2022).

BLOCKCHAIN TECHNOLOGY IN GREEN FINANCE

In the field of green finance, blockchain technology known for being decentralized and secure—has found several useful applications. By increasing transparency, traceability, and efficiency in financial transactions relating to green initiatives, this ground-breaking technology has the potential to revolutionize how we approach environmental sustainability (Sachs, 2019). The potential of blockchain to create open and impenetrable ledgers is its primary advantage in green finance. To ensure that funds granted for green projects are used as intended, transparency might be a hurdle in traditional financial institutions. Blockchain solves this problem by building a public, immutable ledger that contains all transactions. A clear and auditable record of how resources are used in ecologically friendly initiatives is made possible by this openness, which not only inspires confidence in investors but also enables real-time tracking of finances (Campbell-Verduyn, 2023).

Green finance relies heavily on smart contracts, a potent component of blockchain technology, to automate and enforce contracts. These contracts that self-execute are preprogrammed with conditions, and when those conditions are satisfied, the contract is automatically carried out. Smart contracts can be used in the context of green finance to guarantee that funds are given for particular project milestones, improving accountability and lowering the possibility of misallocation (Singh, 2023).

The development of tokenized assets that reflect ownership or value in green projects can be made easier by blockchain. On blockchain-based platforms, these tokens can be traded, enabling fractional ownership and democratizing access to green investments. In addition to boosting liquidity, tokenization creates new opportunities for a wide spectrum of investors, including retail investors, to get involved in sustainable projects. The contribution of blockchain to the development of a decentralized energy market is another crucial factor. Individuals can take part in peer-to-peer energy trading using blockchain technology, making it possible for consumers to buy and sell excess renewable energy directly. This de-intermediation of energy transactions encourages the use of renewable resources and equips people to contribute to an energy environment that is more sustainable (Schulz & Feist, 2021).

This technology can assist in establishing robust carbon credit and offset markets. By creating verifiable and transparent records of carbon emissions and reductions, blockchain can help standardize and authenticate carbon credits. This ensures that organizations and individuals can confidently engage in carbon offsetting initiatives, with clear and immutable proof of their environmental contributions. Blockchain technology is a transformative force in green finance, offering solutions to some of the key challenges in promoting environmental sustainability. Its ability to provide transparency, automate processes through smart contracts, enable tokenization, and support decentralized energy markets positions blockchain as a cornerstone technology for fostering a greener and more sustainable financial landscape. As the world intensifies its focus on combating climate change, the integration of blockchain in green finance stands as a testament to the technology's potential to drive positive environmental impact through innovative financial solutions (Kalaiarasi & Kirubahari, 2023).

Fundamental Principles of Blockchain Technology in FinTech and Unlock Mobilization of Green Finance

Blockchain technology, at its core, operates on several fundamental principles that have profound implications for the financial technology (FinTech) sector. One primary principle is decentralization. Unlike traditional financial systems that rely on centralized authorities like banks, blockchain distributes the control and validation of transactions across a network of nodes. This decentralization not only enhances security by eliminating a single point of failure but also fosters trust among participants in the financial ecosystem (Chueca Vergara & Ferruz Agudo 2021). This principle streamlines and enforces the execution of contractual obligations without the need for intermediaries. In FinTech, smart contracts can automate complex financial processes, reducing costs and increasing the speed of transactions.

Transparency is a core tenet of blockchain technology as all participants in a blockchain network have access to a shared ledger that records all transactions. This transparency not only ensures accountability but also enables real-time tracking of financial activities. This visibility is particularly valuable in the FinTech space, where trust is paramount, and stakeholders require clear and immediate information.

The application of blockchain technology in the financial sector, particularly in the context of green finance, has the potential to unlock new dimensions of mobilizing capital for sustainable initiatives. The decentralized and transparent nature of blockchain addresses critical challenges in green finance, driving positive environmental impact. Blockchain facilitates the mobilization of green finance is by providing transparency in the supply chain. In industries such as sustainable agriculture or renewable energy, blockchain can be used to trace the origin and impact of products or energy sources. This transparency assures investors that their funds are genuinely contributing to environmentally responsible projects, building trust and attracting more capital to the green finance sector (Schoenmaker & Volz, 2022).

Tokenization, enabled by blockchain, allows for the fractional ownership of assets. In the realm of green finance, this means that individuals can invest in small portions of large-scale sustainable projects, such as wind farms or solar energy installations. Tokenization not only democratizes access to green investments but also increases liquidity, making it easier for investors to buy and sell their holdings. Additionally, blockchain can revolutionize the carbon credit market. By creating a transparent and immutable ledger of carbon credits, blockchain establishes a standardized and trustworthy system for tracking and trading carbon offsets. This, in turn, encourages organizations to participate in carbon offset programs, contributing to a more sustainable and low-carbon economy.

Blockchain Overcome Barriers in Green Finance (e.g., Transparency, Traceability and Security)

The concept of transparency, traceability, and security are just a few of the challenges that blockchain technology has emerged as a potent way to address in order to overcome significant obstacles in green finance. Transparency is crucial in the field of environmental sustainability, and blockchain's decentralized ledger offers a permanent and transparent record of financial transactions. The public and investors may track the flow of funds and confirm that they are truly being used for green initiatives thanks to this transparency, which guarantees it. Additionally, the traceability offered by blockchain improves the ability to monitor projects' environmental impact by producing a transparent and verifiable audit trail of sustainability activities. (Singh, 2022).

Blockchain's smart contracts automate and enforce agreements based on predefined conditions, streamlining processes and reducing the need for intermediaries. This automation not only enhances the efficiency of financial transactions but also ensures that funds are disbursed according to predetermined sustainability criteria.

By overcoming barriers related to transparency, traceability, and security, blockchain technology is poised to revolutionize green finance, fostering a more transparent, accountable, and secure ecosystem for environmentally sustainable investments (Sharma & Singh, 2022).

FACILITATING ACCESS TO FOSTER NEW INVESTMENT AVENUES

FinTech and blockchain technologies are revolutionizing the financial landscape by facilitating access to new sources of finance. Through crowdfunding platforms and tokenization of assets, these innovations democratize investment opportunities, allowing individuals and smaller businesses to tap into previously inaccessible pools of capital. This broadened access not only diversifies funding sources but also fosters innovation and entrepreneurial ventures in various sectors, including green finance. By lowering entry barriers and connecting investors with promising projects, FinTech and blockchain play a pivotal role in reshaping the way we fund and support initiatives that drive economic growth and sustainability (Dell'Erba, 2021).

FinTech and Blockchain: Open up New Avenues for Financing Green Projects

Financial technology (FinTech) and blockchain has opened up unprecedented avenues for financing green projects, ushering in a transformative era for sustainable investments. Robo-advisors, powered by artificial intelligence and machine learning algorithms, provide personalized investment strategies tailored to environmental sustainability. This enables a broader range of investors, including individuals and small businesses, to actively participate in funding green projects, breaking down traditional barriers and fostering a more inclusive financial ecosystem (Bin Amin et al., 2022).

In parallel, blockchain technology has emerged as a cornerstone in the realm of green finance. The decentralized and transparent nature of blockchain ensures the traceability and accountability of financial transactions related to sustainable initiatives (Singh, 2022). This transparency builds trust among stakeholders, a crucial factor in attracting capital to environmentally responsible projects. Blockchain's smart contracts automate and enforce agreements, streamlining processes and reducing the need for intermediaries. This not only expedites fund disbursement but also ensures that financial resources are allocated based on predefined sustainability criteria, adding an unprecedented level of efficiency to green financing mechanisms (Puaschunder, 2023).

The most notable contributions is the innovation in funding models. Crowdfunding platforms, often powered by FinTech, allow a diverse group of individuals to contribute to green projects, pooling resources to support initiatives aligned with environmental objectives. Tokenization, enabled by blockchain, facilitates the fractional ownership of assets, allowing investors to hold stakes in large-scale sustainable projects. This not only democratizes access to green investments but also enhances liquidity, making it easier for investors to buy and sell their holdings (Vikas, 2022).

The synergy between FinTech and blockchain is particularly evident in the creation of new financial instruments such as green bonds and carbon credit platforms. FinTech streamlines the issuance and management of these instruments, while blockchain ensures transparency and security in their trading and tracking. As these technologies bring about immense opportunities, they are not without challenges. Regulatory uncertainties, scalability issues, and concerns related to the environmental impact of certain blockchain networks must be addressed to fully unlock their potential (Macchiavello, 2023). Nevertheless, the collective impact of FinTech and blockchain in opening up new avenues for financing green projects is undeniable. Together, these technologies are driving a paradigm shift in how we fund, manage, and invest in projects that contribute to a more sustainable and environmentally conscious future.

Impact on Traditional Financial Institutions and Emergence of New Technologies: Fintech

The financial industry has been undergoing significant changes in recent years, driven by technological advancements, regulatory developments, and changing consumer preferences. This transformation has had a profound impact on traditional financial institutions and has led to the emergence of new players in the market (Marke & Sylvester, 2018). The financial services are becoming more integrated into broader ecosystems. This includes collaborations between financial institutions, fintech firms, and other industries, creating a more interconnected and seamless experience for consumers. The financial industry is experiencing a dynamic shift, with traditional players adapting to technological changes and new entrants bringing fresh perspectives and innovative solutions (Udeagha & Ngepah, 2023).

INVESTMENT OPPORTUNITIES AND TRENDS: SURMOUNT BARRIERS

The investment opportunities and trends are dynamic reflections of the ever-evolving global economic landscape. In recent years, several key themes have shaped the investment landscape. Technology, being a perennial driver, continues to offer compelling prospects. Artificial intelligence, robotics, and cybersecurity present avenues for growth as societies become more reliant on digital infrastructure. The renewable energy sector has gained prominence due to increased environmental consciousness and a shift toward sustainable practices. With advancements in healthcare and biotechnology, investments in innovative medical solutions, genomics, and pharmaceuticals are on the rise (Hassan et al. 2020). The growing importance of ESG (Environmental, Social, Governance) criteria has led to increased interest in socially responsible investing. Fintech, including blockchain and digital currencies, is another area witnessing rapid developments. Emerging markets, driven by demographic shifts and rising consumer classes, offer attractive investment opportunities. It's crucial for investors to stay attuned to geopolitical developments, regulatory changes, and societal trends to navigate the complex and ever-changing landscape effectively. Diversification, risk management, and a keen understanding of long-term trends remain essential in identifying and capitalizing on promising investment opportunities (Fenwick & Vermeulen, 2020).

Investment Opportunities in Intersection of FinTech, Blockchain and Green Finance

The convergence of finTech, blockchain, and green finance has created a dynamic intersection that presents exciting investment opportunities. FinTech innovations are revolutionizing the financial sector, enhancing efficiency and accessibility. Blockchain, with its decentralized and secure ledger technology, is disrupting traditional financial processes and introducing transparency. In tandem, the rise of green finance, driven by a global push for sustainability, is reshaping investment priorities towards environmentally responsible initiatives. Investing in companies at the crossroads of these trends can yield significant returns. FinTech firms incorporating blockchain for secure and transparent transactions in green finance are gaining traction. This includes platforms facilitating green bonds, carbon trading, and sustainable investment portfolios (Nenavath & Mishra, 2023). Cryptocurrencies are being utilized to fund renewable energy projects, offering decentralized and efficient funding mechanisms. Additionally, financial technology is streamlining the monitoring and reporting of ESG criteria, contributing to the growth of sustainable investments. Investors exploring opportunities in this intersection should consider companies at the forefront of developing innovative solutions, from blockchain-based carbon credits to finTech platforms fostering sustainable financial practices (Schulz, 2020). As the world increasingly emphasizes environmental responsibility, investments in fintech and blockchain with a green finance focus not only align with societal values but also position investors at the forefront of transformative trends shaping the future of finance (Moro-Visconti, 2020).

BENEFITS AND LIMITATIONS: INTERSECTION OF FINTECH AND BLOCKCHAIN IN GREEN FINANCE

The intersection of FinTech and blockchain in green finance presents a dual-sided landscape of benefits and limitations. On the positive side, FinTech innovations enhance accessibility, enabling a broader range of investors to engage in green finance initiatives. Platforms offering robo-advisors provide personalized, environmentally conscious investment strategies, while crowdfunding facilitates the democratization of funding for sustainable projects (Marke, 2018). Blockchain technology brings transparency and traceability, assuring investors that their funds are genuinely advancing green goals. However, challenges persist. Regulatory uncertainties, particularly concerning blockchain, may impede widespread adoption. Scalability issues and energy consumption associated with certain blockchain networks pose environmental concerns (Hoang et al., 2022).

Examining Benefits, Potential Limitations, Risks, and Challenges

Financial technology (FinTech) and blockchain have ushered in a new era for green finance, offering a myriad of benefits that enhance accessibility, efficiency, and transparency. FinTech solutions, such as robo-advisors, leverage advanced algorithms to provide tailored investment strategies aligned with environmental sustainability. This democratizes access to green investments, breaking down traditional barriers and allowing a diverse range of investors, from individuals to institutions, to actively participate in supporting environmentally responsible projects. Crowdfunding platforms, another facet of FinTech, introduce innovative funding models that empower communities to collectively contribute to sustainable initiatives, fostering a sense of shared responsibility and engagement (Schloesser & Schulz, 2022).

Blockchain, a decentralized ledger technology, contributes significantly to the transparency and traceability of green finance. Its immutable and transparent nature ensures that financial transactions related to green projects are securely recorded, creating a tamper-resistant record that investors can trust. This transparency not only builds confidence among stakeholders but also provides real-time visibility into the utilization of funds (Singh, 2020). Automation through smart contracts streamlines the execution of agreements, reducing the need for intermediaries, and expediting the flow of funds to support the implementation of sustainable projects. Overall, the synergy between FinTech and blockchain amplifies the positive impact of green finance, aligning financial practices with environmental objectives (Harris, 2018).

However, alongside these benefits, FinTech and blockchain technologies also have potential limitations, risks, and challenges that necessitate careful consideration. Regulatory uncertainty is a significant hurdle, as the rapid evolution of these technologies often outpaces regulatory frameworks. Striking a balance between fostering innovation and ensuring consumer protection and market integrity poses a complex challenge for policymakers. Scalability issues within certain blockchain networks present obstacles to handling a high volume of transactions efficiently, potentially hindering the widespread adoption of these technologies in financial systems (Shih et al., 2023). Moreover, energy consumption is a notable concern, particularly in the context of blockchain. The energy-intensive proof-of-work consensus mechanism employed by some blockchain networks contradicts the principles of green finance, requiring a shift towards more sustainable alternatives. Integration challenges with existing financial infrastructures can lead to complexities and security risks, as legacy systems may not seamlessly interface with these innovative technologies. Ensuring robust cybersecurity measures becomes imperative as financial transactions and sensitive data become increasingly digitized, exposing FinTech and blockchain platforms to potential cyber threats (Ozili, 2023).

Market volatility, especially in the realm of blockchain-associated cryptocurrencies, introduces an additional layer of risk. The fluctuating values of these digital assets can impact investor confidence, potentially affecting projects funded through initial coin offerings (ICOs) or other blockchain-based fundraising methods. Striking a delicate balance between embracing innovation and mitigating risks is paramount for the long-term success and sustainability of green finance platforms leveraging FinTech and blockchain technologies (Bayram et al., 2022).

However, a nuanced examination reveals a set of challenges that require proactive strategies and collaborations to address. As these technologies continue to evolve, stakeholders must navigate regulatory landscapes, enhance scalability, address energy concerns, fortify cybersecurity measures, and manage market volatility to ensure the enduring positive impact (Micaroni, 2020).

REGULATORY LANDSCAPE

The regulatory landscape plays a crucial role in shaping the business environment, ensuring fair practices, and safeguarding the interests of various stakeholders. In the financial sector, stringent regulations are in place to maintain stability and protect consumers. In recent years, there has been a notable shift in the regulatory landscape, driven by technological advancements and evolving business models. The emergence of fintech and digital currencies has prompted regulators to reassess existing frameworks to accommodate innovation while addressing potential risks (Nikolaou, 2018).

There is continual discussion about striking the proper balance when it comes to regulations, which are crucial for upholding order and safeguarding interests. Regulating organizations around the world are faced with the difficult challenge of striking a balance between promoting innovation and protecting against potential hazards. The regulatory environment will probably change as technology develops to address new problems, ensuring that companies act morally and sustainably in a constantly shifting global economy.

Current Regulatory Landscape and Potential Regulatory Challenges

The contemporary regulatory landscape is defined by a complicated web of laws and regulations that control numerous industries, with a focus on adjusting to technology improvements and the dynamics of the global market. Regulators are struggling to understand how finTech, blockchain, and digital currencies will disrupt the banking industry.

In order to stimulate innovation while also safeguarding consumers' interests and maintaining financial stability, governments and regulatory authorities must strike a difficult balance. A dedication to fostering competition and preserving data privacy is shown in initiatives like open banking rules and GDPR compliance. But, this regulatory landscape is not without its challenges because the notable challenge is the rapid pace of technological innovation, which often outstrips the ability of regulators to formulate and implement effective rules. FinTech, for instance, operates on the cutting edge of finance, pushing boundaries and creating novel business models that may not neatly fit into existing regulatory frameworks. Striking the right balance between encouraging innovation and mitigating risks requires regulators to be agile and adaptive. The another challenge arises from the global nature of many businesses. As companies operate across borders, regulatory arbitrage becomes a concern, wherein firms might exploit regulatory differences to gain a competitive advantage. Harmonizing regulations on an international scale is a formidable task, given the diverse legal and cultural contexts of different nations.

The advent of decentralized technologies like blockchain and cryptocurrencies introduces unique regulatory challenges. Regulators are faced with the task of ensuring investor protection, preventing financial crimes, and maintaining market integrity in a landscape that often operates beyond traditional regulatory jurisdictions.

The current regulatory landscape reflects a commitment to adapt to the evolving economic and technological landscape. However, addressing the challenges posed by rapid innovation, global operations, and decentralized technologies requires a collaborative and forward-thinking approach from regulatory bodies worldwide. Balancing innovation with risk mitigation will remain a critical challenge as regulatory frameworks continue to evolve.

Regulatory Framework: Support Responsible Development of FinTech and Blockchain in Green Finance

The regulatory framework plays a pivotal role in fostering the responsible development of fintech and blockchain within the realm of green finance. As financial technology continues to reshape traditional financial services and blockchain introduces decentralized and transparent systems, regulators must ensure that these innovations align with sustainability goals. Regulatory bodies can support responsible development by providing clear guidelines that encourage the integration of fintech and blockchain solutions to facilitate green finance initiatives (Bhowmik, 2022). Striking a balance between innovation and risk management, regulators can establish frameworks that promote the use of technologies to enhance transparency in green investments, streamline processes, and improve the overall efficiency of sustainable financial practices. Additionally, regulatory support can include incentives for businesses and startups engaging in environmentally conscious fintech and blockchain applications, encouraging the development of solutions that contribute positively to environmental goals. By addressing potential risks and ensuring compliance with environmental standards, a robust regulatory framework can create an environment where fintech and blockchain innovations serve as catalysts for the growth and sustainability of green finance (Rizzello & Kabli, 2020).

CONCLUSION AND FUTURE SCOPE

The intersection of finTech, blockchain, and green finance represents a transformative force with the potential to reshape the financial landscape while contributing to environmental sustainability. The amalgamation of financial technology and blockchain not only enhances the efficiency of financial processes but also introduces novel solutions to address challenges in green finance. Regulatory frameworks, crucial in guiding the responsible development of these technologies, need to strike a delicate balance between encouraging innovation and mitigating potential risks. As the financial industry undergoes this paradigm shift, collaboration between traditional financial institutions, fintech startups, blockchain developers, and regulatory bodies will be pivotal in realizing the full potential of these converging trends.

The future scope of this convergence is promising. FinTech, with its data-driven insights and user-centric models, can contribute to the creation of innovative financial products that align with environmental, social, and governance (ESG) criteria. Blockchain's decentralized and transparent ledger technology can enhance trust and accountability in green finance transactions. The emergence of decentralized finance (DeFi) platforms leveraging blockchain can offer inclusive financial services for sustainable development. Moreover, the tokenization of assets on blockchain could unlock new avenues for green investments, providing fractional ownership and liquidity to a broader investor base. The future of this convergence also hinges on advancements in technologies like artificial intelligence and the Internet of Things (IoT), which can further enhance the accuracy of ESG data, automate sustainable investment strategies, and improve the monitoring of environmental impacts.

Privacy concerns and data security, especially in the era of digitized financial services, remain paramount. Additionally, fostering financial inclusivity in the green finance space is a challenge that demands attention to ensure that the benefits of these innovations are accessible to all.

FinTech, blockchain, and green finance holds immense promise for creating a more sustainable and technologically advanced financial ecosystem. While challenges exist, the ongoing collaboration between innovators, regulators, and industry participants is essential to realizing a future where finance not only facilitates economic growth but also contributes positively to environmental and social well-being. The journey ahead involves navigating complexities, refining regulatory frameworks, and harnessing the potential of technology for the greater good.

REFERENCES

Bayram, O., Talay, I., & Feridun, M. (2022). Can FinTech promote sustainable finance? Policy lessons from the case of Turkey. *Sustainability (Basel)*, *14*(19), 12414. doi:10.3390/su141912414

Bayram, O., Talay, I., & Feridun, M. (2022). Can Fintech Promote Sustainable Finance? Policy Lessons from the Case of Turkey. *Sustainability (Basel)*, *2022*(14), 12414. doi:10.3390/su141912414

Bhowmik, D. (2022). An Introduction to Climate Fintech. *European Journal of Science. Innovation and Technology*, *2*(4), 24–35.

Bin Amin, S., Taghizadeh-Hesary, F., & Khan, F. (2022). Facilitating green digital finance in Bangladesh: Importance, prospects, and implications for meeting the SDGs. In *Green Digital Finance and Sustainable Development Goals* (pp. 143–165). Springer Nature Singapore. doi:10.1007/978-981-19-2662-4_7

Campbell-Verduyn, M. (2023). Conjuring a cooler world? Imaginaries of improvement in blockchain climate finance experiments. *Environment and Planning C: Politics and Space*. Springer. 23996544231162858.

Chen, Y., & Volz, U. (2021). *Scaling up sustainable investment through blockchain-based project bonds.* (Special Working Paper Series). ADB-IGF..

Chueca Vergara, C., & Ferruz Agudo, L. (2021). Fintech and sustainability: Do they affect each other? *Sustainability (Basel)*, *13*(13), 7012. doi:10.3390/su13137012

Dell'Erba, M. (2021). Sustainable digital finance and the pursuit of environmental sustainability. *Sustainable Finance in Europe: Corporate Governance, Financial Stability and Financial Markets*.

Dorfleitner, G., & Braun, D. (2019). Fintech, digitalization and blockchain: possible applications for green finance. *The rise of green finance in Europe: opportunities and challenges for issuers, investors and marketplaces*, 207-237.

Fenwick, M., & Vermeulen, E. P. (2020). Banking and regulatory responses to FinTech revisited-building the sustainable financial service'ecosystems' of tomorrow. *Singapore Journal of Legal Studies*.

Harris, A. (2018). A conversation with masterminds in blockchain and climate change. In *Transforming climate finance and green investment with blockchains* (pp. 15–22). Academic Press. doi:10.1016/B978-0-12-814447-3.00002-1

Hassan, M. K., Rabbani, M. R., & Ali, M. A. M. (2020). Challenges for the Islamic Finance and banking in post COVID era and the role of Fintech. *Journal of Economic Cooperation & Development*, *41*(3), 93–116.

Hoang, T. G., Nguyen, G. N. T., & Le, D. A. (2022). Developments in financial technologies for achieving the Sustainable Development Goals (SDGs): FinTech and SDGs. In *Disruptive technologies and eco-innovation for sustainable development* (pp. 1–19). IGI Global. doi:10.4018/978-1-7998-8900-7.ch001

Jaiwant, S. V., & Kureethara, J. V. (2023). Green Finance and Fintech: Toward a More Sustainable Financial System. In *Green Finance Instruments, FinTech, and Investment Strategies: Sustainable Portfolio Management in the Post-COVID Era* (pp. 283–300). Springer International Publishing. doi:10.1007/978-3-031-29031-2_12

Kalaiarasi, H., & Kirubahari, S. (2023). Green finance for sustainable development using blockchain technology. In *Green Blockchain Technology for Sustainable Smart Cities* (pp. 167–185). Elsevier. doi:10.1016/B978-0-323-95407-5.00003-7

Liu, H., Yao, P., Latif, S., Aslam, S., & Iqbal, N. (2022). Impact of Green financing, FinTech, and financial inclusion on energy efficiency. *Environmental Science and Pollution Research International, 29*(13), 1–12. doi:10.1007/s11356-021-16949-x PMID:34705207

Marke, A. (Ed.). (2018). *Transforming climate finance and green investment with blockchains*. Academic Press.

Marke, A., & Sylvester, B. (2018). Decoding the current global climate finance architecture. In *Transforming climate finance and green investment with blockchains* (pp. 35–59). Academic Press. doi:10.1016/B978-0-12-814447-3.00004-5

Micaroni, M. (2020). *Sustainable Finance: Addressing the SDGs through Fintech and Digital Finance solutions in EU* (Doctoral dissertation, Politecnico di Torino).

Migliorelli, M., & Dessertine, P. (2019). The rise of green finance in Europe. *Opportunities and challenges for issuers, investors and marketplaces. Cham. Palgrave Macmillan, 2*, 2019.

Moro-Visconti, R., Cruz Rambaud, S., & López Pascual, J. (2020). Sustainability in FinTechs: An explanation through business model scalability and market valuation. *Sustainability (Basel), 12*(24), 10316. doi:10.3390/su122410316

Naderi, N., & Tian, Y. (2022). Leveraging Blockchain Technology and Tokenizing Green Assets to Fill the Green Finance Gap. *Energy Research Letters, 3*(3).

Nassiry, D. (2018). *The role of fintech in unlocking green finance: Policy insights for developing countries* (No. 883). ADBI working paper.

Nenavath, S., & Mishra, S. (2023). Impact of green finance and fintech on sustainable economic growth: Empirical evidence from India. *Heliyon, 9*(5), e16301. doi:10.1016/j.heliyon.2023.e16301 PMID:37234625

Ozili, P. K. (2023). Assessing global interest in decentralized finance, embedded finance, open finance, ocean finance and sustainable finance. *Asian Journal of Economics and Banking*, *7*(2), 197–216. doi:10.1108/AJEB-03-2022-0029

Puaschunder, J. M. (2023). The Future of Resilient Green Finance. In *The Future of Resilient Finance: Finance Politics in the Age of Sustainable Development* (pp. 185–210). Springer International Publishing. doi:10.1007/978-3-031-30138-4_6

Rizzello, A., & Kabli, A. (2020). Social finance and sustainable development goals: A literature synthesis, current approaches and research agenda. *ACRN Journal of Finance and Risk Perspectives, 9.*

Sachs, J. D., Woo, W. T., Yoshino, N., & Taghizadeh-Hesary, F. (2019). Importance of green finance for achieving sustainable development goals and energy security. Handbook of green finance: Energy security and sustainable development, 10, 1-10.

Schloesser, T., & Schulz, K. (2022). Distributed ledger technology and climate finance. In *Green Digital Finance and Sustainable Development Goals* (pp. 265–286). Springer Nature Singapore. doi:10.1007/978-981-19-2662-4_13

Schoenmaker, D., & Volz, U. (2022). *Scaling up sustainable finance and investment in the Global South*. CEPR Press.

Schulz, K., & Feist, M. (2021). Leveraging blockchain technology for innovative climate finance under the Green Climate Fund. *Earth System Governance*, *7*, 100084. doi:10.1016/j.esg.2020.100084

Schulz, K. A., Gstrein, O. J., & Zwitter, A. J. (2020). Exploring the governance and implementation of sustainable development initiatives through blockchain technology. *Futures*, *122*, 102611. doi:10.1016/j.futures.2020.102611

Sharma, A., & Singh, B. (2022). Measuring Impact of E-commerce on Small Scale Business: A Systematic Review. *Journal of Corporate Governance and International Business Law*, *5*(1).

Shih, C., Gwizdalski, A., & Deng, X. (2023). *Building a Sustainable Future: Exploring Green Finance*. Regenerative Finance, and Green Financial Technology.

Singh, B. (2019). Profiling Public Healthcare: A Comparative Analysis Based on the Multidimensional Healthcare Management and Legal Approach. *Indian Journal of Health and Medical Law*, *2*(2), 1–5.

Singh, B. (2020). GLOBAL SCIENCE AND JURISPRUDENTIAL APPROACH CONCERNING HEALTHCARE AND ILLNESS. *Indian Journal of Health and Medical Law*, *3*(1), 7–13.

Singh, B. (2022). Understanding Legal Frameworks Concerning Transgender Healthcare in the Age of Dynamism. *ELECTRONIC JOURNAL OF SOCIAL AND STRATEGIC STUDIES*, *3*(1), 56–65. doi:10.47362/EJSSS.2022.3104

Singh, B. (2022). Relevance of Agriculture-Nutrition Linkage for Human Healthcare: A Conceptual Legal Framework of Implication and Pathways. *Justice and Law Bulletin*, *1*(1), 44–49.

Singh, B. (2022). COVID-19 Pandemic and Public Healthcare: Endless Downward Spiral or Solution via Rapid Legal and Health Services Implementation with Patient Monitoring Program. *Justice and Law Bulletin*, *1*(1), 1–7.

Singh, B. (2023). Blockchain Technology in Renovating Healthcare: Legal and Future Perspectives. In Revolutionizing Healthcare Through Artificial Intelligence and Internet of Things Applications (pp. 177-186). IGI Global.

Singh, B. (2023). Federated Learning for Envision Future Trajectory Smart Transport System for Climate Preservation and Smart Green Planet: Insights into Global Governance and SDG-9 (Industry, Innovation and Infrastructure). *National Journal of Environmental Law*, *6*(2), 6–17.

Singh, B. (2024). Legal Dynamics Lensing Metaverse Crafted for Videogame Industry and E-Sports: Phenomenological Exploration Catalyst Complexity and Future. *Journal of Intellectual Property Rights Law*, *7*(1), 8–14.

Singh, V. K. (2022). Regulatory and Legal Framework for Promoting Green Digital Finance. In *Green Digital Finance and Sustainable Development Goals* (pp. 3–27). Springer Nature Singapore. doi:10.1007/978-981-19-2662-4_1

Thomason, J., Ahmad, M., Bronder, P., Hoyt, E., Pocock, S., Bouteloupe, J., & Shrier, D. (2018). Blockchain—powering and empowering the poor in developing countries. In *Transforming climate finance and green investment with blockchains* (pp. 137–152). Academic Press. doi:10.1016/B978-0-12-814447-3.00010-0

Udeagha, M. C., & Ngepah, N. (2023). The drivers of environmental sustainability in BRICS economies: Do green finance and fintech matter? *World Development Sustainability*, *3*, 100096. doi:10.1016/j.wds.2023.100096

Vikas, N., Venegas, P., & Aiyer, S. (2022). Role of Banks and Other Financial Institutions in Enhancing Green Digital Finance. In *Green Digital Finance and Sustainable Development Goals* (pp. 329–352). Springer Nature Singapore. doi:10.1007/978-981-19-2662-4_16

Yan, C., Siddik, A. B., Yong, L., Dong, Q., Zheng, G. W., & Rahman, M. N. (2022). A two-staged SEM-artificial neural network approach to analyze the impact of FinTech adoption on the sustainability performance of banking firms: The mediating effect of green finance and innovation. *Systems, 10*(5), 148. doi:10.3390/systems10050148

Yang, Y., Su, X., & Yao, S. (2021). Nexus between green finance, fintech, and high-quality economic development: Empirical evidence from China. *Resources Policy, 74*, 102445. doi:10.1016/j.resourpol.2021.102445

Zhang, X., Aranguiz, M., Xu, D., Zhang, X., & Xu, X. (2018). Utilizing blockchain for better enforcement of green finance law and regulations. In *Transforming climate finance and green investment with blockchains* (pp. 289–301). Academic Press. doi:10.1016/B978-0-12-814447-3.00021-5

Chapter 12
The Nexus of Smart Contracts and Digital Twins Transforming Green Finance With Automated Transactions in Investment Agreements:
Leveraging Smart Contracts for Green Investment Agreements and Automated Transactions

K. Balaji
https://orcid.org/0000-0002-3065-3294
Presidency University, India

ABSTRACT

In recent years, the integration of digital twins and smart contracts has become a revolutionary force in the field of green finance. The purpose of this chapter is to examine how smart contracts and digital twins are interwoven, particularly in relation to how they have significant influence in the field of green finance. It looks into the way these innovations work together to transform agreements regarding investments by making automated transactions possible and maximising effectiveness and transparency. This investigation demonstrates how working together can simplify complicated financing processes and increase responsibility and dependability for sustainable investment projects. The chapter demonstrates the real-world use of digital twins and smart contracts via case studies and theoretical insights, highlighting their revolutionary influence on changing the face of green finance.

DOI: 10.4018/979-8-3693-1878-2.ch012

INTRODUCTION

Green finance is undergoing a major transformation because to the usage of digital twins and smart contracts, that take advantage of automated transactions throughout agreements regarding investments. Smart contracts optimise financial processes by enabling the secure, computerised, as well as accessible operation of agreements through the utilisation of blockchain-based technology. Digital twins provide information and prediction powers which alter making choices in sustainable initiatives when used in tandem alongside tangible resources or operations (26). Together, these innovations will strengthen financial agreements, promote transparency, and raise output within the sustainable finance industry. Smart contracts as well as digital twins, which automate complex financial procedures and ensure credibility, offer a dependable and innovative basis for long-term investment agreements. Green finance practices are subsequently advanced and altered as a result of this (Swan, M, 2015).

BACKGROUND

Smart contracts are essential to the cryptocurrencies space, particularly the ones that Ethereum invented. They are the building blocks of non-fungible token (NFT) and decentralised financial technologies. Utilising its fully Turing-complete Solidity language, Vitalik Buterin built over Nick Szabo's initial concepts for smart contracts within the 2014 Ethereum white paper (Greenspan, G, 2015). Unlike typical contractual relationships represented as intelligent contracts of law in readable by machines code, these agreements are performed in code and automated transactional procedures, allowing the frictionless exchange of assets or cryptocurrencies (Zou, W, et.al, 2019).

Smart contracts have computerised procedures that simplify payments responsibilities or currency funding transfers, or they can be used to perform duties that result from contracts. Nick Szabo first proposed them in the 1990s. The characteristics of code languages and the manner in which it may influence their legality is a topic of continuous discussion. The phrase "smart contract" has come to refer explicitly to universal computations on blockchains or distributed databases since the foundation of Ethereum in 2015. A smart contract is defined by the US National Institute of Standards and Technology as a set of data and instructions that is implemented on a distributed ledger called blockchain through by encryption verified exchanges. The foundation behind Ethereum and IBM define smart contracting as a computer programme that is run and verified by the platform itself, preserving, auditing, as well as proving unchangeable once it is placed in a system known as a blockchain or distributed ledger. This is in contrast to the traditional contract notion (Ream, J. et.al, 2017).

In 2017, Belarus achieved a significant milestone by enacting the Decree on Advancement of the Internet of Things, making electronic contracts legal. The legal basis for smart contracting was introduced in this order by Denis Aleinikov, a lawyer from Belarus. Countries including Arizona, Nevada, Tennessee, and Wyoming have passed laws pertaining to the use of smart contracts. Furthermore, in the month of April 2020, the Senate and House of Congress in Iowa acknowledged the legal validity of electronic contracts (Szabo, N,1997). The UK Jurisdiction Group has unveiled the Electronic Dispute Settlement Standards (Digital DR Rules) in the month of April 2021 with the goal of addressing blockchain and cryptocurrency-related legal issues in Britain as quickly as possible (Taherdoost, H.A, 2022).

"Digital twins" are digital replicas of real-world structures, operations, or objects. Such replications, that are built employing information, sensors, and algorithms, allow the observation, analysis, and simulation of the actions and outcomes of the original object. Digital twins have a lengthy history, having originated in the production and technical domains. Big data analytics, Internet of Things devices, and simulated techniques gained popularity as they developed. Over numerous years in design and manufacturing, digital twins are being produced in tandem with technological advancements. The term "digital twin" was first used in 2002 by Dr. Michael Grieves of the University of Michigan, but the idea had started taking shape decades earlier (Eenmaa-Dimitrieva, H. et.al, 2019).

Originally introduced as virtual replicas of physical assets or systems, digital twins were primarily used in the management of product life cycles for planning and research. Improvements in the field of sensors with the emergence of the Internet of Things (IoT) during the middle of the 2000 substantially accelerated the emergence of digital twins (Zheng, Z. et.al (2020). Instantaneous data collection via physical assets has been rendered feasible by the widespread application of integrated sensors in an extensive variety of technologies and devices, which aided in the creation of greater precise and vibrant electronic replicas. Numerous sectors, like production, automobiles, aerospace, medical care, and electrical power, found simpler for them to gradually embrace the use of digital twins as a result of the breakthrough (Destefanis, G, et.al, 2018).

Businesses like General Electric Company (GE), Siemens, and Airbus spearheaded this embrace by using digital replications to figure out maintenance needs, improve processes, and boost efficiency throughout a variety of sectors. In addition, in the past few years, there has been a substantial convergence of big data analytics, machine learning, artificial intelligence (AI), and digital twins (Marchesi, L.; et.al,2020). This combination has greatly widened the possibilities of digital twins by utilising AI algorithms to understand enormous quantities of data collected by sensors. Consequently, very intricate and prognostic digital models are generated, facilitating before unattainable instantaneous making choices and optimisation throughout various sectors.

(Vieira and Zhang, 2021) evaluated the influence of smart contracts on microgrid energy trade in order to examine the efficiency of transactions between individuals. Their investigation found the importance of smart agreements for productive, safe energy trade, minimising middlemen, improving grid durability, and encouraging community engagement for decentralised electric environments inside microgrids.

(Androulaki et al, 2018) proposed Hyperledger Fabric, emphasising its position as a blockchain with permissions systems that also serves as an operating system for distributed systems. The major results focused on the permission-based blockchain approach, which ensures restricted access and greater confidentiality for corporate applications. Furthermore, the platform's modular framework enables for flexibility element integration, which improves customisation based on individual business requirements. The Hyperledger Fabric blockchain prioritises stability and productivity, exceeding some blockchains with restricted access. Furthermore, the implementation of endorsements criteria enables transactional validity.

(Buterin, 2017) presented Ethereum's smart contract and decentralised programme (DApp) platform, with the goal of explaining its characteristics and potential. The primary results emphasised Ethereum's network being the centre for developing digital applications, employing smart contract technology to provide decentralised functionality. Turing Complete, its programming language, enabling the creation of complicated and multifunctional smart agreements with a wide range of capabilities. The Virtual Machine for Ethereum (EVM) and Gas mechanisms handle processing and transaction expenses effectively inside the Ethereum environment, guaranteeing uninterrupted operation (Taherdoost, H, 2023). Furthermore, Ethereum's system demonstrates the exciting possibilities of blockchain technology smart contracts, showcasing their ability to execute agreement and payments throughout a wide range of businesses, indicating a significant change in existing operations.

(Sklaroff, J.M,2018) attempts to analyse smart contracts, exposing their unpredictability and rigidity) in a article released by the University of Pennsylvania Law Journal. It investigates their constraints, emphasising the difficulties in reacting to unanticipated events or changing agreements, which may result in transactions delays or disagreements (D. Macrinici, 2018) carried out a methodical mapping investigation in Telematics and Informatics in 2018 to categorise as well as organise current studies on smart contract development in the area of blockchain technology. The paper offers special perspectives regarding this sector by providing a complete analysis of technology uses, ramifications, including the growing environment of powered by blockchain contracts.(M. Madanchian and colleagues, 2022) publication in "Riding Transformational Development in E-Business using Applied Intelligence and Innovative Technology" investigates the effect of digitization on organisational shifts in online businesses, including an emphasis on applied intelligence and new innovations.

The research looks at the implications of the digital revolution on organisational structures and tactics, emphasising the significance of new innovations including artificial intelligence in changing e-commerce companies and associated operating systems (Rouhani, S.; Deters, 2019). (Teisserenc and Sepasgozar,2021) investigate the "The Implementation of Blockchain Technologies via Digital Twins within Construction Sector 4.0: A PESTELS Approach" in Building. Researchers use a PESTELS paradigm to study whether blockchain-based technologies might be incorporated into digital twins within the real estate sector, emphasising financial, social, technological, environmental, legal, and moral issues. (Wang, Guo,2022) present "Deep Learning for Evaluation of Ecological Quality Using BIM Big Information in Energies Efficient Building Digital Twins" in Sustainable. Energy Technologies. Assessing. Their research shows the use of deep learning in assessing contextual delight using building data modelling (BIM). (Abioye,et al, 2021) publish an in-depth assessment of "Artificial Intelligence in the Construction Industry" in J. Building Engineering. Their study looks into the existing state, potential advantages, including anticipated challenges of implementing artificial intelligence (AI) in the constructing industry. (Lee, et,al, 2021) put forward a "Combined Digital Twin with Blockchain technology Architecture for Promoting Responsible Disclosure of Information in Construction Works". Researchers present an approach that combines digital twins and blockchain-based technology, with an objective of facilitating safe and transparent exchange of data across diverse players associated with building ventures (Gatteschi, V, et.al,2018).

FOCUS OF THE CHAPTER

Leveraging Smart Contracts for Green Investment Agreements

Blockchain-based smart contracts represent a cutting-edge development in both finance and technology. They constitute autonomous agreements that carry out their obligations without the assistance of intermediaries (Politou, E, et.al,2019). They have particular requirements inscribed in them. Nick Szabo, a computer scientist, initially introduced such agreements during the 1990s, which eventually gained practical importance during the 2015 launching of Ethereum. Ethereum enabled Solidity-based smart contracts and decentralised applications (dApps) upon its blockchain (Pan, J.; et. al, 2018). These kinds of agreements accelerate up interactions, save expenses and enhance safety by automating tasks in a range of businesses, from banking to supply chain management. Since they're visible as well as unchangeable, smart contracts continue to revolutionise industry by offering secure, efficient, more accessible partnerships (Nugent, T, et.al,2023).

Types of Smart Contracts

Smart contracts come in a variety of forms and businesses, and their levels of complexities as well as flexibility vary. The following are a few typical types:

- **Financial Contracts**: These facilitate a range of financial operations, including financing processes, the development of decentralised exchanges (DEX), executing of loans, including the trading for cryptocurrency (Griggs, K.N.; et.al,2018).
- **Escrow Contracts**: Acting as middlemen, they protect assets or funds until specific conditions are fulfilled, fostering trust in a variety of operations, including those involving online platforms and land.
- **Decentralised Autonomous firms (DAO) contracts**: These agreements automate decisions and processes of governing firms which are run through shareholders voting. They also redistribute the ability to vote thus enable decentralised managerial processes (Wang, S,2019).
- **Supply Chain Contracts**: Applied to supply chain management, these agreements offer accountability through automated fund releases, level of stock surveillance, including products validity checks.
- **Insurance contracts**: These agreements specify terms of protection and trigger automatic payments depending on factors like climate or flight delays, automating insurer processes.
- **Legal Contracts and Notary Services:** They handle accessible, immutable legal processes for agreements that need to be notarized, like wills and real estate titles.
- **Gaming and Gambling Contracts**: These contractual arrangements within the gaming sector ensure open and impartial playing and lessen reliance upon central authority for trust through automatic stakes, settlements, as well as gaming guidelines.

Crucial Elements of Smart Contracts

Smart contracts contain an assortment of crucial components which are necessary for their execution, including:

- **Blockchain**: A smart contract is a software application that runs on a distributed ledger called blockchain which acts as the basis to implement the terms of the agreement between the parties.
- **Smart Contract Code**: The conditions of the agreement are represented by the device's software in this section. It has a detailed explanation of each clause and responsibility in the agreement as well as is composed in a specific computer language (Chang, S.E.; et.al, 2019).
- **Triggering Mechanism**: Smart contracts are activated upon the fulfilment of specific conditions. These triggers typically have external origins, like settlements or deadlines.
- **Digital Signatures**: These serve as a means of verifying both parties' legitimacy. Every participant guarantees blockchain technology validation via executing the contract using their unique secret key.
- **Consensus Mechanism**: A system of consensus verifies every single transaction that occurs on the distributed ledger, including ones that involve smart contracts. This method ensures consensus and identification across the whole network.

Theories Supporting Smart Contracts

Several theories and concepts lend assistance to the application and functioning of smart contracts:

- **Game Theory**: Game theory concepts are taken into consideration while designing the reward mechanisms found in smart contracts. It concentrates on devising mechanisms which incentivize partners to act in a manner that promotes the objectives stated in a contract, ensuring that self-serving parties cooperate to achieve gains that are advantageous for both of them. The field of crypto economics combines elements of the field of economics game theory, and cryptography to design and assess financial structures enabled by cryptography technologies (Perera, S.; et.al,2020). Smart contracts on blockchain systems generate rewards, safety precautions (such proof-of-stake or proof-of-work), as well as financial frameworks based on crypto economic principles (Ream, J.; et.al, 2017).
- **Distributed Systems**: smart agreements are based upon the concepts of networked systems. Distributed systems are used to save and execute code among multiple nodes, offering redundant operation, resilience to failure (Namasudra, S. et.al, 2021).

- **Concurrency Theory**: This framework deals with managing and controlling multiple processes at once. To ensure the multiple transactions can occur concurrently with no interacting with each other, smart contracts have to oversee concurrent operations (Chen, Y.;et.al,2020).
- **Legal Theory and Contract Law**: By combining aspects of both conventional legal concepts and contractual law, smart contracts aim to record binding commitments and obligated arrangements in an electronic format. Investigation into aligning smart contracts with regulatory structures is ongoing to ensure enforcement and conformity to prevailing laws (Sharma, P.et.al,2023).
- **Security & Cryptography**: The fundamental principles of encryption are crucial to ensuring the reliability as well as privacy of smart contract software. Electronic signatures, hashing algorithms, encrypted public keys, including zero-knowledge proofs are some of the techniques that are crucial to smart contract transaction safety.
- **Economic Theory:** Smart contracts' incentive structures and financial frameworks were created with an understanding of monetary principles. Concepts such as demand-supply dynamics, the tokenomics process, as well as market processes are used to create distributed structures that are durable and productive.
- **Behavioural Economics**: The design of electronic contracts is influenced by our awareness of human conduct and decision-making. The principles of behavioural economists enable agreements which are customised to individual views as well as reactions to rewards so as to guarantee customer acquisition as well as participation (Rouhani, S.; Deters,2019).

Programming Smart Contracts

A specific programming language can be required, according to the platform for blockchain technology that you choose. Some of the most prevalent programming languages are Solidity, Java, and Rust. Solidity is frequently employed to develop agreements and apps over the network of Ethereum. However, Rust is used by blockchains such as Polkadot and Solana (Feng, T.; et.al,2019).

Smart Contract Management System

The blockchain validation process becomes more challenging and time-consuming as the network gets larger. To get around this problem, we decided to construct two distinct blockchains: one for handling transactions and another for smart contract storing and execution (22). The terms of the engagement must initially be agreed upon by everyone involved, after their decisions are transformed into autonomous agreements, or smart contracts. It is demonstrated ways to store and run smart contracts. The process of storing and executing smart contracts is shown in the figure 1.

Figure 1. Smart contract management system

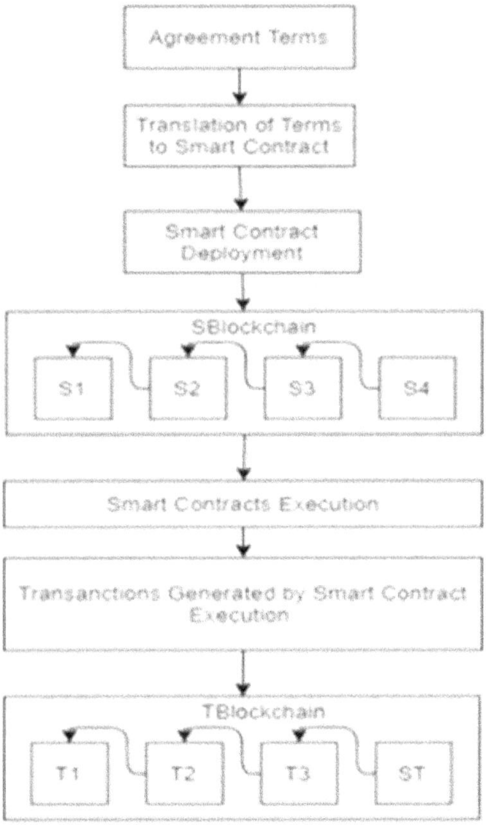

The Smart Contract Management System is seen in illustration 1 above. A chosen nodes operating on behalf of any one of both parties is responsible for posting the agreement into the S Blockchain. The smart contract is securely stored on the S Blockchain once the transaction is finished, ensuring it difficult for both sides to revoke it away. The contract becomes mechanically operative upon fulfilment of its conditions (Chakraborty, P. et.al,2018).

Once individuals fulfil the conditions, a deployed node has the authority to provide implementation privileges for another node or group of networks from the participants to the agreement (Ante, L. 2021). The final client is the person whom can fulfil the contract and make the payment if the item arrives earlier than expected.

Smart Contract Deployment Process

The deployment of smart contracts is a systematic process which commences with selecting a suitable blockchain system, such as Ethereum or the Binance Smart Chain, according to the needs of the venture (Hewa, T.;et.al, 2021). The illustration below shows the mechanics for the Smart contract deployment procedure.

Figure 2. Smart contract deployment process

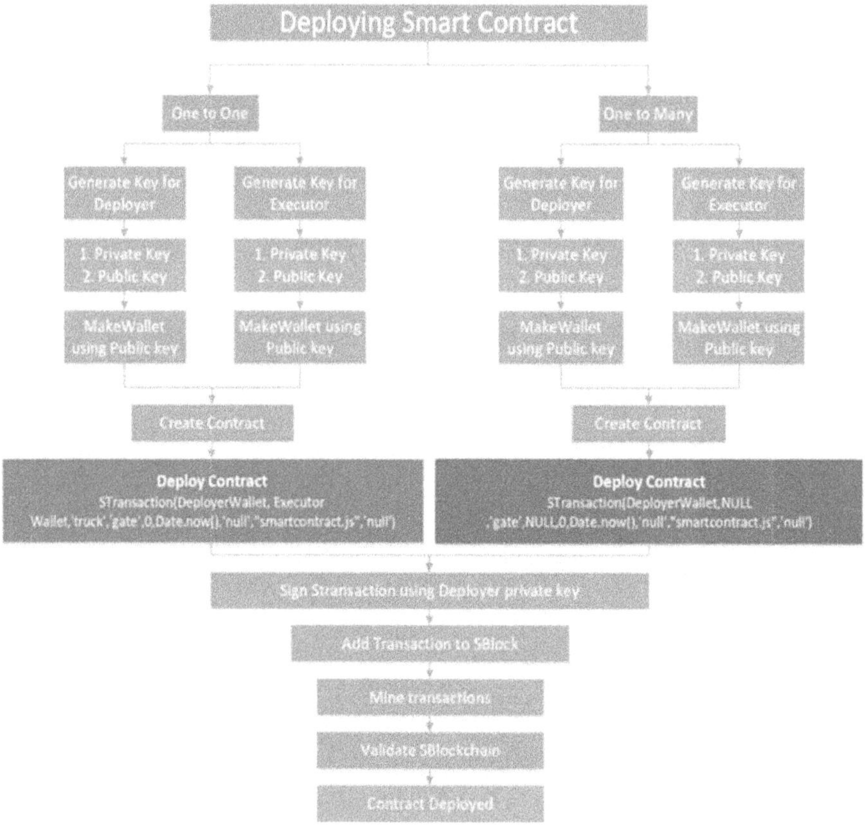

The procedure of deploying smart contracts is depicted in the above figure 2. The implementation of a smart contract involves several critical steps that require an in-depth comprehension of the blockchain system and the chosen system, like

Ethereum or Binance Smart Chain ((Khan, S.N.; et.al, 2021). In the beginning, it's critical to select the appropriate blockchain architecture and coding language (such as Solidity for Ethereum). The agreement is then coded, authenticity checked, compiled through bytecode, and thoroughly tested on test networks to detect and fix issues. The next step is implementation, that necessitates using technologies like Truffle or Remix to communicate with the system on either a testnet or the mainnet. Fuel prices and congestion in networks have a direct effect on transactions approval, which is crucial following implementation (Davidson, S.;et.al, 2016). Clients may communicate with the contract's terms via dApps, wallets, or explorers. Ongoing repairs, updates, security inspections, and complete records guarantee the reliability of the agreement, especially for those which involve confidential data and are publicly accessible.

Smart Contracts and Automated Transactions

Without any requirement for middlemen, smart contracts which are put straight into code and operate on blockchain networks autonomously carry out specified actions when certain criteria are met. They ensure open and unreliable transactions by using the randomised design of blockchains (Liebenau, J.; Elaluf-Calderwood, S,2021). These agreements allow for automated transactions that happen when predetermined requirements are met. For instance, whenever a seller transfers rights to property and a buyer completes payment, ownership changes hands instantly. Payment commitments trigger automatic fulfilment in the financial domain based on specified parameters. This kind of technology is used in numerous sectors such as supply chain management, real estate, gaming, and finance. It provides effectiveness, openness, and secure completion of transactions (Finck, M.2018).

Smart Contracts for Green Investment Agreements

Enabling and enforcing contracts related to sustainable investments through the use of smart contracts self-executing contracts created on blockchain networks is referred to as "leveraging smart contracts for green investment agreements." These agreements contain specified conditions and clauses related to green investments, which, this upon fulfilment of predefined sustainability criteria, set off automated activities. For instance, smart contracts have the ability to release funds for energy efficiency projects in response to the fulfilment of specific benchmarks, like energy output rates or reductions in carbon emissions. Utilising intelligent agreements ensures sustainable targets regulation, boosts openness, and promotes a more successful and accountable strategy for sustainable investment by fostering trust across stakeholders in sustainable finance initiatives (Khatoon, A,2020).

Role of Smart Contracts in Green Investment Agreements

Smart contracts have the potential to significantly increase the transparency, efficacy, and trust in green investment agreements. Such electronic autonomous agreements, which are based on blockchain technology, can automate carrying out the clauses and circumstances of contracts relating to green investments (Khatoon, A,2020). Listed below are some methods by which smart contracts can be used in green investment agreements:

- **Automated Execution**: Smart contracts may be used for automating agreements for investments in the sustainability sector. For instance, they have the ability to start operations or distribute funds immediately when specific predefined requirements are met. The investment procedure is streamlined, inefficiencies are reduced, and intermediaries are used less frequently because to this technology.
- **Transparency and Traceability**: A blockchain-based smart contracts provide accessibility by recording every transaction's detail on an immutable ledger.
- **Verification of Compliance**: Smart contracts can be programmed to monitor the fulfilment of environmental regulations and standards. For example, funds may only be disbursed upon the fulfilment of specific criteria for sustainability or the achievement of environmentally beneficial standards.
- **Lower Costs and Time**: By automating processes and eliminating the necessity of intermediaries, smart contracts can reduce managerial expenses as well as the duration required to create, monitor, and uphold green investment agreements.
- **Risk Mitigation**: Smart contracts might include integrated risk mitigation measures for investments in greenery. For instance, they may rapidly distribute money in the case of unforeseen sustainability issues or failures in projects.

Application Areas of Smart Contracts for Green Investment Agreements

In green investment agreements, smart contracts provide real-time applications that improve reliability, effectiveness, and openness for ecologically sustainable efforts:

- **Investments in Renewable Energy**: Investment procedures in renewable energy projects can be automated with the use of smart contracts. These make sure the funds is only disbursed when certain conditions are met, such reaching predetermined energy generation targets or complying with environmental laws for emission reductions.

- **Carbon Credits and Emission Reduction**: Smart contracts enable the trade of carbon credits by instantly confirming and carrying out payments contingent on the achievement of predetermined environmental targets or a quantifiable decrease in carbon emissions.
- **Supply Chain Sustainability**: Smart agreements may track as well as authenticate the sustainability merits of goods or materials used in the course of the supply chain management process. Sustainable procedures can be followed at different phases of manufacturing, shipment, and transit with the help of automatic agreements.
- **Tracking effect Investments**: Smart contracts make it possible to transparently monitor effect expenditures, guaranteeing that money is given to initiatives that satisfy predetermined requirements for the environment. Based on current information demonstrating favourable impacts on the environment, businesses can implement initiatives.
- **Recycling and Waste Management**: Appropriate waste disposal and recycling techniques can be encouraged by contracts. For example, they have the ability to initiate the process of paying recycling firms based on how much waste gets reused or disposed of in an eco-friendly way.
- **Conservation of Natural Resources**: Smart contracts may be employed in contracts pertaining to conservation campaigns, such as the safeguarding of biodiversity or the preservation of forests. They might make sure that the funding is allotted after specific preservation benchmarks are reached.
- **Green Bonds and Financing**: By linking money disbursement to certified sustainable initiatives, smart contract management and automated green bond issuing can provide openness regarding fund utilisation.

Smart Contracts-Automated Transactions in Cryptocurrencies

With the advancement of the blockchain system, smart contracts have become more and more prevalent. Even before blockchain-based applications were created, during the middle of the 1990 smart contracts were initially characterised as "an accumulation of commitments, laid out in electronic form, encompassing procedures that regulate how both parties perform the aforementioned promise" (Dolgui, A, et.al,2020).

Smart contracts are utilised in cryptocurrency systems for a number of purposes, such as facilitating transferring assets, keeping track of user agreements, and expediting transactions (Lee, D. et.al, 2021). In the context of cryptocurrencies, smart contracts are essentially algorithms composed of code capabilities that enable secure, verifiable settlements on a distributed ledger called blockchain. They constitute independent contracts with predetermined terms and conditions written in them. A smart contract goes through four phases in its lifetime, as shown in Figure 1 [(Hasan, H.R.; Salah, K, 2019)]. The creation, deployment, execution, and completion phases of putting smart contracts into practice are shown in figure 1. Few Notable examples of blockchain-based systems allowing smart contracts is depicted in the table 1.

Table 1 shows the notable examples of blockchain-based systems allowing smart contracts. Hence, smart contracts have its wide applications in ongoing digital space.

Table 1: Notable example of blockchain-based systems allowing smart contracts

<table>
<tr><th>Name of Cryptocurrency</th><th>Summary</th></tr>
<tr><td>Ethereum</td><td>Ethereum, a well-known smart contract platform, introduces a syntax that is Turing-compliant within its blockchain technology.</td></tr>
<tr><td>Bitcoin</td><td>In order to create customised smart contracts on the basis of Bitcoin, such as multi signature user accounts, payout methods, escrows, time locks, instantaneous cross-chained trade, oracles, or multi-party lotteries without an administrator.</td></tr>
<tr><td>Binance Smart Chain</td><td rowspan="7">A blockchain platform for smart contracts</td></tr>
<tr><td>Cardano</td></tr>
<tr><td>Solana</td></tr>
<tr><td>Avalanche</td></tr>
<tr><td>Tron</td></tr>
<tr><td>EOS.IO</td></tr>
<tr><td>Tezos</td><td>An on-chain management architecture allows the blockchain system to change its own regulations having the least amount of network interruption possible. Prominent instances of blockchain systems</td></tr>
</table>

Compiled By: Author. **Source:** From Review of literature

Real-Time Applications of Blockchain Technology and Smart Contracts in the Insurance Sector

Smart contracts and blockchain-based systems possess the potential to revolutionise the insurance business by introducing effectiveness, safety, and openness to a variety of processes. Listed below are some of the reasons why the insurance industry has real-time incorporated these technologies:

- **Automated Claims Processing:** Smart contracts have the ability to handle claims automatically by performing predefined actions. When certain conditions (like inclement weather or a delayed flight) are met, the insured receives payment from the smart contract. This reduces the likelihood of scams, expedites claims payment, and eliminates the need for human intervention.

- **Transparency and Trust:** An unchangeable, comprehensive database of records is provided by the technology known as blockchain. The openness helps to reduce bogus claims, increase trust between consumers and insurance firms, and verify the validity of insurance. Parametric insurance, whereby payment are provided autonomously in accordance with specified circumstances (such as the occurrence of a natural disaster or specific weather conditions), has become available via smart contracts. For instance, smart contracts within the agriculture sector can start insurance reimbursements when weather sensors detect bad weather affecting crops (Nakamoto, S, (2008).
- **Fraud Prevention:** The randomised and unchangeable nature of blockchain reduces the likelihood of fraud within the insurance sector. Documentation of all transactions and policy details is ensured by creating a secure environment that is unaffected by manipulations or tampering.
- **Streamlined Reinsurance**: Blockchain increases the transparency and efficacy of insurance processes by providing reinsurers with the ability to access actual time policy information. This may streamline the reassurance process by lowering mistakes and discrepancies in the information exchange among reinsurers and insurers.
- **Customer Verification and Underwriting**: Blockchain speeds up the client authentication procedure by safely conserving and disseminating consumer data among different organisations while preserving confidentiality. Furthermore, smart contracts may streamline underwriting processes by analysing established standards and granting insurance based on their conclusions.
- **Healthcare Insurance and Data Sharing:** Using blockchain technology, doctors, hospitals, insurance firms, and consumers can safely exchange medical records while maintaining the confidentiality and accuracy of the information. Processing of claims can be automated using smart contracts according to predetermined health criteria.
- **Identity Verification**: Blockchain-based verification of identity solutions can streamline Know Your Customer (KYC) processes, making it easier for insurance to verify the identities of clients and thwart fraud and theft of identities.

Stakeholder collaboration, compliance with regulations, and technical hurdles must all be addressed when attempting to carry out these kinds of applications. But by enhancing security, effectiveness, and transparency across the board, smart contracting and blockchain-based systems have the potential to fundamentally alter the field of insurance.

Applications of Smart Contracts and Blockchain Technology in Real-Time for the Stock Exchange Industry

Blockchain technology and smart contracts hold the potential to enhance the stock exchange sector in a variety of aspects.

- **Settlement and clearing**: Conventional stock exchanges have lengthy settlement timeframes. Blockchain-based settlement platforms can provide immediate clearance and development, reducing risks associated with counterparty and doing away with the requirement for middlemen. Smart contracts have the ability to ensure quick payment and automate trading procedures under specific conditions.
- **Asset Tokenization:** Through tokenizing a range of assets, particularly stocks, blockchain permits limited ownership and the trading of assets in smaller amounts. A wider range of customers may benefit from greater availability and liquidity as a result.
- **Greater Transparency**: The distributed ledger technology used by blockchain enables transactional traceability. Instantaneous recording and verification of each transaction, ownership exchange, and dividend distribution reduces the possibility of mistakes and exploitation.
- **Proxy voting**: Blockchain-based approaches can speed and secure the virtual voting process by ensuring open and immutable voting data. Smart contracts may automate voting procedures, improving their efficacy and lowering fraud.
- **Regulatory Compliance**: Blockchain technology helps exchanges for stocks maintain legal compliance. Immutable documents on the distributed ledger can support adherence to regulations, disclosure, auditing, and assurance.
- **Enhanced Security**: Transactions safety is improved by the decentralised architecture and cryptography concepts behind blockchain technology, which reduces the likelihood of fraud as well as cyberattacks in the stock market sector.
- **Global Accessibility**: Due to time zone differences or regulatory limitations, trade on the distributed ledger is feasible 24/7, providing traders from every corner of the globe with the opportunity to trade marketplaces that were previously inaccessible.

Legal and Ethical Dimensions for Smart Contracts

Smart contracts provide automated processes, productivity, as well as accountability but also bring legal difficulties. Enforcement is crucial; for an act to be supported in court, its terms must correspond with the law. A number of rules relating to investments, agreements, confidentiality, and safeguarding consumers must be observed, necessitating adherence to the existing legal structures. Because of jurisdiction concerns, accountability recognition for code flaws, uncertainty in code comprehension, strong safety precautions to prevent abuse, and other factors, legal explanation and involvement are additionally necessary (Adel, K.; Elhakeem, A.2022).

It remains morally necessary to create a compromise among confidentiality and accessibility so as to safeguard delicate information and preserve blockchain accessibility. Concerns about inclusion as well as accessibility highlight the need to resolve technological disparities so as to encourage fair involvement.

Considerations regarding morals additionally encompass the responsibility of programmers to create agreements that respect ethical standards, promote a greater good, and prevent damage, as well as consumers' freedom and comprehension of integrated contract terms and unbiased processes for making decisions. Such multidimensional legal as well as ethical factors underline the requirement for an extensive structure which blends principles of ethics, compliance with the law, and technological advancements in creation and use of smart contracts.

Future Trends in Smart Contracts and Green Investments

Future smart contract developments and sustainable investment will probably intersect, promoting innovative and sustainable practices across the financial and ecological sectors:

- **Environmental Impact metrics**: It's likely that ecological impact metrics will be included in smart contracts, thereby enabling automated validation and verification of sustainable investments. Established provisions regarding objectives for sustainability, lower emissions, or adherence to ecological laws may be included in these contracts. Through doing this, investors will have empowered to ensure that their funds are supporting projects with measurable ecological advantages, increasing the openness and responsibility of green investments.
- **Tokenization of green assets**: Green potential investments ought to grow more readily available as well as accessible through the use of smart contracts that tokenize ecological assets. Assets such as carbon credits, renewable energy projects, or green buildings can be stored on blockchain systems.

- **Automated Environmental, Social, and Governance (ESG) Reporting and Compliance:** As investment choices are made, consideration of ESG issues is becoming more crucial. Sustainability compliance may be automated via contracts for investments that have incorporated smart contract requirements. These agreements have the potential to start processes that ensure ongoing compliance with environmental, social, and governance (ESG) requirements and streamline disclosure to stakeholders and regulators using data in real time.
- **Green finance through Decentralised Finance (DeFi):** When DeFi procedures are combined via green finance programmes, new avenues for growth may open up. Smart contracts in decentralised finance might allow peer-to-peer green loans, crowdsourcing for eco-friendly projects, or distributed carbon trading systems by cutting out intermediaries and improving effectiveness in sustainable financing.
- **Blockchain-enabled carbon markets**: Smart contracts on blockchain-enabled platforms possess the power to totally revolutionise carbon trading by providing complete and immutable records of carbon credits. By automating operations according to predefined conditions, intelligent contracts could improve the efficiency and credibility of the purchase, sale, and monitoring of carbon credits.
- **Regulatory Compliance and Standardisation:** Smart agreements are expected to evolve in tandem with sustainable finance laws and regulations. Compliance with evolving environmental laws may be facilitated by smart contracts that incorporate standardised designs or processes, ensuring that disclosure obligations and legal responsibilities are fulfilled.

Automating Transactions in Green Finance Through Digital Twins

Introduction

Digital twins are computer-generated images based on actual procedures, frameworks, or items which allow instantaneous evaluation, tracking, and modification. Such virtual versions replicate the characteristics and actions of those in the real world by modelling behaviours, foreseeing issues, and evaluating potential improvements. The simulators combine data from sensors, Internet of Things gadgets, and additional sources (Hunhevicz, J.J.; Hall, D.M,2020). The technique aids in operational optimised performance, scheduled upkeep, including sound choices in a number of industries, like production, transport, infrastructure, and medical. It does these by creating exact replicas. Numerous sectors are undergoing a change thanks to the development of electronic twin's designs, which promote creativity and allow for data-driven choices ((Abioye, S.O. et.al 2021). These can provide useful knowledge, cut minimise interruptions, and boost performance.

"Digital twins" are digital replicas of real-world structures, operations, or objects. Such replications, that are built employing information, sensors, and algorithms, allow the observation, analysis, and simulation of the actions and outcomes of the original object. Digital twins have a lengthy history, having originated in the production and technical domains (Taherdoost, H.A.2022). Big data analytics, Internet of Things devices, and simulated techniques gained popularity as they developed. Over numerous years in design and manufacturing, digital twins are being produced in tandem with technological advancements. The term "digital twin" was first used in 2002 by Dr. Michael Grieves of the University of Michigan, but the idea had started taking shape decades earlier (Nakamoto, S.2008).

Originally introduced as virtual replicas of physical assets or systems, digital twins were primarily used in the management of product life cycles for planning and research. Improvements in the field of sensors with the emergence of the Internet of Things (IoT) during the middle of the 2000 substantially accelerated the emergence of digital twins. Instantaneous data collection via physical assets has been rendered feasible by the widespread application of integrated sensors in an extensive variety of technologies and devices, which aided in the creation of greater precise and vibrant electronic replicas (Adel, K, et.al 2022). Numerous sectors, like production, automobiles, aerospace, medical care, and electrical power, found simpler for them to gradually embrace the use of digital twins as a result of the breakthrough (Piasecki, P.J,2016).

Businesses like General Electric Company (GE), Siemens, and Airbus spearheaded this embrace by using digital replications to figure out maintenance needs, improve processes, and boost efficiency throughout a variety of sectors (Teisserenc, B. et.al 2021). In addition, in the past few years, there has been a substantial convergence of big data analytics, machine learning, artificial intelligence (AI), and digital twins. This combination has greatly widened the possibilities of digital twins by utilising AI algorithms to understand enormous quantities of data collected by sensors (Wang, W. et.al 2022). Consequently, very intricate and prognostic digital models are generated, facilitating before unattainable instantaneous making choices and optimisation throughout various sectors.

Components of Digital Twins

Common digital twin elements are as follows:

- **Physical Entity or thing:** The real structure, procedure, or object which the digital twin replicates is this one. It is equipped with sensors and instruments for gathering information.
- **Sensors and Data Collection:** The actual object is equipped with sensors that gather information in immediate form on a range of attributes, such as humidity, pressure, temperature, movements, and other associated metrics.
- **Data processing and analytics:** By interpreting, examining, and applying the information gathered, a computerised representation that mimics the characteristics and actions of the real thing is produced.
- **Visualisation and Simulation:** Productivity assessment, projections, and optimisation are made feasible by the virtual twin paradigm's ability to visualise and simulate a real-world entity.

Process of Leveraging Digital Twins

Leveraging digital twins entails the following steps:

- **Gathering Data:** At this stage, sensors use the actual thing to get data.
- **Data processing:** Gathered information is assessed and analysed in order to create a computer-generated depiction.
- **Model Creation:** the actions and characteristics of an actual object are represented digitally.
- **Monitoring and Optimisation:** The digital twin is used to replicate, track, as well as improve the operation of its original counterpart.

Real-Time Applications of Digital Twins by Global Companies

Global businesses are using digital twins in real-time across a range of industries:

- **Manufacturing:** Companies like Siemens and General Electric (GE) use digital replicas in their factories to increase efficiency of machinery, predict maintenance needs, as well as streamline manufacturing procedures.
- **Energy and Utilities:** Schneider Electric and ABB employ virtual twins in the energy sector to track along with manage electrical lines, ensuring effective energy distribution and maintenance.
- **Healthcare:** In the area of personalised medicine, Philips develops digital twins for patients to replicate and improve treatments.
- **Aviation:** In order to optimise energy savings, monitor planes efficiency, and anticipate maintenance needs, makers of aircraft, like Boeing and Airbus, utilise digital twins. In order to increase effectiveness, sustainability, and

disclosure across a variety of initiatives, digital twins—digital replicas of actual systems or assets—are utilised to streamline operations in the sustainable finance industry.

Digital twins are being used by a few multinational corporations for automating green finance operations.

- **Siemens:** Digital twins are used by Siemens in the energy sector, particularly for smart grids. Siemens uses these "digital twins" to monitor, evaluate, and improve the flow of energy within power networks. The system allows the company to streamline grid actions, which enhances energy conservation and makes it easier to integrate sources of clean electricity (37).
- **Bosch:** Bosch employs virtual twins in its production procedures to create sustainable output. Thanks to such electronic copies, Bosch has the ability to help their green efforts by maximising resource utilisation, reducing waste, and automating energy-associated transactions and manufacturing automating.
- **General Electric (GE):** GE is using digital twins in its aviation industry to enhance flight dynamics and save money on fuel. GE employs digital twin technology to promote greener aircraft operations by optimising engine efficiency, reducing the use of fuel, and automation activities related to preventive maintenance.
- **Schneider Electric:** Schneider Electric uses digital twins for managing buildings and intelligent infrastructure. By creating digital images of infrastructure and buildings, they facilitate proactive upkeep, streamline HVAC systems, and automate energy-related transactions. Energy is saved as a result, and the damage to the environment is lessened.

Role of Digital Twins

These global firms give instances of the ways companies have integrated digital twins within their operations to streamline interactions within green finance programmes. Digital twins enhance decision-making, optimise utilisation of resources, and foster sustainability across several sectors, ultimately resulting in a more environmentally conscious perspective to financing and company operations.

Digital twins are crucial tools for automation of operations in sustainable investments as they offer virtual replicas of real items or activities connected to sustainability initiatives (38). In the realm of green finance, these virtual twins are crucial for monitoring, assessing, and optimising a number of environmentally friendly project-related processes.

They enable mechanisation in several important ways. Firstly, digital twins gather information in instantaneous fashion on critical sustainability variables such as emission levels, resources and usage of energy, and others since they are equipped with sensors. This data is analysed to identify areas of inefficiency and development potential, which automates operations-focused operations (36).

Automating Transactions With Digital Twins for Green Investments

Digital twins are crucial for automated operations in green investments as they provide an electronic replica of real assets or activities related to initiatives to promote sustainability. In the setting of sustainable finance, virtual twins are used to monitor, assess, and enhance many aspects of green initiatives.

Such digital copies enable electronic transactions in a number of ways.

- **Effective Monitoring and Analysis:** Real-time data on emission levels, usage of energy, and other indicators of sustainability are collected by digital twins equipped with sensors. Through data analysis, opportunities for optimisation and redundancy are identified, and actions related to operational enhancements are mechanised.
- **Automated Reporting and Compliance:** Digital twins facilitate reporting on ecological effects and adherence to sustainability requirements. They automate the collection and verification of data required for tracking, ensuring transparency and dependability in activities related to abiding by green rules.
- **Smart Contract Integration:** By integrating digital replicas with intelligent agreements on blockchain-based systems, computerised transactions can be executed in accordance with preset conditions or sustainability standards. Smart agreements, for example, can be used to immediately begin paying for energy from renewable sources or carbon offsets.

The following are real-world instances of digital twins automating transactions in green investments:

- **Smart Grids:** By proactively modifying electrical power according to current information from sources such as wind and solar, utilities use digital twins to optimise distribution of energy, reducing wastage and boosting network performance.
- **Renewable Energy Management:** Digital twins analyse and optimise the performance of wind or solar power generators while automating chores such as changing panels orientation or turbine speeds for optimal the production of energy.

- **Sustainability of the Supply Chain:** By ensuring adherence to ecologically friendly supply chain protocols, businesses use electronic devices to automate operations by tracking and verifying resources or items that originate sustainably.

All things considered, digital replicas assist in automating transaction in investments in sustainability and facilitate faster, clearer, and legally acceptable actions in the marketplace by providing accurate, immediate information into sustainable procedures.

SOLUTIONS AND RECOMMENDATIONS

Give comprehensive connectivity instructions so that digital twins and smart contracts can collaborate effortlessly in the sustainable finance space. Strong security standards, data uniformity, as well as laws and regulations that validate these agreements ought to be highly prioritised in these recommendations. Promote educational campaigns which will increase participants' understanding. Future studies ought to concentrate on interoperability and scale enhancements to manage massive volumes of environmental data across multiple platforms. Analyse AI's potential for integration, impact quantification, and ethical implications to enhance environmentally friendly financial making decisions and sustainability adoption techniques.

FUTURE RESEARCH DIRECTIONS

Future research in the realm of digital twins and smart contracts in sustainable finance should focus on these three important topics. Initially, investigators will look into solutions that are scalable and interoperable breakthroughs for handling enormous quantities of environmental information across multiple platforms, with a focus on enhanced speed and systems compatibility. In order to improve automation, predictive analytics, and making choices in the area of green finance, secondly, techniques for precise impact evaluation and reporting are going to be created. Additionally, the integration of artificial intelligence (AI) and machine learning would be investigated. Lastly, an essential field of study will be assessing the legal, social, and ethical implications of employing digital twins and smart contracts in green finance. Through the mitigation of risks, prejudices, and unanticipated outcomes, this evaluation aims to furnish an equitable and accountable framework for sustainable development.

CONCLUSION

By automating transactions and changing investing contracts, the integration of digital twins and smart contracts opens up a fresh chapter in sustainable financing. Green finance could benefit greatly from the integration of digital twins, that are digital replicas of actual infrastructure or assets, and smart contracts, that are programmed contracts run on blockchain-based networks. The inclusion of current information via IoT devices within smart contracts linked to digital twins allows stakeholders to track as well as validate the ecological effects of green investments with previously unheard-of openness, accuracy, and certainty. This integration guarantees compliance to sustainable goals, streamlines processes, reduces the cost of administration, and ushers in an age of productivity and responsibility. As smart contracts and digital twins continue to advance, their transition in the field of green financing signifies an important step into a more sustainable future where clear, automated, as well as verified transactions help both the environment and add value for investors as well as the greater ecosystem.

REFERENCES

Androulaki. (2018), ledger fabric: A distributed operating system for permissioned blockchains. In *Proceedings of the Thirteenth EuroSys Conference*; Association for Computing Machinery: New York, NY, USA, pp. 1–15.

Ante, L. (2021). Smart contracts on the blockchain–A bibliometric analysis and review. *Telemat. Information 2023, 14,*117-119.

Buterin, V. (2017). Next-generation smart contract and decentralized application platform. (White Paper, 3).

Chakraborty, P. (2018), Understanding the software development practices of blockchain projects: A survey. In *Proceedings of the 12th ACM/IEEE International Symposium on Empirical Software Engineering and Measurement; Computing Machinery*, (pp. 1–10). IEEE. 10.1145/3239235.3240298

Chang, S. E., Chen, Y.-C., & Lu, M.-F. (2019). Supply chain re-engineering using blockchain technology: A case of smart contract-based racking process. *Technological Forecasting and Social Change*, *144*, 1–11. doi:10.1016/j.techfore.2019.03.015

Chen, Y.;et.al.(2020), Research on the risk of block chain technology in Internet finance supported by wireless networkers. *J. Wirel. Commun. Netw., 71.*

Davidson, S. (2016). Disrupting Governance. *The New Institutional Economics of Distributed Ledger Technology.*, *57*, 101519.

Destefanis, G. (2018). Smart contracts vulnerabilities: A call for blockchain oftware engineering? In *Proceedings of the 2018 International Workshop on Blockchain Oriented Software Engineering IWBOSE*), Campobasso, Italy. 10.1109/IWBOSE.2018.8327567

Dolgui, A., Ivanov, D., Potryasaev, S., Sokolov, B., Ivanova, M., & Werner, F. (2020). Blockchain-oriented dynamic modelling of smart contract design and execution in the supply chain. *International Journal of Production Research*, *2020*(58), 2184–2199. doi:10.1080/00207543.2019.1627439

Eenmaa-Dimitrieva, H., & Schmidt-Kessen, M. J. (2019). Creating markets in no-trust environments: The law and economics of smart contracts. *Computer Law & Security Report*, *35*(1), 69–88. doi:10.1016/j.clsr.2018.09.003

Finck, M. (2018). Blockchains and data protection in the European Union. *Eur. Data Prot. L. Rev.*, *4*(1), 17–35. doi:10.21552/edpl/2018/1/6

Gatteschi, V., Lamberti, F., Demartini, C., Pranteda, C., & Santamaría, V. (2018). Blockchain and smart contracts for insurance: Is the technology mature enough? *Future Internet*, *10*(2), 20. doi:10.3390/fi10020020

Greenspan, G. (2015). *Smart Contracts: The Good, the Bad and the Lazy*. data science.

Griggs, K. N., Ossipova, O., Kohlios, C. P., Baccarini, A. N., Howson, E. A., & Hayajneh, T. (2018). Healthcare blockchain system using smart contracts for secure automated remote patient monitoring. *Journal of Medical Systems*, *42*(7), 1–7. doi:10.1007/s10916-018-0982-x PMID:29876661

Hasan, H. R., & Salah, K. (2019). Combating deepfake videos using blockchain and smart contracts. *IEEE Access : Practical Innovations, Open Solutions*, *7*, 41596–41606. doi:10.1109/ACCESS.2019.2905689

Hewa, T., Ylianttila, M., & Liyanage, M. (2021). Survey on blockchain based smart contracts: Applications, opportunities and challenges. *Journal of Network and Computer Applications*, *177*, 177–187. doi:10.1016/j.jnca.2020.102857

Khan, S. N., Loukil, F., Ghedira-Guegan, C., Benkhelifa, E., & Bani-Hani, A. (2021). Blockchain smart contracts: Applications, challenges, and future trends. *Peer-to-Peer Networking and Applications*, *14*(5), 2901–2925. doi:10.1007/s12083-021-01127-0 PMID:33897937

Khatoon, A. (2018). A blockchain-based smart contract system for healthcare management. *Electronics 2020, 9*, (94).

Liebenau, J. (2016). *Blockchain Innovation beyond Bitcoin and Banking*. Research Gate.

Macrinici, D., Cartofeanu, C., & Gao, S. (2018). Smart contract within blockchain technology: A systematic mapping study. *Telematics and Informatics, 35*(8), 2337–2354. doi:10.1016/j.tele.2018.10.004

Madanchian, M. (2022). Impact of Digital Transformation Development on Organizational Change. In *Driving Transformative Change in E-Business through Applied Intelligence and Emerging Technologies* (pp. 1–24). IGI Global. doi:10.4018/978-1-6684-5235-6.ch001

Marchesi, L. (2020), *Design patterns for gas optimization in Ethereum*. In proceedings of the 2020 IEEE International Workshop on Blockchain Oriented Software Engineering (IWBOSE), London. 10.1109/IWBOSE50093.2020.9050163

Namasudra, S., Deka, G. C., Johri, P., Hosseinpour, M., & Gandomi, A. H. (2021). The revolution of blockchain: State-of-the-art and research Challenges. *Archives of Computational Methods in Engineering, 28*(3), 1497–1515. doi:10.1007/s11831-020-09426-0

Nugent, T. (2020). Improving data transparency in clinical trials using blockchain smart contracts. *F1000Research 016, 5,* (25-41).

Pan, J., Wang, J., Hester, A., Alqerm, I., Liu, Y., & Zhao, Y. (2019). Edge Chain: An edge-IoT framework and prototype based on blockchain and smart contracts. *IEEE Internet of Things Journal, 6*(3), 4719–4732. doi:10.1109/JIOT.2018.2878154

Perera, S., Nanayakkara, S., Rodrigo, M. N. N., Senaratne, S., & Weinand, R. (2020). Blockchain technology: Is it hype or real in the construction Industry? *Journal of Industrial Information Integration, 17*, 100–125. doi:10.1016/j.jii.2020.100125

Politou, E., Casino, F., Alepis, E., & Patsakis, C. (2019). Blockchain ability: Challenges and proposed solutions. *IEEE Transactions on Emerging Topics in Computing, 9*(4), 1972–1986. doi:10.1109/TETC.2019.2949510

Rouhani, S. (2019). Performance, and applications of smart contracts: A systematic survey. *IEEE Access, 7*, 50759–50779.

Sharma, P. (2010). Blockchain-based decentralized architecture for cloud storage system. *J. Inf. Secur. Appl., 62*, 102–970.

Sklaroff, J. M. (2018). Smart contracts and the cost of inflexibility. *University of Pennsylvania Law Review*, 166–263.

Swan, M. (2015). *Blockchain: Blueprint for a New Economy*. O'Reilly Media, Inc.

Szabo, N. (1997). The idea of smart contracts. *Nick Szabo's Pap. Concise Tutor.*, *6*, 199.

Taherdoost, H. (2023). An Overview of Trends in Information Systems: Emerging Technologies that Transform the Information Technology industry. *Cloud Comput. Data Sci.*, *4*, 1–16. doi:10.37256/ccds.5120233284

Vieira, G., & Zhang, J. (2021). Peer-to-peer energy trading in a microgrid leveraged by smart contracts. *Renewable & Sustainable Energy Reviews*, *143*, 110900. doi:10.1016/j.rser.2021.110900

Wang, S., Ouyang, L., Yuan, Y., Ni, X., Han, X., & Wang, F.-Y. (2019). Blockchain-enabled smart contracts: Architecture, applications, and future trends. *IEEE Transactions on Systems, Man, and Cybernetics. Systems*, *49*(11), 2266–2277. doi:10.1109/TSMC.2019.2895123

Zheng, Z., Xie, S., Dai, H.-N., Chen, W., Chen, X., Weng, J., & Imran, M. (2020). overview on smart contracts: Challenges, advances and platforms. *Future Generation Computer Systems*, *105*, 475–491. doi:10.1016/j.future.2019.12.019

Zou, W., Lo, D., Kochhar, P. S., Le, X.-B. D., Xia, X., Feng, Y., Chen, Z., & Xu, B. (2019). Smart contract development: Challenges and opportunities. *IEEE Transactions on Software Engineering*, *47*(10), 2084–2106. doi:10.1109/TSE.2019.2942301

ADDITIONAL READING

Abioye, S. O., Oyedele, L. O., Akanbi, L., Ajayi, A., Davila Delgado, J. M., Bilal, M., Akinade, O. O., & Ahmed, A. (2021). Artificial Intelligence in the Construction Industry: A Review of Present Status, Opportunities and Future Challenges. Journal of Building Engineering, 44, 103299. doi:10.1016/j.jobe.2021.103299 doi:10.1016/j.jobe.2021.103299

Adel, K., Elhakeem, A., & Marzouk, M. (2022). Decentralizing Construction AI Applications Using Blockchain Technology. Expert Systems with Applications, 194, 116–548. doi:10.1016/j.eswa.2022.116548 doi:10.1016/j.eswa.2022.116548

Hunhevicz, J. J., & Hall, D. M. (2020). Do You Need a Blockchain in Construction? Use Case Categories and Decision Framework for DLT Design Options. Advanced Engineering Informatics, 45, 101094. doi:10.1016/j.aei.2020.101094 doi:10.1016/j.aei.2020.101094

Lee, D., Lee, S. H., Masoud, N., Krishnan, M. S., & Li, V. C. (2021). Integrated Digital Twin and Blockchain Framework to Support Accountable Information Sharing in Construction Projects. Automation in Construction, 127, 103688. doi:10.1016/j.autcon.2021.103688 doi:10.1016/j.autcon.2021.103688

Nakamoto, S. (2008). Bitcoin: A peer-to-peer electronic cash system. Decentralized Bus. Rev., 2, 12–60.

Piasecki, P. J. (2016). Gaming self-contained provably fair smart contract casinos. Ledger, 1, 99–110. doi:10.5195/ledger.2016.29 doi:10.5195/ledger.2016.29

Taherdoost, H. A. (2022). Review of Blockchain Acceptance Models—Blockchain Technology Adoption Frameworks and Applications. Computers, 2022(11), 24. doi:10.3390/computers11020024 doi:10.3390/computers11020024

Teisserenc, B., & Sepasgozar, S. (2021). Adoption of Blockchain Technology through Digital Twins in the Construction Industry 4.0: A PESTELS Approach. Buildings, 11(12), 670. doi:10.3390/buildings11120670 doi:10.3390/buildings11120670

Wang, W., Guo, H., Li, X., Tang, S., Xia, J., & Lv, Z. (2022). Learning for Assessment of Environmental Satisfaction Using BIM Big Data in Energy Efficient Building Digital Twins. Sustainable Energy Technologies and Assessments, 50, 101897. doi:10.1016/j.seta.2021.101897 doi:10.1016/j.seta.2021.101897

KEY TERMS AND DEFINITIONS

Decentralised Autonomous Organisations (DAOs): Computer code and smart contract-governed entities that function independently of a central authority. DAOs use consensus processes that are carried out by code and token holders to manage decision-making and operations.

Decentralised finance (DeFi): Financial services and apps based on blockchain networks that do away with middlemen and allow peer-to-peer transactions without the use of conventional banks or financial institutions.

Digital Twins: Digital copies or representations of real-world systems, processes, or objects. They are designed to resemble their physical counterparts in terms of behaviour, attributes, and performance utilising simulations and real-time data.

Environmental, Social, and Governance (ESG): Framework to assess a company's performance in relation to its social responsibility, environmental impact, and governance standards.

Green Finance: A financial services model that prioritises sustainable investments while taking environmental, social, and governance (ESG) factors into account. It encourages funding for programmes and projects that address climate change or lessen their negative effects on the environment.

Initial Public Offerings (IPOs) and Initial Coin Offerings (ICOs): IPOs entail selling tokens to investors in order to raise money for cryptocurrency projects, whereas ICOs entail first presenting shares of a company to the public in order to allow it to raise money by going public.

Internet of Things" (IoT): A network of electronically linked items, sensors, or other devices that have been implanted with technology to gather and share data. IoT devices converse and engage with one another.

Smart Contracts: Self-executing programmes that have predetermined parameters encoded into the code. They use blockchain technology to conduct contracts and enforce them automatically when certain circumstances are satisfied.

Chapter 13
The Future of Green Finance:
Artificial Intelligence-Enabled Solutions for a More Sustainable World

Syed Noorul Shajar
https://orcid.org/0000-0002-0042-0190
Vellore Institute of Technology, India

Mohammad Kashif
https://orcid.org/0000-0002-4940-8264
Graphic Era University, India

Jintu George
Vellore Institute of Technology, India

Sibghatullah Nasir
B.S. Abdur Rahman Crescent Institute of Science and Technology, India

ABSTRACT

The convergence of artificial intelligence (AI) and green finance is revolutionizing the interconnection between the fields of finance and sustainability. AI-powered solutions have the capability to facilitate risk assessments, find investment opportunities, and spread resources with greater precision for financial institutions. The integration of artificial intelligence (AI) with green finance enables the utilization of information-driven methods to decision-making, thereby offering opportunities for a future characterized by improved environmental sustainability and financial stability. Artificial intelligence plays an integral role in facilitating the shift towards a global economy and the attainment of sustainable development goals.

DOI: 10.4018/979-8-3693-1878-2.ch013

INTRODUCTION

There has been a rising acknowledgement of the crucial need to address about climate change and encourage sustainability around the world in the recent years. Hence, the effective role of artificial intelligence (AI) is fetching more prominence in a world where finance and sustainability interconnect each other. The synergical integration between green finance and AI is creating an innovative-solutions towards a more sustainable future. With the surge in demand for environmentally responsible investments, AI-powered tools are enabling financial institutions to conduct in-depth risk assessments, identify promising investment opportunities, and allocate capital with a greater degree of accuracy (Alonso et al., 2023). The conjunction of AI and green finance marks a transformative shift in our approach to environmental issues and investment decisions. The fusion of AI and green finance equips us with the power to harness data-driven insights for transformative decision-making, paving the way for a more environmentally responsible and financially secure future of the world. As we explore the far-reaching implications of AI in green finance, we uncover the opportunity to cultivate a more sustainable and robust global economy. Moreover, Green finance has a substantial role to play in driving the transition towards world economy (Debrah et al., 2022). And the emergence of artificial intelligence (AI) has equipped the world with powerful tools to transform green finance and expedite the realization of sustainable development goals (SDGs). Therefore, this article is an attempt to delve into finding the transformative role of AI-enabled solutions in creating the future of green finance and ushering the world towards a more sustainable future.

UNDERSTANDING GREEN FINANCE AND ITS IMPORTANCE

Green finance refers to financial products and services that promote a shift towards an economy that is less reliant on carbon, utilizes resources more efficiently, and is environmentally sustainable. It plays a pivotal role in directing financial resources towards sustainable investments and projects which contributes in climate change mitigation, environmental goals and adaptation (Maria et al., 2023). This technique stands in line with the rising mindfulness of environmental issues and the growing emphasis towards corporate social responsibility. Chang et al., (2022) emphasised the sustainable finance literatures and viewed the value implications of ESG and CSR practices using the discounted cash flow valuation framework, and found that the ESG and CSR have increased the firm value by motivating employees, strengthening customer supplier relationships, boosting long-term growth, increasing dividends, and reducing financing costs. The significance of green finance stems from its ability to foster positive environmental outcomes along-with generating financial returns. It also serves as a catalyst for stimulating private capital towards sustainable initiatives, which is indispensable for attaining global sustainability goals. Moreover, as the sustainable investing gains impetus, the assimilation of environmental, social, and governance (ESG) aspects into investment decisions has become gradually prevalent, contributing a substantial shift in the financial sector towards more accountable and sustainable practices. Businesses and investors can play a vital role in shaping a more buoyant and environmentally sensible economy by adopting green finance, which in turn not only addresses unrelenting environmental concern but also opens new avenues for growth and innovation.

The Role of Artificial Intelligence in Green Finance

Artificial intelligence (AI) has transformed the field of green finance by providing sophisticated tools to analyse voluminous datasets, unearth hidden patterns, and enhance decision-making processes. So, the application of deep reinforcement learning in smart finance can significantly improve the efficiency and effectiveness of financial analysis and decision-making processes (Chen and Zhou, 2021). In the milieu of sustainable finance, AI aids as a powerful instrument for fetching actionable insights from complicated environmental, social, and financial datasets (Chen 2021; Natanelov et al., 2022). AI also allows financial institutions to evaluate environmental risks, appraise the sustainability initiatives impact, and develop investment strategies to bring into line with ESG principles with the help of machine learning algorithms and predictive analytics. Moreover, integration of AI in green finance spreads beyond data analysis which encircles numerous applications such as predictive modelling, natural language processing and algorithmic trading resulting in enhancing the efficacy and precision of sustainable investment approaches, which in turn authorize financial institutions to balance their financial performance with environmental responsibility (Xu et al., 2020). Studies by Chen (2021), Guo C. et al. (2021), Guo H. et.al., (2022) collectively explore the development of smart finance accounting management models under the perspective of artificial intelligence. Chen's work specifically focuses on meeting new financial management requirements for enterprise groups, emphasizing the direct and indirect effects of AI-infused accounting management models. Both studies underscore how AI technology significantly promotes the development of smart accounting management model architecture, fostering advancements in financial management. Moreover, AI technologies have not only improved the competence and precision of sustainable investment approaches but have also simplified the automation of compliance processes, safeguarding adherence to growing governing standards and endorsing transparency in sustainable practices. Green finance can attain more accuracy in evaluating environmental impacts, classifying opportunities of investment with constructive sustainability outcomes, and augmenting the apportionment of capital to build a more sustainable and robust global economy by leveraging Artificial intelligence (AI).

Advantages of AI-Enabled Solutions in Green Finance

The combination of AI-enabled solutions with green finance has unlocked a new frontier of opportunities, offering diverse range of advantages which has spread across numerous facets of sustainable investing and financial decision-making. One of the prime advantages of AI is the capability to boost the precision and efficacy of Environmental, Social, and Governance (ESG) data analysis. Financial institutions can utilize data analytics to identify companies with robust environmental, social, and governance (ESG) performance and make their investments in these companies using AI algorithms. Moreover, AI also empowers enterprises to categorize and measure complex sustainability risks, allowing proactive management of risk to align with ESG principles. By measuring and attenuating environmental and social risks, financial institutions can safeguard their investment portfolios from probable losses while positioning their investments with sustainable development goals. Furthermore, AI-enabled predictive modelling technique improves the identification of evolving sustainability movements and market prospects, driving proactive investment approaches which capitalise on evolving environmental and social dynamics (Liu et al., 2021). Additionally, AI-powered solutions in green finance enable the formation of customized sustainable investment portfolios as per individual investors' preferences and goals. Financial institutions may also offer tailored investment solutions that align with the values and sustainability goals of their clients by integrating AI algorithms to analyse individual ESG preferences and risk profiles. By customizing sustainable investment strategies to meet specific investor needs improves their engagement, gratification, and the widespread acceptance of sustainable investment practices across several market sections. The advantages of AI-powered tools in green finance promotes enhancing more transparent and accountable approach to sustainable investment practices. By employing AI-enabled reporting and monitoring systems, financial institutions can facilitate stakeholders with comprehensive facts on the environmental and social implications of their investments, endorsing better transparency and conviction in sustainable finance activities. In addition, AI simplifies real-time tracking of ESG performance, allowing dynamic adjustments to investment strategies for changing sustainability factors and market conditions. Hence, by leveraging AI's capabilities, green finance can enhance the precision, efficacy, and effectiveness of sustainable investment strategies, propelling the movement towards a more robust and environmentally sensible monetary ecosystem.

AI Applications in Sustainable Investments

Financial institutions' evaluation, selection, and management of sustainable investment prospects are revolutionized by the application of artificial intelligence (AI) in sustainable investments, which encompasses a variety of functionalities. AI-powered data analytics are essential for evaluating the environmental, social, and governance (ESG) performance of companies, empowering investors to make well informed decisions that support sustainability goals. AI algorithms may find hidden relationships between ESG variables and financial performance through sophisticated data processing and pattern identification, offering significant insights into the long-term sustainability potential of investment opportunities. AI powered applications are also used in impact investing, where tools with AI capabilities make it easier to track and evaluate the effects that investment portfolios have on the environment and society. The findings of Dong et al., (2022) emphasised that the green finance significantly promotes green innovation with a more profound effect on green utility model patents compared to green invention patents. Also, it has the positive role of policy in fostering green innovation within the corporate landscape, aligning with sustainable finance objectives (Tang M et al., 2022; Wang K et al., 2022). Through the utilization of machine learning algorithms, financial institutions may monitor and measure the favourable results of sustainable investments, consequently enhancing the transparency and accountability of impact investing endeavours. This feature enables investors to channel funds towards initiatives that yield measurable social and environmental value, leading to a more effective approach to sustainable finance. AI applications in sustainable investments include predictive modelling and risk assessment features, in addition to ESG analysis and impact measurement. Financial institutions may optimize investment strategies to traverse changing environmental and societal dynamics by anticipating sustainability-related risks and opportunities with AI-powered predictive analytics. Artificial Intelligence (AI) enables proactive risk management techniques that protect financial returns while supporting sustainable development goals by enabling the identification of possible sustainability concerns through scenario analysis and predictive modelling. Additionally, AI is being used in sustainable investing to optimize portfolios and allocate assets. In these contexts, AI-driven algorithms assist in building buoyant and diversified investment portfolios that adhere to ESG standards. Financial institutions can customize investment strategies to prioritize sustainability considerations while enhancing financial performance by applying advanced optimization techniques provided by AI. This facilitates the integration of sustainable investment practices across various asset classes and investment vehicles. The various ways that artificial intelligence (AI) is being applied to sustainable investments highlight how groundbreaking this technology can be in advancing the incorporation of sustainability factors into investment decision-making, changing the face of sustainable finance, and promoting a more resilient and ecologically sensible financial system.

Enhancing Risk Management With AI in Green Finance

The incorporation of artificial intelligence (AI) into green finance presents a transformative advancement to improve risk management practices, enabling financial institutions to detect, evaluate, and address sustainability-related risks with high accuracy and efficiency. Advanced data analytics and predictive modelling are used by AI-powered risk management tools to assess the environmental, social, and governance (ESG) performance of businesses and investment portfolios thereby improving the detection and evaluation of sustainability risks and opportunities (Hemanand et al., 2022). The ability of AI to process and analyze voluminous amounts of ESG data enables financial institutions to obtain comprehensive insights into the sustainability performance of their investment portfolios. AI makes it easier to identify links between ESG factors and financial performance by utilizing machine learning algorithms allowing for proactive risk assessment that support sustainability goals. This capacity enables businesses to foresee and address sustainability related risks that could affect financial performance, while simultaneously advancing social and environmental imperatives. Furthermore, scenario analysis and predictive modelling are supported by AI-driven risk management tools, which help financial institutions in evaluating the possible effects of market dynamics and sustainability-related events on their investment portfolios. By employing a forward-thinking approach to risk assessment enables organizations to establish robust risk management strategies which consist of sustainability concerns, effectively protecting financial returns and advancing the attainment of sustainable development objectives. Additionally, AI fosters the real-time monitoring of ESG performance enabling financial institutions to modify their risk management plans in response to shifting market conditions and sustainability dynamics. The automation of compliance procedures, where AI-powered solutions assist in the monitoring and enforcement of legal requirements pertaining to sustainable finance, is another area in which risk management and artificial intelligence are integrated. Financial institutions can accelerate the identification of sustainability-related compliance issues and ensure alignment with dynamic regulatory landscapes by utilizing AI algorithms for compliance monitoring. Through improving the accountability and transparency of sustainable investment practices, this proactive approach to compliance management builds trust and confidence of the stakeholders. Trukhachev et al., (2022) done a theoretical study on the peculiarity of green finance in the AI era, and suggested that the green finance can reach its full development potential only by relying on smart technology. Also, the increased use of AI based technologies will increase the competitiveness of decision making in the green finance and it accelerates the uses in the economy and environmental management. The advancements in risk management facilitated by AI in green finance underscore its transformative potential in enhancing the precision, efficiency, and impact of sustainability risk assessment and mitigation, thereby contributing to the flexibility and sustainability of the global financial ecosystem.

Innovations in AI-Enabled Sustainable Banking

The integration of artificial intelligence (AI) in sustainable banking represents a transformative leap towards redefining the role of financial institutions in driving positive environmental and social impact. AI-enabled sustainable banking solutions leverage advanced data analytics, machine learning algorithms, and automation capabilities to offer a comprehensive suite of services that align with sustainability objectives. From ESG data analysis to impact measurement and personalized sustainable investment offerings, AI-driven innovations are reshaping the landscape of sustainable banking, propelling the sector towards a more impactful and environmentally conscious paradigm (Shajar & Farooqi 2016; Akhtar et al., 2023). An important development in the domain of AI-enabled sustainable banking concerns the creation of customised sustainable investment alternatives. Sustainable banks can provide tailored investment options that align with the values and sustainability objectives of their clients by utilizing artificial intelligence algorithms to assess individual environmental, social, and governance (ESG) preferences and risk profiles. The enhancement of investor involvement and contentment is facilitated by the deployment of a personalised approach, which in turn encourages the adoption and utilisation of sustainable investment methods. Moreover, this methodology promotes the growth of a more extensive and heterogeneous investor base, distinguished by its inclusiveness and diversification. Furthermore, the application of artificial intelligence (AI) in the field of impact measurement and reporting is becoming increasingly prevalent. Sustainable banks are applying sophisticated data analytics techniques to screen and assess the social and environmental outcomes resulting from their investment portfolios (Nishant et al., 2020). By giving stakeholders clear and thorough insights into the sustainability performance of their investments, sustainable banks can gain stakeholder trust and confidence in their sustainable banking operations. Furthermore, the utilization of AI-enabled impact measurement facilitates the advancement of novel financial products and services that place emphasis on sustainability factors while generating financial gains simultaneously. Within the field of risk management, the utilization of artificial intelligence (AI) in sustainable banking solutions enables the proactive evaluation and reduction of sustainability risks, and protecting financial returns while simultaneously supporting the goals of sustainable development. Artificial intelligence (AI)-powered risk management solutions facilitate compliance monitoring, scenario analysis, and predictive modelling, allowing sustainable banks to create robust risk management plans that comply with ESG principles and regulatory requirements. The implementation of a proactive risk management strategy contributes to the improvement of the resilience and long-term viability of sustainable banking activities, hence cultivating increased trust and assurance among investors and stakeholders. AI-enabled sustainable banking has the potential to revolutionize financial institutions' role in achieving good environmental and social impact, creating a more robust and comprehensive global financial ecosystem.

Challenges and Considerations in Implementing AI in Green Finance

The incorporation of artificial intelligence (AI) into the field of green finance holds significant potential for revolutionary outcomes. However, this integration also brings up a range of problems and considerations that financial institutions must carefully navigate to fully capitalize on the advantages offered by AI-powered tools (Minh et al., 2022). Since AI algorithms rely on enormous volumes of high-quality data to produce precise insights and predictions, one of the main challenges is data availability and quality. Hence, obtaining trustworthy environmental, social, and financial datasets is a major challenge because it can be challenging for companies to find, standardize, and validate the data needed for AI-driven research. Furthermore, the issue of interpretability and transparency in AI models within the context of green finance presents significant concerns. The intricate nature of AI algorithms has the potential to impede stakeholders' understanding of the underlying reasoning behind the insights and decisions made by AI. Desalegn and Tangl (2022) systematically analyse green finance in all its forms, instruments, and measurements, to highlight overall research trends to enhance green finance for inclusive green investment and its results shows that the green financing gap is frequently observed due to low finance levels, pro green project management, risk and return trade-off, and a lack of analytical tools and expertise in identifying and assessing green project risks. To improve accountability and transparency in sustainable investment practices and to build more confidence among stakeholders and investors, it is imperative that the interpretability of AI models be addressed. Furthermore, since AI-driven decisions may have far-reaching effects on financial, social, and environmental results, it is imperative to ensure the ethical and responsible usage of AI in green finance. Concerning regulatory compliance and risk management, the incorporation of AI into green finance presents obstacles, as organizations must navigate dynamic regulatory frameworks and guarantee that AI-powered processes comply with sustainability guidelines and standards. To reduce the risks involved with using AI while adhering to sustainable finance principles, necessitates for the creation of strong governance frameworks and compliance systems to mitigate the risks associated with the implementation of artificial intelligence. In addition, to promote a fair and inclusive method of making sustainable investment decisions, it is imperative to prioritize the resolution of issues pertaining to bias, impartiality, and accountability in AI algorithms. An additional factor to be considered when using artificial intelligence (AI) in the realm of green finance is the issue of scalability and the seamless integration of AI-powered solutions into pre-existing financial systems and operational frameworks. To fully utilize AI in promoting sustainable finance initiatives, financial institutions require to evaluate how well AI technologies fit with their existing personnel, procedures, and infrastructure (Zhou et al., 2020). This requires ensuring scalability and seamless integration. This requires the implementation of strategic planning, allocation of resources towards AI expertise and skills, and continuous creativity to effectively utilize the revolutionary potential of AI in reforming the domain of green finance. It is imperative to acknowledge and address these issues and concerns to fully harness the capabilities of artificial intelligence (AI) in promoting sustainable finance. This will assist in the development of a more robust, equitable, and sustainable global financial ecosystem.

Investing in AI for Green Finance: Opportunities and Risks

Financial institutions must manage an array of opportunities and risks while integrating artificial intelligence (AI) with green finance to fully capitalize on the revolutionary potential of AI-enabled solutions. AI-driven technologies provide enormous opportunity to improve accuracy, efficacy, and effect of sustainable finance activities, ranging from sophisticated data analytics and predictive modelling to personalized sustainable investment solutions. Financial institutions may use AI to open new channels for discovering investment possibilities, analysing sustainability risks, and streamlining capital allocation to promote a more sustainable and environmentally conscientious global economy. Furthermore, the allocation of resources towards artificial intelligence (AI) in the realm of green finance has the potential to augment the transparency and responsibility of sustainable investment methodologies, hence cultivating greater trust and assurance among stakeholders and investors (Enam, et al., 2023; Shajar S.N. 2017; Akhtar et al., 2021). The utilization of AI-driven impact assessment and reporting systems empowers financial institutions to offer thorough analysis about the environmental and social consequences of their investments. This, in turn, improves disclosure and promotes a climate of ethical and sustainable financing. Furthermore, artificial intelligence (AI) plays a crucial role in enabling the continuous monitoring of environmental, social, and governance (ESG) performance. This capability allows for timely modifications to investment strategies, considering the ever-changing dynamics of sustainability and market circumstances. Nevertheless, the allocation of resources towards artificial intelligence (AI) in the context of green finance is not without its inherent hazards.

CONCLUSION

The AI-enabled solutions are closely intertwined with the future of green finance. Through the utilization of artificial intelligence (AI), it is possible to speed up transitioning towards a more sustainable global environment. This advancement may simultaneously stimulate economic progress while mitigating the adverse effects of greenhouse gas emissions and minimizing overall environmental harm. Artificial intelligence (AI) is now changing several critical areas, such as precision agriculture and smart mobility, by facilitating the adoption of more efficient and sustainable techniques (Musleh et al., 2022; Vinuesa et al., 2020). The ethical and responsible utilization of artificial intelligence (AI) in the realm of green finance is of the utmost significance (Peng et al., 2023). It is imperative to address concerns pertaining to data privacy, bias in algorithms, and transparency to ensure the appropriate implementation of AI technology (Sustainable Investments in Green Finance, 2023). By engaging in this practice, we may effectively utilize the whole capabilities of artificial intelligence to achieve a future that is environmentally and socially sustainable.

REFERENCES

Akhtar, S., Alam, M., & Ansari, M. S. (2021). Measuring the performance of the Indian banking industry: Data envelopment window analysis approach. *Benchmarking*, *29*(9), 2842–2857. doi:10.1108/BIJ-03-2021-0115

Akhtar, S., Alam, M., Khan, A., & Shamshad, M. (2023). Measuring technical efficiency of banks vis-à-vis demonetization: An empirical analysis of Indian banking sector using CAMELS framework. *Quality & Quantity*, *57*(2), 1739–1761. doi:10.1007/s11135-022-01431-8

Akhtar, S., Alam, M., & Khan, M. M. (2021). YES Bank Fiasco: Arrogance or Negligence. *Emerging Economies Cases Journal*, *3*(2), 95–102. doi:10.1177/25166042211061003

Alonso, A., Carbó, J. M., & Marqués, J. M. (2023). *Machine Learning methods in climate finance: a systematic review.*

Ansari, M. S., Akhtar, S., Khan, A., & Shamshad, M. (2022). Consequence of Financial Crisis on Liquidity and Profitability of Commercial Banks in India: An Empirical Study. *Studies in Economics and Business Relations*, *3*(2), 36–50. doi:10.48185/sebr.v3i2.367

Chang, X., Fu, K., Jin, Y., & Liem, P. F. (2022). Sustainable finance: ESG/CSR, firm value, and investment returns. *Asia-Pacific Journal of Financial Studies*, *51*(3), 325–371. doi:10.1111/ajfs.12379

Chen, C., & Zhou, Y. (2021). Application of deep reinforcement learning algorithm in smart finance. *Front. Artif. Intell. Appl.*, *341*, 40–48. doi:10.3233/FAIA210230

Chen, Y. (2021). Framework of the smart finance and accounting management model under the artificial intelligence perspective. *Mob. Inf. Syst. 2021 (SI)*, 4295191–4295211.

Debrah, C., Chan, A. P. C., & Darko, A. (2022). Green finance gap in green buildings: A scoping review and future research needs. *Building and Environment*, *207*, 108443. doi:10.1016/j.buildenv.2021.108443

Dong, Z., Xu, H., Zhang, Z., Lyu, Y., Lu, Y., & Duan, H. (2022). Whether green finance improves green innovation of listed companies-evidence from China. *International Journal of Environmental Research and Public Health*, *19*(17), 10882. doi:10.3390/ijerph191710882 PMID:36078597

Enam, M., Shajar, S. N., & Das, N. (2023). Non-Monotonic Relationship between Corporate Governance and Banks' Operating Performance—The Moderating Role of CEO Duality: Evidence from Selected Countries. *Sustainability (Basel)*, *15*(7), 5643. doi:10.3390/su15075643

Guo, C.-Q., Wang, X., Cao, D.-D., & Hou, Y.-G. (2022). The impact of green finance on carbon emission-analysis based on mediation effect and spatial effect. *Frontiers in Environmental Science*, *10*, 844988. doi:10.3389/fenvs.2022.844988

Guo, H., Gu, F., Peng, Y., Deng, X., and Guo, L. (2022). Does digital inclusive finance effectively promote agricultural green development? – A case study of China. *Int. J. Environ.*

Hemanand, D., Mishra, N., Premalatha, G., Mavaluru, D., Vajpayee, A., Kushwaha, S., & Sahile, K. (2022). Vajpayee, & Sahile, K. (2022). Applications of intelligent model to analyze the green finance for environmental development in the context of artificial intelligence. *Computational Intelligence and Neuroscience*, *2022*, 1–8. doi:10.1155/2022/2977824

Liu, Z., Song, J., Wu, H., Gu, X., Zhao, Y., Yue, X., & Shi, L. (2021). Impact of Financial Technology on Regional Green Finance. *Computer Systems Science and Engineering*, *39*(3), 391–401. doi:10.32604/csse.2021.014527

Maria, M. R., Ballini, R., & Souza, R. F. (2023). Evolution of Green Finance: A Bibliometric Analysis through Complex Networks and Machine Learning. *Sustainability (Basel)*, *15*(2), 967. doi:10.3390/su15020967

Minh, D., Wang, H. X., Li, Y. F., & Nguyen, T. N. (2022). Explainable artificial intelligence: A comprehensive review. *Artificial Intelligence Review*, 1–66.

Musleh Al-Sartawi, A. M., Hussainey, K., & Razzaque, A. (2022). The role of artificial intelligence in sustainable finance. *Journal of Sustainable Finance & Investment*, 1–6. doi:10.1080/20430795.2022.2057405

Natanelov, V., Cao, S., Foth, M., & Dulleck, U. (2022). Blockchain smart contracts for supply chain finance: Mapping the innovation potential in Australia-China beef supply chains. *Journal of Industrial Information Integration*, *30*, 100389. doi:10.1016/j.jii.2022.100389

Nishant, R., Kennedy, M., & Corbett, J. (2020). Artificial intelligence for sustainability: Challenges, opportunities, and a research agenda. *International Journal of Information Mang*.

Peng, G., Han, M., & Yuan, H. (2023). Artificial Intelligence Drives the Coordinated Development of Green Finance and the Real Economy: Empirical Evidence from Chinese Provincial Level. *Journal of the Knowledge Economy*, 1–39. doi:10.1007/s13132-023-01506-3

Shajar, S. N. (2017). Relationship between working capital management and profitability of automobile companies in India: A paradigm shift towards economic strengthening. *International Journal of Trade. Economics and Finance*, *8*(4), 210–216.

Shajar, S. N., & Farooqi, S. A. (2016). Impact of working capital management on the profitability of automobile industry in India-an empirical study of selected automobile companies. *Pac. Bus. Rev. Int*, *8*, 197–203.

Sustainable Investments in Green Finance. (2023, November 14). *Advances in Finance, Accounting, and Economics Book Series*. IGI Global. doi:10.4018/979-8-3693-1388-6

Vinuesa, R., Azizpour, H., Leite, I., Balaam, M., Dignum, V., Domisch, S., & Fuso Nerini, F. (2020). The role of artificial intelligence in achieving the Sustainable Development Goals. *Nature Communications*, *11*(1), 1–10. doi:10.1038/s41467-019-14108-y PMID:31932590

Xu, H., Mei, Q., Shahzad, F., Liu, S., Long, X., & Zhang, J. (2020). Untangling the impact of green finance on the enterprise green performance: A meta-analytic approach. *Sustainability (Basel)*, *12*(21), 9085. doi:10.3390/su12219085

Zhou, X., Tang, X., & Zhang, R. (2020). Impact of green finance on economic development and environmental quality: A study based on provincial panel data from China. *Environmental Science and Pollution Research International*, *27*(16), 19915–19932. doi:10.1007/s11356-020-08383-2 PMID:32232752

Chapter 14
Blockchain Technology for Sustainable Investment: A Comprehensive Review and Future Prospects

Anjli Gupta
Maharaja Agrasen Institute of Technology, Rohini, India

Ritu Gupta
Maharaja Agrasen institute of Technology, India

Kiran
Apeejay Institute of Management and Engineering Technical Campus, India

Sharuti Choudhary
Woxsen University, India

ABSTRACT

The purpose of this review is to provide a comprehensive analysis of how blockchain technology can enhance sustainable investment practices. The authors aim to assess the current applications, benefits, and challenges of blockchain in sustainable investment and identify opportunities for future development. They conducted a thorough review of existing literature and case studies to analyze the current landscape of blockchain technology in sustainable investment. This involved examining various blockchain platforms and applications, as well as assessing their impact on transparency, security, and efficiency in sustainable investment. This analysis reveals that blockchain technology offers significant advantages for sustainable investment, including improved transparency, reduced fraud, and increased accessibility for smaller investors. However, challenges such as scalability and regulatory hurdles persist. The review also highlights successful cases and real-world examples of blockchain implementation in sustainable investment.

DOI: 10.4018/979-8-3693-1878-2.ch014

INTRODUCTION

Blockchain technology has garnered significant attention in recent years for its potential to revolutionize various industries, including finance and investment. This comprehensive review explores the use of blockchain technology in sustainable investment, examining its current state and future prospects. Sustainable investment seeks to align financial returns with environmental and social impact, making it an area of growing interest.

The purpose of this review is to provide a comprehensive analysis of how blockchain technology can enhance sustainable investment practices. We aim to assess the current applications, benefits, and challenges of blockchain in sustainable investment and identify opportunities for future development.

We conducted a thorough review of existing literature and case studies to analyze the current landscape of blockchain technology in sustainable investment. This involved examining various blockchain platforms and applications, as well as assessing their impact on transparency, security, and efficiency in sustainable investment.

Our analysis reveals that blockchain technology offers significant advantages for sustainable investment, including improved transparency, reduced fraud, and increased accessibility for smaller investors. However, challenges such as scalability and regulatory hurdles persist. The review also highlights successful cases and real-world examples of blockchain implementation in sustainable investment.

Looking ahead, the integration of blockchain technology in sustainable investment holds great promise. It has the potential to enable more inclusive and responsible investment practices, attracting a wider range of investors and enhancing the overall impact of sustainable investments. However, addressing scalability, regulatory, and interoperability issues will be crucial for realizing this potential.

In conclusion, blockchain technology offers a compelling framework for advancing sustainable investment by enhancing transparency and security. Despite challenges, the future prospects for blockchain in sustainable investment are promising, with the potential to drive positive social and environmental impact while delivering financial returns. Embracing blockchain technology in this context is a step toward a more sustainable and equitable financial ecosystem.

Blockchain

A blockchain is a distributed, decentralized, and chronological chain ledger that stores data in a network of linked blocks. After a block is added to the chain, it becomes irrevocable and impervious to changes (Crosby et al., 2016). Each block comprises an accumulation of transactions or data. Without the need for a central authority, this sort of technology operates on a network composed of peers, where multiple devices or nodes verify and preserve the information. This guarantees transparency, security, and dependability (Ali et al., 2020).

Consensus mechanisms, or protocols that guarantee that all participants concur on the legitimacy of operations prior to when they are submitted to the blockchain (Carrara et al., 2020), are the backbone of blockchain technology. Several popular consensus techniques, each with a distinctive approach for verifying transactions and preserving network integrity, are Proof of Work (PoW), Proof of Stake (PoS), and their variants.

The incorporation of blockchain-based technologies into frameworks for sustainable investments has the possibility to foster greater reliability, transparency, and efficiency in the assessment and administration of environmental, social, and governance (ESG) factors (Saxena et al., 2023). This combination of sustainable investment and blockchain technology creates prospects for novel solutions to critical worldwide problems, aligning economical goals with ecological and social goals.

Blockchain technology has enormous promise, and as it advances and becomes increasingly prevalent, it will continue to establish new paradigms in an assortment of industries while providing a wealth of alternatives for effectiveness, inventiveness, and trust in the age of digital media.

Sustainable Investment

Sustainable investment, occasionally referred to as environmental, social, and governance (ESG) or socially conscious investing (SRI), is an approach to investing that takes into consideration not solely financial returns but also environmental, social, and ethical considerations (Talan & Sharma, 2019).

Here's an overview of key components of sustainable investment:

Environmental Considerations: Making an investment in corporations or campaigns which advocate environmental sustainability is the principal objective of this group of interests (Paliwal et al., 2020). It entails evaluating elements including a business's energy effectiveness, use of energy from renewable sources, handling of trash, and initiatives to mitigate greenhouse gas emissions.

Social obligation: investments that are sustainable investigates how corporations oversee the relationships they have with their vendors, clients, workers, and communities (Aյan et al., 2016). It considers things like equitable compensation, advancement of communities, diversity and inclusion, human rights, labor practices, and sustainable procurement.

Governance Practices: The way businesses are run, governed, and controlled is referred to as governance (Turnbull, 2002). Aspects like compensation for executives, anti-corruption efforts, transparency, board independence, and adherence regarding ethical principles are all reviewed as components of sustainable investment (Fulton et al., 2013).

Investing in businesses, associations, or campaigns that vigorously advocate favorable social or environmental results is known as "positive impact investing." It could entail funding endeavors related to sustainable farming, clean energy, medical research, or education.

Negative Screening: Certain types of sustainable investment strategies call for the exclusion of certain specific businesses or sectors if they do not meet sustainability or ethical criteria (Berry & Junkus, 2013). This may entail steering clear of investments in sectors that consist of tobacco, weapons, fossil fuels, or businesses with subpar labor standards.

Engagement and Campaigning: Investors interact with businesses, leveraging their stake in the company as they advocate for improved ESG procedures (O'Rourke, 2003). The organization might push for adjustments to business operations, policies, or openness so that they coincide with goals for sustainable development.

The dual goals of sustainable holding investments are money-making opportunities and beneficial effects on the environment or society. It reflects the growing recognition that a company's impact on the environment and society, alongside or in addition to the company's financial performance (Lin et al., 2009), is a crucial component of creating long-term value.

When adopting sustainable investment strategies, investors frequently use third-party evaluations, ESG ratings, along with sustainability reports from companies as an outline. The purpose of this program is to prioritize funding toward companies and projects that exhibit an allegiance to sustainable practices and build ideal social or environmental accomplishments.

BACKGROUND OF BLOCKCHAIN

The origins of blockchain technology can be traced to a paper written in 2008 under the pseudonym Satoshi Nakamoto by an individual or group (Nakamoto, 2008). In this paper, the concept of a decentralized digital currency called Bitcoin and the blockchain technology that underpinned it were unveiled.

Bitcoin is the earliest and most well-known use of blockchain technology. It was developed as a peer-to-peer electronic cash system that does not require middlemen such as banks to facilitate transactions (Hellani et al., 2018). To maintain security and transparency, every transaction made using Bitcoin is recorded on its blockchain.

How Blockchain Operates

A distributed ledger system as a whole blockchain allows for the construction and upkeep of a continually growing collection of records, or blocks, that are linked together and preserved by encryption methods. This is a review of how blockchain functions:

Figure 1. Functioning of blockchain
(Ali et al., 2020)

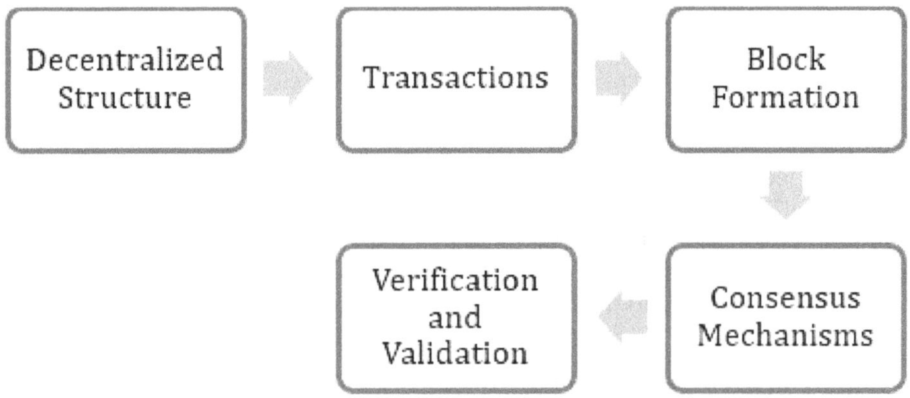

Decentralized Structure: Blockchain runs on a global network of computers, or nodes, without the presence of a central authority or middleman to verify and record transactions. A replica of the perform blockchain remains stored on each node (Gamage et al., 2020).

Transactions: Blocks are collections regarding transactions that are associated (Li et al., 2019). Depending on the intended use of the blockchain specifically, these transactions may encompass numerous types of knowledge in addition to banking transactions.

Block Formation: Upon confirmation that an accumulation of transactions is grouped in tandem and verified by network participants. The procedure is known as block formation. A cryptographic hash of the previous block is typically included in every fresh block in order to establish an affiliation between them at all times (Xiao et al., 2020).

Consensus Mechanisms: the nodes of a network have to agree on a block before it is permitted to be introduced to the chain (Carrara et al., 2020). Nodes reach a consensus on the legitimacy of transactions and the particular order in which they ought to be added to the blockchain by means of an assortment of consensus methodologies (such as Proof of Work, Proof of Stake, etc.).

Verification and Validation: The nodes within the network must verify the transactions contained in a recommended block (Bodkhe et al., 2020). They check that the transactions adhere to the blockchain's role in guidelines and are accurate, authentic, and in compliance.

In Proof of Work platforms like Bitcoin, mining entails resolving challenging mathematical puzzles. This is particularly true for particular blockchains. The first miner successful in figuring out the answer wins the privilege of adding the block to their respective chain as they compete to find it. Transaction fees and cryptocurrency have been distributed to them as rewards.

Immutability: Due to the geographically distributed character of the blockchain, it is practically impossible to alter a block once it was originally added to the chain because executing therefore would necessitate modifying every block that has been added since and then (Nawari & Ravindran, 2019).

Security: One of among the most essential components of blockchain security has become cryptography. A chain can be created by each block having a distinct cryptographic hash of the one before its contents. Any attempt to alter a block would result in a change to its hash, making the network immediately cognizant of any alteration.

Each member of a blockchain network possesses a private key as well as a public key. Private keys convey access to confidential data, while publicly accessible keys are employed to generate IP addresses for data sent and received. Secure transactions are ensured by this asymmetric encryption.

Blockchain technology is suitable during an extensive spectrum of applications beyond cryptocurrencies, which include handling supply chains, voting systems, healthcare, and more. It offers reliability, safety, and decentralization.

HISTORY OF INTEGRATION OF FINANCES WITH BLOCKCHAIN

Blockchain technology gained attention for investment purposes with the rise of Bitcoin and other cryptocurrencies around 2009 when Bitcoin was introduced (Sharma et al., 2019). However, blockchain's integration into investment beyond cryptocurrencies started to gain momentum later.

The idea of using blockchain beyond digital currencies emerged gradually, and its potential in various sectors, including finance, supply chain, healthcare, and more, became evident in the following years.

In the investment realm, blockchain's integration began to gain traction around 2016-2017 when Initial Coin Offerings (ICOs) became popular. ICOs allowed startups to raise funds by issuing their own digital tokens or coins based on blockchain (Jonathan & Wright, 2018). This introduced a new form of investment, enabling people to invest in projects and companies using cryptocurrencies.

Subsequently, the concept of tokenization emerged, where traditional assets like real estate, art, or commodities were represented as digital tokens on a blockchain. This facilitated fractional ownership and easier trade of assets that were traditionally less liquid (Heines et al., 2021).

Moreover, the rise of security tokens, which represent ownership in real-world assets and comply with relevant securities regulations, contributed to blockchain's integration into investment. Security tokens provide a more regulated and compliant way for investors to participate in tokenized assets.

Today, blockchain technology continues to evolve and is being explored for various investment vehicles, including decentralized finance (DeFi) platforms, non-fungible tokens (NFTs), digital securities, and more (Kong & Lin, 2021). Its potential to improve transparency, reduce intermediaries, and streamline processes continues to attract interest from investors and financial institutions seeking innovative opportunities.

KEY ASPECTS OF BLOCKCHAIN

As of last update in January 2022, blockchain technology continued to make significant strides across various industries. Here are some key aspects of the current status of blockchain:

Figure 2. Key aspects of blockchain
(Seebacher & Schüritz, 2017)

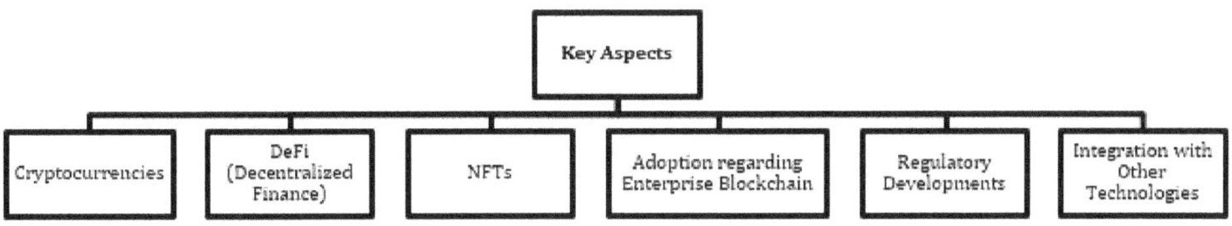

Cryptocurrencies

Bitcoin remains the most well-known cryptocurrency, but numerous others (Ethereum, Binance Coin, Solana, etc.) have gained prominence (Makarov & Schoar, 2022). The crypto market experienced fluctuations in value and continued to attract attention from investors, institutions, and governments.

DeFi (Decentralized Finance)

These mobile applications, that supply financial services without any requirement for standard intermediaries, are still expanding. Lending, borrowing, yield farming, decentralized exchanges, and various other services have been incorporated in this list. While there was a lot of innovation in the DeFi space, there were also difficulties like security weaknesses and regulatory scrutiny (Makarov & Schoar, 2022).

Non-Fungible Tokens

or NFTs, are very popular in the gaming, collectibles, art, and other industries. They serve as distinctive digital possessions and have opened through exciting opportunities for virtual real estate, music, digital art, and other products.

Adoption regarding Enterprise Blockchain: A great deal of companies have investigated blockchain for a number of software, which includes identity verification, supply chain management, provenance tracking, and transparent record-keeping. Industry and blockchain platform pilot projects and collaborations grew.

Regulatory Developments

Throughout the entire globe, governments and regulatory organizations continue to experience challenges figuring out how to govern blockchain technology and cryptocurrencies (Smith, 2008). whereas some nations approved of the groundbreaking developments of blockchain technology, others tightened requirements because of worries about consumer protection, money laundering, and financial stability.

Technological Recent Developments

Blockchain systems have made progress in sustainability, scalability, and interoperability (Qin & Gervais, 2018). Aims were set on improving the current protocols, creating additional layer 2 solutions, and progressing toward consensus mechanisms that use less energy (like Ethereum's transition to Proof of Stake in Ethereum 2.0).

Integration With Other Technologies

precisely blockchain technology became more closely associated with AI, IoT, and big data, it opened up novel possibilities for seamless workflows, secure data exchange, and enhanced capabilities in an assortment of industries.

The evolution of blockchain technology remains dynamic, with ongoing research, development, and real-world implementation. However, the landscape is continually changing, so there might have been further advancements or shifts in the status of blockchain and cryptocurrencies since my last update.

PRACTICAL APPLICATION OF BLOCKCHAIN IN VARIOUS FIELDS

Blockchain technology has diverse applications across various industries due to its unique features like decentralization, transparency, and immutability. Here are some notable blockchain use cases:

Bitcoin and Other Cryptocurrencies

The most well-known application of the technology known as blockchain is in facilitating the development of sound, decentralized digital currencies, among which are those who were found in the digital currencies Bitcoin and Ethereum (Tschorsch & Scheuermann, 2016).

Supply Chain Management

By when logging every financial transaction and items posture, blockchain utilizes the manufacturing processes easily accessible and observable. This indicates authenticity mitigates fraud, and enables customers to keep tabs on the provenance of merchandise.

Smart Contracts

Autonomous execution arrangements built on blockchain technology that, in response to specific events, take swift action and enforce every clause of an agreement. They diminish the need for middlemen in a variety of industries, including real estate, insurance, and contracts.

Voting Systems

By delivering an impermeable to document of votes, blockchain technology can provide safe and upfront voting systems, guaranteeing the integrity of elections (Küfeoğlu, 2022).

Healthcare Statistics Management

It provides an interoperable, safe platform for handling medical records, making sure accessibility, privacy, and data integrity.

Decentralized Finance (DeFi)

Without the use by conventional banks, DeFi applications employ blockchain technology for building financial issues services and products (Garg, 2023). These encompass yield farming, decentralized exchanges, lending, and borrowing.

Tokenization of Assets

By permitting fractional ownership, blockchain technology makes it achievable to tokenize stocks, commodities, real estate, and creations, expanding accessibility to a broader demographic of investors.

Protection of Intellectual Property

By using the blockchain system to timestamp and authenticate internet content, intellectual property, and patents, plagiarism and counterfeiting can be dipped.

Peer-to-peer energy trading has been made possible by it, enabling people to buy as well as sell excess renewable energy, strengthening energy distribution, and cutting dependability on centralized systems (Tushar et al., 2021).

Identity Management

By enabling confidential and distributed identity verification, blockchain-based identity solutions reduce the danger of identity theft and give humanity control over their confidential data (Lim et al., 2018).

The distribution regarding assistance and charitable donations can be rendered more transparent through the application of blockchain technology, which at first guarantees that contributions are made to the right people and are put into constructive use.

These use cases draw attention to the wide-ranging versatility of blockchain technology across industries and demonstrate how it may modify standard processes by putting efficiency, security, and full disclosure.

INTEGRATION OF BLOCKCHAIN WITH SUSTAINABLE INVESTMENT

Blockchain technology has drawn enthusiasm compared to sustainable investment, a commonality considering it has the ability to completely transform an assortment of industries through enhanced efficiency, traceability, and transparency . Here's an in-depth evaluation:

Being forthcoming and Obligation: Transparency is ensured by the immutable and decentralized nature of blockchain, which keeps a timeless record of business transactions. This can be extremely crucial in sustainable investing to track currency, validate impact announcements, and make sure the requirements for social responsibility, governance, and the environment (ESG) are came across (Akhtar et al., 2022).

Supply Chain Tracking

Employing blockchain-based technologies, merchandise and raw materials can be tracked all the way through the supply chain. This is critical for sustainable investing because it enables buyers to confirm the trustworthiness (Centobelli et al., 2022) that products were sourced ethically, guaranteeing moral behavior and reducing the negative environmental impact.

Crowdfunding and Tokenization

Blockchain generates fractional ownership achievable through tokenization, which allows investors to invest a part in assets or sustainable projects that would otherwise be out of reach. This may encourage global sustainable initiatives by way of a variety of entails, which might include carbon credits, impact-driven startups, or renewable energy projects.

Impact Measurement and Smart Arrangements

Smart contracts allow for the automation of agreements and the self-execution of contracts under certain predetermined conditions (Möslein & Marburg, 2020). This might be employed to construct impact-driven contracts, in wherein funding is released in anticipation of accomplishing predetermined standards or objectives regarding sustainability.

The Cutting Process Intermediaries and Expenses

Blockchain eliminates intermediary companies compared to transactions, lowering expenses and potential risks that come with suffering a third party associated. This can directly allocate extra funds to worthwhile projects or initiatives in sustainable investments.

Blockchain-based systems can be employed for securely handling ESG data, that guarantees its accuracy and reliability (Fulton et al., 2013). This makes it easier when evaluating the environmental and social repercussions of investments, restoring investors an in-depth comprehension to help their interests make decisions that are in accordance with their values.

Voting and Governance

To offer stakeholders an immediate say in decisions pertaining to sustainable practices and initiatives, blockchain's transparent and secure nature can be utilized to facilitate upfront shareholder representation and governance in sustainable investment portfolios (O'Rourke, 2003).

Considerations and Challenges

even though blockchain technology has great potential, there are still issues with seamless integration, scalability, regulatory uncertainty, and consumption of electricity (in some consensus mechanisms like Proof of Work). For sustainable investment to be widely implemented, these obstacles must be addressed.

The prospect for blockchain technology to be incorporated into sustainable investment is considerable as it cultivates more thoroughly. To maximize its beneficial impacts, however, cooperation among technology developers, financiers, government agencies, and sustainability trained professionals is required to feed its successful implementation.

FORMS OF SUSTAINABLE INVESTMENT FACILITATED BY BLOCKCHAIN

Through several regarding approaches and applications blockchain technology has proven its promise for advancing sustainable investment practices:

Figure 3. Forms of sustainable investment facilitated by blockchain
(Paliwal et al., 2020)

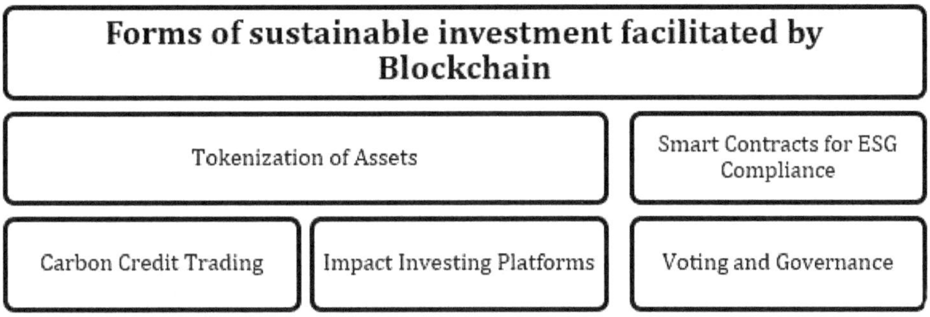

Transparency and Traceability

Supply chains and transactions can be transparently monitored owing to blockchain technological devices. This describes the technique known as environmentally friendly investing, which involves making sure that the funds is allocated to corporations or campaigns that adhere to environmental, social, and governance (ESG) standards. Blockchain implies the accurate and transparent logging of transactions, which at first may boost assurance and demonstrate the outcomes of decisions regarding investments.

Tokenization of Assets

Real estate, projects that generate electricity from renewable sources, and carbon credits are several instances of assets that may be entirely or acquired in part through the tokenization process made achievable by blockchain technology. This can encourage liquidity in these economies and make it more straightforward for investors to become involved in sustainable undertakings.

Smart Contracts for ESG Compliance

Smart agreements are capable of being configured to operate solely as a reaction to the fulfillment of specific ESG prerequisites. To guarantee investment decisions are in alignment with goals for sustainable development, earnings for a project, for illustration, could only be published if tailored sustainability benchmarks are encountered.

Carbon Credit Trading

By streamlining and verifying the steps involved, blockchain-based platforms can create an unchangeable, transparent ledger of greenhouse gas emissions and credits (Woo et al., 2021). This might encourage businesses to lessen emissions while establishing a carbon market that may be far more efficient.

Impact Investing Platforms

Investors with impact investments will be able to connect with projects that have quantifiable optimistic outgoing or environmental impacts through platforms powered via blockchain. The concept of transparency, accountability, and traceability to earn impact investments are the stated objectives of these platforms.

Voting and Governance

Implementing blockchain technology for governance, companies may deliver transparent yet secure voting procedures for their shareholders (O'Rourke, 2003). This guarantees that stakeholders have a voice in the decision-making procedure especially when it pertains to ESG.

Cutting Out the Intermediaries and Expenses

Blockchain innovation can lower costs and enhance accessibility to sustainable investments by doing separate alongside middlemen. This has the potential to attract additional funding to environmentally conscious projects.

Blockchain technology has the potential for boosting sustainable investment, nevertheless there are still challenges that get that must be resolved, including scalability worries, unclear regulation, and the requirement for standards from the industry and concurrence on ESG reporting and measurements.

EXAMINING READ-WORLD'S BLOCKCHAIN AND SUSTAINABLE INVESTING EXAMPLE

The adoption of blockchain technology in the carbon credit marketplace is a noteworthy real-world example of sustainable investment.

Carbon credits, which can be swapped to offset the emissions of other entities, can frequently be acquired by businesses and projects that push themselves to reduce carbon emissions (Woo et al., 2021). On the other conjunction, difficulties with credit legitimacy, verification, and transparency have plagued the carbon credit market.

Blockchain offers an opportunity to track the creation, exchange, and retirement of emissions reduction credits in an open, unchangeable ledger. Veridium, for illustration, is tokenizing carbon credits using blockchain technology with the goal of rendering them transparent and easily tradeable (Shrivas & Yeboah, 2019).

Each carbon credit is embodied by a digital asset with a distinct identity that corresponds to an identifiable amount of carbon reduction because of to the tokenization of credits for carbon reduction on a blockchain. Because they ought to are preserved on a blockchain, it has become relatively easy to trace the beginnings, ownership as well as and historical transactions of these tokens.(Bondarenko et al., 2019)

By boosting the legitimacy and transparency of carbon credits, this application makes confident that consumers are able to validate the authenticity and environmental impact of the credits their bodies buy. Additionally, it makes trading those credits easier, which might encourage more companies and shareholders to volunteer to take part in carbon offsetting software applications.

Furthermore, fraud or the double counting of carbon credits, that's resulted in problems with the conventional carbon credit market, can be avoided with the help of blockchain's transparency. Overall, this use case demonstrates how blockchain technology can contribute to sustainable investment by creating a more transparent, efficient, and trustworthy marketplace for carbon credits and environmental offsets.

The second finest illustration is the tokenization of real estate assets is one application of blockchain technology in the real world during investment purposes.

Representing ownership of tangible assets (such as real estate, artwork, or commodities) as digital tokens on a blockchain is known as tokenization (Heines et al., 2021). Through this procedure, ownership of an asset can be split into smaller, exchangeable units, thereby rendering it conceivable for investors to purchase and sell fractional ones of these assets.

A multimillion-dollar real estate property, for instance that could be transformed into tokens into smaller fractions (Giannoni et al., 2023). Investors can afterward purchase these smaller amounts, which are displayed on a blockchain as digital tokens. On a platform constructed using blockchain technology, investors have the opportunity to pick up or sell tokens, each of whose value represents a certain amount of the property.

Benefits of tokenizing real estate assets using blockchain include:

a. Fractional Ownership: This characteristic provides it with possible for investors to own a certain amount of extremely valuable assets, establishing more diversified and economically viable investment options conceivable.

b. Liquidity: By facilitating quicker and more straightforward transactions on blockchain-based platforms, tokenization possesses the potential to elevate liquidity for assets wholly or partially typically illiquid, for instance real estate (Benedetti et al., 2023).
c. Security and Disclosure: Blockchain keeps track of ownership and transaction history on a permanent, unalterable ledger, thereby fostering transparency. By streamlining operations like rent distribution, smart contracts could enhance security and eliminate paperwork.

Access to International Markets: Investors are able to participate in real estate investments lacking considering their spot as a result of blockchain-based platforms.

Blockchain technology has been adopted by an abundance of platforms along with companies to implement or investigate real estate tokenization. By making real estate investment opportunities more accessible and liquid for a broader spectrum of investors, these initiatives desire to promote equal the accessibility of real estate investment opportunities.

Let's investigate a concrete example of how Bitcoin, the initially created and most well-known cryptocurrency, incorporates blockchain technology.

Another real-world example is Bitcoin and Blockchain, both of which possess the following traits such as:

a. Decentralized Exchanges: Peer-to-peer transactions are made possible by Bitcoin's implementation of blockchain technology, which eliminates the need over centrally located entities like the financial institutions (Gamage et al., 2020). A transaction is announced to the network when someone desires to send Bitcoin to another client.
b. Verification regarding Transactions: Each of the Bitcoin network's nodes examine and assure these transactions. They make certain the transaction adheres according to the network's consensus rules and that the sender possesses a sufficient quantity of Bitcoin to send.
c. Block Establishment and Mining: Transactions that have been independently examined are compiled into blocks. Miners compete to find solutions to challenging mathematical puzzles (Miller et al., 2015). They are network participants who contribute computational power. The block is eligible for addition to the blockchain by the very first miner who completes the puzzle. Mining is an operation that adds additional transactions to a distributed ledger and serves as vital for safeguarding the network.
d. Blockchain Structure: The blocks are coupled with the previous one in a chain that is arranged chronologically (Tschorsch & Scheuermann, 2016). A distinct cryptographic hash of the previous block's contents has been incorporated in

each new block so as to ensure immutability and resistance to tampering. The history of every Bitcoin transaction, attending all across time back to the first one, is contained in the following set of blocks.

e. Security via Cryptography: Cryptography protects the network. Digital signatures have been generated using public keys as well as private keys to demonstrate ownership and transaction authorization. The private key is necessary to execute transactions, and these keys are archived in digital wallets.

This real-world illustration demonstrates that blockchain technology, which powers Bitcoin, enables safe, dispersed, and transparent transactions. The Bitcoin virtual currency simplifies peer-to-peer transactions without the need for intermediary companies, along with the blockchain makes certain the integrity of the entire transaction history.

EVOLUTION OF INVESTMENT USING BLOCKCHAIN

Investment using blockchain has seen significant growth and evolution in recent years. Here are some facts and figures related to blockchain-based investments:

Initial Coin Offerings (ICOs)

ICOs were a popular fundraising method for blockchain projects. In 2017, ICOs raised around $6 billion (Canidio et al., 2021). However, this fundraising method faced regulatory scrutiny due to concerns about investor protection and fraudulent schemes.

Security Token Offerings (STOs)

STOs emerged as a more regulated form of token sales (Castro et al., 2022). Unlike ICOs, STOs are compliant with securities regulations, aiming to represent ownership in real-world assets. The global STO market was valued at over $1 billion in 2018.

Venture Capital Investment

Venture capital investment in blockchain and crypto-related startups has been substantial. In 2021, blockchain and cryptocurrency startups received around $27 billion in venture capital funding, indicating growing interest from institutional investors.

Cryptocurrency Market Capitalization

The total market capitalization of cryptocurrencies reached its peak in 2021, exceeding $2 trillion (Barna, 2021). Bitcoin, the first and most well-known cryptocurrency, has often dominated a significant portion of this market capitalization.

DeFi (Decentralized Finance) Ecosystem

The DeFi sector has witnessed substantial growth, offering various financial services without traditional intermediaries. Total value locked (TVL) in DeFi protocols surpassed $200 billion in 2021, showcasing increased adoption of decentralized lending, borrowing, and trading platforms.

NFTs (Non-Fungible Tokens)

NFTs gained popularity in 2021, representing unique digital assets like art, collectibles, and music (Kong & Lin, 2021). The NFT market saw transactions worth billions of dollars, with some high-profile digital artworks selling for tens of millions of dollars.

Institutional Involvement

Institutional interest in cryptocurrencies and blockchain technology has grown. Notable financial institutions and corporations have begun investing in cryptocurrencies, exploring blockchain solutions, and offering crypto-related services to clients.

Global Blockchain Spending

Corporate and government spending on blockchain solutions continues to increase. The global blockchain technology market was projected to reach over $23 billion by 2023, demonstrating a growing appetite for blockchain solutions across industries.

These figures highlight the rapid growth and interest in blockchain-based investments, showcasing both the potential and the evolving nature of this nascent industry. As blockchain technology matures and regulatory frameworks become clearer, further growth and innovation in investment using blockchain are expected.

LATEST BLOCKCHAIN TRENDS RELATED TO INVESTMENT

Investment trends associated with the blockchain fluctuate swiftly Several significant trends were influencing investment strategies in the decentralized ledger and cryptocurrency space as of my most recent update in early 2022:

Adoption by Institutions

Institutional interest in and investment in blockchain technology and cryptocurrencies has grown substantially. Companies, hedge funds, and firmly established financial institutions began investing a sizeable sum of money in blockchain projects and cryptocurrency assets (Varma, 2019).

Growth of Decentralized Finance (DeFi)

DeFi protocols intrigued substantial financing and preserved development. Due to their potential for immense yield farming, decentralized exchanges (DEXs), liquidity provision, and lending platforms captured attention.

NFT Market Surge

Investments in digital art, collectibles, gaming assets, and intellectual property have turned to Non-Fungible Tokens (NFTs), which saw substantial expansion (Kong & Lin, 2021). In this nascent market for distinctive digital assets, investors hunted for opportunities.

Solutions Concerning Layer-2 and Scalability

Investment interest was drawn to projects that used Layer-2 solutions or competing blockchains to increase scalability of the blockchain and transaction speeds (Vilà Brualla, 2022). The scalability problems with large networks, such as Ethereum, were the focus of these solutions.

Investments have been made in projects that investigate the idea of the metaverse and simulated property in blockchain-based virtual environments. The potential for fully immersive experiences and controlling digital assets made these projects prominent.

Sustainable and Eco-Friendly Projects

As anticipated regarding the way blockchain technology might impact the environment, money has been directed toward eco-friendly initiatives and cryptocurrencies that use energy-efficient consensus methodologies.

Regulatory Adaptation: Investors kept a careful eye on changes to the regulations. Investments frequently took consideration of assets or projects that adhered with changing regulatory requirements, since institutional participation in regulatory clarity became progressively crucial.

Blockchain Infrastructure and Development

Projects related to blockchain infrastructure, developer tools, and interoperability have sparked increased interest from investors in a bid to render it more simple for decentralized applications (dApps) to be developed across chains.

Central Bank Digital Currencies (CBDCs) and Stablecoins

As governments investigated digitizing traditional currencies, CBDC-related projects and research attracted attention (Clarke & Hrnjic, 2022), while stablecoins' stability and extending utility attracted funding.

Security and Privacy Solutions

Amid increasing concerns about data protection and confidentiality, projects aimed at boosting blockchain security, privacy, and identity solutions sketched interest from investors.

The aforementioned trends are indicative of the dynamic investment landscape pertaining to blockchain technology, which has been influenced by factors such as market demand, legislative developments, investor preferences, and technological advancements. Investment strategies in the blockchain space are dictated by the dynamic nature of the space, which frequently results in the emergence of new trends or the improvement of traditional approaches.

RECENT ADVANCEMENTS IN INVESTMENT DUE TO BLOCKCHAIN TECHNOLOGY HAVE CONTINUED TO EVOLVE, BRINGING ABOUT SEVERAL NOTABLE DEVELOPMENTS

Tokenization of Assets

Blockchain facilitates the tokenization of traditionally illiquid assets such as real estate, art, and commodities. This process allows fractional ownership, increased liquidity, and accessibility to a wider pool of investors.

DeFi Yield Farming and Staking

Decentralized Finance (DeFi) protocols offer opportunities for yield farming and staking, allowing users to earn rewards or interest by providing liquidity or locking up their cryptocurrencies in smart contracts.

NFTs and Digital Ownership

Non-Fungible Tokens (NFTs) have expanded beyond art and collectibles, entering realms like music, gaming, and virtual real estate (Kong & Lin, 2021). These tokens represent unique digital ownership, enabling creators to monetize digital assets and providing new investment avenues.

STOs and Regulatory Compliance

Security Token Offerings (STOs) have emerged as a regulated form of fundraising, tokenizing assets while complying with regulatory frameworks (Hughes et al., 2019). This advancement offers investors opportunities for fractional ownership of securities backed by tangible assets.

Cross-Border Transactions and Remittances

Blockchain facilitates faster and more cost-effective cross-border transactions and remittances (Naderi, 2021). This capability has the potential to revolutionize the way money is transferred globally, reducing fees and transaction times.

Institutional Investment in Crypto Assets

Institutional investors, including hedge funds, asset managers, and corporations, are increasingly allocating funds to cryptocurrencies and blockchain-based assets, contributing to market maturity and mainstream adoption.

Sustainable Investing and ESG Integration

Blockchain technology supports sustainable investing by enabling transparent tracking of funds and ensuring compliance with Environmental, Social, and Governance (ESG) criteria. This helps investors allocate capital to projects aligned with sustainability goals.

Smart Contracts and Automated Investments

Smart contracts automate investment processes, enabling conditional and programmable agreements that execute when predefined conditions are met. This automation streamlines investment procedures and reduces administrative overhead.

Blockchain-Based Funds and ETFs

Investment products based on blockchain technology, including blockchain-focused exchange-traded funds (ETFs) and funds investing in crypto assets, provide traditional investors with exposure to the blockchain and cryptocurrency markets.

These advancements showcase the growing integration of blockchain technology into the investment landscape, offering new opportunities, increased efficiency, and diversified investment avenues for both retail and institutional investors.

BENEFITS

Blockchain investments can offer several potential benefits to the general public:

Financial Inclusion:

Blockchain technology has the potential to provide access to financial services for the unbanked or underbanked populations worldwide. By bypassing traditional financial intermediaries, blockchain-based services can enable people to participate in the global economy more easily (Swan, 2017).

Figure 4. Research classification framework
(Developed from Ali et al., 2020)

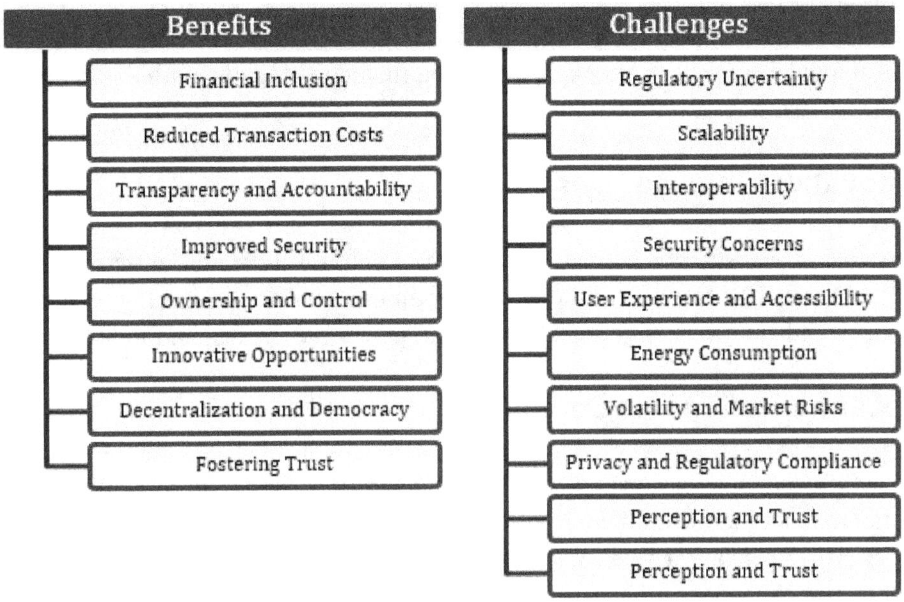

Reduced Transaction Costs

Blockchain-based transactions can significantly reduce transaction fees compared to traditional banking and financial systems. This can make financial transactions more affordable, particularly for cross-border payments and remittances.

Transparency and Accountability

Blockchain's transparent and immutable nature can enhance trust in various sectors. For instance, in supply chains, consumers can trace the origin of products, ensuring ethical sourcing and authenticity (Centobelli et al., 2022). In charitable donations, blockchain can provide transparency on where funds are being utilized.

Improved Security

Blockchain's cryptographic security features can enhance data security and protect personal information. Users have more control over their data, reducing the risks of identity theft and data breaches.

Ownership and Control

Blockchain-based assets, such as cryptocurrencies and tokenized assets, give individuals more direct ownership and control over their assets (Lee, 2019). This can empower people to manage their wealth independently without relying on intermediaries.

Innovative Opportunities

Blockchain investments offer opportunities for innovation and entrepreneurship (Morabito, 2017). They can stimulate the development of new technologies, business models, and solutions, potentially leading to economic growth and job creation.

Decentralization and Democracy

Decentralized applications (dApps) built on blockchains can promote a more democratic and fair digital environment (Wu & Gladyshev, 2020). They can allow for peer-to-peer interactions without centralized control, promoting open access and fair participation.

Fostering Trust

Blockchain's trust-building features can facilitate trust between parties who might not trust each other traditionally. Smart contracts and transparent transactions can help build trust in business dealings and agreements.

While these benefits are promising, it's important to note that blockchain technology is still evolving, and its widespread adoption faces challenges, including scalability issues, regulatory hurdles, and technological limitations. However, as the technology matures, it has the potential to positively impact various aspects of society by providing more accessible, transparent, and secure systems.

Challenges of Blockchain With Respect to Investment

Certainly, while blockchain presents numerous opportunities for investment, it also faces several challenges:

Regulatory Uncertainty

Regulatory frameworks around blockchain and cryptocurrencies vary widely across jurisdictions and are continually evolving (Cumming et al., 2019). Lack of clear regulations can create uncertainty for investors and businesses, impacting investment decisions and market growth.

Scalability

Scalability remains a significant challenge for many blockchain networks. As the number of users and transactions increases, some networks experience congestion and slower transaction speeds, hindering widespread adoption for certain applications (Gadekallu et al., 2019).

Interoperability

Different blockchain platforms often operate in isolation, lacking interoperability to communicate and share data seamlessly. This limits the potential for collaboration and efficient integration between various blockchain networks.

Security Concerns

While blockchain is known for its security features, it's not entirely immune to vulnerabilities. Smart contract bugs, hacking attempts, and security breaches on exchanges can lead to significant losses for investors and erode trust in the technology (Zamani et al., 2020).

User Experience and Accessibility

Blockchain technology can be complex for average users, creating a barrier to entry. Improving user interfaces, enhancing accessibility, and providing better education about blockchain are essential to broader adoption.

Energy Consumption

Some blockchain networks, particularly those using Proof of Work (PoW) consensus mechanisms like Bitcoin, consume substantial amounts of energy. This issue has raised concerns about the environmental impact and sustainability of such networks.

Volatility and Market Risks

Cryptocurrency markets are highly volatile, experiencing rapid price fluctuations. This volatility poses risks for investors and can discourage mainstream adoption due to concerns about market stability.

Privacy and Regulatory Compliance

Balancing privacy with regulatory compliance is a challenge in blockchain systems. Ensuring data privacy while complying with regulations, especially in industries like finance and healthcare, remains a complex issue.

Perception and Trust

Despite the potential benefits, blockchain technology still faces skepticism and lack of trust in some circles due to its association with cryptocurrencies, past scams, and misconceptions about its capabilities.

Addressing these challenges will require collaboration among stakeholders, ongoing innovation, regulatory clarity, and improvements in technology infrastructure to realize the full potential of blockchain in the investment landscape.

MAJOR LIMITATIONS

Investing in blockchain-based assets or projects involves various risks, similar to any other investment. Here are some common risks associated with blockchain investments:

Volatility

Cryptocurrencies, which are a primary application of blockchain, are known for their high volatility. Prices can fluctuate significantly within short periods, leading to substantial gains or losses for investors (Makarov & Schoar, 2022).

Regulatory Uncertainty

Regulatory landscapes for cryptocurrencies and blockchain projects are still evolving in many jurisdictions. Changes in regulations or government policies can impact the legality and viability of investments in this space (Smith, 2008).

Cybersecurity Threats

Blockchain is considered secure due to its cryptographic principles. However, vulnerabilities in smart contracts, hacking incidents, or security breaches on exchanges can lead to theft or loss of assets (Zamani et al., 2020).

Liquidity Risks

Some tokens or digital assets may suffer from low liquidity, making it challenging to buy or sell them without significantly affecting their market price.

Market Risks

The blockchain and cryptocurrency market can be influenced by various factors such as technological advancements, market sentiment, adoption rates, and competition among projects. These factors can impact the value of investments.

Project Viability

Many blockchain projects are startups with innovative ideas but unproven business models. There's a risk that the project might not deliver on its promises or fail due to lack of adoption, technical issues, or mismanagement.

Token Utility and Value

The utility of tokens or digital assets issued by blockchain projects may not align with their perceived value. Changes in the utility, purpose, or demand for these tokens can affect their value significantly (Ansari et al., 2023).

Exit Scams and Fraud

The decentralized and pseudonymous nature of blockchain can make it a breeding ground for fraudulent schemes and scams. Investors might fall victim to Ponzi schemes, fake projects, or misleading information.

To mitigate these risks, it's essential for investors to conduct thorough research, understand the technology and project fundamentals, diversify their investments, only invest what they can afford to lose, and stay updated on market trends and regulatory changes. Seeking advice from financial experts and staying cautious while navigating the blockchain investment landscape can help manage these risks.

SUSTAINABLE INVESTMENT: FUTURE ASPECTS

Blockchain innovation appears to have an exceptionally promising future in ventures, with an abundance of trends and developments shaping its course:

Asset Tokenization

Conventional assets such as real estate, artwork, commodities, and more are capable of being digitized through the application of blockchain technology (Kong & Lin, 2021). Through the conversion of ownership rights into digital tokens, this process makes for centuries illiquid markets more accessible and enables fractional ownership.

Decentralized Finance (DeFi)

DeFi applications, encompassing yield farming, lending, borrowing, and decentralized exchanges, are disrupting traditional financial services (Makarov & Schoar, 2022). These based on blockchain technology platforms elevate financial transaction efficiency, accessibility, and transparency.

The issuance of security tokens backed by real-life assets, which might include stocks, bonds, or residential property, has been rendered possible by Security Token Offerings (STOs), which are a controlled type of tokenization. These digital currencies ensure legal compliance while adhering to regulatory frameworks, which could eventually give rise to new avenues for investment (Akhtar et al., 2023).

Integration With Conventional Finance

Conventional financial institutions are progressively incorporating blockchain technology (Ashta & Herrmann, 2021). Blockchain has been investigated by a number of banks as well as financial service providers in an effort to boost cross-border transactions, settlement procedures, and payment systems (Akhtar et al., 2021).

Institutional Adoption

Blockchain technology and cryptocurrencies are attracting the curiosity of institutional investors more and more. More money is flowing into the blockchain space as as a consequence of hedge funds, asset managers, and corporations considering which includes crypto-assets in their portfolios of assets.

Regulatory Clarity

Regulatory frameworks around blockchain and cryptocurrencies are evolving. Governments are working on establishing clearer regulations, which could potentially reduce uncertainty and encourage more mainstream adoption of blockchain-based investment products.

Focus on Sustainability

With growing concerns about climate change and sustainability, blockchain technology is being harnessed to facilitate and verify investments in sustainable and socially responsible projects (Fulton et al., 2013). This includes tracking carbon emissions, supporting renewable energy projects, and enabling transparent supply chains.

Interoperability and Scalability

Efforts are underway to enhance blockchain networks' scalability and interoperability, addressing limitations to accommodate larger transaction volumes and facilitate seamless communication between different blockchains (Akhtar et al., 2023).

The future of blockchain in investment hinges on resolving existing challenges, such as scalability, regulatory hurdles, and user experience, while capitalizing on its strengths in transparency, security, and decentralization. Continued innovation, industry collaboration, and regulatory clarity will likely shape how blockchain transforms the investment landscape in the years to come.

CONCLUSION

In conclusion, blockchain technology offers a compelling framework for advancing sustainable investment by enhancing transparency and security. Despite challenges, the future prospects for blockchain in sustainable investment are promising, with the potential to drive positive social and environmental impact while delivering financial returns. Embracing blockchain technology in this context is a step toward a more sustainable and equitable financial ecosystem.

REFERENCES

Akhtar, S., Alam, M., & Khan, M. M. (2021). YES Bank Fiasco: Arrogance or Negligence. *Emerging Economies Cases Journal*, *3*(2), 95–102. doi:10.1177/25166042211061003

Ali, O., Ally, M., Clutterbuck, & Dwivedi, Y. (2020). The state of play of blockchain technology in the financial services sector: A systematic literature review. *International Journal of Information Management*, *54*(July), 102199. doi:10.1016/j.ijinfomgt.2020.102199

Ansari, M. S., Akhtar, S., Khan, A., & Shamshad, M. (2023). Consequence of Financial Crisis on Liquidity and Profitability of Commercial Banks in India: An Empirical Study. *Studies in Economics and Business Relations*, *3*(2), 36–50. doi:10.48185/sebr.v3i2.367

Ashta, A., & Herrmann, H. (2021). Artificial intelligence and fintech: An overview of opportunities and risks for banking, investments, and microfinance. *Strategic Change*, *30*(3), 211–222. doi:10.1002/jsc.2404

Aɿan, Y., Kuzey, C., Acar, M. F., & Açikgöz, A. (2016). The relationships between corporate social responsibility, environmental supplier development, and firm performance. *Journal of Cleaner Production*, *112*, 1872–1881. doi:10.1016/j.jclepro.2014.08.090

Barna, B. J. (2021). *B LOCKCHAIN AND C RYPTOCURRENCIES.*

Berry, T. C., & Junkus, J. C. (2013). Socially Responsible Investing: An Investor Perspective. *Journal of Business Ethics*, *112*(4), 707–720. doi:10.1007/s10551-012-1567-0

Bodkhe, U., Tanwar, S., Parekh, K., Khanpara, P., Tyagi, S., Kumar, N., & Alazab, M. (2020). Blockchain for Industry 4.0: A comprehensive review. *IEEE Access: Practical Innovations, Open Solutions*, *8*, 79764–79800. doi:10.1109/ACCESS.2020.2988579

Bondarenko, O., Kichuk, O., & Antonov, A. (2019). the Possibilities of Using Investment Tools Based on Cryptocurrency in the Development of the National Economy. *Baltic Journal of Economic Studies*, *5*(2), 10. doi:10.30525/2256-0742/2019-5-2-10-17

Carrara, G. R., Burle, L. M., Medeiros, D. S. V., de Albuquerque, C. V. N., & Mattos, D. M. F. (2020). Consistency, availability, and partition tolerance in blockchain: A survey on the consensus mechanism over peer-to-peer networking. *Annales Des Telecommunications. Annales des Télécommunications*, *75*(3–4), 163–174. doi:10.1007/s12243-020-00751-w

Centobelli, P., Cerchione, R., Del Vecchio, P., Oropallo, E., & Secundo, G. (2022). Blockchain technology for bridging trust, traceability and transparency in circular supply chain. *Information & Management*, *59*(7), 103508. doi:10.1016/j.im.2021.103508

Clarke, G., & Hrnjic, E. (2022). *National Study on Central Bank Digital Currency and Stablecoin in the Maldives*. 1–68.

Crosby, M., Pattanayak, P., Verma, S., & Kalyanaraman, V. (2016). BlockChain Technology: Beyond Bitcoin. *Applied Innovation Review*, *2*, 6–19.

Cumming, D. J., Johan, S., & Pant, A. (2019). Regulation of the Crypto-Economy: Managing Risks, Challenges, and Regulatory Uncertainty. *Journal of Risk and Financial Management*, *12*(3), 126. doi:10.3390/jrfm12030126

Fulton, M., Kahn, B. M., & Sharples, C. (2013). Sustainable Investing: Establishing Long-Term Value and Performance. SSRN *Electronic Journal, June*. doi:10.2139/ssrn.2222740

Gamage, H. T. M., Weerasinghe, H. D., & Dias, N. G. J. (2020). A Survey on Blockchain Technology Concepts, Applications, and Issues. *SN Computer Science*, *1*(2), 1–15. doi:10.1007/s42979-020-00123-0

Garg, R. (2023). Blockchain for Decentralized Finance: Impact, Challenges and Remediation. *International Journal of Computer Science and Information Technologies*, *17*(March), 225–237.

Giannoni, C., Medda, F., & Bartolucci, S. (2023). Blockchain Technologies and Art: Opportunities and Open Challenges. SSRN *Electronic Journal*. doi:10.2139/ssrn.4439318

Heines, R., Dick, C., Pohle, C., & Jung, R. (2021). The Tokenization of Everything: Towards a Framework for Understanding the Potentials of Tokenized Assets. *Proceedings of the Pacific Asia Conference on Information Systems (PACIS), July*, 1–14. https://widgets.ebscohost.com/prod/customerspecific/ns000290/authentication/index.php?url=https%3A%2F%2Fsearch.ebscohost.com%2Flogin.aspx%3Fdirect%3Dtrue%26db%3Dedb%26AN%3D151674974%26amp%3Blang%3Dpt-pt%26site%3Deds-live%26scope%3Dsite

Hellani, H., Samhat, A. E., Chamoun, M., El Ghor, H., & Serhrouchni, A. (2018). On BlockChain Technology: Overview of Bitcoin and Future Insights. *2018 IEEE International Multidisciplinary Conference on Engineering Technology, IMCET 2018*, (pp. 1–8). IEEE. 10.1109/IMCET.2018.8603029

Hughes, L., Dwivedi, Y. K., Misra, S. K., Rana, N. P., Raghavan, V., & Akella, V. (2019). Blockchain research, practice and policy: Applications, benefits, limitations, emerging research themes and research agenda. *International Journal of Information Management*, *49*(February), 114–129. doi:10.1016/j.ijinfomgt.2019.02.005

Jonathan, R., & Wright, A. (2018). Blockchain-based token sales, initial coin offerings, and the democratization of public capital markets. *The Hastings Law Journal, 70*, 463.

Kong, D.-R., & Lin, T.-C. (2021). Alternative investments in the Fintech era: The risk and return of Non-Fungible Token (NFT). SSRN *Electronic Journal*. doi:10.2139/ssrn.3914085

Küfeoğlu, S. (2022). Emerging Technologies. In *Emerging Technologies, Sustainable Development Goals Series*. https://doi.org/10.1007/978-3-031-07127-0_2

Lee, J. Y. (2019). A decentralized token economy: How blockchain and cryptocurrency can revolutionize business. *Business Horizons, 62*(6), 773–784. doi:10.1016/j.bushor.2019.08.003

Li, Q. L., Ma, J. Y., Chang, Y. X., Ma, F. Q., & Yu, H. B. (2019). Markov processes in blockchain systems. *Computational Social Networks, 6*(1), 1–28. doi:10.1186/s40649-019-0066-1

Lim, S. Y., Fotsing, P. T., Almasri, A., Musa, O., Kiah, M. L. M., Ang, T. F., & Ismail, R. (2018). Blockchain technology the identity management and authentication service disruptor: A survey. *International Journal on Advanced Science, Engineering and Information Technology, 8*(4–2), 1735–1745. doi:10.18517/ijaseit.8.4-2.6838

Lin, C. H., Yang, H. L., & Liou, D. Y. (2009). The impact of corporate social responsibility on financial performance: Evidence from business in Taiwan. *Technology in Society, 31*(1), 56–63. doi:10.1016/j.techsoc.2008.10.004

Makarov, I., & Schoar, A. (2022). Cryptocurrencies and Decentralized Finance (DeFi). *Brookings Papers on Economic Activity, 2022-Sprin*, 141–215. doi:10.1353/eca.2022.0014

Miller, A., Kosba, A., Katz, J., & Shi, E. (2015). Nonoutsourceable scratch-off puzzles to discourage bitcoin mining coalitions. *Proceedings of the ACM Conference on Computer and Communications Security*. IEEE. 10.1145/2810103.2813621

Morabito, V. (2017). Business Innovation Through Blockchain. In Business Innovation Through Blockchain. doi:10.1007/978-3-319-48478-5

Möslein, F., & Marburg, P. (2020). S. Legal Boundaries of Blockchain Technologies: Smart Contracts as Self-Help? (Möslein). *Digital Revolution - New Challenges for Law, February 2000*, 313–326. Springer. doi:10.17104/9783406759048-313

Naderi, N. (2021). Utilizing Blockchain Technology in International Remittances for Poverty Reduction and Inclusive Growth. In Poverty Reduction for Inclusive Sustainable Growth in Developing Asia (pp. 149–163). doi:10.1007/978-981-16-1107-0_7

Nakamoto, S. (2008). *Bitcoin: A Peer-to-Peer Electronic Cash System*. Decentralized Business Review.

Nawari, N. O., & Ravindran, S. (2019). Blockchain and the built environment: Potentials and limitations. *Journal of Building Engineering, 25*(October 2018). doi:10.1016/j.jobe.2019.100832

O'Rourke, A. (2003). A new politics of engagement: Shareholder activism for corporate social responsibility. *Business Strategy and the Environment, 12*(4), 227–239. doi:10.1002/bse.364

Paliwal, V., Chandra, S., & Sharma, S. (2020). Blockchain technology for sustainable supply chain management: A systematic literature review and a classification framework. *Sustainability (Basel), 12*(18), 1–39. doi:10.3390/su12187638

Qin, K., & Gervais, A. (2018). An overview of blockchain scalability, interoperability and sustainability. *Hochschule Luzern Blockchain Lab, 15*. https://www.eublockchainforum.eu/sites/default/files/research-paper/an_overview_of_blockchain_scalability_interoperability_and_sustainability.pdf

Saxena, A., Singh, R., Gehlot, A., Akram, S. V., Twala, B., Singh, A., Montero, E. C., & Priyadarshi, N. (2023). Technologies Empowered Environmental, Social, and Governance (ESG): An Industry 4.0 Landscape. *Sustainability (Basel), 15*(1), 309. doi:10.3390/su15010309

Sharma, G. D., Jain, M., Mahendru, M., Bansal, S., & Kumar, G. (2019). Emergence of Bitcoin as an Investment Alternative: A Systematic Review and Research Agenda. *International Journal of Business and Information, 14*(1), 47–84. doi:10.6702/ijbi.201903

Shrivas, M. K., & Yeboah, T. (2019). The Disruptive Blockchain: Types, Platforms and Applications. Texila International Journal of Academic Research (TIJAR) Special Edition, 17–39. doi:10.21522/TIJAR.2014.SE.19.02.Art003

Smith, A. (2008). Regulatory Issues in Blockchain Technology Purpose-Blockchains. *Journal of Financial Regulation and Compliance, 16*(2), 13. doi:10.1108/JFRC-08-2016-0068

Swan, M. (2017). Anticipating the Economic Benefits of Blockchain. *Technology Innovation Management Review, 7*(10), 6–13. https://timreview.ca/article/837. doi:10.22215/timreview/1109

Talan, G., & Sharma, G. D. (2019). Doing well by doing good: A systematic review and research agenda for sustainable investment. *Sustainability (Basel), 11*(2), 353. doi:10.3390/su11020353

Tschorsch, F., & Scheuermann, B. (2016). Bitcoin and beyond: A technical survey on decentralized digital currencies. *IEEE Communications Surveys and Tutorials, 18*(3), 2084–2123. doi:10.1109/COMST.2016.2535718

Turnbull, S. (2002). *A New Way to Govern Organisations and Institutions Network, 14*. Corporate Governance.

Tushar, W., Yuen, C., Saha, T. K., Morstyn, T., Chapman, A. C., Alam, M. J. E., Hanif, S., & Poor, H. V. (2021). Peer-to-peer energy systems for connected communities: A review of recent advances and emerging challenges. *Applied Energy, 282*(PA), 116131. doi:10.1016/j.apenergy.2020.116131

Varma, J. R. (2019). Blockchain in Finance. *Vikalpa, 44*(1), 1–11. doi:10.1177/0256090919839897

Vilà Brualla, M. (2022). *Blockchain Layer 2 scalability solutions: a framework for comparison.*

Woo, J., Fatima, R., Kibert, C. J., Newman, R. E., Tian, Y., & Srinivasan, R. S. (2021). Applying blockchain technology for building energy performance measurement, reporting, and verification (MRV) and the carbon credit market: A review of the literature. *Building and Environment, 205*(July), 108199. doi:10.1016/j.buildenv.2021.108199

Wu, Q., & Gladyshev, V. (2020). *Design for the Decentralized World: Democratization of Blockchain-Based Software Design*. Design, User Experience, and Usability. Design for Contemporary Interactive Environments: 9th International Conference, Copenhagen, Denmark.

Xiao, Y., Zhang, N., Lou, W., & Hou, Y. T. (2020). A Survey of Distributed Consensus Protocols for Blockchain Networks. *IEEE Communications Surveys and Tutorials, 22*(2), 1432–1465. doi:10.1109/COMST.2020.2969706

Zamani, E., He, Y., & Phillips, M. (2020). On the Security Risks of the Blockchain. *Journal of Computer Information Systems, 60*(6), 495–506. doi:10.1080/08874417.2018.1538709

Chapter 15
Disrupting Financial Services:
A Case Study on Capital One's Fintech Odyssey

N. Naseema
Woxsen University, India

Shakeb Akhtar
https://orcid.org/0000-0003-2069-6669
Woxsen University, India

Asila Abdullah Al Hinai
University of Technology and Applied Science, Nizwa, Oman

ABSTRACT

This book chapter aims to ferret into the ever-evolving landscape of financial technology through a comprehensive case study of Capital One- A disruptor of financial services by using big data. It involves a broad range of technological applications, including software, mobile applications, artificial intelligence, block chain, big data and other emerging technologies, to enhance and streamline various financial activities such as banking, payments, investments, and insurance. This book chapter explores the journey of "Capital One" in adopting fintech innovations to enhance its financial services offerings and increasing profitability by reducing the risk. Capital One is recognized as one of the early adopters of fintech in the banking industry. As a leading financial institution, Capital One has strategically integrated fintech solutions to improve operational efficiency, customer experience, and overall competitiveness in the dynamic financial landscape.

DOI: 10.4018/979-8-3693-1878-2.ch015

INTRODUCTION

The objective of this Case study titled *Disrupting Financial Services: A case study on Capital One's Fintech Odyssey*. is to provide the readers with a detailed exploration of the evolution, successes, challenges and the lessons learned by Capital One, a financial institution which is Known for its differential practices and approach based on customers. Right from its simple beginnings as a credit card company to its current business as a diversified financial services provider, the Capital One's story is a live example of the power of the right use of technology, long term decision-making, and a deep focus on the customer experience. The case study delves into the company's initial years, the milestones, innovative practices adopted, and the lessons that other companies can learn from the success of Capital One's

By analyzing the important mile stones, strategic decisions, and the combination of modern technologies, the chapter aims to uncover the factors that are underlying and have boosted Capital One's growth and prominence in the financial industry. By deep diving into the company's historical movements, decision-making that is driven by data, and commitment of the company to personalized customer experiences, the chapter seeks to give valuable lessons for industry professionals, academics, researchers and business enthusiasts. Additionally, the chapter addresses the challenges that are faced by Capital One, which includes regulatory compliance and cybersecurity incidents in 2019, also offering insights into how the company navigated these those hurdles and emerged stronger day by day. At the last, the chapter serves as a source of inspiration and an ocean of knowledge, encouraging the readers to understand meaningful lessons from the journey of Capital One in shaping the future of financial services. This case study would take the readers through the beautiful journey and also through the obstacles of Capital one.

OBJECTIVES OF THE CASE STUDY

This Case Study Seeks To

- To examine the evolution of Capital One and its strategic shifts.
- To analyze the key factors that contributed to the Capital One's success in the financial services industry.
- To explore Capital One's interest innovative technologies and data-driven decision-making.
- To discuss challenges faced by Capital One and lessons learned for other organizations

BACKGROUND OF THE STUDY

Capital one has long history dating back to the year 1988 when it was founded by two young entrepreneurs and data scientists Mr. Richard Fairbank and Mr. Nigel Morris. At first they established business as a single line credit card company. Capital One aimed to be unique itself through a data-driven approach to credit risk management and personalized the customer offerings. Capital One is a financial services company which has managed to emerge as a distinguished player in the banking and financial services industry, renowned for its unique approach to consumer finance and financial services driven by data. This case study showcases the strategies that have contributed to the success of the financial service provider Capital One by focusing on its transformative use of advanced technology in financial services, customer-centric strategies, and risk management practices to tackle the obstacles.

Capital One gained its popularity as a credit card issuer in the United States, using advanced technology in its financial services such as big data analytics to revolutionize the way risky customers are differentiated from the non-risky ones (Ansari et al. 2022). This was the unique strategy that made Capital one successful by considering the credit cards to the less-riskier customers. The company strategically diversified its offerings in to banking and financial services after recognizing the potential.

Historical Evolution

Early adopters make important decisions on innovations even though their benefits and losses are still not clearly defined (Harrison and Waite, 2006). In the early nineties, two data scientists wanted to use predictive modeling to help banks determine the best terms to offer credit card clients. Richard Fairbank and Nigel Morris are the two heroes of early fintech adoption of this story. Both had backgrounds in finance and consulting. Richard Fairbank was a Stanford graduate holding Masters in Business Administration degree and had experience of working at Strategic Planning Associates which is a company in to management consultancy. Whereas Nigel Morris is a graduate of Oxford University, had experience in financial services consulting.

The "Heroes of Capital One"

Richard Fairbank

Richard Fairbank is the co-founder and CEO of Capital One. Richard Fairbank was a prominent figure who is considered as a backbone in developing the Capital One's vision and strategy. Richard Fairbank is known for his innovative approach and he was instrumental in transforming Capital One into a most popular technology based financial service provider.

Nigel Morris

Nigel Morris is considered as another prominent figure along with Richard Fairbank in shaping the vision and Strategy of Capital One. Nigel Morris was the chief operating officer of Capital One. He has contributed significantly to its early development and success. His role in Capital one was to make decisions on Operational and strategic plans. His expertise helped capital one in becoming a Successful financial service provider in the Banking industry of United States.

Richard Fairbank and Nigel Morris were two bussing Entrepreneurs who envisioned the dream of using technology and data analytics to bring in the revolution in the way banks operate and Credit card services are disseminated to the customers. They focused on decision making that is driven by data analytics and consumer centric innovations took their business beyond just selling credit cards and making Capital one a pioneer in the banking industry. Their skills and vision had made Capital One what it is today.

Founder's Expertise That Acted as a Catalyst for Capital One's Journey

As discussed in previous part of the chapter, Richard Fairbank and Nigel Morris both had backgrounds in finance and consulting. Capital one was a brain child of Richard Fairbank and Nigel Morris and this is through their deep analysis and observations of the credit card industry in the United States. After their deep investigation and market research they analyzed the high potential for the new start up. Richard Fairbank and Nigel Morris initially approached numerous banks with their idea of transforming the credit card industry through data-driven decision-making. The traditional banks they approached, however, were hesitant to embrace the innovative approach they were proposing. The rejection from traditional banks led Fairbank and Morris to pursue an alternative route: they decided to start their own company.

The key insight that Fairbank and Morris had was that by utilizing data and technology, they could make more accurate credit decisions and provide personalized credit offerings to consumers. This approach was a departure from the conventional risk assessment methods employed by traditional banks at the time. The decision to form their own company, which eventually became Capital One, proved to be a pivotal moment. Capital One's innovative use of data analytics and technology transformed the credit card industry and set new standards for how financial services could leverage technology for more efficient and customer-focused operations.

The rejection they faced from traditional banks ultimately fueled their entrepreneurial spirit, leading to the creation of a company that would become a leader in the financial services industry, known for its commitment to innovation and technology-driven solutions.

From Signet Financial Corporation to Capital One

Prior to Capital One's inception, Fairbank and Morris were involved in the formation of Signet Financial Corporation. Signet Financial was a regional bank holding company based in Richmond, Virginia.

- *Spin-Off and Formation of Capital One (1994)*: In 1994, Fairbank and Morris managed the spin-off of Signet Financial Corporation's credit card division as a separate entity. This new entity was named Capital One.
- *Initial Public Offering (IPO):* On July 27, 1994, Capital One made an initial public offering (IPO), becoming an independent company. The IPO provided the necessary capital for the newly formed Capital One to pursue its vision of transforming the credit card industry.

Leadership and Vision

Richard Fairbank served as the CEO, and Nigel Morris held the role of Chief Operating Officer during the early years of Capital One. Their leadership and strategic vision played a crucial role in the company's growth and success. Richard Fairbank and Nigel Morris' vision for Capital One as a technology-driven and customer-centric financial services company has had a profound impact on the industry. Their innovative approach and commitment to leveraging data analytics set the stage for Capital One's evolution into a major player in the financial services sector (Utami, 2021).

Key Milestones of Capital One

1988: Inception

At its inception, emphasis was given on the data driven approach to the risk management in credit card business. This has set the foundation for the success of Capital One. In the early nineties, two data scientists wanted to use predictive modeling to help banks determine the best terms to offer credit card clients. Richard Fairbank and Nigel Morris are the two heroes of early fintech adoption of this story. With their backgrounds in finance and consulting. With their expertise from their past careers they were successful in inculcating the technology in to traditional banking business.

1990s: Rapid Growth

In 1994, Fairbank and Morris orchestrated the spin-off of Signet Financial Corporation's credit card division as a separate entity. This new entity was named as Capital One. Capital One experienced tremendous growth as a credit card issuer, becoming one of the largest in the banking industry. Introduction of innovative marketing strategies and personalized credit offerings.

2000-2005: Diversification into Banking

Capital One now entered in to the era of expansions. The founders now felt the need for the expansion to sustain the market competition. Capital one now expands its services beyond credit cards, entering the banking sector. To make this possible, Capital one started acquiring big banks like Hibernia National Bank, marking a strategic move into traditional banking services. Recognizing the changing landscape of financial services, Capital One strategically expanded beyond credit cards into banking. This expansion not only aimed at diversifying the portfolio of Capital one but also involved introducing technology in its most of the banking services.

One of the example for such diversification is offering Online and Mobile Banking Services. Capital One was early bird in the financial services industry to introduce online banking and mobile banking services, providing customers with convenient and user-friendly digital interfaces for managing their accounts. The bank's mobile app offerings further confirmed its commitment to providing tech-savvy solutions for customers.

2006-2010: Technology Integration

Capital One after introducing online banking and mobile banking services, it embraces technological advancements, incorporating data analytics and machine learning into its operations. Apart from these advancements, it launches online banking platforms and advanced mobile applications for enhanced customer convenience. The company's commitment to technology became evident in its embrace of data analytics, machine learning, and AI (Jafar et al, 2023a). These innovations not only streamlined processes but also enhanced customer experiences.

2011-2015: Continued Expansion

The next five years Capital One saw the continued expansions as it went on acquiring its competitors such as ING Direct, marking a significant step in expanding its reach into online banking. Capital One in this stage introduced innovative products such as Spark Business to cater to the requirements of the small businesses.

2016-2020: Customer-Centric Focus

Capital One at this phase felt the need of emphasis on customer-centricity, for which Capital one did not delay further in introducing personalized services and experiences to its customers. At this point, Capital One invests in digital transformation to streamline its operations and enhance the overall customer journey. Shifting towards a customer-centric philosophy, Capital One utilized customer data to tailor better services to the customers. Memorable marketing campaigns by Capital one made the image of capital one stronger as an institution and it aimed at carrying out the business with simplicity and transparency. This is also the phase where Capital one faced the biggest hurdle of Data threat in the year 2019 where there was a cyber-attack and it witnessed a big failure in data privacy which shook the business.

2020-Present: Navigating Challenges

Capital One, like any other organizations, faces many challenges such as regulatory compliance and cybersecurity incidents. The company's robust response mechanisms demonstrate resilience and an unwavering commitment to customer data protection. This is where Capital one recognized the need of involving celebrities in the ad campaigns. Capital One's marketing campaigns, featuring prominent personalities, became synonymous with the brand. This approach contributed significantly to its brand recognition and innovative image.

Ongoing: Innovations and Future Outlook

Capital One continues to lead in technological innovation, exploring blockchain and other emerging technologies. The company maintains a focus on sustainability, financial inclusion, and adapting to the evolving needs of the digital age.

RISK MANAGEMENT PRACTICES AT CAPITAL ONE

Capital One's robust risk management framework, driven by analytical approaches to credit risk assessment, proved vital during economic downturns, maintaining a healthy portfolio.

Diverse Product Portfolio

Capital One's diversification in to the portfolio of services beyond credit cards into banking and other financial services played a role in its resilience. Though credit cards are a significant part of Capital one's business, the company's exposure to other sectors helped the company to sustain the competitive world.

Conservative Lending Standards

Capital One was known for maintaining relatively conservative lending standards compared to some other financial institutions and this was possible by data analytics in its lending business. This conservative approach contributed to a more stable credit portfolio during times of economic stress. Through the help of Data analytics, capital one was able to focus on low risk customers.

Early Recognition of Risks

Capital One is proactive in recognizing potential risks associated with the economic downturn. The company took early steps to address issues such as rising non-performing loans and also it survived through the subprime crisis.

Strategic Acquisitions

Prior to the crisis, Capital One made strategic acquisitions, including the purchase of North Fork Bancorporation in 2006. These acquisitions contributed to the company's overall stability and sustainability during the times of crisis. Strategic acquisitions such as ING Direct, facilitated entry into online banking, enhancing the market presence and reinforcing its multifaceted identity. Capital One strategically expanded its market presence through acquisitions. The purchase of ING Direct in 2012 facilitated entry into the online banking sector, broadening the company's reach. The acquisition of companies like Hibernia National Bank and North Fork Bank strengthened Capital One's position in key markets.

Capital Adequacy

Capital One maintained strong capital levels, and this is also one of the contributing factor which provided a buffer against potential losses. Having adequate capital allowed the company to absorb shocks and maintain its financial stability during its difficult stages.

Focus on Customer-Centric Solutions

This is one of the uniqueness of capital one that made capital one stand different in the market. Capital One's emphasis on understanding and meeting customer needs and developing the products and services tailor made to customer needs helped it navigate challenges during the crisis. By focusing on customer satisfaction and attracting the brand loyalty, capital one was able to position itself better in the market and not only retain its existing customers but also attract new customers. Capital One differentiated itself from its competitors by adopting a customer-centric philosophy. The company's commitment to understanding the needs and preferences of the customers has been acting as a driving force towards its product development and creating new marketing strategies. We can say that by analyzing customer data effectively, Capital One tailors its offerings to meet the diverse financial needs of its existing customers which makes it easy to retain its customers.

Adaptability and Innovation

Desmarais (2020) in their paper "The technological revolution in financial services" emphasized the importance of importance of transforming the financial services by the use of technology. Adaptability to the changing customer needs, upgrading the technology and innovating new products and services while implementing modern technologies is what makes capital one unique in its own way. The commitment to innovating the financial services by being the first one in the market to introduce innovative products make the capital one unique.

It is worth to mention that during subprime crisis when whole banking system was facing challenges, Capital One was able to fare relatively well. The subprime crisis gave significant lessons to the financial institutions in terms of risk management practices and regulatory changes. The ability of capital one to navigate the crisis affirmed its reputation as a company with risk conscious approach.

Disruption in Financial Services

Disruption of traditional banking and financial services is the mantra to the success of Capital One. This was possible because of the technological advancements and a customer centric approach influencing the whole of banking system in the United States. This forced the competitors to adopt the technology based approach.

Branding and Marketing

Another feather in the crown of capital one is its memorable marketing campaigns featuring personalities like Samuel L Jackson and Jenifer Garner has become a building block in building brand recognition of Capital One. The marketing strategy of the company aligns with the innovative image of Capital One reinforcing its commitment to simplicity and transparency.

Fintech Partnerships and Acquisitions

Fintech has brought ways to realize this for some of the poorest countries in the world. Scholars are still trying to investigate the factors that lead some firms to success in extending financial inclusion for these people. One study found that among the factors, are network effects, customer centricity, the appropriateness of the commercial strategy used by the firm (Soriano, 2017). Mergers and Acquisitions are the steps in the ladder of success of Capital One. Capital One has actively engaged with financial technology through partnerships and acquisitions. It has invested in and collaborated with different startups to incorporate smart technologies into its operations, enhancing the customer experience and internal processes.

Focus on Customer-Centric Innovation

Fintech holds enormous potential for the underbanked and unbanked populations across the world (Salampasis and Mention, 2018). Capital one has consistently focused on customer centric approach and it goes beyond operational efficiency. The company always strives to put forth the products and services based on customer requirements and their ease. The journey of this innovative company illustrates the integration of fintech in its DNA since inception. The continuous commitment of the company to technological innovation keeping in mind the customer needs and demands has allowed the company to stay ahead of the competition.

Financial Performance

Capital One has always shown strong financial performance over the years which has impressed its shareholders. The revenue, earnings and operational efficiency have shown positive growth over the years. The company's early adoption of innovative technologies has allowed the company to stay ahead of the competition and show profitable financial performance over the years.

Brand Recognition

Capital one's constant efforts in renovating its products and services, bringing in new products, strong presence of memorable marketing campaigns has made a strong brand presence.

Digital Banking Services

Capital One's seamless innovation in its services, going digital has positioned it as a preferred choice for the customers. As discussed earlier, Capital one was one of the early birds to introduce digital banking and online banking services for the customers.

Community Engagement

Capital One has been actively involved in corporate social responsibility. With the tagline of "Developing future Engineers", Capital one has been providing training to the students. It follows a sustainability approach in its corporate social responsibility.

CHALLENGES FACED BY CAPITAL ONE

Any company faces challenges throughout its life, and Capital one is not an exception to that. Right from the inception, Capital one has been facing hurdles. Let us study those challenges. Hyun-sun Ryu (2018) in their paper "Understanding benefit framework of Fintech adoption: Comparison of early adopters and late adopters"

Industry Skepticism

Capital One's unconventional approach created skepticism on its performance and sustainability. There was a huge resistance from the successful banks. The traditional successful banks were not even ready to accept the fact that this idea would ever work.

Lack of Track Record

As Capital one was newly formed company, it had no well-established track record or reputation in the financial service industry. Attracting new customers and convincing the customers to stick on was taxing on the company at the beginning.

Funding and Capitalization

As it is not surprising to know that startups find it difficult to find the funding fr the very obvious reason that the investors are skeptical about the success of the business. The founders Richard Fairbak and Nigel had to navigate the complexities of raising funds and private investments. Later on the company went for the Initial public offering in the year 1994.

Regulatory Environment

These are the biggest challenges or hurdles faced by Capital One. The regulatory requirements and compliance standards in the financial industry posed challenges. Following the regulations along with implementing innovative practices posed additional challenge to capital One.

Technological Infrastructure

It was not easy to develop necessary technological infrastructure to support the data driven decision making. Capital one needed huge investments on technological infrastructure to handle and analyze large volume of data. Technological infrastructure was quiet taxing on the company at the initial stage if inception

Competing With Established Banks

Competing with well-established big dinosaurs which were well settled and had strong market presence was not a simple task. Capital one had to compete with big banks which were positioned strategically since long time. Getting customers out of those trusted traditional banks posed a big Challenge to Capital one.

Economic Conditions

Economic conditions bring in challenges to any institution. But an extra level challenge to the financial institutions. Surviving the economic downturn as well as financial crisis was an unamicable challenge to Capital One.

Educating Consumers

Attracting customers from the traditional and most trusted banks and educating them on the advantages of technology and bringing trust in the data driven financial services was as challenging task for capital one. AT the initial stages, customers were reluctant to accept the change. There was a resistance towards adoption of technology for financial services for the sole reason of data privacy. It required huge efforts and effective marketing strategies to educate the customers.

Despite these challenges, Capital One's founders, Richard Fairbank and Nigel Morris, demonstrated resilience and determination. Their commitment to innovation and the use of technology in financial services allowed Capital One to overcome initial obstacles and establish itself as a pioneering force in the credit card and broader financial services industry. The company's success in navigating these challenges laid the foundation for its subsequent growth and expansion. Capital One weathered the subprime mortgage crisis (often associated with the 2008 global financial crisis) better than many other financial institutions. Several factors contributed to Capital One's resilience during this challenging period.

WHAT MADE CAPITAL ONE SUCCESSFUL?

Capital One's business strategy has evolved over the years, but some key elements of their approach include:

Data-Driven Decision Making

Capital One has been a pioneer in using data analytics and technology for decision-making. From its early days, the company focused on leveraging data to assess credit risk, personalize financial products, and enhance customer experiences. "Fintech extends beyond alternative financing mechanisms like P2P lending to include the financing of technology itself (e.g. via crowdfunding) and the use of technology in financial transactions such as algorithmic trading" (Arner et al., 2016).

Customer-Centric Innovation

The company places a strong emphasis on understanding customer needs and preferences. Capital One strives to offer innovative and personalized financial solutions that align with the evolving expectations of its customers.

Diversification of Products and Services

Fintech refers to innovators and disruptors that offer more security, flexibility, opportunities, and efficiencies (Gabor and Brooks, 2017). Capital One has strategically diversified its product portfolio beyond credit cards. This includes banking services, auto loans, mortgages, and more. This diversification helps the company balance its revenue streams and cater to a broader range of financial needs.

Technology and Digital Transformation

Capital One has been at the forefront of digital transformation in the financial industry. A "plethora of brilliant technologies" of the fourth industrial revolution (4IR) are fundamentally transforming ways of creating value for customers (Brynjolfsson and McAfee, 2014). The Company has invested heavily in technology to provide seamless online and mobile banking experiences, making it convenient for customers to manage their finances.

Strategic Acquisitions

Capital One has pursued strategic acquisitions to enhance its capabilities and market presence. Notable acquisitions include ING Direct, which facilitated entry into online banking, and various fintech companies to integrate cutting-edge technologies.

Risk Management Excellence

The company places a strong emphasis on risk management. Capital One's risk management practices involve a careful assessment of credit risk, a conservative approach to lending standards, and a focus on maintaining a healthy and resilient credit portfolio.

Brand Marketing and Recognition

Capital One is known for its memorable and effective brand marketing. Engaging advertising campaigns featuring well-known personalities have contributed to the company's brand recognition and market presence.

Community and Social Responsibility

Capital One actively engages in community and social responsibility initiatives. This involvement aligns with the company's commitment to making a positive impact on the communities it serves.

Agile and Adaptive Culture

Capital One fosters an agile and adaptive organizational culture. This culture encourages innovation, flexibility, and a willingness to adapt to changing market conditions.

Focus on Financial Education

Capital One has demonstrated a commitment to financial literacy and education (Azmi and Akhtar, 2023). The company provides resources and tools to help customers make informed financial decisions, aligning with its customer-centric approach. Capital One's business strategy reflects a commitment to innovation, technology, customer satisfaction, and risk management. The company's ability to adapt to industry trends and its proactive approach to leveraging technology have contributed to its success in the dynamic financial services landscape.

Data-Driven Decision Making

Central to Capital One's success is its commitment to leveraging data and analytics for informed decision-making. This section explores the company's data-centric approach, highlighting how it enabled better risk management and personalized customer experiences.

Technological Innovation

Capital One has been at the forefront of technological innovation in the financial sector. This part of the case study investigates the company's adoption of cutting-edge technologies such as artificial intelligence, machine learning, and mobile banking applications (Akhtar, 2021). An important form of user innovation–Internet-supported collaborative design of new products and services by user communities–is likely to progressively supplant producer product and service design in many fields (von and Jin, 2008).

Customer-Centric Approach

Personalization and Customization Capital One's focus on customer satisfaction is analyzed in this section, emphasizing how the company has excelled in tailoring products and services to meet individual customer needs (Alam et al. 2023). Case studies of specific initiatives and their outcomes are discussed.

Customer Feedback and Engagement

The case study evaluates Capital One's strategies for collecting and utilizing customer feedback. It explores the role of customer engagement in shaping product development and service improvements.

LESSONS LEARNED

Regulatory Challenges as with any financial institution, Capital One has faced regulatory challenges. This section explores specific instances, how the company navigated them, and the lessons learned for maintaining compliance while fostering innovation. The case study addresses notable cybersecurity incidents that Capital One experienced and analyzes the company's response.[1] It delves into the lessons learned regarding cyber Capital One's success story is marked by various challenges and lessons learned that have contributed to its growth and prominence in the financial industry. While specific details may evolve over time, here are some general insights as of my last knowledge update in January 2022.

Capital One's Data Breach

On July 19, 2019, Capital one determined that an outside individual gained unauthorized access and obtained certain types of personal information about Capital One credit card customers and individuals who had applied for credit card products. As per Khan et al (2022) in their paper "A systematic analysis of Capital one data breach: Lessons learned": The 2019 Capital One data breach was one of the largest data breaches impacting the privacy and security of personal information of over a 100 million individuals.

The company immediately fixed the issue and promptly began working with federal law enforcement. The outside individual who took the data was captured by the FBI. The government has stated they believe the data has been recovered and that there is no evidence the data was used for fraud or shared by this individual. Capital one then invested heavily in cybersecurity and has incorporated the learnings from this incident to further strengthen cyber defenses (Jafar et al. 2023b).

The 2019 Capital One data breach was one of the largest data breaches impacting the privacy and security of personal information of over a 100 million individuals. In most reports about a cyberattack, you will often hear that it succeeded because a single employee clicked on a link in a phishing email or forgot to patch some software, making it seem like an isolated, one-off, trivial problem involving maybe one person, committing a mistake or being negligent. But that is usually not the complete story. By ignoring the related managerial and organizational failures, you are leaving in place the conditions for the next breach.

Capital One paid an $80 million penalty to the OCC for "failure to establish effective risk assessment processes prior to migrating significant information technology operations to the public cloud environment," and for failing to fix the deficiencies quickly (Wajid et al. 2022). Beyond the credit card application data, the individual obtained portions of credit card customer data, including:

- Customer status data, e.g., credit scores, credit limits, balances, payment history, contact information.
- Fragments of transaction data from a total of 23 days during 2016, 2017 and 2018.

This information has been shared on Capital One's website, servicing portal, press release and 8K filing. The individual also obtained the following data:

- About 140,000 Social Security numbers of our credit card customers.
- About 80,000 linked bank account numbers of our secured credit card customers.

The case was settled in the year 2022 and compensation was paid to all those who suffered from the data breach incident. Capital One has learned lesson on the following parameters:

Customer-Centric Approach is the Main Pillar of Success

Capital One's success is often attributed to its customer-centric approach. Understanding customer needs and preferences, and tailoring products and services accordingly, is a key lesson. "In the last decade, a new form of competitor has emerged that represents a serious threat to the traditional banking model and is revolutionizing the entire banking sector (Nocera, 2022).

Constant Innovation and Technology

Fintech innovations can sometimes overcome specific market failures (e.g. by reducing information asymmetries or transaction costs) (Frost, 2020). Embracing innovation and leveraging technology is crucial for staying ahead. Capital One's emphasis on digital banking and data analytics underscores the importance of technology in the financial sector.

Risk Management Practices

Effectively managing risks, both in terms of financial products and cybersecurity, is vital. Capital One's risk management practices have been integral to its stability and growth. "Customers were less likely to adopt fintech services if they had higher reported levels of concern with security, information secrecy, limited government control, and high levels of reported service intuitiveness obstacles" (Mahmud et al. 2022).

Data-Driven Decision Making

Capital One has been known for its sophisticated use of data analytics. The ability to gather, analyze, and derive actionable insights from data is a critical competency in the modern business landscape. The speed of diffusion of an emerging service with new technologies depends not only on the characteristics of the service itself, but also on the characteristics of the user who adopt it (Teo et al. 2008).

Agility and Adaptability

The business environment is dynamic, and the ability to adapt quickly to changing market conditions is essential (Akhtar et al. 2021). Capital One's success story underscores the importance of agility and flexibility. It's important to note that the business landscape is subject to change, and Capital One's challenges and lessons learned may evolve over time. Keeping abreast of the latest developments and industry trends will provide a more accurate and up-to-date understanding of their success story.

FUTURE OUTLOOK OF CAPITAL ONE

The Future of Capital One: CEO Richard Fairbank's Strategy; "Digital is who we are and how we do business,"; "We need to make digital how we do business not only with our customers, but also how we operate the company". These are the words by the long time CEO of the company Richard Fairbank. Capital One Financial Corporation ("Capital One") has acquired Velocity Mobile Limited ("Velocity Black"), a leading digital concierge company that delivers travel, entertainment, shopping and dining offerings to consumers globally. Velocity Black has built a unique customer experience — its proprietary platform deploys cutting edge technology and human experts to offer inspiration, recommendation and fulfillment in one place, making it an integral part of customers' lives. In retail banking, Capital One punches above its weight in brand recognition. By total assets, the Virginia-based bank is number 11 in the U.S. However, based on brand value, it ranks number six, according to Brand Finance's latest ranking — well ahead of U.S. Bank, PNC and Truist, all larger banks.

- Capital One partnered closely with Hopper to build Capital One Travel, a frictionless travel booking experience that delivers smart features not found anywhere else in the credit card industry.
- Capital One acquired Wikibuy, an Austin, Texas-based company whose automated digital shopping tool used intelligent, real-time technology to help people save time and money when shopping online. The expertise and tech from Wikibuy has been central in powering Capital One Shopping, a tool that matches premium retailers with consumer shoppers to drive meaningful engagements and considerable financial benefits for all.
- Capital One collaborated with Seven Rooms to Capital One Dining which unlocks special access to hard-to-get reservations at a collection of highly curated restaurants, along with exclusive culinary experiences for cardholders.

CONCLUSION

The case study summarizes key takeaways, highlighting Capital One's journey from a credit card issuer to a diversified financial services provider. It underscores the pivotal role of innovation, data-driven decision-making, and customer-centricity in the company's success, offering valuable insights for organizations seeking to thrive in the dynamic financial industry.

REFERENCES

Akhtar, S. (2021). *Comparative study of Performance evaluation of select private and foreign Banks in India*. Research Gate.

Akhtar, S., Alam, M., & Khan, M. M. (2021). YES Bank Fiasco: Arrogance or Negligence. *Emerging Economies Cases Journal*, *3*(2), 95–102. doi:10.1177/25166042211061003

Alam, M., Akhtar, S., & Al-Faryan, M. A. S. (2023). Do Indian banks perform better in corporate governance than other SAARC nations? An empirical analysis. *Corporate Governance: The International Journal of Business in Society*.

Ansari, M. S., Akhtar, S., Khan, A., & Shamshad, M. (2022). Consequence of Financial Crisis on Liquidity and Profitability of Commercial Banks in India: An Empirical Study. *Studies in Economics and Business Relations*, *3*(2), 36–50. doi:10.48185/sebr.v3i2.367

Arner, D. W., Barberis, J., & Buckley, R. P. (2016). 150 years of Fintech: An evolutionary analysis. *Jassa*, (3), 22–29.

Azmi, S. N., & Akhtar, S. (2023). Interactions of services export, financial development and growth: Evidence from India. *Quality & Quantity*, *57*(5), 4709–4724. doi:10.1007/s11135-022-01566-8

Brynjolfsson, E., & McAfee, A. (2014). *The second machine age: Work, progress, and prosperity in a time of brilliant technologies*. WW Norton & Company.

Desmarais, P. III. (2020). *The technological revolution in financial services: how banks, fintechs, and customers win together*. University of Toronto Press.

Frost, J. (2020). The economic forces driving fintech adoption across countries. *The technological revolution in financial services: how banks, fintechs, and customers win together, 838*, 70-89.

Gabor, D., & Brooks, S. (2020). The digital revolution in financial inclusion: international development in the fintech era. In *Material Cultures of Financialisation* (pp. 69–82). Routledge. doi:10.4324/9781351002103-6

Harrison, T., & Waite, K. (2006). A time-based assessment of the influences, uses and benefits of intermediary website adoption. *Information & Management*, *43*(8), 1002–1013. doi:10.1016/j.im.2006.09.004

Jafar, S. H., Akhtar, S., El-Chaarani, H., Khan, P. A., & Binsaddig, R. (2023a). Forecasting of NIFTY 50 Index Price by Using Backward Elimination with an LSTM Model. *Journal of Risk and Financial Management*, *16*(10), 423. doi:10.3390/jrfm16100423

Jafar, S. H., Akhtar, S., & Johl, S. K. (2023b). AI in Insurance. In *Artificial Intelligence for Business* (pp. 164–173). Productivity Press. doi:10.4324/9781003358411-10

Khan, S., Kabanov, I., Hua, Y., & Madnick, S. (2022). A systematic analysis of the capital one data breach: Critical lessons learned. *ACM Transactions on Privacy and Security*, *26*(1), 1–29. doi:10.1145/3546068

Mahmud, K., Joarder, M. M. A., & Muheymin-Us-Sakib, K. (2022). Adoption factors of FinTech: Evidence from an emerging economy country-wide representative sample. *International Journal of Financial Studies*, *11*(1), 9. doi:10.3390/ijfs11010009

Nocera, G. (2022). *Fintech revolution and traditional banks-what factors influence members of generation Z to place their trust in Fintech companies, specifically neobanks, over traditional banks as banking and financial service providers?: a case study on the banking application of the Swiss neobank Yuh*. Academic Press.

Ryu, H. S. (2018). *Understanding benefit and risk framework of fintech adoption: Comparison of early adopters and late adopters*.

Salampasis, D., & Mention, A. L. (2018). FinTech: Harnessing innovation for financial inclusion. In Handbook of Blockchain, Digital Finance, and Inclusion, Volume 2 (pp. 451-461). Academic Press.

Soriano, M. A. (2017). *Factors driving financial inclusion and financial performance in Fintech new ventures: An empirical study*.

Teo, T., Lee, C. B., & Chai, C. S. (2008). Understanding pre-service teachers' computer attitudes: Applying and extending the technology acceptance model. *Journal of Computer Assisted Learning*, *24*(2), 128–143. doi:10.1111/j.1365-2729.2007.00247.x

Utami, A. F., Ekaputra, I. A., & Japutra, A. (2021). Adoption of FinTech products: A systematic literature review. *Journal of Creative Communications*, *16*(3), 233–248. doi:10.1177/09732586211032092

von Hippel, E., & Jin, C. (2008). The major shift towards user-centred innovation: Implications for China's innovation policymaking. *Journal of Knowledge-based Innovation in China*, *1*(1), 16–27. doi:10.1108/17561410910912896

Wajid, A., Sabiha, A., Akhtar, S., Tabash, M. I., & Daniel, L. N. (2022). Cross-Border Acquisitions and Shareholders' Wealth: The Case of the Indian Pharmaceutical Sector. *Journal of Risk and Financial Management*, *15*(10), 437. doi:10.3390/jrfm15100437

ENDNOTES

1 https://www.capitalone.com/digital/facts2019/

Compilation of References

Abhilash, S., Shenoy, S. S., Shetty, D. K., Lobo, L. S., & N, S. K. (2023). Green Bond as an Innovative Financial Instrument in the Indian Financial Market: Insights from Systematic Literature Review Approach. *SAGE Open*, *13*(2), 21582440231178783. doi:10.1177/21582440231178783

Abideen, A. Z., Sundram, V. P. K., Pyeman, J., Othman, A. K., & Sorooshian, S. (2021). Digital twin integrated reinforced learning in supply chain and logistics. *Logistics*, *5*(4), 84. doi:10.3390/logistics5040084

Abu-Elezz, I., Hassan, A., Nazeemudeen, A., Househ, M., & Abd-Alrazaq, A. (2020). The benefits and threats of blockchain technology in healthcare: A scoping review. *International Journal of Medical Informatics*, *142*, 104246. doi:10.1016/j.ijmedinf.2020.104246 PMID:32828033

Aggarwal, S., Chaudhary, R., Aujla, G. S., Kumar, N., Choo, K. K. R., & Zomaya, A. Y. (2019). Blockchain for smart communities: Applications, challenges and opportunities. *Journal of Network and Computer Applications*, *144*, 13–48. doi:10.1016/j.jnca.2019.06.018

Agrawal, P., Narain, R., & Ullah, I. (2019). Analysis of barriers in implementation of digital transformation of supply chain using interpretive structural modelling approach. *Journal of Modelling in Management*, *15*(1), 297–317. doi:10.1108/JM2-03-2019-0066

Ahmad, D., Lutfiani, N., Ahmad, A. D. A. R., & Rahardja, U. (2021). Blockchain Technology Immutability Framework Design in E-Government. [Public Administration Journal]. *Jurnal Administrasi Publik*, *11*(1), 32–41.

Ahmad, R. W., Hasan, H., Jayaraman, R., Salah, K., & Omar, M. (2021). Blockchain applications and architectures for port operations and logistics management. *Research in Transportation Business & Management*, *41*, 100620. doi:10.1016/j.rtbm.2021.100620

Akhtar, S. (2021). *Comparative study of Performance evaluation of select private and foreign Banks in India*. Research Gate.

Akhtar, S., Alam, M., & Ansari, M. S. (2022). Measuring the performance of the Indian banking industry: Data envelopment window analysis approach. *Benchmarking*, *29*(9), 2842–2857. doi:10.1108/BIJ-03-2021-0115

Akhtar, S., Alam, M., Khan, A., & Shamshad, M. (2022, June 9). Measuring technical efficiency of banks vis-à-vis demonetization: An empirical analysis of Indian banking sector using CAMELS framework. *Quality & Quantity*, *57*(2), 1739–1761. doi:10.1007/s11135-022-01431-8

Akhtar, S., Alam, M., & Khan, M. M. (2021, December). YES Bank Fiasco: Arrogance or Negligence. *Emerging Economies Cases Journal*, *3*(2), 95–102. doi:10.1177/25166042211061003

Alam, M., Akhtar, S., & Al-Faryan, M. A. S. (2023). Do Indian banks perform better in corporate governance than other SAARC nations? An empirical analysis. *Corporate Governance: The International Journal of Business in Society*.

Alam, M., Akhtar, S., & Al-Faryan, M. A. S. (2023, November 8). Do Indian banks perform better in corporate governance than other SAARC nations? An empirical analysis. *Corporate Governance: The International Journal of Business in Society*. doi:10.1108/CG-02-2023-0059

Alamsyah, A., & Muhamad, I. F. (2023). Revealing Market Dynamics Pattern of DeFi Token Transaction in Crypto Industry. *2023 IEEE International Conference on Data Science and Advanced Analytics*. IEEE. 10.1109/ICoDSA58501.2023.10276473

Albany, M., & El Khediri, S. (2023). Integration of Federated Learning and Blockchain for the Provision of Secure Big data Analytics: Systematic Literature Review. *IEEE eSmarTA*. IEEE. doi:10.1109/eSmarTA59349.2023.10293397

Ali, O., Ally, M., Clutterbuck, & Dwivedi, Y. (2020). The state of play of blockchain technology in the financial services sector: A systematic literature review. *International Journal of Information Management*, *54*(July), 102199. doi:10.1016/j.ijinfomgt.2020.102199

Ali, O., Momin, M., Shrestha, A., Das, R., Alhajj, F., & Dwivedi, Y. K. (2023). A review of the key challenges of non-fungible tokens. *Technological Forecasting and Social Change*, *187*, 122248. doi:10.1016/j.techfore.2022.122248

Aliperti, G., Sandholz, S., Hagenlocher, M., Rizzi, F., Frey, M., & Garschagen, M. (2019). Tourism, crisis, disaster: An interdisciplinary approach. *Annals of Tourism Research*, *79*, 102808. doi:10.1016/j.annals.2019.102808

Aljaed, S. (2024). *The Impacts of Bitcoin on the Financial Market*. Computational Finance and Decision Journal., doi:10.21608/cfdj.2024.324085

Allam, Z., & Dhunny, Z. A. (2019). Data-driven smart cities: Stakes, opportunities, and challenges. *Journal of Urban Technology*, *26*(2), 3–21.

AlmansooriA.NobaneeH.NobaneeH. (2019). How Sustainability Contributes to Shared Value Creation and Firms' Value. SSRN. https://ssrn.com/abstract=3472411 or http://dx.doi.org/doi:10.2139/ssrn.3472411

Almasan, P., Ferriol-Galmés, M., Paillisse, J., Suárez-Varela, J., Perino, D., López, D., & Barlet-Ros, P. (2022). *Digital twin network: Opportunities and challenges*. arXiv preprint arXiv:2201.01144.

Alonso, A., Carbó, J. M., & Marqués, J. M. (2023). *Machine Learning methods in climate finance: a systematic review.*

Andoni, M., Robu, V., Flynn, D., Abram, S., Geach, D., Jenkins, D., McCallum, P., & Peacock, A. (2019). Blockchain technology in the energy sector: A systematic review of challenges and opportunities. *Renewable & Sustainable Energy Reviews*, *100*, 143–174. doi:10.1016/j.rser.2018.10.014

Androulaki. (2018), ledger fabric: A distributed operating system for permissioned blockchains. In *Proceedings of the Thirteenth EuroSys Conference*; Association for Computing Machinery: New York, NY, USA, pp. 1–15.

Anggara, M. R. H. (2022). The presence of commercial banks in Metaverse's financial ecosystem: Opportunities and risks. *Journal of Commercial Law and International Commerce*. doi:10.21098/jcli.v1i3.28

Anna, V., Andrea, D. S., Visaggio, C. A., & Gerardo, C. (2021). A systematic literature review of blockchain and smart contract development: Techniques, tools, and open challenges. *Journal of Systems and Software*, *174*, 110891. doi:10.1016/j.jss.2020.110891

Ansari, M. S., Akhtar, S., Khan, A., & Shamshad, M. (2023, March 31). Consequence of Financial Crisis on Liquidity and Profitability of Commercial Banks in India: An Empirical Study. *Studies in Economics and Business Relations*, *3*(2), 36–50. doi:10.48185/sebr.v3i2.367

Antal, C., Cioara, T., Anghel, I., Antal, M., & Salomie, I. (2021). Distributed ledger technology review and decentralized applications development guidelines. *Future Internet*, *13*(3), 62. doi:10.3390/fi13030062

Ante, L. (2021). Smart contracts on the blockchain–A bibliometric analysis and review. *Telemat. Information 2023, 14,*117-119.

Antonopoulos, A. M. (2014). *Mastering Bitcoin: Unlocking Digital Cryptocurrencies*. O'Reilly Media.

Arin, I. A., Murad, D. F., Hendric, H. L., & Warnars, S. (2023). A Systematic Literature Review of Recent Trends and Challenges in Digital Twin Implementation. *2023 IEEE International Conference on Information Systems and Software Technologies*. 10.1109/ICISS59129.2023.10291219

Arner, D. W., Barberis, J., & Buckley, R. P. (2016). 150 years of Fintech: An evolutionary analysis. *Jassa*, (3), 22–29.

Ashta, A., & Herrmann, H. (2021). Artificial intelligence and fintech: An overview of opportunities and risks for banking, investments, and microfinance. *Strategic Change*, *30*(3), 211–222. doi:10.1002/jsc.2404

Atana, R., Razali, F. A., Said, J., & Zainun, S. (2016). Environmental, Social, and Governance (ESG) Disclosure and Its Effect on Firm's Performance: A Comparative Study. *IJEM*, *10*(S2), 355–375.

Aıan, Y., Kuzey, C., Acar, M. F., & Açikgöz, A. (2016). The relationships between corporate social responsibility, environmental supplier development, and firm performance. *Journal of Cleaner Production*, *112*, 1872–1881. doi:10.1016/j.jclepro.2014.08.090

Atlas, L. G., Kumar, C. M., Rajakumari, & Hamsagayathi, P. (2020). Applications with blockchain technique. *Cryptocurrencies and blockchain technology applications*, 157-179.

Azmi, S. N., & Akhtar, S. (2023). Interactions of services export, financial development and growth: Evidence from India. *Quality & Quantity*, *57*(5), 4709–4724. doi:10.1007/s11135-022-01566-8

Bagria, V. K., & Meena, B. (2023). Analysis of FinTech Enablers and Role of Future Internet of Things (IoT) in the New-Age Business World. *International Journal of Management and Decision Sciences*. doi:10.53983/ijmds.v12n07.004

Balachandran, P. A., & Padmanabhan, K. V. K. (2023). Integrated Operations System: Implementation of a Truly Integrated Digital Oil Field and Development of Digital Twin. *Offshore Technology Conference*. One Petro. 10.4043/32841-MS

Ballandies, M. C., Dapp, M. M., & Pournaras, E. (2022). Decrypting distributed ledger design—Taxonomy, classification and blockchain community evaluation. *Cluster Computing*, *25*(3), 1817–1838. doi:10.1007/s10586-021-03256-w PMID:35601685

Banerjee, S., Das, D., Chatterjee, P., & Ghosh, U. (2023). Blockchain-enabled Digital Twin Technology for Next-Generation Transportation Systems. *2023 IEEE International Symposium on Real-Time Computing (ISORC)*. IEEE. 10.1109/ISORC58943.2023.00040

Bariev, E. Y. (2017). Blue Brain Project. In Recent Achievements and Prospects of Innovations and Technologies (pp. 126-128).

Barna, B. J. (2021). *B LOCKCHAIN AND C RYPTOCURRENCIES.*

Batty, M., Axhausen, K. W., Giannotti, F., Pozdnoukhov, A., Bazzani, A., Wachowicz, M., Ouzounis, G., & Portugali, Y. (2019). Smart cities of the future. *The European Physical Journal. Special Topics*, *214*(1), 481–518. doi:10.1140/epjst/e2012-01703-3

Bayram, O., Talay, I., & Feridun, M. (2022). Can FinTech promote sustainable finance? Policy lessons from the case of Turkey. *Sustainability (Basel)*, *14*(19), 12414. doi:10.3390/su141912414

Begum, A., Tareq, A., Sultana, M., Sohel, M., Rahman, T., & Sarwar, A. (2020). Blockchain attacks analysis and a model to solve double spending attack. *International Journal of Machine Learning and Computing*, *10*(2), 352–357.

Bellini, P., & ... (2023). Mobility and Transport Data for City Digital Twin Modeling and Exploitation. *2023 IEEE International Smart Cities Conference (ISC)*. IEEE. 10.1109/ISC257844.2023.10293300

Belu, M. G. (2019). Application of blockchain in international trade: An overview. *The Romanian Economic Journal*, *22*(71), 2–15.

Berry, T. C., & Junkus, J. C. (2013). Socially Responsible Investing: An Investor Perspective. *Journal of Business Ethics*, *112*(4), 707–720. doi:10.1007/s10551-012-1567-0

Bhowmik, D. (2022). An Introduction to Climate Fintech. *European Journal of Science. Innovation and Technology*, *2*(4), 24–35.

Bhutta, M. N. M., Khwaja, A. A., Nadeem, A., Ahmad, H. F., Khan, M. K., Hanif, M. A., Song, H., Alshamari, M., & Cao, Y. (2021). A survey on blockchain technology: Evolution, architecture and security. *IEEE Access: Practical Innovations, Open Solutions*, *9*, 61048–61073. doi:10.1109/ACCESS.2021.3072849

Bilberg, A., & Malik, A. A. (2019). Digital twin driven human–robot collaborative assembly. *CIRP Annals*, *68*(1), 499–502. doi:10.1016/j.cirp.2019.04.011

Bin Amin, S., Taghizadeh-Hesary, F., & Khan, F. (2022). Facilitating green digital finance in Bangladesh: Importance, prospects, and implications for meeting the SDGs. In *Green Digital Finance and Sustainable Development Goals* (pp. 143–165). Springer Nature Singapore. doi:10.1007/978-981-19-2662-4_7

Bisht, D., Singh, R., Gehlot, A., Akram, S., Singh, A., Montero, E., Priyadarshi, N., & Twala, B. (2022). Imperative Role of Integrating Digitalization in Firms Finance: A Technological Perspective. *Electronics (Basel)*, *11*(19), 3252. doi:10.3390/electronics11193252

Bodkhe, U., Tanwar, S., Parekh, K., Khanpara, P., Tyagi, S., Kumar, N., & Alazab, M. (2020). Blockchain for Industry 4.0: A comprehensive review. *IEEE Access: Practical Innovations, Open Solutions*, *8*, 79764–79800. doi:10.1109/ACCESS.2020.2988579

Bondarenko, O., Kichuk, O., & Antonov, A. (2019). the Possibilities of Using Investment Tools Based on Cryptocurrency in the Development of the National Economy. *Baltic Journal of Economic Studies*, *5*(2), 10. doi:10.30525/2256-0742/2019-5-2-10-17

Boros, A., Lentner, C., Nagy, V., & Tózser, D. (2023). *Perspectives by green financial instruments – a case study in the Hungarian banking sector during COVID-19*. Banks and Bank Systems. doi:10.21511/bbs.18(1).2023.10

Boschert, S., & Rosen, R. (2016). Digital twin—The simulation aspect. *Mecademia*, *11*(1), 123–133.

Breslin, S., & Wadhwa, B. (2018). Gender and Human-Computer Interaction. The Wiley Handbook of Human Computer Interaction, 1, 71-87. Wiley. doi:10.1002/9781118976005.ch4

Brown, A., & Patel, M. (2019). Blockchain and Digital Twins: Revolutionizing Green Investments. *Journal of Sustainable Finance*, *12*(3), 45–62.

Brynjolfsson, E., & McAfee, A. (2014). *The second machine age: Work, progress, and prosperity in a time of brilliant technologies*. WW Norton & Company.

Busch, T., & Lewandowski, S. (2018). Sustainability accounting and reporting in the industry 4.0. *Journal of Cleaner Production*, *188*, 972–986.

Buterin, V. (2014). *Ethereum: A Next-Generation Smart Contract and Decentralized Application Platform.* White Paper.

Buterin, V. (2017). Next-generation smart contract and decentralized application platform. (White Paper, 3).

Cabada, Estrada, M. L. B., Hernández, F. G., Bustillos, R. O., & Reyes-García, C. A. (2018). An affective and Web 3.0-based learning environment for a programming language. *Telematics and Informatics*, *35*(3), 611–628. doi:10.1016/j.tele.2017.03.005

Caldecott, B., & McDaniels, J. (2014). *Stranded assets: A climate risk challenge.* Smith School of Enterprise and the Environment, University of Oxford.

Campbell-Verduyn, M. (2023). Conjuring a cooler world? Imaginaries of improvement in blockchain climate finance experiments. *Environment and Planning C: Politics and Space.* Springer. 23996544231162858.

Cao, L., Yuan, G., Leung, T., & Zhang, W. (2020). Special Issue on AI and FinTech: The Challenge Ahead. *IEEE Intelligent Systems*, *35*(3), 3–6. doi:10.1109/MIS.2020.2983636

Cao, X., & ... (2022). BDTwins: Blockchain-based Digital Twins Lifecycle Management. *2022 IEEE International Conference on Smart World, UIC, ATC, ScalCom, DigitalTwin, PriComp, Metaverse.* IEEE. 10.1109/SmartWorld-UIC-ATC-ScalCom-DigitalTwin-PriComp-Metaverse56740.2022.00290

Caprari, G., Castelli, G., Montuori, M., Camardelli, M., & Malvezzi, R. (2022). Digital Twin for Urban Planning in the Green Deal Era: A State of the Art and Future Perspectives. *Sustainability (Basel)*, *14*(10), 6263. doi:10.3390/su14106263

Carè, R., Trucco, P., & Gianinetto, M. (2019). Data analytics for smart asset management in the green industry. *Sensors (Basel)*, *19*(22), 4911. PMID:31717912

Carrara, G. R., Burle, L. M., Medeiros, D. S. V., de Albuquerque, C. V. N., & Mattos, D. M. F. (2020). Consistency, availability, and partition tolerance in blockchain: A survey on the consensus mechanism over peer-to-peer networking. *Annales Des Telecommunications. Annales des Télécommunications*, *75*(3–4), 163–174. doi:10.1007/s12243-020-00751-w

Castellini, M., & Riso, V. (2023). Risk Management in Practice: A Multiple Case Study Analysis in Italian Municipalities. *Journal of Risk and Financial Management*, *16*(1), 30. doi:10.3390/jrfm16010030

Castro, M., & Liskov, B. (2002, November). Practical byzantine fault tolerance and proactive recovery. *ACM Transactions on Computer Systems*, *20*(4), 398–461. doi:10.1145/571637.571640

Catalini, C., & Gans, J. S. (2016). Some simple economics of the blockchain. *MIT Sloan Research Paper No. 5191-16*. MIT.

Centobelli, P., Cerchione, R., Del Vecchio, P., Oropallo, E., & Secundo, G. (2022). Blockchain technology for bridging trust, traceability and transparency in circular supply chain. *Information & Management*, *59*(7), 103508. doi:10.1016/j.im.2021.103508

Chakraborty, P. (2018), Understanding the software development practices of blockchain projects: A survey. In *Proceedings of the 12th ACM/IEEE International Symposium on Empirical Software Engineering and Measurement; Computing Machinery*, (pp. 1–10). IEEE. 10.1145/3239235.3240298

Challapalli, S. R. (2023). Benefits and Constraints Associated with the Harmonization of Financial Regulations: An Overview. *Asian Journal of Economics, Business and Accounting*. doi:10.9734/ajeba/2023/v23i151015

Chang, S. E., Chen, Y.-C., & Lu, M.-F. (2019). Supply chain re-engineering using blockchain technology: A case of smart contract-based racking process. *Technological Forecasting and Social Change*, *144*, 1–11. doi:10.1016/j.techfore.2019.03.015

Chang, V., Baudier, P., Zhang, H., Xu, Q., Zhang, J., & Arami, M. (2020). How Blockchain can impact financial services–The overview, challenges and recommendations from expert interviewees. *Technological Forecasting and Social Change*, *158*, 120166. doi:10.1016/j.techfore.2020.120166 PMID:32834134

Chang, X., Fu, K., Jin, Y., & Liem, P. F. (2022). Sustainable finance: ESG/CSR, firm value, and investment returns. *Asia-Pacific Journal of Financial Studies*, *51*(3), 325–371. doi:10.1111/ajfs.12379

Chang, Y. W. (2018). Examining interdisciplinarity of library and information science (LIS) based on LIS articles contributed by non-LIS authors. *Scientometrics*, *116*(3), 1589–1613. doi:10.1007/s11192-018-2822-7

Chatterjee, P., Das, D., & Rawat, D. B. (2023). Next Generation Financial Services: Role of Blockchain enabled Federated Learning and Metaverse. *2023 IEEE/ACM 23rd International Symposium on Cluster, Cloud and Internet Computing Workshops (CCGridW)*, (pp. 69–74). IEEE. 10.1109/CCGridW59191.2023.00025

Chen, Y. (2021). Framework of the smart finance and accounting management model under the artificial intelligence perspective. *Mob. Inf. Syst. 2021 (SI)*, 4295191–4295211.

Chen, Y., & Volz, U. (2021). *Scaling up sustainable investment through blockchain-based project bonds*. (Special Working Paper Series). ADB-IGF..

Chen, Y.;et.al.(2020), Research on the risk of block chain technology in Internet finance supported by wireless networkers. *J. Wirel. Commun. Netw., 71*.

Chen, C., & Zhou, Y. (2021). Application of deep reinforcement learning algorithm in smart finance. *Front. Artif. Intell. Appl.*, *341*, 40–48. doi:10.3233/FAIA210230

Chen, D. (2018). Selecting Ponzi Schemes on Ethereum: Towards Healthier Blockchain Technology. *Proceedings of the World Wide Web Conference*, (pp. 1409–1418). ACM. 10.1145/3178876.3186046

Chen, D., Doumeingts, G., & Vernadat, F. (2008). Architectures for enterprise integration and interoperability: Past, present and future. *Computers in Industry*, *59*(7), 647–659. doi:10.1016/j.compind.2007.12.016

Chen, J., Lv, Z., & Song, H. (2019). Design of personnel big data management system based on blockchain. *Future Generation Computer Systems*, *101*, 1122–1129. doi:10.1016/j.future.2019.07.037

Chen, M., & Patel, R. (2017). Decentralized Payroll Systems: A Case Study of Blockchain Implementation. *Journal of Financial Technology*, *9*(1), 56–72.

Chen, X., Cheng, Q., & Luo, T. (2023). The economic value of blockchain applications: Early evidence from asset-backed securities. *Management Science*. doi:10.2139/ssrn.4077443

Chen, Y., & Volz, U. (2021). Scaling up sustainable investment through blockchain-based project bonds. *Development Policy Review*, *40*(3), e12582. doi:10.1111/dpr.12582

Chillakuri, B., & Attili, V. P. (2022). Role of blockchain in HR's response to new-normal. *The International Journal of Organizational Analysis*, *30*(6), 1359–1378. doi:10.1108/IJOA-08-2020-2363

Chohan, U. W. (2021). Non-Fungible Tokens: Blockchains, Scarcity, and Value. *Critical Blockchain Research Initiative, Notes on the 21st Century.*

Choudhari, S., Das, S., Parasher, S., & Gangwar, D. (2021, April). Sub-contractor life cycle management in enterprise system using blockchain technology. In *2021 6th International Conference for Convergence in Technology (I2CT)* (pp. 1-7). IEEE. 10.1109/I2CT51068.2021.9417981

Chueca Vergara, C., & Ferruz Agudo, L. (2021). Fintech and sustainability: Do they affect each other? *Sustainability (Basel)*, *13*(13), 7012. doi:10.3390/su13137012

Ciampi, F., Marzi, G., Demi, S., & Faraoni, M. (2020). The big data-business strategy interconnection: A grand challenge for knowledge management. A review and future perspectives. *Journal of Knowledge Management*, *24*(5), 1157–1176. doi:10.1108/JKM-02-2020-0156

Cimino, C., Negri, E., & Fumagalli, L. (2019). Review of digital twin applications in manufacturing. *Computers in Industry*, *113*, 103130. doi:10.1016/j.compind.2019.103130

Clarke, G., & Hrnjic, E. (2022). *National Study on Central Bank Digital Currency and Stablecoin in the Maldives*. 1–68.

Collomb, A., & Sok, K. (2016). Blockchain/distributed ledger technology (DLT): What impact on the financial sector? *Digiworld Economic Journal,* (103).

Colombo, A. W., Karnouskos, S., Kaynak, O., Shi, Y., & Yin, S. (2017). Industrial Cyberphysical Systems: A Backbone of the Fourth Industrial Revolution. *IEEE Industrial Electronics Magazine*, *11*(1), 6–16. doi:10.1109/MIE.2017.2648857

Colomo-Palacios, R., Sánchez-Gordón, M., & Arias-Aranda, D. (2020). A critical review on blockchain assessment initiatives: A technology evolution viewpoint. *Journal of Software (Malden, MA)*, *32*(11), e2272. doi:10.1002/smr.2272

Cooper, C., Booth, A., Varley-Campbell, J., Britten, N., & Garside, R. (2018). Defining the process to literature searching in systematic reviews: A literature review of guidance and supporting studies. *BMC Medical Research Methodology*, *18*(1), 1–14. doi:10.1186/s12874-018-0545-3 PMID:30107788

Cooper, C., Garside, R., Varley-Campbell, J., Talens-Bou, J., Booth, A., & Britten, N. (2020). "It has no meaning to me." How do researchers understand the effectiveness of literature searches? A qualitative analysis and preliminary typology of understandings. *Research Synthesis Methods*, *11*(5), 627–640. doi:10.1002/jrsm.1426 PMID:32495989

Crosby, M., Pattanayak, P., Verma, S., & Kalyanaraman, V. (2016). BlockChain Technology: Beyond Bitcoin. *Applied Innovation Review*, *2*, 6–19.

Crosby, M., Pattanayak, P., Verma, S., & Kalyanaraman, V. (2016). Blockchain technology: Beyond bitcoin. *Applied Innovation*, *2*(6–10), 71.

Cucari, N., Lagasio, V., Lia, G., & Torriero, C. (2022). The impact of blockchain in banking processes: The Interbank Spunta case study. *Technology Analysis and Strategic Management*, *34*(2), 138–150. doi:10.1080/09537325.2021.1891217

Cuevas, P. E. G., Davidson, P. M., Mejilla, J. L., & Rodney, T. W. (2020). Reminiscence therapy for older adults with Alzheimer's disease: A literature review. *International Journal of Mental Health Nursing*, *29*(3), 364–371. doi:10.1111/inm.12692 PMID:31984570

Cui, Y., Idota, H., & Ota, M. (2022). Reforming Supply Chain Systems in Metaverse. *2022 ACM International Conference on Information Technology for Social Good (GoodIT)*. ACM. 10.1145/3561278.3561289

Cumming, D. J., Johan, S., & Pant, A. (2019). Regulation of the Crypto-Economy: Managing Risks, Challenges, and Regulatory Uncertainty. *Journal of Risk and Financial Management*, *12*(3), 126. doi:10.3390/jrfm12030126

D'OrazioA.PopoyanL. (2019). Artificial intelligence, algorithmic pricing and collusion. *Available at* SSRN 3461165.

Damiano, D. F. M., Mori, P., & Ricci, L. (2019). A blockchain based approach for the definition of auditable Access Control systems. *Computers & Security*, *84*, 93–119. doi:10.1016/j.cose.2019.03.016

Damle, M., & Kulkarni, P. (2023). Blockchain Technology in Talent Retention and Capability Development in HRM, *5th International Conference on Inventive Research in Computing Applications (ICIRCA)*, Coimbatore, India. 10.1109/ICIRCA57980.2023.10220633

DasS. (2023). Digital Twins: The Key to Unlocking Industry 4.0 and beyond. SSRN, p. https://ssrn.com/abstract=4426592 or doi:10.2139/ssrn.4426592

Davidson, S. (2016). Disrupting Governance. *The New Institutional Economics of Distributed Ledger Technology.*, *57*, 101519.

Debrah, C., Chan, A. P. C., & Darko, A. (2022). Green finance gap in green buildings: A scoping review and future research needs. *Building and Environment*, *207*, 108443. doi:10.1016/j.buildenv.2021.108443

Dell'Erba, M. (2021). Sustainable digital finance and the pursuit of environmental sustainability. *Sustainable Finance in Europe: Corporate Governance, Financial Stability and Financial Markets.*

Deren, L., Wenbo, Y., & Zhenfeng, S. (2021, March 29). Smart city based on digital twins. *Computational Urban Science*, *1*(1), 4. Advance online publication. doi:10.1007/s43762-021-00005-y

Deshmukh, P., Sharma, D., & Sharma, P. (2022). Do Socially Responsible Indices Outperform the Market During Black Swan Events: Evidence from Indian Markets During Global Financial and COVID-19 Crises. *Australasian Accounting. Business and Finance Journal*, *16*(5), 19–37.

Desmarais, P. III. (2020). *The technological revolution in financial services: how banks, fintechs, and customers win together*. University of Toronto Press.

Destefanis, G. (2018). Smart contracts vulnerabilities: A call for blockchain oftware engineering? In *Proceedings of the 2018 International Workshop on Blockchain Oriented Software Engineering IWBOSE*), Campobasso, Italy. 10.1109/IWBOSE.2018.8327567

Dewey and Patil. (2023). *Blockchain & Cryptocurrency Laws and Regulations 2024.* Global Legal Insights. https://www.globallegalinsights.com/practice-areas/blockchain-laws-and-regulations

Dhayal, K. S., Giri, A. K., Kumar, A., Samadhiya, A., Agrawal, S., & Agrawal, R. (2023). Can green finance facilitate Industry 5.0 transition to achieve sustainability? A systematic review with future research directions. *Environmental Science and Pollution Research International*, *30*(46), 102158–102180. doi:10.1007/s11356-023-29539-w PMID:37695480

Di Pierro, M. (2017). What is the blockchain? *Computing in Science & Engineering*, *19*(5), 92–95. doi:10.1109/MCSE.2017.3421554

di Prisco, D., & Strangio, D. (2021). Technology and financial inclusion: A case study to evaluate potential and limitations of Blockchain in emerging countries. *Technology Analysis and Strategic Management*, 1–14. doi:10.1080/09537325.2021.1944617

Di Vaio, A., & Varriale, L. (2020). Blockchain technology in business and information systems research: A systematic literature review. *Business Process Management Journal.*

Diamantopoulos, G., Tziritas, N., Bahsoon, R., & Theodoropoulos, G. (2022, December). Digital Twins for Dynamic Management of Blockchain Systems. In 2022 Winter Simulation Conference (WSC) (pp. 2876-2887). IEEE. doi:10.1109/WSC57314.2022.10015447

Dietz, M., & Pernul, G. (2020). Unleashing the Digital Twin's Potential for ICS Security. *IEEE Security and Privacy, 18*(4), 20–27. doi:10.1109/MSEC.2019.2961650

Dinesha, D., & Balachandra, P. (2023). Decentralized Token Exchanges in Blockchain Enabled Interconnected Smart Microgrids. *2023 IEEE PowerTech.* IEEE. doi:10.1109/PowerTech55446.2023.10202994

Dolgui, A., Ivanov, D., Potryasaev, S., Sokolov, B., Ivanova, M., & Werner, F. (2020). Blockchain-oriented dynamic modelling of smart contract design and execution in the supply chain. *International Journal of Production Research, 2020*(58), 2184–2199. doi:10.1080/00207543.2019.1627439

Dong, Z., Xu, H., Zhang, Z., Lyu, Y., Lu, Y., & Duan, H. (2022). Whether green finance improves green innovation of listed companies-evidence from China. *International Journal of Environmental Research and Public Health, 19*(17), 10882. doi:10.3390/ijerph191710882 PMID:36078597

Donthu, N., Kumar, S., Mukherjee, D., Pandey, N., & Lim, W. M. (2021). How to conduct a bibliometric analysis: An overview and guidelines. *Journal of Business Research, 133*, 285–296. doi:10.1016/j.jbusres.2021.04.070

Dorfleitner, G., & Braun, D. (2019). Fintech, digitalization and blockchain: possible applications for green finance. *The rise of green finance in Europe: opportunities and challenges for issuers, investors and marketplaces*, 207-237.

Dowling, M. (2021). Is non-fungible token pricing driven by cryptocurrencies? *Finance Research Letters, 44*, 102097. doi:10.1016/j.frl.2021.102097

Eenmaa-Dimitrieva, H., & Schmidt-Kessen, M. J. (2019). Creating markets in no-trust environments: The law and economics of smart contracts. *Computer Law & Security Report, 35*(1), 69–88. doi:10.1016/j.clsr.2018.09.003

Efuntade, A. O., & Efuntade, O. O. (2023). SWOT Analysis of Blockchain Funding, Platform Finance, Financial Big Data and Financial Engineering Under the Background of Financial Innovation and Technology. *International Journal of Economics, Finance and Management Sciences.* doi:10.56201/ijefm.v8.no4.2023.pg18.38

El Saddik, A. (2018, April-June). Digital Twins: The Convergence of Multimedia Technologies. *IEEE MultiMedia, 25*(2), 87–92. doi:10.1109/MMUL.2018.023121167

Elisa, Yang, L., Chao, F., Naik, N., & Boongoen, T. (2023). A Secure and Privacy-Preserving E-Government Framework Using Blockchain and Artificial Immunity. *IEEE Access : Practical Innovations, Open Solutions, 11*(99), 1–1. doi:10.1109/ACCESS.2023.3239814

Enam, M., Shajar, S. N., & Das, N. (2023). Non-Monotonic Relationship between Corporate Governance and Banks' Operating Performance—The Moderating Role of CEO Duality: Evidence from Selected Countries. *Sustainability (Basel), 15*(7), 5643. doi:10.3390/su15075643

Erol, T., Mendi, A. F., & Doğan, D. (2020). *The Digital Twin Revolution in Healthcare*. 2020 4th International Symposium on Multidisciplinary Studies and Innovative Technologies (ISMSIT), Istanbul, Turkey. 10.1109/ISMSIT50672.2020.9255249

Esmat, A., de Vos, M., Ghiassi-Farrokhfal, Y., Palensky, P., & Epema, D. (2021). A novel decentralized platform for peer-to-peer energy trading market with blockchain technology. *Applied Energy, 282*, 116123. doi:10.1016/j.apenergy.2020.116123

Etemadi, N., Van Gelder, P., & Strozzi, F. (2021). An ism modeling of barriers for blockchain/distributed ledger technology adoption in supply chains towards cybersecurity. *Sustainability (Basel), 13*(9), 4672. doi:10.3390/su13094672

European Commission. (2018a). *Action plan: Financing sustainable growth*. EC. https://eur-lex.europa.eu/legal-content/EN/TXT/PDF/?uri=CELEX:52018DC0097&from=EN

Evans, T. M. (2019). Cryptokitties, cryptography, and copyright. *AIPLA Quarterly Journal, 47*, 219.

Fachrunnisa, O., & Hussain, F. K. (2020). Blockchain-based human resource management practices for mitigating skills and competencies gap in workforce. *International Journal of Engineering Business Management, 12*, 1847979020966400. doi:10.1177/1847979020966400

Farahani, B., Firouzi, F., & Luecking, M. (2021). The convergence of IoT and distributed ledger technologies (DLT): Opportunities, challenges, and solutions. *Journal of Network and Computer Applications, 177*, 102936. doi:10.1016/j.jnca.2020.102936

Farnaghia, M., & Mansouriana, A. (2022). Blockchain, an enabling technology for transparent and accountable decentralized public participatory GIS. *Cities, 105*.

Far, S. B., & Rad, A. I. (2022). Applying digital twins in metaverse: User interface, security and privacy challenges. *Journal of Metaverse, 2*(1), 8–15.

Feng, M., & Wang, R. (2019). Blockchain technology for smart city and smart tourism: Latest trends and challenges. *Asia Pacific Journal of Tourism Research, 24*(5), 457–468.

Fenwick, M., & Vermeulen, E. P. (2020). Banking and regulatory responses to FinTech revisited-building the sustainable financial service'ecosystems' of tomorrow. *Singapore Journal of Legal Studies*.

Fernandez-Vazquez, S., Rosillo, R., Meijueiro, L., Alonso Alvarez, R., & De La Fuente, D. (2023). A comparative study of blockchain's largest permissionless networks. *Technology Analysis and Strategic Management, 35*(4), 409–423. doi:10.1080/09537325.2021.1976748

Finck, M. (2018). Blockchains and data protection in the European Union. *Eur. Data Prot. L. Rev., 4*(1), 17–35. doi:10.21552/edpl/2018/1/6

Firzli, M. N. J., Weeks, D., & Sherry, N. (2021). *ESG, Green Growth and Employee Capitalism: G7 Roadmap for the Fifth Industrial Revolution.*

Fridgen, G., König, C., Urbach, N., Böhm, M., & Guggenmos, F. (2018). Digital transformation in the energy sector: A systematic review of the business and economics literature. *International Journal of Energy Sector Management, 12*(1), 2–29.

Frizzo-Barker, J., Chow-White, P. A., Adams, P. R., Mentanko, J., Ha, D., & Green, S. (2020). Blockchain as a disruptive technology for business: A systematic review. *International Journal of Information Management, 51*, 102029. doi:10.1016/j.ijinfomgt.2019.10.014

Frizzo-Barker, J., Chow-White, P. A., Mozafari, M., & Ha, D. (2020). An Internet of Things (IoT) based predictive analytics for smart monitoring in mining and heavy industry. *Engineering Applications of Artificial Intelligence, 87*, 103312.

Frost, J. (2020). The economic forces driving fintech adoption across countries. *The technological revolution in financial services: how banks, fintechs, and customers win together, 838*, 70-89.

Fuessler, J., León, F., & Mock, R. (2018). *Navigating blockchain and climate action.* Gold Standard. https://www.goldstandard.org/sites/default/files/documents/cli_report_dec18.pdf

Fulton, M., Kahn, B. M., & Sharples, C. (2013). Sustainable Investing: Establishing Long-Term Value and Performance. SSRN *Electronic Journal, June.* doi:10.2139/ssrn.2222740

Gabor, D., & Brooks, S. (2020). The digital revolution in financial inclusion: international development in the fintech era. In *Material Cultures of Financialisation* (pp. 69–82). Routledge. doi:10.4324/9781351002103-6

Gamage, H. T. M., Weerasinghe, H. D., & Dias, N. G. J. (2020). A Survey on Blockchain Technology Concepts, Applications, and Issues. *SN Computer Science, 1*(2), 1–15. doi:10.1007/s42979-020-00123-0

Gan, Q., Lau, R. Y. K., & Hong, J. (2021). A critical review of blockchain applications to banking and finance: A qualitative thematic analysis approach. *Technology Analysis and Strategic Management*, 1–17. doi:10.1080/09537325.2021.1979509

Gao, L., Guo, K., & Wei, X. (2023). Dynamic relationship between green bonds and major financial asset markets from the perspective of climate change. *Frontiers in Environmental Science, 10*, 1109796. doi:10.3389/fenvs.2022.1109796

Garcia-Arroyo, J., & Osca, A. (2021). Big data contributions to human resource management: A systematic review. *International Journal of Human Resource Management, 32*(20), 4337–4362. doi:10.1080/09585192.2019.1674357

Garcia, R., & Patel, S. (2022). Optimizing Sustainable Outcomes: The Synergy of Blockchain and Digital Twins in Green Projects. *Environmental Innovation and Societal Transitions, 18*, 120–135.

Garg, P., Gupta, B., Chauhan, A. K., Sivarajah, U., Gupta, S., & Modgil, S. (2021). Measuring the perceived benefits of implementing blockchain technology in the banking sector. *Technological Forecasting and Social Change*, *163*, 120407. doi:10.1016/j.techfore.2020.120407

Garg, R. (2023). Blockchain for Decentralized Finance: Impact, Challenges and Remediation. *International Journal of Computer Science and Information Technologies*, *17*(March), 225–237.

Gatteschi, V., Lamberti, F., Demartini, C., Pranteda, C., & Santamaría, V. (2018). Blockchain and smart contracts for insurance: Is the technology mature enough? *Future Internet*, *10*(2), 20. doi:10.3390/fi10020020

Gawusu, S., Zhang, X., Ahmed, A., Jamatutu, S. A., Miensah, E. D., Amadu, A. A., & Osei, F. A. J. (2022). Renewable energy sources from the perspective of blockchain integration: From theory to application. [Part B]. *Sustainable Energy Technologies and Assessments*, *52*, 52. doi:10.1016/j.seta.2022.102108

Gervais, A., Karame, G. O., Wüst, K., Glykantzis, V., Ritzdorf, H., & Capkun, S. (2016, October). On the security and performance of proof of work blockchains. In *Proceedings of the 2016 ACM SIGSAC conference on computer and communications security* (pp. 3-16). ACM. 10.1145/2976749.2978341

Ghenai, C., Husein, L. A., Al Nahlawi, M., Hamid, A. K., & Bettayeb, M. (2022). Recent trends of digital twin technologies in the energy sector: A comprehensive review. *Sustainable Energy Technologies and Assessments*, *54*, 102837. doi:10.1016/j.seta.2022.102837

Giannoni, C., Medda, F., & Bartolucci, S. (2023). Blockchain Technologies and Art: Opportunities and Open Challenges. SSRN *Electronic Journal*. doi:10.2139/ssrn.4439318

Glaessgen, E., & Stargel, D. (2012). The digital twin paradigm for future NASA and US Air Force vehicles. In *Proc. 53rd AIAA/ASME/ASCE/AHS/ASC Struct. Struct. Dyn. Mater. Conf.*, (pp. 23-26). Reston: Reston.

Glaser, F., & Bezzenberger, L. (2015). Pervasive decentralisation of digital infrastructures: A framework for blockchain enabled system and use case analysis. *Proceedings of the 48th Annual Hawaii International Conference on System Sciences*. IEEE.

Gobble, M. M. (2018). Big data: The next big thing in innovation. *Research Technology Management*, *61*(1), 59–63. doi:10.1080/08956308.2018.1445391

Gopal, S., Gupta, P., & Minocha, A. (2023). Advancements in Fin-Tech and Security Challenges of Banking Industry. *2023 International Conference on Innovations in Electrical and Electronics Engineering (ICIEM)*. IEEE. 10.1109/ICIEM59379.2023.10165876

Goumopoulos, C., & Mavrommati, I. (2020). A framework for pervasive computing applications based on smart objects and end user development. *Journal of Systems and Software*, *162*, 110496. doi:10.1016/j.jss.2019.110496

Govinda, G., Kunal, C., Sudhanshu, G., Rahul, J., Ketan, K., & Om, M. Parasha Deepak r & Mulay Preeti (2023). Payroll Management Using Blockchain. *International Conference on Innovative Computing and Communications. ICICC 2023. Lecture Notes in Networks and Systems*. Springer, Singapore.

Goyal, A., kanyal, H. S., & Sharma, B. (2023). Analysis of IoT and Blockchain Technology for Agricultural Food Supply Chain Transactions. *International Journal of Recent Technology and Engineering (IJRTE)*. doi:10.17762/ijritcc.v11i3.6342

Greenspan, G. (2015). *Smart Contracts: The Good, the Bad and the Lazy*. data science.

Grieves, M., & Vickers, J. (2017). Digital Twin: Mitigating Unpredictable, Undesirable Emergent Behavior in Complex Systems. Kahlen, J., Flumerfelt, S., Alves, A. (eds) Transdisciplinary Perspectives on Complex Systems. Springer. doi:10.1007/978-3-319-38756-7_4

Grieves, M. (2014). *Digital Twin: Manufacturing Excellence through Virtual Factory Replication*. Springer International Publishing.

Griggs, K. N., Ossipova, O., Kohlios, C. P., Baccarini, A. N., Howson, E. A., & Hayajneh, T. (2018). Healthcare blockchain system using smart contracts for secure automated remote patient monitoring. *Journal of Medical Systems*, *42*(7), 1–7. doi:10.1007/s10916-018-0982-x PMID:29876661

Gromov, A. Y., Petrovskaia, T. A., Suslina, A. A., Khizriyeva, N. I., & Stepanov, M. A. (2018, June). Human resources intelligent selection algorithm with improvement of data validity. In *2018 7th Mediterranean Conference on Embedded Computing (MECO)* (pp. 1-4). IEEE. 10.1109/MECO.2018.8406036

Grover, P., Kar, A. K., & Janssen, M. (2019). Diffusion of blockchain technology: Insights from academic literature and social media analytics. *Journal of Enterprise Information Management*, *32*(5), 735–757. doi:10.1108/JEIM-06-2018-0132

Guo, H., Gu, F., Peng, Y., Deng, X., and Guo, L. (2022). Does digital inclusive finance effectively promote agricultural green development? – A case study of China. *Int. J. Environ.*

Guo, C.-Q., Wang, X., Cao, D.-D., & Hou, Y.-G. (2022). The impact of green finance on carbon emission-analysis based on mediation effect and spatial effect. *Frontiers in Environmental Science*, *10*, 844988. doi:10.3389/fenvs.2022.844988

Gupta, S., Sinha, S., & Bhushan, B. (2020, April). Emergence of blockchain technology: Fundamentals, working and its various implementations. In *Proceedings of the international conference on innovative computing & communications (ICICC)*. IEEE.

Gupta, A., & Chen, W. (2022). Enhancing Employee Onboarding Through Blockchain Technology. *Journal of Emerging Technologies in HR*, *6*(3), 120–138.

Hakimi, O., Liu, H., Abudayyeh, O., Houshyar, A., Almatared, M., & Alhawiti, A. (2023). Data Fusion for Smart Civil Infrastructure Management: A Conceptual Digital Twin Framework. *Buildings*, *13*(11), 2725. doi:10.3390/buildings13112725

Halpin, H., & Piekarska, M. (2017). *Introduction to Security and Privacy on the Blockchain. 2017 IEEE European Symposium on Security and Privacy Workshops (EuroS&PW)*, Paris, France. 10.1109/EuroSPW.2017.43

Harari, M. B., Parola, H. R., Hartwell, C. J., & Riegelman, A. (2020). Literature searches in systematic reviews and meta-analyses: A review, evaluation, and recommendations. *Journal of Vocational Behavior, 118*, 103377. doi:10.1016/j.jvb.2020.103377

Harris, A. (2018). A conversation with masterminds in blockchain and climate change. In *Transforming climate finance and green investment with blockchains* (pp. 15–22). Academic Press. doi:10.1016/B978-0-12-814447-3.00002-1

Harrison, T., & Waite, K. (2006). A time-based assessment of the influences, uses and benefits of intermediary website adoption. *Information & Management, 43*(8), 1002–1013. doi:10.1016/j.im.2006.09.004

Hasan, H. R., & Salah, K. (2019). Combating deepfake videos using blockchain and smart contracts. *IEEE Access : Practical Innovations, Open Solutions, 7*, 41596–41606. doi:10.1109/ACCESS.2019.2905689

Hashimy, L., & Sandner, P. (2020). The Impact of Financial Regulation on the Development of Distributed Ledger Technology (DLT) Firms. *Front. Blockchain, 3*, 21. doi:10.3389/fbloc.2020.00021

Hassan, M. K., Rabbani, M. R., & Ali, M. A. M. (2020). Challenges for the Islamic Finance and banking in post COVID era and the role of Fintech. *Journal of Economic Cooperation & Development, 41*(3), 93–116.

Hawashin, D., Salah, K., Jayaraman, R., & Musamih, A. (2023). Using Composable NFTs for Trading and Managing Expensive Packaged Products in the Food Industry. *IEEE Access : Practical Innovations, Open Solutions, 11*, 10587–10603. doi:10.1109/ACCESS.2023.3241226

Heines, R., Dick, C., Pohle, C., & Jung, R. (2021). The Tokenization of Everything: Towards a Framework for Understanding the Potentials of Tokenized Assets. *PACIS 2021 Proceedings*, 40. Research Gate.

Heines, R., Dick, C., Pohle, C., & Jung, R. (2021). The Tokenization of Everything: Towards a Framework for Understanding the Potentials of Tokenized Assets. *Proceedings of the Pacific Asia Conference on Information Systems (PACIS), July*, 1–14. https://widgets.ebscohost.com/prod/customerspecific/ns000290/authentication/index.php?url=https%3A%2F%2Fsearch.ebscohost.com%2Flogin.aspx%3Fdirect%3Dtrue%26db%3Dedb%26AN%3D151674974%26amp%3Blang%3Dpt-pt%26site%3Deds-live%26scope%3Dsite

Hellani, H., Samhat, A. E., Chamoun, M., El Ghor, H., & Serhrouchni, A. (2018). On BlockChain Technology: Overview of Bitcoin and Future Insights. *2018 IEEE International Multidisciplinary Conference on Engineering Technology, IMCET 2018*, (pp. 1–8). IEEE. 10.1109/IMCET.2018.8603029

Hemanand, D., Mishra, N., Premalatha, G., Mavaluru, D., Vajpayee, A., Kushwaha, S., & Sahile, K. (2022). Vajpayee, & Sahile, K. (2022). Applications of intelligent model to analyze the green finance for environmental development in the context of artificial intelligence. *Computational Intelligence and Neuroscience*, *2022*, 1–8. doi:10.1155/2022/2977824

Heslop, J., Lu, W., & Gray, A. (2019). Digital twin: Enabling technologies, challenges, and opportunities. *IEEE Access : Practical Innovations, Open Solutions*, *7*, 167653–167662.

Hewa, T., Ylianttila, M., & Liyanage, M. (2021). Survey on blockchain based smart contracts: Applications, opportunities and challenges. *Journal of Network and Computer Applications*, *177*, 177–187. doi:10.1016/j.jnca.2020.102857

He, X., Tu, Z., Xu, X., & Wang, Z. (2021). Programming framework and infrastructure for self-adaptation and optimized evolution method for microservice systems in cloud–edge environments. *Future Generation Computer Systems*, *118*, 263–281. doi:10.1016/j.future.2021.01.008

Hj. (2022). Addressing Accountability and Transparency Challenges in Waqf Management Using Blockchain Technology. *Journal of Islamic Monetary Economics and Finance*, *8*. doi:10.21098/jimf.v8i0.1413

Hoang, T. G., Nguyen, G. N. T., & Le, D. A. (2022). Developments in financial technologies for achieving the Sustainable Development Goals (SDGs): FinTech and SDGs. In *Disruptive technologies and eco-innovation for sustainable development* (pp. 1–19). IGI Global. doi:10.4018/978-1-7998-8900-7.ch001

Hoffecker, L. (2020). Grey literature searching for systematic reviews in the health sciences. *The Serials Librarian*, *79*(3-4), 252–260. doi:10.1080/0361526X.2020.1847745

Höhne, N., Khosla, S., Fekete, H., & Gilbert, A. (2012). *Mapping of green finance delivered by IDFC members in 2011*. Ecofys.

Hughes, L., Dwivedi, Y. K., Misra, S. K., Rana, N. P., Raghavan, V., & Akella, V. (2019). Blockchain research, practice and policy: Applications, benefits, limitations, emerging research themes and research agenda. *International Journal of Information Management*, *49*(February), 114–129. doi:10.1016/j.ijinfomgt.2019.02.005

Hu, J., & Lykourentzou, I. (2023). TONIC: A teamwork simulator and digital twin for organizational innovation challenges. *ACM SIGCHI Conference on Human Factors in Computing Systems*. ACM. 10.1145/3594806.3596549

Ibrahim, D. (2023). Opportunities, Challenges and Implications of Blockchain Technology for Accounting: An Exploratory Study. *Alexandria Journal of Accounting Research*, *7*(3), 173–220.

Ibrar, Y., Salah, K., Jayaraman, R., & Al-Hammadi, Y. (2021). Blockchain for healthcare data management: Opportunities, challenges, and future recommendations. *Neural Computing & Applications*, *34*(14), 11475–11490. doi:10.1007/s00521-020-05519-w

IFC. (2013). *Mobilizing Public and Private Funds for Inclusive Green Growth Investment in Developing Countries - An Expanded Stocktaking Report Prepared for the G20 Development Working Group*. IFC Climate Business Department.

Industry Forum. (2023). *2023 IEEE/ACM 45th International Conference on Software Engineering Companion (ICSE-Companion)*. IEEE. 10.1109/ICSE-Companion58688.2023.00009

Inshakova, A., & Osadchenko, E. (2023). *Green Bonds and Industrial Mortgages as Key Financial Instruments for Digital Sustainability Institutions*. Legal Concept., doi:10.15688/lc.jvolsu.2023.1.19

International Finance Corporation (IFC). (2017). *Green finance. A bottom-up approach to track existing flows*. IFC.

Intizar Ali, M., Patel, P., Breslin, J. G., Harik, R., & Sheth, A. (2021). Cognitive Digital Twins for Smart Manufacturing. *IEEE Intelligent Systems*, *36*(2), 96–100. doi:10.1109/MIS.2021.3062437

Jabbar, N. A. A., & Breesam, H. K. (2023). Risk Management in The Oil Sector / Oil Exploration Company as A Case Study. *Journal of Petroleum Research and Studies*. doi:10.52716/jprs.v13i3.686

Jadhav, J. S., & Deshmukh, J. (2022). A review study of the blockchain-based healthcare supply chain. *Social Sciences & Humanities Open*, *6*(1), 100328. doi:10.1016/j.ssaho.2022.100328

Jafar, S. H., Akhtar, S., El-Chaarani, H., Khan, P. A., & Binsaddig, R. (2023, September 25). Forecasting of NIFTY 50 Index Price by Using Backward Elimination with an LSTM Model. *Journal of Risk and Financial Management*, *16*(10), 423. doi:10.3390/jrfm16100423

Jafar, S. H., Akhtar, S., & Johl, S. K. (2023b). AI in Insurance. In *Artificial Intelligence for Business* (pp. 164–173). Productivity Press. doi:10.4324/9781003358411-10

Jaiwant, S. V., & Kureethara, J. V. (2023). Green Finance and Fintech: Toward a More Sustainable Financial System. In *Green Finance Instruments, FinTech, and Investment Strategies: Sustainable Portfolio Management in the Post-COVID Era* (pp. 283–300). Springer International Publishing. doi:10.1007/978-3-031-29031-2_12

Jiang, Y., Yin, S., Dong, J., & Kaynak, O. (2020). A Review on Soft Sensors for Monitoring, Control, and Optimization of Industrial Processes. *IEEE Sensors Journal*, 12868–12881.

Jia, Z., Chen, Y., Lang, J., & Li, P. (2023). The Analysis of Asset-Backed Security Backed by Online Consumer Loan. *Asia-Pacific Journal of Accounting & Economics*, *4*(1), 292–302. doi:10.54254/2754-1169/4/20221078

Jing, Y., Chen, C., Dong, J., & He, Z. (2023). Blockchain-Embedded Strategic Options for Satellite Operators: Sell, SataaS, or Dual [MDPI AG.]. *Systems*, *11*(11), 550. doi:10.3390/systems11110550

Jonathan, R., & Wright, A. (2018). Blockchain-based token sales, initial coin offerings, and the democratization of public capital markets. *The Hastings Law Journal*, *70*, 463.

Jones, D. (2020). Characterising the Digital Twin: A Systematic Literature Review. *CIRP Journal of Manufacturing Science and Technology, 29*. . doi:10.1016/j.cirpj.2020.02.002

Jones, L., & Smith, K. (2021). Smart Contracts in Green Investments: A Blockchain-Digital Twin Perspective. *Sustainable Development Journal, 25*(4), 287–305.

Kadlec, P., Grbić, R., & Gabrys, B. (2011). Review of adaptation mechanisms for data-driven soft sensors. *Computers & Chemical Engineering, 35*(1), 1–24. doi:10.1016/j.compchemeng.2010.07.034

Kafi, M. A., & Akter, N. (2023). Securing Financial Information in the Digital Realm: Case Studies in Cybersecurity for Accounting Data Protection. *American Journal of Theoretical and Applied Psychology*. doi:10.18034/ajtp.v10i1.659

Kalaiarasi, H., & Kirubahari, S. (2023). Green finance for sustainable development using blockchain technology. In *Green Blockchain Technology for Sustainable Smart Cities* (pp. 167–185). Elsevier. doi:10.1016/B978-0-323-95407-5.00003-7

Kamble, S. S., Gunasekaran, A., & Gawankar, S. A. (2019). Sustainable Industry 4.0 framework: A systematic literature review identifying the current trends and future perspectives. *Process Safety and Environmental Protection, 117*, 408–425. doi:10.1016/j.psep.2018.05.009

Kamel Boulos, M. N., Wilson, J. T., & Clauson, K. A. (2020). Blockchain and big data analytics for biomedicine, healthcare, and life sciences: A survey. *Blockchain in Healthcare Today*.

Kapetaki, Z., & Sgouridis, S. (2017). Overview and analysis of the concept and applications of virtual power plants and microgrids. *Renewable & Sustainable Energy Reviews, 77*, 193–214.

Karpf, A., & Mandel, A. (2018). Finance and sustainability: The progress of sustainable finance as a new discipline. *Finance Research Letters, 26*, 381–389.

Kasprzak, P. (2021). Blockchain to the Rescue—Tokenization of Residential Real Estate in the Emerging Token Economy. In *H. T.A., & D. J.J., Digitalization, Digital Transformation and Sustainability in the Global Economy* (pp. 21–35). Springer. doi:10.1007/978-3-030-77340-3_3

Kenny, R. (2022). Photovoltaics in 2021. *Solar RRL, 6*(5), 2200288. doi:10.1002/solr.202200288

Khan, A., Priyadarshi, R., Bhattacharya, T., & Rhim, J.-W. (2023). Carrageenan/Alginate-Based Functional Films Incorporated with Allium sativum Carbon Dots for UV-Barrier Food Packaging. *Food and Bioprocess Technology, 16*(9), 2001–2015. doi:10.1007/s11947-023-03048-7

Khan, K. M., Fahim, A., Saleem, D. M., & Jokhio, M. (2022). Empirical Investigation on Blockchain Interoperability. *VFAST Transactions on Software Engineering, 11*(1), 25–36. doi:10.21015/vtse.v10i4.1315

Khan, M. A., Riaz, H., Ahmed, M., & Saeed, A. (2022). Does green finance really deliver what is expected? An empirical perspective. *Borsa Istanbul Review, 22*(3), 586–593. doi:10.1016/j.bir.2021.07.006

Khan, M. A., & Salah, K. (2018). Blockchain's adoption in IoT: The challenges, and a way forward. *Journal of Network and Computer Applications*, *125*, 251–279.

Khan, N., & ... (2018). Blockchain's role in green finance. *Journal of Financial Management*, *36*(4), 784–799. doi:10.24136/oc.2023.021

Khan, S. N., Loukil, F., Ghedira-Guegan, C., Benkhelifa, E., & Bani-Hani, A. (2021). Blockchain smart contracts: Applications, challenges, and future trends. *Peer-to-Peer Networking and Applications*, *14*(5), 2901–2925. doi:10.1007/s12083-021-01127-0 PMID:33897937

Khan, S., Kabanov, I., Hua, Y., & Madnick, S. (2022). A systematic analysis of the capital one data breach: Critical lessons learned. *ACM Transactions on Privacy and Security*, *26*(1), 1–29. doi:10.1145/3546068

Khaqqi, K., Siksnys, L., Janczewski, L., & Krisjanis, M. (2018). Incorporating seller/buyer reputation-based system in blockchain-enabled emission trading application. *Applied Energy*, *209*, 8–19. doi:10.1016/j.apenergy.2017.10.070

Khatoon, A. (2018). A blockchain-based smart contract system for healthcare management. *Electronics 2020, 9*, (94).

Kietzmann, J., Lee, L. W., McCarthy, I. P., & Kietzmann, T. C. (2020). Deepfakes: Trick or treat? *Business Horizons, 63*(2), 135e146.

Kim, H. W., & Jeong, Y. S. (2018). Secure authentication-management human-centric scheme for trusting personal resource information on mobile cloud computing with blockchain. *Human-centric Computing and Information Sciences*, *8*(1), 1–13. doi:10.1186/s13673-018-0136-7

Kim, T. H., Kumar, G., Saha, R., Rai, M. K., Buchanan, W. J., Thomas, R., & Alazab, M. (2020). A privacy preserving distributed ledger framework for global human resource record management: The blockchain aspect. *IEEE Access : Practical Innovations, Open Solutions*, *8*, 96455–96467. doi:10.1109/ACCESS.2020.2995481

King, S., & Nadal, S. (2012). *PPCoin: Peer-to-Peer Crypto-Currency with Proof-of-Stake.*

Kong, D.-R., & Lin, T.-C. (2021). Alternative investments in the Fintech era: The risk and return of Non-Fungible Token (NFT). SSRN *Electronic Journal*. doi:10.2139/ssrn.3914085

Konstantinidis, I., Siaminos, G., Timplalexis, C., Zervas, P., Peristeras, V., & Decker, S. (2018). Blockchain for business applications: A systematic literature review. In Business Information Systems: 21st International Conference, BIS 2018, Berlin, Germany, July 18-20, 2018 [Springer International Publishing.]. *Proceedings*, *21*, 384–399.

Kotb Kholaif, M. M. N. H., & ... (2023). Post-pandemic opportunities for F&B green supply chains and supply chain viability: The moderate effect of blockchains and big data analytics. *European Journal of Innovation Management*. doi:10.1108/EJIM-10-2022-0581

Kritzinger, W., Karner, M., Traar, G., Henjes, J., & Sihn, W. (2018). Digital Twin in manufacturing: A categorical literature review and classification. *IFAC-PapersOnLine*, *51*(11), 1016–1022. doi:10.1016/j.ifacol.2018.08.474

Krosinsky, C. (2012). *Sustainable investing: The art of long-term performance*. Routledge. doi:10.4324/9781849773959

Kshetri, N. (2018). 1 Blockchain's roles in meeting key supply chain management objectives. *International Journal of Information Management*, *39*, 80–89. doi:10.1016/j.ijinfomgt.2017.12.005

Küfeoğlu, S. (2022). Emerging Technologies. In *Emerging Technologies, Sustainable Development Goals Series*. https://doi.org/10.1007/978-3-031-07127-0_2

Kumar, K. S., Kumar, T. A., Radhamani, A. S., & Sundaresan, S. (2020). Blockchain technology: an insight into architecture, use cases, and its application with industrial IoT and big data. In *Blockchain Technology* (pp. 23–42). CRC Press.

Kumar, N. M., & Mallick, P. K. (2018). Blockchain technology for security issues and challenges in IoT. *Procedia Computer Science*, *132*, 1815–1823. doi:10.1016/j.procs.2018.05.140

Labatt, S., & White, R. R. (2007). *Carbon finance: The financial implications of climate change*. John Wiley & Sons.

Labazova. (2019). Towards a Framework for Evaluation of Blockchain Implementations, Association for International System. *ICIS 2019 Proceedings*, *18*. AIS. https://aisel.aisnet.org/icis2019/blockchain_fintech/blockchain_fintech/18

Lanza, S., & Neag, N. P. (2023). *Safety and Ergonomic Risk Management for Visual Stress. A Theoretical and Experimental Case*. International Transactions on Visual Arts. doi:10.59168/ITVA8408

Lee, J. Y. (2019). A decentralized token economy: How blockchain and cryptocurrency can revolutionize business. *Business Horizons*, *62*(6), 773–784. doi:10.1016/j.bushor.2019.08.003

Lee, S., & Yigitcanlar, T. (2019). Advanced data analytics in green finance decision-making. *Journal of Environmental Management*, *246*, 267–278. doi:10.3390/s22176619

Lehner, O. M., Harrer, T., Silvola, H., & Weber, O. (Eds.). (2023). *The Routledge Handbook of Green Finance*. Taylor & Francis. doi:10.4324/9781003345497

Le, V. T., & ... (2022). Blockchain Powered QA Process Management for Digital Twins. *2022 IEEE International Conference on System Reliability and Safety (ICSRS)*. IEEE. 10.1109/ICSRS56243.2022.10067396

Li, Z., Wang, P., Han, X., & Shang, D. (2023). Research on Digital Twin Technology of Port Structure Safety based on Floating 3D Display. *2023 IEEE 9th International Conference on Industrial and Business Engineering (ICIBE)*. IEEE. 10.1109/ICIBA56860.2023.10165263

Li, D., & Li, J. Y. (2023). Big data of enterprise supply chain under green financial system based on digital twin technology. *Kybernetes*. doi:10.1108/K-02-2023-0291

Liebenau, J. (2016). *Blockchain Innovation beyond Bitcoin and Banking*. Research Gate.

Li, G., Wang, L., Li, Z., & Guo, Z. (2023). Has pilot zones policy for green finance reform and innovations improved the level of green financial development and environmental quality? *Environmental Science and Pollution Research International*, *30*(26), 68667–68676. doi:10.1007/s11356-023-27243-3 PMID:37126176

Li, L., Aslam, S., Wileman, A., & Perinpanayagam, S. (2021). Digital twin in aerospace industry: A gentle introduction. *IEEE Access : Practical Innovations, Open Solutions*, *10*, 9543–9562. doi:10.1109/ACCESS.2021.3136458

Lim, S. Y., Fotsing, P. T., Almasri, A., Musa, O., Kiah, M. L. M., Ang, T. F., & Ismail, R. (2018). Blockchain technology the identity management and authentication service disruptor: A survey. *International Journal on Advanced Science, Engineering and Information Technology, 8*(4–2), 1735–1745. doi:10.18517/ijaseit.8.4-2.6838

Lin, C. H., Yang, H. L., & Liou, D. Y. (2009). The impact of corporate social responsibility on financial performance: Evidence from business in Taiwan. *Technology in Society*, *31*(1), 56–63. doi:10.1016/j.techsoc.2008.10.004

Lin, G., Lam, J. F. I., Shi, Y., Chen, H., & Chen, H. (2023). Revisiting the linkage between green finance China's sustainable development: Evidence from the pilot zones for green finance reform innovations. *Frontiers in Ecology and Evolution*, *11*, 1264434. doi:10.3389/fevo.2023.1264434

Li, Q. L., Ma, J. Y., Chang, Y. X., Ma, F. Q., & Yu, H. B. (2019). Markov processes in blockchain systems. *Computational Social Networks*, *6*(1), 1–28. doi:10.1186/s40649-019-0066-1

Liu, H., Yao, P., Latif, S., Aslam, S., & Iqbal, N. (2022). Impact of Green financing, FinTech, and financial inclusion on energy efficiency. *Environmental Science and Pollution Research International*, *29*(13), 1–12. doi:10.1007/s11356-021-16949-x PMID:34705207

Liu, J., Li, J., Wang, J., Uddin, M. M., & Zhang, B. (2022). Research on the application of blockchain technology in coal supply chain finance. *Sustainability (Basel)*, *14*(16), 10099. doi:10.3390/su141610099

Liu, J., Zhang, L., Li, C., Bai, J., Lv, H., & Lv, Z. (2022). Blockchain-Based Secure Communication of Intelligent Transportation Digital Twins System. *IEEE Transactions on Intelligent Transportation Systems*, *23*(11), 22630–22640. doi:10.1109/TITS.2022.3183379

Liu, M., Fang, S., Dong, H., & Xu, C. (2021). Review of digital twin about concepts, technologies, and Industrial Applications. *Journal of Manufacturing Systems*, *58*, 346–361. doi:10.1016/j.jmsy.2020.06.017

Liu, Xu, Z., Li, R., Zhao, H., Jiang, H., Yao, J., Yuan, D., & Chen, S. (2021). Applying blockchain for primary financial market: A survey. *IET Blockchain*, *1*(2-4), 65–81. doi:10.1049/blc2.12009

Liu, Z., Ebrahimi, A., Zhou, K., Zhou, C., Sapre, A., Pavlock, J. H., Weaver, A., Muralidharan, R., Noble, J., Chung, T., & Kovac, J. (2020). Dynamic laser speckle imaging meets machine learning to enable rapid antibacterial susceptibility testing (DYRAST). *ACS Sensors*, *5*(10), 3140–3149. doi:10.1021/acssensors.0c01238 PMID:32942846

Liu, Z., Song, J., Wu, H., Gu, X., Zhao, Y., Yue, X., & Shi, L. (2021). Impact of Financial Technology on Regional Green Finance. *Computer Systems Science and Engineering*, *39*(3), 391–401. doi:10.32604/csse.2021.014527

Lu, Q., Parlikad, A. K., Woodall, P., Don Ranasinghe, G., Xie, X., Liang, Z., Konstantinou, E., Heaton, J., & Schooling, J. (2020, May). Developing a Digital Twin at Building and City Levels: Case Study of West Cambridge Campus. *Journal of Management Engineering*, *36*(3), 05020004. doi:10.1061/(ASCE)ME.1943-5479.0000763

Macrinici, D., Cartofeanu, C., & Gao, S. (2018). Smart contract within blockchain technology: A systematic mapping study. *Telematics and Informatics*, *35*(8), 2337–2354. doi:10.1016/j.tele.2018.10.004

Madanchian, M. (2022). Impact of Digital Transformation Development on Organizational Change. In *Driving Transformative Change in E-Business through Applied Intelligence and Emerging Technologies* (pp. 1–24). IGI Global. doi:10.4018/978-1-6684-5235-6.ch001

Mahmud, K., Joarder, M. M. A., & Muheymin-Us-Sakib, K. (2022). Adoption factors of FinTech: Evidence from an emerging economy country-wide representative sample. *International Journal of Financial Studies*, *11*(1), 9. doi:10.3390/ijfs11010009

Mahmudnia, D., Arashpour, M., Bai, Y., & Feng, H. (2022). Drones and Blockchain Integration to Manage Forest Fires in Remote Regions. *Drones (Basel)*, *6*(11), 331. doi:10.3390/drones6110331

Makarov, I., & Schoar, A. (2022). Cryptocurrencies and Decentralized Finance (DeFi). *Brookings Papers on Economic Activity, 2022-Sprin*, 141–215. doi:10.1353/eca.2022.0014

Maldonado-Ruiz, D., Torres, J., & Madhoun, N. E. (2022). Fundamentals of Blockchain Technology. In Principles and Practice of Blockchains (pp. 3-25). Cham: Springer.

Malhotra, A., O'Neill, H., & Stowell, P. (2021). Thinking strategically about blockchain adoption risks and risk mitigation. *Business Horizons, 65*(2), 159e171.

Malik, G., Parasrampuria, K., Reddy, S. P., & Shah, S. (2019), Blockchain Based Identity Verification Model,*International Conference on Vision Towards Emerging Trends in Communication and Networking (ViTECoN)*, Vellore, India.

Mandolla, C., Petruzzelli, A. M., Percoco, G., & Urbinati, A. (2019). Building a Digital Twin for Additive Manufacturing through the Exploitation of Blockchain: A case analysis of the aircraft industry. *Computers in Industry*, *109*, 134–152. doi:10.1016/j.compind.2019.04.011

Marchesi, L. (2020), *Design patterns for gas optimization in Ethereum.* In proceedings of the 2020 IEEE International Workshop on Blockchain Oriented Software Engineering (IWBOSE), London. 10.1109/IWBOSE50093.2020.9050163

Maria, M. R., Ballini, R., & Souza, R. F. (2023). Evolution of Green Finance: A Bibliometric Analysis through Complex Networks and Machine Learning. *Sustainability (Basel), 15*(2), 967. doi:10.3390/su15020967

Marke, A. (Ed.). (2018). *Transforming climate finance and green investment with blockchains*. Academic Press.

Marke, A., & Sylvester, B. (2018). Decoding the current global climate finance architecture. In *Transforming climate finance and green investment with blockchains* (pp. 35–59). Academic Press. doi:10.1016/B978-0-12-814447-3.00004-5

Marra, A., Gerbino, S., Greco, A., & Fabbrocino, G. (2021). Combining integrated informative system and historical digital twin for maintenance and preservation of artistic assets. *Sensors (Basel), 21*(17), 5956. doi:10.3390/s21175956 PMID:34502848

Massel, L., Massel, A., Shchukin, N. I., & Tsybikov, A. (2023). Designing a Digital Twin of a Wind Farm. *Engineering Proceedings, 33*(1), 30.

Matharoo, I. (2023). *Economics unchained: Investigating the role of cryptocurrency, blockchain and intricacies of Bitcoin price fluctuations*.

Matytsin, D. (2023). *The Legal Regulation Development of Key Technologies of Industry 4.0: Digital Tokens as Special Investment Instruments*. Legal Concept., doi:10.15688/lc.jvolsu.2023.2.14

Melesse, T. Y., Pasquale, V. D., & Riemma, S. (2020). Digital Twin Models in Industrial Operations: A Systematic Literature Review. *Procedia Manufacturing, 42*, 267–272. doi:10.1016/j.promfg.2020.02.084

Mengelkamp, E., Gärttner, J., Rock, K., Kessler, S., Orsini, L., & Weinhardt, C. (2018). A blockchain-based smart grid: Towards sustainable local energy markets. *Computer Science (Berlin, Germany), 33*(1–2), 207–214. doi:10.1007/s00450-017-0360-9

Meng, X. (2022). Risk assessment and analysis in supply chain finance based on blockchain technology. *Journal of Sensors, 2022*, 1–11. doi:10.1155/2022/1985803

Mettler, M. (2016). Blockchain technology in healthcare: The revolution starts here. In *2016 IEEE 18th International Conference on e-Health Networking, Applications and Services (Healthcom)* (pp. 1-3). IEEE. 10.1109/HealthCom.2016.7749510

Micaroni, M. (2020). *Sustainable Finance: Addressing the SDGs through Fintech and Digital Finance solutions in EU* (Doctoral dissertation, Politecnico di Torino).

Michael, J., & Anjali, G. (2013). Contracts for Employee Work Agreements: Legal Implications. *The Journal of Law and Technology, 12*(4), 213–230.

Migliorelli, M., & Dessertine, P. (2019). The rise of green finance in Europe. *Opportunities and challenges for issuers, investors and marketplaces. Cham. Palgrave Macmillan, 2*, 2019.

Milani, F., García-Bañuelos, L., & Dumas, M. (2016). Blockchain and business process improvement. *BP Trends newsletter* (October 2016).

Miller, A., Kosba, A., Katz, J., & Shi, E. (2015). Nonoutsourceable scratch-off puzzles to discourage bitcoin mining coalitions. *Proceedings of the ACM Conference on Computer and Communications Security*. IEEE. 10.1145/2810103.2813621

Minerva, R., Crespi, N., & Lopes, R. V. (2018). Digital Twin in Industry: State-of-the-Art. *IEEE Transactions on Industrial Informatics*.

Minh, D., Wang, H. X., Li, Y. F., & Nguyen, T. N. (2022). Explainable artificial intelligence: A comprehensive review. *Artificial Intelligence Review*, 1–66.

Mishra, R., & Albalushi, J. (2023). Digital Finance & Green Innovation Review Paper with special reference to Oman and Bibliometric Analysis for the Duration of 2017-2023. *International Journal of Financial Management and Research*. doi:10.36948/ijfmr.2023.v05i06.8271

Misra, N., Gupta, S., Sidhu, K. S., Kumar, A., Anandaram, H., Rao, T. J., Singh, R., Gehlot, A., Akram, S., & Joshi, K. (2023). *Role of Blockchain Technology Integration for Green Bonds Issuance with Sustainability Aspect. International Journal of Recent Technology and Engineering*. IJRTE. doi:10.17762/ijritcc.v11i6.7300

Mohammed, A. H., Abdulateef, A. A., & Abdulateef, I. A. (2021, June). Hyperledger, Ethereum and blockchain technology: a short overview. In *2021 3rd International Congress on Human-Computer Interaction, Optimization and Robotic Applications (HORA)* (pp. 1-6). IEEE.

Monetary Authority of Singapore. (n.d.). Securities and Futures Act (Cap. 289) *Notice on Risk Based Capital Adequacy Requirements for Holders of Capital Markets Services Licenses*. MAS. https://www.mas.gov.sg/-

Monrat, A., Schelén, O. & Andersson, K. (2019). Survey of Blockchain from the Perspectives of Applications, Challenges and Opportunities. *IEEE Access*. IEEE. . doi:10.1109/ACCESS.2019.2936094

Morabito, V. (2017). Business Innovation Through Blockchain. In Business Innovation Through Blockchain. doi:10.1007/978-3-319-48478-5

Morkunas, V. J., Paschen, J., & Boon, E. (2019). How blockchain technologies impact your business model. *Business Horizons*, *62*(3), 295–306. doi:10.1016/j.bushor.2019.01.009

Moro-Visconti, R., Cruz Rambaud, S., & López Pascual, J. (2020). Sustainability in FinTechs: An explanation through business model scalability and market valuation. *Sustainability (Basel)*, *12*(24), 10316. doi:10.3390/su122410316

Möslein, F., & Marburg, P. (2020). S. Legal Boundaries of Blockchain Technologies: Smart Contracts as Self-Help? (Möslein). *Digital Revolution - New Challenges for Law, February 2000*, 313–326. Springer. doi:10.17104/9783406759048-313

Mougayar, W. (2016). *The Business Blockchain: Promise, Practice, and Application of the Next Internet Technology*. John Wiley & Sons.

Moztarzadeh, O., Jamshidi, M., Sargolzaei, S., Jamshidi, A., Baghalipour, N., Malekzadeh Moghani, M., & Hauer, L. (2023). Metaverse and Healthcare: Machine Learning-Enabled Digital Twins of Cancer. *Bioengineering (Basel, Switzerland)*, *10*(4), 455. doi:10.3390/bioengineering10040455 PMID:37106642

Mozumder, M. A. I., A, T. P. T., Sumon, R. I., Uddin, S. M. I., Athar, A., & Kim, H.-C. (2023). The Metaverse for Intelligent Healthcare using XAI, Blockchain, and Immersive Technology. *2023 IEEE International Conference on Metaverse Computing (MetaCom)*. IEEE. 10.1109/MetaCom57706.2023.00107

Mukherjee, P., Barik, R. K., & Pradhan, C. (2021). *A Comprehensive Proposal for Blockchain-Oriented Smart City. Security and Privacy Applications for Smart City Development.308*. Springer. doi:10.1007/978-3-030-53149-2_4

Musleh Al-Sartawi, A. M., Hussainey, K., & Razzaque, A. (2022). The role of artificial intelligence in sustainable finance. *Journal of Sustainable Finance & Investment*, 1–6. doi:10.1080/20430795.2022.2057405

Mustapha, Z., Kunhibava, S. B., & Muneeza, A. (2020). Legal and Sharīʿah non-compliance risks in Nigerian Islamic finance industry: A review of the literature. *International Journal of Law and Management*, *63*(02), 275–299. doi:10.1108/IJLMA-03-2020-0075

Mylrea, M., Zhang, C. Y., Tyler Cohen Wood, C. I. S. S. P., & Thornley, B. (2023). Impact of Blockchain-Digital Twin Technology on Precision Health, Pharmaceutical Industry, and Life Sciences Conv2X 2023 Report. *Blockchain in Healthcare Today*, *6*(2).

Naderi, N. (2021). Utilizing Blockchain Technology in International Remittances for Poverty Reduction and Inclusive Growth. In Poverty Reduction for Inclusive Sustainable Growth in Developing Asia (pp. 149–163). doi:10.1007/978-981-16-1107-0_7

Naderi, N., & Tian, Y. (2022). Leveraging Blockchain Technology and Tokenizing Green Assets to Fill the Green Finance Gap. *Energy Research Letters*, *3*(3).

Naher, K., & Uddin, M. S. (2023). *Exploring the influence of Blockchain in the financial services: Quick assessment of its applications across various financial domains*. Financial Services Journal. doi:10.24294/fsj.v6i1.2228

Nakamoto, S. (2008). *Bitcoin: a Peer-to-Peer Electronic Cash System*. Bitcoin. https://bitcoin.org/bitcoin.pdf

Nakamoto, S. (2008). *Bitcoin: A Peer-to-Peer Electronic Cash System*. Bitcoin. https://bitcoin.org/bitcoin.pdf

Nakamoto, S. (2019). *Bitcoin: A peer-to-peer electronic cash system*. Manubot.

Nakamoto, S. (2008). *Bitcoin: A Peer-to-Peer Electronic Cash System*. Decentralized Business Review.

Namasudra, S., Deka, G. C., Johri, P., Hosseinpour, M., & Gandomi, A. H. (2021). The revolution of blockchain: State-of-the-art and research Challenges. *Archives of Computational Methods in Engineering, 28*(3), 1497–1515. doi:10.1007/s11831-020-09426-0

Narayanan, A., Bonneau, J., Felten, E., Miller, A., & Goldfeder, S. (2016). *Bitcoin and Cryptocurrency Technologies: A Comprehensive Introduction*. Princeton University Press.

Nassiry, D. (2018). *The role of fintech in unlocking green finance: Policy insights for developing countries* (No. 883). ADBI working paper.

Natanelov, V., Cao, S., Foth, M., & Dulleck, U. (2022). Blockchain smart contracts for supply chain finance: Mapping the innovation potential in Australia-China beef supply chains. *Journal of Industrial Information Integration, 30*, 100389. doi:10.1016/j.jii.2022.100389

Nawari, N. O., & Ravindran, S. (2019). Blockchain and the built environment: Potentials and limitations. *Journal of Building Engineering, 25*(October 2018). doi:10.1016/j.jobe.2019.100832

Negri, E., Fumagalli, L., & Macchi, M. (2017). A review of the roles of digital twin in CPS-based production systems. *Procedia Manufacturing, 11*, 939–948. doi:10.1016/j.promfg.2017.07.198

Nenavath, S., & Mishra, S. (2023). Impact of green finance and fintech on sustainable economic growth: Empirical evidence from India. *Heliyon, 9*(5), e16301. doi:10.1016/j.heliyon.2023.e16301 PMID:37234625

Neshenko, N., Bou-Harb, E., Crichigno, J., Kaddoum, G., & Ghani, N. (2019). Demystifying IoT Security: An Exhaustive Survey on IoT Vulnerabilities and a First Empirical Look on Internet-Scale IoT Exploitations. *IEEE Communications Surveys and Tutorials, 21*(3), 2702–2733. doi:10.1109/COMST.2019.2910750

Ng, A. K., & Mahkeswaran, R. (2021, August). Emerging and disruptive technologies for urban farming: A review and assessment. [). IOP Publishing.]. *Journal of Physics: Conference Series, 2003*(1), 012008. doi:10.1088/1742-6596/2003/1/012008

Ng, T.-H., Lye, C.-T., Chan, K.-H., Lim, Y.-Z., & Lim, Y.-S. (2020). Sustainability in Asia: The Roles of Financial Development in Environmental, Social, and Governance (ESG) Performance. *Social Indicators Research, 150*(1), 17–44. doi:10.1007/s11205-020-02288-w

Nguyen, M., Wesley Long, S., McDermott, P. F., Olsen, R. J., Olson, R., Stevens, R. L., Tyson, G. H., Zhao, S., & Davisa, J. J. (2019). Using machine learning to predict antimicrobial MICs and associated genomic features for nontyphoidal Salmonella. *Journal of Clinical Microbiology, 57*(2), e01260-18. doi:10.1128/JCM.01260-18 PMID:30333126

Ng, W. Y., Tan, T. E., Movva, P. V., Fang, A. H., Yeo, K. K., Ho, D., & Ting, D. S. (2021). Blockchain applications in health care for COVID-19 and beyond: A systematic review. *The Lancet. Digital Health, 3*(12), e819–e829. doi:10.1016/S2589-7500(21)00210-7 PMID:34654686

Niavis, H., Laskari, M., & Fergadiotou, I. (2022). *Trusted DBL: A Blockchain-based Digital Twin for Sustainable and Interoperable Building Performance Evaluation*. 7th International Conference on Smart and Sustainable Technologies (SpliTech), Croatia. 10.23919/SpliTech55088.2022.9854287

Nikolaev, S., Gusev, M., Padalitsa, D., Mozhenkov, E., Mishin, S., & Uzhinsky, I. (2018). Implementation of "digital twin" concept for modern project-based engineering education. In Product Lifecycle Management to Support Industry 4.0: 15th IFIP WG 5. Springer.

Nishant, R., Kennedy, M., & Corbett, J. (2020). Artificial intelligence for sustainability: Challenges, opportunities, and a research agenda. *International Journal of Information Mang.*

Nocera, G. (2022). *Fintech revolution and traditional banks-what factors influence members of generation Z to place their trust in Fintech companies, specifically neobanks, over traditional banks as banking and financial service providers?: a case study on the banking application of the Swiss neobank Yuh*. Academic Press.

Nofer, M., Gomber, P., Hinz, O., & Schiereck, D. (2017). Blockchain. *Business & Information Systems Engineering*, *59*(3), 183–187. doi:10.1007/s12599-017-0467-3

Nugent, T. (2020). Improving data transparency in clinical trials using blockchain smart contracts. *F1000Research 016, 5,* (25-41).

Ny, B. (2022). Blockchain in Impact Investing: The Potential of Impact Tokens on SDGs. *Medium*. https://medium.com/@Godswisdomtoday/blockchain-in-impact-investing-the-potential-of-impact-tokens-on-sdgs-767ad67b4f3

O'Dwyer, K. J., & Malone, D. (2014). Bitcoin mining and its energy footprint. *IET Conference Publications, 2014*(CP655). IEEE.

O'Rourke, A. (2003). A new politics of engagement: Shareholder activism for corporate social responsibility. *Business Strategy and the Environment*, *12*(4), 227–239. doi:10.1002/bse.364

Onwubiko, A., Singh, R., Awan, S., Pervez, Z., & Ramzan, N. (2023). Enabling Trust and Security in Digital Twin Management: A Blockchain-Based Approach with Ethereum and IPFS. *Sensors (Basel)*, *23*(14), 6641. doi:10.3390/s23146641 PMID:37514938

Oyewobi, L., Okanlawon, T. T., Ibrahim, K., & Jimoh, R. A. (2023). Influence of blockchain adoption barriers and drivers on potential application areas in the construction lifecycle: Partial least squares structural equation modelling (PLS-SEM) approach. *Engineering, Construction, and Architectural Management*. doi:10.1108/ECAM-07-2023-0746

OziliP. K. (2020). Blockchain finance: Questions regulators ask. *Available at* SSRN 3542307.

Ozili, P. K. (2023). Assessing global interest in decentralized finance, embedded finance, open finance, ocean finance and sustainable finance. *Asian Journal of Economics and Banking*, *7*(2), 197–216. doi:10.1108/AJEB-03-2022-0029

Ozturan. (2019). Assessment of Blockchain Technology Readiness Level of Banking Industry. *International Journal of Business Marketing and Management(IJBMM),4*(12),01-13, http://www.ijbmm.com/paper/Dec2019/2115167856.pdf

PadmavathiV.KanimozhiR. (2023). Pandemic Alert with Smart Covid-19 Using Blockchain-Powered Digital Twins' Collaboration. Research Square, [https://doi.org/10.21203/rs.3.rs-3028917/v1].

Paliwal, V., Chandra, S., & Sharma, S. (2020). Blockchain technology for sustainable supply chain management: A systematic literature review and a classification framework. *Sustainability (Basel), 12*(18), 1–39. doi:10.3390/su12187638

Panagopoulos, A., & Tzionas, I. (2023). The Use of Sustainable Financial Instruments In Relation To The Social Impact Investment. ESG Policies, Capital Markets' Approach and Investors' Protection. An Innovative Perspective. SSRN *Electronic Journal*. doi:10.2139/ssrn.4131735

Panda, R. (2003). Trends in Prices and Production of Agricultural Commodities in Orissa in the Post-Liberalisation Period-Some Thoughts for Policy. *Indian Journal of Agricultural Economics, 58*(3), 404.

Pan, J., Wang, J., Hester, A., Alqerm, I., Liu, Y., & Zhao, Y. (2019). Edge Chain: An edge-IoT framework and prototype based on blockchain and smart contracts. *IEEE Internet of Things Journal, 6*(3), 4719–4732. doi:10.1109/JIOT.2018.2878154

Peng, G., Han, M., & Yuan, H. (2023). Artificial Intelligence Drives the Coordinated Development of Green Finance and the Real Economy: Empirical Evidence from Chinese Provincial Level. *Journal of the Knowledge Economy*, 1–39. doi:10.1007/s13132-023-01506-3

Perera, S., Nanayakkara, S., Rodrigo, M. N. N., Senaratne, S., & Weinand, R. (2020). Blockchain technology: Is it hype or real in the construction Industry? *Journal of Industrial Information Integration, 17*, 100–125. doi:10.1016/j.jii.2020.100125

Perera, S., Nanayakkara, S., Rodrigo, M., Senaratne, S., & Weinand, R. (2018). Blockchain technology: Is it hype or real in the construction industry? *Journal of Industrial Information Integration, 13*, 15–24.

Phillip, A., Chan, J., & Peiris, S. (2018). Predictive models for decision support in the blockchain era. *Journal of Risk and Financial Management, 11*(4), 79.

Picone, M., Mariani, S., Virdis, A., & Castagnetti, P. (2023). Digital Twin & Blockchain: Technology Enablers for Metaverse Computing. *IEEE International Conference on Metaverse Computing, Networking and Applications (MetaCom)*, (pp. 1-8). IEEE. 10.1109/MetaCom57706.2023.00017

Pilkington, M. (2016). Blockchain technology: principles and applications. In *Research handbook on digital transformations*. Edward Elgar Publishing. doi:10.4337/9781784717766.00019

Piroumian, V. (2021). Digital Twins: Universal Interoperability for the Digital Age. *Computer, 54*(1), 61–69. doi:10.1109/MC.2020.3032148

Politou, E., Casino, F., Alepis, E., & Patsakis, C. (2019). Blockchain ability: Challenges and proposed solutions. *IEEE Transactions on Emerging Topics in Computing*, *9*(4), 1972–1986. doi:10.1109/TETC.2019.2949510

Proof of Elapsed Time (PoET). 2022). Investopedia. Available from: https://www.investopedia.com/terms/p/proof-elapsed-time-cryp tocurrency.asp#citation-1

Puaschunder, J. M. (2023). The Future of Resilient Green Finance. In *The Future of Resilient Finance: Finance Politics in the Age of Sustainable Development* (pp. 185–210). Springer International Publishing. doi:10.1007/978-3-031-30138-4_6

PwC. (2018). *Building block(chain)s for a better planet*. PxC. https://www.pwc.com/gx/en/sustainability/assets/blockchain-f or-a-betterplanet.pdf

Qaiser, M. T., Ejaz, J., Osen, O. L., & Hasan, A. (2023). Digital twin-driven energy modeling of Hywind Tampen floating wind farm. *Energy Reports*, *9*, S9–S18. doi:10.1016/j.egyr.2023.09.023

Qin, K., & Gervais, A. (2018). An overview of blockchain scalability, interoperability and sustainability. *Hochschule Luzern Blockchain Lab*, *15*. https://www.eublockchainforum.eu/sites/default/files/researc h-paper/an_overview_of_blockchain_scalability_interoperabili ty_and_sustainability.pdf

Qin, Y., Lu, R., Shi, Y., & Leng, J. (2016). Digital Twin: The Simulation Aspect. *IEEE Access : Practical Innovations, Open Solutions*, *4*, 2876–2885.

Qi, Q., Tao, F., Hu, T., Anwer, N., Liu, A., Wei, Y., Wang, L., & Nee, A. (2021, January). Enabling technologies and tools for digital twin. *Journal of Manufacturing Systems*, *58*, 3–21. doi:10.1016/j.jmsy.2019.10.001

Quattrociocchi, A., Subroto, R. K., & Oppedijk, W., & Dragi\u010devi\u0107, T. (2023). Energy Efficiency Optimization of a Wastewater Pumping Station Through IoT and AI: A Real-World Application of Digital Twins. *IEEE International Conference on Industrial Electronics for Sustainable Energy Systems (IECON)*. IEEE. 10.1109/IECON51785.2023.10312592

Raj, A. T., Shobana, J., Nassa, V. K., Painuly, S., Savaram, M., & Sridevi, M. (2023). Enhancing Security for Online Transactions through Supervised Machine Learning and Block Chain Technology in Credit Card Fraud Detection. *2023 International Conference on Intelligent Sustainable Systems (I-SMAC)*. IEEE. 10.1109/I-SMAC58438.2023.10290462

Raj, P., & Surianarayanan, C. (2020). Digital twin: The industry use cases. [). Elsevier.]. *Advances in Computers*, *117*(1), 285–320. doi:10.1016/bs.adcom.2019.09.006

Ramachandran, R., Babu, V., & Murugesan, V. P. (2023). The role of blockchain technology in the process of decision-making in human resource management: A review and future research agenda. *Business Process Management Journal*, *29*(1), 116–139. doi:10.1108/BPMJ-07-2022-0351

Rashid, A., Masood, A., Abbas, H., & Zhang, Y. (2021). Blockchain-Based Public Key Infrastructure: A Transparent Digital Certification Mechanism for Secure Communication. *IEEE Network, 35*(5), 220–225. doi:10.1109/MNET.101.2000532

Rats, O., & Alfimova, A. (2023). *Green bonds as a perspective financial instrument for bank investment in Ukraine*. Development Management. doi:10.57111/devt/1.2023.08

Ravikiran, A. S. (2023). *Merkle Tree in Blockchain*. Simplilearn. https://www.simplilearn.com/tutorials/blockchain-tutorial/me
rkle-tree-in-blockchain

Regner, F., Schweizer, A., & Urbach, N. (2019). NFTs in Practice — Non-Fungible Tokens as Core Components of a Blockchain-based Event Ticketing Application. In *Fortieth International Conference on Information Systems*.

Riegelman, A., Harari, M. B., Parola, H. R., & Hartwell, C. J. (2023). *Literature searches in systematic reviews and meta-analyses: A review, evaluation, and recommendations*.

Rijal, S., & Saranani, F. (2023). The Role of Blockchain Technology in Increasing Economic Transparency and Public Trust. [TACIT]. *Technology and Society Perspectives, 1*(2), 56–67. doi:10.61100/tacit.v1i2.51

Rizzello, A., & Kabli, A. (2020). Social finance and sustainable development goals: A literature synthesis, current approaches and research agenda. *ACRN Journal of Finance and Risk Perspectives, 9*.

Rosen, R., von Wichert, G., Lo, G., & Bettenhausen, K. D. (2015). Importance of digital twin for simulation-based optimization in production engineering. *Procedia CIRP, 37*, 141–146.

Rouhani, S. (2019). Performance, and applications of smart contracts: A systematic survey. *IEEE Access, 7*, 50759–50779.

Rozas, D., Tenorio-Fornés, A., Díaz-Molina, S., & Hassan, S. (2021). When Ostrom meets Blockchain: Exploring the potentials of blockchain for commons governance. *Sage publications. SAGE Open, 11*(1), 1–14. doi:10.1177/21582440211002526

Ryu, H. S. (2018). *Understanding benefit and risk framework of fintech adoption: Comparison of early adopters and late adopters*.

Saari, A., Junnila, S., & Vimpari, J. (2022). Blockchain's Grand Promise for the Real Estate Sector: A Systematic Review. *Applied Sciences (Basel, Switzerland), 12*(23), 11940. doi:10.3390/app122311940

Sachs, J. D., Woo, W. T., Yoshino, N., & Taghizadeh-Hesary, F. (2019). Importance of green finance for achieving sustainable development goals and energy security. Handbook of green finance: Energy security and sustainable development, 10, 1-10.

Sadri, H., Yitmen, I., Tagliabue, L., Westphal, F., Tezel, A., Taheri, A., & Sibenik, G. (2023). Integration of Blockchain and Digital Twins in the Smart Built Environment Adopting Disruptive Technologies—A Systematic Review. *Sustainability (Basel)*, *15*(4), 3713. doi:10.3390/su15043713

Salah, K., Rehman, M., Nizamuddin, N., & Al-Fuqaha, A. (2019). Blockchain for AI: review and open research challenges. *IEEE Access, 7.*

Salampasis, D., & Mention, A. L. (2018). FinTech: Harnessing innovation for financial inclusion. In Handbook of Blockchain, Digital Finance, and Inclusion, Volume 2 (pp. 451-461). Academic Press.

Sangsuwun, S., Phakdeekul, W., & Kedthongma, W. (2023). In-Patient Costs Of Coronavirus Disease 2019 With Financial Regulations And Heath Economy. *Russian Law Journal*. doi:10.52783/rlj.v11i6s.920

Sankar, J., Ilangovan, K., Arokiaraj, D., & Ganeshkumar, C. (2022). Adoption Of Blockchain Technology In HRM. *Korean Review Of International Studies*, *15*(40), 5–7.

Sasikumar, A., Vairavasundaram, S., Kotecha, K., Indragandhi, V., Ravi, L., Selvachandran, G., & Abraham, A. (2023). Blockchain-based trust mechanism for digital twin empowered Industrial Internet of Things. *Future Generation Computer Systems*, *141*, 16–27. doi:10.1016/j.future.2022.11.002

Sawada. (2016). Digital Assets Policy and Regulatory Challenges In Asia. *Asian Development Bank, 43.* file:///C:/Users/rnabh/OneDrive/Desktop/working%20papers/web%203/distributed-ledger-technology-digital-assets-asia.pdf

Saxena, A., Singh, R., Gehlot, A., Akram, S. V., Twala, B., Singh, A., Montero, E. C., & Priyadarshi, N. (2023). Technologies Empowered Environmental, Social, and Governance (ESG): An Industry 4.0 Landscape. *Sustainability (Basel)*, *15*(1), 309. doi:10.3390/su15010309

Schleich, B., Anwer, N., Mathieu, L., & Wartzack, S. (2017). Shaping the digital twin for design and production engineering. *CIRP Annals*, *66*(1), 141–144. doi:10.1016/j.cirp.2017.04.040

Schloesser, T., & Schulz, K. (2022). Distributed ledger technology and climate finance. In *Green Digital Finance and Sustainable Development Goals* (pp. 265–286). Springer Nature Singapore. doi:10.1007/978-981-19-2662-4_13

Schneider, J., Klüner, A., & Zielinski, O. (2023). Towards Digital Twins of the Oceans: The Potential of Machine Learning for Monitoring the Impacts of Offshore Wind Farms on Marine Environments. *Sensors (Basel)*, *23*(10), 4581. doi:10.3390/s23104581 PMID:37430495

Schoenmaker, D., & Volz, U. (2022). *Scaling up sustainable finance and investment in the Global South.* CEPR Press.

Schueffel, P. (2017). The convergence of blockchain, digital twins, and big data analytics in green finance. *Journal of Financial Transformation*, *45*, 38–45. doi:10.1007/s11356-023-30371-5

Schulz, K. A., Gstrein, O. J., & Zwitter, A. J. (2020). Exploring the governance and implementation of sustainable development initiatives through blockchain technology. *Futures*, *122*, 102611. doi:10.1016/j.futures.2020.102611

Schulz, K., & Feist, M. (2021). Leveraging blockchain technology for innovative climate finance under the Green Climate Fund. *Earth System Governance*, *7*, 100084. doi:10.1016/j.esg.2020.100084

Semeraro, C., Lezoche, M., Panetto, H., & Dassisti, M. (2021, September). Digital twin paradigm: A systematic literature review. *Computers in Industry*, *130*, 103469. doi:10.1016/j.compind.2021.103469

Sepasgozar, S. M. (2020). Digital twin and web-based virtual gaming technologies for online education: A case of construction management and engineering. *Applied Sciences (Basel, Switzerland)*, *10*(13), 4678. doi:10.3390/app10134678

Shahriar, F., Katibur, R. S. M., & Sharfuddin, M. (2023). Blockchain: A Comparative Study of Consensus Algorithms PoW, PoS, PoA, PoV. [IJMSC]. *International Journal of Mathematical Sciences and Computing*, *9*(3), 46–57. doi:10.5815/ijmsc.2023.03.04

Shajar, S. N. (2017). Relationship between working capital management and profitability of automobile companies in India: A paradigm shift towards economic strengthening. *International Journal of Trade. Economics and Finance*, *8*(4), 210–216.

Shajar, S. N., & Farooqi, S. A. (2016). Impact of working capital management on the profitability of automobile industry in India-an empirical study of selected automobile companies. *Pac. Bus. Rev. Int*, *8*, 197–203.

Shariawi, S., Panjaitan, M. Y. T. B., & Nathanael, A. (2023). Meminimalisir Resiko Perubahan Valuta Asing Melalui Lindung Nilai (Hedging) Terhadap PT. Petrosea Tbk. *Journal of Accounting. Business Economics (Cleveland, Ohio)*, *2*(2), 30–36. doi:10.30630/jabei.v2i2.187

Sharma, A., Kosasih, E., Zhang, J., Brintrup, A., & Calinescu, A. (2022). Digital Twins: State of the art theory and practice, challenges, and open, research questions. *Journal of Industrial Information Integration*, *30*, 100383. doi:10.1016/j.jii.2022.100383

Sharma, A., & Singh, B. (2022). Measuring Impact of E-commerce on Small Scale Business: A Systematic Review. *Journal of Corporate Governance and International Business Law*, *5*(1).

Sharma, G. D., Jain, M., Mahendru, M., Bansal, S., & Kumar, G. (2019). Emergence of Bitcoin as an Investment Alternative: A Systematic Review and Research Agenda. *International Journal of Business and Information*, *14*(1), 47–84. doi:10.6702/ijbi.201903

Sharma, P. (2010). Blockchain-based decentralized architecture for cloud storage system. *J. Inf. Secur. Appl.*, *62*, 102–970.

Shavshukov, V., & Zhuravleva, N. (2023). National and International Financial Market Regulation and Supervision Systems: Challenges and Solutions. *Journal of Risk and Financial Management*, *16*(6), 289. doi:10.3390/jrfm16060289

Shelhamer, E., Long, J., & Darrell, T. (2017). Fully Convolutional Networks for Semantic Segmentation. *IEEE Transactions on Pattern Analysis and Machine Intelligence*, *39*(4), 640–651. doi:10.1109/TPAMI.2016.2572683 PMID:27244717

Shen, J., Ridwan, L. I., Raimi, L., & Al-Faryan, M. A. S. (2023). Recent developments in green hydrogen–environmental sustainability nexus amidst energy efficiency, green finance, eco-innovation, and digitalization in top hydrogen-consuming economies. *Environment and Planning C: Politics and Space*. doi:10.1177/0958305X231153936

Sheth, H., & Dattani, J. (2019, April 16). OVERVIEW OF BLOCKCHAIN TECHNOLOGY. *ASIAN JOURNAL OF CONVERGENCE IN TECHNOLOGY*, *05*(01), 1–4. doi:10.33130/AJCT.2019v05i01.013

Shih, C., Gwizdalski, A., & Deng, X. (2023). *Building a Sustainable Future: Exploring Green Finance*. Regenerative Finance, and Green Financial Technology.

Shrivas, M. K., & Yeboah, T. (2019). The Disruptive Blockchain: Types, Platforms and Applications. Texila International Journal of Academic Research (TIJAR) Special Edition, 17–39. doi:10.21522/TIJAR.2014.SE.19.02.Art003

Shrivastava, G. (2020). Cryptocurrencies and Blockchain Technology Applications. *Wiley eBooks*. doi:10.1002/9781119621201

Shuai, Z. (2022). *Financial Instruments for Attracting Investments in the Real Estate Market*. International Business and Economics Studies., doi:10.22158/ibes.v4n4p18

Sidhardhan, A. S. K., & Kannimoola, J. M. (2023). Weaponizing Real-world Applications as C2 (Command and Control). *2023 IEEE International Conference on Innovations in Data Science and Communication (ICIDCA)*. IEEE. 10.1109/ICIDCA56705.2023.10100279

Singh, B. (2023). Blockchain Technology in Renovating Healthcare: Legal and Future Perspectives. In Revolutionizing Healthcare Through Artificial Intelligence and Internet of Things Applications (pp. 177-186). IGI Global.

Singh, B. (2019). Profiling Public Healthcare: A Comparative Analysis Based on the Multidimensional Healthcare Management and Legal Approach. *Indian Journal of Health and Medical Law*, *2*(2), 1–5.

Singh, B. (2020). GLOBAL SCIENCE AND JURISPRUDENTIAL APPROACH CONCERNING HEALTHCARE AND ILLNESS. *Indian Journal of Health and Medical Law*, *3*(1), 7–13.

Singh, B. (2022). COVID-19 Pandemic and Public Healthcare: Endless Downward Spiral or Solution via Rapid Legal and Health Services Implementation with Patient Monitoring Program. *Justice and Law Bulletin*, *1*(1), 1–7.

Singh, B. (2022). Relevance of Agriculture-Nutrition Linkage for Human Healthcare: A Conceptual Legal Framework of Implication and Pathways. *Justice and Law Bulletin*, *1*(1), 44–49.

Singh, B. (2022). Understanding Legal Frameworks Concerning Transgender Healthcare in the Age of Dynamism. *ELECTRONIC JOURNAL OF SOCIAL AND STRATEGIC STUDIES*, *3*(1), 56–65. doi:10.47362/EJSSS.2022.3104

Singh, B. (2023). Federated Learning for Envision Future Trajectory Smart Transport System for Climate Preservation and Smart Green Planet: Insights into Global Governance and SDG-9 (Industry, Innovation and Infrastructure). *National Journal of Environmental Law*, *6*(2), 6–17.

Singh, B. (2024). Legal Dynamics Lensing Metaverse Crafted for Videogame Industry and E-Sports: Phenomenological Exploration Catalyst Complexity and Future. *Journal of Intellectual Property Rights Law*, *7*(1), 8–14.

Singh, V. K. (2022). Regulatory and Legal Framework for Promoting Green Digital Finance. In *Green Digital Finance and Sustainable Development Goals* (pp. 3–27). Springer Nature Singapore. doi:10.1007/978-981-19-2662-4_1

Sirenko, N. N., Atamanyuk, I., Volosyuk, Y., Poltorak, A., Melnyk, O., & Fenenko, P. (2020). Paradigm Changes that Strengthen the Financial Security of the State through FINTECH Development. *2020 IEEE 11th International Conference on Dependable Systems, Services and Technologies (DESSERT)*. IEEE. 10.1109/DESSERT50317.2020.9125026

Sklaroff, J. M. (2018). Smart contracts and the cost of inflexibility. *University of Pennsylvania Law Review*, 166–263.

Smith, A. (2008). Regulatory Issues in Blockchain Technology Purpose-Blockchains. *Journal of Financial Regulation and Compliance*, *16*(2), 13. doi:10.1108/JFRC-08-2016-0068

Sobik, B. (2023). Green bonds—Financial innovation for sustainability financing: The case of the Polish green bonds market and their development barriers. *Central European Economic Journal*, *10*(57), 287–303. https://doi.org/doi:10.2478/ceej-2023-0017

Soriano, M. A. (2017). *Factors driving financial inclusion and financial performance in Fintech new ventures: An empirical study.*

Spratt and Griffith-Jones. (2013). *Mobilising Investment for Inclusive Green Growth in Low-Income Countries.* Federal Ministry for Economic Cooperation and Development, GIZ. https://stephanygj.net/papers/MobilisingInvestmentforInclusiveGreenGrowth2013.pdf

Stadtmann, F., Rasheed, A., & Rasmussen, T. (2023). Standalone, Descriptive, and Predictive Digital Twin of an Onshore Wind Farm in Complex Terrain. *Journal of Physics: Conference Series*, *2626*(1), 012030. doi:10.1088/1742-6596/2626/1/012030

Suhail, S., Hussain, R., Jurdak, R., Oracevic, A., Salah, K., Hong, C., & Matulevičius, R. (2022). Blockchain-Based Digital Twins: Research Trends, Issues, and Future Challenges. *ACM Computing Surveys*, *54*(11s), 1–34. Advance online publication. doi:10.1145/3517189

Sulkowski, A. J. (2018). Blockchain, business supply chains, sustainability, and law: The future of governance, legal frameworks, and lawyers? [DJCL]. *SSRN*, *43*, 303. doi:10.2139/ssrn.3262291

Sustainable Investments in Green Finance. (2023, November 14). *Advances in Finance, Accounting, and Economics Book Series*. IGI Global. doi:10.4018/979-8-3693-1388-6

Swan, M. (2015). *Blockchain: Blueprint for a New Economy*. O'Reilly Media.

Swan, M. (2017). Anticipating the Economic Benefits of Blockchain. *Technology Innovation Management Review*, *7*(10), 6–13. https://timreview.ca/article/837. doi:10.22215/timreview/1109

Szabo, N. (1996). Smart contracts: building blocks for digital markets. *EXTROPY: The Journal of Transhumanist Thought, 18*(2), 28.

Szabo, N. (1997). Formalizing and securing relationships on public networks. *First Monday*, *2*(9). https://firstmonday.org/ojs/index.php/fm/article/view/548/469. doi:10.5210/fm.v2i9.548

Szabo, N. (1997). The idea of smart contracts. *Nick Szabo's Pap. Concise Tutor.*, *6*, 199.

Szewczyk, P. (2020). Mangement of blockchain based digital assets in industry and services. *Zeszyty Naukowe. Organizacja i Zarządzanie/Politechnika Śląska*, (150), 267-277.

Taherdoost, H. (2023). An Overview of Trends in Information Systems: Emerging Technologies that Transform the Information Technology industry. *Cloud Comput. Data Sci.*, *4*, 1–16. doi:10.37256/ccds.5120233284

Tahi, S., & Farissi, I. E. (2023). Credit Derivatives: Main Concepts and Pricing. *Journal of Economics, Finance and Management Studies*. doi:10.47191/jefms/v6-i11-03

Talan, G., & Sharma, G. D. (2019). Doing well by doing good: A systematic review and research agenda for sustainable investment. *Sustainability (Basel)*, *11*(2), 353. doi:10.3390/su11020353

Tao, F., Cheng, J., Qi, Q., Zhang, M., Zhang, H., & Sui, F. (2018). Digital twin-driven product design, manufacturing, and service with big data. *International Journal of Advanced Manufacturing Technology*, *94*(9-12), 3563–3576. doi:10.1007/s00170-017-0233-1

Tao, F., Zhang, H., Liu, A., & Nee, A. Y. (2018). Digital twins and cyber–physical systems toward smart manufacturing and Industry 4.0: Correlation and comparison. *Engineering (Beijing)*, *5*(4), 653–661. doi:10.1016/j.eng.2019.01.014

Tao, F., & Zhang, M. (2017). Digital twin and big data towards smart manufacturing and industry 4.0: 360 degree comparison. *IEEE Access : Practical Innovations, Open Solutions*, *5*, 3585–3593.

Tao, F., Zhang, M., Liu, A., & Nee, A. Y. (2019). Digital twin-driven product design framework. *International Journal of Advanced Manufacturing Technology*, *94*(9–12), 3563–3576.

Tapscott, A., & Tapscott, A. D. (2017, March 1). Blockchain solutions for cybersecurity. *Harvard Business Review*, *21*, 9–11.

Tapscott, D., & Tapscott, A. (2016). *Blockchain revolution: how the technology behind bitcoin is changing money, business, and the world*. Penguin.

Tapscott, D., & Tapscott, A. (2016). *Blockchain revolution: How the technology behind bitcoin is changing money, business, and the world.* Penguin.

Team, G. C. (2021, December 14). *HPE Helps EPFL Blue Brain Project Unlock the Secrets of the Brain.* HPE. https://www.hpe.com/us/en/newsroom/press-release/2018/07/hpe-helps-epfl-blue-brain-project-unlock-the-secrets-of-the-brain.html

Teo, T., Lee, C. B., & Chai, C. S. (2008). Understanding pre-service teachers' computer attitudes: Applying and extending the technology acceptance model. *Journal of Computer Assisted Learning*, *24*(2), 128–143. doi:10.1111/j.1365-2729.2007.00247.x

Thomason, J., Ahmad, M., Bronder, P., Hoyt, E., Pocock, S., Bouteloupe, J., & Shrier, D. (2018). Blockchain—powering and empowering the poor in developing countries. In *Transforming climate finance and green investment with blockchains* (pp. 137–152). Academic Press. doi:10.1016/B978-0-12-814447-3.00010-0

Thompson, S. (2021). *Green and sustainable finance: Principles and practice* (Vol. 6). Kogan Page Publishers.

Tian, Y., Minchin, R. E., Chung, K., Woo, J., & Adriaens, P. (2021). Towards Inclusive and Sustainable Infrastructure Development through Blockchain-enabled Asset Tokenization: An Exploratory Case Study. *IOP Conference Series: Materials Science and Engineering,* Volume 1218.

Tozanlı, Ö., Kongar, E., & Gupta, S. (2020). Evaluation of Waste Electronic Product Trade-in Strategies in Predictive Twin Disassembly Systems in the Era of Blockchain. *Sustainability (Basel)*, *12*(13), 5416. doi:10.3390/su12135416

Treleaven. (2022). Web 3.0 Tokenization and Decentralized Finance (DeFi), SSRN,19. http://dx.doi.org/ doi:10.2139/ssrn.4037471

Trivedi, S., Mehta, K., & Sharma, R. (2021). Systematic Literature Review on Application of Blockchain Technology in E-Finance and Financial Services. *Journal of Technology Management & Innovation*, *16*(3), 89–102. doi:10.4067/S0718-27242021000300089

Truby, J. (2018). Decarbonizing Bitcoin: Law and policy choices for reducing the energy consumption of Blockchain technologies and digital currencies. *Energy Research & Social Science*, *44*, 399–410. doi:10.1016/j.erss.2018.06.009

Tschorsch, F., & Scheuermann, B. (2016). Bitcoin and beyond: A technical survey on decentralized digital currencies. *IEEE Communications Surveys and Tutorials*, *18*(3), 2084–2123. doi:10.1109/COMST.2016.2535718

Tseng, M. L., Tan, P. A., Jeng, S. Y., Lin, C. W. R., Negash, Y. T., & Darsono, S. N. A. C. (2019). Sustainable investment: Interrelated among corporate governance, economic performance and market risks using investor preference approach. *Sustainability (Basel)*, *11*(7), 2108. doi:10.3390/su11072108

Turnbull, S. (2002). *A New Way to Govern Organisations and Institutions Network, 14*. Corporate Governance.

Tushar, W., Yuen, C., Saha, T. K., Morstyn, T., Chapman, A. C., Alam, M. J. E., Hanif, S., & Poor, H. V. (2021). Peer-to-peer energy systems for connected communities: A review of recent advances and emerging challenges. *Applied Energy, 282*(PA), 116131. doi:10.1016/j.apenergy.2020.116131

Udeagha, M. C., & Muchapondwa, E. (2023). Green finance, fintech, and environmental sustainability: Fresh policy insights from the BRICS nations. *International Journal of Sustainable Development and World Ecology, 30*(6), 633–649. doi:10.1080/13504509.2023.2183526

Udeagha, M. C., & Ngepah, N. (2023). The drivers of environmental sustainability in BRICS economies: Do green finance and fintech matter? *World Development Sustainability, 3*, 100096. doi:10.1016/j.wds.2023.100096

Uhlemann, T. H.-J., Lehmann, C., & Steinhilper, R. (2017). The digital twin: Realizing the cyber-physical production system for Industry 4.0. *Procedia CIRP, 61*, 335–340. doi:10.1016/j.procir.2016.11.152

UNEP. (2021). *Making Peace with Nature [R]*. United Nations Environment Programme. https://wedocs.unep.org/handle/20.500.11822/34807

United Nations Environment Programme (UNEP). (2016, September). *Definitions and concepts. Background note.* Inquiry working paper 16/13.

Utami, A. F., Ekaputra, I. A., & Japutra, A. (2021). Adoption of FinTech products: A systematic literature review. *Journal of Creative Communications, 16*(3), 233–248. doi:10.1177/09732586211032092

Uzsoki, D., & Guerdat, P. (2019). *Impact Tokens: A blockchain-based solution for impact investing*. International Institute for Sustainable Development.

Varma, J. R. (2019). Blockchain in Finance. *Vikalpa, 44*(1), 1–11. doi:10.1177/0256090919839897

Vasiliu, L. A., Roman, D., & Prodan, R.-C. (2023). Extreme and Sustainable Graph Processing for Green Finance Investment and Trading. *Proceedings of the 2023 ACM/SIGAPP Symposium on Applied Computing*. ACM. 10.1145/3578245.3585337

Vieira, G., & Zhang, J. (2021). Peer-to-peer energy trading in a microgrid leveraged by smart contracts. *Renewable & Sustainable Energy Reviews, 143*, 110900. doi:10.1016/j.rser.2021.110900

Vikas, N., Venegas, P., & Aiyer, S. (2022). Role of Banks and Other Financial Institutions in Enhancing Green Digital Finance. In *Green Digital Finance and Sustainable Development Goals* (pp. 329–352). Springer Nature Singapore. doi:10.1007/978-981-19-2662-4_16

Vilà Brualla, M. (2022). *Blockchain Layer 2 scalability solutions: a framework for comparison.*

Vinuesa, R., Azizpour, H., Leite, I., Balaam, M., Dignum, V., Domisch, S., & Fuso Nerini, F. (2020). The role of artificial intelligence in achieving the Sustainable Development Goals. *Nature Communications*, *11*(1), 1–10. doi:10.1038/s41467-019-14108-y PMID:31932590

von Hippel, E., & Jin, C. (2008). The major shift towards user-centred innovation: Implications for China's innovation policymaking. *Journal of Knowledge-based Innovation in China*, *1*(1), 16–27. doi:10.1108/17561410910912896

Wajid, A., Sabiha, A., Akhtar, S., Tabash, M. I., & Daniel, L. N. (2022). Cross-Border Acquisitions and Shareholders' Wealth: The Case of the Indian Pharmaceutical Sector. *Journal of Risk and Financial Management*, *15*(10), 437. doi:10.3390/jrfm15100437

Wamba. (2018). Bitcoin, Blockchain, and FinTech: A Systematic Review and Case Studies in the Supply Chain. *Production Planning and Control*, *31*(6), 115–142. doi:10.1080/09537287.2019.1631460

Wang, B., Lai, J., Liu, M., Jin, F., Peng, Y., & Yao, C. (2022). Electronic Source Data Transcription for Electronic Case Report Forms in China: Validation of the Electronic Source Record Tool in a Real-world Ophthalmology Study. *JMIR Formative Research*, *6*(12), e43229. doi:10.2196/43229 PMID:36525285

Wang, S., Ouyang, L., Yuan, Y., Ni, X., Han, X., & Wang, F.-Y. (2019). Blockchain-enabled smart contracts: Architecture, applications, and future trends. *IEEE Transactions on Systems, Man, and Cybernetics. Systems*, *49*(11), 2266–2277. doi:10.1109/TSMC.2019.2895123

Wang, S., & Wang, C. (2023). How do Fintech and green bonds ensure clean energy production in China? Dynamics of green investment risk. *Environmental Science and Pollution Research International*, *30*(57), 120552–120563. doi:10.1007/s11356-023-30491-y PMID:37940828

Weber, O. (2018). *Green finance: Theory and practice*. Springer.

Wei, W., An, B., Qiao, K., & Shen, J. (2023). A Blockchain-Based Multi-Users Oblivious Data Sharing Scheme for Digital Twin System in Industrial Internet of Things. *IEEE Journal on Selected Areas in Communications*, *41*(10), 3318–3332. doi:10.1109/JSAC.2023.3310105

White, R., & Black, P. (2022). Challenges and Opportunities in Blockchain-Digital Twin Integration for Sustainable Development. *International Journal of Green Technology*, *15*(1), 78–95.

Wilson, K. B., Karg, A., & Ghaderi, H. (2021). Prospecting non- fungible tokens in the digital economy: Stakeholders and ecosystem, risk and opportunity. *Business Horizons*, *65*(5), 657e670.

Woo, J., Fatima, R., Kibert, C. J., Newman, R. E., Tian, Y., & Srinivasan, R. S. (2021). Applying blockchain technology for building energy performance measurement, reporting, and verification (MRV) and the carbon credit market: A review of the literature. *Building and Environment*, *205*(July), 108199. doi:10.1016/j.buildenv.2021.108199

World Economic Forum. (2013). *The Green Investment Report*. World Economic Forum. https://reports.weforum.org/green-investing-2013/

Wright, S. A. (2023). IoT Blockchains for Digital Twins. In X. H. P. Yu (Ed.), *Opportunities and Challenges of Industrial IoT in 5G and 6G Networks* (pp. 244–260). IGI Global. doi:10.4018/978-1-7998-9266-3.ch011

Wu, Q., & Gladyshev, V. (2020). *Design for the Decentralized World: Democratization of Blockchain-Based Software Design.* Design, User Experience, and Usability. Design for Contemporary Interactive Environments: 9th International Conference, Copenhagen, Denmark.

Wu. (2022). Financial Crimes in Web3-empowered Metaverse: Taxonomy, Countermeasures, and Opportunities. *Open Journal of Computer Society*, *24*. doi:10.48550/arXiv.2212.13452

Xiao, Y., Zhang, N., Lou, W., & Hou, Y. T. (2020). A Survey of Distributed Consensus Protocols for Blockchain Networks. *IEEE Communications Surveys and Tutorials*, *22*(2), 1432–1465. doi:10.1109/COMST.2020.2969706

Xu, B., Wang, J., Wang, X., Liang, Z., Cui, L., Liu, X., & Ku, A. Y. (2019). A case study of digital-twin-modelling analysis on power-plant-performance optimizations. *Clean Energy*, *3*(3), 227–234. doi:10.1093/ce/zkz025

Xu, H., Mei, Q., Shahzad, F., Liu, S., Long, X., & Zhang, J. (2020). Untangling the impact of green finance on the enterprise green performance: A meta-analytic approach. *Sustainability (Basel)*, *12*(21), 9085. doi:10.3390/su12219085

Yakubi, Y., Basuki, B., Purwono, R., & Usman, I. (2022). The Impact of Digital Technology and Business Regulations on Financial Inclusion and Socio-Economic Development in Low-Income Countries. *SAGE Open*, *12*(3). doi:10.1177/21582440221116112

Yan, C., Siddik, A. B., Yong, L., Dong, Q., Zheng, G. W., & Rahman, M. N. (2022). A two-staged SEM-artificial neural network approach to analyze the impact of FinTech adoption on the sustainability performance of banking firms: The mediating effect of green finance and innovation. *Systems*, *10*(5), 148. doi:10.3390/systems10050148

Yang, F., Zhou, W., Wu, Q., Long, R., Xiong, N. N., & Zhou, M. (2019). Delegated Proof of Stake With Downgrade: A Secure and Efficient Blockchain Consensus Algorithm With Downgrade Mechanism. *IEEE Access : Practical Innovations, Open Solutions*, *7*, 118541–118555. doi:10.1109/ACCESS.2019.2935149

Yang, Y., Su, X., & Yao, S. (2021). Nexus between green finance, fintech, and high-quality economic development: Empirical evidence from China. *Resources Policy*, *74*, 102445. doi:10.1016/j.resourpol.2021.102445

Yaqoob, I., Khaled, S., Uddin, M., Raja, J., Omar, M., & Imran, M. (2020). Blockchain for Digital Twins: Recent Advances and Future Research Challenges. IEEE. doi:10.1109/MNET.001.1900661

Yasanur, K., & Nachiappan, S. (2022). Blockchain Interoperability Issues in Supply Chain: Exploration of Mass Adoption Procedures. In *A. a. EMROUZNEJAD, Big Data and Blockchain for Service Operations Management. Studies in Big Data* (pp. 309–328). Springer.

Yi, C. S. S., Yung, E., Fong, C., & Tripathi, S. (2020). Benefits and Use of Blockchain Technology to Human Resources Management: A Critical Review. *International Journal of Human Resource Studies*, *10*(2), 2–6. doi:10.5296/ijhrs.v10i2.16932

Yi, L., Glatt, M., Ehmsen, S., Duan, W., & Aurich, J. C. (2021). Process monitoring of economic and environmental performance of a material extrusion printer using an augmented reality-based digital twin. *Additive Manufacturing*, *48*, 102388. doi:10.1016/j.addma.2021.102388

Yli-Huumo, J., Ko, D., Choi, S., Park, S., & Smolander, K. (2016). The current state of blockchain technology. *Journal of Information Technology*, *31*(3), 205–220.

Yoo, S., & Managi, S. (2021). Disclosure or action: Evaluating ESG behavior towards financial performance. *Finance Research Letters*, 102108.

You, M., Wang, Q., Sun, H., Castro, I., & Jiang, J. (2022). Digital twins based day-ahead integrated energy system scheduling under load and renewable energy uncertainties. *Applied Energy*, *305*, 117899. doi:10.1016/j.apenergy.2021.117899

Zadek, S., & Flynn, C. (2013). Redefining the financial system. *Solutions*, *4*(1), 15–20.

Zadorozhnyi, Z., Desyatnyuk, O., Muravskyi, V., & Shevchuk, O. (2023). Combination of Digital Twin Technology and FinOps in Management Accounting Modeling. *2023 IEEE 12th International Conference on Advanced Computer Information Technologies (ACIT)*. IEEE. 10.1109/ACIT58437.2023.10275621

Zamani, E., He, Y., & Phillips, M. (2020). On the Security Risks of the Blockchain. *Journal of Computer Information Systems*, *60*(6), 495–506. doi:10.1080/08874417.2018.1538709

Zeng, W., Sharma, S., & Shull, T. (2021). Quantum Computing: Impact on Blockchain Technology and Cybersecurity. *IEEE Transactions on Engineering Management*.

Zhang, C., Zhu, L., & Xu, C. (2023). BSDP: Block Chain Based Smart Parking for Digital-Twin Empowered Vehicular sensor Networks with Privacy Protection. *IEEE Transactions on Industrial Informatics*, *19*(5), 7237–7246. doi:10.1109/TII.2022.3223211

Zhang, S., Li, L., & Deng, B. (2023). *Sensing digital twin technology helps upgrade power equipment of new power system equipment*. SPIE. doi:10.1117/12.2669433

Zhang, X., Ai, X., Wang, X., Zong, G., & Zhang, J. (2023). A Study on the Effects of Digital Finance on Green Low-Carbon Circular Development Based on Machine Learning Models. *Mathematics*, *11*(18), 3903. doi:10.3390/math11183903

Zhang, X., Aranguiz, M., Xu, D., Zhang, X., & Xu, X. (2018). Utilizing blockchain for better enforcement of green finance law and regulations. In *Transforming climate finance and green investment with blockchains* (pp. 289–301). Academic Press. doi:10.1016/B978-0-12-814447-3.00021-5

Zhang, X., Shen, J., Saini, P. K., Lovati, M., Han, M., Huang, P., & Huang, Z. (2021, June 21). Digital Twin for Accelerating Sustainability in Positive Energy District: A Review of Simulation Tools and Applications. *Frontiers in Sustainable Cities*, *3*, 663269. doi:10.3389/frsc.2021.663269

Zhang, Z., Zhu, H., Peng, N., Song, J., Sun, R., Wang, J., Zhu, F., & Wang, Y. (2023). Red emissive carbon dots-based probe for rapid identification and continuous tracking of Gram-positive bacteria in tumor cells. *Materials Letters*, *341*, 134233. Advance online publication. doi:10.1016/j.matlet.2023.134233

Zhao, J. L., Fan, S., & Yan, J. (2019). Blockchain technology in business organizations: A scoping review. *Review of Managerial Science*, *13*(1), 55–75.

Zhao, Y., Yue, Y., & Wei, P. (2021). Financing advantage of green corporate asset-backed securities and its impact factors: Evidence in China. *Frontiers in Energy Research*, *9*, 696110. doi:10.3389/fenrg.2021.696110

Zheng, X., Zhou, Y., & Iqbal, S. (2022). Working capital management of SMEs in COVID-19: Role of managerial personality traits and overconfidence behavior. In *Economic Analysis and Policy* (Vol. 76, pp. 439–451). Elsevier B.V. doi:10.1016/j.eap.2022.08.006

Zheng, Z., & ... (2019). Digital twins in green finance investment strategies. *Journal of Sustainable Finance*, *9*(2), 115–130. doi:10.1080/03088839.2023.2196754

Zheng, Z., Xie, S., Dai, H. N., Chen, W., Chen, X., Weng, J., & Imran, M. (2020, April). An overview on smart contracts: Challenges, advances and platforms. *Future Generation Computer Systems*, *105*, 475–491. doi:10.1016/j.future.2019.12.019

Zheng, Z., Xie, S., Dai, H. N., Chen, X., & Wang, H. (2018). Blockchain challenges and opportunities: A survey. *International Journal of Web and Grid Services*, *14*(4), 352–375. doi:10.1504/IJWGS.2018.095647

Zheng, Z., Xie, S., Dai, H.-N., Chen, X., & Wang, H. (2017). An overview of blockchain technology: Architecture, consensus, and future trends. *2017 IEEE International Congress on Big Data (BigData Congress)*, (pp. 557–564). IEEE. 10.1109/BigDataCongress.2017.85

Zhou, X., Tang, X., & Zhang, R. (2020). Impact of green finance on economic development and environmental quality: A study based on provincial panel data from China. *Environmental Science and Pollution Research International*, *27*(16), 19915–19932. doi:10.1007/s11356-020-08383-2 PMID:32232752

Zhou, X., Wang, Y., Zhu, Q., Mao, J., Xiao, C., Lu, X., & Hui, Z. (2020). A Surface Defect Detection Framework for Glass Bottle Bottom Using Visual Attention Model and Wavelet Transform. *IEEE Transactions on Industrial Informatics*, *16*(4), 2189–2201. doi:10.1109/TII.2019.2935153

Zou, W., Lo, D., Kochhar, P. S., Le, X.-B. D., Xia, X., Feng, Y., Chen, Z., & Xu, B. (2019). Smart contract development: Challenges and opportunities. *IEEE Transactions on Software Engineering*, *47*(10), 2084–2106. doi:10.1109/TSE.2019.2942301

Zribi, H., Elloumi, A., Hani, Y., & Elmhamedi, A. (2023). Industry 4.0: Digital Twin's Industrial Applications. *9th International Conference on Control, Decision and Information Technologies (CoDIT)*. IEEE. 10.1109/CoDIT58514.2023.10284310

About the Contributors

Syed Hasan Jafar is an Area Chair/ HOD of Finance at Woxsen University. He has around 14 Years of experience in the field of Finance and worked as a Deputy Research Head and Corporate trainer before joining academics. He comes on several national & International media channels, including CNBC, AajTak, BizTak, ET, The Finance World, Dubai, and others, as a financial expert to share his view on the Financial market. He is a contributing writer for "The Economic Times" on various Finance topics. He shares his opinion on the global magazine "The Finance World," published in the Middle East and diverse countries, including India. He is a Board member of various corporate and a financial advisor for multiple companies. His areas of expertise are Security Analysis, Equity and Derivative Research, and Valuation. He has taken several sessions at top universities in India and abroad. He was awarded Best Faculty of the Year 2020-21 and best faculty of corporate alignment in the Year 2022-23 at Woxsen University. He conducted over 50 Investor awareness programs nationwide and was awarded the best Research Analyst multiple times during his corporate journey.

Raul Villamarin Rodriguez is the Vice President at Woxsen University. He holds a Ph.D. in Artificial Intelligence and Robotics Process Automation Applications in Human Resources from San Miguel University, Mexico. Under his leadership, Woxsen University has partnered with 50+ Leading Universities in 35 countries across 6 continents. He has been instrumental in bringing International Exchange Programs & Research opportunities with the said global partner universities for students and faculty. His areas of expertise span across the domain of Artificial Intelligence and Quantum Artificial Intelligence, Natural Language Processing, Computer Vision, Robotic Process Automation, Multi-agent Systems, Data Analytics (Big Data), Cybersecurity Management and Knowledge Engineering. Dr. Raul has been part of significant research during his tenure, primarily through RRBM, GRLI, and PRME. He has also played vital roles in organizing renowned educational symposiums for institutions like the Oxford Brookes University, UK and European Union-government bodies in Brussels, Belgium. A young achiever, Dr. Raul, has recently been awarded in the Europe India 40 under 40 Leaders and nominated in Forbes 30 Under 30 Europe 2020. His achievements also highlight him as a registered expert in Artificial Intelligence, Intelligent Systems, and Multi-agent Systems at the European Commission. Treading the path of thought leadership in the education domain, Dr. Raul has made his place as a member of international bodies such as GRLI Deans and Directors cohort, Harvard Business Review Advisory Council, and the Institute for Robotics Process Automation & Artificial Intelligence (IRPA AI). As a staunch knowledge contributor to his field of expertise, Dr. Raul is frequently seen as the keynote speaker and panel moderator at various national and international conferences. In addition, he has co-authored two reference books: 'New Age Leadership: A Critical Insight' and 'Retail Store'e' and has more than 70 publications to his credit. He is also a weekly contributing writer to various magazines, a notable journal reviewer, and an associate editor in renowned publications such as IEEE.

Hemachandran Kannan holds the Area Chair of the Analytics Department at Woxsen University. Dr. Hemachandran is an Advisory board member at APT AI Labs, LLC. He has been a passionate teacher with 15 years of teaching experience and 5 years of research experience. He served as an effective resource person at various national and international scientific conferences and also gave lectures on topics related to Artificial Intelligence. He was bestowed as Best faculty at Woxsen University in 2021-2022 and also in Ashoka Institute of Engineering & Technology in 2019 – 2020. He is having rich working experience in Natural Language Processing, Computer Vision, Building Video recommendation systems, Building Chatbots for HR policies and Education Sector, Automatic Interview processes, and Autonomous Robots. He is working on various real-time use cases and projects in collaboration with Industries such as Advertflair, LLC, Course5i and Apstek Corp. He has organized many International Conferences, Hackathons and Ideathon. An open-ended positive person who has a stupendous peer-reviewed publication record with more than 35 journals and international conference publications.

Shakeb Akhtar is currently Assistant Professor, Program Director (MBA-FS) and Research Coordinator (SOB) at Woxsen University. He holds an MFC and Ph.D. in Banking and Finance from Aligarh Muslim University, India. He specializes in accounting and finance related courses and has over 10 years teaching experience in accounting and finance at both tertiary and senior high school levels. His research interest is in banking industry, behavioral economics, and secondary data analysis techniques namely; static panel estimation, dynamic panel estimation, ARDL panel modulation and time series estimation, efficiency analysis, sustainability and SDG's with seven years of research experience. He has 17 publication, published in ABDC, ABS, Scopus and Web of Science journals.

Philipp Plugmann has been Professor of Interdisciplinary Periodontology and Prevention in the Bachelor's degree program in Dental Hygienist at the Leverkusen campus of the SRH University of Applied Sciences since February 1, 2020. After studying dentistry at the University of Cologne and passing the state examination in 2000, he received his doctorate in 2005 from the University Hospital of Cologne in the Department of Oral and Maxillofacial Surgery. In addition, he completed his doctoral studies in medical sciences (grade: very good) at the Private University of the Principality of Liechtenstein (UFL) in 2013. He holds a Master of Science in Periodontology and Implant Therapy from DGParo (grade 1.6), Master of Business Administration with a focus on Health Care Management and Master of Science in Business Innovation. In total, he has published 95 papers in the fields of dentistry, innovation and technology and edited 12 german and English-language books. His first book on future trends in medical technology was reviewed in 2012 by CISCO, a major U.S. technology company. His second book in 2018 "Shaping Innovation Environments" published by Springer Gabler Verlag had over 30,100 chapter downloads in the first 000 months. During his 23 years of dental professional activity, he has also founded 2 companies dealing with prevention and services in healthcare, the development of surgical software for dental surgeries and digital technologies. He has presented research results on innovations in healthcare at conferences at Harvard University (USA), the Max Planck Institute for Innovation and Competition (Munich) and Nanyang Tech University (Singapore), among others. Parallel to his practice, Prof. Dr. Dr. Philipp Plugmann was active for 12 years at universities in Karlsruhe, Cologne and Bielefeld, where he was also able to accompany master's theses as a supervisor and first examiner. From 2007 to 2016 he was a lecturer in the field of innovation at the Karlsruhe University of Applied Sciences and was awarded by the Rector for outstanding teaching. Since 2013, he has been a Research Fellow at the University Clinic of Dentistry Marburg in the Department of Periodontology, where he has also been honored for outstanding commitment due to his case reports, lectures and international research presentations.

* * *

Mahfooz Alam is working as a Faculty Instructor in the Department of Business Administration at the University of the People, Pasadena, CA, USA. He holds MBA and Ph.D. in the area of Finance from Aligarh Muslim University, India. Prior to joining UoPeople, he worked at GLA University, Mathura and The ICFAI University, Dehradun as an Assistant Professor with over 4 years of academic experience. His research interests include Asset Pricing, Behavioural Finance, Mutual Funds performance and Islamic Banking and Finance. He has 12 publications in international and national journals of repute such as the International Journal of Emerging

Markets, Journal of Asset Management and International Journal of Islamic and Middle Eastern Finance and Management.

K. Balaji is an Assistant Professor in Commerce and Economics, Presidency University, Bangalore. He did Ph.D. from KLU Business School, KL University,Vijayawada. He is having 12 years of teaching experience. He has to his credit 23 Research Articles published in reputed National and International Journals. He has participated and presented more than 12 papers in both National and International Seminars/Conferences and also attended more than 50 workshops/FDPS organized by various reputed organizations. He has also participated in more than 50 seminars / webinars organized by various reputed organizations. He has also attended in 6 Short Term Training programs.He has successfully conducted 3 webinars, one 5 day FDP and one International Conference on Reimaging marketing in New Normal. He is a ratified as Assistant Professor by both JNTUH, JNTU Anantapur and Sri Venkateswara University,Tirupati. His specialized areas include, Accounting and Financial management, Marketing Management, Retailing Management, Consumer Behavior studies, Entrepreneurship and Business Laws.

Sharuti Choudhary is an accomplished professional serving as a Professor, COE-Digital Transformation & Customer Experience specializing in Marketing and Branding at Woxsen University in Hyderabad, India. With over 18 years of extensive experience in teaching, training development, and research, Dr. Choudhary holds a Doctorate Degree obtained in 2015, focusing on innovative marketing strategies. Her academic journey includes a Master's in Business Administration, a Master's in Computer Application, and an M.Sc in Information Technology. Dr. Choudhary's expertise extends to the realms of Marketing and Technology, where she has made significant contributions to the research field. Her work is evidenced by numerous international and national publications, featuring in reputable ABDC/ Scopus Journals, as well as numerous edited book chapters. Beyond academia, Dr. Choudhary has played a pivotal role in conducting Management Development Programs (MDP), Faculty Development Programs (FDP), and training sessions for multinational companies, showcasing her commitment to bridging the gap between academia and industry.

Prashant Chougule, Assistant Professor, Dept. of Finance, School of Business, Woxsen University, Hyderabad, India. His research areas include Fintech, Financial Analytics, Financial Econometrics, Cryptocurrencies, Volatility Analysis, Volatility Prediction and integration of Data Science and Machine Learning with Finance.

Saumendra Das presently working as an Associate Professor at the School of Management Studies, GIET University, Gunupur, Odisha. He has more than 20 years of teaching, research, and industry experience. He has published more than 52 articles in national and international journals, conference proceedings, and book chapters. He also authored one book on advertising effectiveness. Dr Das has participated and presented many papers in seminars, conferences, and workshops in India and abroad. He has organized many FDPs and workshops in his career. He is an academician, author, and editor. He has also published two patents also. He is an active member of various professional bodies such as ICA, ISTE and RFI. In the year 2023, he has been awarded as the best teacher by Research Foundation India.

Anjli Gupta is currently working as an assistant professor in Department of Management at Maharaja Agrasen Institute of Technology, Rohini, Delhi, also Serving as Associate NCC Officer and ranked as Leutinent and specialised in Finance and Business analytics with five years of teaching experience. She has contributed 3 research papers, granted 2 international patents and 1 national patent and published 2 books chapters and further working upon 2 UK design patents in the field of fintech.

Ritu Gupta, working as Assistant Professor, at Department of Management (MBA), Maharaja Agrasen Institute of Technology, Rohini, New Delhi. She has a rich teaching experience of more than 16 years. Her area of specialization is Accounting and finance. She has also conducted more than 20 workshops as a resource person of Securities Exchange Board of India. She has contributed 13 research papers , granted 2 National patent, 1 international patent, , More than 50 conferences & workshops/FDP's participation. She is also empaneled as supervisor at K R Manglam, University and one scholar has successfully submitted the thesis. (6141b0a4-bee4-4d96-a5f8-a1d1a80214e6)

Kavitha Reddy Gurrala, Assistant Professor, Operations and Marketing, School Of Business, Woxsen University, is an Innovative and passionate educator with a strong desire to apply technical knowledge gained through multidisciplinary research for long-term sustainable and economic development. Moreover, she is a dedicated professional with over fifteen years of experience in the supply chain domain gained from working for both Industry and academia who is into the realization of Innovative Ideas for continual improvements. Her research interests include: application of decision making tools and models for Supply Chain Performance Enhancement and digital Transformation within Supply Chains.

Jintu George is an Assistant Professor in the Department of Commerce at VIT Vellore. Her research areas are Stock Market, Renewable Energy, Green finance etc. She is a very active scholar and academician.

Mohammad Kashif is a distinguished academician and researcher in the area of finance, economics and international business at Graphic Era Deemed to be University, Dehradun, India . He has several publications indexed in WoS, Scopus and ABDC. He authored a book titled Financial Management for undergraduate students. He is guiding PhD scholars in his area of expertise. Besides he is a member of several professional bodies at university level. He has been awarded many academic and research awards by reputed organizations.

Christian Kaunert is Professor of International Security at Dublin City University, Ireland. He is also Professor of Policing and Security, as well as Director of the International Centre for Policing and Security at the University of South Wales. In addition, he is Jean Monnet Chair, Director of the Jean Monnet Centre of Excellence and Director of the Jean Monnet Network on EU Counter-Terrorism ().

Kiran, is current working as an Assistant Professor in School of Management at Apeejay Institute of Management and Engineering Technical Campus at Jalandhar, Punjab. She has 5 years of teaching experience and 3 years of research experience. She has contributed 3 research papers, 1 book chapter publications and 3 research paper presentations at national conferences. She is also pursuing PhD from Guru Nanak Dev University, Punjab.

Naseema N. is a research scholar at Woxsen University. Her area of specialization include Fintech, Digital transformation.

Ch Siddharth Nanda, Associate Professor in School of Business, Woxsen University, Telangana is a distinguished professional with over 17 years of extensive experience in his field. Previously he was Deputy Director and Associate Professor at Amity University, Kolkata. He has made significant contributions to the academic and research community, showcasing his expertise through a multitude of research papers published in prestigious journals indexed in Scopus and ABDC (Australian Business Deans Council) databases. His commitment to advancing knowledge is evident in the quality and quantity of his scholarly works. In addition to his prolific research output, Dr. Nanda has been recognized for his thought leadership and has been invited as both a session and keynote speaker at various international conferences. His presentations reflect a deep understanding of his subject matter and a keen ability to communicate complex ideas effectively to diverse audiences.

Sibghatullah Nasir is an Assistant professor (Senior Grade) in the Department of Commerce at BSA Crescent Institute of Science and Technology. Dr Nasir is an expert in the domain of Finance and Economics with teaching experience of around 7.5 years. His research areas are Microfinance, Renewable energy and Green finance.

Jyotikanta Panda presently working as an IT Professional at Tata Consultancy Services, Bhubaneswar, Odisha. He has more than 20 years of industry experience in delivery and project management in Cognitive Business Operations, cyber security, Internet Of Things and Cloud Computing.He has participated and presented many papers in seminars, conferences, and workshops in India and abroad. Has been certified as ITIL V3 Expert, CCNP, Ethical Hacker, PRINCE2 Practitioner, MCSE in MS Windows server and MS Azure and Certified Information Systems Auditor(CISA).

Moushami Panda presently working as an IT Professional at Tata Consultancy Services, Bhubaneswar, Odisha. She has more than 20 years of industry experience in Digital Transformation Services, cyber security practice and ELearning. She has participated and presented many papers in seminars, conferences, and workshops in India and abroad. Has been certified as ITIL V3 Expert, CCNP, Ethical Hacker, PRINCE2 Practitioner, MCSE in MS Windows server,MS Azure and Certified Information System Auditor (CISA).

Tapaswini Panda is presently working as Guest Faculty at Model Degree College, Rayagada, Odisha. She has completed Master of Business Administration from GIET University, Gunupur, India. Her research interest is on Work Life Balance, Quality of Work Life and Human Resource Information System. She has published three patents in India and abroad. She is a passionate researcher and a true academician teaches the subject such as Principles of Management, Human Resource Management, Organizational Development and Change. She has published one paper in National Journal and two book chapters.

Udaya Sankar Patro is presently working as a Lecturer at Rayagada Autonomous College, Rayagada, Odisha. He has completed a Master of Business Administration from GIET University, Gunupur, India. His research interest is on Workplace Spirituality, Work life Integrity and Human Resource Management. He has published three patents in India and abroad. He is a passionate researcher and a true academician who teaches the subjects such as Management and Theory Practices, Managerial Economics, and Human Resource Management. He has published one paper in National Journal and two book chapters.

Dulu Patnaik is presently working as the Principal, Govt. Engineering College, Bhawanipatna, Odisha. He has more than 30 years of teaching, research and industry experience. He is an active member of various professional bodies such as IE (I), ISTE, IETE, TSI, BMESI, IIIE, INSC, ISOI, BMESI and ICA He has chaired/organized and attended various STTPs, workshops, seminars, conferences etc. and acted as a resource person/giest faculty and delivered invited talks. He has published many research papers and is also Reviewer and Consulting Editor of some National and International repute. He received (08)awards from IE(1), IETE and the Rajalaxmi Memorial "Best Engineering College Teacher" in 2011 from ISTE, New Delhi. He is actively enagaged in consultancy and project works. He has worked in different capacities for different committees of BPUT, Odisha, Academic Advisor of NCSS, New Delhi as well as BoG, BoS member of different Universities &Autonomous Institutions. Beside this he is also associated with DR. A P J kalam Foudation Trust, Kalahandi for social service.

Afzalur Rahman is a distinguished academic and a seasoned finance and business analytics professional, currently serving as a Professor at Presidency University in Bengaluru, India. With a rich background that spans over twelve years in academia and industry, Dr. Rahman is celebrated for his expertise in finance education, research, and the practical application of business analytics. He earned his Ph.D. from Patna University in 2011, demonstrating a profound commitment to academic excellence. His educational journey also includes an MBA from VM University and a Master's in Commerce from Patna University, further solidifying his credentials in the fields of finance and commerce. Dr. Rahman's professional journey is marked by diverse experiences, ranging from academia to corporate training. Before his current role, he has imparted knowledge and leadership at institutions like B.S. Abdur Rahman Crescent University, Chennai, and Bakhtar University, Kabul, among others. His teaching methodology, deeply rooted in practical application, is complemented by his proficiency in a range of technical skills including Python, Golang, R programming, and various database and cloud technologies. An advocate of digital education and innovative teaching methods, Dr. Rahman has developed numerous online courses and educational resources. His website, clickuniv.com, stands as a testament to his commitment to making education accessible and engaging. Additionally, his proficiency in algo-trading and his developments on platforms like Kite-Zerodha highlight his practical application skills in the rapidly evolving finance sector. Dr. Rahman's research work is equally commendable, with numerous publications and a significant presence in academic circles, as evidenced by his citation index and h-index. His contributions extend beyond classroom teaching to guiding Ph.D. and M.Phil candidates, further showcasing his dedication to nurturing future scholars. Outside the classroom, Dr. Rahman is a dynamic figure, actively involved in organizing international conferences, workshops, and being a part of various educational initiatives. His efforts in modernizing the Department of Commerce with IT technologies and his forward-thinking approach in curriculum development have been pivotal in shaping contemporary education in his field. With a blend of academic rigor, industry relevance, and a passion for teaching and research, Dr. Afzalur Rahman continues to inspire students and peers alike, contributing significantly to the fields of finance and business analytics.

Nayan Kanwal's life traces an international pathway that makes him an asset to any organisation, especially an academic institution, which can only gain from his broad outlook, considerable cultural exposure and vast life experience. Born in India in 1958, Nayan left the country at the young age of 11 for a stint in Kenya, where his father served a United Nations (UNDP/ILO) Chief Technical Adviser. Upon his return to India to begin secondary school, Nayan was enrolled in one of the country's best schools in the capital city, the Delhi Public School. While Nayan's academic background is in agriculture management, he has accumulated extensive professional experience in publishing. In 1982, he obtained his Bachelor's degree in agriculture from the University of Papua New Guinea/Queensland University, Australia. He went on to receive his Master's degree, also in Agriculture, in 1985 from the same university, and worked there as a research associate for a year. In 1987, he went freelance to work in Singapore. He later obtained his doctorate in 2005 from France. Nayan lays claim to almost 36 years of professional experience primarily in Communication, Scholarly Journal publishing and Research and Development Management & Administration. His research expertise is in the following areas: Languages, Linguistics, Management, Environmental sciences, etc Nayan is an experienced senior Executive Editor, Editor-in-Chief, Author, Reviewer and a Professor, with a demonstrated history of working in the publishing industry. Skilled in Academic Publishing, Publications, Creative Writing, and Text Editing. Strong media and communication professional with substantial experience in Communications, Media, Print Design with a strong scholarly journal publishing background. He has written on a wide range of subjects beyond his area of study, agriculture. He has published articles in different publications as well as book chapters in his long academic and professional career. He has also authored and co-authored several research and development books. The subjects he has written on range from management and administration of research to information technology. Nayan is described as a man with conviction and commitment, responsible for the education of countless postgraduate students from all over the world. He is a brilliant and intelligent communicator who has devoted himself for the promotion of academic publications not only for Malaysia, but also for the developing world and for the entire humanity. There must be some method to his madness that single-handed he has created this mammoth publishing impact. He is full of surprises and his level of energy is very high and contagious". Professor Nayan Kanwal has authored and co-authored numerous academic books and journals, served as a reviewer to many SCOPUS-indexed journals. He has also served as an external examiner/ evaluator for PHD thesis with several universities around the globe. He has delivered countless lecturers, invited by universities in Malaysia, Thailand and Indonesia; attended copious Seminars/Workshops/Courses and has been invited as a Special Guest at more than a hundred Plenary/ Keynote/ Invited Talks. In addition, he has also been involved in research consultancies in Indonesia, Thailand, Vietnam and Malaysia. He is a Fellow of the Royal Society of Arts (FRSA), United Kingdom, a Life Member of the British Institute of Management (BIM), United Kingdom, an Associate Member of the Marketing Institute of Singapore (AMIS) and an Associate Member of the Australian Institute of Agricultural Science and Technology (AIAST).

Saibabu Neyyila currently working as an Assistant Professor department of Management Studies at Aditya Institute of Technology & Management, Tekkali. He is having more than 16 years of teaching experience in various management and engineering colleges. He has published many articles in journals and conference proceedings. He did post graduation in M.Com, MBA from Andhra University, PGDIM from Pondicherry University and he he had completed his Ph.D from Acharya Nagarjuna University. He had also qualified Andhrapradesh State Eligibility Set (APSET) both Commerce and Management. He is an enthusiastic learner and active academician.

Syed Noorul Shajar is an Assistant Professor in the Department of Commerce at VIT University, Vellore. He has 5 years of post-Ph.D. teaching and research experience in the domain of Accounting and Finance. His research interests include Corporate Finance, Working Capital management, Corporate Governance, Renewable energy, and Green Finance. He has published 9 papers in journals indexed in Web of Science, Scopus, and ABDC etc. He has also received grant from Government of India to present his research paper in an International conference in Japan. Moreover, he has presented several research papers at seminar and conferences in India. He has been an active member of the Board of studies, Syllabus Committee and several other committees for 3 different organizations. Dr. Syed Noorul Shajar is a passionate educator and researcher. He is committed to teaching students the skills and knowledge they need to succeed in their careers and make a positive impact on the world. He is also very keen and committed to conducting research that advances the field of Corporate Governance, Green finance, and renewable energy.

Muhammad Usman Tariq has more than 16+ year's experience in industry and academia. He has been working as a consultant and trainer for industries representing six sigma, quality, health and safety, environmental systems, project management, and information security standards. His work has encompassed sectors in aviation, manufacturing, food, hospitality, education, finance, research, software and transportation. He has diverse and significant experience working with accreditation agencies of ABET, ACBSP, AACSB, WASC, CAA, EFQM and NCEAC. Additionally, Dr. Tariq has operational experience in incubators, research labs, government research projects, private sector startups, program creation and management at various industrial and academic levels. He is Certified Higher Education Teacher from Harvard University, USA, Certified Online Educator from HMBSU, Certified Six Sigma Master Black Belt, Lead Auditor ISO 9001 Certified, ISO 14001, IOSH MS, OSHA 30, and OSHA 48. He is a Principal Fellow of Advance HE UK, Chartered Fellow of CIPD, Certified Business and Management Educator, and member of SEDA.

Koppala Venugopal, a professor in Management Studies at Aditya Institute of Technology and Management at Srikakulam, A.P. has had an adroit experience of academic, Research and community service. He has contributed 5 Projects, 2 patents, 10 books, 70 publications, 48 paper presentations, 56 resource talks and 12 memberships. He is guiding 4 scholars from various universities. His exceptional interest industry interface has made his efforts dexterous.

Mohamadi Begum Y. holds a Doctorate in Computer Science & Engineering, and with over 29 years of teaching and research experience. Her current areas of research include Cloud resource management, Blockchain technology, machine learning and information management.

Index

A

B

C

D

E

F

G

H

I

T

V

W

www.ingramcontent.com/pod-product-compliance
Lightning Source LLC
LaVergne TN
LVHW080119011026
849160LV00013B/1134
* 9 7 9 8 3 6 9 3 4 6 5 5 6 *